Neither Led nor Driven

Neither Led nor Driven

Contesting British Cultural
Imperialism in
Jamaica, 1865–1920

~

Brian L. Moore
and
Michele A. Johnson

University of the West Indies Press
Jamaica • Barbados • Trinidad and Tobago

University of the West Indies Press
1A Aqueduct Flats   Mona
Kingston 7   Jamaica
www.uwipress.com

© 2004 by The University of the West Indies Press

All rights reserved. Published 2004

08 07 06 05 04   5 4 3 2 1

CATALOGUING IN PUBLICATION DATA

Moore, Brian L.
Neither led nor driven: contesting British cultural imperialism in
 Jamaica, 1865–1920 / Brian L. Moore and Michele A. Johnson
p. cm.
Includes bibliographical references.

ISBN: 978-976-640-155-9 (cloth). – 978-976-640-154-2 (pbk.)

1. Jamaica – Civilization – British influences. 2. Jamaica – Civilization –
African influences. 3. Social classes – Jamaica. 4. Jamaica – Social life and customs.
5. Politics and culture – Jamaica. 6. Social conflict – Jamaica – History.
I. Johnson, Michele A. II. Title.

F1886.M668 2004   972.9704

Cover illustration: Passengers embarking from a quay, St Ann's Bay, Jamaica.
From John Henderson, *The West Indies* (London: Adam and Charles Black, 1905).
Courtesy of A&C Black (publishers) on behalf of John Henderson (author) and
A.S. Forrest (artist).

Book and cover design by Robert Harris.
Set in Adobe Garamond 11/14 x 27.
Printed in the United States of America.

For Kamau Brathwaite
and
Nigel Bolland
whose ideas, theories and scholarship on Creolization in the
Caribbean have tremendously influenced our own conceptualization
and analysis of the cultural fabric of post-emancipation Jamaica.

Contents

	List of Illustrations	viii
	Preface	ix
	Introduction	xi
1	In the Shadow of Morant Bay: Jamaica, 1865–1920	1
2	Afro-Creole Belief System I: Obeah, Duppies and Other "Dark Superstitions"	14
3	Afro-Creole Belief System II: Folk Religions	51
4	Sex, Marriage and Family: Attitudes and Policies	96
5	"Manners Maketh (Wo)Man": Transforming the Jamaican Character	137
6	Christianizing Jamaica: The Quest for a Moral Culture	167
7	Schooling for God and Empire: The Ideology of Colonial Education	205
8	Proselytizing the Asian Immigrants	245
9	The Cult of Monarchy and Empire: Moulding British Colonial Subjects	271
10	Britannica versus "Africana": Contestation and Negotiation	311
	Appendix 1 Governors of Jamaica, 1864–1920	326
	Appendix 2 Population Statistics, 1861–1920	327
	Appendix 3 Legal Marriages, 1879–1920	329
	Appendix 4 "Illegitimate" Births, 1878–1920	331
	Appendix 5 Education Statistics	334
	Appendix 6 Conversion Statistics of Indian Immigrants	338
	Notes	340
	Bibliography	435
	Index	459

Illustrations

1	Map of Jamaica	*facing page 1*
2	Silk cotton tree	*47*
3	Possessed by spirits	*48*
4	Healing pool in a Revival mission ground	*49*
5	Balm-yard procession	*49*
6	Alexander Bedward	*50*
7	The faithful and the curious at August Town	*50*
8	Three generations and their homestead	*105*
9	A mother and her children	*118*
10 & 11	Portraits of proud defiance	*following page 156*
12	Awaiting trial at the courthouse	*following page 156*
13	A West India Regiment soldier	*following page 156*
14	Market women	*following page 156*
15	Going to church	*following page 156*
16	Church congregation after Sunday service	*179*
17	Sunday Wesleyan procession, Savanna-la-Mar	*189*
18	Elementary schoolroom	*210*
19	Montego Bay High School	*233*
20	Jamaica High School	*234*
21	Barbican School for Girls	*237*
22	Martha B. Croll	*251*
23	Indian catechist Kangaloo and two converts	*255*
24	First Indian converts of Scottish Presbyterians	*256*
25	Indian congregation at Paul Island, Westmoreland	*257*
26	Chinese immigrants	*269*
27	A westernized Chinese gentleman	*269*
28	Statue of Queen Victoria	*283*
29	God, King and Empire	*287*
30	Coronation Day in Mandeville	*288*
31	Coronation Day military parade	*288*
32	Royal arch of welcome for Princess Louise	*291*
33	Concert performers draped in the Union Jack	*305*

Preface

THIS BOOK HAS BEEN LONG IN the making. In 1997 we commenced our work with the award of a Mona Research Fellowship from the University of the West Indies, Jamaica, and since then this project has taken on a life of its own. Never did we expect to uncover the mass of materials that we found in various archives and libraries across the Atlantic. And yet there remain frustrating gaps that seemingly cannot be filled. Nevertheless, we are sanguine that this book will provide readers with rich new data and perspectives about the sociocultural experiences of the people of Jamaica in the years after the massacre of Morant Bay, and will also shed some light on British colonial policies in the Caribbean before the First World War.

As one might expect, over the long period of research and writing, we have incurred enormous debts of gratitude to many individuals and institutions. We thank first Lorna Murray, who encouraged us to apply for the research fellowship in the first place, and the Mona campus of the University of the West Indies, which awarded it to us. Without the two years of time off from teaching, this work would not have been possible. We are also indebted to the School of Graduate Studies and Research of the University of the West Indies for a small grant to copy documents and photographs connected with this work.

Our research was conducted at several libraries and archives which we would like to acknowledge and thank. Most of our work was done at the National Library of Jamaica, whose vast resources of newspapers, books, articles and photographic collections proved invaluable. In particular, we especially thank Eppie Edwards and John Aarons for putting up with us for over a year and providing access to materials that we might otherwise have missed. We also thank the staff of the Jamaica Archives in Spanish Town for their friendly assistance during several months of work there. The Main Library and the Sir Arthur Lewis Institute of Social and Economic Studies of the University of the West Indies, Mona, were also major resource centres for our research. Thanks to the librarians of both.

In the United Kingdom, we wish to thank the following institutions: the Public Record Office; the British Library; the School of Oriental and African Studies, University of London; Partnership House library, and the Society of Jesus (English Province), in London; the Angus Library of Regent's Park College, and Rhodes House Library, Oxford University; and New College Library, Edinburgh. These institutions provided a wealth of data not available in Jamaica.

This book has also benefited enormously from a rich body of contemporary photographs and sketches. All of these have been taken from previous publications whose authors and publishers we acknowledge and thank profusely. But in particular, we would like to express our gratitude to A&C Black of London, publishers of John Henderson's *The West Indies* (1905). This is the source of the colour prints (including the cover picture) which were painted by his travel companion, A.S. Forrester. Special mention must be made, too, of the Methodist Publishing House for granting us permission, on behalf of the Trustees of the Methodist Church Purposes, to reproduce some of their fine photographs.

We would like to express our sincere gratitude to Bridget Brereton of the University of the West Indies, St Augustine, and Barry Higman of the Australian National University, who so kindly and willingly read early drafts of this manuscript. Without their stern critiques and constructive suggestions for improvement, this book would not have attained the quality that we hope it has.

Publishers far too often are taken for granted, but we are especially happy that this work is being produced by the University of the West Indies Press. Small though it might be, the quality of its editorial staff is unsurpassed. We would like to pay special tribute to Rachel Mordecai, the copy editor who worked on this book. Thorough would be an understatement for what she has done. But a special word of thanks must be reserved for Shivaun Hearne, Linda Speth and the Board of the Press for consenting to publish a book of this size. We can only hope that the credits will justify the confidence that they have placed in our scholarship.

Ultimately, we take full responsibility for what appears on the pages that follow, including the errors.

Brian L. Moore
Michele A. Johnson

Introduction

ONE OF THE STRANGE PECULIARITIES OF Jamaican historiography has been the scant attention paid to the period after the cataclysmic outbreak at Morant Bay in 1865. Most scholars have concentrated their efforts on the heady period dating from the late eighteenth century to 1865, arguably the most eventful period of "modern" Jamaican history, encompassing the agitation over the abolition of the slave trade and slavery itself, the Sam Sharpe rebellion of 1831 and the tense years after 1838, and culminating at Morant Bay. By comparison, not much appeared to happen in the placid years of the late nineteenth and early twentieth centuries, at least not until the violent upsurges of 1938 that marked another major turning point in Jamaica's history. A classic example of this historiographical imbalance is Thomas C. Holt's prize-winning *The Problem of Freedom: Race, Labor, and Politics in Jamaica and Britain 1832–1938*, which devotes only about one-fifth of the text (two of ten chapters) to seventy-three years of Jamaica's history (1866–1938), while over three-quarters of the book (eight chapters) is devoted to the previous thirty-four years (1832–65).

Nevertheless, since the Second World War, aspects of Jamaica's post-1865 history have been examined in some depth. Gisela Eisner's *Jamaica 1830–1930: A Study of Economic Growth* still remains a very useful economic history, although some of its findings have been challenged by Veront M. Satchell's more recent *From Plots to Plantations: Land Transactions in Jamaica 1866–1900*. Political developments have been examined by Roy Augier, H.A. Will, Graham Knox, James Carnegie and, of course, Holt.[1] Early nationalist figures, especially Marcus Garvey but also Robert Love and Claude McKay, have been the focus of study by both historians and political scientists.[2] The white and Jewish elite populations have been studied by Patrick Bryan and Thomas August respectively.[3] Subordinate ethnic minorities in Jamaica have also received some attention: Walton Look Lai, Howard Johnson, Jacqueline Levy and Patrick Bryan have examined the Chinese community after emancipation, and Verene Shepherd the East Indians.[4]

However, the area of culture in the late nineteenth and early twentieth centuries has been sadly underexplored. This is not confined to Jamaica: in anglophone Caribbean historiography the study of culture has traditionally been treated as an appendage to social history, and it is only recently that historians of the region have begun to treat cultural history as a distinct area of historical investigation.[5] Globally, Bill Schwarz asserts that although there are still relatively few practitioners, cultural history is now rising to the forefront of professional history; its visibility is high in part because

> everywhere we are confronted with the concentration on symbolic and linguistic systems that had done much to erode the authority of older, inherited positivism. In part, this can also be explained by the breathtaking accelerations of the culture industries, representing a quantum acceleration in the symbolic worlds we all inhabit. This reordering of lived experience is reflected in the sorts of questions that historians are prompted to ask of the past, seeing new things in the past that had been previously invisible.[6]

For Jamaica, most scholarly work on the post-emancipation cultural past has been done by anthropologists like Martha Beckwith, Joseph John Williams, George Eaton Simpson, W.F. Elkins, Barry Chevannes and Diane Austin-Broos, who have researched various aspects of Afro-Christian religion such as Revival sects, Rastafari and Pentecostalism.[7] The historical work of Philip Curtin, Mary Turner, Monica Schuler, Robert J. Stewart and Catherine Hall also has strong cultural content, but they all focus on the period before 1865.[8] Very little work has been done on the secular culture of Jamaicans.

Patrick Bryan's *The Jamaican People 1880–1902* is the only major social history of late-nineteenth-century Jamaica. While it provides readers with vignettes or glimpses of the cultural landscape of Jamaica, much of that landscape still remains unexplored. Nevertheless, his analysis of Jamaican society is most valuable in demonstrating that the fundamental social configuration of Jamaica, based on race/colour and class, was preserved into the early twentieth century, although individual blacks and coloureds (that is, racially mixed persons) made significant social progress.

Bryan convincingly shows that the ruling elites were able to maintain their hegemony by manipulating "the law, the control or influence upon the political and constitutional order, by the control of land resources, and by the projection of the indispensability of white leadership for the progress of the colony". Further, he argues correctly that in the absence of the forms of direct control that the old ruling oligarchy had exercised over the people during slavery, they were obliged "to adopt policies that would ensure consent, and project a principle of tolerance and the sanctity of British legal institutions". This was effected largely through a system of education that not only "promoted opportunities for *individual* [our emphasis] social mobility, [but also] encouraged values that legitimated the system of domination". Thus, "The evolution of a black middle class was not an anomaly in the pattern of hegemony. On the contrary, the achievement of European culture and education became an end in itself for probably most members of the black middle class."9

This book builds on the foundation laid by Bryan by examining in detail the sociocultural strategies and methods employed by the ruling elites to preserve their hegemony. It does not attempt, nor does it pretend, to be a full-fledged or comprehensive cultural history aimed at filling the glaring lacuna in the study of Jamaica's cultural past after 1865. Instead, it offers a highly focused examination of the efforts of the Jamaican social elites and their British imperial masters to impose a new sociocultural religious and moral order, based on British imperial ideologies and middle-class Victorian ideas, ideals, values and precepts, on the Jamaican people, particularly on the subordinate black population who already possessed a stable, functioning cultural matrix, born in Africa and refashioned on the Jamaican plantation, that had survived the rupture of the Middle Passage and the rigours and brutality of slavery.10 This work treats the latter as the *mainstream* (though not *dominant*) culture, which the British reformers and their local allies were seeking to change through the superimposition of their imported, *alternative* cultural system, which they perceived as superior. It therefore analyses the agency of the people as they struggled for cultural self-determination in the face of resolute efforts from above to transform them into model British colonial subjects. It examines the cultural agenda of those who identified key aspects of the culture of the Jamaican people as major "problems" for civilized society and thus as primary targets for assault, with a view to casting them into oblivion. It also analyses the complex process of negotiation and contestation that ensued. Finally, it looks at the efforts to "civilize" the new Indian and Chinese immigrant minorities whose distinctive cultures were also considered inferior.

While we concur with Raymond Williams's three-pronged conceptualization of "culture" as the general process of intellectual, spiritual and aesthetic development, the particular way of life of a people, a period or a group, and the works and practices of intellectual and artistic activity,[11] we focus here specifically on those elements that dominated the cultural policies of the period under study: belief systems, sexuality, marriage and family, morality, and social behaviour. We plan to produce a second volume that will examine other aspects of Jamaican culture such as food and dress, architecture and furniture, music and dance, theatre and cinema, arts and craft, language and literature, sports and entertainment, festivals and holidays, gambling, alcohol and narcotic consumption for pleasure, and the rites of passage. Together these two works should provide a fairly comprehensive account of the Jamaican cultural landscape in the late nineteenth and early twentieth centuries, and thereby add substantially to the body of knowledge on Caribbean cultural history.

This study takes into account what would have been termed the "proper culture" or "high culture" of the Victorian elites (among both expatriates and locals) in Jamaica between 1865 and 1920. In their anxiety to replicate the dominant, middle-class culture of the mother country (Britain), many Jamaican elites sought to import and to impose what nineteenth-century scholar Matthew Arnold would have described as "the best that has been thought and said, as well as that body of knowledge and the application of that knowledge to the 'inward condition of the mind and spirit' ".[12]

These elites, like Arnold, were horrified by the prospect of the ascendancy of the people's culture. But where Arnold sought the restoration of a mythical, shared and common English culture, albeit through educating the masses in "proper" British culture, many in the Jamaican upper and middle classes could not find anything worthy of reviving in the island's indigenous creole culture, whether rooted in the rural, aristocratic, planter tradition or in the "lowly" Afro-creole tradition. Instead, they sought to transform or eliminate significant aspects of those two traditions and to replace them with imported Victorian culture. No matter the point of origin, however, these reformers in both Britain and Jamaica pressed for a "culture and civilization" tradition premised on their own middle-class values and morality to save the society, since they equated an embrace of the people's culture with anarchy of the "raw and uncultivated . . . masses".[13] A proper "cultural education" (indoctrination), especially of the black lower classes, would maintain class deference, prepare the unwashed rabble for their inclusion in the political process, and "would bring to the working class a 'culture' which would in turn remove the temptations of trade-unionism, political agitation, and working-class culture.

In short, culture would remove popular [people's] culture."¹⁴ The "civilizing mission" was thus similar in both Britain and Jamaica, except that in the colony racism reinforced the class prejudices with which the mission arrived.

This volume analyses those aspects of the culture of the "ordinary people"¹⁵ that were regarded by these sociocultural reformers as "problems for civilized society", and the efforts to change or eradicate them. But while it is the reformist Victorian cultural agenda that undoubtedly sets the parameters of this study, the culture and behaviour of the Jamaican people are examined, not merely as responses or in reaction to British cultural dominance, but as part of their own independent programme aimed at fashioning a world that suited their self-determined social and cultural criteria and needs. These set the stage for a dynamic and very complex process of contestation and negotiation among the three major cultural forces: the newly imported, Victorian reformist (aimed at anglicizing the whole society); the old, conservative plantocratic (determined to preserve some of its rural, aristocratic values and customs); and the Afro-creole and lower-class (seeking to assert its own value system as perhaps the most important element in an ongoing process of creolization). The situation is made even more complex by the introduction of Asian immigrants, mainly from India and China, whose cultural influence in some aspects of Jamaican life far exceeded their small numbers. The core of this work thus centres on the interplay among these several contending cultural forces, with a view to determining the evolution of Jamaica's cultural identity by the end of the First World War.

Many modern cultural studies have their theoretical foundation in the neo-Gramscian theory of "hegemony", which argues that notwithstanding class exploitation in capitalist societies, elite cultural institutions, beliefs and traditions are valued by the masses even if they do not actively participate in them, and that the masses are ultimately incorporated through "negotiation" into the dominant power structure to produce societal consensus. Indeed, John Storey cites the British Caribbean as a classic example of Gramscian-like hegemony at work. He argues that British Caribbean culture is the product of negotiation between the dominant and subordinate groups involving both "resistance" and "incorporation".¹⁶ The existence, however, of three competing cultural traditions, two of which were "elite" (not to mention those of the Asian immigrants), suggests that Jamaican and West Indian reality was far more complex than that.

The process of creolization lies at the heart of this work. For ultimately, in their efforts to "civilize" lower-class Jamaicans, the Victorian cultural reformers engaged in a complex process that, while seeking to eradicate most traces of African-derived culture, introduced new cultural elements from Britain that they (the elites) sought to adapt to the local sociocultural environment. Edward Kamau Brathwaite attempted to address this complexity by seeing it as the consequence of "an historically affected socio-cultural continuum, within which . . . there are four inter-related and sometimes overlapping orientations", namely European, Euro-creole, Afro-creole (or folk) and creo-creole (or West Indian). "A common colonial and creole experience is shared among the various divisions, even if that experience is variously interpreted." All subsequent waves of immigrants, in his view, were thrown into this creole matrix and creolized. But none, not even the original African and European groups that constructed it, was completely creolized.[17]

Sociologist Nigel Bolland, however, argues that Brathwaite and others (mainly historians) use the term "creolization" in an imprecise, ambiguous, inconsistent way that deprives it of its potency. What he thinks it needs is a good dose of rigorous dialectical theory. According to him,

> The dialectical analysis of society draws attention to the interrelated and mutually constitutive nature of "individual", "society", "culture", and of human agency and social structure. Dialectical theory conceives of social life as essentially *practical* activity, and of people as essentially *social* beings. Hence, society consists of the social relation in which people engage in their activities, and is not reducible to individuals. . . . Culture in the form of traditions, ideas, customs, languages, institutions, and social formations, shape [sic] the social action of individuals, which in turn maintains, modifies, or transforms social structure and culture. This mutually dependent relationship between social structure and human agency has been referred to as the "dialectics of structuring". Dialectical theory draws attention in particular to conflicts in social systems as the chief sources of social change. Many important social relationships are defined and differentiated in terms of power, between the dominant and the subordinate.[18]

This definitional polarization between the dominant and the subordinate in dialectical theory is problematic. Not only is it inadequate for dealing with the competing cultural traditions among the elite classes themselves but, as conceived by Bolland, dialectical analysis is essentially a theory of domination/hegemony versus subordination/resistance. This, however, threatens to straitjacket the historical analyst, because it does not apparently lend itself to nuances in the power relationship. This is further demonstrated in Bolland's treatment of the relationship between colony and metropolis.

Here he notes that "Dialectical theory draws attention, *unequivocally* [our emphasis], to the elements of resistance that are inherent in the domination/subordination relationship between the metropole and the colony, and shows how resistance and conflict are therefore constituent aspects of the cultures and social and economic structures of the colonial society."[19]

William A. Green, however, is particularly wary of this "abiding theme [of] black resistance to white domination", which he considers subjective and thus risky.[20] Nor does he like twinning dialectical analysis with the creolization approach. Regarding the dialectic as "a dualistic concept of struggle that pits haves against have-nots, whites against blacks, and planters against plantation workers", he claims that "it cannot accommodate the extraordinary plurality of Caribbean society without artificially fusing groups that possessed little conscious identity on a comprehensive range of societal issues". He further admonishes dialectical creolists for elevating Afro-Caribbean culture to a position of equality in a bipolar struggle: "The historical record continuously confronts us with behaviour that defies the notion of perpetual resistance or of universal Afro-Caribbean solidarity. . . . Not all West Indians who might be classified with an Afro-Caribbean culture group were defiant."

While admitting that the old imperial historians did err "by ignoring the depth and tenacity of Afro-Caribbean culture", Green thinks that modern dialectical creolists also err

> by superimposing on the West Indies an analytical structure that fails to accommodate the kaleidoscopic diversity of human motives and forces that influenced the course of life in the western tropics. The inherent logic of the dialectic is to emphasize the operation of two conflicting forces. Once this scheme is imposed on the historical landscape, it becomes difficult for a researcher to avoid fitting his data into preconceived packages.[21]

While we certainly do not share Green's views on the creolization approach, there is some validity in his strictures on dialectical analysis, for as this book will show, the Jamaican cultural landscape was/is much too diverse and complex to be viewed through the lenses of such a binary. Likewise this volume does not, as seems integral to the dialectical analysis of Caribbean history, conceptualize Afro-creole culture as *intrinsically* a culture of resistance to British "cultural imperialism" or dominance. This is not to say that resistance is not an important issue discussed; indeed this is done particularly in relation to the hypothesis advanced by Richard D.E. Burton. But the issue of resistance is not treated as part of any hard-and-fast theoretical construct.

As regards Burton's hypothesis, there are some fundamental problems relating to the peculiar definitions he employs. He defines resistance as "those forms of contestation of a given system that are conducted from *outside* that system, using weapons and concepts derived from a source or sources other than the system in question". Thus, he argues that Afro-creole culture was not a culture of resistance, certainly not after emancipation, because it utilized cultural elements borrowed from the dominant system itself, contested that system on its own ground, and did not overthrow or fundamentally alter that system. Accordingly, he labels it a culture of "opposition" rather than resistance.[22]

What is striking is that both Bolland and Burton draw some of their intellectual inspiration from the same source, Michel de Certeau,[23] even though they have diametrically opposed notions of the importance of resistance in Caribbean history and culture. Be that as it may, however, Burton's definition seems so narrow and contrived that it rules out from the very outset any action that Afro-Caribbean people may have adopted to counter British cultural dominance after emancipation, simply on the ground that they utilized cultural elements borrowed from the British themselves. This was not resistance, he argues, but opposition. Afro-Caribbean peoples did not overthrow the dominant system; they engaged in oppositional "play" within the parameters defined by the dominant power system.[24]

But did Afro-Jamaicans have to combat the dominant system directly in order for this to qualify as resistance (in Burtonian terms)? Does resistance manifest itself in only one way? And does it necessarily have to lead to the overthrow or fundamental change of the dominant system? Do the appropriation, reinterpretation and creolization of imported British cultural items not qualify as resistance? And what if Afro-Jamaicans simply ignored what was being thrust upon them, and literally "did their own thing"? Should that be classified within the narrow binary of opposition-resistance? These are some of the issues that will be addressed in this work.

Reconstructing the cultural past is a difficult and painstaking exercise because the data are often patchy, fragmented and dispersed. For this work we made use of a vast range of documents taken from several archival depositories in Jamaica, the United Kingdom and the United States: official documents (including governors' correspondence with the Colonial Office, interdepartmental correspondence, laws, department reports, censuses); church and missionary reports, letters, registers, and journals; newspapers and magazines; private letters and diaries; and, not least of all, photographs, "magic lantern" slides and sketches. The major "problem" with these sources is that they were, with few exceptions, generated by the very persons who were seeking to impose the new moral order on Jamaica. Very often these people were unsympathetic towards and quite ignorant of the cultures of the working people, although a few did occasionally take the time and make the effort to try to ascertain what ordinary Jamaicans thought and felt about certain issues. But by and large these sources are the voice of the educated elites, local and foreign, and present a skewed picture of the cultural past. Thus, while we conceive Afro-creole culture as the mainstream system in post-emancipation Jamaica, very often the sources render it impossible to provide a holistic picture of the internal dynamics of that culture.

However, there were three sets of sources that reflected the voices of the people. The first was a collection of 312 letters gathered by the *Gleaner* in November 1959 in response to a competition that it sponsored. For a first prize of twenty-five pounds (and other smaller prizes), Jamaicans were encouraged to write about their recollections of life in the island fifty years earlier. Many of these letters, now housed at the Jamaica Archives under the title "Jamaica Memories", were written by ordinary people from town and country in their own style and language, and provide very useful data and insights from their perspectives. The second set of sources was ninety transcripts of interviews conducted by Dr Erna Brodber, noted social historian and novelist, on life in early-twentieth-century Jamaica. Housed at the Sir Arthur Lewis Institute of Social and Economic Studies, University of the West Indies, Mona, these transcripts of oral histories also provide valuable insights from below into social and cultural life. Finally, we found fragments of original pamphlets, generated by obeah practitioners or their allies, that detailed their exploits over long periods of time. These papers demonstrated a spirit of defiance, pride and a sense of accomplishment in their profession at a time (the 1890s) when the colonial authorities were instituting harsh legal penalties for obeah.

Despite the fragmentary nature and class bias of most of the sources, with careful use and analysis it has been possible to capture the cultural tone of the times under study, important aspects of the culture of the Jamaican people, and the motivations behind the policies, ideologies and values that the local elites and their imperial allies sought to impose on Jamaica. And, very often reading between the lines, we have been able to discern why their "lesser subjects" reacted in the way they did.

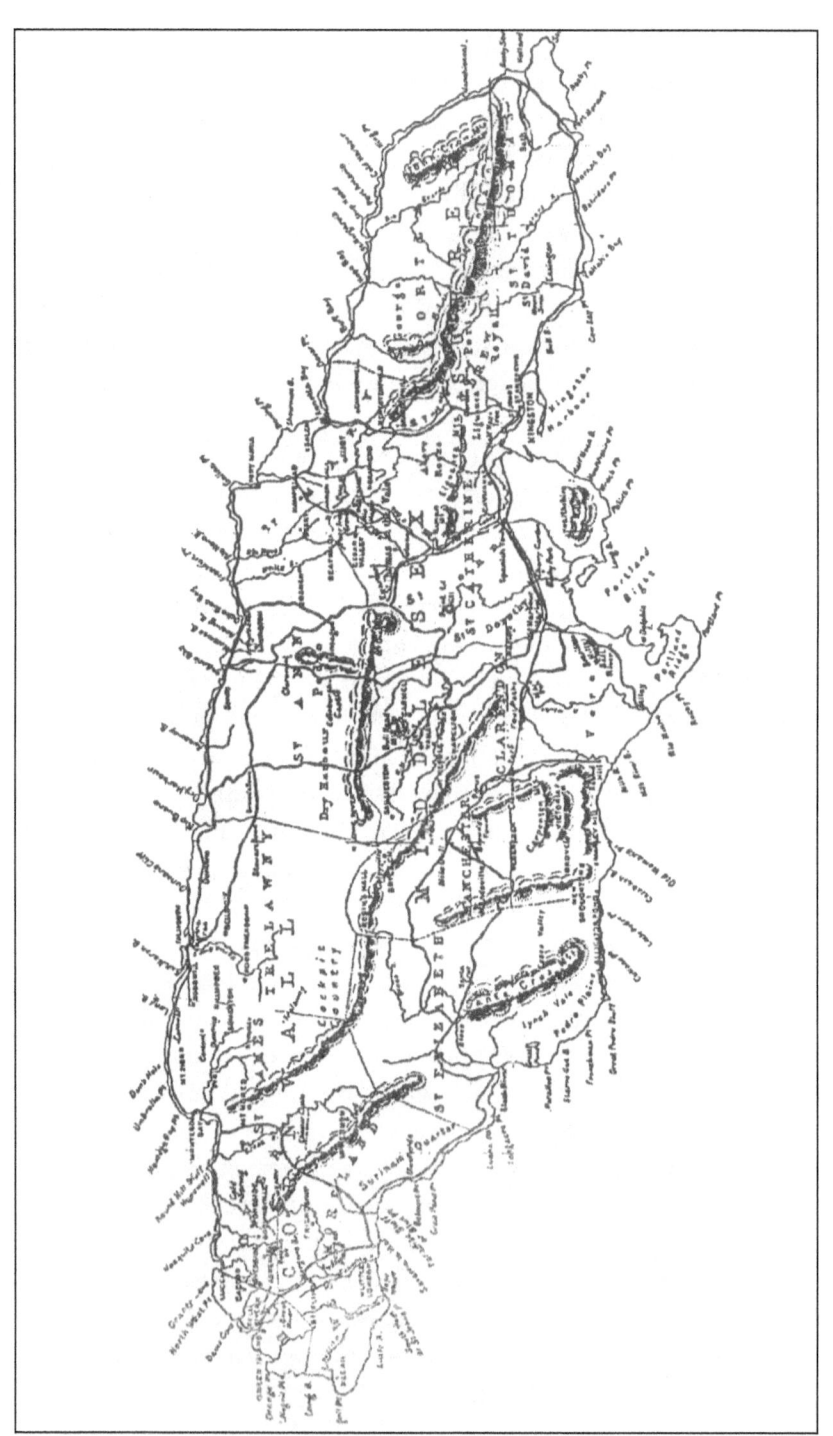

Figure 1. Map of Jamaica
Source: United Presbyterian Church, Minutes of Foreign Mission Board, 1890–91.

Chapter 1

In the Shadow of Morant Bay
Jamaica, 1865–1920

THE YEAR 1865 WAS PERHAPS THE most cataclysmic in Jamaica's postemancipation history prior to the First World War. That year was marked by a dramatic uprising among the peasants of the township of Morant Bay in the parish of St Thomas-in-the-East; the uprising was brutally suppressed by the colonial government. But the Morant Bay disturbance was merely the high point of a struggle among the ex-slaves that had persisted ever since emancipation in 1838, and was to continue for at least another seventy years. That struggle sought to translate the legal freedom won by the slaves into the language of equality – social, political and economic – and to share the same civil rights and privileges that white inhabitants of the island had always enjoyed. It manifested itself in the quest for the vote and representation in the assembly; for fair and liveable wages, and decent conditions of work on the plantations; for freehold land not only to establish a claim on the soil that the ex-slaves and their ancestors had worked unremittingly for centuries, but as the basis of a material improvement in their way of life; for an education by which they could qualify themselves and their progeny for social advancement and an equal voice in the affairs of the country; and for social respectability as free and equal subjects of Her Majesty.

On the other side of the coin, however, the old plantocracy and their merchant allies sought to preserve the status quo of white dominance and black servitude. Emancipation might have freed the slaves but it was not, as far as this group was concerned, intended to usher in an egalitarian society. For them, the social order characterized by white privilege had to be preserved at all costs. "Civilization" itself depended on the preservation of the status quo. White dominance of the political, economic and social institutions had to be maintained, for the alternative was seen as "black barbarism". Emancipation, therefore, did not change their attitude to the black majority (or, for that matter, to the "uppity" coloured middle group). They considered the ex-slaves an ignorant, potentially vengeful and vicious populace, who had to be kept in their place lest mayhem ensue. As far as possible the latter had to be excluded from the political process lest another Haiti, with all its political upheavals and instability, be courted. Everything had to be done to keep them actively employed on the plantations, both to ensure the continued economic prosperity of that institution upon which white dominance was premised, and to prevent the ex-slaves from becoming idle and dissolute, and from "reverting to barbarism". Nothing ought to be done to raise their expectations or encourage them in the mistaken belief that they were the social equals of whites.

These diametrically opposed attitudes meant that from 1 August 1838, "two Jamaicas"[1] were set on a collision course, for white hegemony could only be maintained by denying black aspirations. The first quarter century after emancipation thus witnessed a growing conflict as the two sides jostled each other. It manifested itself in the attempts to coerce the ex-slaves to continue working on the estates for low wages in poor working conditions; in restricting their access to freehold land in order to prevent them from withdrawing their labour from the estates and establishing an independent existence; in denying them political rights by imposing high income and property qualifications for the franchise and membership in the assembly; in taxing common consumer items to bear heavily on the ex-slave population, making them dependent on wage-labour income; and in the refusal to fund adequate social services such as schools, hospitals, roads, bridges and so forth that might facilitate their social and economic progress.[2]

This growing tension reached a climax at Morant Bay in October 1865. When Paul Bogle and his followers marched from Stony Gut to Morant Bay on 11 October, they brought to the courthouse all their accumulated grievances and frustrations, but they came face to face with the obstinacy and obduracy of the planter authorities. This was a showdown between the two Jamaicas, both equally intransigent and standing their ground. Thus, when Bogle and his people refused to disperse as instructed by the custos, Baron von Ketelhodt, the militia was ordered to fire at them. The killing of seven of their number infuriated the people, who felt compelled to retaliate, killing the custos and a few other whites in the ensuing mêlée. What followed was a massacre, as the rioters and their sympathizers were ruthlessly hunted down and killed or summarily executed, leaving almost 450 blacks dead. Over six hundred others, both men and women, were flogged, and over a thousand peasant huts destroyed.[3] It was a savage retribution by the state, intended to send a clear message to the black population that they should never again attempt any such outbreak of violence.

Morant Bay was an important watershed in the post-emancipation history of Jamaica. It demonstrated, *inter alia,* that the small, white, planter-merchant oligarchy was unfit to continue exercising political power over the large black majority, and that political change was essential. It also should have indicated that the persistent stifling of black aspirations could not continue indefinitely. That second message, however, was masked by a third, shared by the officers of the imperial government itself and by the local white elites, many coloureds, and even some socially aspiring blacks: that the ex-slaves and their descendants (mainly black) had hardly advanced as civilized beings. It was this that determined what "reforms" would be instituted after the uprising and massacre of 1865.

Out of fear of black ascendancy, the Jamaican assembly was persuaded to transfer its power to the British crown. Crown colony government was thus instituted the following year. All power was vested in the officials appointed by the Colonial Office under the autocratic authority of the governor. Insofar as Jamaicans were allowed a voice in their own affairs, it took the form of persons of "substance" and "influence" (that is, the same wealthy white planters and merchants who had misruled in the old assembly) nominated by the governor to sit in the new Legislative Council. Under this pure form of crown colony government, there were no elections: all Jamaicans, white, coloured and black, were disenfranchised. This political regression was made imperative by a consensus of opinion among the local elites and imperial officials that the franchise could not be extended to the black majority, who had just demonstrated their incapacity to govern by their "barbarity" at Morant Bay. That catastrophic event indicated (to the elite mind) that white leadership was essential for the well-being of Jamaica. In the official mind, such leadership should come from Britain rather than from the local whites, who were considered inept, narrow-minded and selfish.[4] The latter were willing to surrender their time-honoured exercise of power because they were terrified by the violence, and were no longer willing to accept full responsibility for governing "unruly" blacks in the wake of the events at Morant Bay.

Although the local ruling class had been prevailed upon by their new-found hero and saviour, Governor Edward John Eyre, to cede their power to the crown, they soon became disenchanted with crown rule. Through the nominated members they could still influence government policy, but they found the early crown colony governors, in particular John Peter Grant (1866–74), highly autocratic and unwilling to be guided by their interests in all matters. By the early 1880s they and other politically aspiring groups, such as the coloured and black middle classes, were demanding a more active voice in the colony's affairs. Eventually, in 1884, the Colonial Office acquiesced by reintroducing limited elected representation based on qualifications similar to those that existed before 1865 (males paying direct taxes of ten shillings or earning a minimum salary of fifty pounds per annum). Nevertheless, owing to the economic advances that some coloureds and blacks had made in the intervening two decades, the electorate was predominantly black (50.7 per cent in 1885), with coloureds comprising over a third (34.6 per cent). Even then the electorate comprised only about 1.3 per cent of the total population (1881 census). More significant was the fact that although whites comprised just 2.5 per cent of the population in 1881, their proportion of the electorate was 13.4 per cent in 1885, and as Thomas Holt has observed,

> In the elections immediately following these reforms . . . not only were no Afro-Jamaicans elected to the new Legislative Council but all the councilmen were either planters or merchants, and only five were even natives of Jamaica. . . . [And in the elections] that followed over the next several decades, not only were spokesmen for the people scarce but a majority of the legislative seats were not even contested.[5]

Blacks were further disqualified by the imposition of a literacy test in 1893. Thus, as Patrick Bryan observes, "representation in the Legislative Council was dominated by spokesmen of the landed and business interests", just as it had been before 1865.[6] That remained the case beyond the end of the First World War.

Government and politics in Jamaica up to the end of the First World War were exclusively male activities, as women – regardless of race, colour or class – were denied the vote. It was not until 1918 that a campaign for the female franchise was launched. Initiated by H.A. Leslie Simpson, coloured member of the Legislative Council and former mayor of Kingston, the movement was given an enormous fillip through the support of the governor's wife, Lady

Probyn, and ultimately resulted in the franchise being extended to middle- and upper-class women in May 1919.[7]

In the minds of the representatives of imperial power, metropolitan white leadership was necessary for good governance and also to "civilize" Jamaicans, not only the "ignorant, barbaric" blacks and the socially aspiring coloured population, but also the whites themselves, whose morality and manners had been "perverted" by centuries of depraved existence in a slave society. As Catherine Hall has so brilliantly shown, the mission of the nonconformist missionaries to civilize black and coloured Jamaicans had begun even before the end of slavery. Their mission was not merely to christianize the ex-slaves, but to civilize them, in accordance with British middle-class moral ideas and conventions. These ideas and conventions were also being pursued (albeit less vigorously) by the elite churches (such as the Churches of England and Scotland, and the Roman Catholic Church) among their congregations, which included a significant percentage of upper- and middle-class Jamaicans.

However well intentioned these missionaries were, they too believed that the newly freed blacks were inferior and required white tutelage, which (in their own opinion) they were only ones with the moral authority to provide. They also shared the view of secular whites both in the colonies and in Britain, that African and Afro-creole cultural forms, expressions and institutions did not fall within the ambit of civilization, and therefore had to be eradicated. Hall shows that this ultimately brought them into collision with black Jamaicans, whose confidence the missionaries began to lose from as early as the mid-1840s. The events at Morant Bay, however, following on outbreaks of Afro-creole religious "revival madness"[8] a few years earlier, were devastating for the missionaries. These occurrences seemed to unravel everything they had worked so hard to achieve for over half a century, the efforts both to christianize and to civilize. With specific reference to the British Baptists, who had the largest mission in the island, Hall records their utter disillusionment with this turn of events, and their gradual withdrawal from the island thereafter.[9]

Morant Bay may have brought about a major change in the form of government, but it did not fundamentally alter the policies and attitudes of the colonial authorities. However disillusioned the Baptist (and other) missionaries may have been by the events of 1865, as in India after the "Mutiny" of 1857–58, the disturbances seemed to reinforce in the official mind the necessity of British rule as the only way to bring law, order, justice and civilization to Jamaica, and to the entire British Caribbean. Indeed, by the mid-1870s, they were patting themselves on the shoulder for having restored utter calm and stability in Jamaica, attributing that to the "even-handed" and "judicious" exercise of British justice and the rule of law.[10]

Yet there was always some disquiet and anxiety about the apparent capacity for violence among the "uncultured" blacks. Everyday street brawls and small outbreaks of rioting in Montego Bay in 1902, in Kingston in 1912, and against Chinese shopkeepers in St Catherine in 1918 served as reminders of this latent and dangerous potential. To snuff it out before it got out of hand a new police force, the Jamaica Constabulary, was established in 1867 to replace the old militias that had played such a critical role at Morant Bay. The force was armed and placed under the centralized command of an inspector general and officers who were white. It was supported in the rural areas by a Rural Police Force under the supervision of the white constabulary officers.[11]

A law of 1879 established new volunteer militias in various parts of the island under the supervision of the military. Their membership was drawn mainly from the propertied middle and upper classes. But as Bryan notes, the qualification of blacks and coloureds for service soon led to a decline in popularity of these militias among white Jamaicans. In his words, "The elected members of the [Legislative] Council, representing the views of parts of the white establishment, were averse to the creation of a militia which would put arms into the hands of people whom they viewed as their race or class enemies."[12] Although these militias came under the supervision of the military, control over them and over the distribution of arms was loose. This was quite different from the situation in the police force and the West India Regiments (see below), whose rank and file, although predominantly composed of blacks and coloureds, were directly under the close supervision of white officers.

Jamaica also always enjoyed the "protection" of British imperial forces stationed in the island. There were generally two West India Regiments stationed at Up Park Camp in Kingston, composed mainly of blacks but under white British officers, as well as true "blue-blooded" British troops at Port Royal and Newcastle in St Andrew. This combined military and police presence, although never numerically overwhelming, was sufficient to put down localized disturbances, and served as a show of force with the knowledge that there was always the full coercive power of the British Empire, symbolized by the annual visit of the British North American and West Indian Squadron, that could be unleashed if things got out of hand.

The two Jamaicas that clashed at Morant Bay represented the two primary racial groups in the island: one black, the other white. The mixed or coloured population always occupied an ambivalent position between these two groups. Seeing themselves as a distinct social group with their own interests, and as the only truly "indigenous" Jamaicans, they were inclined to pursue their interests in alliance with one or other of the primary groups as circumstances warranted. Often, however, they were divided on issues, and Morant Bay was no different. Some, like the prominent coloured politician George William Gordon, a political associate of Paul Bogle, sympathized with the plight of the peasants; Gordon paid for that sympathy with his life. Others, however, either kept their distance (and their lives), or supported Governor Eyre's drastic action.[13]

These socioracial distinctions persisted long after 1865, although population changes and socioeconomic developments in the late nineteenth and early twentieth centuries increasingly blurred the lines of division. According to the 1861 census, Jamaica had a population of 441,264, of whom whites numbered 13,816 (3.1 per cent of the total), coloureds 81,065 (18.4 per cent) and blacks 346,374 (78.5 per cent). By 1921 the population had almost doubled, to 858,118. The white population then numbered 14,476 (declining to 1.7 per cent of the whole), coloureds 157,223 (remaining virtually constant at 18.3 per cent) and blacks 660,420 (a marginal decline to 77 per cent). To these were added new immigrants: by 1921 there were 18,610 Indians (2.2 per cent), 3,696 Chinese (0.4 per cent) and 3,693 others not specified (0.4 per cent). In the total population, women numbered 227,743 (51.6 per cent) in 1861, increasing to 456,145 (53.2 per cent) in 1921. Among the whites, they formed 47.2 per cent in 1861, and increased to 49.4 per cent by 1921. Coloured women formed 52.8 per cent of that social category in 1861, increasing to 55.6 per cent by 1921, and black women composed 51.7 per cent of that group in 1861, increasing to 53.1 per cent in 1921. The greatest gender disparity was among the new immigrants, the Indians and especially the Chinese, who experienced an acute shortage of women.[14]

Each of the three principal socioracial groups in Jamaican society, as Bryan notes, was internally stratified. Although whiteness had special meaning that translated itself into social superiority, there were differences in wealth, privilege and status among whites. At the apex were colonial officials and senior army officers, born in Britain and representing the imperial power. Although many local whites found some of these bureaucrats and military men aloof and pompous, they nevertheless placed enormous social value on socializing with them, since it was considered a mark of distinction in colonial society. In turn, some of these officials invested in landed property in the island, thereby identifying even more closely with the economic interests of the local elites.[15]

Despite the decline of sugar production after emancipation, sugar planters (including attorneys representing absentee plantation owners, and estate managers) formed the core of the traditional Jamaican white upper class – for example, Michael Solomon, E.J. Saddler, Colonel. C.J. Ward, and the Farquharsons (A.W., C.S., J.M., M.S., W.H., F.H., H.M. and C.M.). But as Veront Satchell has shown, with the growth of the banana industry after 1880, the ranks of the planters were diversified by the inclusion of merchants and professionals who invested in banana plantations.[16] Bryan notes that some merchant capital also went into sugar enterprises in the late nineteenth century, thus blurring the old class distinctions between planters and merchants.[17] A very important element in this socioeconomic transformation was the accession of Jewish merchants and large landholders into the white upper class. Bishops, archdeacons, canons and others in the upper echelons of the major churches (the Churches of England and Scotland and the Roman Catholic Church) also formed part of this social elite.

A middle class of whites was composed mainly of professionals, police officers, low-ranking clergymen and missionaries, school inspectors, journalists, owners or managers of small businesses, and what Bryan calls "medium farmers" who owned farms of up to about fifty or sixty acres. Below them were office and store clerks, and plantation overseers and bookkeepers. The ranks of the small number of poor whites were swollen by the addition of German immigrants, who were encouraged during the 1840s to settle in Jamaica to form a middle class of white small farmers in the interior of the island. Most of those who came settled in and around Seaford Town, Westmoreland, but never prospered. They thus constituted a rural, poor white enclave in the heart of the island.[18]

The status of white women was usually tied to that of their fathers or husbands, but some did own landed property, albeit usually inherited from deceased male relatives; while others somewhat lower down the social ladder pursued independent occupations such as tavern keepers and guest-house operators. By the late nineteenth century those who were unable to find mates to support them in marriage for life, or who needed to supplement their husbands' incomes, worked as teachers, nurses, postmistresses, secretaries and store clerks. As a rule, though, like their counterparts in Europe and North America, elite white women opted for marriage to a suitable male and remained at home where their primary role was to bear and rear children, care for their husbands and families and either keep house or supervise their domestic servants. Their primary activities outside of the home were largely philanthropic, usually for church societies and other charities.[19] As shown above, it was not until 1919 that some "earned" the right to participate in the political process, but only as voters.

The coloured population was also differentiated internally by wealth, education, occupation and culture. By the late nineteenth and early twentieth centuries, coloured men such as S.C. Burke (magistrate), William Plant (headmaster of Titchfield High School), Reverend William Webb (Baptist pastor, teacher and politician), D.A. Corinaldi (politician), H.A. Leslie Simpson (lawyer and politician), Astley Clerk (musician) and Dr J.J. Cameron, to name a few, were at the upper end of the coloured section and interacted professionally and, on a limited scale, socially with elite whites. Several were highly successful professionals (especially lawyers and doctors), or prominent and wealthy businessmen and landowners such as Peter A. Moodie (banana producer and trader) and George Steibel (businessman). Coloureds formed a substantial part of the middle class and held similar occupations to whites of equal social status: white-collar jobs in the civil service, in the church and in teaching, journalism and small business; clerical jobs in offices and stores; and jobs as plantation overseers, bookkeepers and small farmers. Middle-class coloured women, like their white "sisters", were socialized to prefer marriage and domestic life to working outside of the home, but in spite of that aspiration many had to earn a living for themselves and their families in a variety of jobs such as teachers, nurses, secretaries, telegraph operators, tavern keepers and guest-house operators, store attendants, and seamstresses. Many coloureds were, however, quite poor and their existence differed in no way from that of working-class blacks.[20]

The black majority too was differentiated along class lines. Education was their principal means of social mobility, and this made access to high-status occupations – such as the liberal professions (law and medicine), the civil service, the priesthood and teaching – possible for a few. Some became very prominent by the turn of the twentieth century – for example, Samuel Josiah Washington (teacher and pastor), Claude McKay (poet), Marcus Mosiah Garvey (political thinker and leader) and Hector Josephs (lawyer). Dr Robert Love, a black Bahamian, was able to find a home and enjoy social prominence in Jamaica as an influential journalist and politician.

These people formed a black intelligentsia and shared middle-class status alongside coloureds and whites. Yet their position in a white-dominated colonial society was ambiguous, for although highly successful in their chosen fields, they were nevertheless not quite accorded the same degree of respect as whites with equivalent qualifications. That notwithstanding, Hector Josephs, for instance, was able to build a highly successful legal career in the government service, reaching the height of acting attorney general before being substantively confirmed to that post in British Guiana in 1925.[21] The barriers of race and colour, therefore, while still very much present up to and during the 1920s, were gradually being broken down by individual blacks.

Those blacks who were able to make significant social progress on account of their educational accomplishments were a very small minority of the black population. But in addition, economic success in small business, small farming (especially bananas, citrus, pimento and coffee for export), and as "master tradesmen" (highly skilled artisans) enabled others to claim a place in the lower ranks of the middle class; as Bryan observes, policemen also formed part of this class.[22] The vast majority of blacks, however, remained desperately poor and at the bottom of the social structure, whether as plantation workers or peasant farmers in the rural areas, or as dwellers in the fast-growing urban slums of Kingston and Montego Bay, doing low-paying or odd jobs to eke out a living.[23]

The growth of the peasantry – on public and private lands, occupied legally and illegally – was phenomenal during the first four decades after emancipation. But since most of the flatter, low-lying and fertile arable land was already in the hands of the sugar plantations, a significant measure of this peasant development took the form of migration to and settlement in the mountainous interior of the island.[24] Much of this terrain, characterized by steep, forested hill slopes and deep ravines, was very difficult at the best of times and, although the crown colony administrations after 1866 made some effort to develop interior roadways and bridges,[25] large parts of the hinterland remained relatively isolated from "civilized" society well beyond the First World War. This not only affected the ability of these inland settlers to market their produce, but also served to confine them to a more pristine form of peasant life (with all the attendant social "dangers" of that, not least of all a probable "relapse into barbarism"), and insulated them from many of the "progressive" social and cultural developments taking place in the urban centres.

Satchell notes, however, that the peasantry began to stagnate after 1880 as the plantation sector, in decline since emancipation, was revived. This revival, ironically, began precisely when the cane sugar economy entered perhaps its most prolonged global depression of the nineteenth century, as subsidized beet sugar produced in Europe flooded the world market and reduced prices, and the McKinley tariff curtailed access for West Indian sugar to the American market. The impetus to the Jamaican plantation sector came instead from the fruit trade to the United States, particularly in bananas and, to a lesser extent, citrus. This led to new investment by local merchants and professionals with capital to purchase abandoned sugar estates, and by American interests, most notably Captain Lorenzo D. Baker and his Boston Fruit Company (later the United Fruit Company). The growing profitability of banana cultivation also encouraged some traditional sugar planters to convert part or all of their sugar lands into bananas. Satchell argues that these developments made it much more difficult for peasants and small farmers to purchase either public or private land after 1880; as a result of this, as well as the fragmentation of their existing holdings and poor agricultural practices, the black peasantry began to stagnate by the turn of the century.[26]

That process, according to Holt, intensified in the early twentieth century. This was particularly so after the First World War, when the sugar economy itself regained some of its old vigour because of higher prices following war damage to the European beet industry and a fundamental reorganization (via amalgamation and mechanization) of the surviving Jamaican sugar plantations. Notwithstanding a favourable change in government policy towards the peasant sector from the mid-1890s, these developments gradually forced many peasants to become a rural proletariat working once more on the plantations for wages, or migrants to Kingston, Montego Bay and overseas (Panama, Costa Rica, Cuba, the United States).[27]

Many of those who moved to the two major urban centres ended up in slums where housing and living conditions were often atrocious, sanitation poor or nonexistent, and disease rampant, while their dreams of high-paying jobs, a better way of life, and social mobility were quickly dashed. There was instead rising un- and underemployment, malnutrition, crime and violence, and prostitution, as people crowded together in squalor in substandard tenement yards. Most of the men were doing odd jobs to survive: as semi-skilled artisans, labourers, porters, stevedores and gardeners; the women were more often than not coal-women, street and market vendors, brick-breakers or prostitutes. The "lucky" ones were domestic servants.[28]

Notwithstanding the fact that the vast majority of black Jamaicans remained at the bottom of the social hierarchy at the end of the nineteenth century, that a small number of educated ones were able to break down the barriers of race and colour that had characterized Jamaican society ever since the days of slavery meant that new criteria were needed to maintain class distinctions. Hence, "culture" increasingly became an important determinant of social status in Jamaica. Culture, however, meant British-derived cultural attributes, and those who came closest to emulating them were accorded the highest social status. Culture, therefore, supplemented race and colour in determining one's social position by the late nineteenth century, and a premium was placed on the acquisition of the "appropriate" cultural characteristics: speech (the "queen's/king's English", not Jamaican creole); Western/British-style dress; Christian beliefs and practices; legal, monogamous marriage and the nuclear family; British customs, ideas, values and morals, sports and entertainments, arts and music, furnishings, societies and associations, and so forth.

In late-nineteenth- and early-twentieth-century Jamaica, however, the boundaries of race/colour and culture were not coterminous. While most upper- and middle-class whites strove to emulate their British cousins culturally, and could legitimately be considered the "cultural elites" of Jamaica (in keeping with the exalted status accorded to British culture), some could also be quite "vulgar". On the other hand, many socially aspiring coloureds and blacks did their utmost to acquire the essentials of British culture, to qualify themselves for the social respectability and mobility they so desperately craved in colonial society. As Bryan has observed, "in cultural terms they cannot, at the upper level, be distinguished from whites".[29] Thus, notwithstanding their (upper) middle-class *social* status, these anglophile coloureds and blacks could legitimately be considered part of the cultural elites as well, for they shared the same cultural attributes, and tried (as far as economic resources permitted) to engage in the same cultural pursuits, as upper- and middle-class whites (theatre, opera, music, literature, sports and games, religion, and so forth). They literally spoke the same language as the white social elites. Indeed, as Bridget Brereton observes for Trinidad, although they were not part of the ruling class, these middle-class coloureds and blacks placed enormous emphasis on British culture "because [with few notable exceptions] they had no other valuable or valued possession to hold on to. They were not wealthy. They owned few businesses and no large ones. With some exceptions, they were not landowners and no large ones."[30]

At the other end of the cultural spectrum was the mass of working-class blacks, some coloureds, a few poor whites and, as the immigration schemes expanded, Indian and Chinese "heathens" too, all of whom were collectively considered coarse and vulgar, loud and lewd: in a word, "uncultured". When one adds to these the African-derived "superstitions" of the majority black working and peasant classes, it was translated to mean "barbarism". This was what the missionaries had been fighting ever since the last days of slavery. It was against this that a new, concerted thrust would be launched after the Morant Bay debacle, no longer only by the churches and the schools under their control, but joined by the state under crown rule, the colonial press, and public opinion formed by those "cultured" whites and coloureds, and later by a few black *evolués* too, who comprised the middle and upper echelons of Jamaican society. It is this loose coalition of culturally anglophile interests that are referred to throughout this book as the cultural elites. Their boundaries were much wider than those of the upper class – the social elites.

These cultural elite interests considered all forms of non-Western cultural expression as signs of uncivilized behaviour, and thus as social problems that had to be eradicated. They therefore devised new strategies, policies and propaganda methods after Morant Bay with a view to standardizing Jamaican cultural norms in accordance with their ideals. This would intensify the struggle for the cultural heart and soul of Jamaica. It is this renewed thrust to civilize Jamaica, and the cultural policies, imperial ideologies and Victorian moral codes that accompanied it in the late nineteenth and early twentieth centuries, that this book will examine and analyse, centring on those areas of Jamaican cultural life deemed particularly problematic by the cultural elites: belief systems, sex, marriage and family life, morality, and social behaviour.

Chapter 2

Afro-Creole Belief System I
Obeah, Duppies and Other "Dark Superstitions"

THE VAST MAJORITY OF BLACK AND coloured Jamaicans had a functional cultural system rooted in Africa and reshaped (creolized) on the slave plantations, which also had an influence on the white population. It encompassed their entire world view. In the minds of those who feared "black power", however, these retained cultural beliefs and practices, linked with the "darkness" of Africa and thus deemed inherently barbaric, had to be eradicated if Jamaica was ever to become a civilized society by their definition.

The Afro-creole belief system was the embodiment of the cultural mind of the Jamaican people. The very foundation of the Afro-Jamaican world view, it was integral to the process of rationalizing and ordering their lives, both spiritually and materially. Like its West African antecedent cosmology, it made no distinction between the secular and the sacred, but rather formed an intricately interwoven mosaic embracing all aspects of Afro-Jamaican life. Vilifying it as superstition, paganism and savagery, therefore, was a direct attack on the psyche of its adherents. This is precisely what the missionaries and other Victorian reformers did in the nineteenth and early twentieth centuries in their attempts to eradicate Afro-creole beliefs and practices, or at least to limit their allegedly baneful influence. This was a quest to control the minds of the people, for whither the mind, so went the body. For analytical purposes, although the belief system of Afro-Jamaicans formed one indistinguishable, integrated whole, we have divided our examination of it into two chapters.

Obeah

In many ways, the fight against the belief in and practice of obeah came to symbolize the focus of the thrust to "civilize" Jamaica. By the late nineteenth century obeah – perhaps best defined as witchcraft, magic and sorcery – had been a part of the Caribbean cultural landscape for centuries. As part of the culture that the Africans had been able to transport across the Middle Passage, the complicated beliefs – which included ideas about the power of the ancestors, spirits, benevolence and malevolence, and the possibility of explaining and controlling life's circumstances – were an important part of the daily lives of the people. Belief in and fear of the supernatural powers of obeah practitioners continued to exercise a powerful influence over the minds of the majority of Afro–West Indians after emancipation. The practitioners had been long been revered for their expertise and dextrous use of herbal poisons, and not least for their ability to manipulate the spirits for good or bad. Moreover, obeah practitioners could also use their enormous influence in the Afro-creole cultural complex for para-political purposes. In Guyana, for instance, they had been credited with maintaining the solidarity of two colony-wide labour strikes by the ex-slaves against wage cuts in 1842 and 1848.[1] Breaking the influence of the obeah practitioner was thus vital to gaining control over the minds of the black people.

Monica Schuler observes that in traditional African belief systems, people who prospered in a world where resources were limited were suspected of doing so at the community's expense, by practising magic or sorcery – by manipulating malevolent forces in the universe against others. Thus, the ills of individuals and of society at large were believed to be caused by sorcery,[2] in Jamaica by obeah. According to Mary Turner, obeah was believed to make use of charms that protected both individuals and property; it functioned as a means of divination and was controlled by obeah practitioners.[3]

In October 1904, with interest growing in the subject, the *Gleaner* (Jamaica's leading newspaper, which generally represented white elite opinion) attempted to explain the origins of obeah, linking it to the belief systems of West Africa. The newspaper's explanation delineated four classes of gods among the West Africans, three of which spawned orders of priests and priestesses. It was the fourth, the lowest class, which could be accessed by the layman who was connected to obeah. "A private individual may procure for himself the service of one these minor gods, but in doing so is attended with grave risks. For these gods are supposed to be subordinate to one of the most malicious and terrible deities [a *suhman*] worshipped on the West Coast of Africa, and their principal purpose is to work evil." With the discouragement of all classes of gods in the Caribbean during slavery, it was the fourth pantheon that survived underground. And it was here that the obeah(wo)men made their mark.4

According to American Jesuit anthropologist Joseph John Williams, who did his research during the 1920s, Jamaican obeah has its roots in Asante witchcraft – *obayifo*. But whereas the Asante made important distinctions between the herbalists (*sumankwafo*) and those who practised witchcraft (*obayifo*), these distinctions were lost in Jamaica because African religion was outlawed. The obeah practitioners, however, thrived in secrecy that was guaranteed by the universal fear generated by their expert use of poisons. And even though just before and after emancipation they were challenged by the Myalists (see chapter 3), they disguised themselves and remained very influential by adopting some of the Myalists' anti-obeah and healing practices. So the same person who "set" obeah often also removed it.5

The account of "the craft" by Martha Beckwith, another American anthropologist who conducted her research in Jamaica just after the First World War, pointed to its function in the community. It was used, she said, "to cope successfully with the shadow world", a world where many did not see a clear distinction between the sacred and the profane, between spirit and flesh. The easy accessibility to the lower deities meant that anyone could "set" obeah for another, once the proper rituals were followed, but almost always an obeah(wo)man had to be sought to set it properly and either an obeah(wo)man or Myal(wo)man had to remove it. It was, according to Beckwith, the unique power of the obeah(wo)men to control the spirit world which was the source of their extraordinary influence in the community.6

The Obeah Practitioner

As in other parts of the Caribbean, the person of the obeah(wo)man attracted hostile attention from many elite observers.7 Some commentators perpetuated stereotypes, conflating the alleged evil with the physical appearance of the practitioner. According to Thomas Banbury, one of a small number of black and coloured Anglican clergymen in the late nineteenth century, "he is the agent incarnate of Satan . . . the embodiment of all that is wicked, immoral and deceptious." He was described as sinister, with a slouching gait; he seldom looked anyone in the face, was of a dirty appearance and had a sore foot.8

Magistrate Charles Rampini considered the obeah(wo)man to be part of the guild or fraternity of crime:

> Hardly a criminal trial occurs in the colony in which he is not implicated in one way or another. His influence over the country people is unbounded. He is the prophet, priest, and king of his district. . . .
>
> As an outward and visible sign of his power the obeah man sometimes carries about with him a long staff or wand, with twisted serpents or the rude likeness of a human head carved round the handle. He has his cabalistic book, too, full of strange characters, which he pretends to consult in the exercise of his calling. . . . With a dirty handkerchief bound tightly round his forehead and his small, bright, cunning eyes peering out from underneath it.

There are no equivalent descriptions of obeahwomen, but they and their male counterparts struck fear in the hearts of many people.[9] Obeah(wo)men were allegedly "dangerous characters", disturbers of the peace of the community, obstacles to social progress: "in a word, they demoralize a community and should be punished when legitimately caught in their nefarious practice".[10]

The direct connection between Africa and the practice of obeah was quite firm in many minds. As elsewhere in the Caribbean, those who were African, such as those "liberated" from the slave ships of the mid-nineteenth century or imported as indentured labourers directly from West Africa, could command more respect in this spirit world of beliefs since their association with the source of power was so clear. In an 1892 account by Marianne North, a white visitor, "two African niggers" tried to sell her some obeah or charmsticks. They had been "liberated" by the English from a Spanish ship that was bound for Cuba, and each made a living of twelve shillings per week by carving these sticks for charms.[11]

While the majority of the practitioners seem to have come from among the most marginal people in Jamaican society – poor, black, dispossessed – there were a few instances where practitioners emerged from elsewhere. This was brought home in stark fashion in September 1893 when David Elisha Bates was charged in the Morant Bay Court with practising obeah. The case attracted a great deal of excitement "on account of the position once occupied by the accused; he was once schoolmaster and local preacher and at the time of his arrest was assistant Inspector of Poor for the eastern division of the parish, and because he is a light colored brown man, a *rara avis* among the brethren". Bates was accused of claiming to solve the problems of Grace Kelly, who said she was being stoned by duppies (spirits).[12] Kelly explained how she had sought help from a Haitian woman in Kingston who was unable to stop the stoning, whereupon Bates, who had previously sought to have a relationship with her, offered his services at a charge of three pounds. With a "stock in trade" that included rice, rum, two yards of white calico and a cock (rooster), as well as a number of white plates, Bates proceeded, in the full view of several witnesses, to work the obeah. The newspaper gave a great deal of detail on how this was done, including killing the cock, catching its blood and encouraging Kelly to consume the blood (which she refused to do), cooking the meat, consuming it (without "cracking the bones"), undressing Kelly, "boxing" her and passing her over an open flame. Bates was found guilty and sentenced to twelve months with hard labour in the General Penitentiary, as well as thirty lashes (fifteen at the beginning of his sentence and fifteen in the last month of his incarceration).[13] That this middle-class man was caught indulging in such "degrading" practices must have brought great discomfort to those who championed the civilizing mission, particularly since he had been both a schoolmaster and a preacher, occupations closely tied to that mission.

Obeah Paraphernalia

Some writers saw obeah as part of a general set of activities, referred to as "the black art", that included "revivalism, obeahism (proper), myalism and bush-doctoring" (see chapter 3). "Obeahism" in Jamaica, as in Guyana, made use of a wide range of paraphernalia:

> It consists of snakes, lizards, weeds, teeth, skulls, hair, etc. After mixing the rum with some of his charms he drinks the decoction, while he mutters certain unintelligible words. The fowl (generally a white one) is killed and after a great deal of juggling the client is given to understand that the charm has "worked" satisfactorily, and his desires, whether they be for death of an enemy, the love of a girl, the possession of riches or anything else, will be attained.[14]

Since the materials of obeah were well known by many, there was a fear of anything which might be connected to obeah:

> An egg seen on the road or anywhere would not be touched. People would not walk near it. Even money would not be picked up by the superstitious. There is a notion that it was used by the obeahman in the washing of some diseased person and cast in the road to transfer the distemper to anyone taking it up. . . . [The egg] is considered an *embodiment* of obeah. There are very few of the people who would have the courage to steal eggs even out of the nest.[15]

So when Jane Patterson was observed burying an egg in Smith's Village in 1893, she was accosted by another resident of the area. She told him that she was trying to gain some luck, since she had been very unfortunate in business. For her trouble, Patterson was sentenced to six months in jail.[16]

Of course, with the paraphernalia of the art being made up of more or less ordinary items that could be acquired by almost anyone, obeah could be widely practised, and since some basic rituals were known well enough across the community, it sometimes did not require a specialist. Thus, ordinary people could take it upon themselves to set obeah against their enemies.

Services Provided

Obeah was used for a wide range of purposes. People believed that the obeah(wo)man, as magician, could "work" on a coin so that it could "draw" away money; if such a coin was put among other money, that coin would have "the power of extracting the other moneys into his pocket".[17] Obeah practitioners sometimes mirrored the Myalists as "duppy catchers" (see chapter 3). In 1881, for instance, great excitement was generated in Princess Street, Kingston, where spirits had "interfered" with a young man and a lady, both of whom had fallen into fits. An obeahman who was called in attempted to seal the duppies in a bottle, but they escaped. As the crowd gathered over several nights, watching for the duppies, the police had a difficult task in trying to clear the streets.[18]

The obeah(wo)man was also a healer of illnesses believed to be caused by spirits: "All the herbs used to 'drive duppy' are so used because of the relation believed to exist between them and the activities of human life." According to the district medical officer for St Mary in 1911, because the peasantry believed that fevers were due to evil spirits, they sought to get rid of them by employing obeah(wo)men who exorcized the fever with the fumes of burning cloth. Other forms of treatment included beating the patient with wet calico and ramming the abdomen with clenched fists, in order to expel whatever spirit was the cause of the illness.[19]

Obeah was also reputedly worked by winding up "materials" with thread, or placing them in a vial or in the ground. Certain words were spoken that converted the materials into the elements of obeah, which were then given to the applicant for burial in the yard of the intended victim; these magically entered the victim's body, where they wreaked havoc. Another important service of the obeah(wo)man was to influence one person's mind to another's advantage. Called "turning his eyes" ("tun him yeye"), it was allegedly used primarily by females to prevent their sweethearts, paramours or husbands from leaving them for other women. Alternatively, a woman might use it to secure a man who did not normally pay her any attention. In some cases, the obeah(wo)man gave love potions – called "tempting powder" and described as "a very nauseous draught" that was sometimes dangerous.[20] But there were other methods. For instance, in 1899 Samuel Leslie was employed by Edmund Graham to restore the affection of his former love, Agnes Beckford. With sixpence worth of proof rum, a reel of black thread (worth one and a half pence), withes, and a plait of her hair, Leslie worked to "tie" Beckford to Graham.[21]

Obeah practitioners also provided assistance in the judicial system. Litigants often hired both lawyers and obeah(wo)men. The latter sometimes "worked" the case from afar, but at times they accompanied their clients to court "to stop the prosecutor's mouth", "to control the witnesses' words", and to influence the judge and jury. In 1909 Agnes Francis, who was brought up on charges of larceny in the Kingston Court, allegedly on the advice of "a diminutive old man in a peculiar uniform" who was observing the court's proceedings, "sprinkled the judge's desk with some yellow powder" composed of a combination of "assofoetida, camphor, oil of rignum and human hair", in the hope of influencing his decision.[22]

In the largely agricultural communities of the rural areas, the obeah(wo)man had an important role in preventing praedial larceny. According to British anthropologist Bessie Pullen-Burry, who did her research just after the turn of the twentieth century, in order to prevent midnight raids upon their "plantain and cocoa patches and to check the besetting sin of theft", farmers employed one of the "rascals" to "mutter some mystic formula in the orchard requiring his protection". Bottles purportedly containing salt water, a dead cockroach or two and a little washing blue were hung on the branches of the trees, after which "only the most hardened sceptic of a black man would dare approach the place by night, otherwise he may be 'stoned by duppies' or 'swell up and burst,' or be killed by ferocious snakes let loose by the Obi-man". Mrs T.B. Butcher, an English visitor, claimed that two sticks crossed or a black bottle hung from a tree was enough to protect one's property from interference. Not only small peasant farmers made use of this expertise, but whites as well, although some of them made the symbols of obeah themselves, well aware as they were that the population, including their peers, had great respect for the craft.[23]

In the universe of obeah, said the black middle-class newspaper the *Jamaica Advocate,* there was an attempt to control the deities of everyday life in such a way that luck might come to the devotees, and it might be in their power to appoint ill-luck to anyone whose progress they desired to impede. The obeah(wo)man, it was believed, could help to give success in business, to make provision grounds yield in abundance and to cause crops to find a ready sale.[24]

Obeah could also be used maliciously by an unfriendly party to induce insanity or unsociable behaviour. In October 1891 Henrietta Davis's husband told the police court that she had been made "mad" by an old African man who lived in the yard with them, and who had been instructed to do so by the landlord after a quarrel with Henrietta. According to Banbury, "a man may kill himself, steal, commit murder, rape etc. when under an *obeah spell*". It has the effect of "making him turn [good] for nothing", and "a vagabond".[25]

The obeah was usually set at night. When the victims awakened to see the "dreaded insignia" of the obeah(wo)man and realized that obeah was being worked against them, they often gave up. The bottle with the turkey's or cock's feather stuck into it, accompanied by parrots' beaks, drops of blood, coffin nails and empty eggshells were the indicators that one was the target of the obeah(wo)man. Reverend Warrand Carlile claimed that upon discovering the paraphernalia of obeah, a "perfect panic" usually ensued, and many persons allegedly became ill and even died of mere fright.[26]

Beckwith noted that it was usually for purposes of "revenge" that the obeah(wo)man's skills were most sought: "At this Obeah Man's yard there may be three flags – white, red, and black. The client chooses the white one if he wishes merely to 'turn down somebody, can't come to nothing', the red one for blood, the black for murder. He bargains for his price and lays down his money." The obeah(wo)man then devised a plan to execute on the client's behalf. He or she might decide to "put a shadow", which meant that a shadow or duppy was put to work: "To secure the duppy you should go to a graveyard at night and visit the grave of some friend or some member of your family, preferably your mother. Take an egg, rice, and rum, and mash the egg at the grave. The duppy will come up and feed upon the egg and the food which you bring; thus you pay him to help you." The practitioner might, instead, choose to use poisonous herbs to complete the task. According to Banbury, it was in the uses of poisons that the obeah(wo)man was most feared: "He is known to make a . . . decoction of these poisons and soak the undergarments of people taken to him, which when taken back, and put on by the unsuspecting owner, the poison is absorbed along with the perspiration, and engender some directed disease in the system."[27]

The wide range of services offered by obeah(wo)men spoke to the attempt by the people to explain, control and direct their worlds. From encouraging prosperity, preventing larceny, curing illnesses and ensuring love affairs, to catching shadows and harming enemies, obeah practitioners answered many of the needs of ordinary Jamaicans as they went about their daily lives. In a universe that did not recognize any real divisions between the spiritual and the material worlds, the spiritual cause of material conditions was easy to ascertain. Attempts to right wrongs, to direct fortunes and to live in relative health and prosperity led many Jamaicans to seek expert assistance. Obeah(wo)men were essential operators in the quest for equilibrium and improvement among the Jamaican people.

Obeah Literature

In the 1890s the fame of the workers of obeah was given an immense boost when "obeah literature" began to circulate in the community. All over the island there were tracts relating to John Nugent's activities that declared that among his workings, he had killed Robert Campbell (because Campbell had cut a bunch of plantains on Nugent's father's plantation) as well as George Reid (at the behest of George Williamson), while James Bennet paid him "to put a frog in Eliza Blake's belly and make her carry it in her womb for two years". The tract dedicated to George Elleth referred to his own genealogy; he was "a [sic] African, his father was a [sic] Obeah man, his Grand Father the greatest obeah man in his country", and it claimed that he had killed 241 men and injured 655 others during his forty-two years' practice in the "art".[28]

The workings of Old Mother Austin, who called herself "Fire Rush" and operated out of Llandewy, also caught the public's attention. The tract claiming to capture her confession said that she had killed twenty-five babies as well as a number of men and women, and that she had learned her trade by "giving her body" to several male practitioners, including John Nugent who was 'paid' "four times" for his expertise. The tract entitled "Death and Confession of Daniel Hart", as well as those detailing the confessions of Hannah Grant (alias Mrs Bywater) and Richard Daly, captured the imagination of the Jamaican public, and the tracts sold quickly and well.[29]

The *Gleaner* pressed for a law to control the printing and selling of these publications and for the substitution of a purer literature in their stead.[30] In particular, the Elleth pamphlet drew a response from Reverend T.P. Russell stating that these pamphlets – purporting to give an account of the career of an obeahman who had allegedly worked for shopkeepers, cake sellers, butchers and planters, some of whom were church members – were dangerous. He warned,

> This is not a solitary instance of the sale of these tracts; in all parts of the Island similar low-class publications are disposed of from time to time and are eagerly bought up and read by the literate, who retail the particulars to the less intelligent who, again, discuss the matter among themselves. The statements they contain are believed in, no matter how absurd they are, and serve only to intensify the superstition already too rampant among the lower classes.[31]

When tracts with the confessions of Dennis Spaulding of Kingston were sold, they were found to contain the names of some "decent" persons. David P. Mendes of Spanish Town was alarmed that such obeah literature was readily available on the streets, resulting in "respectable citizens being the butt and target of the ignorant and lower classes who received what was stated therein as gospel truth". He too urged the Legislative Council to pass a law to imprison the printers of such literature. The *Gleaner* was further aghast, in 1894, when a legal technicality obliged the governor to release several convicted obeahmen from prison, for it seemed to send the wrong message to the people: that His Excellency was afraid of obeah's power, or that he was himself a believer in the craft. In 1898, however, a law was passed (No. 5) that prohibited the composition, publication and distribution of obeah pamphlets, and so effective was its enforcement that a decade later all the revelations and confessions by obeah(wo)men had disappeared.[32]

Obeah literature recorded the exploits of obeah practitioners for Jamaicans who had an interest in these things. And since the records were produced in the language of the elite and in a medium (the printed word) that the elite promoted as almost sacrosanct, the influence of the literature was bound to be great. As people *read* (by the 1890s over half the population above age five was officially listed as literate) about the confessions of those who operated in the nether world, not only did these activities seem more real (than if they had simply been relayed orally, especially since important details were included), but they explained things that the people may have wondered about, and made the services offered by the obeah practitioners appear more legitimate.

Elite and Christian Believers

It is clear from the evidence that it was not only the poor, black, uneducated masses who believed in obeah. In 1872 the coloured middle-class newspaper, the *Morning Journal*, asserted that "we may venture to affirm that were the obeah practitioners able to write, and were in the habit of keeping books, shewing their dealings with their clients, some revelations would be made that would rather startle the examiners in the names and positions in life of some of the persons implicated". Likewise, Banbury declared that "we do not wish to leave the impression . . . that it is only the black people of the country that have faith in [obeah] . . . the majority of the coloured people also come under the category of the superstitious, and even some of the white people are not exempted".[33]

Some devout members of the Christian denominations were also obeah believers. Even some church elders and leaders, said the *Gleaner*, were not free from "the power of the evil"; this was later confirmed by the obeah(wo)men's own "confessions". The missionaries were especially "pained" when a "spirit filled man backslides into these things".[34] In 1898 S.H. Brown of Portland claimed that it was no uncommon thing for members of Christian churches to be proven guilty of consulting the obeahman, by whose incantations and devices they sought to obtain "either prosperity in this world's goods, the hurt of their fellow creatures, the highest positions in the church locally, or to exercise a dominant influence over the local church and over those who rule it, or to effect a cure for themselves, their friends or relatives in trivial or aggravated ailments".[35] Obeah, in other words, pervaded the aisles of the church.

The Quakers, one of the newer missionary bodies (with headquarters in Ohio, United States), expressed grave concern at the apparent ease with which people moved between what these missionaries saw as competing systems of belief. A report in 1899 spoke of a female church member in good standing who fell ill a few months after her wedding. Believing that her husband's former sweetheart had "put duppy pon her", she paid an obeahman to remove the duppy, but to no avail. The community then believed that the vengeance of the jilted love was to be found in an alligator that was sent to torment her:

> The ugly feature of this is that these people are fairly intelligent and have for years been members in good standing in a certain denomination. We have sometimes to deal with cases of this kind in our own church. Yet, in spite of ridicule from those

who know better, denouncement from the pulpit, and the penalty of loss of church membership for the practice of such things, it is the *few* [our emphasis] only who triumph through Christ to the putting away of a belief in the supernatural power of the obeah man.[36]

The problem, as far as "Truth" was concerned, was that the "dark night of superstition is mixed with the Gospel and reigns in many of our Churches among men who hold great positions".[37]

Throughout the period the missionaries continued to comment on the persistence of the belief in obeah: "Superstition still lingers in some parts of Jamaica and has wrought mischief in . . . our churches." In 1870 the United Brethren claimed that "the majority of the people in the Savanna . . . possess more superstition than religion", so that even their anxiety to baptize their children was about securing "protection" from obeah. The Wesleyan Methodists lamented in 1907 that "hereditary forms of African superstition" were just as strong as ever. This "relic of heathen barbarism", according to the Presbyterians in 1912, had a very strong hold on the people. In 1918 the Quakers' exasperation could be heard in Alma Swift's lament: "Some of the people do not understand why they are so broken down financially and their minds revert to the old African superstition that it is the work of man hindering them and they consult the Obeah man – thus giving him the only pittance they have and bringing again a reign of darkness." The Quakers thus had to wage "war on Superstition, intemperance, and immorality in the name of the Master with some results". In 1920 they told of the experiences of "[o]ne man just recovering from malaria fever [who] was in a weak condition and had pain in the back of his head and back. . . . The community in which he lived was full of Obeahism. They talked all the time in this man's hearing that it was his mother-in-law's ghost, duppy, on his back – till the man became so alarmed and being weak – went insane."[38] There was also the case in 1890 of a man and wife, communicants and office bearers in the Moravian Church, who had lived together many years and raised eleven children. They separated and the wife, desiring to get the husband permanently out of the way, engaged an obeahman to kill him. However, the scheme came to light and the two were arraigned before the law and tried. They were freed and the matter hushed up, after which the husband left the house and moved to another parish, leaving all his property behind. The wife celebrated her victory with a great dance in her yard on the night after Christmas. Obeah, said the Moravians, was powerful in the community and "a great deal of money that ought to go to the church goes into this channel".[39]

The ability to move between competing belief systems – as the missionaries regarded them – or along a spiritual continuum – in the view of the people – gave to the latter a range of answers for the business of life. While the Christian church encouraged absolute reliance on prayer and faith (which many persons endorsed), obeah provided a means of activism that was also very appealing. Since everybody "knew" that evil spirits operated across the world, and that they needed to be controlled and even "cast out" (as in biblical times),[40] obeah provided access to immediate solutions to problems. This did not mean that many of the persons who believed in the power of obeah did not also believe in the power of God; those in the church who believed in both systems were opening a wider range of possibilities that addressed their concerns.

The Prevalence of the "Scourge" of Obeah

It seemed to some that obeah was on the increase towards the turn of the century, and the proliferation of obeah laws between 1892 and 1903 was reflective of that perception among the lawmakers (see below). There appeared to be considerable evidence that its influence was growing all over the island, particularly from the 1890s onwards.[41] In 1894 "Hypothesis" claimed that obeah practice had reached levels since the beginning of 1893 that had never been seen before in the history of the island. In St Elizabeth, in particular, "there are hundreds [of obeahmen] who are practising daily the Black Art". S.H. Brown claimed the same distinction for Clarendon and Portland, where "the Black Art is the favourite resort of the majority of the peasantry", as each district had its "four-eyed man" or "runkuss doctor" (see chapter 3). The middle-class *Jamaica Times* opined in 1900 that "there can be no healthy national growth and progress when a cankerworm . . . obeahism . . . is vigorously eating out the very vitals of Jamaican Society".[42]

At the same time there were some conflicting reports, suggesting that obeah might not in fact have increased much after 1865. In 1868 the *Morning Journal* expressed concern lest newspapers fall into a state of "monomania about obeah" by their reports "feign[ing] lest it be believed that obeah is rampant in Jamaica". The apprehension of two obeahmen ought not, in its view, to have caused much excitement since "two obeahmen no more prove the wide prevalence of obeah practices, than do two swallows make a summer".[43] One generation later the *Jamaica Advocate* more cautiously declared that "in spite of the great revival of what is called Obeahism, in spite of Bedwardism, in the face of the present wave of revivalism [see chapter 3] . . . the people of Jamaica are *not* retrograding; on the contrary, they are advancing". Indeed, "No one who has read anything of the superstitious, heathenish practices of one hundred years ago, will dream of saying that we have not advanced on them to-day."[44]

Some people even perceived a decline; Pullen-Burry thought that was due to the spread of "enlightenment and education". For W.P. Livingstone, editor of the *Gleaner* in the late 1890s, in addition to the influence of Christianity there was an increasing sense of shame among the Jamaican people at being associated with obeah beliefs: "The negro is very sensitive to the ridicule of the white, and he was beginning to feel himself morally naked, and to be ashamed. Obeahism was less openly acknowledged and practised and larger numbers of obeah men were being brought to punishment. The influence of Christianity was freely mingling with and modifying the old beliefs."[45] Given the proliferation of reports to the contrary, however, these overtly optimistic images smack of collective denial and self-delusion on the part of some cultural elites. If the belief in and practice of obeah were indeed declining, why would the lawmakers have felt obliged to pass several pieces of anti-obeah legislation in the last decade of the nineteenth century?

Controlling Obeah

As in other British colonies in the region, after emancipation the local authorities responded to the practice of obeah (and Myal) by passing various laws that imposed heavy fines, imprisonment and flogging on those convicted of the offence.[46] Act 19 Victoria c.30 (1856) made obeah- and Myalmen liable to twelve months' imprisonment with hard labour and seventy-eight lashes. Act 21 Victoria c.24 (1857) made anyone who consulted an obeah- or Myalman liable to a fine of forty shillings or thirty days' imprisonment without hard labour. "The Obeah and Myalism Acts Amendment Law" (No. 28) of 1892 gave clear power to the resident magistrates' courts to try obeah cases, where the abolished district courts had tried many of these cases previously. With respect to punishment, the law reduced the period of imprisonment to six months and, under instruction from the Colonial Office, the maximum number of lashes was halved to thirty-nine "on the bare back with a cat-of-nine tails". Women, however, were exempted from flogging. In 1893 this was reduced further to thirty-six lashes for persons over sixteen years old, and eighteen lashes if under sixteen years, thus bringing it in line with the general flogging law for other offences.[47]

The Obeah Law (No. 5) of 1898 repealed all others in an attempt to simplify what was described as a "technical and somewhat involved" process that debilitated the police in their attempts to secure convictions. In addition, as already indicated, the composition, publication and distribution of obeah pamphlets, which had caused a "good deal of mischief . . . amongst the more ignorant black population", were placed in the same category as publishing obscene works – that is, punishable by a fine of twenty pounds or six months' imprisonment with hard labour. The law defined a person practising obeah as "any person who, to effect any fraudulent or unlawful purpose, or for gain, or for the purpose of frightening any person, uses, or pretends to use any occult means, or pretends to possess any supernatural power or knowledge". The penalty for those who consulted obeah practitioners was also significantly raised, to a fine of fifty pounds or twelve months' imprisonment with hard labour. The prison term for practising obeah was increased to twelve months with hard labour, although the flogging penalty was reduced. Those who were sixteen or older were liable to receive eighteen lashes; those under sixteen years, twelve lashes; children between ten and twelve, six lashes; while those under ten, and women, were not to be flogged.[48]

The problem of definition was carried over into the 1899 amendment law (No. 18), which made it sufficient in the charge to state that a person was practising obeah. This could include anyone, although it was felt by some that the law had street preachers in mind. Quite apart from innocent persons being taken before the courts, some people were concerned that the impression would be given that the scourge of obeah was more rampant than it actually was. This was considered undesirable especially if these reports reached foreign journals, for it would cast a shadow over Jamaica as an uncivilized island. The *Jamaica Advocate* opined that instead of spending time defining obeah, which by logic did not exist, the authorities would be much better off concentrating on the fraud that was being perpetrated by obeah practitioners and protecting people from the deceit.[49]

As further amended in 1903 (Law 8), the law provided that resident magistrates could order that persons convicted of obeah who had served twelve months with hard labour be subject to police supervision for seven years after their sentences ended. If they failed to report personally at the police station every month or changed address without notifying the authorities, they were liable to an additional two years' imprisonment with hard labour.[50]

With the laws in place, the authorities used the police, the courts, jails and the cat-o'-nine tails to try to rid the society of the "scourge of obeah". The public were also encouraged to assist the police in apprehending obeah practitioners. Thus, in 1894 the *Gleaner* reported that "the people themselves are lending willing aid in securing the capture of these miscreants animated by a desire to free their country from so discreditable a superstition". Several reports of such collaboration between citizens and police were reported.[51] For instance, Margaret Gordon of Regent Street, Hannah Town, said to be an obeahwoman of some repute, was arrested in March 1901. Charles Campbell had visited her and related a long story about his misfortunes and how much he needed her help. She had agreed to fix the situation for eight shillings, had rubbed his skin with some ointment and given him a parcel that contained "luck". When Campbell returned to pay his fee, the police were with him; they rushed in and arrested Gordon, carting her off to the Sutton Street police station.[52] In 1907 Francis Harmit, "a one-armed man, lame, blind in one eye and beginning to get gray", was charged with practising obeah when he offered to help James Ramsay to get two hundred pounds at King's House (the governor's residence). Ramsay returned with police sleuths, who participated in the rituals. Harmit produced a set of playing cards and gave instructions that would secure a lucrative job offer: "Put nickol seeds in your mouth and don't move your eyes from the gentleman till he turns away. Take these carbolic balls and bury them right and left of King's House Gate." After various oils had been produced and both Ramsay and Detective Campbell had paid, they were assured of the success of the process. Harmit was promptly arrested.[53]

The courts also became increasingly active with obeah cases. In 1865 a "notorious character" named William Cunningham was sentenced to hard labour for eighty days in Falmouth District Prison. In 1868 Alexander Martin was sentenced to three months' hard labour and warned that if charged again he would be liable to twelve months and seventy-eight lashes. In 1892 a sixty-year-old obeahman was sentenced to two months' imprisonment in Brown's Town, while in 1893 a man named Sterling was sentenced to ninety days with hard labour. In the same year Deggy was sentenced to eight months' hard labour and eighteen lashes; Shelley was captured at Moneague while practising obeah, tried at Ocho Rios, found guilty and sentenced to twelve months as well as eighteen lashes at the beginning of his sentence and eighteen more at its end. Noting that he was an old man, the *Gleaner* wondered if Shelley would survive the floggings.[54]

These floggings were accompanied by a certain perverse ceremony. When the preparations were put in place for his flogging in December 1893, Thomas Mason broke down and wept. He was marched out in the presence of prison officials, the prison surgeon and the wielder of the "cat", then, judged fit to undergo the punishment, was strapped down. On receiving the first three or four lashes he yelled loudly enough to be heard in adjoining houses, but after that, apart from wincing, he remained perfectly quiet. The surgeon checked after each lash to see if he could withstand the punishment, and at the end he was taken to the hospital. William Richards and his son were treated in like fashion. The father "bore his castigation courageously", although when the last lash had been administered he was so weak that he had to be taken to the hospital. His son, however, yelled as every lash was administered and frequently called on the doctor to have mercy; he too was conveyed to the hospital. This was in keeping with the administration's caution that "the greatest care" should be exercised that the prisoner was in a physical condition to bear the punishment without injury to health. In an unusual move in April 1899, the court in Savanna-la-Mar convicted James Murray to twelve months in the St Catherine District Prison and to twelve lashes with the cat-o'-nine tails. In this case, "the catting [was] to be inflicted on the premises of Ephraim Campbell, at Delve Land, the place where the offense was committed".[55]

Although the sentence applied against those found guilty of practising obeah usually included flogging, there were some instances when convicted

Table 2.1 Statistics of Floggings for Obeah, 1897–1906

Year	Cases	Total Lashes	Average Lashes
1897–1898	4	69	17.25
1900–1901	13	184	14.15
1901–1902	12	171	14.25
1903–1904	2	22	11.00
1905–1906	2	22	11.00

Sources: Returns of flogging sentences for obeah, enclosed in Hemming to Chamberlain, 12 April 1898, No. 140, CO 137/589; Hemming to Chamberlain, 21 October 1901, No. 620, CO 137/622; Hemming to Chamberlain, 29 April 1902, No. 210, CO 137/627; Hemming to Chamberlain, 21 July 1903, No. 417, CO 137/635; and Swettenham to Elgin, 29 May 1906, No. 262, CO 137/651.

persons were exempted, generally on account of old age or gender. Thus in 1894 James Smith, an old man "of respectable appearance", was sentenced to nineteen months' hard labour, but on account of his age no lashes were administered. In 1898 two old black men, aged seventy and eighty years respectively, were caught at Morgan's Bridge, Westmoreland, "when they were killing the white cock and mixing the rum". One was sentenced to five months, the other to six months, in the Hanover District Prison, but no lashes were ordered for either. In 1909 Samuel Garvey, who reputedly had practised obeah for over forty years and had twelve previous convictions (his first in 1872 and his last in 1907, when he got twelve months and eighteen lashes), was not imprisoned by Magistrate Richard Reece at the Porus Court because he was blind and frail, but he was expelled from the parish and instructed not to return.[56]

Flogging, however, became increasingly controversial by the turn of the century. Many officials and the upper- and middle-class cultural elites favoured it. In 1880 Inspector General of Police Hartwell stated that what was needed were "public floggings" that would "disabuse the minds of the poor people as to the powers of the Obeahman". Flogging, according to Livingstone, was appropriate because it was "a punishment greatly dreaded by the negroes and coloured class". In 1893 the *Gleaner* also argued that imprisonment was not enough and that the "rascality of the Obeahman is such that he is rightly singled out for a special kind of punishment". The newspaper thus argued that "a good licking has its place".[57]

But there were equally strong opinions against flogging. S.C. Morris stated that although three members of his own family had been poisoned by an obeah practitioner in 1887, he objected to "catting" on the principle that a beating only encouraged the obeahman to be more careful in the future in order to prevent discovery. Abraham Emerick held that the belief in obeah was so ingrained that even the drastic punishment of the lashes of the cat-o'-nine tails was not enough to prevent obeah from flourishing.[58] But increasingly the issue was one of civilization, and this posed a serious dilemma for elite society. Obeah might be considered uncivilized, but so too, by the turn of the century, was brutal flogging with the cat-o'-nine tails. W.F. Jones hit the nail on the head in 1909 when he said, "The practice of obeah is not by any means so heinous an offence as many other practices which exist around and about us and of which the law takes no cognizance[,] and civilisation and professing Christianity will ever stand condemned, so long as the Divine law of Brotherhood is allowed to be outraged without protest." The *Jamaica Times* endorsed this, arguing that it was an indication of the island's "degradation" that the lash was resorted to as punishment, and that since obeah amounted to an entanglement with "superstitious nonsense" and obtaining money under false pretences, it was foolish that the legislature could not see the anachronism in flogging: "Men used to burn old women for witchcraft once, to the glory of Heaven, and the good of the State. We smile now at their folly; or we sigh over their sin; but we lash the obeahman, and for what? He believes, poor fool, that he can do this and undo that by the manipulation of a white cock's blood, and rum and cow's horn. . . . We can never lash out superstition. We must displace it with knowledge."[59]

By 1909 even the *Gleaner* was seeing things differently, through the lens of "enlightened civilization". It referred to Richard Aiken, who had been convicted by the courts for practising obeah, served time in prison, been lashed, and yet upon his release had resumed his practice. Said the newspaper, "we should like to ask whether the lash is really a preventive in the majority of cases". Indeed,

> to lash a man until his back is a mass of bloody weals, until the skin swells and breaks and the instrument of torture becomes red with his blood, may be very excellent evidence of our civilization and Christianity, but is no testimony whatever to the intelligence we are so fond of thinking we possess. . . . we brutalise judge and executioner by making flogging a part of our means of correction.[60]

Colonial opinion, however, was way behind that of the metropolitan government. Ever since 1862 opinions within the Colonial Office had tended away from the continuation of flogging, on the grounds that the circumstances of Jamaica (that is, the attitude of the ruling class) made it likely that the punishment would be abused. Furthermore, since the foundation of obeah practices was considered to be "abject credulity", officials thought that to treat them so seriously with special and severe legislation did a great deal to *strengthen* the belief in them. Still, the Colonial Office allowed flogging to remain on the statute books as an "issue of domestic interest".[61] But thirty years later they insisted that the maximum number of lashes for obeah should be significantly reduced, continued to ask questions about its desirability, and required that future floggings should be closely monitored and reported on.[62]

In 1901 puisne judge Dr Charles Frederick Lumb stirred things up locally by arguing that while crime was not directly traceable to obeah, the practice was very dangerous to the peace and order of the island. But he was convinced that flogging was no remedy for the practice, that the culprits were generally old men, and that such an exceptional form of punishment applied to them might increase belief in their supernatural power. Flogging had had a long trial and it had not been an effective check, hence it should be abandoned.[63] But Governor Hemming claimed that Lumb's concerns were not shared by most people with experience in the West Indies, who saw obeah as "lamentable, dangerous [with] far reaching influence". Most agreed that flogging was the "only punishment which will deter obeahmen".[64]

In 1909 Lumb proposed that the stocks should be revived as a substitute for flogging. He argued that flogging had not proven to be an effective deterrent because many who had been charged, convicted and flogged were repeat offenders. Since there was no real fear of the "cat", he thought that the ridicule inherent in the stocks would be a better sort of punishment, especially since it would indicate to the public that the obeah practitioner had no power: "There is nothing that cuts deeper than ridicule; in England it cuts to the quick, in Jamaica it kills."[65] However, there was little enthusiasm among local officials for a revival of this "ancient form of punishment", and there was still some hesitance to end the flogging for fear that the repeal of the law and the removal of corporal punishment would have an undesired effect on the number of convictions for the offence.[66]

Local opinion remained divided on the issue.[67] However, in 1910 the magistrates agreed to refrain from issuing sentences that included floggings in order to test whether or not the discontinuance would have any effect on this crime.[68] By 1911 official local opinion seemed to be moving in greater harmony with their metropolitan bosses, in seeing obeah more as a sort of confidence trick than a real source of evil. Accordingly the severe punishments came under more scrutiny, and some people began to argue that the harshness of the penalty only served to magnify the office of the obeahman. Finally in 1919, in *Rex v. Bulgin,* it was settled that the mere possession of paraphernalia that might be used in obeah was not enough for prosecution.[69]

The attempts by the authorities to control the activities of obeah(wo)men spoke in large measure to the aspiration of the elite to have the island's claim as a civilized nation ratified. Since the people seemed bent on retaining and preserving the "barbarous" and "superstitious" ways of their ancestors, and the ruling classes and civilizers were anxious to cast those ways aside, the penalties for indulging in the "black art" (by black people) were quite harsh. Extended prison sentences and floggings with the "cat" contained echoes of an allegedly past time, when corporal punishment was seen as a means of exemplifying the folly of disobedience.

Old Hige

If obeah practitioners were of both sexes, the "old hige" lore (*ole haig* in Guyana, *soucouyant* in Trinidad) was associated exclusively with old women. The old "hag" was a witch who reputedly constituted a menace to infants; she craved and sucked their blood.[70] Beckwith located the old hige in "the skin-changing witch of European folk tales". More likely, however, belief in the old hige was rooted in the African tradition described by Nadel among the Nupe.[71] In Jamaica, as in Guyana and Trinidad, the witch was supposed to be a living person who could shed her skin and, in her search for blood, moved "as swift as lightning, with blazes of fire rising out of her armpits". Her approach was suspected when an irresistible drowsiness came over those gathered to protect the child, and with the flickering of the light. If those on watch succumbed and fell asleep, the infant was in grave danger. The hag entered the dwelling and sucked the child; the child would cry out and, upon awakening, the watchers would witness that the child was overcome with "locked-jaws", would refuse to suckle its mother's breast and was considered doomed.[72]

The fear of the old hige led families to go to great lengths to protect their young ones from her grasp. They made a blue cross on the door of the dwelling on the ninth night after a child's birth, and grain was strewn before the door. The old hige (also called "blow-fire") was kept at bay when knives and forks and sometimes the Bible were placed at the infant's head, and the doors were marked all over with chalk. The story was commonly told of the child who watched the witch slip out of her skin and who rubbed pepper on the skin or else burnt it, so that the witch could not resume it on her return. This led to her destruction. This method of capturing the witch was also subscribed to in other parts of the Caribbean.[73]

The persistent belief in the evil of the old hige rendered some old women potential targets of community violence. For instance, in 1902 the *Jamaica Times* reported:

> Those who think that the old ideas about witches have entirely disappeared are mistaken. One of our country correspondents this week wrote us of a case in which a certain woman was regarded by the whole district as a "witch", going about at nights sucking young babies. Not very long since she was caught by some people who beat her very badly. She went to look for fresh blood but she got something else.[74]

In Jamaica and the wider Caribbean, as people tried to explain their misfortunes, especially the inexplicable illness or death of a child, the myth of the old hige answered anxieties and painful questions. There was something perversely reassuring about knowing the cause of tragedy, and if the source could be isolated and perhaps even dealt with, then the proactive nature of the people's culture was once again in evidence. The old hige was simply part of a wider, more complex set of beliefs that many of the Jamaican people upheld and perpetuated.

River Mumma

One of the distinctive beliefs that observers commented on in the period was the "river mumma" or "ribba mumma" (*watermamma* in Guyana, *watramamma* in Suriname). Banbury, who referred to her as the "Rubba Missis", argued that she was the Jamaican version of the mermaid or water nymph of England.[75] Williams disagreed with Banbury's assessment, claiming instead that the river mumma was a residue of old Ashanti/Asante myths about the divine origin of water, as well as

> a reflexion of what constitutes the very basis of Ashanti theological beliefs . . . namely, the accepted relation of every important body of water in Ashanti to the Supreme Being as being "a son of God." Ashanti consider all waters as containing power or spirit of Divine Creator and thus as being a great life-giving force.[76]

In Guyana the watermamma was linked to the Afro-creole religious rituals of *Cumfo*, which are rooted in the West African worship of the river gods.[77]

According to Banbury, the river mumma was believed to inhabit "every fountainhead of an inexhaustible and considerable stream of water in Jamaica". As a result, the sources of such streams were worshipped and sacrifices were offered to the river mumma. The river mistress was occasionally seen sitting composedly by a fountain, combing her long black tresses. She always made her appearance at midday and when approached, she immediately disappeared. If an intruder should see her first, and their eyes should meet, that unlucky person was doomed, but otherwise no harm would come to them. The comb of the river mumma was sometimes found at the fountain heads; food was taken to the river head for her and, at particular times, songs and dances were held in her honour. In some communities, where the river mumma made her appearance, people did not eat the fish that came from these rivers, because they were believed to be the children of the river goddess and whoever ate them would suffer.[78]

The respect for water, as giver of life and in some communities as potential taker of life, was implicit in the stories about the river mumma. Reappearing in some Euro-Christian rituals such as baptism, which gained prominence among the Afro-Christian groups, and in aspects of the healing that occurred in balm-yards across the island, water was seen as a source of life, purification and a part of the ritual that spoke to salvation, among other things. However, in Jamaican communities where the power of water was in evidence in the rivers that ran through them, there were other aspects to the personality of water that were well known. When the rivers became swollen after heavy rainfall, and crops, animals and people were washed away, the might that could be contained in water was apparent. And a goddess who could be appealed to in such circumstances represented yet another attempt to deal with the reality of the circumstances within which Jamaican people had to operate. The legend of the river mumma was not constructed outside of a context; she had been spotted in the communities where her presence might make a difference. She was honoured and appealed to because she was thought to be a potential ally in a world that could be harsh and that seemed to offer few advocates.

Duppies

According to Banbury, duppies (*jumbi* in Guyana, *zumbi* in Brazil, *zambi* in Haiti) were persons who had died and whose souls returned to earth and haunted their "habitations", or else remained near to where their bodies were buried.[79] For Williams the links to Ashanti/Asante beliefs were clear: the Asante believed that when a person died, his spirit or *saman* immediately appeared before the Supreme Being or subordinate deity and ascertained whether or not it would go to the spirit world or haunt earth for a time (or even permanently). Such a spirit became a "wait-about" spirit. Food was constantly put aside for the *saman*; when it was visible to the naked eye, it was described as white or dressed in white.[80] Alice Spinner observed that the duppy was not simply the local equivalent of the English ghost:

> To be exact, true "Duppy," although an apparition, is not the spirit or soul, but only the shadow of the departed. The soul being perfectly distinct from its Duppy, going to heaven or hell as the case may be, leaving its shadow behind on earth where, unless exorcised by certain ceremonies, it may work mischief, or at least, cause annoyance to the living.[81]

The duppies were believed capable of returning for any relatives or friends, or to anyone who had injured them in life. For those they intended to harm, they "put hand" or "knocked". The duppies ate and drank like living beings; the people, in their fear of possible malevolence if the duppies were displeased, left food and drink for them. According to Emerick, duppies amused themselves by "haunting houses, frightening people by slamming doors, upsetting chairs, drawing bed curtains, etc.".[82]

According to Rampini, the belief in ghosts/duppies was universal among the people: "The natives of Jamaica are childishly and ridiculously superstitious; every action, word, and thought is full of the supernatural. They are horribly and unmistakably afraid of spirits . . . the fear is everywhere – not confined to hundreds of thousands, but universal in the breast of every black man, woman and child in Jamaica, educated and ignorant." Alice Spinner echoed these sentiments when she claimed that, after some time in Jamaica, she came to understand that "in the daily life of the negro population 'Duppies' occupied a very considerable and, indeed, dignified position, and were not only recognized as a serious fact, but were to be spoken of – if, indeed, it was advisable to speak of them at all to strangers – with fitting reverence".[83]

So ingrained were the beliefs that at dusk, when the spirits were thought to be about to go abroad, people reputedly flocked home from their provision grounds. "Nothing would tempt the negro to go out of sight of the light burning in his hut on a dark night" for fear that the duppies would "trouble him". Emerick's observations were similar; according to him, on Friday nights before market day and on Saturday nights after market, the roads were lined with people who filed along with a muffled tread, in perfect silence, due to a fear that a duppy might be encountered on the roads at night.[84] According to Rampini, the signs that the duppies were close by were many:

> If your horses blow or prick their ears when travelling at night, if, in passing through a lonely wood, you perceive the odour of musk, ghosts are either beside you, or near at hand; if, in some desolate country region, you notice the faint smell of cooking, the negroes say, "it duppy pumpkin", – it is duppies preparing their food; if a rat bites you during sleep, if an owl flaps its wings heavily, evil of a serious nature is approaching; if the wind has a "sough" in its tone, it is the heralding of evil tidings; if bats cross each other diagonally in the crimson stream of sunset, some powerful fiend will shortly be at variance with you; and if you set a duppy at defiance, going towards it in the endeavour to prove that the supernatural appearance is caused by some undulation of light, or by the shadow flickering on the curtainfold, illness of a dangerous or perhaps fatal nature will surely follow.[85]

Duppies did not always take forms that made them immediately recognizable. They could assume animal or other forms, especially the "ghost with a rope around his neck", a "Chinese or Coolie ghost", the "three-foot horse", "two pickney duppies" (spirits of dead children) and the "rolling calf", which was worse than others. The three-foot horse galloped through the moonlight, faster than any living steed, and its breath was fatal to anyone upon whom it fell. The two pickney duppies were "whooping boy" and "Long-bubby Susan". The former rode the three-foot horse, whooping like a human being and dancing on twigs in the woods. Long-bubby Susan ("long bubbies" in Guyana) was characterized by breasts which touched the ground and which she threw over her shoulders when attacked.[86]

The worst possible sort of duppy was reputed to be the rolling calf (also in Guyana). It was "a spirit who haunts the city by night with a flaming eye, trailing a long chain behind him", and was bent on destruction. One person described the rolling calf as something which appeared in the form of a hornless goat, black, white or spotted, with a collar about its neck to which was attached a short chain that dragged upon the ground. It had red eyes which at night looked like blazing fires; its tail curled over its back; one of its front feet was shaped like a horse's hoof and the other like a human foot, while the back feet were goat-shaped. The creature left a bad smell like a billy-goat.[87]

According to Banbury, these creatures, called "rollen calves" or "roaring calves", appeared as cats, dogs, hogs, goats, horses, bulls. They were said to be very dangerous when they appeared in the feline form, and of a black or brindled colour. During the day they lived at the roots of cotton trees, in bamboos and in caves; at night, when they roamed, they were often attacked by dogs, which were their bitter enemies. They possessed the extraordinary capacity to grow suddenly from the size of a cat or dog to that of a horse or bull. They were fond of molasses (and could be found about sugar estates at night) and were partial to cattle (and so broke into cow pens, causing terror among the animals). Escape could be achieved by sticking an open penknife in the ground and running without glancing backward; by using one's left hand to flog the rolling calf with a tarred whip, at which point the creature cried out, "Me dead two time, oh"; by running up a slope because although it was incredibly swift on level ground, the rolling calf could not run up a hill; or perhaps by marking a Roman cross (X) on the ground since no rolling calf could stand that.[88]

In 1903 Charles Distin gave a detailed account of "a remarkable experience" that he had had fifty-two years previously. Born into the sort of family which sent him to "the Mother Country" for his education, he grew up knowing nothing about "the duppies, rolling calves etc., etc., so firmly believed on in Jamaica". A few years after returning to Jamaica, he had an encounter in a field with "a figure that [he] took to be a cow from its size and general appearance". That conclusion was soon put to flight:

> [I]t got up and came directly to me, almost touching me, humped up its back and ran around me some three or four times, then started away into the bush a few yards off, returned again and performed the same feat over and over just as a favourite dog does with his master when he comes out of the house in the morning.

The creature was finally chased away by dogs. When Distin told his story to his granduncle he was assured that the same thing had been seen by several people, "just in the same shape, and that the spot where I saw it was used as a burial ground for the soldiers who had died at the Barracks".[89]

Those who could see duppies were believed to be gifted. One indication of the gift was when a child was born "with caul" over its face. However, twins, especially if they were of the opposite sex, were automatically "protected"[90] as one could look out for the other.

Duppies were known to have their favourite haunts, such as the Salt Ponds near Spanish Town. They were also believed to inhabit the roots of cotton trees, which were held in veneration. According to Banbury, it was difficult to get cotton trees cut down, as the people believed that the "deaths" who lived in the tree would harm them. Duppies were also said to live in bamboo thickets and to feed on bamboo roots, "fig" leaves and a vine called "duppy pumpkin".[91]

Reports of duppy incidents were numerous during the period. A favourite pastime of duppies was supposedly stone throwing, and whenever the source of the stones could not be ascertained, duppies (poltergeists) were believed to be the culprits. Hence, reports were quite common of persons and buildings being stoned by them. In 1873 when, despite the presence of the police, Miss Robertson's house was being stoned, the police themselves attributed the act to duppies since the windows were closed and the stones were falling from the ceiling. In February 1878 there was a suspicion that supernatural forces were at work when stones fell on William Bryan's house in Wild Street, Allman Town. Later in the year, showers of stones were pelted into an "eating house" in West Queen Street, breaking glasses, plates, saucers and other items. The black proprietor believed that he was suffering from the malicious persecution of his enemies, who were using "supernatural effects produced by witchcraft".

In 1900, at Lamb's River, Westmoreland, the duppy of a boy who had allegedly been murdered was believed to have stoned one of his alleged killers. The young woman in question had her head broken with the stones, and fears were entertained that she would "lose her reason" over the matter.[92]

Because the belief existed that duppies could stone, some people took advantage of this and carried out their own stonings, hoping that duppies would be blamed. In 1875, when a young woman was caught stoning houses in Upper Church Street and charged, the *Morning Journal* opined that she should be punished as a deterrent; it hoped that the case would "tend to dispel the silly superstition of those fools who are always but too ready to attribute to some cause any phenomenon, however simple, for which their shallow brains cannot afford a natural explanation".[93] Similarly, in 1903 the *Jamaica Times* reported that a man and his wife were convicted for throwing stones into another man's yard; prior to the arrest, the people of Falmouth had believed that the stoning was carried out by duppies.[94]

Newspaper reports seemed to confirm the pervasiveness of the belief in duppies. The *Gleaner* reported that there were "strange appearances" in King Street in 1877, when showers of sand descended on the heads of those within a certain residence, while hot gravel was thrown into one boy's face; at times tumblers and pickle bottles on the sideboard were thrown down and broken. The police had reportedly searched the house without finding any human being. In 1879 a black man died suddenly in St Andrew after declaring that duppies had got hold of him. The post-mortem found that he had suffered a heart attack. Reports of a duppy in Princess Street in 1881 encouraged a large crowd to gather in the expectation of seeing it. A small black snake caused quite a stir in Bowden in July 1899 since, as the people said, "mangoose eat alla snake, ha way di one cum from? It mus' be some one sen' him." Later, in August 1899, a woman in Negril named Hylton was reported to believe that her illness was the result of being "kicked in the head" by a duppy.[95]

In 1901 a man named McKail took it upon himself to go to Roehampton bent on killing green lizards, which he labelled "Iniquity" in the belief that they were the causes of distress and sickness in the district.[96] In 1903 "a curious phenomenon" was reported in Bunker's Hill, where

> at a certain home two children had begun to vomit things like glass bottles, hair pins, safety pins, small pocket knives, etc. The tables and other household utensils had been removed from the house by unseen hands and thrown outside, breaking glassware etc. Next followed the throwing of stones hitting everyone who happened to speak a rash word against these curious proceedings.[97]

When a young girl became ill in 1904, her mother lamented, "duppy, duppy, duppy, come out of my house, a weh me do you mek you come fe killed [*sic*] mi daughter". Her father hired the services of a "four eye [Myal] man", who advised him that although the duppy was probably the girl's sister who would not harm her, he should nevertheless get a guard (amulet) in case it was "a coolie duppy of the worst kind".[98]

One "duppy case" in St Ann spoke to the lengths to which families would go to prevent duppies from harming one of their own. In 1904, as a sick girl was "troubled by duppies", her relatives shot into the room with a gun to "shoot the duppy". According to the sick girl, who used a mirror to track its activities, the enraged duppy changed forms many times (rat, bat, and such things) and a double cow whip was brought into service, but to no avail. While the "catchers" lamented "lard you ting [think] im no smart!", the duppy escaped through the coffee trees. In the meantime a kerosene tin containing cow horns and eyes and sulphur was kept burning and the girl's father sharpened his machete and chopped at the duppy without success. Although the reporter was "ashamed to live among such people", for many Jamaicans this spirit world where the division between sacred and profane, where the lines between material and spiritual worlds were, at best, blurred, was simple reality.[99]

It was not only lower-class Jamaicans who believed in duppies. According to Alice Spinner, "Even the more educated were not above a lurking belief in their existence; while for the ordinary negro, that there were Duppies around him was as undoubted a truth as the clear sunlight in which he lived."[100] Said Makin:

> While educated Jamaicans are apt to protest loudly against the belief in duppies, there are few of them who will not reveal in the darkness of the bush or within the walls of some haunted house, a dreaded respect for this West Indian spirit world. "Duppy say, 'Day fe you, night fe me,'" is an old Jamaican saying. And because of it, the people . . . will keep at nights to the familiar and lamplit interiors.[101]

Since duppies were such a part of the belief system, and there was great fear of incurring their wrath, it is not surprising that a number of rituals emerged to ward them off. Children and infants were thought to be especially susceptible, so the caul which enveloped some infants at birth was dried, pounded, mixed with their pap and fed to them. A bit of the caul was also sewn in a piece of black ribbon with garlic, camphor, asafoetida and other strong-smelling drugs and tied around the children's necks. When the water for children's baths was placed in the sun to remove the chill, there was a fear that spirits would "play" with it, so two sticks in the sign of a cross were placed across the tub to scare the spirits.[102] If one of a set of twins died, the surviving baby was handed over the coffin of the other and back again, lest the dead child should return for the survivor.[103] It was widely believed that if a baby was not christened before it was six months old, duppies could steal it away. To keep them at bay, said Isabel MacLean, a pair of scissors and a Bible were placed on the baby's pillow; the scissors, when open, formed another cross (X) that was supposed to ward off evil.[104]

To prevent the return of a duppy, red peas or banana suckers were planted at the grave of the deceased person. If a person died with his eyes open, it was feared that he was "looking back" for someone; the counteraction to this was to place cut limes over the eyes. According to Beckwith, precautions included wearing black string or ribbon about the neck; tying camphor, garlic and asafoetida, sewn together in black cloth; the use of musk powder; making a cross in the road and sticking a penknife in it; and turning clothing (such as a jacket or cap) inside out. To keep duppies away, some effort was taken to sprinkle sand or throw rice, grain or pebbles out of the door for the duppies to count. Since they could not count beyond three, this had the effect of delaying them indefinitely. The cracking of a whip with the left hand, the burning of things with strong odours, and certain herbs smoked in a pipe, burnt in a pan or rubbed on the body all had the effect of keeping the spirits at bay. Rosemary (*Croton lineans*), parrot or spiritweed (*Eryngium foetidum*), worm weed or see-me-contact (*Chenopodim ambrosioides*), guinea weed (*Letineria alliacea*) and water weed (*Medilia gracilis*) were all used for this purpose.[105]

Sharing a belief system that was distinct from the nineteenth-century European beliefs which identified body and soul, and saw the temporal world as the only one with which people had to contend on a daily basis, the majority of Jamaicans inhabited a world where the dead walked freely among the living. Those who died did not simply leave the earth and their loved ones (or enemies) behind; rather they moved among them and had to be acknowledged and dealt with. And since it was never clear if a spirit simply "walked" or was sent on a mission on behalf of a person in the community who had sought its intervention (for good or evil), it was important to appease it, to encourage its goodwill and to guard against its potentially malevolent activities. Duppies, in whatever form, were not to be taken lightly, and the communities responded to their own preoccupation with "all those who had gone before": they saw them, spoke with them, left food for them, conducted rituals which focused on them and implored them to help or, at least, not to act against them, in the constantly shifting circumstances that existed in their spiritual/material world.

Jamaican "Superstitions"

Apart from the beliefs already dealt with, there were others which many middle- and upper-class contemporaries referred to as "Jamaican superstitions". According to Rampini, there was a general belief in "the evil eye". He reported having seen a woman come to the magistrate's court with "a piece of pink ribbon tied to one arm and piece of blue on the other to ward off its malign influence".[106]

In keeping with the belief that there was a causal relationship between action and result, there was a set of beliefs governing what one should or should not do in order to produce desirable circumstances. According to Rampini's account, it was unlucky to praise an infant too much, or to say that it closely resembled its father or mother. If one carried pepper in one's pocket, then one could expect to be poor. It was believed that to give a thing and take it back would give a stye in the eye, and that to kill a large black (Anancy) spider would inevitably result in some sort of domestic misfortune. The spilling of salt at mealtime denoted imminent confusion, while the breaking of a mirror signified seven years of bad luck.[107]

> Crossing of weapons, or the opening of an umbrella, [means] bad luck; and the dropping of a san-pattern, or shoe, [signifies] the losing of a lover. The precedence of a forthcoming visitor, [is] indicated by means of a little insect shedding forth an unsteady light, called a candle-fly. Another insect named the newsmonger, on entering one of their huts and buzzing in the ears of any particular person, is attributed to good or bad intelligence coming to them from afar; owing to the distinction in colour. [There is n]o worse fatality than the presence of a rat-bat within a dwelling, or the piercing screams of the owl at nights. . . . A person's face coming in contact with web spun by the active spider, is the foreboding of a good or evil spirit, enjoining them to proceed on their journey, no further, or ill luck betides them.[108]

According to Pullen-Burry, the birds that fed on carrion, called "John Crows", were regarded with great superstition. Children, in particular, were discouraged from looking at them, and no one dared to throw stones at this bird – if anyone did a fever would result.[109]

Some of the beliefs were focused on the main means by which people earned their living: agriculture. Some beliefs surrounded attempts to maximize production; certain phases of the moon were thought to be favourable for planting crops. For example, All Fools' Day (1 April) was thought to be best for sowing corn, and 15 April was thought to be best for sowing peas. Other beliefs, also linked to agriculture, were concerned with preventing negativity. If a person pointed at a young pumpkin his finger would drop off; also, it was unlucky to inspect the soil when tobacco had been sown, before it appeared above the surface.[110]

The Afro-creole belief systems were by no means concerned only with the prevention of bad luck or with the invitation to good luck. The systems functioned in the community as a means of regulating behaviour. Where wrongdoing was discovered, the community relied on these beliefs as corrective measures. In one case reported in the *Falmouth Post,* Isaac Brown received some money in cheques and silver to pay wages; he entrusted a one-pound cheque to Robert Green, who left it at George Porter's cottage. When the cheque could not be found, the "broom-weed" or "book-and-key" method was used to discover the culprit. A tub was prepared with water, ashes and a "fig-penny", and incantations were said. Although the report did not say if the thief was discovered, the process of investigation was notable.[111] In 1890, according to the *Colonial Standard,* "a respectable pauper (a Polish woman)" was accused of stealing a gold ring by "a number of lewd women":

> They took with them several broom sticks and cordage and pulled up a quantity of broom weed which they fastened to the unfortunate woman's neck, while they chanted several lines of an incantation frequently heard among superstitious persons invoking the aid of St. Paul to restore to them the lost property or to discover the thief. They also had with them a pack of playing cards which they dealt around and a part of which they left when called to by neighbours who interfered.[112]

The allegedly superstitious nature of the Jamaican people was by no means confined to those in the lower classes. Frank Cundall, for instance, commented that those who "sneered" at the lower classes for their unfounded beliefs "declin[ed] to sit to a table of thirteen and fanc[ied that] ill-luck will follow the spilling of salt".[113] "Superstition" was pervasive throughout the society.

"Panya Jars"

Another aspect of Jamaican folklore focused on enchanted Spanish jars ("Panya jars") that were believed to be huge and bearing enormous treasure. Banbury observed, "There are stories of them being seen above ground, but as soon as discovered they sink down immediately. [On one occasion a] duppy sitting on top of one was seen; the ghost is said to be that of the person killed by the depositor, to watch the treasure, and hence the enchantment."[114]

The way to break the enchantment was to cast a hat, knife, handkerchief or anything else quickly over or on to the "Panya jar". Some people believed that the treasure could not be recovered without the assistance of an obeah(wo)man; from time to time there were reports that persons professing to be able to retrieve the "Panya jars" were paid large sums to do so. When they failed at the attempt, the reason was invariably that the jars had sunk beyond the point of retrieval, or else that the ghostly guard prevented them from taking the treasure.[115]

In 1869 at Lucea, Hanover, a number of obeahmen were hired to recover a Spanish jar that had reportedly been found, and thought to contain a large quantity of gold coins. A "black man named Johnson" on whose land this jar was supposed to be located supplied the obeahmen with food and liquor, paid them ten pounds for their services, and provided the wherewithal for "superstitious rites" to be carried out. They sacrificed goats and pigs, and "a white cock" (rooster) was killed. The *Falmouth Post*'s correspondent reported that someone in the crowd that had gathered further advised that "human blood must be used, for nothing else would answer". When, however, a constable and a Clerk of the Peace intervened, the area where the jar was supposed to be was found to contain "a clayed cooking utensil, called a Yabba, and a common water jar, both of which had been evidently placed in the newly-excavated earth by Johnson and his associates". But the crowd of about four hundred men, women and children preferred to believe that "the Jar began to sink down as soon as the white people began to trouble it". Johnson and some others were charged, but the three obeahmen disappeared, perhaps further confirming their power in the minds of spectators. [116]

Conclusion

Obeah and "duppyism" formed integral parts of a cosmology derived from West Africa in which the spirit world interacted with and influenced all aspects of life, sacred and secular, for good or bad. Obeah might have been bad magic, but for many people it seemed to empower them to shape their own existence by manipulating the spirits, both benevolent and malevolent. Besides, in a context where neither the much-vaunted "superior" religious belief system of Christianity, nor the "rational ethic" of nineteenth-century Western secularism proved sufficient to explain all of life's mysteries or problems, and the "scientific method" of Western medicine did not cure all illnesses, obeah, the spirit world and herbalism (see chapter 3) seemed to provide effective answers and cures, or at least comparatively effective ones.

The persistent pervasiveness of these Afro-creole beliefs that were collectively labelled "dark superstition" and "uncivilized" is clear testimony that the Jamaican people held on strongly to their traditional belief system throughout the period, and were not prepared to be dictated to by the cultural elites of the upper and middle classes – whether white, coloured or indeed black – in this sphere of their lives. Some of the cultural elites were themselves ambivalent towards this culture that they labelled "debased", since they had been nurtured in a pre-existing Jamaican culture in plantation society and also shared a belief in the power of obeah and the wanderings of duppies. Although the dominant imperial order through its institutions (legislature, police, courts and jails), the churches, schools, press and the opinion of segments of the cultural elites coerced, bullied and cajoled the people to renounce their "heathen" beliefs and practices, they remained resilient (resistant) and, in the process, not only made the law an ass, but rendered the entire ethical system that it bolstered irrelevant and unworkable. They had no wish or ambition to get rid of or overturn the dominant system. Rather, they simply chose to ignore it where it impinged on their fundamental beliefs, a course of (in)action made possible particularly by those who were isolated in remote rural villages in the mountainous interior of the island. The preservation of their traditional Afro-creole belief system further served to confirm their intention to determine *for themselves* what was culturally apposite and what was not. It was a positive assertion of cultural self-determination in the face of hostile pressure from above.

Figure 2. Silk cotton tree: symbol in Jamaican folk belief systems
Source: James H. Stark, *Stark's Jamaica Guide* (Boston: James H. Stark, 1898). Courtesy of the National Library of Jamaica.

Figure 3. Possessed by spirits
Source: Martha Beckwith, *Black Roadways* (Chapel Hill: University of North Carolina Press, 1929). Courtesy of the National Library of Jamaica.

Figure 4. Healing pool in a Revival mission ground
Source: George Eaton Simpson, *Religious Cults of the Caribbean* (Río Piedras: University of Puerto Rico Press, 1980).

Figure 5. Balm-yard procession
Source: Martha Beckwith, *Black Roadways* (Chapel Hill: University of North Carolina Press, 1929). Courtesy of the National Library of Jamaica.

Figure 6. Alexander Bedward

Figure 7. The faithful and the curious at the August Town healing stream
Source (for figures 6 and 7): Martha Beckwith, *Black Roadways* (Chapel Hill: University of North Carolina Press, 1929). Courtesy of the National Library of Jamaica.

Chapter 3

Afro-Creole Belief System II
Folk Religions

RELIGION WAS AN INTEGRAL ASPECT OF the belief system of Afro-Jamaican people. Their so-called superstitions and obeah were parts of a broad cosmology about the relationship between God, mankind and ancestral spirits that determined the very essence of human existence. This was an interactive relationship in which humans could attempt to assume control of their lives by propitiating God and the spirits in direct ways, and using them to bring about equilibrium in everyday life. The clearest manifestation of this interaction between man and the spirit world was "spirit possession", which was a central feature of the religious expression of Africans and their descendants in Jamaica and the diaspora. The adoption or grafting on of aspects of Christian belief did not fundamentally alter either their world view or their manner of spiritual expression. Rather, Christianity was "Africanized", manifested in Jamaica after emancipation especially by the growth of a new Afro-creole Revivalist movement.

Myal/Revival

What became known as Revival had its roots in the black American Baptist proselytization conducted in Jamaica from the late eighteenth century. The most prominent of these black missionaries were George Lisle/Leile, George Gibb and Moses Baker, whose scriptural interpretations varied significantly from those of the white Baptist missionaries who arrived later. Breakaway sects, often under illiterate leaders, fostered further doctrinal "unorthodoxy". According to Philip Curtin, "The characteristic doctrinal departure from orthodoxy in the early Native Baptist groups was the emphasis on 'the spirit' and a corresponding neglect of the written word. Most of the leaders could not read in any case, and the shift accorded with the remnants of African religious attitudes."[1] Mary Turner further states,

> There were sects which mortified the flesh and sects where the spirit spoke in tongues. Some repudiated the Bible on the strength of the text "the letter killeth, but the Spirit giveth Life." Followers were expected to be possessed of "the spirit" before they were admitted to baptism, and the spirit was sought by penances, fasting, sleeping in the bush. The baptism ceremony itself took on a new significance; it was no longer a symbol of grace but an extension of grace itself. Conversion, therefore, meant not embracing a strict code of Christian morality but being above morality.[2]

The third personality in the Christian trinity, the Holy Spirit, fit all too well into the cosmos of spirits that the Afro-creole culture had recognized and nurtured. That possession by this spirit was a crucial and necessary part of the Afro-creole Christian experience is understandable within the context of possession by other spirits. Further, that the "spiritual" nature of the conversion should be given more weight than the "word" spoke of a process not only of assimilation but also of inversion. The word of God was something that only the educated had access to, but the spirit of God was available to all who sought it, and since the Word could be interpreted in many ways (witness the wide variety of denominational doctrines), it was the spirit which indicated the authentic experience. This was the true conversion. And having been immersed in the "Truth", touched by the spirit of the living God, one was, indeed, superior to those who had not had that experience but relied mainly upon words in a book in order to have communion with God. "The children of the book" were to be pitied; they had not "met" God. "The children of the spirit" had had the true experience and were the true children of God.

Robert Stewart identifies that aspect of Native Baptist worship in which "communication with the spirit world did not rely on the mediation of minister or book" as "a Jamaican syncretism of African spirit belief and apocalyptic Christianity" called Myal. Although he seems to make a clear distinction between Myalists and Native Baptists, he nevertheless recognizes links between them, noting that some Myal leaders and their followers persisted in identifying themselves as Baptists or Wesleyans.[3] Monica Schuler, however, asserts that the Myalists and the Native Baptists were more or less identical, arguing that "Europeans didn't recognize this, and tended to call the more 'African' behavior of Native Baptists 'Myalism' ". While admitting the separate genesis of Myal in the eighteenth century, she claims that after 1791 it absorbed "certain congenial aspects of the Baptist version of Christianity", most notably "the inspiration of the Holy Spirit, and Baptism, in the manner of John the Baptist, by immersion – because they seemed to correspond with beliefs or symbols already familiar to them"; and thereafter the two became virtually indistinguishable.[4] Curtin argues that because these Native Baptist (or Myal) preachers had enjoyed a forty-year head start on the orthodox teachings of the mainstream white missionaries, who really began in earnest during the 1820s, the Native Baptist interpretation of Christianity had had an opportunity to take root among the slaves. Hence, "By 1830 the doctrine and organization of the Native Baptists [and/or Myalists] had become a thoroughly integrated part of Negro culture – another religion competing with the Christianity of the European missionaries."[5]

Anthropologist Diane Austin-Broos argues that Revival was

> not simply a "mixing" of elements, but rather a redefinition of the form of Christianity that the missionaries had brought to Jamaica. Limited literacy made it difficult for missionaries to purvey a text-centered Christianity that focused on moral rules, and the cultural differences between the missionaries and their followers meant that their ethical rationalism would have had a limited meaning for Afro-Jamaicans. . . . [Hence] the complex called "myal" by missionary observers was not simply a nativistic movement or even a consistent millennialism. It was rather a complex of rite and belief that sought to sustain the logic of affliction by assimilating elements of Christianity to it.[6]

That "logic of affliction" related to the Afro-creole belief that social or personal ill could be caused by witchcraft, sorcery or ancestral spirits, and required holistic treatment of both the moral and physical being. This had to be performed by experts who were both spiritual and herbal healers – "Myalmen".[7] Myal's conceptualization of sin as sorcery, "an offense not against God but against society, made it far more this-world oriented than the Baptist faith". For Schuler, therefore, Myal ritual offered a cure for society's ills by its use of anti-sorcery (anti-obeah) ritual.[8]

Myal/Revival incorporated two key features of the Baptist faith, namely, baptism by immersion *à la mode* of John the Baptist, and the inspiration of the Holy Spirit. According to Curtin, baptism seen as an extension of grace itself

> led to practices that the white missionaries condemned as antinomianism. The revivalists believed that they had achieved superior spiritualism based on their direct connection with the spirit of God. Having accepted the basic doctrine of Protestant salvationism, they claimed a special connection to the god who had saved them and that connection gave them a certain authority and power. The Spirit spoke through them and they were God's "pickney".[9]

Martha Beckwith stated that the Revivalists were influenced by "myal angels".[10] Schuler notes that the Myalists had three grades of membership: archangels, angels and ministering angelics:

> The archangels, both men and women, were the leaders whose chief function was that of divination. . . . The angels spoke readily of their visions and their ability to detect obeah and its devotees. The ministering angelics usually operated in groups of nine to twenty people and performed the work of making converts, digging up buried obeah charms, and catching shadows.[11]

According to anthropologist Joseph G. Moore, the ranking of the spirits was as follows: God the Father, God the Son, God the Holy Spirit (who was the chief energizing spirit), the archangels and prophets, the four evangelists, the great disciples, and leading ancestral shepherds/shepherdesses.[12]

There were public upsurges of Myal fervour during the 1840s which, according to Curtin, even invaded the orthodox churches, some of whose members were Myal participants. These were later referred to as "Revivalists",[13] and manifestations of their style of worship peaked during the Great Revival of 1860–62, which had originally been promoted by the missionaries themselves. Curtin, Schuler and Stewart agree that the missionaries lost control of that Revival to the Myalists, who introduced spirit possession, dancing, flagellation, dreams and trances, prophesies and revelations, shouting and groaning. But Shirley Gordon more cautiously asserts that the Revival "was vigorously adopted by the native Baptists and other black independent groups, in association with those Myal practices which they already maintained in different degrees according to each group's particular disposition"; she further argues that Myal-related activities were probably "more observable than the less demonstrative practices of the same groups".[14]

There were subsequently other similar, albeit smaller, public manifestations of Revival fever: in 1874 and 1886.¹⁵ Then in 1906–7, just before and after the calamitous earthquake, a major Revival was reported in the press. According to the *Jamaica Times,* a "stirring revival" broke out in July 1906 at the Wesleyan Church in Ocho Rios. There were crowded meetings with people arriving from all over. "They do not seem gospel-hardened, for they flock to the altar rails to be converted by the dozens; in fact it is said that one night there were fully 100 penitents, most of them weeping bitterly." As soon as the meetings started, the rum shops in the district were deserted and eventually forced to close. Similar manifestations were exhibited at the Waltham Baptist Church in St Ann during one week of meetings in September, when "about three hundred men, women and children decided for Christ, amid great rejoicing. Many big men were smitten down by the power of God, some in the road when on their way from meetings." Clarendon was another major centre of this Revival: at the Zion Baptist Church, for instance, 450 were registered as "converted", while members of the Smithville Baptist Church marched to the Farm Church to start a Revival there and 350 converted, "including some of the worst characters of the district". Similar Revival scenes were witnessed in other parts of the island.¹⁶

Since much of this Revival activity was centred around the Baptist churches, that denomination treated it as a genuine "Christian revival" (that is, more respectable than its manifestations outside the walls of the church) and credited it with increasing their membership to heights seen only during similar Revival upsurges in 1842 and 1861. According to them, the 1907 Revival led to 9,242 new members in the Baptist congregation, with a net increase of 5,915 and a total of 39,103. They attributed this in part to the shock effect of the earthquake.¹⁷

Revival was thus a fixed feature of the Jamaican religio-cultural landscape by the later nineteenth century. However, anthropologists Edward Seaga and Barry Chevannes have observed that two broad Revival sects emerged from the Great Revival, namely, Zion and Puk(k)umina/Pocomania, with the latter having some links with the purely African religion of Kumina (see below). According to Chevannes, while Zion emerged first in 1860 and "retained a closer resemblance to Christianity, in the way the Native Baptists did" by making "greater use of the Bible and other Christian symbols" and refusing to dabble with "belligerent and dangerous spirits", Pukumina emerged in 1861 and was "closer to traditional African religions in which there is no equivalent of the evil spirit Christians call Satan; all spirits can possess and therefore deserve respect, an attitude also found in Vodun [Haiti] and Orisa (Shango)

[Trinidad]".[18] But most contemporary observers were never able to look beyond their prejudices to recognize any difference between these two sects. On those rare occasions when they did, they were just as disgusted as W.D. Townsley, for whom "Pokomania" was sheer superstition, to be treated in the same way as obeah and Myal. This and other "superstitions" were "the great enemy against which all the agencies of civilization in this island have to wage unending war".[19]

Beckwith claimed that the "Pukkumerians" owed their name to their preoccupation with detecting and picking up obeah – "pick-them-there".[20] William Makin regarded Pocomania as "a West African Voodoo dance" with its "blood cult", mired in "whispers of human sacrifice".[21] Others thought that the term "Pocomania" was a Spanish derivative that aptly captured the "mad frenzy" of the sect's adherents – "a little madness". These reflect some of the biases with which Revival was regarded by elite society.

Seaga and Joseph Moore state that the similarities between Zion and Pukumina included the bands in which they were organized, their mission grounds (where they gathered for worship) with the seal (a specially consecrated area where the religious rites were conducted) and water pool for ritual baths, feasting tables and altars, prayer and street meetings, spirit possession (including speaking in tongues), healing and digging up of obeah (a symbolic act signifying the rooting out of evil). But Seaga also notes important differences. In Zion the seal (sacred area) is in the mission house; in Pukumina it is in the centre of the mission ground. Possession occurs, and is referred to, in different ways: in Zion it is called "receiving messages"; in Pukumina, "travel" in the spirit world. In the latter, rituals begin on Sunday nights, whereas in Zion that is not necessarily so. In Zion the leader is called Captain or Shepherd if male, and Mother or Shepherdess if female; in Pukumina the leader is almost always male and is called the Shepherd. Most importantly, at the doctrinal level,

> *Zionists* deal primarily with Heavenly spirits, and with Apostles and Prophets of the "Earthbound" group. They believe in the existence of the other powers of the pantheon [ground spirits], but consider them evil, and therefore useful only for evil purposes. . . . On the other hand, *Pukkumina* followers work primarily with "Ground" spirits and "Fallen Angels", who in their value system are not considered evil. They maintain that these spirits are more useful than those used by Zion, since they are nearer to them and more easily contacted . . . .

These doctrinal differences colour the perceptions of each sect towards the other: "Zionists regard Pukkumina people as better practitioners of obeah, since they deal with 'ground' spirits constantly and these are considered evil by the Zion cult; on the other hand, Pukkumina regard Zionists as more experienced in matters of healing."[22] As we shall see below, however, these subtle differences were entirely absent from the contemporary records, and consequently the descriptions of Revival are generic.[23]

According to Joseph Moore, Revival groups held two kinds of services – public and private. The first took place in the streets, whereas the second were held in private yards. The roadside meeting was simple, with just a small table covered with a white cloth upon which a lantern and a Bible were placed; the service consisted of hymn singing, scripture reading and preaching. During the singing the leader and an acolyte would dance around the table in a counter-clockwise direction. At the end money contributions were solicited and a benediction sung.[24] The description of H.G. De Lisser, a leading contemporary journalist and literary figure, of a meeting in Kingston attended by women, all dressed in white with white head-dresses that looked like turbans,[25] is a good example of a public service. At this meeting the leader was a woman (which suggests that it was Zionist), who led the meeting into a well-known hymn, "moving slowly a few paces to and fro as she utter[ed] the words". Like most of his contemporaries, De Lisser was sarcastic: "Shrill, shrill and ear-piercing, the hymn is intended as a call to the neighbourhood to come out and be saved; and the neighbourhood does come forth, not to be saved, but to enjoy itself by singing." As the crowd thickened, the admonition that "Jesus was coming" was repeated several times, while the leader shook a little whip. "Oh! my brothers and sisters . . . are you prepared to meet Him on Judgement Day; are you ready for the bridegroom, you who are standing on the blazing brink of hell? The devil is waiting for you! Oh, prepare, prepare, ere it be too late – too late, too late!" An impassioned chant followed, with encouragement and cries from the gathered crowd.[26]

Joseph Moore observed that private services were conducted by the head of the band and featured what he called full "trumping", "labouring" and spirit possession.[27] Beckwith described one such service, a Revival service that she attended in Lacovia, St Elizabeth. She described the dress (which featured the white turban), and a table covered with a white cloth on which lay a Bible, a glass of water, and a bunch of red and white roses. She spoke of the "peculiar" singing of hymns from the "Moody and Sankey" collection,[28] the use of the drum, and the movement that accompanied the rhythmic dance ("trumping" or "trooping"):

This was done by raising first one foot and then the other, at the same time lifting the arms and letting the body sway into line with the planted foot. Those who carried rods swayed them up and down with the rocking motion . . . [and they] began to breathe with a short sharp intake that sounded like the bark of a dog, an exercise that is called "trooping" and which, if persisted in, will produce in the worker that semiconscious condition so favorable to the communication of spirits, and hence so coveted at a really successful Revivalist meeting.[29]

Beckwith recognized that most Revivalists were also "good church members" and that their services featured "the beauty of biblical phrases", prayers and exhortations.[30] Thus, in a Revival meeting in 1897 the style of prayer, although Christian, seemed to have its own ritual:

> [S]he started off and took up a position on a sort of dunghill or refuse heap near by, and repeated the Lord's Prayer while gazing at the sun that was rising in the east. She afterwards turned to the other three points of the compass, repeating it in each position in a very impressive manner indeed.[31]

The use of the doctrines and rituals of the Euro-Christian church in ways that suited the Afro-Christian Revivalists was a source of great distress for the missionaries who observed them, for they were observing the inversion of the means by which they had intended to bring the "lost sheep" into the fold.

Myal as Anti-Obeah Ritual

One of the principal features of Myal/Revival ritual was the rooting out of evil, symbolized in particular by obeah. It was generally believed that "what the obeahman did the myal doctor could undo". But elite contemporary commentators oft-times regarded Myal as an integral part of the complex of obeah itself, practised by the same persons: "In public . . . he might become a myalist doctor, while in secret he was still the obeah-man. He could apply the healing properties of herbs to counteract the very poisons he had occultly administered. Together with the vile concoctions devised at the mid-night hour for harm and ruin, he might fashion the protective fetish as a counter-irritant."[32] This was more in keeping with the practice in Guyana, where no discernible distinction was made between obeah (bad magic) and Myal (good magic), but instead the obeah practitioner combined both functions, and also served as "bush doctor" (herbalist). Even in Jamaica the law treated both Myal and obeah as "one and the same meaning and the like offence".[33]

However, Reverend Hope Waddell, described as "one of the missionaries of the Emancipation period", warned against conflating the two phenomena: "Myal must not be confounded with obea, to which indeed it was wholly opposed; it affected to cure the illness, and remove other evils, which the obea produced. The Myal practitioners counted themselves angels of light, and called those of the opposite craft angels of darkness."[34]

Claiming that the core of Afro-Jamaican culture was derived from the Asante, American Jesuit anthropologist Joseph Williams argued that the latter made important distinctions between the *okomfo* (priesthood) who supervised all religious rites and practices relating to birth, marriage and death; the *sumankwafo* (medicine man) whose herbs cured people of their illnesses (white magic); and the *obayifo* (wizard) who practised witchcraft aimed at harming individuals. Although these distinctions were maintained for some time after the crossing, the outlawing of African religion during slavery reduced the visibility of the priesthood, who had to go underground, and allowed for the secret practice of obeah to thrive among the slaves, backed by the fear of its use of poison. But the *okomfo* never became extinct; rather, they survived in modified form (perhaps incorporating the functions of the *sumankwafo*) to become Myalmen who intensified their counter-obeah role, and re-emerged after emancipation in the form of Native Baptists seeking to reassert their religious authority by declaring war on obeah.[35]

However credible this explanation may or may not be, it is clear that one of the main functions of Myal/Revival was perceived to be the fight against evil (obeah). According to the *Gleaner* in 1904, the object of Myal "was to discover 'the wickedness' [of obeah] and to hinder its effects". Bessie Pullen-Burry treated it as "counter-witchcraft", and Williams termed it "white magic" carried out for the welfare of the community. An important difference between the two sets of activities was that while obeah was practised in secret, Myal was practised in the open.[36]

Reverend Thomas Banbury provided a detailed description of how the Myalists "pulled" obeah. They did so either from the ground or from the skin. In the first case, the "puller" went to a spot and fixed his eyes on it, to prevent it from escaping: "It is believed to have the power of *running* when approached to be taken up." The puller stooped over the spot, muttered some words, looked into his *amber*[37] and predicted exactly what was below the surface. He then marked out a circle, stuck knives and forks all around, rolled up his sleeves, got some ashes and waste, and saturated the ground as he dug. The leaves of the cotton bush[38] were thrust under the soil, the obeah felt for and then extracted. The obeah was then thrown into a basin and lime squeezed over it, along with sprinkled ashes: "No one would dare to touch an obeah unless first so treated. It is called 'killing' the obeah."[39]

To pull the obeah from the skin, the puller consulted his amber and made a few chalk marks on a table. He then surveyed the victim in order to identify where the obeah was lodged, caught up the area with his fingers and gave it a slight score or two with a razor or knife in order to take the obeah out. Applying the mouth to the spot – "it does not matter what part" – he "pretended" to suck the obeah out, spat it into a basin, then treated it in the same way as the obeah which was extracted from the ground. "Pieces of glass bottles, nails, pins, needles, teeth of cats, serpents, bits of bones, shells, small vials, lizards, spiders and other small insects, all have been known to come out of the skin." This practice was identical to what was done in Guyana, albeit by obeah practitioners.[40]

Although Myal practices were intended for the good of the community, they sometimes generated conflict. This was illustrated in 1901 in the case of Anderson, who began Revival meetings at Melin Hall, otherwise called Perfume Hill. His mission concentrated on the "Elect daughters of Zion – God pickney", whom he sought to send to a Zion school in Kingston. Among his "chosen few", Bunchy and Ada, sisters of Zion, received the gift of unknown tongues. But as good Myalists, their attempt in June 1901 to keep "the dirty face" – that is, all who dealt in the "black art" of obeah – out of Perfume Hill brought them into conflict with Bunchy's mother, who then sought redress from the custos (the chief executive officer of the parish). Ada was arrested, but Anderson assured her that no harm could befall "Zion Pickney", and she called on him to speak on her behalf at her trial. Anderson, however, attempted to convert Judge Cole, who ordered him to stand down. When he refused he had to be removed by three policemen, while Ada was fined forty shillings and costs. Anderson was subsequently charged with contempt and sentenced to thirty days "in His Majesty's Model Farm at Hog Hole".[41]

Shadow Catching

According to Stewart, "After the great Myalist revival that gathered force upon full emancipation, the catching of shadows became almost as important a Myal function as the digging up of Obeah." He traces Myal theology to Akan beliefs regarding the human soul. In this belief system, the *sunsum* (the individual spirit that determines one's character and personality) can get hurt or become ill and affect the body. There is also a malevolent element to the *sunsum* (*sasa* in Asante, *shadow* or *duppy* in Jamaica) which, according to Stewart, can be dissociated from the rest of the personality through witchcraft (obeah).[42] Jesuit Father James Splaine noted the preservation of this belief in Jamaica:

> Mrs. Colliard told me yesterday that many of the people believe they have two souls, one to be saved & the other to be damned. . . . Speaking of the size of the soul, she said it was big when it was going to heaven, but small when going to hell; "as him tek de road", she said, "him come down smaal so", holding the palms of her hands concave towards each other; "but when him go a heaven him big, bi-i-ig so," stretching her arms out as wide as she could. When questioned as to how she knew all that, she exclaimed, "hy! My own judgment tell me. De glory no mek him so? No one person, when him happy, look bigger 'an somebody. . . ."[43]

Hence Stewart says, "It was a function of the Myal man in Jamaica to regain a lost or wandering shadow lest the person it belonged to waste away to death. This shadow is also very demanding at death and must be properly laid or it will remain to annoy the living."[44]

Myal practitioners, therefore, had to possess the ability to see spirits and to converse with them. Consequently they were said to be "fo-yeyed" (four-eyed). Although Myal was supposed to be benign, Banbury argued that its practitioners could also cause harm by "depriving persons of their 'shadows'", and it was believed that "after the shadow of any one is taken he is never healthy; and if it be not caught, he must pine away until he dies". (Presumably in situations like this the Myal(wo)man doubled as obeah(wo)man or vice versa.) When the shadow was taken it was nailed to a cotton tree, whence it could be rescued by the Myal(wo)man.[45] The cotton tree was thus central to shadow catching.

Banbury described the process of shadow catching in the later nineteenth century. The victim was dressed in white, with a white kerchief about the head. Eggs and fowls, along with cooked food, were used in the ceremony, which took place at a cotton tree. The Myalmen, who had white cloths over their shoulders, paraded in front of the tree, singing and dancing; the tree was pelted with eggs, and the necks of the fowls were wrung off and the bodies also thrown at the tree. This, said Banbury, was done "to propitiate the . . . 'duppies' that have the shadow enthralled at the tree". The singing and dancing continued, and became more vigorous as the shadow showed signs of leaving the tree. A white basin with water was held up to receive the shadow; suddenly the victim was "caught up" and the group ran home with him or her, affirming that the shadow had been caught and was covered in the basin. Upon reaching the home, a cloth was immersed in the (shadow) water and applied to the head of the patient. The shadow was then restored.[46]

Revivalists' reputation as "shadow catchers" was well known in the society. According to one correspondent from Grange Hill in 1903, the "noisy and most disagreeable" business of the "Duppy Catchers" or Revivalists, which was to be heard for most of the night, had only been brought under control with the intervention of the rector. Ethel Symmonett described their activities: "[T]hey sing, feast, dance and shout in their native tongue" with one intention, that "the spirit of the deceased may not return to earth transformed into animals, to haunt the living". "Curious" wrote to the *Jamaica Times* about the strong belief in "Obeahism [and] Duppyism" which prevailed in Duncans: "Lately there was a so-called 'revivalist' proclaiming himself to be filled with the Holy Ghost, and telling of wonders that will soon happen, and at the same time introducing himself as a physician for Duppyism and Obeahism."[47]

Healing

Often at issue was the healing provided by Myalists through the use of various herbs, and ceremonies where oils were used to anoint in the name of God. The people often resorted to "bush teas" and "bush baths", frequently accompanied by the anointing of oils, to attend to their illnesses.[48] In 1900 a "Revival Doctor" named Brown was reportedly active in Askenish, Hanover, where he boiled "Bush medicine" for thousands who sought his assistance.[49] The Moravians, in 1908, reported on the activities of a "Medicine Woman" who had set up a "Balm" in Mizpah, Manchester, which was so popular that the church even had to abandon a communion service one Sunday.[50] In the field of folk medicine, however, the lines between the Myal and obeah practitioner were blurred. Both functioned as "bush doctors and doctresses".

At a time when the Western practice of medicine by certified doctors was still quite rudimentary and largely ineffective in the treatment of most tropical diseases, Jamaicans of all classes routinely resorted to herbal curatives. For Susan Gunter, the reasons that the people turned to the "bush" were very clear – there was a shortage of doctors and in some places there were no dispensaries, so the people did what they had to. They used nature's bounty that had proved itself time and again. According to Gunter, "Leaf-of-Life, Man to man . . . Garden Balsam, Spirit-weed, Fresh cut Pepper-Elder and many others" could be used as "first aid" remedies for a number of illnesses.[51] Pullen-Burry further observed that there was a "patent treatment for fever, called the 'bush bath'." This consisted of equal proportions of the leaves of the following plants: ackee, soursop, jointwood, pimento, cowfoot, elder, lime-leaf and liquorice. The patient was plunged into the bath when it was very hot, and was covered with a sheet. When the steam penetrated the skin, the patient was removed from the bath and covered with warm blankets, leaving the skin undried. The treatment usually resulted in a refreshing sleep and "a very perceptible fall in temperature".[52]

However, some of the attempts at cures provided by folk practitioners had potentially dangerous consequences. For example, in an attempt to cure yaws, said Pullen-Burry, the patient's feet were held in boiling water; apart from the possibility of scalding, this could, she believed, even lead to pneumonia.[53] On one occasion in 1899, Catherine Allen who was suffering from yaws sought an "unconventional" cure. A hole was dug in the ground and horse dung and a duck ants' nest placed into it; the whole thing was set on fire. Allen was to lower both feet into the hole but, unable to stand the pain, she ran. Bystanders caught her and brought her back, and Robert Henry and Mary Brown helped to hold her in her cure. Allen's feet were very badly burnt and, eventually, both had to be amputated. Henry and Brown were charged with "assault occasioning bodily harm".[54]

In 1881 the *Gleaner* reported that there was a belief that for the stings of wasps, scorpions, and centipedes, the injured area was to be rubbed with raw onion and salt. However, the newspaper's own scepticism on the matter was clear when it advised those who believed this to begin with the sting of the black scorpion.[55] In 1902, when a large crocodile was shot in George's Plain, Westmoreland, the *Jamaica Times* reported that the reptile was skinned and "a large amount of fat was taken from it to be used medicinally".[56]

While it is true that folk medicine was mostly associated with poorer Jamaicans, there was a certain segment of the upper classes that subscribed to the healing properties of herbs. C.A. Jeffrey-Smith, for instance, pointed to his own experiences with measles and jaundice as a child, and as a parent who sought a cure for his daughter's fever. In the first instance, Jeffrey-Smith said that he had been under the care of the esteemed Drs Bowerbank and Campbell, but although no cure was accomplished, he had been stuck with a large bill. Sent to the country, he came under the care of "an old woman" who gave him a large pan of bush tea which she later told him included "the leaves and branches of Marigold, Susumber leaves, and blades of the Guinea grass, boiled to make a strong tea". He was cured. His daughter, at ten days old, developed a terrible fever; she was placed under the care of "a leading M.D., alive and practising" who ordered that she was to have nothing but vervain tea; her fever was broken. Jeffrey-Smith went a step further to validate his position on the efficacy of herbs by referring to various publications which came from London, and which, therefore, were perhaps given the status of gospel. *The Complete Herbalist* by Professor Brown spoke highly of vervain, while Murray's *Materia Medica*, volume 2, described how to prepare a number of herbal preparations to cure various ailments.[57]

Many of the elements of this healing system could, in fact, be found in some of the island's drug stores. This was especially true for the various oils which were used for anointings and some of the powders that were mixed. According to Mrs B. Jolly, one of the premier drug stores (sometimes called "doctor shops") was "kingkade" (Kinkead's) on King Street.[58] It was at these "doctor shops" or "chemists' shops" that various concoctions were mixed in order to dispense "pick-me-ups, opiates and draughts". The demand for pick-me-ups came primarily from persons who were feeling "tired" or "nervous" and could include combinations such as "cardamums, gentian, and sal-volatile" or "cardamums, hydrocyanic acid, and tincture of capsicum", or else the popular combination of "liquor strychnia, tincture of orange and disulphate of quinine", all of which were self-prescribed.[59]

For generations the Jamaican people had been helped and cured by the various concoctions that herbalists, "balmists" and "doctors" of various sorts administered to them. In a community where a significant portion of the population was poor, the access to relatively cheap consultations and medicines from traditional sources was a great relief. They had seen their grandmothers' aches and pains relieved by the bushes that were soaked, boiled, applied or consumed, and had seen their friends and neighbours benefit from the bush baths and anointments. They *knew* that these things were real and effective. Consequently, herbal practitioners were very popular all over Jamaica. At Prospect, St Elizabeth, according to the *Jamaica Times* in 1899, there was "a quack who is carrying on a large business in bush-doctoring under the misnomer of 'Doctor'". Hundreds flocked to him daily and although he dispensed the same medicine for all complaints, his patients expressed faith in him.[60] At the Roehampton "Balm", John Scott dispensed medicine in a complex of buildings which included "hospitals" where some of the worst cases resided.[61] Lucea also boasted its own "so-called Doctor" who administered medicine, while at Ulster Spring, Trelawny, the *Gleaner* reported that there was a man "practising medicine unlawfully". Although there were two "regular doctors" in the district, "the craze is spreading over the entire parish and people come from Falmouth and Rio Bueno to Warsop, where the imposter has taken up his abode in a hut".[62] In 1905, despite the objections of the "cultured" classes, according to the *Jamaica Times*, at Gayle in St Mary, a "miraculous Healer" was drawing enormous crowds, including "the blind, the lame, the deaf and the crippled".[63]

In 1902 "Doctor Reid" was fined fifteen pounds for breaches of the medical laws. The case drew some interest since Reid's partner in his practice, an ex-soldier named Da Costa, claimed that he had a licence from the governor to dispense medicines, and produced a letter from the colonial secretary Sydney Olivier (who was the acting governor), to that effect. According to the letter, there was "no objection" to Da Costa's selling "Balm Oil and other harmless mixtures".[64] The *Gleaner* thus asked:

> [W]ho gave the power to the Acting Governor to dictate what people can sell in the way of medicine? . . . We have never credited Mr. Olivier with an intimate knowledge of the social conditions in Jamaica. . . . If he knew the people he would have thought twice before giving what is nothing more than a license to an irresponsible man to do anything he likes. . . . He may have done it out of good nature but there is no question that letters of this kind become in the hands of charlatans and imposters very strong weapons in persuading ignorant persons of the legality of their acts and the strength of their representation.[65]

But since in the new thrust to advance towards civilization Afro-creole herbalism was increasingly tainted with the "curse of primitivism", sometimes these unauthorized medical practices brought the "bush doctors and doctresses", who generally operated on the margins of "proper" Jamaican society, into conflict with the law. The herbalists were often accused of practising obeah (an accusation which seemed, in some cases, entirely justifiable). In 1899 the *Jamaica Times* complained that a self-styled "French Doctor" was making the rounds in Moore Town, Portland, and was dispensing medicine after he "cut" playing cards to determine the source of the illnesses which were brought to him.[66] In Gordon Town, a man named Price was fined five pounds for selling medicine without a licence. He claimed that this was not true, that he had himself been ill and had received a vision which featured a white man who showed him certain grasses that he should boil and drink. After his own recovery, he had made this concoction available to others who offered him "something" for his trouble.[67]

Because the practice of herbal folk medicine formed an integral part of their spiritual belief system, many practitioners operated in fierce defiance of the law as an exercise of cultural self-determination. For instance, in 1870 a sick child died and another was dangerously ill ostensibly because, instead of administering medicine to them, their relatives consulted a Myal doctor. The arrested Myalman, however, was unrepentant:

> "The word of God tells me to pray, and that if any are sick, let him send for the elders of the church to anoint the sick with oil and pray over him. This is what I believe in, and what I have done . . . it is the Lord's will that it should die." When asked about the name of his denomination, he replied, "Just what the Bible says we are, 'a chosen and a peculiar people, holy unto the Lord.' We are not ashamed of our name. . . ."[68]

They knew that their ways were neither understood nor embraced, but they answered detractors by situating themselves in a zone of "peculiarity". While the elite might have agreed (using quite another definition of "peculiar") it was the claim of being holy and chosen that gave to the Revivalists a confidence that was perhaps not usually available to the children of ex-slaves. There was no reliance here on the status ascribed by the cultural elites; the people were constructing, maintaining and advocating a distinctive world view and culture of their own.

The balm-yards where healing took place were a source of curiosity and consternation. In 1897 the *Gleaner* sent a correspondent into Darliston, Westmoreland, to investigate why sick people went there from miles around every Wednesday "to be 'balmed' and to have their wounds attended to". At Mother Ackinson's balm-yard, he was shown a pot which contained the bush medicine that had been boiled. But, she said, it was "prayer that people want, and not physic. . . . There is only one that can heal [that] is Jesus Christ."[69] In 1898 when a *Jamaica Times* correspondent visited Mother Ackinson's balm-yard, "victims of consumption, of ulcers, of even leprosy, paralytics and rheumatics" were there, and "all were of the poorer class of the island, not a light skin showing among them".[70]

In 1902 the Moravians complained that a "bush doctor" who had been operating in Carisbrook left the district "in search of other fields more favourable to his superstitions and money making craft, still his evil influence remains, as many still believe in and fear him, keeping away from the house of God, and either attend the meetings kept up by his so-called 'soldiers' or remain at home sunken into utter carelessness". Even after he was sent to prison in July, there was still "a deplorable lack of interest in spiritual [Christian] things" among people in the district.[71]

The hostility of some elites to the practice of spiritual and herbal healing seems to suggest that the people who had been taught to regard Christ as the great healer and comforter had taken the lesson to places never intended. When the healers and balmists invoked the name of Jesus to heal the sick in the midst of an anointment or bush bath, it signified a coalescence of a fundamental Christian practice with their own traditions. Missionary denunciations must thus have seemed hypocritical. But this was a complex cultural environment in which the competing (and complementary) world views of Euro-Christianity and Afro-creole beliefs in the ancestors, spirits and herbs were in continual negotiation.

Further, when some members of the elite endorsed the use of herbs, those who would deny the efficacy of the bushes were placed in a quandary – inasmuch as the use of herbs had ties to an African and slave past that the elite would rather ignore or forget, the herbs' apparent efficacy made it difficult to deny at least this aspect of the creole culture. However, since so many aspects of the herbalist's practice resembled or were linked with obeah and Myal, the outright embrace of herbal remedies by the upper- and middle-class cultural elites was not possible. So, whereas there was widespread acceptance of herbs among the people, among the elites, as in so many other facets of creole culture, there was ambivalence. They were well aware of the possible benefits, but had a well-developed need to distance themselves from anything associated with a "barbarous past". Herbal medicines fell uneasily into such a categorization.

Spirit Possession

> "And they were all filled with the Holy Ghost, and began to speak with other tongues, as the Spirit gave them utterance."[72]

Spirit possession was at the heart of Revival worship. According to Waddell, the worshippers formed a ring "around which were a multitude of onlookers. . . . Inside the circle some females performed a mystic dance, sailing round and round with outspread arms and wild looks and gestures. Others hummed or whistled a low monotonous tune to which the performers kept time, as did the people around also, by hands and feet and the swaying of their bodies." Drummond observed that "They were yelling, wheeling round, and striking against one another in a frightful manner. . . . One young man was beating himself and spinning about, till he fell down in convulsions. Afterwards, several men and women went reeling and staggering about, moving and striking themselves. All this they did when possessed by 'the spirit'." According to the *Gleaner,* "some people declare that when they 'confess' it is the Holy Spirit speaking through them! This shows at once how Christianity has become mixed up with absurd savage rites; and probably it is because these revival dances have some semblance of genuine religious meetings that they have been allowed to continue so long."[73] Perhaps, instead, what it showed was how Christianity had been incorporated into a pre-existing world of spirits and ancestors.

In Patrick Town, according to a missionary in 1901, church work was impeded by a "strange and curious kind of religious fanaticism":

> You will find men, women and even children who profess to get the spirit and who say that their eyes are opened now. These groan and shout, jump and kick, and very often are worked up to a state of frenzy. Many of them have no taste for the services held in the church and if they join, they cease from paying church subscriptions. They are now fond of going from place to place keeping meetings especially in the night, and it is astonishing to see many running after them. It is almost useless to reason with them and to show them that that is not conversion.[74]

Likewise, in 1922, in the midst of the Prospect community of St Mary, there was a large booth where "old time revival of being possessed by a spirit (evil spirit) has been carried on", and African dances "so low and vile" were put on and supported. The Quakers were forced to admit that "we find the task of undoing prevailing ideas of what constitutes conversion and Christianity more difficult than where the soil is virgin. In this community they have been feeling after God but in their own way, with contortions of the physical – vision, messages while in a trance, rolling on the ground, and loud cries."[75] Having partaken of "superior spiritualism", many persons found the staid Anglo-American method of worship unsatisfying.

Often described as "frenzied", the Revivalists were observed to "tarry"[76] for as many as seven days and nights for the anointing of the Holy Spirit. According to Charles Rampini, "Some fed on grass; others crouched on all-fours like beasts; others went about prophesying that obeah was hidden under the threshold of the church. Immorality, under such circumstances, was much more rife than religion."[77] Far more usual in the contemporary descriptions were reports that while they awaited holy anointing, the people made "the hideous noise" called "trooping" which sounded like a rhythmic guttural grunt.[78] It was this trooping that was often described as animalistic. At Mount Ward in 1874 there were reports of "fanatical meetings" which began in the house of a leader and local preacher:

> [W]hat began in the evening as a prayer-meeting soon became a dance, called trooping, which was often followed in the early hours of the morning by certain superstitious practices similar to Obiaism; and it is well known that among those who take part in these meetings are more cases of fornication than is common. Mixed up with these proceedings a few persons who take a very prominent part in the Meetings, pretend to receive direct revelations from God, which they make known either in English or in a gibberish they call the unknown tongue.[79]

Further, according to one report from Shortwood, St James, they had "queer practices" such as "scattering corn, beating drums etc." which drew "foolish people" into the fold.[80]

The Revivalists also purportedly prophesied, and warned those within earshot of events which were to follow. "Girls 'get the spirit,' and display it in noisy prophesy. Ignorant men speak in 'unknown tongues,' and are listened to with awe and astonishment. Lengthy meetings are kept at night, often accompanied by the drum and ending in vulgar amusement."[81] In July 1897 a "warner" admonished the city to "Beware! fornicators, beware! False professors, beware! The Lord is coming quickly. He is coming as a judge." In August 1899 a Revivalist from Negril arrived at the Hope Wharf with a divine warning to a young fisherman, that he would shortly be drowned. Said the *Jamaica Times,* "We wait for the fulfilment of this prophesy." According to one interviewee in Smith's Village in 1914, there was every reason to believe in the divine connection of one particular warner, who claimed to be Jesus and to have been crucified, because he had predicted the 1907 earthquake. Generally speaking, however, Revivalist claims of "spiritualism and clairvoyance" were dismissed by many as "a great deal of rubbish".[82]

However, in a society which by the late nineteenth century relied on many of the Western indicators of status (wealth, education, occupation – in a word, class), the Revivalists gained a different sort of status from a different set of values. Usually marginalized men and women were listened to, and the community created for them the space and place that they were not otherwise able to command. Their apparent connection to a spiritual world of power elevated them, and they had every reason to speak, "as the Spirit gave them utterance".[83]

Water Rituals

Many of the activities that Revivalists were involved in included wonders worked with consecrated water. Time and again water featured in the Revival ceremonies, whether for anointment or for baptism. Rivers and the worship of river gods form a very important aspect of most West African religions,[84] and the rite of Christian baptism fitted naturally into the existing belief system of Afro-Jamaicans. Baptism by immersion was essential for initiation into Revival sects. Immersion was also used for healing and washing away sin. In 1895 a "healing spring" was discovered in Williamsfield, St Catherine. Led by a woman called Cole, whose father had been born in Africa, the group waited for the water to be "troubled" by spirits, when it was pronounced blessed and holy, and then hundreds of devotees rushed into the stream in a "nude condition"; according to the *Gleaner*, "disgusting scenes" followed. A similar situation occurred in 1899 when "President Dan" and his Revival group engaged in "Fountainism", drinking water consecrated by themselves.[85]

Without doubt the most famous of the "fountainists" was Alexander Bedward (see below), whose healing stream became the subject of folk knowledge and song.[86] But many were they who were compared to him. In 1899 "another Bedward" named Simm Bygrove appeared in Croft's Hill, pitched a tent, and displayed a banner with a black cross and the words "The banner of our Lord Jesus Christ" inscribed. He blessed the water from a little spring in the community, and his followers claimed that the water took on medicinal properties. In 1905 Elder Raymond was reported to be involved in "faith healing". Hundreds flocked to his three daily services, and his baptismal services also attracted those who were already members of the Free Methodist, Baptist and Church of England congregations. Likewise, in 1906, Alexander Crawford offered "a new fountain" in Bath, St Thomas, which had healing properties. He claimed to have encountered a lizard-like animal (the size of a mongoose) at a spot nearby. When the lizard retreated, it reputedly left behind "an unreadable writing" and water flowed from the spot. As the news spread, "the halt, the blind, the good, the bad, the indifferent" flocked to see the new wonder. In short order, services of prayer and hymn singing sprang up around the dispensation of the "holy water" (which Crawford prohibited from being removed).[87]

The cleansing properties of water and its necessity for life made it an understandable part of Revival rituals. And since many of the established Christian churches used it too, there was little that could be done to dissuade people from the idea that, ultimately, it must be a good thing. If the elite Anglicans used a few drops of water on a baby's forehead in a ritual of purification and inclusion in the heavenly community, how much greater a claim on spirituality and inclusion in the Kingdom of Heaven was to be had from the total immersion of baptism in water and its ingestion?

"Mad Revivalists"

One of the generally assumed adverse effects of Revival was its inducement of insanity. According to R. Edward Foulkes, Revivalist meeting places were "nurseries for the Lunatic Asylum".[88] In 1860 three persons (a man and two women) were sent from Porus, Manchester, to the lunatic asylum under police escort. They were committed by the parish magistrate for indulging in "revival practices" to such an extent as to be considered of unsound mind. At a jury inquest in 1899, it was stated that the subject's death was due "mainly to the excited shouting he had indulged in at a revival meeting". The jury went further, calling for legislative interference for the suppression of the Revival meetings, "as they were responsible for a large percentage of lunatics, paupers and criminals". These ideas were supported by at least one resident magistrate, who could not recollect a single case of insanity brought before him "which has not been directly attributable to revivalism".[89]

By June 1899 the idea that there was a clear connection between Revival and insanity led the *Gleaner* to launch an investigation. This purported to show that the number of inmates at the lunatic asylum had increased "by leaps and bounds" during the 1890s. Citing the resident magistrate and the inquest jury (above), the newspaper also noted that the parochial board of St Elizabeth had passed a resolution "That in the view of the increasing insanity in [the] parish, and the heavy Lunatic charges on the funds of the parish, and it having been creditably ascertained that the increase is attributed to so-called revival meetings in a great measure; that the Government be asked to take some legal steps for the prevention of these meetings". There was also special concern that the female inmates of the asylum were "victims of revivalism".[90]

But Dr Plaxton, who worked at the lunatic asylum, labelled this a "mistaken view". According to him, that impression was gained from the fact that many of the asylum's inmates did talk about religion, but he took the view that "the masses of Jamaica have nothing to occupy their leisure except religious exercises". For him, one of the major causes of insanity was heredity. Although this caused the *Gleaner* to concede that since there was no better authority on the matter than Plaxton, "the belief that revivalism is fast producing lunatics is a fallacy",[91] the link between Revival and lunacy was retained in the public mind. And when in 1919 Dr D.J. Williams, medical superintendent of the lunatic asylum, listed "religious excitement" as one of the four main reasons for growing numbers of persons suffering from insanity, because "persons of unstable nervous organizations who generally revelled in revival meetings and 9th night orgies, usually terminate their careers within the walls of the lunatic asylum", the argument seemed sealed.[92] If further confirmation were needed, there was always Alexander Bedward, the best-known Revival leader, who was officially certified insane and spent his last years confined to the asylum (see below).

Since the Revivalists were almost invariably black, a racial aspect was added to this issue. "An occasional contributor" to the *Jamaica Post* contended that "of all nations comprising the great family of mankind, we have no hesitation in asserting that those belonging to the African race are the people most hopelessly the prey to the deepest horror and depravity of superstitious observances". For him or her, the practices of the Revivalists constituted "wild and wicked superstition" and a sort of "inherent barbarism" which affected mental and moral progress among the people. A white physician "of long acquaintance with the Negro temperament" corroborated this view, noting that the "emotional instability of the Negroes . . . would be unbelievable to an Anglo-Saxon".[93]

The lines separating sanity from insanity are, to some extent, socially constructed. Behaviour which falls outside of the "norm" is held up for interrogation and where, as in this situation, it could not be explained logically, it was labelled insane. It is no surprise, therefore, that much of the conduct of the Revivalists should come under close scrutiny since, among other things, they flouted the "acceptable" standards of dress (with their flowing robes and turbans), of worship (with their trooping and "setting of tables"), and of their place in Jamaican society (with their claims of spiritual superiority and "godliness"). Their beliefs and behaviour were held in suspicion and derision. Insanity seemed a good explanation for those who dreamed dreams, saw visions, rooted out evil, tarried for the Holy Spirit, called upon the name of Jesus as they cast out demons, caught straying shadows, and healed with water, with oil, by the laying on of hands and the use of herbs.

Within the context of Victorian and Edwardian Jamaica these were, indeed, "mad people".

Female Revivalists

Again and again, reference was made to the many women who dominated the congregations of the Revival movement. According to "Omega" in 1861, Kingston, "the commercial metropolis of Jamaica, the focus of intelligence, knowledge and wealth of the island . . . witnessed to its shame, nay to its disgrace, a host of incongruous, prejudiced and bigoted fanatics . . . pastors, laymen and office-bearers, among whom are WOMEN, who are strictly forbidden to be heard in public by their Bibles", and who presented scenes of "inconceivable confusion".[94] The only explanation that could account for women's presence in the streets as members of such "disreputable" religious groups was sex. Hence, it was claimed that these women were "allured to path[s] of vice", and "tempted to yield to the lusts of the men, they [were] the ready and lost victims to sexual concupiscence".[95]

Some of these women were Revival leaders called "mothers" (Zion) or "shepherdesses" (Pukumina). But most were ordinary devotees who, it seems, were often most affected by the anointing of the spirit. For instance, in 1862, at the corner of John Street and Kelly Lane in Allman Town was a large yard, covered with coconut boughs and owned by one Delaney, where "error, superstition and all manner of devilment" were in evidence, and "most of the 'stricken' [were] young women". Among these women were "Soldiers Mammees" or "Revival Girls" who, when given the signal, fell down, beating and thumping themselves, chasing people with sticks and stoning them away.[96] The *Gleaner*'s description of a meeting in West Queen Street in 1897 was typical; over two hundred persons, "principally women", were gathered. The meeting opened with a prayer and a hymn from Sankey's. Then

> a woman, who had been sitting on one of the benches fell forward suddenly and began bawling at the top of her voice . . . she appeared to be a raving lunatic and was jumping about the place and throwing herself on the ground in a manner that led me to believe that she was destitute of feeling. . . . Not long after this woman had fallen, another followed her example. . . . A while later, another woman went down and began calling upon the Lord to save her. . . . One by one girls and women fell down until about 7 or 8 had fallen.[97]

The *Falmouth Post,* however, "understood" why women were most susceptible to spirit possession: "[I]t is by no means strange that females only are subjected to the 'convulsions' for which Revivalism is remarkable, as nervous excitement is a part of the composition of the weaker sex, to be reduced to a great state of nervousness by constitutional disorganisations."[98]

In a patriarchal society such as Victorian Jamaica, that Revival created a space for women is partly what made it so potentially powerful and disruptive. According to the tenets of Victorian gender ideology, "ideal women" were expected to be pious, obedient, submissive and chaste/virtuous. The women who were engaged in Revival meetings across the island appeared not to fulfil many of the criteria for the label "true women"; in the execution of their spiritualism they seemed to flout many of the conventions of the Victorian ethos, and were therefore harshly criticized.[99]

Revival Preachers

It was a novel sight to see
A coloured man named Captain C,
With stockings nearly to his knee,
And big drum twice as big as me.

. . . With rod and Bible in his hand,
Away he went to Johnson's land;
And scarcely did he take his stand
Before he gave his first command:

"If anybody dem nabor kill
I gwine fe mek dem all stan' still;
Ram too too, la de yard is full
Wid ebery sort ob deb'lish ill.

"I gwine to show you wonders to-night
I want fe see a few more light;
Sacree nah Joe nah sacree vite;
I see some angel all in white."

This thing continued till half-past ten,
Till all the women, girls, and men
Began to yawn and say "Oh then
I think I must go to me den."

"De obeah-man you go last week,
To kill you bredda dat's what you seek;
See how you tan op deh so meek,
You guilty 'til you cannot 'peak

"Soo too la ge, jist lok an see
At Revelation twenty-three;
De verses dem's not told to me,
But read de chapter, Sas ta ta be"

He called for water, poured it out,
And then they all began to shout;
A few were standing who were in doubt
About the doings of this lazy lout.

The shouting grew into a yell;
Ah well, said I, the hosts of hell
Have hired hands and big bomb shell,
Because there was a nasty smell.

Oh Gospel Preachers, Christian Friend,
Your hearts and hands and voices lend
Our Saviour's Kingdom to defend
For to these acts there's awful end.[100]

In many cases Revival groups were led by colourful nomadic preachers, who competed with each other and with the churches for the privilege of leading persons to Jesus. In 1879 the Moravians complained bitterly about a group of "wild fanatics" that was robbing them of members. The group's "shepherd" told the Moravians' members that they were wrong to go to a church whose ministers were guilty of taking filthy lucre, even though he (the shepherd) was supported by voluntary subscriptions of his followers. Early on Sunday mornings he climbed to the top of a tall tree and "like a Muslim muezzin", called his followers to worship: "This consists mainly of the singing of some most absurd songs. The scene ends with howling, accompanied by contortions of the body and other improprieties which cannot be mentioned."[101] In November 1897 the *Gleaner* reported that "an army of street preachers" congregated about the northwestern and western sides of the Victoria Gardens in Kingston. The sites selected were "the northern and western gates of the Park, Orange and Sutton Street, Heywood Street and Luke Lane, the south-western corner of the Parade, Princess and West Queen Streets and West Queen Street near West Street". The meetings lasted for about four hours and were well attended, including those who gathered to ridicule.[102]

In Warsop, Trelawny, open-air services held in 1902 by a street preacher were said to be responsible for the "dry rot" which lurked in the community. In Oracabessa in 1903, "Itinerant street preachers seems [*sic*] to be on the increase as we are visited every week by one or two. Indeed it is no uncommon sight to see two different sets about a chain or two apart holding forth at the same time, and seemingly vying with each other as to who can send forth the loudest and most unmelodious sounds and attract the biggest crowd." In the same village, "religious fever" seemed to have affected a young man who started preaching at two in the morning one Sunday in 1903. He was determined "to deliver a message he had in the form of a dream much to the disgust of the tired and sleepy residents along the route of his march". Some citizens, however, grew increasingly concerned about the violent language that was allegedly used by some street preachers to abuse "the Ministers, and other Authorities including the Governor, and it is abuse the most violent and indecent". According to the *Jamaica Times,* "The fanatics deny restraint, claim inspired prerogative, roam where they please, speak and utter what they please."[103]

By the turn of the century, therefore, Revival street preachers were not just a nuisance to the "respectable" public, but potential political agitators.

Not surprisingly, in November 1903 the governor in Privy Council, under the provisions of the Kingston Police Laws (1881–87) and the Amendment Law (1902), approved regulations for controlling street preaching in Kingston. These were, in turn, adopted by the mayor and council. But, even in the face of laws, the preachers continued in their calling, creating a spectacle that could not be ignored by sceptical observers:

> With hands clasped and head uplifted they pour their inexhaustible torrent into the ears of the assembled crowd as uninterruptedly as if it were being produced by the turning of the handle at the back of them. Every now and then a voice in the crowd responds, repeating perhaps the last words of a sentence. . . . The recipe seems to be a thorough and inherent knowledge of the Scripture, and a good wind. There is no home-made eloquence about it; it is simply stringing beads with an instinct for matching the colours.[104]

In spite of the attempts at control, the street preachers continued to create a "disturbance", especially in Kingston. Small wonder that in 1907 over two hundred persons, "among them prominent doctors, lawyers, merchants and clergymen", signed a petition to remedy this "evil". Nothing, however, came of this.[105]

Charles Higgins

One of better known of these street preachers was Captain Charles C. Higgins, B.A.E. (British and American Evangelist), a self-styled "Orator, Preacher, Dictator, and Instigator, and though last but not least sailor and soldier". He returned from England in 1897 and immediately began street preaching before forming his Royal Millennium Baptist Missionary Society and associated Millennium Hospital for herbal treatment of illness in 1899. He also aligned himself with the even more (in)famous Alexander Bedward (see below), and together they conducted mass baptisms in the Hope River at August Town.[106]

He earned the sobriquet "Warrior" Higgins on account of his fiery denunciations of the mainstream churches and the colonial civil authorities, which were described as outrageous to decency and common sense. Said the *Jamaica Times*, "We can testify that the conglomeration of nonsense, abuse, and indecent expression is not at all exceptional on the part of Higgins." He called the Anglican bishop "a damn lazy idle dog", castigated the same bishop and the pope as "damn confounded liars", called ministers and judges fools, and even mocked the king.[107] "Higginsism" was also tainted with violence. For instance, in 1901 Father Kayser, a Catholic priest, was attacked by "a Militant Higginite" in Chestnut Lane, Kingston. Again in 1901 a "fanatic" dressed in "full regalia" entered the Holy Trinity Cathedral and sat quietly through the service, but at the end "chose a convenient spot outside and lavished the most virulent abuse on the departing worshippers". Likewise, the open-air gospel meetings of the Salvation Army were also disrupted. Higgins and his followers aroused not only elite hostility, but also that of some ordinary people, and they got as good as they gave. He was himself physically attacked on a few occasions, and eventually died in July 1902 following a severe beating.[108]

But Higginsism did not die, for one of his followers, W.F. Dougal, took up his mantle (as well as the sword he had used). In 1905 the police still considered Higginsism a problem, and the so-called respectable public had become so fed up that the Kingston City Council considered "putting its foot down" on Higginsism.[109]

Under the mantle of Revivalism, Higgins attacked some of the bastions of colonial authority in the period. The bishop and other ministers, judges and even the king came into his line of fire, and it was no wonder that the authorities wanted him and his followers silenced. If part of the civilizing mission was the acknowledgement of Britain's cultural power, then the assault on the head of the Church of England, the representatives of English law and the sovereign of the British Empire was potentially dangerous, and consequently these attacks had to be suppressed.

"Modern Messiahs"

According to "R.W.T.", a *Gleaner* correspondent, by 1914 Smith's Village was a centre for the Revival movement. There the Reverend Hewitt, dubbed a "Modern Messiah", had a large following. His meetings were attended by a great number of "women of the labouring and peasant class" who were dressed in white frocks and turbans, while the "prophet" himself dressed in a white shirt and collar, a black sailor's tie, a stole, a white gown and white boots and gloves. There were three stands with kerosene oil lamps and a table covered with a white cloth, on which lay the Bible. Hewitt was considered one of the most violent preachers around. At one meeting he is quoted as saying:

> You know I have caused a commotion in Kingston. They follow everything I do. ... They put me – the Lord's anointed – in Sutton Street gaol. Yes my own people do it. ... But their day is coming. They say I am black art, but if it was not for Christ I would show them something. They ask me why ah wear white gown. I am sent by God to do his work. White mean purity, and it is Christ who give me the right to wear white gown.[110]

Another Revival preacher, the Reverend Dr Bell, who was "tried by the Gentiles", also had a massive following in Smith's Village. In 1914 he was involved in a "sensational crucifixion play" which had apparently made a great impression on the people. That excitement, according to "R.W.T.", was added to by Bell's "medicinal ministrations" at his headquarters, at the corner of Tulip and Bread lanes, which was marked by banners on which scriptural texts were transcribed in red and white. There the "prophet, evangelist and healer" met "the great unwashed" who attended his services. Central to the proceedings was a table, covered with a white cloth, on which there were some flowers, a Bible and other books. This "modern Messiah" was described as being about five feet tall and dark in complexion, with an amiable countenance. He dressed in a wonderful costume of red, green and yellow and "wore a band, covered profusely with beads, spangles and brilliants". He also carried a fine walking stick, which he used as a baton or prophet's rod as the occasion demanded. "Thus we witness the firm grip which superstition has upon the minds of a large section of our people, and these are not all of the lowest class."[111]

In 1896 the Quaker missionaries in Morant Bay reported that a Mr Harrison, a quite well-to-do *white* Jamaican who owned a coffee plantation,

> represents himself as having lived a wicked life until a year ago, when he professes to have been converted, and received a call to preach. ...
>
> He claims to have direct revelations, and says that neither Paul nor any man that ever lived knew what he does about the spiritual being of man, the future life, etc. He also foretells future happenings. He drives about the country with two or more black women, – one of them he calls Mary Magdalene and the other the Virgin Mary, – all dressed in white, and holds open-air meetings, which are attended by multitudes of people.[112]

The Quakers described his meetings and the general behaviour of his congregation as "hideous, ludicrous, blasphemous, by turns". Harrison also claimed that he could raise the dead. Thus, when a female member of his flock allegedly died suddenly, was placed in a coffin, and was put into an open grave on Wednesday, he was supposed to raise her on Friday. But the authorities intervened, and when the district medical officer raised the lid of the coffin, the woman was found to be alive.[113] Harrison's claims of conversion and direct spiritual revelations, as well as his travels with the white-clad "Mary Magdalene" and "Virgin Mary", placed him closer to the Revivalist end of the Christian continuum than was usual for men of his hue. And the fact that he was white might have been a greater source of consternation for the observing elite: not only had he "let down" other whites, but in an island where whiteness was privileged, he might have been thought to be lending legitimacy to Revival.

Alexander Bedward

> Dip dem Bedward, dip dem
> Dip dem in the healin' stream,
> Dip dem sweet but not too deep
> Dip dem fe cure bad feelin'.[114]

The best known of the Revival preachers, however, was Alexander Bedward. Born in 1848, he was described by the *Gleaner* as "an ignorant black man living somewhere in the Long Mountain" who had managed to construct a movement that was alternately the source of derision, concern and consternation. Ordained as an elder in the Jamaica Baptist Free Church in 1876, Bedward began to experience disturbing dreams which eventually led to his being declared insane by Drs Bronstorph and Ogilvia in 1892. Another tumultuous spiritual episode led to his being informed that "the water of the Hope River would be miraculously converted into medicine for soul and body".[115]

Bedward's first test was with a woman who had long been ill. He administered the water to her and allegedly cured her. The news of this healing spread, and people flocked from all over the island to partake of the miracle. The jar which contained the blessed water had to be refilled so many times per day, and the "Prophet" was spending so much time on his ministrations, that another spiritual encounter directed a change in tactics and turned "the whole of the river near August Town into a healing stream, to cure people not only of their bodily ailments but of their sins . . . [and] Bedward selected Wednesday as the day for his grand demonstration".[116]

Bedwardism was increasingly regarded as "one of the most painful and saddening [phenomena] that could possibly be witnessed by anyone of ordinary intelligence, who has his country's good at heart . . . . [T]he seething mass of ignorance . . . congregates in the vicinity without a blush of shame at the credulity and infatuation which is [*sic*] on every side exhibited."[117] Large numbers of people went to August Town carrying "bottles, calabashes, demijohns, cans, or some other utensil, in fact anything capable of holding water", while near the site of the "healing stream" the scene "baffled description":

> Stalls, booths, and small shops had been created at intervals where "coffee, tea, chocolate, pudding or beer" could be obtained by the thirsty traveller. Higglers were present in hundreds, selling bread, fish, fruit and everything else necessary for the refreshment of the inner man . . . there was a constant stream of buggies, buses, horses, mules, donkeys, pedestrians, passing along in the direction of the river. . . . There were lepers, people with running sores, the crippled and deformed, blind, consumptive, asthmatic and in fact every complaint known in the medical world was well represented.[118]

On one occasion it was estimated that between ten and twelve thousand people were gathered to participate in the mass healing. When Bedward arrived and blessed the water at nine in the morning, "every consideration of decency was lost" and the very foundation of Victorian codes of behaviour was overturned:

> Women undressed on the bank and went into the water stark naked, among the men and children . . . the banks were crowded with women; on the left naked men and women bathed together indiscriminately. . . . The spectacle was a most discreditable one and it is safe to say that there is more harm done in five minutes at Hope River than can be undone by all the preachers in Jamaica in five years.

The *Gleaner* expressed concerns about the healthy and diseased persons bathing together, "rubbing against one another", heightening the risk of contagion and infection in scenes that would "turn the stomach of most individuals". As the people were distinctly enjoined by the prophet "to bath[e] first and drink afterwards", the report declared it "terrible to think of the amount of disease that must be spread. . . . the muddier and dirtier the water appears to be, the more readily people drink it".[119] Testimonies as to the healing power of the water spread and Bedward's popularity increased, especially in the rural areas, where "they are completely oblivious of the trend of intelligent opinion in the metropolis".[120] Demands for an end to these activities resounded in the island's newspapers.

The *Gleaner* called for an analysis of the water to be done by the St Andrew

Parochial Board, especially since some were willing to put forward "pseudo scientific" arguments about the possible healing powers of the water due to its mineral content. The paper argued that the water was ordinary river water without any peculiar properties whatever.[121] It also called on the churches to get involved with the containment or elimination of the "Bedward menace"[122] and, in particular, demanded a position and direction from the Most Reverend Enos Nuttall, the Anglican bishop of Jamaica. When the good bishop was asked if he thought the government should interfere with the proceedings at August Town, His Lordship replied:

> Well, there being no disorder or breach of the public peace I do not see how the government could interfere except so far as the matter affects public decency and the public health. . . . I think it would be wrong in principle, practically useless, and likely also to create resistance that would involve danger to the general peace, if the public authorities in any way interfered with the movement so far as it is only a question of religious or superstitious belief and practice. Knowing as I do the temper of our people and the way in which they can usually be managed and controlled without difficulty (if they are led and not driven) I should say that the government might reduce to a minimum the physical and moral mischiefs by firm and kindly representations to Bedward in the first instance as to his duty and what they would require him to do and then by a sufficient force of constables to regulate the matter accordingly.

When asked if the churches should interfere, the bishop declared that he did not have faith in the wisdom of denunciation, although he did advise that those who were caught up with the Bedwardites should be prevented from participating in communion. This wave of fanaticism, he believed, would do less harm if allowed to run its course. When the claims that Bedward made were proven to be false, the people would drift away.[123] The *Gleaner*, however, did not agree with this prescription; it argued that any overtures to Bedward would be "misconstrued by the deluded people and [would] give their leader a false importance in their eyes as well as in his own".[124]

The Roman Catholic bishop, Charles Gordon, took a different view. While the Catholic Church believed in miracles and miracles were still possible, the church owed it to its members to be definitive in its rejection of Bedwardism since the doctrines and activities of that group pointed to "a palpable fraud", and the persons involved with the movement were being "deluded". He was bound to denounce the fraud inherent in the superstition of Bedwardism and to warn Catholic members away from any contact with the phenomenon.[125]

As the discussion and concerns about Bedwardism mounted, the focus turned to Bedward's own capacity for leadership, his alleged ignorance and mental illness. In October 1893 Dr Bronstorph broke any pretence of confidentiality and issued a statement on his examination of Alexander Bedward. He said that late in 1892

> two or three women brought a black man into his office in Harbour Street for examination. They said that the man (whom they called Bedward) had gone mad, and had threatened to kill his wife and children. He had gone on in the most extravagant manner, said he was a man sent from God, that God had appeared to him in a dream, and that he possessed miraculous powers.

After his examination Bronstorph declared Bedward insane, "dangerously so – and suffering from religious monomania". His family, however, was too poor to go through the process of having him privately committed to the asylum, so Bronstorph advised that Bedward be allowed to go loose on the street where he would be arrested by the police "and would be confined by the Government".[126] However, since the police did no such thing, Bedward was left to carry on his ministrations. When he visited Kingston in November 1893, hundreds of persons surrounded him in Orange Street. The *Gleaner* claimed that "he exhibited unmistakable signs of lunacy and carried on a series of antics with two pans which he carried".[127]

In 1894, as the "Bedward craze" continued unabated, the *Gleaner* criticized the positions of the government and Bishop Nuttall, whose prescription of ignoring the movement had, in the paper's estimation, failed. Hundreds still gathered every Wednesday for the blessing of the water, and the stalls to supply the pilgrims were doing a thriving business. Further, the movement was being formalized with the erection of a "Temple": "the establishment of a regular form of service has, in a measure, solemnized the farce and brought the proceedings to be called purely religious". The Bedwardites now had "their own prophet, their own martyr, their own creed, their own form of worship". Said the *Jamaica Times*, "Bedwardism seems to be a nondescript denomination, as it is neither one known thing or another. When will our people open their eyes to see that they have only been 'following cunningly devised fables' and that Bedwardism is a farce?"[128] But it was Bedward's sociopolitical message that caused the *Gleaner* the most concern as, according to its correspondents, the "Prophet" had begun to denounce the rich "who grabbed the substance of the poor".[129] This represented a potential threat to social order and wealth, and it was these concerns with Bedward's language and message that brought the confrontation between the worlds of Victorian Christianity and Afro-creole Bedwardism.

On 16 January 1895 Bedward spoke to his followers on the banks of the Hope River. The *Gleaner*'s report of the proceedings resulted in the charge of seditious language being laid against him. According to the official version of the events, which was based almost entirely on the *Gleaner*'s report,

> He told them that after baptism they had undertaken to throw off the oppression cast upon them by the white people and the Government. He spoke in the most insulting way of the Governor, the Government and the Clergy, designating the latter as vagabonds, thieves, robbers and liars, saying that they had filled our hospitals, almshouses and prisons, that they were blasphemers and scoundrels who were worshipping Anti-Christ. . . . He called upon the people to drive out the white population who were oppressing them, holding out to them the fires of hell as their doom if they neglected to do it and reminding them of the Morant Bay rebellion. He referred to the black population as the "black wall" and the white as the "white wall" saying that the white wall had long enough oppressed the black wall and the time had now arrived when the black wall must knock down and oppress the white.[130]

At Bedward's trial in April 1895, an all-white jury (given the fact that whites formed only about 2 per cent of Jamaica's population, it must have been very carefully selected) in the circuit court returned a verdict of not guilty by reason of insanity, and Bedward was committed to the Bellevue Asylum. On 21 May 1895 he was released after a successful appeal by Philip Stern, a Jewish lawyer with political ambitions. As the *Gleaner* put it, the "Prophet" and the people were once again united.[131]

For the rest of the 1890s Bedwardism continued, largely undisturbed. Thousands continued to gather at the Hope River, but in 1899 some changes as to the decorum of the "dippers" were noted. All who entered the water were "properly clothed", and when they emerged sheets were wrapped around them.[132] But the newspaper campaign against the movement continued unabated. In 1907 the *Jamaica Times* pointed out that Bishop Nuttall's advice to leave the movement to run its course had not borne fruit, since in the aftermath of the earthquake, "far from diminishing, Bedwardism has increased, one risks little in saying prodigiously". In 1910 when "W.A.S." visited Bedward on behalf of the *Gleaner*, the impressive chapel was almost complete, as were the other buildings on the compound. The number of candidates coming forward for baptism was still very large, and Bedwardism was a "settled" institution in August Town.[133]

The influence of the Bedwardites also spread well beyond August Town, not only because of the constant movement of persons, but because efforts were made by some of the ordained Bedwardite pastors to propagate the faith. In 1901 a *Jamaica Times* report from Swift River spoke of the arrival of Reverend Dawson, a Bedwardite; a large crowd gathered to hear him, and four candidates (two children and two "frenzied women") joined the group. From Arcadia came a report that the Bedwardites had held a lively service in April 1901, which had ended in a "revival" with a baptism expected to follow. In Trinityville, St Thomas, the meetings in 1905 also made an impression. The response might not have been so positive in Mavis Bank when the Bedwardites held a service there in June 1903, but they were able to take a small collection of 2s. 3¾d.[134]

In spite of the perceived challenge to the institutions of authority and to Victorian culture, there were some in the community who were quite vocal about their support for Bedward's right to worship and about the possibility that his were positive works. In 1902 "A Well Wisher" warned, "Take heed to yourselves what ye intend to do as touching him [Bedward] and let him alone lest haply ye be found even to fight against God. . . . The Bedwardites are the most prayerful sect and they always have something to say in honour of Jesus['] name."[135] While "I Cor. 13:13" agreed that the movement was making strides, he argued that it was not simply a lack of education that attracted people to the movement, but the fact that the traditional churches lacked spiritual power and spiritual love, and that the focus on dress and "refined" language did little to attract those who had neither:

> As to whether people get much good who join the Bedwardites I cannot say very well. . . . They themselves ought to be the best judges, and they look, I must confess, much happier in their faces than many church Christians that I know, and they do not indulge in drinking, card-playing and "questionable amusements." If they are a bit too noisy, well, many Christians are not noisy enough, and if they pray too loud, well, many do not, and cannot, pray at all.[136]

C.E.A. Roberts went further, arguing that Bedward seemed to be "blessed by God . . . although great men of this world condemn him and look down on him". Although he was "poor and despised", that meant little since the Redeemer had been in the same position: "If Bedward was a learned man with great title, men would not condemn him so much." And for "Leo the Saint", Bedward's movement had only come under pressure because it was "a manger of Black progress".[137]

In 1920 "Prophet" Bedward dreamed that the millennium was at hand; he had received a message that he would ascend to heaven on Friday 31 December 1920 at ten o'clock in the morning. The *Gleaner* scoffed, and declared, "A man does not openly proclaim that he is going to be caught up to Heaven on a certain date if he is not persuaded of the truth of what he says; and it is because he is so emphatic on his translation, and gives the date of it, that Bedward has impressed his ignorant and credulous followers."[138] Since only those gathered at the compound would be saved, thousands made the journey to August Town and made preparations to be "caught up". According to the *Gleaner*, many had disposed of their earthly goods: "houses and lands, live stock, furniture, jewellery and even articles of clothing were, it is reported, sold for a song and Bedwardites in singles, couples, in tens and in hundreds turned their faces toward the new Mecca and trekked for August Town". The tailor shop there worked full-time to provide the white garments which were necessary for the faithful, and the West India Regiment, rather than the police, arrived to control what was expected to be a chaotic occasion. Martha Beckwith, who visited Bedward on 26 December 1920, stated that even "intelligent whites" thought that something extraordinary was about to happen; some "feared a Negro uprising"[139] – which explains why the soldiers and not the police were deployed.

At the appointed hour (ten o'clock), word came that Bedward's departure was postponed until noon. When the ascent still did not occur and the word came that Bedward would no longer "go up" in the flesh, but in the spirit at three o'clock in the afternoon (and then later at ten in the evening) disappointment settled on the gathered faithful and the movement began to unravel. Eventually, those who remained were told that the spiritual ascent would take place at a later date. Many Bedwardites thus returned home disappointed.[140]

But this was not the end of Alexander Bedward. Within a few months he had an open confrontation with the authorities when, on 28 April 1921, over six hundred of his followers responded to a call to join him in a "manifestation" in Kingston. Early on the morning of that day the police and soldiers ambushed him and his followers, and warrants, including one for "threatening to commit a breach of the Peace in Kingston and for inciting others to do the same", were issued for his arrest. Within three days all those arrested, except Bedward and four others, were released. Bedward was again placed on trial on 4 May 1921, and acquitted by reason of insanity, but this time, out of a fear that his followers would see his release as another intervention from heaven, the authorities incarcerated him in the Bellevue Asylum until his death in 1930.[141]

For more than thirty years the authorities struggled to contain Alexander Bedward. His promotion of a distinctive world view and belief system (albeit related to Christianity), with its own doctrines and rituals, resulted in a massive national following of a man who the medical (and other) authorities had declared insane. Whether or not he was indeed batty, he was in any event liable to be so labelled (like the other "mad Revivalists") because he behaved in ways that many people simply did not understand. But for many *other* persons, his behaviour was no more strange than celebrated personalities in the Bible. Had not the great John the Baptist "had his raiment of camel's hair, and a leathern girdle about his loins; and his meat was locusts and wild honey"?[142] Bedward's very "strangeness", then, gave him authenticity among his followers.

Bedward offered a message of healing to those who were desperate for some sort of ministration, and he spoke in the "water language" that had been long understood and appreciated, as he made his gift of healing available to all who could come into contact with the Hope River. The outpouring of support among humble Jamaicans for Bedwardism in particular and Revival in general is indicative of the social as well as the cultural functions that these movements served. Revival spoke to and for the masses who had neither the fine clothes nor the language that marked so many of the established churches. It attracted those who sought more spiritualism and certainly more power than could be had from meekly listening to the admonitions of missionaries and priests. And because those who led these movements came from the people, lived with them, endeavoured to address their concerns, looked like them, spoke like them, and were themselves poor and despised, the support for Bedward and other Revival leaders was, in fact, an invocation of self-acceptance and celebration. The people's prophets came from among them, and the people were willing to bear the ridicule of the social and cultural elite in order to support their spiritual leaders and the messages that they delivered. That Bedward also advocated social insurgency made him a potential threat to the authorities who, after waiting for the movement's fire to wane and witnessing his failed attempt to "fly", finally resorted to the law and a colonial institution (Bellevue) to contain a man who had defied them for decades.

Cultural Elite Reactions to Revival

Missionary and elite Jamaican reactions to Afro-Christian Revival were universally hostile and disparaging. Many shared the American Jesuit Abraham Emerick's opinion that "the Revivalists masquerade as a Christian sect and cover themselves with a glamor of christianity". They accused the Revivalists of "committing acts of most indecent nature", and their meetings were labelled "orgies". The *Falmouth Post* reported in 1863 that the Revivalists in Hanover assembled nightly, and at the end of their "debauchery" they slept together under a large shed which they had erected. The suggestions of sexual impropriety were clear, and calls were made for police suppression. Two years later the *Post* reported that the movement in Hanover, Westmoreland and other parts of the island featured "the miserable superstition". Further, said the newspaper, Revival was accompanied by "idleness and prostitution, robberies and vagabondism, and depravity of every description" and ought to be curbed. Throughout the period there were regular reports of nightly Revival meetings in Rum Lane, Humbug Lane, Passmore Town near Victoria Gardens, Allman Town, Patrick Town and several other parts of Kingston "consisting chiefly of yells and screeching", where there were "certain disgraceful and abominable scenes" that kept "respectable" citizens awake well into the early morning. In 1873 the *Falmouth Post* described the large numbers of persons who usually attended these meetings as "utterly demoralized as vagabonds and prostitutes", and largely supported by contributions obtained from stealing the property of industrious and respectable families. In 1900 C. Wesley-Gammon accused the Revivalists of being "as uncivilized as were there [sic] forefathers who came from Africa" who had indulged in "fearful orgies". The Wesleyan Methodists agreed in 1907 that there was a "prevalence of fanatical revivalism in some places".[143]

The majority of the criticisms that were levelled at the Revival movement came from "decent respectable citizens" who were disturbed or threatened by its activities. Many of these were coloured and black people, whose only qualification for the label of respectability was their embrace of the imported British middle-class mores advocated by their social "betters". They thus considered themselves a part of that loose category referred to here as the cultural elites, although socially they might not qualify as elite. But even among the lower classes there was occasional hostility to Revivalists. For instance, in one incident in Market Street, Spanish Town, in 1863, a "country woman" began to have "violent contortions" and broke out into "incoherent vociferations" to the effect that she was "in hell". A female spectator was affected as well, and the market crowd began shouting and hooting and pelting oranges and other things at them. According to the *Falmouth Post*, this soon convinced "the infatuated ladies" that they were "on terra firma"; they took to their heels "perfectly revived from their revivalism".[144] By their own means of definition, which were not always clear, the people determined for themselves who to accept as authentic Revivalists. Not every warner was embraced, not every message heeded.

The Official Position

By 1867 public concerns about the persistence of Revival were so very strong that the bishop of Kingston reported that he had received news from Cornwall county of "filthy, blasphemous idolatrous" activities, and claimed that the Revivalists were performing "much mischief among the people, disturbing their minds, unsettling their habits, causing them to neglect the cultivation of the land, and to live in idleness and in consequence essentially by plunder". Further, there was alleged evidence of blasphemy, such as when a woman rode about on a donkey that she called "Jesus Christ", and when the blood of a goat was used instead of wine for Holy Communion. The bishop commented, "I believe that since the Rebellion and those unfortunate proceedings by which the minds of the people have been excited afresh, both obeahism and Revivalism, have been on the increase, and it will need the energetic and judicious use of all available legal and moral and religious influences, to prevent their further extension."[145]

This prompted Governor Grant to require the custodes of the parishes in Cornwall, and the inspector general of police, to enquire into these allegations. However, opinion was divided among the local officials: while those in St James could not corroborate the bishop's claims,[146] the reports from St Elizabeth and Trelawny were different. John Salmon, custos of St Elizabeth, claimed that the Revival groups there were brought together by "lewd men and women", and their popularity was maintained by "the licentiousness of their proceedings" as well as with food. While he did not think that they were a threat to the peace of the country, he objected strongly to the conduct of the leader, "John the Baptist", who reportedly left a "brothel" where the congregation had spent the night, accompanied by a woman called "the Virgin Mary" and mounted on an ass before which branches were strewn.[147]

I.W. Fisher, senior magistrate, and Presbyterian Reverend John Aird of

Trelawny substantiated those views. According to Aird, in the "negro villages" such as Duan Vale, Sawyers and Perth the people had stopped attending churches and were instead "giving themselves up to vagrant revivalists, who are encouraged to settle down and carry on their mal-practices in their midst". Aird was particularly distressed by those who "professed" to be members of established churches, but were strident members of the Revival bands and involved in "nonsensical practices with fearful bawlings and yellings, thus disturbing the rest of peaceful and orderly families". He thought the situation was extremely serious since "the moral power of the Ministers of religion is disregarded; so that recourse must be had to the constituted power of law".[148]

Such views were reiterated throughout the period. In 1902 the *Jamaica Times* expressed grave concern about what it regarded as "a combination of Religion and Devilism", and advocated the removal of the offending Revivalists through the Vagrancy Law. It was argued that the use of the law would convince "even the most recalcitrant and stubborn of supernatural beings that a British Colony is not exactly the place for him to incite people to break the peace in". The *Gleaner* asserted in 1905 that the intervention of "a sturdy policeman" would have a calming effect upon the spirit-possessed person, and "he would exorcise the Spirit in double-quick time".[149] And, from time to time, the police did indeed intervene in Revival meetings. Thus, in 1867 five female Revivalists were taken to the Falmouth Police Court and charged with disorderly conduct for "speaking, singing, and praying aloud, accompanied with contortions of the body, thereby disturbing the peace and quietness of the neighbours around". They were severely reprimanded and discharged with a warning. The eight women and two men against whom identical charges were made in 1870, however, were not so lucky: they were sentenced to ten days with hard labour in the Falmouth District Prison.[150]

The case of *Regina v. Frances Stines* in 1890 focused on a woman who was accused of keeping "a noisy, ill-governed and disorderly yard, where persons of ill-fame frequent and remain singing and shouting and misbehaving themselves unlawfully, thereby creating a common nuisance to all Her Majesty's liege subjects". Despite the attempts of the defence, and the testimony of several persons that there had been no such meeting, the judge ruled that "the ringleaders of this mockery, and who deceived the ignorant people, should be put down". Stines was fined ten pounds or two months' imprisonment with hard labour.[151] In 1904, when four members of a band of Revivalists were taken to the lock-up in Port Maria charged with disorderly conduct, their yells, groans and "peculiar movements" (especially the women) caused a crowd to gather. But their behaviour convinced the court of their guilt, and each was fined forty shillings or thirty days' imprisonment.[152]

The law was particularly utilized when Revivalists engaged in violent activities. In 1864 a Revivalist "shepherd" was jailed for leading his flock at Lilliput in "stoning the clergy as false prophets". In June 1881 the testimony of a police constable in the court of petty sessions was to the effect that, at a Revival meeting in Fletcher's Town, "while the women bellowed and kept up a great noise which he heard half a mile off, the men fought with each other". The accused, six men and three women, were all fined. Six Revivalists (three men and three women) who had engaged in a "free fight" at a meeting in Black River in 1884 were likewise fined for assault.[153]

But the resort to law was not always considered prudent, nor was it always successful. First, there was a concern that if the police were routinely used against Revival a greater evil might be precipitated, since "the ignorant auditors would consider the Prophets persecuted for righteousness['] sake and in their superstitious emotionalism might give no end of trouble".[154] Beyond that, however, some persons in authority did recognize the legal right of the Revivalists to worship, no matter how inappropriate their mode of worship was deemed. For instance, in 1872 Governor Grant himself disclaimed any authority to prevent a group of Revivalists from meeting near Craighton, despite complaints. According to Marianne North, "When I told the governor about these things, he said he had no more right to prevent their amusing themselves in that way than he had to stop the white people from giving balls and keeping polkas and waltzes going till the small hours of the morning, preventing all near neighbours from sleeping; and that seemed just." In 1889 even the *Gleaner* recognized that there was no law against the Revival scenes of "debauchery and hideous caterwauling", and that the police had no orders to interfere. Likewise, because there was a tendency to twin Revival with obeah, in 1901 "Climaticus" reminded the readers of the *Jamaica Times* that the Obeah Act could not be used to suppress Revival; rather, it was the Religious Toleration Act which gave them licence.[155]

The Revivalists' legal right to worship as they chose was also occasionally upheld by the courts. For instance, in 1876 the *Gleaner* called the attention of the authorities to several parts of Kingston, especially the upper part of Rum Lane, immediately behind the Mico premises, where "from time to time . . . midnight orgies, commonly known as 'revivalism'" were held in Mrs Bruce's yard. At her trial, however, Mrs Bruce's lawyer designated the gatherings "religious worship", and because of that "legal flaw" the case was withdrawn.[156] Similarly, in the case of *Loza v. Church* (1889), the "mistaken sympathies of an ignorant or prejudiced jury" punished Loza (a policeman) for his "interference" in Church's Revival meeting. No wonder the *Gleaner* inveighed against those "pettifogging lawyer[s]" who were inclined to bring legal action and win damages against the police when they interfered.[157] Even so, however, judicial decisions in favour of Revivalists were not frequent; more often than not when they were taken before the courts they were punished, usually for "disorderly conduct".

The Revivalists, however, very often benefited from the refusal of some policemen, perhaps themselves connected with Revival bands or with the communities where they were popular, to interfere with their meetings. Again and again, reference was made to the non-interference of the police in dealing with Revival. In 1889, for instance, "Taxpayer" complained of the "disgraceful scenes" of the Revival meetings, where these "religious Arabs . . . with their bawling or singing" annoyed and disturbed the Torrington Bridge community. On one occasion, as "Taxpayer" was passing the yard where the meetings were taking place, he or she had encountered a constable on the beat, who was calmly observing the proceedings. When "Taxpayer" challenged him to quiet the people, he declined on the grounds that he had no instruction to do so, and advised "Taxpayer" to report the matter to the police station if he or she thought it a nuisance.[158]

By 1899 the ineffectiveness of the police and the courts in curbing Revival led the parochial boards to urge the police to watch the progress of the movement closely. Although the majority of the boards were hesitant to ask for any new, specific laws against Revival, fearing that they might provoke social disorder, those of St Elizabeth, Portland, Clarendon and Trelawny decided to launch a "campaign against revivalism".[159] That campaign, however, was clearly no more effective in suppressing it than previous efforts had been.

Some people thought that only education would ultimately lead to the eradication of the Revival "scourge". The *Jamaica Times* argued that "education alone can help us to get the better of such diseases of ignorance as 'Revivalism'". Ignorance was seen to be at the root of "Revivalism, Obeahism, Higginsism and Bedwardism", and until it was dispelled, legislation would have little effect. The newspaper also pointed to the lack of "rational recreation" for the people, and argued for "[m]ore schools then, and the start of methods for providing or helping the people to provide healthy and really interesting amusements; these are the things that, helped by wisely framed laws, will rid us of revivalism". Specifically, "a band of enlightened

Christian workers" should be encouraged to go among the people in order to combat the influences of the movement.[160]

But the *Gleaner* thought that the issue was much more complex. The numbers and frequency of the Revival meetings pointed to the fact that the churches had failed the people in an important aspect of their spiritual needs:

> It is plain that the people have some part of their nature unsatisfied. They seek dimly for relief in the rude chanting of sentimental hymns and lugubrious "amens," often in something worse, and the church looks calmly on. Why does it not recognize the importance of the movement and use it for its own purposes? Under sane and responsible guidance the emotions of the people would obtain higher, if less congenial satisfaction.[161]

The *Gleaner* had identified an aspect that seemed to be lost on most of the ruling class: that there was *something* about the beliefs and practices of Revival that was attracting a significant proportion of the people, and that instead of trying to identify what about the spiritualism and rituals of the Revivalists was proving so enticing, the authorities were trying to stifle it in the name of civilization. They were, as has been seen, singularly unsuccessful. Yet it must be said that despite the cultural elite's hostility to Revival, the Jamaican legislature did not go as far as two of its counterparts in the eastern Caribbean which outlawed similar Afro-creole religious expressions, in the form of the Shakers of St Vincent in 1912, and the Shouters of Trinidad in 1917.[162]

Kumina

One of the striking mysteries of the archival documents for the nineteenth and early twentieth centuries is the almost total silence about the Central African religion of Kumina, which was brought by immigrants from that region after emancipation. Schuler (and Stewart) rely heavily on the anthropological fieldwork of Joseph Moore, done during the 1950s, to reconstruct the structure and rituals of that religion; Moore's work is supplemented in Schuler's case by oral evidence.[163] One explanation for the documentary silence may be that because Kumina was associated largely with newly arrived Africans, it was dismissed (and confused) by elite contemporaries simply as obeah, Pukumina, or African fetish. It is also probable that the silence might be related to the "underground" practice of Kumina, as was the case with Orisa/Shango in Trinidad.

Both Moore and Schuler have shown that, despite the small number of Kongos who were taken to Jamaica,[164] Kumina was preserved as a complex, well-organized religion. But Schuler points out that, since these African communities existed in a wider plantation creole society,

> almost from the beginning Central Africans had one foot in "the African world" and the other in the Jamaican world, although as long as they lived primarily in their own communities, the greater part of their religious life was likely to be focused on the cult of spirits of recently deceased ancestors – *min 'kuyu* – the shades.

Kumina involved dancing, drumming and singing, culminating in possession by the shades, who were primarily, but not exclusively, deceased ancestors said to ride or dance with relatives, friends or disciples. Adherents also revered other spirits, including those bound to the earth and to the sky.[165]

All spirits, however, were those of deceased persons, and consequently considerable emphasis was placed in Kumina on "memorial rituals for the dead". Like the Myalists, Kumina practitioners believed that each individual had two souls or spirits: "the personal spirit, which contains his or her personality; and the duppy, the individual's shadow. The personal spirit dwells with a person during life, while the duppy or shadow walks alongside, just like a shadow on a wall." Although at death the personal spirit went to *Nzambi Mpungu* (God Almighty) and never returned to earth, the shadow (duppy) remained in the grave with the corpse and, if a proper burial had not been done, would wander around and create evil among the living. Every Kumina band required an expert, generally male, to supervise the feeding of the spirits and prepare for the ceremony. Schuler also noted that a queen and her disciples controlled Kumina ritual secrets and paraphernalia, which included two drums: "Drums are indispensable in both the private sessions and the public ritual of Kumina, for they call the spirits."[166]

Kumina seemed to be influenced only marginally by Christianity, whether the dominant Euro- form or the "vulgar" Afro-creole variant. It thus represented a classic example of cultural resistance by Central Africans and their descendants in an alien cultural environment characterized by hostility from the Euro-Christian tradition, and by the more openly assimilative influence of the Afro-Christian Revival. Since, as Joseph Moore has shown, obeahmen did play a major role as leaders in many Kumina rituals, Kumina may have attracted some antagonism from Zion Revivalists in their zeal to root out the "evil" of obeah.[167] On the other hand, notwithstanding initial negative perceptions that Africans held of Creoles, the presence of Kumina within the cultural landscape of creole Jamaica may have served to reinforce the pre-existing elements of Africana in the Creole belief system, and perhaps in Pukumina as well. In short, Kumina was an Africanizing force whose strength might have belied the small size of the African population.

Conclusion

That the Jamaican people had managed to construct an entire world, complete with its signs and wonders, outside of the control of the cultural elites was, as far as the latter were concerned, a matter of grave concern and consternation. These were beliefs that the elite neither understood nor directed; here were people who could declare, as did Paul, "[W]e wrestle not against flesh and blood but against principalities, against powers, against the rulers of the darkness of this world, against spiritual wickedness in high places."[168] Ancestors, spirits, herbs, balms and baptisms gave ordinary Jamaicans another frame of reference, transported them into another world where Christ was relevant insofar as he was powerful enough to deal with the evil that obeah visited upon the world. For those who moved between and among the systems of belief, their utility was one of the important aspects that determined their value. Believing simply for belief's sake was far less important when there were people's spirits to save, shadows to be returned, evil to be rooted out, and a spirit world to explain, control and perhaps subdue. Within this cosmos the Myal(wo)man was a person deserving of respect; the Revivalist generated a power that the community understood. None of the elite's standards of achievement mattered here. The Revivalist might be unable to read, might be materially deprived, but he or she could root out evil and restore equilibrium to the lives of persons who often had no other sources of justice, no other advocates or supporters. This was phenomenal empowerment, both for the Revivalists and for those who consulted them.

If Kumina represented African cultural resistance, Revival was an Afro-creole expression of cultural self-determination. Black creole Jamaicans appropriated Christian, mainly Baptist, doctrine and rituals into their own religious belief system and created a new Afro-Jamaican Christianity which openly challenged the cultural hegemony claimed by Euro-Christianity. Their zeal for rooting out evil did not target Afro-creole obeah alone, but also extended in some respects to Euro-Christianity itself and to the colonial civil authorities. Indeed, they claimed to possess a purer form of Christianity than the missionaries, some of whom they denounced as false prophets. This was largely because the spirituality which marked their interpretation of "holiness" was not demonstrated by the Euro-Christian church. Moreover, as Chevannes observes, "To a far greater extent than most people realize, Myal and its later manifestation, Revival, have shaped the world view of the Jamaican people, helping them to forge an identity and a culture by subversive participation in the wider polity."[169] This was an early manifestation of cultural nationalism, at a time when nationalist *political* activity was stifled by the crown colony regime.

This was not mere opposition, as Richard Burton argues.[170] It may not have led to the overthrow of the dominant system, as he would have it do in order to be classified as resistance; but then, even the word "resistance" does not encapsulate the real significance of Afro-Christianity. It was much more than resistance: it was a positive, creative expression of Afro-creole cultural self-determination that sought to establish, and in large measure succeeded in establishing, its independence of the colonial religio-cultural power structure. It placed itself *outside* the control of the Euro-Christian religious complex and the supporting secular institutions, even while its members had a relationship with those very institutions. In this sense, the objective was not to *change* the dominant power structure, but rather to render it *impotent* where it tried to impinge on what they believed was their superior spiritualism. Through Revival, Afro-Jamaicans made it strikingly clear that on matters of faith they were not prepared to be dictated to; they were determined to decide for themselves what was appropriate and suitable for them.

Chapter 4

Sex, Marriage and Family
Attitudes and Policies

IF THE "SPIRITUALISM" CENTRAL TO THE belief system of Afro-Jamaicans differed markedly from the "scientific rationalism" of the nineteenth-century Western secular world view and the religious doctrines of Victorian Christianity, their attitudes to sex, marriage and family conflicted sharply with British middle-class religious and moral values, which the nonconformist missionaries in particular sought to embed in Jamaica. Indeed, issues of sex and marriage were placed at the very heart of the agenda of the British civilizing mission. Both the missionaries and the civil authorities exhibited a virtually obsessive interest in the sexual proclivities of the Jamaican people, and sought to bring them under their moral control. As part of the British-controlled and -influenced empire of the nineteenth century, those who attempted to guide and shape the social institutions in Jamaica sought to import and impose the ideals of Victorian Christianity on the Jamaican people, encouraging them to take religio-legal vows declaring their lifelong commitment to their mates. These vows also bolstered the gender hierarchy of the prevailing patriarchal order by conceiving wives to be the property of their husbands, who in turn were legally bound to provide material support and protection for the members of the families that they headed.

The ideal of legal Christian monogamous marriage was an integral part of an entire ideology of what constituted morality and civility and, inasmuch as it provided the only "appropriate" context within which sexual intercourse should occur, it was the basis for the "legitimacy" of sexual relationships and for the issue of those unions.¹ The principal purveyors of this "ideology of respectability", as Karen Fog Olwig labels it, were the nonconformist missionaries. The male-headed nuclear family was one linchpin of this ideology, which arose among the European middle class during the eighteenth century.² According to Catherine Hall, after emancipation the missionaries sought to create a new Jamaican society based on "a proper gender order, in which men worked for money and women stayed at home, caring for children and household". This new society was to be modelled on that of the English middle classes, and was encapsulated in a sermon by Baptist missionary David East in 1856:

> [H]usbands should love wives, wives submit to their husbands, children honour and obey their parents, servants be obedient. . . . The humblest Christian cottage should be a model home, clean and bright, comfortable and proper, with separate sleeping quarters for parents and children, sons and daughters, and decent chairs and tables. Families should sit down to meals together rather than "the wife standing like a slave while the tyrant master downs his food". It was essential that fathers should act as ministers of their own households.³

For those who embraced such tenets of Victorian Christian morality, sex, marriage and family were key indicators of the progress of civilization in Jamaica after emancipation. They were used to measure the "improvement" of a people whose experiences during slavery had been such that they were believed to have been "shapen in iniquity; and in sin did [their] mother[s] conceive [them]".⁴ But despite the promulgation of the ideal, and the benefits which were allegedly attendant on the state of legal marriage, the majority of the Jamaican people continued to avoid the institution and chose instead to live and love in non-legal relationships disparagingly labelled "concubinage", producing children who were branded "bastards" and causing untold consternation to the cultural elites who, despite the sexual misconduct of some of their own (see below), encouraged others – or else tried to coerce them – into "civilized behaviour".⁵

Non-legal Marriage

Within the Jamaican culture there were several means by which the people constructed conjugal relationships. According to Patrick Bryan, there were two main sorts of unions: those "founded on . . . the civil, Christian or Jewish rites of marriage", and others formed through "the pragmatic, functional marriage often referred to as 'faithful concubinage' ".[6] Jean Besson, however, takes the analysis further by identifying two types of non-legal relationships: those established by "consensual cohabitation", and others created through "extra-residential conjugal relations". These two forms of unions and their variants, collectively and disparagingly referred to as "concubinage", constituted the main types of conjugal relationships in the island. However, Besson's conclusion that these were "Creole transformations of European legal marriage and social stratification based on Eurocentric respectability"[7] is questionable. The Jamaican concept of marriage, shaped largely by conditions of life on the slave plantations, was quite simply *different* from the English model. But her estimation that those persons who were labelled "concubines", and the "bastards" that resulted from the relationships, had founded a system which they controlled and which seemed to work for them is eminently sound. That these domestic units had their own rules, internal dynamics and, therefore, legitimacy, was an idea unrecognized by most contemporary commentators.

In Jamaica, as elsewhere in the Caribbean, contemporary elite commentators during the late nineteenth and early twentieth centuries repeatedly observed that the people did not get married legally, and that they preferred to "live together in sin", in "concubinage", without the blessing of the church and the sanction of the law. As the people put it themselves, they were "married but not parsoned".[8] Thus, the missionaries asserted that legal "marriage is the exception, and living in a state of uncleanness the rule". This "base and barefaced uncleanness of the people" did not meet the approval of the clergy, who inveighed against it both from pulpit and in their daily visitations to the people's houses.[9] Still the legal marriage rates were generally below those in Britain, Europe and the white empire, although on par with sister Caribbean territories such as Trinidad and Barbados.[10] As the table in appendix 3 shows, the rate rose from 3.7 per thousand of population in 1879–80 (when statistical recording began) to a peak of 7.4 in 1907–8 (the year of the great earthquake), then declined to a nadir of 3.0 in 1914–16 (during the First World War).

Despite the overall low marriage rates in the period, there were intervals of "improvement" that provided encouragement to those persons who assumed the role of society's moral guardians, some of whom were inclined to think that a small "moral" and cultural revolution was in the making. In 1867 Methodist Richard Harding at Beechamville regarded the unusual number of legal marriages recently celebrated as a hopeful sign: "Some of this class when under conviction, have been sorely troubled on this account [the "evil sin of concubinage"], and were preparing to be married without the publishing of bans [*sic*] as the law requires. . . . we regarded the feeling as an evidence of the sincerity of their convictions, and contrition." In 1871 George Lockett at Duncans claimed that legal marriage was honoured by all: "The people are evidently ashamed of living in open sin, and I have had an unusual number of marriages this year which is generally considered a good sign."[11]

At the end of the century, the Quakers too felt that a comparatively large number of legal marriages was proof that "[t]he conscience of the people increasingly feels [concubinage] to be a sin", and that cohabitation was declining. Likewise the Moravian missionary at Carisbrook in 1912 thought that "[t]he influence of the church is gradually being felt. . . . Very few of those who were in concubinage three years ago are to be found in that condition today"; but he did warn that "while such marriages are taking place others are entering into those same relationships:– though perhaps, not so many as before".[12] White journalist W.P. Livingstone was most effusive about this new "trend":

> It is noticed that those irregularly related are more sensitive as to their position, and readier to listen to argument on the subject. An appreciation of right relations is spreading, and although the number of marriages is not rising in proportion to the population, there is a better knowledge of all that the ceremony involves. It means, in addition to the legal advantages, elevation in the social scale, respectability, and the possession of all the privileges connected with the Church. These are the simple objects of negro ambition, and . . . along with economic prosperity they will act more and more as a magnet to draw them into a proper conjugal condition.[13]

The benefits that legal marriage was supposed to offer to its adherents were clear, and any people who made a claim to and a pretence of civilization were bound to uphold the institution as an ideal. If this was the case, then according to the statistics the Jamaican people were decidedly uncivilized. On the other hand, that many lower-class Jamaicans did go to great lengths to marry legally (see below), albeit in middle age after they had cohabited for several years and had formed families, offers strong evidence that legal Christian marriage might have been held as a desirable ideal to work towards.

The people thus appeared to be sending mixed signals that were difficult to interpret. That the legal marriage rate peaked in 1907, the year of the devastating earthquake, to reach parity with the leading European countries, could have suggested at first glance that the people did recognize that they had indeed been living "in sin", and that God had visited them with a terrible vengeance as a censure. If so this was only a partial, although not unimportant, explanation. The registrar general's statistics showed that the upward trend had begun in the last quarter of 1906, *before* the earthquake, although it did peak in the second and third quarters of 1907, *after* that calamitous catastrophe.[14] Those rates declined steadily thereafter, and in fact they went to the other extreme during the First World War.

According to Bryan, several explanations have been advanced about the apparently universal reluctance to marry legally, "ranging from black moral turpitude, to white example, to the breakdown of African family practices, and to the low self-esteem of the black population".[15] Based on the contemporary discussions, however, there seemed to be essentially two schools of thought seeking to explain the failure, unwillingness or refusal of the people to get legally married. One held that the costs – which included the governor's licence, the marriage officer's fee, and all the ingredients considered essential for a "proper wedding" (trousseau and feast) – were a major deterrent: "It matters not how many years a couple have lived together when at last they marry, the rule is – a great display so far as dress and feasting are concerned." "The custom of generations has been to make this one great display of their lives, and it seems impossible to induce them to brave the sneer – 'too poor to make a wedding' and be married in a simple way." Livingstone considered this to be the result of the black population's desire to emulate the whites, and because they were unable to afford the costs they simply cohabited.[16]

According to this body of thought, despite the absence of the sanction of the church or the law, the conjugal pair had no intention of separating. Having cohabited for some time, the necessity of legal marriage appeared to them not very great. Also, in their case, it was claimed that the marriage ceremony was connected with some feeling of shame, especially since it entailed the prior reading of banns which, as Anglican priest C.H. Coles put it, called attention to their improper relation.[17] So they never got married at all.

Journalist H.G. De Lisser, on the other hand, argued that "the simple truth is that no disgrace attaches to members of the labouring and peasant class who do not choose to get married".[18] This view was endorsed by some other observers, including Jesuit Father James Splaine, who observed "no sign of shame or confusion anywhere". When, for instance, he challenged some people at May River in April 1872 "about living in concubinage", the men replied that it was necessary to live so for a time in order to find whether their tempers were compatible. To all arguments against the sin they replied that God was merciful, & they could not help it. I was particularly struck by one girl who said she was not living with any man, & backed me up when I urged on Wilson that he ought to get married, *especially* as he had tried his lady for three years. Then she added that she would not give any man more than three months. I took her to task for that & asked her if it was not a sin to live for three months in concubinage. She only turned her eyes sideways up to the sky and asked me no mus' beg de Lard? – They seem to think there is less sin on the whole in living together for a time unmarried to see how they get on, than to marry at once & have to separate for peace sake.[19]

This suggests that the people had their own criteria for what constituted unacceptable moral behaviour and, despite the efforts of the authorities and the clergy, cohabitation was not one of them.

But uncertified cohabitation did not mean rejection of the "ideal" of legal marriage, and many couples resolved to find the money and conform to "civilized" convention, however long that took. According to Splaine,

> Still it must be borne in mind that there is *some* code of morality. If two people live together it is supposed that sometime or other when everything is prepared, those two will marry. And there is a kind of faithfulness, as of man & wife, very often, and unfaithful conduct gives a kind of scandal. So that these alliances bear a certain likeness to marriage contracted where a clergyman cannot be had. It is also to be remarked that although there is so much freedom or license in this matter, there seems to be, according to *my* experience, much less, very much less, of that morbid immorality one hears of in Europe, unnatural sins, filthy tricks, &c.[20]

Said Livingstone, "Half a lifetime frequently passes away before the intention is realized, and it is no uncommon thing to witness a marriage where the bridesmaids are the grown-up daughters of the family." In one case the couple had lived together for twenty-four years, and in another for thirty-five years, before getting legally married – clear testimony of the stability of some of these unions.[21] This also brings into sharp focus the place of legal marriage in the realm of supposedly correct and appropriate behaviours that the populace was aware of, and perhaps even hankered after (for all of the alleged benefits), but that they did not *practise,* for one or another reason. Legal marriage may, in fact, have been taken with such seriousness and may have been viewed with such solemnity that there was great hesitation about entering into it, particularly given its irrevocability under the law.

This links with the other main contemporary school, which argued that the people's failure to "tie the knot" legally was related to the unwillingness of the parties to be bound for life to any one person ("for better or for worse"). The stereotyped version was that legal marriage "was opposed to the whole bent of their nature. . . . They loved freedom and licence, and were not sufficiently trustful to place their lives permanently in each other's keeping." De Lisser noted that many men did not want to be tied to one woman because, apart from the responsibility of legal marriage, they were aware that they might not get on very well with their wives. Livingstone observed a reluctance in some men of the artisan class who, while inclined to marry legally and settle down, did not want to be tied to a woman of the same class "because of her lack of training and domestic qualities". In fact, he attributed the failure of many unions to this want of Victorian female domesticity.[22]

But such disinclination was by no means a male prerogative. Women seemed to entertain even clearer notions about marriage, and felt no shame about cohabiting with a man out of wedlock. Bryan argues that, in keeping with the pattern of female subordination in Victorian marriage, there was a concern among women that "formal marriage would lead to a reduction of female independence". Hence, one woman reportedly said, "If we love each other, what need is there of marrying? If we don't, we are able to leave each other." Women seemed far more reluctant to bind themselves for life to men who might turn out to be lazy, good-for-nothing, and a burden requiring support along with the children. They preferred a relationship which could, if necessary, give them their freedom at any time. "Me get tired of him, sah, and he get tired of me", was a common refrain. They claimed that as long as they were not married the man worked for them, and if he did not they were free to get rid of him and have one who would. But, quite contrary to the Victorian model promoted by the missionaries, they said that once they got married the woman would have to support and perhaps maintain the man, and sooner or later might follow his sexual promiscuity, neglect or desertion. In fact, Bessie Pullen-Burry asserted that desertion was most dreaded by black women,[23] although some commentators believed that the dissolution of non-legal unions was effected with consummate casualness.[24]

The church considered sacred marriage a permanent institution of God prescribed by Holy Scripture, and it lost no opportunity to instruct its followers "to avoid fornication, [and] let every man have his own wife, and let every woman have her own husband".[25] Librarian and historian Frank Cundall asserted that blacks preferred "concubinage to marriage" because it was "more conducive to faithfulness". Livingstone too reflected the Jamaican reality when he opined that as long as these unions remained open-ended they could be permanent: "When casual, necessity for mutual kindness and forbearance establishes a condition that is the best guarantee of permanence." But if made legal and indissoluble, the risk was that they would become intolerable and cease by one of the parties leaving the other. This situation prompted Winifred James to express the radical view that whites "who call it morality to tie together two comparative strangers so hideously bound or else wade in the mud to get free" could learn many lessons from the blacks in their domestic relationships.[26] The black Jamaican population had constructed a radically different culture, where the assumed "insecurity" of non-legal cohabitation in fact engendered better relationships which featured more negotiation than the legal marriages of their middle- and upper-class counterparts, aware as the parties were that the possibility of uncomplicated severance acted as a check on inappropriate behaviours.

Given the narrow ideological and moral motives of those who generated the historical documentary sources, most are preoccupied with vilifying and castigating the Jamaican people for failing to get legally married and thus giving birth to "little black and brown bastards", rather than commenting on the black family structure and relationships. Hence, considerable reliance has to be placed on the modern work of sociologists and anthropologists to reconstruct the Jamaican family of the late nineteenth and early twentieth centuries. While evidence produced by historians B.W. Higman and Michael Craton shows that the nuclear family was not uncommon among slaves in Jamaica and the Bahamas in the early nineteenth century,[27] modern sociologists of the Caribbean have stressed the prevalence of the matrifocal lower-class black family. Indeed, Raymond Smith, Nancie Solien and some others have argued that the term "household" is a more appropriate label for the lower-class West Indian family. For whereas the nuclear family is comprised of a conjugal couple plus their offspring, a household is a wider domestic unit, embracing kinship relationships that may or may not contain a family unit, which is not unusual in the Caribbean.[28]

Smith asserts that the household is started when a man and a woman set up house together. What gives the unit its matrifocal structure is the fact that child care, the central function of the domestic organization, is the primary responsibility of the woman. Although she and the children might be dependent on the man for support, he does not participate very much in child care or spend much time at home. The matrifocality of the household is seen "whether the husband-father is present or not, and although the proportion of women who are household heads increases with age – principally because of widowhood – matrifocality is a property of the internal relations of male- as well as female-headed households".[29] Thus, matrifocality is not incompatible with the nuclear family structure.

According to Martha Beckwith, who did anthropological fieldwork in Jamaica just after the First World War, many times the parties to the conjugal relationship were not strangers at all. They more often than not came from the same district, from the same or neighbouring villages, and might even be related. As she observed, "It is considered a good match for cousins to marry – 'cousins boil good soup', says the proverb. But second cousins should not think of such an alliance; that is, the children of brothers and sisters may marry freely, but not the children of such unions." During the courtship the man was expected to spend money on the girl, while the girl was to look out for a man who would support her in return for her favours, and set up a house for her to keep for him.[30] Both contemporary observers, as noted above, and modern scholars confirm that many of these non-legal unions were stable and long lasting.

Since many lower-class families lived in desperately cramped conditions, often single-room huts in the rural areas or single-room apartments in tenement yards in the towns, much of their socialization took place in the yard amidst a wider community of people. Privacy was a luxury in such an environment, where people cooked, ate, washed (their utensils, clothes and themselves), played and entertained in the open air.[31] Such open community/yard life encouraged gregariousness and competition in interpersonal relations. Elite commentators alleged, however, and without much evidence, that "loose" sexual attitudes were nurtured by the fact that male and female, adult and child, all had to sleep huddled together in the same small room.[32]

Within the household unit, as in any family, relations between the primary conjugal couple, as well as among other members of the wider kinship group, varied from cordial to abusive. The family or household unit, especially in the rural areas, functioned as a cooperative unit as adults, both male and female, often had to work to support the unit. Once the children were old enough, they too were drafted into the production process which, however, adversely affected their attendance at school. This labour-sharing arrangement meant that women enjoyed rather more independence and authority *vis-à-vis* their partners than their middle- and upper-class "sisters"; this was reflected in their disinclination to put up with men who were unwilling to contribute

Figure 8. Three generations and their homestead
Source: Brian L. Moore and Michele A. Johnson, "*Squalid Kingston*", *1890–1920* (Kingston: Social History Project, 2000). Courtesy of the National Library of Jamaica.

financially to the upkeep of the household, or who were unfaithful ("womanizers"). Under these circumstances their preference not to marry legally before they were satisfied with the stability of the domestic situation and the loyalty of their partners was very practical, because before 1879 there was no possibility of dissolving a legal marriage; and although divorce was available after that, it was very difficult to obtain.[33]

The longevity of non-legal marriages is to some degree suggestive of cordial relationships between the conjugal couple as they raised a family around them and supported other kin. In 1897 Quaker missionary Anna M. Farr spoke approvingly about a

> transformation of many homes. . . . Where once the members of the family never sat down together around the table to partake of their meals, or met for daily family devotion, now they do both, and quite a number of parents are making an effort to have suitable books and papers in their homes for their children to read.[34]

This certainly corresponded to the model middle-class family that the missionaries had long promoted. But there was also discord and even violent abuse between the conjugal partners, sometimes requiring the intervention of the police (see chapter 5).

The authority of women within the household was further enhanced by their bearing the principal responsibility for child rearing. Several contemporary writers attested to the devoted attention, care and protection provided to their children by black mothers.[35] Children were carefully treated throughout infancy, which lasted until age three or four, and taught not to steal, lie or be disrespectful to others. From age five they were introduced into household chores such as sweeping the yard, feeding the animals or picking coffee. Boys would later accompany their parents to the provision ground, help with the weeding and run errands. By age nine a boy was encouraged to cultivate his own little garden, and whatever money he earned went to his parents. He also attended school, but not necessarily on a regular basis. At age fourteen or fifteen he entered the adult world of work, and might be apprenticed to learn a trade such as carpentry, masonry, shoemaking, cabinetmaking, blacksmithing, coopering, tailoring, baking and so on. Girls were generally taught to wash, sew and cook. And from about age twelve, both boys and girls would accompany their parents to dances.[36]

Living in an urban yard or small rural village meant that "parenting" assumed a community character. As Mary Lawrence of Hanover recalled, "One man's child was another man's child and [he] had the right to reprimand or scold or even whip anyone if he caught him misbehaving in the absence of his parents; and better still the child stood the chance of receiving a second [whipping] if a complaint were handed in." Likewise, C.G. Bailey recollected that "[c]hildren also had great respect for their parents which in many instances amounted to fear, and to disobey any instruction however trivial was a great offence and would be dearly paid for".[37] This emphasis on corporal punishment of children for misdemeanours, however, could be overdone and sometimes led to the physical abuse and even injury of children.[38] As shown in chapter 5, this became a source of concern among reform-minded cultural elites at the turn of the century.

Within a society built on the precepts of racial difference and deference, race also presented a substantial obstacle to legal marriage. Whereas there were sexual relationships between whites and blacks, marriages were rare in these cases. Quaker missionary Naomi George Swift observed that while it was not uncommon for white and black to live together, it was rare that they legally married, for fear on the part of the white man (for that was the usual nature of the relationships) of ostracism by fellow whites. A good example was an Englishman named Jones who lived with a black woman in Manchioneal, Portland, for about eight or ten years and had four "illegitimate" mulatto children by her. Their marriage in November 1890 was an aberration and caused quite a stir in the community; as Swift put it, "[I]t will make the English hate him for marrying her. . . . I think eternal punishment has been staring him in the face and to escape he has felt that he must either give up his wife and children, or bear humiliation in the sight of all the prejuadiced [sic] whites."[39] What was at issue was the "legitimacy" that he offered his black partner and their so-called bastards. Such episodes unmasked an underlying hypocrisy in Jamaican society, which permitted the campaign for moral "upliftment" to be sacrificed on the altar of racism.

Bryan labels these intimate relationships between individuals from different races/classes "elite concubinage", and notes that they were qualitatively different from the so-called concubinage practised by the peasants. "Elite concubinage" was in fact a feature of old planter tradition and values that persisted well beyond the end of slavery, despite the yearning to hold on to the coat-tail of Mother England. Karen Fog Olwig locates it within a patriarchal cultural tradition that was established when the English first settled in the Caribbean during the seventeenth century. As it related to sex, marriage and family, this tradition created intimate, sometimes long-term "establishments" with female slaves alongside a hierarchical, legal family structure dominated by a patriarch.[40] The mission to civilize Jamaica, therefore, had to deal not only with lower-class non-legal unions, but with upper-class patriarchal plantocratic customs and values as well, which were often at odds with the new Victorian middle-class ethos emanating from Britain.

Relying on Gardner's assertion that gentlemen in Jamaican society in the 1870s had "concubines" as an "all but universal appendage",[41] Bryan argues that the "arrangement" was usually between a white or coloured male and a coloured or black woman who maintained his house (usually as a housekeeper, ostensibly responsible for supervising and performing the domestic chores), and who made way for a white wife when the "right time" arrived. These unbalanced relationships did not compare well, in Bryan's eyes, with those among the peasants or working class, where "men and women . . . were economic partners in day to day survival". He claims that, in a situation where lower-class women provided labour on the sugar, coffee and banana estates of the island, worked on their own provision grounds, and dominated the marketing networks that linked the island's agriculturally productive areas with the main residential centres, women entered into relationships of "partnership rather than domination". Further, he agrees with Livingstone that the economic contributions that women made to their unions gave them "a certain power . . . over the men", and at the same time removed them from the "prevailing concept of femininity, domesticity, [and] the woman's role as mother".[42]

What Bryan does *not* take cognizance of is the fact that while these economic realities may have increased female authority within the household, they did not abrogate the larger patriarchal structures or the Victorian ideal of "true womanhood". Even in the case of non-cohabiting unions (what Besson called "extra-residential conjugal relations") where women and their children constituted the primary unit, men "visited" and women were assumed to be in charge of their own households, according to Morrissey, there is no reason to think that the influence of the "visiting men" over the women was slight. Male authority in such households was to some extent perpetuated by the "emotional and social contributions" of men; even where that authority may have been questioned or apparently lacking, it was in fact "embodied in the patriarchal family [that was] often an ideal" which the community, as a whole, aspired to.[43] Nevertheless, it would be true to say that these households gave women much more effective authority than the alternative Victorian family model.

Marriage and Gender Order

Quite separate, but not altogether unrelated to the question of Christian legal monogamous marriage, was another debate that raged principally among the middle and upper classes over the virtues of marriage and its importance in maintaining the "proper" gender order in Jamaican society. A letter by "Simplicite, Symitric, et Solidite" to the *Gleaner* in 1899 suggested that middle-class young men preferred "celibacy" to marriage for several reasons: scarcity of remunerative employment, an unwillingness to burden an innocent woman with their economic distress, fear of marital failure and unhappiness, and a refusal to follow in the iniquitous footsteps of their ancestors.[44] "Bachelor" claimed that the modern young man was much too active socially to contemplate marriage. He had to keep abreast of the latest novels; his hobbies were quite varied – collecting postage stamps, picture postcards, curios, coins and so forth; he played cricket, football, tennis or some other sport; there were concerts, parties and balls, calls, meetings; and there was travel as well. All of these were costly as well as time consuming, and put marriage on the back burner: "I think our youths in Jamaica appreciate as well as anybody the value of a house and the charm of a wife, but it would be simply misery to attempt to keep two, and very shortly a family, on an income that is only capable of meeting the needs of one, in comfort."[45] That these privileged young men may not have wanted to marry in early adulthood is very much in keeping with a trend in other parts of the Caribbean as well as in Britain. Ronald Hyam notes that in Britain the average age of marriage for men was twenty-nine, while about 10 per cent never married at all. In addition to enjoying their youth, most men seemed to seek to become economically and socially established before marrying. This meant that they felt free to "play the field" with single and married women and with prostitutes. "Womanizing" was as much a young elite male pastime in Jamaica as it was in Guyana and elsewhere in the region.[46]

Towards the turn of the century the emergence of the so-called new woman among the middle classes brought new attitudes and challenges to the dominant patriarchal order. Emulating their "sisters at home" (Britain), in Europe and in the United States, some Jamaican women were no longer prepared to conform unquestioningly to the dependent role that had been assigned to them. Growing out of the "traditional" and "accepted" Victorian notions about gender, in the late nineteenth and early twentieth centuries Western women increasingly questioned their ascribed place and status. Where previously they had largely accepted and even perpetuated those notions which limited them to the domestic sphere and which emphasized their role as nurturers, women began to challenge the markers of gender by seeking to reform the wider societies into which their children (and mates) would enter. In Britain and the United States they found their voices (although not without severe criticism) in the abolitionist campaigns and in the agrarian and labour movements.[47] Stirred by the flames of evangelicalism and reformism, women established and ran organizations which sought to address the social "problems" of poverty, prostitution and intemperance. Through the women's rights campaigns they began to argue that the place of women needed to be extended into the public space, so that their moral leadership could be brought to bear on matters affecting the whole society.[48] By the end of the nineteenth century these antecedents had spawned the "new woman": more educated than her mother or grandmother, raised in an atmosphere of women's clubs and activism, she was more willing to question the limitations and expectations that defined the experiences of her sex.[49] And as in Britain and the United States, when they appeared in Jamaica the new women came under intense scrutiny; their very claim of womanhood was questioned or rejected.

This new breed of womankind was not considered by some Jamaicans to be sufficiently "feminine" to make attractive and responsible marriage partners. One commentator claimed that they were competing with men for the same jobs; by accepting less money than men could afford to, they were lowering wages, which made them independent and "mannish" in character.[50] The new woman was also reputed to be instinctively disinclined to marry, or else to be bent on shocking and unacceptable gender-role reversals:

> These women are bent on pleasure at any cost and the subject of marriage is as distant from their ideals as the North is from the South pole; consequently to propose marriage to such women would certainly end in zero, because their natures being of such a masculine turn would fall within the meaning of the well known truism, "two bulls cannot reign in one pen." If these women would play their parts through like men, then surely they ought to propose to us men and then let us out of the difficulty . . . and we would be (I believe to a man) willing to wear the kilts while they wear the bloomers. We will further promise to remain at home and mind the kids, while they go to the clubs, or make the speeches on some political matter, or to attend some banquet. So that to this class, marriage is possible only if things take the reverse of the precedents laid down.[51]

"Young Woman", aged twenty, seemed to epitomize this image of the new woman. She vehemently contested the prevailing notion

> that the be-all and end-all of a woman's life should be to please man! How is it that we never hear of men being educated so as to be our companions? Where, pray, are we to find men to suit us? Why should things continue thus? People talk of higher education as if it existed solely for the purpose of making us suitable companions for man! Surely a woman's proper place in the world is not only at the head of a man's household.[52]

Nor were women "ripe cherries ready to fall into the matrimonial basket the moment an opportunity offers".[53] "Young Woman" felt that marriage worked to women's disadvantage, no matter how educated they were. With the growth of the family through children,

> How is the woman to find time to keep abreast of the times to cultivate her mind so that the "intellectual and emotional" harmony which her lord desires may exist? Talk of the joys of literature! Literature with a fourteen months old body in the house and another on the *tapis*. The result is that the woman becomes merely a "slave" and the man seeks congenial society elsewhere. It is ludicrous for men to sit in their easy chairs and discuss these things. If it were possible for them to exchange

places with women for a year or two they might possibly gain much valuable knowledge, and be able to understand women better.[54]

Marriage was synonymous to her with children, a thought she found unsettling at best: "since babies invariably give much trouble in coming into the world, and in some cases cause loss of life, I shall ever hold that marriage is a handicap". To crown this attitude, she voiced admiration for American women, whom she thought realized the disadvantageous position of married women and opted to remain single: "I know of young women in Jamaica who hold similar views."[55] "A Married Woman" certainly did, although perhaps she had come to her position too late. Based on her experience she could say categorically that the work of a married woman with children was never done, and at times she was cut off from forms of amusement for many months of the year:

> There is no denying the fact that marriage is a handicap, and the young men and women of to-day know it. They are afraid of venturing on the unknown waters and so steer clear of matrimony. We cannot expect every young woman to like all the phases of the married life, and who can say whether the old maids of twenty and thirty years ago did not object to marriage on account of over-refinement.[56]

"A Married Woman", however, was most probably a not-too-well-off middle-class person struggling to raise her children without the usual aids of upper-class domestic life: nannies, wet nurses and maids.

Ideas like these openly challenged the "sacred" institutions of matrimony, the nuclear family, and the overarching patriarchal system which they bolstered. Since the Christian family was the very foundation of Victorian civilization itself, these threats to it aroused a hostile reaction not only from men, but also from some women. Twenty-one-year-old male "Amor" speculated that "Young Woman" might have had a previously unhappy love affair, and was thus bitter towards all men. He blamed her attitude, characterized as being "so hard to please – this tendency of over-refinement and ostentation" shared by "most young women", for the failure of many relationships and "the chief factor of creating the 'Old Maid' ". For him marriage was not based on material considerations; it was a spiritual "union of two souls by invisible links that man cannot sever; links that make 'a man leave his father and his mother and cleave unto his wife.' Children are not a compulsory sequel, but they are optional and desirable, depending on the married parties." Besides, "man" had not found a substitute for marriage. It is ironic that although living in a society with a viable alternative to legal marriage, "Amor" was socially blind to it because it was looked down upon as uncivilized. He would or could not see that the indigenous creole system of non-legal marriage might answer some of the concerns that reluctant parties had about the institution;[57] although, to be fair, it is doubtful that "Young Woman" could either.

"Experience", another male, patronizingly regarded marriage as "the sweetest and best institution in man's life! Is there anything else to make a man so happy as a dear little woman in his home, all his own, much more so, when the dear little toilers begin to stump around and say 'dada'?"[58] Reverend S.R. Brathwaite cited US president Theodore Roosevelt, father of six, who is reported to have said, "[T]he man or woman who deliberately avoids marriage and has a heart so cold as to know no passion and a brain so shallow and selfish as to dislike having children is in effect a criminal against the race and should be an object of contemptuous abhorrence by all healthy people." "A Married Woman", however, responded dismissively: "With respect to President Roosevelt I do not consider him qualified to write on this subject. He, being a man, cannot have any conception of the 'throes of agony' which women endure."[59]

But some women, socialized in and fully supportive of the Victorian patriarchal system, were equally offended by "Young Woman's" attitude to marriage and to children, and took strong exception to her views. "Some Of It" was scathing:

> Those women who prefer a method of worldliness and selfishness to the affection of "children" are devoid of much, so do well to remain "single" – poor would be the man with such a wife or mother for his children . . . no sensible mother could allow love and devotion to her children to interfere with her duty and sociability to their father. Then also, no home-loving or *wise* husband would be so ungenerous and unsympathetic as to deprive her of his presence which she needs to cheer her on, after the day's labour of love.[60]

Eloise Da Costa asserted that it was only "the common everyday woman who can have no conception of marriage in its most sacred and holy ties". The "better class" of women shared their troubles with the men they loved, "and by such unison of soul make marriage what God intended it to be". Children added to the beauty of marriage like *fleurs des jardine*. "A Mother" commented,

> Going to balls and parties, visiting friends, keeping up with the latest style, will not fit a woman to fulfil the duties of a wife and mother. . . . Marriage calls a woman

to a higher sphere of usefulness. The impulses within her for good have a wider scope: then, she realizes that she must play *her* part, and, that well.[61]

The precepts of Victorian Christian marriage were, then, not embraced without question. While the ordinary people took part in that imported cultural ideal when it suited them, and ignored it when it did not, among the upper and middle classes there were at least two other stresses. One was bound to a pre-existing planter cultural tradition that created space for non-legal relationships, out of which emerged children whose links to their fathers, although not legal, were well known. Within those same classes Victorian culture was also under pressure from more modern notions of "ideal" relationships: among young men who defined the parameters differently, and among young women who questioned the very basis of Victorian gender ideology. Caught among several strands of resistance, from above and below, the Victorian ideal of Christian monogamous marriage was severely challenged in Jamaican society.

Controlling Non-legal Marriage

During the nineteenth century and into the twentieth, the colonial authorities made several attempts to curb the Jamaican penchant to live in non-legal unions, claiming that "concubinage" contributed to the destruction of the country's moral fibre. The use of the law in this effort pointed to the mind-set of those who sought to "improve" the society by legislating morality. Until 1879 the law gave power to an authorized clergyman to conduct a legal marriage ceremony after the publication of banns, and without the necessity for any witness to be present. The *Gleaner*, however, observed that the disestablishment of the Anglican Church in 1870 (that is, the church was no longer financially supported out of the colonial budget) produced a curious anomaly "that while the State visited with the heaviest penalties the children of unmarried parents, it left the regulation of the conditions under which marriage could be performed entirely in the hands of a variety of conflicting bodies, over none of which had it any control".[62] In 1879 a new law placed marriage under the full control of the state. A superintendent registrar was appointed in each parish who was responsible for publishing notices of marriage and who could also conduct civil marriage ceremonies. Marriage officers were also to be appointed by the governor, and each wedding required two independent witnesses. A licence fee of ten pounds was also imposed.[63]

This, however, did not sit well with the Anglican Church, which duly protested: first on the grounds that the new law was fundamentally un-Christian and did not recognize marriage as a divine institution, but instead dealt with it as a civil contract. This was especially so because the law required that certain civil declarations should be made before the religious ceremony was performed. This, it was argued, introduced a secular tone to marriage which would reduce its spiritual connection and its importance in the minds of the people. The critics also felt that the law needlessly multiplied obstructions and imposed restraints – not least of all the burdensome licence fee and the restricted hours during which marriages could be performed (ten in the morning to four in the afternoon) – rather than facilitating and encouraging legal marriage. And they objected to its provision (Article 8) which seemed to restrict marriage officers to function only in the parish in which they officiated.[64] Since the Colonial Office added its voice to some of these criticisms, the law was amended in 1880 to extend the hours from six in the morning to eight at night, to reduce the governor's licence fee to five pounds, and to allow marriage officers to operate outside of their parish.[65]

Still, the people showed very little enthusiasm for legal marriage, and the church and elite society in general became obsessed with what was considered a grave sin and social evil in their midst. Some thought that "concubinage" should be outlawed and made a criminal offence "punishable with extreme penalties".[66] Far less draconian, however, was the solution of "An Old Minister", who claimed in 1885 that he used to publish banns of marriage between persons who were living together, without their knowledge or consent, and by so doing he was able to induce a number of couples to be married either in the church or in their houses who would otherwise never have been married: "And no evil consequence of my proceedings has ever come to my knowledge." He therefore suggested that every marriage officer should be authorized to publish banns between persons whom he knew had been living together for three years, and also to declare publicly in church, unless the banns had been forbidden, that the parties were legally married. In his view, "A little coercion would . . . do no harm in this matter." By the end of the century, however, several persons considered the very publication of banns itself to be a deterrent to legal marriage and advocated its removal, because they had an impression that it caused embarrassment to the parties if they were cohabiting out of wedlock.[67]

Another seemingly viable option was to adopt the Scottish marriage code, a step that the *Gleaner* advocated. In Scotland there were two forms of marriage recognized by law: "regular" and "irregular". In both cases it was the deliberate consent or contract of the parties, and not the ceremony, that constituted the marriage. Marriage was a civil contract, and all that was required was consent deliberately expressed or implied: *concensus non concubitus facit matrimonium*. Regular marriages were contracted by a priest after the proclamation of banns. Irregular marriages were not, but although they only required the consent of the two parties, they were binding in law and dissoluble only by divorce or death. The issue therefrom were not deemed "illegitimate" and thus suffered no legal disability. But even the *Gleaner* was ambivalent about whether it would be prudent to treat "mere" living together in Jamaica as marriage:

> We have always to remember that we are dealing with a people who are largely ignorant of the moral principles that govern more advanced peoples. . . . To say to a couple who have been living together that they are legally married would not educate them to a proper sense of the highest relations of life and how these relations should be rightly contracted.[68]

So while committed cohabitation was enough for the Scots, it was argued that among the "immoral" Jamaicans a similar policy might be misread as the state condoning sin. The "unadvanced" Jamaican people may have been able to create longstanding relationships of commitment and nurturance, but they were not to be supported in their "sinful" behaviour by the authorities, who were anxious that they enter into "proper" liaisons. Some part of this concern about the mating patterns of the people had to do with how the elite thought it reflected on themselves, as part of an "uncivilized" community, determined to carry on what they would have labelled as one of the worst elements of the culture of slavery.

The other aspect of this reluctance to get married was the "social evil" of "illegitimacy", the rate of which, as we shall see below, was continuously rising. As a consequence these two problems became the centre of considerable public debate by the turn of the century. So concerned were the elites with these twin "sins" that in 1903 the legislature pressed Governor Hemming to appoint a commission of clergy and laymen to enquire into the working of the marriage and registration laws.[69]

After due investigation the Marriage and Registration Commission reported that the causes of "concubinage" and "illegitimacy" were mainly "temperamental" and economic, and that the remedies must be gradual, via education and industrial progress to improve the moral and living standards of the people. With respect to legal marriage, the commission recommended that the publication of the banns should be reduced from three times to one; that the marriage licence fee should be reduced to two shillings and sixpence; and that the licences should be issuable by any clerk of court or justice of the peace, instead of only by the governor. These recommendations were embodied in Law No. 28 of 1905. Very interestingly, however, without offering reasons, the commission rejected the idea of adopting the Scottish law which would have legitimized cohabitation in Jamaica.[70]

If the *Gleaner* could be regarded as representative of a broad cross-section of elite opinion, then it seems that not many members of the elite thought that the new law would lead to much change, and they were right. The provisions hardly seemed to influence the attitude of the people to legal marriage, as the rates appeared to fluctuate without reference to the legal facilities made available. They continued to live according to their own circumstances, ideas and ideals, without regard to the law. As the *Gleaner* observed, "It is impossible to believe that there can be many persons in the island who have a wish to get married, but are deterred by the expenditure of the few shillings required to secure a legal and binding marriage." The licence fee was but a minute fraction of the cost of covering "numerous carriages, more numerous guests, a silk gown for the bride, a coat for the bride-groom, a big dinner with a lot of wine and other things thrown in. These are considerations that entirely outweigh the legal expenses involved."[71]

The newspaper was correct to believe that the marriage situation would not conform to "civilized" standards unless there was a fundamental alteration in the values of the people, that is, their full acculturation to the Victorian (Christian) culture. Thus, with specific reference to the women, there was a concern that

> their ideas of morality are not as advanced as those of their European sisters; they differ from the latter temperamentally; and the same code of social ethics cannot be applied to them. They are among the majority and are influenced by the ideas and feelings which govern the majority; and until those ideas and feelings undergo some alteration . . . no effective pressure can be brought to bear upon them.[72]

In the latter part of the nineteenth century and into the twentieth, elite society sought to impress upon ordinary Jamaicans the idea that the institution of legal marriage was the only acceptable form of conjugality. For reasons of their own the people formulated distinctive indigenous means of establishing unions, and the majority would not marry legally, or at least not before their mature years. In 1920, therefore, "polite society" was no closer to getting the "unwashed majority" to conform to its ideals of legal marriage than had been the case in 1865.

"Illegitimacy"

Closely linked with non-legal marriage ("concubinage") was the "curse of illegitimacy". As appendix 4 demonstrates, the rate of "illegitimate births" increased steadily from 59.3 per cent in 1878, when the first official registration of births took place, to 72.14 per cent in 1920. The parishes of St Catherine, Clarendon, Hanover, St James, St Mary, and especially St Thomas were consistently above the mean, with the latter reaching a record high of 81.5 per cent in 1920, while St Andrew, Manchester and St Ann were generally below average. On the scale of "civilization", Jamaica ranked "embarrassingly" low, although it was at least on par with, if not "better" than, some of its sister Caribbean colonies. The Jamaican social and religious establishments, however, were not consoled by the island's rating within an equally "depraved" region, but rather were dismayed by its failure to attain the "high moral standards" set by England and her white colonies: "the failure of others does not contribute to our success and we do not seek to emulate their sins".[73]

"Illegitimacy" was deemed a "national sin" by the churches, which battled unsuccessfully with this "social evil". Quaker missionary Mary White noted in 1916, "[I]t is the exception to find anyone married but almost all have families about them, often no two of the children bear the same name."[74] Several elite commentators tried to paint this "immorality" as a black lower-class problem.[75] But it was by no means confined to the poorer classes; it pervaded the whole society. As already shown, old planter customs persisted and competed with the new middle-class Victorian values. Several contemporaries observed that "respectable" elite men, including public officials, often took advantage of poorer women and had "illegitimate" children by them.[76] For instance, R.E. Clarke alleged in 1904 that there was hardly a house in Jamaica where one or more of its members was not then leading, or had not at some previous time led, an "immoral" life:

> The upper and ruling classes have always been, and still are, in great measure responsible for the unsatisfactory moral condition of the masses of the people. To this day large numbers of young men, and indeed too many older ones, and married men also, of the higher class are debased and corrupt in morals, and take

Figure 9. A mother and her children
Source: Alfred Leader, *Through Jamaica with a Kodak* (Bristol: John Wright, 1907). Courtesy of the National Library of Jamaica.

advantage of their position to corrupt and ruin young women of lower station in life simply because they know they can do so with impunity . . . there are large numbers of men who deliberately set themselves to debauch those who might otherwise have led virtuous lives; and yet these very men are received into our drawing rooms and admitted into the society of our sisters, and are accepted as their husbands – men who, very often, are not fit to cross the threshold of any dwelling where decency and morality are held in any repute.[77]

Likewise, outraged Methodist missionary Stephen Sutton forcefully denounced "the secret abominations, which are perpetrated by hundreds yea thousands of barefaced degraded creatures called here the middle and upper classes, who are filling the island with bastards, and like some pestilential blast striking down all purity and modesty whenever they appear". "An Anglican" asked, "[I]s it not truth that the bastards of men in position, high and honoured, are to be met with practically anywhere, the son's name is not the father's, and this simple artifice hides much to those who watch the surface only. Immorality runs to and through every class and colour."[78] Like many others, R.E. Clarke claimed that public officials, including civil servants and magistrates, were among the most "dissolute characters". Reverend John Graham could point "to at least half a dozen of these gentlemen who live in open concubinage, with 'illegitimate' families flaunting in the eyes of custodes and Government. Yet these men are held up as the leaders of society, the administrators of justice, and examples to the people." He and others unsuccessfully urged successive governors to uphold strictly the Queen's Proclamation which debarred immoral men from public office.[79] That in 1909 the Colonial Office was obliged to issue a circular to its officers overseas against entering into concubinary relationships with local women demonstrates how widespread the practice was, or was perceived to be. The circular was not sent to the West India colonies, only because the Colonial Office did not want it to set back white-black race relations by any suggestion of encouraging white aloofness.[80] But British officials enjoyed the same opportunities to indulge in sexual adventurism in the Caribbean as they did in Africa, Asia and the Pacific.

In addition, as already shown, white males who cohabited with black women rarely married them, for fear of social ostracism; hence their children were deemed "illegitimate". Indeed, in 1887 the Jesuits felt obliged to open a girls' industrial school to cater to the female "illegitimate offspring of white fathers, who are well brought up as long as the fathers live, but if they die or fail, must suffer poverty, destitution, and much misery".[81]

It was not only the locals who were touched by this "sin". *Gall's News Letter* asserted that several married men came from Britain posing as bachelors and seduced unsuspecting Jamaican girls.[82] Ronald Hyam has shown that the empire offered greater sexual opportunity for Britons than was available at home, and many indulged lavishly in both male and female "native" flesh.[83] Even the clergy were not exempt; indeed, some of the local parsons were themselves "bastards". Moreover, occasionally church records reflected improprieties allegedly committed by priests, catechists and teachers, some of whom were tried and punished or dismissed. The American Quaker missionaries, with more than a touch of arrogance born of their sense of moral superiority in relation to the clergy of other denominations, boldly alleged that very few of the religious leaders in Jamaica held a high standard of personal purity, a large number were unmarried men, and many had "illegitimate" children themselves.[84] The *Jamaica Advocate* was most explicit in pointing to a white (English) minister "not a hundred miles from Kingston, who has kept a black girl as his mistress, not more than a stone's throw from his wife's residence, and is still keeping her. If she has no illegitimate children for him, it is not his fault." But perhaps the most shocking instance was Benjamin Miller, a thirty-eight-year-old, married preacher, who was actually convicted of carnal abuse of an underaged girl and sentenced to three years' imprisonment. The girl had been entrusted to Miller and his wife to be taught and trained, but on attaining her thirteenth birthday he seduced and impregnated her. She died in childbirth.[85] Generally speaking, however, the churches tried to maintain a veil of silence on such malfeasance by their officers, while conducting a loud public campaign against the "evil" of "illegitimacy".

No one, however, captured the entire social situation more succinctly than "An Anglican", who summarized it thus:

> Lift the black list, and in the steady light of truth read. Names rise from the thousands there and strike you almost with terror. Branch after branch of the Church lifts the shame of years branded with the fall of her members, young and old, her officers, her Ministers; for there is a dark list about which men say little, over which even the man fiercest in his attacks upon the Church does not exult. Ministers tried, honoured, not of a few years service, not of one deed's renown; but their names are here. And men who came from lands of sterner virtue and firmer mind, who stood well and resolutely – but their names are here. Seek back, one by one, see they dropped from their place, and mercifully, quietly, with a chill about their hearts, their comrades closed in the ranks; and so it passed. The evil is gigantic. I pray be sparing of scourge and lash and torture for those within its grip, for the men as well as the women.[86]

This moral problem, as it was perceived, severely tested the authority of the church. While in general disapproving, the clergy had to deal with the reality of children born out of wedlock and to determine whether or not to ostracize them. The Anglicans, Roman Catholics and Wesleyans, for whom baptism was an inalienable sacrament, apparently baptized all children regardless of their legal status, although they did try to exercise some control in the matter. As John Thomson noted,

> I baptize all Illegitimate children brought to me – provided they have Church of England communicants as Godparents. When I know, however, that the child is

> the offspring of persons . . . living in open sin I do all in my power to get the Godparents to refuse standing for the children until the parents themselves either signify their intention of marrying or separate from each other. I do this in order to show the people that I do make some difference between children of lawful marriage, & those born contrary to the law of God.[87]

Officially all churches, the press and so-called respectable society remained openly hostile to this "national disgrace" and inveighed against it as the nineteenth century drew to a close. This was not unique in the Caribbean, but Jamaica perhaps more than the other British colonies seemed to become obsessed with this "disgrace".[88] Various legislative attempts to deal with "illegitimacy" and the maintenance of "illegitimate" children had proven ineffective, and added to the frustration of social reformers as they approached the new century. But there were three principal conceptual and ideological assumptions that underlay the framing of legislation, and hampered its success:

1. Concepts of Christian morality were imported wholesale from bourgeois British Victorian society, principally by the missionaries, and superimposed on the Jamaican people.
2. Legislation had a strong class bias, designed to exempt the upper and middle classes.
3. The laws were also framed with a decided gender bias which placed the burden of responsibility, and the penalty for failure, on women.

The elites were also reluctant to face the probability that the people could hold independent moral views, especially regarding personal life, and might not be prepared to be dictated to on such matters.

Controlling "Illegitimacy"

Three sets of laws pertained to this "social problem": marriage laws (already treated), bastardy and maintenance laws, and registration laws. As early as 1860 the coloured assemblyman, Edward Jordan, had tabled a bill to compel fathers to maintain their "illegitimate" children. It received the support of the *Falmouth Post*,[89] perhaps because its scope was restricted only to men who had lived in open "concubinage" with the mothers previous to or at the time of birth, or who had acknowledged and treated the child as theirs. However, when Governor Sir John Peter Grant, without the "obstacle" of elected members, piloted a maintenance law through the legislature (No. 31, 1869) that for the first time gave women the right to name and sue the putative fathers of their "illegitimate" children for support regardless of whether they lived with the mothers or acknowledged paternity, it aroused a howl of indignation and protest. Both the *Falmouth Post* and the *County Union* denounced it as objectionable, since it allegedly gave "encouragement to lewd women" and would "render respectable families unhappy and miserable by swearing that men of long-established and moral and religious character are the Fathers of their children, for the oath of every harlot . . . will be the test of paternity, be it hazarded against the Governor, the Bishop, or the most sacred names boasted by the colony". The *Post* thought that the governor had gone too far in his effort to stop the evil.[90]

The 1880s, and especially the last years of *pure* crown colony government (1879–84), witnessed a plethora of legislation on social morality relating to marriage (1879, 1880), divorce (1879, 1881), registration (1881, 1882, 1885, 1890), bastardy (1881, 1882) and maintenance (1881, 1887). The 1881 bastardy law, in particular, made it easier for women to claim support for their "illegitimate" children by permitting them to apply to a justice of the peace or the clerk of petty sessions, instead of only the resident magistrate. If proof of the putative father's relation were provided, he could be made to support his child. But the law also punished the mother "as a rogue and a vagabond" for neglecting her children. Under the registration laws, a man's name could not be registered as the father of an "illegitimate" child without his consent; both the father and the mother were required to go together to the registrar's office and sign the register.

Yet these laws did not address the core issue of "illegitimacy", the rates of which continued to rise, much to the chagrin of the moral elites and the churches. In 1885 the Synod of the Church of England, emulating its parent in Britain, established a branch of the Social Purity Society. The objectives of this organization were to promote "purity" among men and women, to cultivate a chivalrous respect for women, to preserve the young from contamination, to do rescue work, and to set a "higher" tone of public opinion. The society worked quietly among both men and women, holding meetings, distributing literature on social purity, and making representations in the form of petitions to the legislature on issues affecting the social life of poor Jamaicans. The house tax was one of its main targets, as it was widely believed that the tax on improvements of houses militated against people enlarging their homes and thus contributed to "immorality", as children and adults were forced to sleep in the same room.91 The synod itself petitioned the legislature on this issue and, as we shall see, was a major player in the debate on registration.

Another major player was the Presbyterian Church. This body took an uncompromising position on non-legal marriage and "illegitimacy" throughout the period, and pressed, most notably, for the compulsory registration of fathers of "illegitimate" children and for the legitimization of children whose parents married after the child's birth. Its Life and Work Committee was very active, pursuing these goals and spreading the mantra of social purity.92 These issues were also prominently featured at the Wesleyan annual conferences, which spoke out for social purity in pastoral sermons and resolutions. In 1897 the Wesleyans even barred "illegitimate" children from admission to their York Castle High School, although this was overturned by the Missionary Committee in London.93 The Baptists, Moravians, Congregationalists (formerly the London Missionary Society) and Friends (Quakers) also added their voices to the general outcry.94

The war against "illegitimacy" was made more poignant because very many influential persons believed that it was the root cause of other social problems, particularly vagrancy, praedial larceny and petty theft. This view was most stridently expressed by Reverend John Robson who, in opening the Presbyterian Synod of 1899, argued that Jamaica was "within measurable distance of a crisis pregnant with disaster". The ramifications of the "evil" were innumerable:

> While some of the class sprung from it have risen to positions of respectability and trust in state and in church, yet the inevitable tendency of it as a whole is to increase that class which rests as an incubus on the Island, sucking the very life out of labour and honest work: that class which is in infancy and childhood a charge on the already over-burdened poor rates, and in manhood a praedatory [sic] class of vagrants subsisting largely by plundering the grounds planted by the industry of honest workers.95

This "social crisis" seemed to stem from the almost universal failure of fathers of "illegitimate" children (regardless of race or class) to support their offspring. Said Rampini:

> The offspring of such connexions – "bye-children", "out-children", or "love-children", as they are called, – generally follow the mother. It is rare that a father thinks himself bound even to provide food for such children. He bears them no affection: he does not recognize any claim they may have upon him. If they lose

themselves, and die in the woods, he does not deem himself bound to go and bury them. It is the woman's look-out, not his.[96]

Robson thus called for the compulsory registration of the names of the fathers of "illegitimate" children as the best way to stem the "evil". This issue of registration was first placed on the political agenda in 1893 by Reverend Henry Clarke, Anglican rector and elected representative for Westmoreland in the Legislative Council,[97] who thereafter annually tabled bills proposing compulsory registration. It was boldly taken up by the editor of the *Gleaner*, W.P. Livingstone, who opened that newspaper to the public as a forum in which a debate on the issue could take place. The *Jamaica Post*, too, came out strongly in favour of compulsory registration of paternity.

Henry Clarke argued that those who were responsible for the birth of "illegitimate" children should be punished and barred from decent society. But, on the other hand, it was no more a shame or a disgrace to a man or a woman to have been born "illegitimate" than to have been born lame: they could not be blamed for their misfortune. Thus, "illegitimate" children should, *as a right*, be protected and maintained by their fathers. This formed an integral part of his demand for gender equality before the law on this issue:

> The point I seek to carry is that the law shall deal with the father of an "illegitimate" child in precisely the same way as it deals with the mother. Any reason which can be used for allowing the father to conceal his paternity, must apply with greater force to the mother, whose shame and suffering and loss from publicity are infinitely greater than the father's.[98]

This, of course, was a Eurocentric view that assumed that in lower-class black Jamaica, disgrace accompanied the conception of a child out of wedlock.

The logic of compulsory registration meant, however, that the woman should be compelled to name the putative father if he failed to come forward; if she refused or simply could not do so, Clarke's bills would make her punishable. So, notwithstanding his objective to achieve gender equality on this issue, Clarke's proposal placed the woman at a disadvantage insofar as she still bore primary liability before the law. This feature was repulsive to his main critic, fellow Anglican clergyman Canon William Simms, who observed, "I believe there is no single case in English law in which the law tries by dint of penalty to compel an offender to betray his accomplice."[99]

Clarke, however, saw no reason why a distinction should be made between the offences of theft (usually, but not exclusively, associated with the lower classes) and adultery (largely a middle- and upper-class phenomenon, if only because they were primarily the ones who were legally married), and blamed the social elites for not legislating on the latter because as a class it did not suit them to do so: "As a member of the old House of Assembly said to me when I was trying to get a Bastardy Law passed in 1860, 'Do you think we are such fools as to cut a stick to flog our own backs?' " In many respects, his was a crusade against a "debauched" aristocracy who perpetuated their customs and values even in the face of the campaign for social reform; hence he felt that "[a]s soon as this crime ceases among the upper class it will soon sink to manageable dimensions among the lower".[100] His call for compulsory registration of fathers was thus meant as much to expose the vices of "gentlemen" as to provide legal and material support for disadvantaged "illegitimate" children.

Clarke was most annoyed that some churches, especially his own Church of England, did not line up solidly behind his call for compulsory registration. If they had done so, he argued, no government could have resisted passing appropriate legislation. He charged that "[t]he registration of the names of both the parents of every child born, is not a question of morals, or religion, or church discipline. It is simply a question of law, and the Christian Church has no duty in respect of it, except to require the Government to do their duty." He attributed the opposition of his (Anglican) church to compulsory registration to

> the wish to furnish a loop hole for men in the higher ranks to indulge their lawless propensities without the risk of exposure and its consequences. But these are just the men whom it is necessary, as well for their own safety, as for the public safety, to catch and restrain, for they have been the originators and upholders of the vile system through all its history.[101]

Without necessarily imputing any immoral motives to the Anglican Church, it is reasonable to assert that Clarke had a point. Although most of its members, like those of the other churches, were lower class, the Anglican Church probably had a disproportionate number of upper-class members, upon whom it was increasingly dependent financially after its disestablishment in 1870. It could not, therefore, afford to alienate such influential people. This was clearly demonstrated when Anglican clergyman Reverend C.H. Coles, in a letter to the *Jamaica Daily Telegraph* (4 April 1903), endorsed the widely held view that many government officials, including several from England, were leading grossly immoral lives. Governor Hemming formally took exception to this, whereupon Archbishop Nuttall promptly issued a strong statement vouching for the morality of the officials.[102] There might thus have been no small degree of self-interest in the Anglican Church's opposition to Clarke's scheme.

Notwithstanding that, however, Clarke's message resonated among a large number of people, and especially the nonconformist churches. Wesleyan minister J. Kissock Braham argued that while "[y]ou cannot make men morally honest by law. . . . you can restrain the vicious by stringent laws. . . . you can lessen acts of immorality by law. Is purity less desirable than honesty? Is virtue to be less protected than bananas, canes and yams?" "W" supported compulsory registration because it would help to create public opinion against the "evil of illegitimacy", which neither legislation nor preaching alone could accomplish, and "A Woman of Jamaica" argued that it was essential for securing the child's maintenance from the right source. "Legitimacy" echoed Clarke's hostility towards the upper classes: "I do not think the Bill will effect any great change among the peasantry; but it has my full sympathy, because it is intended for what is generally called the 'better class;' a class that has a great deal to do with the 60 percent of illegitimate births."[103]

However, it was the *Gleaner* under W.P. Livingstone's editorship, and the *Jamaica Post,* that took Clarke's baton and ran with it in the public arena. Both papers made it very clear that the question was not primarily one of morality, but rather "a question of legal rights – the rights of children. . . . [T]he children of the State possess rights and the State should see that these are secured on their behalf." "Illegitimate" children in Jamaica had no legal status, the *Gleaner* argued; the majority were uncared for and unsupported. Men took more pride in their livestock than in their "illegitimate" children. The *Post* went further, asserting that fathers who repudiated and neglected their children were committing a crime against humanity which the state could not overlook. Hence, "[I]t is the duty of the State to see that every child born in the country has a legal father."[104]

The critical problems as far as the *Gleaner,* the *Post,* Henry Clarke and the social reformers were concerned lay in the gender inequality of the existing laws. In 1903 the *Gleaner* editor penned these words:

> Fathers of legitimate children are responsible for the up-bringing of the latter up to a certain age; in the case of "illegitimate" children the responsibility is placed on the mother. The distinction is unfair and unjust, because the mother in the latter case is less likely to be able to support them than the father. The law is based on

the singular principle that the woman is the greatest sinner and must suffer the greatest punishment. There has always been something irresistibly comical in the thought of the long line of statesmen, judges, and ecclesiastical doctrinaires – all men – who have solemnly declared after the ripest reflection that the sin most serious in a woman is in a man most venial, a principle which is carried out right through the law. . . . If there is a law at all it should apply equally to the father and the mother, or to the father as in the case of legitimate children. . . . This would mean that the name of the father as well as of the mother would be registered so that should the State be compelled to take over the maintenance of the mother or the child, as it often is, the father could be got at and made to perform his duty.[105]

This was heresy to the patriarchal establishment of turn-of-the-century Jamaica, and it might not have been coincidental that Livingstone was replaced the next year (1904) by H.G. De Lisser as editor of the *Gleaner*, and that the newspaper made a sharp volte-face on these issues. But for as long as he was editor, Livingstone left no stone unturned and rebutted all who ventured to oppose the issue of compulsory registration, including the leading clergy of the Anglican Church.

Ever since 1885 the Anglican Synod had been raising the question of "illegitimacy", and had actually petitioned the government, urging legislation to ensure that "illegitimate" children were protected, maintained and educated. Reverend William Gillies, however, went a step further to hint at compulsory registration when he asked, "Is [the country] to wait till these men 'consent' to have their names recorded as fathers? Or till the mothers prove their paternity? Has it no duty to itself in the matter? . . . If the fathers do not choose to acknowledge their obligations, is the country to let them go free?"[106] Henry Clarke took Gillies's radical posture to its logical conclusion with his annual bills during the 1890s.

But when Archbishop Enos Nuttall addressed the synods of 1898 and 1899, rather than support compulsory registration he urged local community action to bring moral pressure to bear on those who transgressed in maintaining their offspring; he claimed that this course was already proving effective, as it had resulted in a considerable number of legal marriages.[107] Furthermore, the 1899 synod approved concrete proposals for changes in the law, as an alternative to the compulsory registration bills tabled annually by Henry Clarke. These proposals were adopted by the government as the basis of the Registration Bill (No. 29 of 1900). The essential features of the Anglican proposals and the subsequent bill were as follows:

1. Either parent could go the registrar's office and state the father's name, or the birth of a child could be attested to by a justice of the peace, clergyman, doctor, or the clerk of the resident magistrate's court and then forwarded to the registrar; but the father's name could not be registered until the registration forms were signed by both parents.
2. Alternatively, the mother could seek a resident magistrate's order declaring any man to be the putative father. This would require her to name the person on the registration form, which would be referred by the registrar to the inspector of the poor for investigation after a lapse of forty-two days (to allow the alleged father to register voluntarily). The inspector of the poor would subsequently submit signed statements from his investigation to the clerk of courts who, if satisfied that a prima facie case had been made against the man, would refer the matter to the resident magistrate. The latter would issue a summons to the alleged father; at the end of the legal proceedings, the magistrate would determine whether or not there was sufficient evidence to declare him the legal father. But the man had the right of appeal; no similar right of appeal was given to the woman if she felt that her case had been inadequately adjudicated.
3. If the woman was found to have made a false allegation of paternity, she was liable to imprisonment for up to two years with hard labour, or to penal servitude for up to three years.[108]

Although these provisions in theory allowed for the "independent" investigation of alleged paternity, they fell short of compulsion and, as in the case of previous bills, they laid the burden of bastardy at the feet of the mother. The Anglican Church, the government and a large body of elite opinion eschewed compulsory registration because they feared that it would lead to blackmail – the names of "upstanding" citizens might be tarnished and their families destroyed by "vicious" women seeking money. Even if the man was exonerated by the court, it was felt, the damage to his reputation would already have been done (essentially the same fears were expressed in 1869 when the first bastardy law was passed). Clarke, perhaps rather naively, responded that he had never heard of an instance of a woman swearing her child to a man who had never had any carnal knowledge of her.[109]

Canon William Simms, principal of Jamaica High School, was the primary spokesman defending the position of the Anglican Church in the press. He indicated that the Anglicans had

> built our recommendations on a careful consideration of a very considerable variety of actual cases, and of the effect that would be produced upon father, mother, child, innocent outsiders (such e.g., as the wife and legitimate children of the father of an "illegitimate" child) and the community at large by the applications of compulsion in every case.

He claimed that their proposals would enable all *willing* fathers to register their paternity, imposed no pains and penalties on anybody in addition to those in the existing law, and amended that law to make it more efficient. There was nothing to be gained by registering the names of married men, or mere boys, or men who were dead, or the fathers of the children of the multitude of married women who were living apart from their husbands who might be abroad or elsewhere in the island. Finally, he contested the view that the church had failed in its mission because of the high rate of "illegitimacy": "[T]he Church may retort by asking . . . what is the explanation of the forty per cent that are not illegitimate."[110]

Other Anglican clergy weighed in in defence of their church as well. Archbishop Nuttall argued that the Anglican proposals had resulted in a bill that improved on the existing law without resorting to compulsory registration, and went further than the laws in any other British country or colony in securing voluntarily, by moral pressure, the registration of the father and his obligation to support his children. He reiterated the view that the work of the church, not legislation, was the only way to exercise effective influence on moral issues.[111]

C.H. Coles, Warden of the Jamaica Church Theological College at Up Park Camp, noted that in its measured moderation, his church eschewed legislation on compulsory registration in very much the same way that the parent church in England stopped short of advocating legislation against intemperance. The reasons were essentially the same: "public" opinion did not favour such reform in practice: "The 60 odd [per cent] of illegitimate births, shows the majority of men [and] women in favour of illegitimacy." Hence, "We say, first educate public opinion, let that first coerce; give individuals the chance of reparation, then let law come in to compel." At the same time, however, he did not think the government should attempt any measures that it could not enforce without much expense and labour.[112]

Addressing, perhaps, a more fundamental issue, William Graham of the Church of Scotland did not believe that compulsory registration could redress the relationship between father and "illegitimate" child: "It is an 'improper' relationship, and must always remain so. Any attempt to give bastard children a status by legal enactments is an injury to the cause of sexual morality."[113] Those who opposed compulsory registration, then, would rather banish the "illegitimate" child than facilitate any sort of "normal" relationship between the child and its parent, because such a relationship would give legitimacy to the association that had resulted in the child's existence.

Livingstone's *Gleaner* was not slow to attack these arguments. It asserted that the Anglican Church was unwilling to endorse compulsory registration from fear of the social consequences that might ensue if every child did have a legal father, responsible for its care and education. It charged that the church was compromising with an unjust and unrighteous state of things, and argued that the laws of the moral world, like those of the physical, were fixed and inflexible: there was no room for compromise. More importantly, it observed that the Anglican proposals would leave untouched "the vast mass of vicious relationships which are undermining the progress of the country"; and it accused the church of giving married men, mainly of "the educated vicious class", "freedom to have as many illegitimate children as they like without incurring any responsibility except that enforced by the mother by a tedious process of law". Persuasion was not enough, according to the *Gleaner*, for under the present law a man might induce a woman to remain quiet for some years and then drop both her and his child, and she would have no redress because it would be difficult for her to prove paternity after so long a period. It was thus necessary to place the father's name permanently on record from the beginning in order to prevent this and to save the woman from falling into deeper shame. As to Canon Simms's allusion to the churches' success in fostering a 40 per cent legitimacy rate, the paper reiterated what his fellow Anglican clergyman, William Gillies, had said in 1886: "Have the moral and religious forces that have secured the forty per cent of legitimate births lost their power to diminish the 60 per cent of illegitimate ones?"[114]

Even some lay members of the Church of England were not entirely convinced by the position taken by that body. For instance, while recognizing the danger of blackmail, "An Anglican" admitted to being persuaded by the "clean cutting straight and fair" exposition of the *Gleaner* in opposition to the church. If "illegitimacy" were a disgrace, the man should bear an equal share with the woman. "An Anglican" observed that although under the bastardy law a woman could name the father and claim child support, "poverty, ignorance, or exceptional circumstances may interfere to prevent [her] employing the law to establish proof of her child's paternity and thus secure its support or partial support by the father, or the rich man, and the cunning man, can make it worth her while to be silent". While recognizing the scope for blackmail of innocent men, the writer thought that the good of the greatest number demanded a compulsory registration law with fair safeguards.[115]

But the Anglican Church found a powerful ally in the *Jamaica Times*, which rebutted the rebel priest Henry Clarke, the *Gleaner*, the *Jamaica Post* and sceptics like "An Anglican". It attacked compulsory registration on three main grounds: that it would hurt many innocent men and their families, would violate the individual rights of citizens, and would not promote pure families. All the "greatest good" could not be set against the evil that a compulsory registration law might cause to wrongly accused men and their families. The *Times* also reiterated Canon Simms's plea for the rights of the individual against the state and, like him, considered the compulsion of a woman to tell the father's name an unwarranted piece of state tyranny:

> Even the Negro woman has rights, and they must be respected. . . . She is not to be prosecuted for the act of bringing an illegitimate child into this world; her perfect legal right to do this is recognized, and the law does not attempt to consider the question in a moral light at all. But she is to be prosecuted for concealing the father's name, and the reason given for this is, that every child should have a "legal father".[116]

This was irony, indeed; black women's rights were being championed as the basis upon which the compulsory registration law should *not* proceed. That these women would, likely, be solely responsible for their children was secondary to the issue of "privacy". And hidden just below the alleged right to the mothers' privacy was the secret of their children's fathers; that was the real privacy that was being upheld.

Hinting that this was tantamount to a witch-hunt against the middle and upper classes, the *Times* asked:

> Well, suppose a woman has a child for one of these men, and he bribes her not to name him as its father, what then? She is brought before the Court, but you cannot send her to prison without the option of a fine. And suppose you do fine her, and inflict an ordinarily heavy fine, say two or three pounds, do you believe it will not be paid by your suspected middle-class and upper-class persons? . . . And why, too, seeing that the law aids her, should not the woman who is forced to tell the name of the father of her child, accept a bribe from one man, and father the child on another?[117]

Nor would, the paper contended, compulsory registration advance the morality of the lower classes, for,

> as a matter of fact, our people are not and have never been immoral – they are simply unmoral. They have in the main no sense of the disgrace attaching to illicit connections, the word "immorality", therefore, has no meaning for them. "Pure" and "impure" family life are terms that do not convey any exact meaning to their minds. How then would you secure a "purer" family life by compulsory registration?[118]

Leaving aside the somewhat superior attitude displayed by the *Times,* the newspaper had, in fact, unveiled an interesting perspective that had been alluded to by others: the Jamaican people had their own set of standards by which they created and maintained families. There was no disgrace attached to the unions that were constructed outside of official sanction, and the children who were produced therein were, very often, welcomed into their families and communities, counted as blessings, cherished, and expected, when growing and grown, to make their contribution to their parents' lives.

The government's position on this issue was enunciated by acting Colonial Secretary Sydney Olivier, in his introduction of the (1900) Registration Bill in the legislature. Considering the high "illegitimacy" rates as evidence that West Indian societies were far removed from what was generally regarded as the necessary foundation of a stable and progressive community, he racialized the issue by viewing it as a *black* problem. However, the government eschewed compulsory registration partly because of the great difficulty of framing such a law but, more particularly, because "they were in the position of one set of people in the Council with one set of mental habits legislating for another set of people with a different set of mental habits".[119] That reservation, however, did not prevent him and his "set of people" from pushing through the government/Anglican registration bill, even though a majority of the elected members claiming to represent and uplift the other "set", led by Reverend Henry Clarke (Westmoreland) and Reverend James Macnee (Hanover), boycotted the sittings of legislature during discussion of the bill. The law was thus passed in their absence.

Like Coles, Olivier argued that if the people had any desire for registration of paternity, it would have been reflected in their habits; he was very chary of going beyond the established habits of the people and trying to force them into a position they did not naturally adopt. If the government went too far in an attempt to compel matrimony or recognition of paternity by legislation, they would be getting themselves into difficulties and, to a certain extent, perverting the natural growth of the island. He further believed that in Jamaica there was no strong desire on the part of either women or men for legal union or legal recognition of paternity. And he shared the view that compulsory registration would be impossible to enforce without often resulting in the naming of a man who was not the father of the child. That was a danger that should not be incurred.[120]

Coles, Olivier and the *Jamaica Times* seemed to recognize that radically different moral systems were extant in Jamaica, although they did ascribe positions of superiority and inferiority to each system. Some of the social elites were seeking to impose a "superior" foreign standard borrowed from Victorian England on the people of Jamaica, even while some of these very elites sought to hold on to the old plantocratic cultural tradition, moulded by the life experiences and values of plantation society. While "concubinage and bastardy" signified social disgrace under the first system, they implied no shame under the second. But the *Jamaica Post* interpreted Olivier's unwillingness to impose the external moral system by legislation as an attempt to lower standards to suit the "inferior" moral practices of the majority and the "decadent" morality of elements of the upper classes. The paper asserted that "the public as a whole" did *not* want a lowering of the standards, but "It would rather say 'set the standard higher, and help us by every means in your power to rise towards it'."[121] The *Post*, in many ways representative of the cultural elite position, could not see that there could be and was a distinctive Afro-creole world view in operation, which ran parallel to a longstanding white upper-class creole culture. As far as it was concerned, only the imported Victorian standard could "uplift" the people (and their "debased" elite counterparts) and lead them into the folds of the "civilized". That they refused to be compelled was regarded only as a sign of their stubborn backwardness, rather than any ability of theirs to fashion a separate, related but competing culture.

Opinion in the Colonial Office was divided over the registration law. But Secretary of State Joseph Chamberlain finally decided that the absence of the elected members from the debate in the legislature was sufficient grounds for its disallowance – because he did not want them using the working of the law as a grievance to agitate for constitutional reform.[122] At least seven years of agonizing soul-searching debate in Jamaica had been abruptly halted by just one month's *ad hoc* deliberations by Colonial Office administrators, and on a point that had absolutely no bearing on the fundamental issue.

Archbishop Nuttall greeted the disallowance as a vindication of his church's position against the drift towards compulsory registration,[123] but the nonconformist churches (Baptists, Wesleyan Methodists, Presbyterians, Congregationalists, Free Methodists and the Christian Church together claiming to represent 250,000 members) used the opportunity to petition the secretary of state in favour of the policy. They also called for a law similar to one passed in New Zealand in 1894, which legitimized the children born before the legal marriage of their parents. There were also public demands for a commission to enquire into the marriage and registration laws and to recommend appropriate amendments.[124]

The 1903 Marriage and Registration Commission that was set up as a result recommended against compulsory registration and in favour of an amended version of the disallowed 1900 voluntary registration law. It also, with some hesitation, favoured a law that would legitimize the children of persons who subsequently married, but proposed to restrict it to persons already married and to those who married within eighteen months of the law coming into operation;[125] this was with a view to containing the incidence of illicit sexual relations and the "bastards" who resulted. But the morality of this attempt at legitimation provoked yet another controversy that rent asunder the fabric of Jamaican society, even though it was permitted by law in several parts of the British Empire, including British Guiana, Trinidad and St Lucia in the Caribbean.[126] Influential persons like Frank Cundall scoffed at the idea: "Calling things legitimate which were previously called illegitimate, will not make a people moral."[127]

Henry Clarke, as expected, was highly critical of the commission's report, but in an amazing volte-face the *Gleaner*, under new editorship, supported it.[128] While welcoming the report as valuable, the Colonial Office was still opposed to the proposed registration procedures. H.B. Cox anticipated that the inspectors of the poor would have plenty of legal proceedings on their hands, as they would be the ones responsible for investigating claims of paternity (see above). In the end, Secretary of State Lyttelton indicated that he would not take exception to laws framed along the lines proposed by the commission if the governor thought the experiments should be made, and the legislature was fairly unanimous on the subject.[129] Therein lay the problem. The island remained sharply divided on both registration and legitimation; within the Legislative Council itself, while the electives favoured compulsory registration and legitimation, they found Governor Swettenham and Attorney General Oughton resolutely opposed.[130] It was not until 1909 that a bill (No.

34) legitimizing children whose parents subsequently married got past the hurdle of official opposition and was put into law. However, that hardly had an impact on the "illegitimacy" statistics, which continued to rise. The stark reality was that the people were forming families out of wedlock, and having done so they would not be persuaded to "legitimize" them by Victorian (Christian) standards until late in life.

Elite Jamaican society, however, never became reconciled to the mountain of "immorality" in its midst. As the "illegitimacy" rates continued to rise uncontrollably, so the social reformers continued to agonize over it. But an effective solution eluded them, and the church continued to take the blame for the society's moral shortcomings. As late as 1918, "Young Bachelor" was still urging compulsory registration of fathers as a prescription.[131] Few, it seems, were willing to concede, let alone accept, that Jamaica and the Caribbean were simply *different* culturally from Britain and Europe. Yet this was precisely what the (new) *Gleaner* editor put on the table in 1908 when he wrote,

> [W]e now see why most persons here view illegitimacy somewhat differently from the newcomer or the stranger who dogmatically criticises our conditions. In Jamaica, speaking generally, we are at a stage where permanent monogamy – that is, the life-long attachment to our wife by means of legal and religious bonds is alien to the spirit and culture of the majority, and where, therefore, it is not quite fair to apply standards of judgement that imply moral condemnation. These standards are out of place here at the present time.[132]

But the editor was not much more enlightened than many of his peers, for he still regarded this difference as an indication of cultural inferiority which he hoped would some day be removed. Even though the reality spoke to a uniquely *creole* culture, the cultural elite continued to reach for a seemingly unattainable Victorian ideal, even while some of their plantocratic counterparts were participants in that same creole culture that they considered debased.

Conclusion

One of the major reasons that the civilizing mission failed in relation to sex, marriage and family was that the Jamaican elites themselves were ambivalent. Many of them (including some clergymen) were living double lives, conforming on one hand to the conventional legal, Christian, nuclear family, while on the other hand keeping mistresses and concubines (correctly labelled in this case) on the side. The old planter-aristocracy's tradition and value system remained alive and well, and competed with the newly imported Victorian moral code. It was elite opposition to compulsory registration of paternity (backed by the Anglican Church, which depended heavily on upper-class support for its continued social influence after its disestablishment in 1870) that made it impossible for any concerted attack to be launched on what was considered "immoral" sexual conduct ("fornication") and the resulting "illegitimacy".

But one should not presume that the ambivalence of the upper and middle classes is sufficient to explain the failure of the civilizing "moral crusade" against non-legal marriage/"concubinage" and "illegitimacy". For ordinary Afro-Jamaicans were not prepared to allow themselves to be unduly pressured into embracing a morality that was alien to their world view. In the private spheres of sexual behaviour, conjugality and family relations, the Jamaican people demonstrated in no uncertain terms that they were the masters of their own lives.

However, their decision not to marry before forming families, not to practise Euro-Christian monogamy steadfastly, nor to adhere strictly to the "ideal" male-headed nuclear family structure should not automatically be construed as resistance to dominant British cultural norms. For many of them did eventually get legally married in church in a conventional manner, and at enormous expense, after cohabiting for several years. But although legal, Christian, monogamous marriage might have been seen as a "respectable ideal" to aspire to, no shame or opprobrium was attached to living together, or forming and raising families, without the sanction of church or state. The people made it absolutely clear that in matters of personal status they had the final word, notwithstanding the denunciations of their lifestyles from the pulpit, the press, or by the state authorities. These were largely ignored, and thus rendered of marginal practical importance to the people's way of life. Sex, marriage and family were, therefore, yet another sphere of Jamaican life that represented a powerful and resilient expression of cultural self-determination.

Chapter 5

"Manners Maketh (Wo)Man"
Transforming the Jamaican Character

A CRITICAL OBJECTIVE OF THE CIVILIZING mission was to "improve" the morals, manners, character and behaviour of the people of Jamaica. Emerging from the dehumanizing conditions of slavery, those who were keen on building a new Jamaican society patterned on that of middle-class Britain believed that the ex-slaves would require a process of instruction in Christian morality and Victorian etiquette, long and sedulously administered, before they could attain the status of civilized beings. But they also believed that the institution of slavery had "lowered" the moral standards and behaviour of the colonial upper class, who were themselves in need of "upliftment" and character training if they were to become true Victorian ladies and gentlemen. As a group riddled with insecurities in the uncertain, post-emancipation social environment, some of these elites were willing candidates for such "upliftment" because they felt a gnawing need to identify more closely with metropolitan British society by adopting its "civilized", middle-class ways. That would also reinforce their claims to superior social status in Jamaican society, by placing them above the "coarseness" of the common people. But there were others who strove to retain not just their elite status in Jamaica, but their traditional aristocratic creole ways and values that were at sharp variance with the imported Victorian value system. This patriarchal plantocratic tradition[1] was patterned on the old English landed aristocracy and characterized by rough, even "coarse" behaviour, a luxurious lifestyle, conspicuous consumption and lavish hospitality, a keen sense of individual male honour, and female subordination (albeit alleviated by a large retinue of domestic servants). The civilizing mission, therefore, encountered resistance as well as competition not just at the bottom of Jamaican society, but also at the top; this was reflected in the manners and behaviour of some in the upper classes.

In the thrust to create a new Jamaican society, however, the idealized middle-class Victorian lady and gentleman were used as models of the civilized being. The ascribed characteristics of these idealized figures were increasingly used as the yardstick for admission into "cultured" society. By the turn of the century, wealth or even birth was no longer sufficient to qualify one for elite status, for many of the rich (both the old planter class and the *nouveaux riches*) were regarded as "degenerates . . . vulgar and far removed from being gentlemen as they can be". The accent was increasingly on "refinement" (cultivated manners) and education. As Agricultural Instructor A.P. Hanson put it, "To know how to act decently, speak properly, how to conduct yourself in the company of refined people, are matters of the first importance to [those] who would be gentlemen and ladies. Rudeness makes you contemptible in the eyes of cultured people; polished manners elevate you in their estimation." Those without refinement "unconsciously offend all the time . . . by disagreeable or uncleanly personal habits (all due to lack of training) or by transgressing the laws of 'good taste' in conversation, or in their way of dressing; which shortcomings, and others . . . debar them from the society of refined persons, – render their presence unwelcome".[2]

But there were important characteristics that differentiated the refined lady from her gentleman. According to the imported Victorian ideas, women were physically weaker, intellectually inferior and, therefore, ordained by nature to a subordinate and dependent position. Constructed on the foundations of an institutionalized patriarchal society, the expectations that surrounded women's roles were embodied in the "cult of true womanhood": the "ideal woman" was to be obedient to institutions and (male) symbols of authority, pious and righteous (shunning all vice identified by the moral institutions). She was depicted as passive, meek, powerless and expected to follow customs that prescribed her place in society. Because women were seen as "physical temptresses", and men wanted to be assured about their paternity, the control of women's bodies was vital; society demanded that they should be chaste or virtuous. The ideal middle-class Victorian lady was domesticated and restricted to the private space of the home, where her focus was to be the creation of a moral, clean and righteous environment for her husband and children.³ And to fulfil her role as a good housewife and mother, she had to possess certain homemaking skills. Even if her husband could afford domestic help, she was expected to know how to cook and bake, clean, and sew. She was also nurse to her family in illness. Here the ideal departed sharply from the norm among women in the Jamaican upper class who, in keeping with long-established plantocratic tradition, handed over practically all domestic tasks to an army of servants. A good, refined wife did, however, have to bear the hallmarks of "accomplished gentility": she ought to be well read, able to make polite conversation on light matters, play a musical instrument and sing, and she was expected to be a gracious hostess.⁴ As Marion Amies put it, "At a social gathering, a lady was expected to provide an accompaniment without hesitation, or add her voice to a duet or quartet. . . . Lack of competence and taste in the performance of accomplishments indicated a lack of gentility."⁵

The Victorian middle-class concept of masculinity which was promoted in Jamaica after emancipation also stood in sharp contrast to many old plantocratic values. As Catherine Hall asserts, according to the new ideal,

> True manliness was derived not from property and inheritance, but from "real religion" – the faith born from religious conversion and a determination to make life anew. True manliness also encompassed a belief in individual integrity and freedom from subjection to the will of another. Furthermore, it encompassed the capacity to establish a home, protect it, provide for it and control it: all these were a part of a man's good standing. . . . True manhood was defined by the capacity to work for oneself in the world, to trust in the dignity of labour, and to make money, rather than live off an existing fortune.⁶

Thus, as head of the family, the gentleman was the "breadwinner" who looked after the material welfare of his wife and children. He was to be kind and gentle, yet strong and resolute: "The gentleman is a man whose bearing is gentle because he is himself self-controlled and the master of his own soul. The calm, self-possessed man will always stand out in sharp antithesis to the violent self-assertive pushing personage." He had to have "a high sense of honour, faithfulness to obligation, absolute sincerity of word and deed; chivalry to women and to the weak; self-control; [and] deliberate consideration of others' feelings".⁷ Given women's frailty and dependence, he was expected to be chivalrous, courteous and respectful to them:

> [Gentlemen] have it in their power to show by innumerable ways their respect and reverence for womanhood. Such small attentions as the giving up of one's seat to

a lady, or opening the door for her ... are based on the ideas of chivalry. It has been well said that until a man has satisfactorily mastered, as the cardinal principle upon which society rests, that a lady shall always take precedence of the gentleman, he can never feel his feet firmly amongst cultured people.[8]

In the peculiar context of Jamaican society where "concubinage" and "illegitimacy" were rife, not least among the upper classes, the gentleman's obligation to provide for his children was specially emphasized: "It was the paramount duty of every father to care for his children", especially since "fathers were very prone even more than mothers to resent things displeasing to them and to treat their children unfairly".[9] These were the basic beliefs that informed the construction of gender relations in the Victorian period. By importing its tenets, apparently intact, many among the middle and upper classes sought to prove themselves "cultured and civilized", and at the same time to spread its civilizing influences to the rest of society, especially those below.

The Upper and Middle Classes

It was against this philosophical background that the churches, in particular, set about the task of "improving" the character of the Jamaican man and woman. By 1860 Governor Darling could report a decided improvement in the behaviour of the island's upper classes, which was most noticeable in their growing inclination to marry, in contrast to "former days". This coincided with an increase in the proportion of white women in the colony, from just 41 per cent of the white population in 1844 almost to parity by 1861. As the number of women increased, the tone and civility of elite life in Jamaica, as elsewhere in the Caribbean and the colonial world, became more refined. White women, working from the moral pedestal on which they were placed in the system of patriarchy where gender roles were clearly defined, were the primary bearers of "decency" and spirituality;[10] according to Ann Stoler, wherever they were introduced in significant numbers they seemed to exert "a civilizing, cultured, and restraining check on the rowdy, crude, and hard-drinking life style" of the rural plantocracy.[11]

As the Jamaican social elites outwardly assumed a more genteel and refined character, they mixed more easily and confidently with "cultured" visitors and expatriate residents. Edgar Bacon and E.M. Aaron observed that "the Creole of position" moved about easily with "his visiting cousin from Europe or the

American continent". He took his place in a first-class carriage, where he was often accompanied by "a pretty girl or two", who were themselves, for the most part, "too demure to notice the stranger who is trying use his eyes to the best advantage".[12]

The adoption of Victorian etiquette by large sections of the upper and middle classes as a critical yardstick of social status, however, meant that considerable emphasis was placed on external forms, rules and conventions and on an outward show of propriety. Particularly for aspiring coloureds and blacks within the middle class, the display of "correct" manners and behaviour was critical to attaining recognition of their social position, and they shared with whites of similar status, both in Jamaica and in other parts of the British Empire, a strong desire "to be rich and successful coupled with a passion for achievement and respectability".[13] As W.P. Livingstone put it, their behaviour was ruled by a kind of egoism which was "an essential principle regulating their lives, and they [sought] mainly their private gain and pleasure".[14]

The *Gleaner* observed that a "cult of respectability" characterized by a high degree of hypocrisy developed among the upper and middle classes, where "[we] must affect to like what we dislike . . . admire what we do not understand, we must do what we do not want to do; it is all 'the proper thing' ".

> [W]hen custom leads to the petrifying of the soul of men, when it makes us a slave to the opinions of others, when it stamps our every spark of individuality in our own bosoms, when it leads to self-righteousness, and makes a religion of selfishness and "proper form," then it becomes something abhorrent, something at which the finer spirit revolts. Fancy that kindness and humane feelings may be atrophied because of cast iron conventions. To think that what is genuine in us should have to give place to what is factitious, to what is external and artificial. And yet this is what the cult of respectability often results in.[15]

"Proper" but insincere behaviour became the order of the day, as the upper and middle classes engaged in what "The Critic" called "mutual admiration societies". For instance, when they visited each other there were sure to be discussions of painting or poetry, mainly of European provenance, whereupon the host/ess would unveil his or her own displays of talent. On such occasions the guiding principle was ritualized social correctness. Thus, on viewing the amateur painting of one of his hosts, "The Critic" was expected to behave true to form:

> At first I took it for a representation of a landscape at sunset, but on a critical examination I changed my mind and inwardly pronounced the thing on canvas

to be an elephant on the rampage. It seems that I was wrong, however, for it was a bunch of flowers and was called "still life." I said it was realistic. If I had been told it was a portrait of the Duke of Wellington, I should have said it was realistic.

The same practice of "friendly duplicity" held for appreciating pieces of writing and music unveiled on these occasions.[16]

This emphasis on form and stylized behaviour rendered hypocrisy a required social skill. It was not unusual for guests to remark in private, after profusely thanking their hostess for the pleasant afternoon, that the entertainment was awfully slow and that they only went because it was something to do. If, as became fashionable by the end of the nineteenth century, tennis and croquet were offered as additional entertainment,[17] then one was obliged

> to watch the tennis players with marked admiration, to clap at intervals when some player of ordinary skill does a little better than usual; and, if you have been playing yourself, at the end of the performance you must declare that you have had a most delightful game, and find any number of complimentary explanations for your beaten opponents. This is absolutely essential and is a mark of good breeding. If you are a man, and if any lady would like "a cup of tea", you should hand it to her yourself if possible; though there will always be some more fitting person to do it instead.... The way to win the favour of your hostess, too, is to take "another bit of cake". It is true the cake might not commend itself to your taste, but you must protest (if an opportunity offers) that it is the best you have ever tasted. This form of appreciation is flattering, but you will win a still greater reputation for intellect if you can show a deep concern in the tale of how one of the little ones recovered from the measels [*sic*].[18]

Upper-class social gatherings were also notorious as occasions for spreading unsavoury gossip about other "high society" people. They

> enable you to criticize the absent ones freely to your dear and sincere friends, who will do the same by you on the first convenient occasion.... [T]he real substantial viands are the small talk about engagements, weddings, servants, the vocal abilities of young ladies "just out", and other highly intellectual topics of the kind.[19]

Against the background of a pre-existing creole culture where "decency" had never been particularly emphasized, the hypocrisy of the Victorian period made for a stylized and predictable social life. However, the social elites were caught in a dilemma: they had to shed their old coarse behaviour, born of a basic life of coercion and violence shared with their human chattel, and to adopt a new but uncomfortable *gentilité* which may have marked them as approaching the civilized ways of their middle-class cousins in England, but which they wore as an ill-fitting cloak.

The general adherence to the cult of respectability was in many cases little more than a veneer that masked several social and character shortcomings. Indeed, some social elites seemed distinctly uncomfortable trying to conform strictly to the stiff Victorian etiquette. Their garden or lawn parties, carnivals, fairs, fêtes and festivals, where "proper" behaviour was expected, were often a greater source of social uneasiness than enjoyment for many of those who attended. According to the *Gleaner*, "[A]t those entertainments the self-consciousness of everyone is painfully apparent, and self-consciousness is the enemy of enjoyment." Greater effort was thus spent in artificially trying to behave "correctly" than in amusing oneself.[20] Many were unable to adhere faithfully to the new imported behavioural code. At the end of the nineteenth century Livingstone declared that although both white and coloured elites had generally kindly feelings and hospitable ways,

> [i]n all the amenities and graces of life they come up short of a reasonable standard. Public spirit is almost unknown. There is neither civic ambition and sense of responsibility, nor efficient administration and service in the interests of tax payers. The streets and lanes, the stores and offices of even the wealthiest merchants . . . are squalid and mean. High principle in business is rare. Order, method, and discipline in the proper sense, are seldom enforced.[21]

Over and above that, many in the upper and middle classes also fell well short of "civilized" Victorian standards by public displays of crass behaviour. Young men in particular seemed to breach the accepted code of conduct regularly, and were consequently described as vulgar cads: "The cad, like the poor, we have always with us." These miscreants were seemingly "heedless alike of the common laws of decency and politeness, as of circumstance and place", and behaved in a raucous manner in public, whether in church, the theatre, the cinema or lectures. They usually succeeded in making

> the more respectable portion of the audiences or congregation as it may be, as uncomfortable as possible. . . . We have seen a clergyman much distressed while preaching, by the continual coughings, droppings of books, and other unpleasant noises made. . . . In the Theatre the rowdy is in his element. There as a "god" he is free to scream out his insulting remarks on those below in the dress circle and pit. Such choice expressions as "white duppy" and "East Street beauty," are much in vogue, whilst the beating of sticks and calls for music add to the Pandemonium.

> ... [At one lecture] [s]everal persons suddenly remembered that they had a cold and those who had not one did their best to make up for the deficiency by holding animated conversations in a low tone.²²

Such unseemly behaviour also took the form of "howling, stamping and irrelevant exclamations" which disrupted performances; "insults [were] hurled at inoffensive persons in the theatre, at circuses and elsewhere". Indeed, it reached the point where anyone who sat among the "gods" was accused of being a ruffian, whether or not he participated in the vulgar activities issuing from that section. The same boorishness was exhibited at the cinemas.²³ The young men who were destined to become social leaders in the society seemed to be so decidedly unaffected by the new "superior" culture that many must have wondered about the possibility of the island ever breaking out of the mould of the old creole culture.

Further, some of the very bearers of the Victorian standard were sometimes lax in their public behaviour:

> Very bad examples are at times set by those whose social position should make them models of conduct. Some readers may recall a small disaster produced some years ago at a Kingston Sacred Concert by the fact that a certain Governor's wife was talking while a Singer was operating. He thought that he was being unfavourably commented on and so far lost his stride as to quit the platform there and then.

Equally deplorable was the tendency of many patrons to rush out at the end of a performance "ere the strains of 'God save the King' [were] even half way through".²⁴ If the "upper crusts" could barely observe the tenets of acceptable behaviour, how were they to convince foreigners, their social "inferiors" and themselves that they deserved to be the cultural leaders that they claimed to be?

Some people, however, felt audiences had a right to make as much noise as they pleased. Ever looking to the metropolis for guidance, they contended that British audiences also behaved badly in London theatres: "[W]e might wait until England set us an example in good manners before we began to insist upon a decent standard of behaviour in public places here." But in rising to the defence of the "motherland", the *Gleaner* claimed that English "public" opinion did not condone "exhibitions of vulgarity. . . . Shrieking and hooting are after all but the way in which savages express their feelings: civilized men should easily be able to find a new method. There is nothing admirable in merely making an obnoxious noise." It took the stationing of policemen inside the theatre, and the arrest and fining of patrons for disorderly conduct, to put an end to this kind of boorish behaviour.[25]

Very often such coarse behaviour among the upper and middle classes was accompanied by the use of "indecent language". According to the *Jamaica Post*, some of them delivered "vile expletives with impunity" and defended the practice by averring "that they swear because the English language provides no expression suitable for the exigencies of the moment", or that sometimes "the comparatively modest big D might . . . be employed in preference to a tyrade [*sic*]".[26]

It was rare, however, that white people were actually charged for using obscene language; for even when they were clearly not elite, their very whiteness conferred a certain privilege in colonial society. Catherine Hall put it succinctly: "Whiteness carries with it authority and power, the legacy of having 'made the modern world', of never being 'strangers anywhere in the world'."[27] So, for instance, although Thomas Trumble was a "full blooded" Irishman (and therefore not a member of the elite), he was entrusted with a limited amount of authority as overseer at the ice factory. Nevertheless, his indiscriminate use of indecent language in public, and his multiple appearances in court for that misdemeanour, threatened to debase whiteness in colonial Jamaica. But his behaviour could be explained, or so his lawyer thought in 1873 (notwithstanding Trumble's guilty plea), by the fact that "he was a man, and had under him forty labourers of the worst class in the country to deal with". He was, in other words, not necessarily vulgar in his own right, but was tainted by his association with blackness. Whatever credence the magistrate gave to that explanation, however, he observed that he could not imagine language more offensive coming from a man's lips "whether the man be black or white"; since this was not the defendant's first offence, he was fined thirty shillings and sixpence.[28]

The social status of dentist Dr Chevers was more elevated than Trumble's, so when in 1875 he employed "the most abominable language" to abuse the city inspector, who had gone into his yard and called attention to a nuisance, it must have been very disturbing to Chevers's friends and neighbours. He was fined the maximum: forty shillings and costs.[29] Yet it speaks volumes that neither of these white offenders (albeit of differing social ranks) was even threatened by the alternative penalty of imprisonment, which was routinely imposed in cases involving nonwhite persons charged with the same offence (see below).

Some upper-class persons also occasionally resorted to public brawling. For instance, the charge preferred in 1889 against Dr Vine of the Government Medical Department, of disorderly conduct and assaulting the police, was rare but not isolated. He pleaded guilty and, according to the *Colonial Standard*, "The Magistrate inflicted a fine of £5, remarking that he did so because he, Dr. Vine, should have known better than to have been guilty of such conduct and should have set a better example to the lower orders."[30] Very significantly, too, the old plantocratic cultural tradition of defending one's honour was still extant in the later nineteenth century. Horsewhipping an opponent was one method of doing so. Thus, on one Saturday afternoon in October 1875, two "gentlemen", Messrs Desnoes and Cespedes, were arrested for fighting at Port Royal and King Streets, "the one with blood running down his face, and armed with a riding whip; and the other, with a pair of knuckle dusters, with which he [was] said to have struck his opponent in the head".[31]

Also in 1875, two elite lawyers – Henry Vendrys and D.P. Nathan – abused and assaulted each other at the end of a case in the Kingston Circuit Court. In an argument that developed as soon as the magistrate vacated the bench, the two actually came to physical blows, causing the magistrate to return to the bench to hear the case of assault. According to Vendrys, who seemed to be aggressor in the incident, "I said to Mr. Nathan I will not take your word any more; he said you are a blackguard and I struck him", whereupon Nathan "doubled his fist" and prepared to fight. Vendrys went on,

> I put it to your Honor, that although the sternness of law, orders me not to strike under any circumstances whatever, a gentleman who is told he is a blackguard, may not, when he resents an insult of that sort, in a manner more intended as a reproof than an assault, be excused. I may tell your Honor that he told me I was only fit to sell rat-poison, an insult, which, I regret, I returned.

They were both fined by the magistrate.[32] Remnants of such old plantocratic traditions and values thus continued to rear their heads in the later nineteenth century in the behaviour of upper-class men, and competed against the new Victorian value system that was being imported to civilize Jamaican society.

Elite "rowdyism" also occurred in the fashionable clubs of Kingston. In what was described as an "exposé" in the resident magistrate's court in March 1896, the extent of this (mis)behaviour was laid bare:

> Here are some young men – gentlemen if you will – who move in the best society and look down with contempt upon all who have a darker skin or wear a shabbier coat than themselves. Yet they stand convicted of conduct which places them on

precisely the same moral and intellectual level with the lowest rowdies who infest the lanes of Kingston.33

Occasionally rowdyism among upper- and middle-class Jamaicans even threatened the public peace. Perhaps one of the most celebrated instances of this was a cricket match between the Falmouth and St James cricket clubs in June 1870, when a dispute arose over the dismissal of a batsman off a no-ball. It was alleged that the umpire was influenced by a bet he had placed on the game. Out went the noble Victorian ideal of unquestioningly obeying the umpire's decision; a fracas ensued between the two teams, and involving their supporters, in which "fists were freely made use of in the presence of a large number of Ladies". It took a platoon of police armed with rifles and fixed bayonets to quell the disorder of these white mobs.34

Apart from the juicy details of domestic discord (including physical abuse) revealed in reportage of elite divorce cases,35 occasionally the newspapers offered glimpses of more serious crimes perpetrated by white people. For instance, in 1902 Annie Wheatle, an Englishwoman of middle-class status, was charged with concealing the birth of her child, whom she had buried among the roses in the garden of her grocery shop in Stony Hill. Granted bail, she vanished mysteriously before her case was tried.36 Even more sensational was the shooting of Kenneth Spencer by his wife, Doris, in May 1920. Unlike Wheatle, these were well-to-do whites who lived in Potter's Lane, Rae Town, and the trial naturally generated much public interest. It lasted just two days, however, before the jury returned a verdict of not guilty on the grounds that the killing was accidental, due to the couple's struggle for the revolver. The question does arise whether the verdict would have been similar were the defendant black and working class.37

Incidents like these were embarrassing to elite Jamaica because, as the self-appointed standard-bearers of civilization, they were expected to "set a better example to the lower orders", as the magistrate told Dr Vine in 1889. Some incidents were clearly lapses which demonstrated that even the cultural elites of the upper and middle classes were somewhat imperfect or ambivalent in their adoption of the Victorian moral and behavioural ethic. Although the cult of respectability became very important to their quest for high social status, very often it was little more than a thin veneer. When from time to time that outer crust tore, it exposed the raw sore of "raucous coarseness" with which they had been infected ever since the days of slavery, where the creole culture which developed had little space for the "decency" that characterized the new Victorian culture. There still remained among some of the upper classes vestiges of the old plantocratic, patriarchal cultural tradition, which competed against the new middle-class Victorian culture. Thus, for several reasons both upper and middle classes fell short of the characteristics of the civilized or cultured Victorian lady and gentleman, and instead behaved in ways that were sometimes indistinguishable from their allegedly coarse, lower-class counterparts, and sometimes were a throwback to the "crude" old ways of the rural plantocracy. Said to be rough and uncultured by middle-class Victorian standards, they were in reality creole Jamaicans.

The Lower Classes

If the success in inculcating civility in Jamaica's elite classes was only partial, the challenge to civilize the mainly black lower classes and to transform their character and behaviour was considered formidable. But two mutually reflecting and reinforcing assumptions underlay fundamental differences in attitude towards these two social categories, based, it must be said, largely on race and colour. Although the behaviour and manners of the lighter-skinned classes may not have corresponded with the ideal Victorian model, by the late nineteenth century the general assumption was that "bad behaviour" and boorishness were the aberration rather than the norm among them. Those who stepped out of line could easily be isolated and ostracized. The reverse, however, was regarded to be the case as far as the "darker" lower classes were concerned, for they were considered to be coming out of the savagery of Africa and slavery and so having an enormous mountain to climb. Uncouth, vulgar, even violent behaviour was thus to be expected as their norm (which is why when they "behaved" at public functions it was cause for comment), and it was not likely to incur any punitive social sanctions among them. After all, they did not know better. So, as regards the lower classes, the focus of attention was in one direction only: to "improve" their manners and behaviour. This analysis pursues that focus, to ascertain if it attained its anticipated logical conclusion: "civilization".

The fundamental assumption that the lower classes were uncivilized stemmed largely from the fact that the civilizers viewed them through the prisms of broad, negative racial stereotypes developed back in the days of slavery. According to Brackette Williams, stereotyping is a common feature of colonial societies, and is largely a product of elite ideological rationalizations or distortions of the prototypical experiences of the various groups in society, based on perceived ethnic differences.³⁸ Hence, in Jamaica, imitation and cunning, rather than creativity or inventiveness, were supposed to be the hallmarks of lower-class, uneducated "negroes". They were "garrulousness and love . . . chatter and argument", albeit illogical; they were given to display, and were capable of strong and deep personal attachments. They were like children in need of guidance and patience: their existence was simple and ruled by elementary laws. They possessed little mental power and lacked self-control. They were religious but not pious and, believing in evil, were superstitious. Ignorant, timid and dependent, they were also sensitive and responsive to sympathy and justice, but when badly treated vacillated between sullenness and rage. Polite, temperate in diet and displaying an unsophisticated humour, they were insensible to noise and unconscious of odours. The working-class "negro" was also thoughtless and thriftless: "He spends his money as he gets it, and makes no provision for meeting his liabilities", although on the occasion that he received high wages, he spent money on his family. Most frustrating, said Mary Eliza Bakewell Gaunt, was that it was very difficult to "enter into the workings of the mind" of these people; their points of view were kept hidden, and one could never discover why they told the lies that they did. Lying was related to their penchant for stealing: "[H]e steals because he is too lazy to work. As he steals, so of course he lies; and as a natural result, he has little idea of the sanctity of an oath."³⁹

In a word, these negative stereotypes spelled "uncivilized", and coloured the image of uneducated black and brown Jamaicans in the eyes of whites. Not surprisingly, the *St James Gazette* in 1885 opined that black people universally had a tendency to "revert to savagery", and

> In Jamaica this tendency to revert to savagery is still more marked and more extraordinary. Most of the black inhabitants have been under the influence of Christianity and civilization for two or three generations; and it might be supposed, therefore, that the negroes were thoroughly leavened with the teaching of their instructors. Not so. Some, no doubt, half-breeds and full blooded negroes alike, have completely overcome the hereditary instincts of their race, and display an ability which is worthy of sincere respect. But the great mass of the enfranchised negroes, where they are left to their own devices, are drifting back to savagery, with its concomitant devotion of Obi.⁴⁰

For those who preferred to think in stereotypical terms, there was always experiential evidence to support their views. In 1875, for instance, a "gentleman" who returned to Jamaica twenty-four years after his first visit noted that although the scenery was "as beautiful as ever . . . the retrogression of the people [was] astounding and undeniable". The days when "the streets were quiet and orderly" and the people displayed "good behaviour and respectful manners" had gone. Instead,

> the first thing that strikes a visitor in returning is the rude, rough and loud deportment of the lower classes – their utter want of respect for any body, and the vile, infamous and beastly language which is poured forth in vollies before and in the ears of people of refined feeling, and before the very constables without check or punishment, and the effect of this is not only pernicious to morality in general, but to the purity of the juvenile mind which proper parents try to preserve. The markets . . . exhibit the true character of the lower classes, for with almost the same breath the women speak of the blessings of God and the sweetness of God's mercies, while they belch forth curses and most filthy expressions on the slightest remark as to the quality of their produce, or the price they may happen to be asking for it. They are . . . indolent in work – improvident in life – lack ambition, and money is only valuable to make a show and a splash until it is spent.[41]

Frank Bullen too observed that, on landing at the Kingston wharf, his first encounter with Jamaicans occurred a hundred feet from the gangway which was "packed with negroes of both sexes, clean and unclean, through which crowd it [was] necessary to bore one's way, [and be] subjected to ribald remarks in volleys, and in absolute danger of personal violence from the lewd negroes of the base sort".[42] Perhaps these visitors were shocked by the loud exuberance of the Jamaican lower classes who, along with their "social betters", had fashioned a demonstrative and functional culture; these were no shrinking violets.

If indecent language was a problem with the upper and middle classes, among the lower classes it was almost a way of life. There were some streets in Kingston which were said to be the haunts of men and women who threw obscenities about with impunity. Residents complained regularly about the verbal assaults that they had to endure in and around the corners of John's Lane and Tower Street, Barry Street and Maiden Lane, Peter's Lane and Tower Street, as well as along the bridge on Tower Street, where "between thirty and forty persons of each sex congregate nightly . . . from about seven o'clock and indulge in the most lewd language". Many of these attacks of "filthy, obscene language" were said to be directed at "ladies" who walked through the city's streets. This "foul" behaviour also occurred on streetcars where persons created disturbances for one reason or another.[43]

As far as the promoters of the new Victorian culture were concerned, especially regarding its dictates about the place and role of women, what was even worse was the fact that lower-class women and children were unashamed principals in this "lewd" culture of profanity. When, for instance, Margaret Henry of Peter's Lane was taken to court in 1882 and charged with using indecent language, she confessed to thirty previous convictions and was given the maximum sentence of forty shillings plus costs or thirty days' imprisonment. She opted for prison and was taken from the court, "but not without firing a volley of bad language as is her custom". She then proceeded to pay her own bus fare *and* that of a constable conveying her to the prison! So infamous were the women for their use of bad language that on one occasion when two men were brought before the police court for abusing each other, the magistrate commented that in all his experience he had never heard such abominable language and "if the purlieus of Princess Street and Peters Lane were to be ransacked, two women could not be found to utter anything more nasty".[44] Although the middle-class-bound Victorian culture never intended to transform lower-class women into "ladies", they were nevertheless expected to be the main sources of decency and respectability among that class of people. By their behaviour, however, they challenged and undermined the idea of what was appropriate conduct for women; as a result they were labelled "dissolute" and, whenever possible, were castigated and punished by the authorities.

Young children were also quite adept in the use of profane language. Said the *Morning Journal* in 1871,

> It is painful as one walks along the streets to hear the beastly obscenity that issues so frequently from the lips of the numerous lawless girls, and boys, by which they are infested. . . . The number of idle, dissolute foulmouthed women and girls, by whom in particular this sort of thing is practised, is very large indeed. . . . They live lives of most disgusting wantonness, and their practice is to parade the streets and taint the atmosphere with their foul breath.[45]

It was the *Gleaner*'s belief that the swarms of outrageous children in the city were made up of a large number of disreputable girls and boys: "They are the most depraved characters and in most cases are distributed in the various taverns about the city, while others take up residence in Peter's Lane and Temple Lane." The girls, in particular, indulged in the most filthy language imaginable. In 1876 a girl who could scarcely be more than twelve was found in the street at nine o'clock at night, "making use of very dirty expressions".

She was sentenced to ten days' imprisonment with hard labour. Two girls about twelve, named Elizabeth Young and Rebecca Brown, were brought before the police magistrate in 1882 for singing an indecent song in the street. When the magistrate asked if the children were known to the police the sergeant replied that they were not, whereupon the magistrate remarked that they were "children in years but women in depravity", and ordered their imprisonment in the penitentiary for ten days. In 1915, at Orange Bay, the children converted the Quaker church into a play-house, running over the seats and using the most abusive language to the day-school teachers. One boy even went so far as to use a pocketknife on the teacher.46 For many observers, the fact that children were involved in producing the "volleys" of curses that were emitted in public places was certainly a mark of social depravity. Children, according to the new Victorian belief, were flawless creatures, as close to the angels as any humans could be. That these Jamaican children could be involved in such behaviour was simply indicative of the corrupting influence of their parents, peers and the society in general.

The use of indecent language by working-class blacks was regarded as clear proof of their lack of civilization, and was particularly embarrassing to those blacks eager not to be "dragged down" by their less "cultured" brethren. Thus, Bahamian-born Robert Love, editor of the black newspaper, the *Jamaica Advocate*, regretfully opined that

> [i]t is *we* [black people], and not others, who are guilty. We make this confession unreservedly, and we denounce the evil publicly because we hope to arouse the sentiment of shame as well as that of regret, in our people, for this cruel wrong to themselves and to the community. We scarcely ever hear obscene language in public from the lips of a *white* man – certainly never from the lips of a *white* woman; whereas our boys and girls, our young men and young women and even our old men and old women are vomiting everywhere, and at all times, the Billingsgate which would surprise, if not shame an English fish-woman.47

While Love's claim that the use of indecent language was confined to black people was clearly erroneous, it is nevertheless true that swearing was an integral part of a culture of noise that emanated from the streets. Certain sections of Kingston were particularly plagued with this "affliction": Pink Lane, Beeston Street, Water and Foster Lanes, Luke Lane, East Queen Street, Tower Street, and Rae Town where boys, men and "lewd" or "disreputable" women gathered nightly in raucous, "indecent" assemblies, preventing "respectable" residents from sleeping at night. Drumming, loud music, "dignity balls" (parties), boisterous arguments, wakes and "revivalist" street preachings formed integral features of this culture of nightly noise.[48] According to the *Gleaner*,

> From about eight to ten o'clock a medley of loose characters will assemble, hitching up against garden fences and garden walls, and laughing and talking at the top of their voices; sometimes also running about the street and screaming. From ten to one, you may have a couple of men or more in the vicinity, talking all the while, and talking so loudly that sleep is impossible to scores of people in the neighbourhood. At two o'clock, one or two persons may pass along the street, singing with foolish loudness and cacophony.[49]

Considered even worse were "night picnics" in the streets and yards, especially on holidays, where men and women engaged in "a hideous dance . . . called the 'Spanish dance,' where the men and women hug each other in the most indecent way possible; calling up memories that all civilized races relegate to the place where their dirty linen is washed".[50]

Gatherings that were characterized by loud laughter, chatter and music disturbed the society, not simply by the literal noise that was made, but by the insistence on carrying on the culture of exuberance, in spite of the disapproval levied against it. The people had learned to construct enjoyment in the midst of the savagery of slavery, and in fact had been somewhat encouraged by their masters to do so (in order to relieve some of the tensions inherent in the system). So their continued determination to "have a good time" was in keeping with a longstanding culture. It was not that *they* had changed or were "depraved"; rather, the importation of the new Victorian culture radically changed the elite perception of these established cultural manifestations. With echoes of seventeenth-century Puritanical beliefs, the new Victorian culture sought "decency" at every turn, and those who promoted it began to fear that "someone, somewhere might be having fun".[51]

In keeping with this mindset, the ultimate sacrilege was committed when church services were disrupted by these so-called lewd people. In one notorious incident in November 1884, there was a "most unseemly affray" at a church on Duke Street during a baptismal service: "At the hour appointed for the ceremony a crowd gathered, put out the gas, and struck several persons with sticks, smashed sashes, and injured plants in the Church yard."[52]

Although members of their own class sometimes behaved in a disorderly manner, many upper- and middle-class Jamaicans expressed shock when this occurred among the lower classes; they announced that they found such raucous behaviour unacceptable, and interpreted it as an indication of a lack of civilization among the people. Said the *Gleaner,* "Now a love of noise is a sign of the savage. It is also an indication of vulgarity. It suggests that those who make it find a sheer delight in barbarous cacophony [*sic*], or desire to annoy others, or wish to attract attention to themselves." The *Gleaner* writer felt that this ought to be stamped out.[53]

It was a short leap from noisy street gatherings where indecent language was used freely to assaults on "respectable" persons. In July 1878, for instance, one of "a band of lawless wretches" who loitered at the corner of Peter's Lane tore a shawl from the shoulders of "a lady of high respectability". In 1902 "a respectable Kingston girl", on her way home with "a woman of equal respectability", was assaulted by a ruffian who struck her violently on the mouth. When this failed to evoke a quarrel, he attacked her further with "a flood of filthy abuse".[54]

Street brawls were also commonplace, and some were particularly vicious. For instance, in August 1862 a man was arrested for having bitten off part of the tongue of another man with whom he was fighting. According to the *Falmouth Post,* he apparently choked his antagonist until his tongue protruded from his mouth and then bit it off. In a similar incident in 1880, John Muir bit a piece out of the right half of William Reid's upper lip. The wound was so severe that Reid had to be hospitalized. Later in that year, at Eleven Miles (east of Bull Bay, on the border of St Andrew and St Thomas), a drunk attacked a man and bit off his upper lip. In 1892 two men of the same name, James Williams, were assaulted in two separate districts of St Mary. One was attacked by Robert Richards who, after mauling Williams, bit off his left ear and allegedly swallowed it. The other Williams had a large piece of his upper lip bitten off and, likewise, allegedly swallowed by his assailant.[55]

Nor was street fighting confined to men. In 1873 Magistrate Rampini witnessed a fight between two coal girls:

> Catching her opponent by the neck, vixen No. 1 commenced the attack by delivering a vigorous "buck" with her head right in front of her antagonist – a compliment which was instantly returned. Now both were wrestling on the ground, legs twined with legs, and arms with arms, and the blood flowing pretty freely on either side. [The fight was stopped by a constable who took] the two termagants bleeding, wounded, and almost naked, [but] hurling abuse at each other all the time, with many tears and many objurgations to the lock-up.[56]

According to the *Gleaner,* the practice of butting heads was common among women of the streets:

> It is said to be a very cruel thing on the part of the butter, who generally lays hold of her victim by the plaits of the hair, draws the party towards her and strikes with great force on the fore head with one side of the head, at [the same] time sending her antagonist into convulsions, leaving her bleeding. . . . It is a common thing to hear a blackguard woman say to some one who she thinks is unprotected "a wi buck you an' pay [a court fine] foo you."[57]

Women were capable of doing more serious damage. For instance, in 1880 Eliza Cottman bit George Wright, a blacksmith, in a fight at a tavern in Tower Street. Wright later died from tetanus. In 1881 Maria Llewellyn, an office woman, was tried for "biting the right eye and one of the fingers of Annieta Lawrence", a ginger-beer seller on the race course. Lawrence was disfigured for life. Street fighting occurred among men, among women, and between men and women.[58] The sight and reports of women, in particular, fighting in the street brought Victorian Jamaica up short. That women could butt, bite and severely injure men and each other served to dispel the notion of the frail and "gentle" woman. Even as they shouted obscene words in the street, danced, argued and fought, Jamaican women regularly invaded the public sphere of men, as defined by the Victorians. And while there they were no mere observers of the street culture that developed; they were full participants who made their presence felt.

The police, symbols of civil authority, were not exempt from the wrath of irate "street women". Indeed, according to the *Jamaica Times,* the people were contemptuous of the police. "[T]he contempt felt by the large class of rowdies for the Constabulary" was due in part to the fact that policemen, with a few exceptions, were allegedly "very unintelligent . . . [and] deficient both in quality and in quantity". The "crass stupidity" of the average policeman was described as "astounding", even as many "wink[ed] the other eye" and seemed not to notice the "dish of bad words" served up around them. Thus, when in 1873 a policeman reprimanded Alberta Henry, a higgler, for breaching the market regulations, she not only abused him verbally but "deliberately tore his clothes to rags, laid hold of him by the head and butted him like an ox, and kicked him, to use the constable's own words, 'like a man'". Again in 1880, when a policeman attempted to arrest another female street vendor for refusing to take her goods to the Sollas (later renamed Jubilee) market, she held on to his jacket, "a clean one he had just put on – and tore off every button, and then became so boisterous as to attract a large crowd" which then followed her to the courthouse. The woman admitted to holding on to the policeman but only, she said, after he had hauled and pulled her about.[59] These women were not about to be intimidated by officers of the state, and their willingness to lay hold of them spoke to a culture that was separate from the class-bound gender ideology of the Victorian period. As persons who had long fended for themselves and defended their own space (with no men to protect them, according to the patriarchal construction), lower-class Jamaican women were not about to retreat from that sense of personhood. And if the source of violation happened to be the representatives of the state (many of whom lived among them), they were not daunted, but rather were willing and ready to defend themselves or even to attempt to subdue those representatives.[60]

"Free fights" involving gangs of men and women were also a feature of lower-class Jamaican behaviour. In 1876 one erupted on King Street near to the Parade; knives were brandished and cries of "Murder!" heard. Another free fight at Pink Lane in February 1909 arose "as usual from an altercation amongst some women, in which there were some forty or fifty participants". Fish-lances, knives, bottles, sticks and stones were freely used and after nearly an hour's quarrel, some of the persons who were involved in the fight were escorted by the crowd to the public hospital.[61]

As in other parts of the Caribbean, free fights also took the form of "stick-licking" ("stick-fighting" in Trinidad), a sort of ritualistic social contest.[62] For instance, at a "Queen's Party" that was held at Juno Pen, a few miles from Annotto Bay, to celebrate the August (emancipation) holidays in 1899, a fight occurred with stick-licking or "roast-wood", a name given to the sticks. By the time the fight had reached its climax, several people had been knocked down, speechless, with blood flowing from their wounds (principally in the head) "like water". Then many of the Annotto Bay folks, who seemed to have had the worst of it at Juno Pen, determined to have revenge as soon as the Juno Pen people went into town: "Having met them as desired, a fight again ensued at a place called 'Marking Stone,' near the railway station, on Thursday night, followed by another on Saturday evening which resulted in many more going to hospital, and the arrest of about nine of the 'ringleaders,' and noted 'warriors'." By the turn of the century the *Jamaica Times* declared, "Stick-licking is becoming a pastime"; in Kingston in October 1902 there was a big stick-licking at Tower and Church Streets that lasted for about forty-five minutes. Sticks, stones and other missiles were freely used by the combatants,

Figures 10 and 11. Portraits of proud defiance

Source: John Henderson, *The West Indies* (London: Adam and Charles Black, 1905). Courtesy of A&C Black (publishers) on behalf of John Henderson (author) and A.S. Forrest (artist).

Figure 12. Awaiting trial at the courthouse

Source: John Henderson, *The West Indies* (London: Adam and Charles Black, 1905). Courtesy of A&C Black (publishers) on behalf of John Henderson (author) and A.S. Forrest (artist).

Figure 13. A West India Regiment soldier

Source: John Henderson, *The West Indies* (London: Adam and Charles Black, 1905). Courtesy of A&C Black (publishers) on behalf of John Henderson (author) and A.S. Forrest (artist).

Figure 14. Market women

Source: John Henderson, *The West Indies* (London: Adam and Charles Black, 1905). Courtesy of A&C Black (publishers) on behalf of John Henderson (author) and A.S. Forrest (artist).

Figure 15. Going to church

Source: John Henderson, *The West Indies* (London: Adam and Charles Black, 1905). Courtesy of A&C Black (publishers) on behalf of John Henderson (author) and A.S. Forrest (artist).

and the event encouraged a large crowd to assemble. "Stoning" was another troubling pastime of the lower classes: young men and women at street corners would throw stones at passersby or at rival "gangs".[63]

By the early twentieth century, however, new concerns were voiced about where this lower-class culture of noise, profanity and violence was leading. The *Jamaica Times* pointed to an ominous development consequent on the growth of urban slums (due to the large influx of people from the country seeking work in Kingston).[64] In times of scarce resources (the Jamaican plantation sector had been in the throes of a chronic depression ever since emancipation), the influx generated an antipathy between the newcomers and the Kingston labourers, made worse by people returning from abroad. Hence, the *Jamaica Times* asserted that "the abundant intercourse of our people with places like the Central and South American republics, and even with parts of the United States itself, has inculcated many of them with the idea that the revolver, the knife, violence instead of Law are very fine and effective things".[65] The impact of outside influences was one explanation for the alleged increase in violence, but those influences fused with a pre-existing circumstance where violence had been used to effect control and to ensure power. This was but a continuation of that trend.

Child care was another area in which the "civilization" of the people was tested, notwithstanding the fact that many upper-class families entrusted the care of their babies and infants to lower-class women as wet nurses and nannies. Nevertheless, the care of children, both legitimate and "illegitimate", came under intense scrutiny in the later nineteenth century. From time to time the newspapers printed stories of the ill-treatment, abandonment and even murder of children that aroused grave concern among the "respectable public". Although these were no more brutal than similar incidents reported in the British, European or American press, they were sufficiently frequent for those Jamaicans who were concerned about the island's image as a civilized colony to call on the authorities to protect the children.[66]

The abandonment of young children was not unusual. For instance, in reporting the discovery of a month-old black infant in June 1875, the *Gleaner* asserted that "[t]hrowing away children seems to be becoming quite a fashion in our midst".[67] The abandonment of an infant sometimes led to its death, but there were also several deliberate cases of infanticide and concealment of birth. This was by no means peculiar to Jamaica; in fact, there was growing concern in Britain about the rise in the number of infanticides during the nineteenth century, which, interestingly, was linked by reformers to "illegitimacy". Women who gave birth to children out of wedlock were generally poor, often could not get the fathers to support the children financially, and were condemned as "fallen women" to a life of shame and disgrace.[68] Whether any of these factors had an influence on instances of infanticide in Jamaica is not clear. But in February 1865, for instance, Rosalie Ward of Metcalfe was charged with the murder of her child. Catherine Eccles of Orange Street, Kingston, threw her newborn baby through the window in January 1877, while Julia Campbell in June 1881 and Louisa Brown in July 1891 threw theirs down latrines. Catherine Satchele/Satchell was charged with murdering her male infant in February 1889; in June 1892 a male infant of about three weeks old was found in Chancery Lane, Kingston, with a wound on his head and marks of violence all over his body. This, as we have seen, was not just a lower-class phenomenon.[69]

Abandonment and infanticide were the most drastic forms of child abuse practised in Jamaica. More common was the everyday physical maltreatment of children as punishment for minor misdemeanours, both at home and in school. Some of these instances were blood-curdling. In 1876, for instance, Susan Barrett of Barry Street severely beat her nine-year-old girl until the child bled. Not satisfied, Barrett reportedly took hold of the child by her plaits, lifted her off the ground and butted her on the forehead "after the manner of a cow". When the girl fell, her mother jumped on her chest three times and then dragged her into the house. The child managed to escape through a window and climbed on the roof of an adjoining house, but her mother threw a brick at her. All this because she claimed that the little girl was "ungovernable". Barrett was sentenced to thirty days' hard labour. In another instance, in May 1890, a woman named Gordon was charged with placing the fingers of her seven-year-old granddaughter into the fire of her stove because the child, whom she had sent on an errand, stayed out longer than expected. In March 1895 Henrietta Laing of Slipe Pen Road was fined forty shillings for tying the hands of her little girl with sash cord, and whipping her about the head and back until she bled.[70] The violence of parents, especially mothers, towards their children, particularly their daughters, spoke to age-old issues of parental authority and frustration, lack of parental skills, and intra-gender contestation. The tendency of Afro-creole parents to use excessive force in punishing their children has also been observed in post-emancipation Guyana and Trinidad. David Trotman explains it partly as an attempt to "restrain them from potential conflict with the ruling class by curbing youthful exuberances", and partly as an unconscious taking out of their own frustrations, created by an oppressive colonial system, on their defenceless children.[71]

In a letter to the press, "Jamaican" asserted that various methods were used to punish children. One was to tie the hands at the wrists and fasten them to the limb of a tree or some spot over the head which left the child helpless, and then with a heavy strap or switch, a strong man or woman would administer thirty or forty stripes with full force until the child was too exhausted even to cry. Thereafter the child was left hanging for hours. This was clearly a leaf taken from the former white slavemasters' manual; slavery had indeed cast a long shadow on the lives and behaviour of the ex-slaves and their descendants. Another method of punishment was for one person to hold the child while another flogged him or her. If no one else was there to assist, the shirt or dress was turned over the child's head and twisted tightly so that the arms and head were confined in a sack, leaving the rest of the body exposed for the assault.[72]

The state of civilization in turn-of-the-century Jamaica was also severely tested by the prevalence of domestic violence between adult couples. This, as already shown, was not confined to any single class of people. Whether marriage was legal or not, the idea prevailed that the man was the boss of the domestic unit and the woman was his property. Those women who married legally were perhaps in a worse situation since they were bound by the vow to "honour and obey" their husbands, many of whom took it as their duty to enforce that pledge by physical force.

Instances of domestic violence were frequent and in some cases quite brutal, but because these were private matters between men and their partners, it was not often that the law intervened. So it was only when it reached the courts that public attention was drawn to this phenomenon. In August 1871, for instance, Joseph Duhaney was charged with "beating and ill-treating" Rosy, his common-law wife. Claiming that she had spoken against him, he sharpened his knife while she ran out of the house bawling for murder. He caught her at the gate, beat and head-butted her. She was rescued by her neighbours; he was sentenced to six months' hard labour. Young Smith was sentenced to three months' hard labour in 1876 for unmercifully beating his "wife" because she had been unfaithful. After terminating their engagement, Mary Ann Dufete in 1880 accosted James McGhie in the street and asked him to return her ring. He grabbed her hair, "drew her to him and butted her like a cow", kicked her and destroyed her dress. Mary, however, was not helpless: she tore up his hat and threatened him with a brick. McGhie was fined twenty-one shillings or thirty days' imprisonment.[73] This type of domestic discord has also been observed in Guyana and Trinidad. Trotman argues that since many Afro-creole wives, whether legal or common law, were either unemployed or marginally employed, they often preferred to suffer brutalization in silence to facing a life of poverty without the financial support of a man.[74] The data in this book, however, do not seem to support the notion of the financially dependent black woman who needed to remain within an abusive relationship for male support. On the contrary, many "battered" women remain in such relationships for a number of complex reasons.[75]

While domestic violence was frequent, it was rare that it threatened life. But in 1880 William Walker, a bread-cart driver, did attempt to kill his wife by cutting her throat, and then tried to commit suicide by the same means. He was unsuccessful in both attempts. In December 1887 James Rugless of Hannah Town was rather more successful. He beat his wife, tore off her clothes and then set her alight with kerosene. That the charge of manslaughter was preferred raises a question about the value the society placed on the lives of its women. Pregnancy was no hindrance to male violence against women. In Ocho Rios in 1899 an eighteen-year-old man, O'Malley, stalked his pregnant, nineteen-year-old "concubine", surnamed Wilmot, urging her to return to his house from her mother's. When she refused he "left her with imprecations on his lips", bought a revolver and cartridges, returned and "solicited an interview with her". Her refusal did not deter him; he waited until she left the house and shot her in the head, eye and abdomen. He then "delivered himself into the hands of the police".[76]

Although men were the principal perpetrators of domestic violence, women were not by any means coy, and they occasionally asserted themselves. In June 1888 Thomas Kelly went home at about ten at night, fell asleep and was rudely awakened by his "wife" Alberta Gonzales, who struck him on the head with a bottle. In November 1905 Rose Francis attacked her husband Cleveland when he returned home one morning after having slept out the night before. They fought, were arrested and each fined two shillings and sixpence or five days' imprisonment. Moore has observed similarly assertive behaviour by black Guyanese women towards their husbands.[77]

The treatment of domestic and commercial animals by lower-class Jamaicans was employed as yet another indicator of the general state of civilization in the island. The many "lean, ragged, half-starved [mongrel] dogs, with ribs protruding out of their thin flesh" seemed to offer testimony of general neglect. But if Magistrate Rampini can be believed, cats were singled out for maltreatment because they were reputed to represent "the evil one".

This superstitious association of cats with evil generated such hostility towards them that it occasionally resulted in acts of horrible cruelty, which reinforced the stereotypical view that black Jamaicans were inherently savage. In 1881, for instance, a case was brought in the police court against Evelina Dollar "for maliciously killing a cat". According to the report, a female allegedly threw the cat on Dollar's daughter. The defendant, "without ascertaining if it were so, caught hold of the cat, and with a large stick continued striking the cat on the head until it died; and then took the dead cat and threw it in the owner's yard". In 1888 three boys were likewise charged with cruelty to two cats that they evidently beat over their heads and bodies with tarred rope while the cats were tied around the necks and legs with a cord. One of the cats died from the blows received. A *Gleaner* report in 1875 indicated that dogs suffered no easier fate. One owner of a dog allegedly decided to put an end to the animal's life by cutting its throat; the carcass was then disposed of by throwing it down "the out-office" (latrine).[78]

Most of the cases of cruelty to animals that were reported, however, had to do with the misuse of mules, donkeys and horses, especially draught animals. In July 1881 John and Charles Steele, father and son, were charged with cruelty to a mule that was unfit to work. In another case in the same month, William Palmer was observed ill-treating a horse suffering severely from what appeared to be a broken hip. When he was advised that he should take the horse for medical attention, he laughed and continued to whip it, whereupon he was served a summons to appear in court. This proved to be no hindrance, since the day after the summons was served Palmer continued to abuse the animal. By 1888 the *Gleaner* claimed that acts of cruelty to animals were on the increase, and these were taken as a further sign of the failure of the Jamaican black to attain civilization. In fact, for Magistrate Rampini, the black man was essentially a savage: "To animals he [the negro] is often most savagely cruel. It is no uncommon thing for a man who has a grudge against another to catch his mule or his horse, and after cutting out its tongue and filling the mouth with leaves, to leave it to die in the most fearful agony."[79] In a society that had been founded on the principle that some lives were without worth, and other lives only counted insofar as they were calculably productive, violence towards beasts went without much comment or concern. Before the introduction of the niceties of Victorian culture, the beating, maiming and slaughter of man and beast occurred on the whim of those who owned both, and often the former was instructed to extract as much labour as possible from the latter. That such behaviour should continue (with some of those same persons owning the beasts and employing the men) should not have been a surprise.

Incidents of violence and cruelty seemed to provide clear proof of the need to civilize working-class Jamaicans and to teach them gentility and decorum. This view was not confined to the white elites, government officials and missionaries but was shared in large part by many of the brown and black middle class. Earlier it was shown that Robert Love's *Jamaica Advocate* deprecated the indiscriminate use of indecent language by the black lower class. Likewise A.P. Hanson, an agricultural instructor, claimed that "a good many of our young men and young women, otherwise intelligent, lacked the carriage that would make them acceptable in good society".[80] Black Presbyterian minister Reverend C.A. Wilson declared,

> There are too many indolent, shiftless people in Jamaica, and these have been the prime cause of much of the scathing criticism which has been passed on the sons of the soil by men who have never done a fair day's manual toil under the burning sun. . . . In a majority of instances mothers are altogether unfit for parental responsibilities. They are either too young, or too simple, or too vicious.[81]

The president of the Universal Negro Improvement Association, Marcus Garvey, asserted in no less a strident manner that

> The bulk of our people are in darkness and are really unfit for good society. To the cultural mind the bulk of our people are contemptible – that is to say they are entirely outside the pale of cultured appreciation. . . . Go into the country parts of Jamaica and you see there villainy and vice of the worse kind; immorality, obeah and all kinds of dirty things are the avocation of a large percentage of our people. . . . Kingston and its environs are so infested with the uncouth and vulgar of our people that we of the cultured class feel positively ashamed. . . . My opinion is that we are too envious, malicious and superficial and because of this we keep back ourselves and eventually keep back the country.[82]

But the very presence of these black and brown critics was testimony that change had taken and was still taking place in Jamaica, because they had all (except Love, who was Bahamian) sprung from the same ranks of Jamaican society whose members they criticized. Indeed, there appeared to be many signs of growing "civility" among the common people, notwithstanding their behaviour described above. But this does not necessarily signify a decline in bawdy behaviour among Jamaican blacks by the turn of the twentieth century, as Downes claims for Barbados; one can, however, broadly concur with him that the evidence of "improving" behaviour "was not so much [an indication] that the black working class [were inclined to repudiate] their 'traditional' Afro-creole festivities, as the fact that [some of them] sought an accommodation within the dominant culture".[83]

One probable indicator of a growing so-called civility was the absence of large-scale disturbances following the Morant Bay uprising. It is true that unrest was reported again in St Thomas-in-the-East a decade later, and that minor rioting occurred in Montego Bay in 1902, Kingston in 1912, and against the Chinese shopkeepers in 1918.[84] But these were piddling by any standard, although the fact that the police were the primary targets of the Montegonians in 1902, and the governor himself, Sydney Olivier, had to beat a hasty retreat in order to escape assault by irate Kingstonians in 1912, did generate momentary concern among the colonial authorities and the local elites.

But on the whole the people were praised for their peacefulness and respect of the law and of authority. While recognizing that the history of political disturbances in the island showed that the "negro" was not always placid and that he was "readily offended", Vaughn Cornish claimed that the general peaceful condition was due to the fact that Jamaican blacks recognized "the unfailing justice which they receive in the Law Courts and appreciate the civility with which they are treated". Likewise American visitor Alpheus Verrill noted how orderly the people were, possessing a true "British" regard and respect for laws and willing to take punishment, without grumbling, if they were in violation of the law[85] – in short, they had even developed the proverbial British "stiff upper lip".

While agreeing that the people did have a high regard for law and order, Frank Cundall opined that this was not simply out of respect for the laws themselves, but because they stood in awe of the power that enforced the law.[86] But senior British army officer Sir Sibbald Scott did not share that view. He did marvel at the profound tranquillity of the island just eleven years after the Morant Bay uprising: "In no part of the world can travelling be accomplished with greater security than in Jamaica. Ladies and gentlemen ride home at night from entertainments and I never heard of anyone taking the precaution of being armed. In private houses . . . doors and windows are left unfastened by day and by night." Although there was a problem of praedial larceny, this did not extend itself into general burglary. Likewise, W. Bellows was amazed that although the blacks and coloureds outnumbered the whites by forty to one (by 1907), an English person could travel without risk to life or property anywhere in the island: "Jamaica is certainly not one of those countries in which the rulers and the ruled are forever coming into conflict."[87]

But, in the opinion of Scott, this could not be attributed simply to the show or use of force, because the military establishment was small (not more than nine hundred men), while the police force numbered just 680. The answer lay in "the harmless nature of the Creoles and the content which pervades all classes", and perhaps more importantly, in "the wisdom of British rule". Bessie Pullen-Burry shared this perspective: it was "testimony of the highest worth to the civilizing agencies at work, let them be Moravian, Wesleyan, Roman [Catholic] or Anglican". While she believed that left to himself the "negro" might revert to a state of savagery, under the influence of the civilizing forces "the black under British rule [was] not an unworthy subject of the Empire".[88]

If British missionaries, British justice (the rule of law) and British rule itself were credited with civilizing the Jamaican people, this was ostensibly further reinforced by the very presence of (white) British people in the island and the inordinate respect, even deference, that blacks allegedly displayed towards them. Cundall observed that "although they may teef [sic] in a small way from their employers, they will as a rule guard his interests from outside attack". Cornish saw the "voluntary respect for white women" as perhaps the black Jamaican's most important characteristic, as far as the white community was concerned. This was fully endorsed by Margaret Newton who, on her visit in 1897, experienced nothing but respect from the "coloured" people, who "[were] more English than in the other islands". In Ocho Rios, in particular, people were most courteous, offering her chairs, bringing her water and holding her umbrella over her. "When I have started to walk alone someone has always been going in the same direction who has offered to guide." And when she visited the church, as the only other white person besides the minister she was "most graciously offered a front seat".[89] Verrill also commented on the reputed respectfulness and deference of Jamaicans to white people:

> The black drivers and conductors of tramcars, busses [sic], etc., are the most respectful, polite and courteous of men, and are particularly noticeable for their kindness, patience and real solicitude when dealing with children, elderly people or the infirm. The black "bobbies" are ever respectful and quiet and possess unlimited patience, while the uniformed attendants in the largest hotels, in government buildings, etc. are invariably courteous and polite. It is perhaps in this universal deference and respect which that Jamaica[n] exhibits toward his superiors – whether white or coloured – that he differs most from our northern negro.[90]

This respect, deference and politeness towards their "social betters" was reflected in other ways too:

> Men and boys quite generally touch the hat (or the forehead in absence of any head-wear) in greeting you; and stand bare-headed in conversation with one he recognized as his superior. Of course, such fine courtesy ... is not absolutely universal. If you are not understood, it is always: "Please, sir?" or "Please, Mam?" If you have done a favour, it is: "Thank you, sir," "Thank you, my good Missus" "God bless you, my good minister", etc., etc. You never want for thanks, sincere and profuse.[91]

Alfred Leader observed that in addition to the salutes and "Mornin' my sweet buckra!", the people displayed their white teeth in broad smiles. On Ella Wilcox's visit in 1909 there were politeness and courtesy, greetings, smiles and bows, and "flowers were flung into carriages". Being white in and of itself seemed to command respect among black and brown Jamaicans. No wonder Jesuit Father James Splaine could smugly assert, "It is wonderful how proud a drop of white blood makes these people."[92]

The etiquette of the people was sometimes seen as quaint, and the extremes to which they went to show "good" manners almost humorous:

> It is quite common for a public speaker, on being called upon to address an audience, first to bow to the chairman and then to the audience, and then to bow again when his speech is over in a way which ... calls to the English mind the thought of a child saying a recitation. But it is courteous – and unEnglish.

Indeed, said Ernest Price, "courtesy is innate in the people of Jamaica"; they have "a sense of the dignified and can add grace to an ordinary act with an ease that is altogether foreign to the English temperament".[93] Had the Jamaican people, or some of them at least, out-mannered the bearers of Victorian etiquette? Perhaps, because when the bearers themselves did not follow the *accepted* or conventions in addressing them, the people interpreted it as an affront, based precisely on those imported standards and forms of etiquette. Hence, according to American Quaker Arthur Swift, "These people are not so ignorant or so utterly void of feeling as they seem to be and now I find I have to be guarded in my expressions and manner as they are very unreasonable and will take affront at anything not pleasant to them if they are in a combative mood."[94]

Conclusion

The civilizing mission might not have succeeded in transforming the average Jamaican into the image of the ideal Victorian lady or gentleman, but given its class-bound nature, it was not intended to do so for the lower classes. Instead it sought to turn the latter into polite, deferential people. In that regard it achieved partial success, since it does seem to have had tremendous influence on their values, although that influence did not always determine their behaviour. Even among the upper and middle classes, there was not a total character transformation. But it does seem that there was a growing consensus of what constituted good and bad behaviour, good and bad manners, proper and improper protocol. These notions, as will be shown, were primarily propagated through the churches and schools and reinforced by the press, and with some effect. Thus Splaine observed, "To call a man a 'black gentleman' is quite the thing."[95] But at the same time there was an undercurrent of resistance among some elements of the lower classes, particularly those who resided in urban slums, which seemed almost consciously to defy the conventions of "polite" society and to render them irrelevant to their own lives. Again, it seems that the people were intent on determining for themselves how they would live their lives. They were not going to be unduly pressured by what the (morally flawed) cultural elites decided was best for them.

Chapter 6

Christianizing Jamaica
The Quest for a Moral Culture

THE ASSAULT ON THE BELIEF SYSTEM, sexual morality, and mating and behavioural patterns of the majority of Jamaicans was not intended simply to eradicate beliefs and practices that were deemed barbarous and immoral. Rather, those beliefs were to be supplanted by an entirely new religio-moral code – buttressed by an ideology that bonded the Jamaican people as loyal British subjects – upon which a new, "civilized", consensual society would be constructed. This new thrust, initiated by the nonconformist missionaries through their chapels and schools, was intensified after the Morant Bay uprising, as the colonial state under crown rule began to play a more active role, reinforced by the elite press. In this chapter we examine the renewed efforts in the late nineteenth and early twentieth centuries to christianize Jamaicans, with a view to exercising influence over their minds.

The Christian Mission to Civilize

Although Christian churches were present in Jamaica from the early sixteenth century, initially they embraced no mission to christianize the working people of the island, but strove simply to serve the religious and spiritual needs of the free white inhabitants. The Church of England (and after 1819 the Church of Scotland too) were content to provide "the planters with the formalities required at birth, marriage, and death, and were generally regarded as a necessary appendage to white society". They simply ignored the slaves, except when occasionally called upon by the planters "to conduct a mass baptism service".[1] As they were not considered human beings, the growing body of African and creole slaves were regarded as "savages without souls", "heathens", whose only role in the life of the island was to work as beasts of burden on the plantations and other agricultural properties; as such, there was no imperative to make Christians of them.

It was not until 1754, with the arrival of the Moravians, that the first organized attempts were made to christianize the slaves. These were followed by other Protestant missions: the black American Baptists (1784), the Wesleyan Methodists (1789), the Scottish Missionary Society (1800), the (British) Baptist Missionary Society (1814), the Church Missionary Society (1825), the Society for the Propagation of the Gospel (1834) and the London Missionary Society (1834).[2] These remained the principal missionary societies operating in Jamaica until the later nineteenth century, when they were joined by new organizations (see below).

The whole purpose of Christian proselytization was to supplant the old Afro-creole belief system, which was deemed pagan and riddled with superstition. As Robert J. Stewart observes, the missionaries "entered an Afro-creole religious world the essential elements of which were what Christian preaching was intended to eradicate".[3] Mary Turner notes that before the arrival of the missionaries, the planters had, within limits, allowed the slaves "to develop, within their villages, a cultural life that included their own religion. Slave culture incorporated many 'African' elements." If the forced crossing and enslavement had isolated them from the indigenous institutions of Africa, they nevertheless carried *within* them traditional African ideas, beliefs and values that were creolized and used to explain, rationalize and order their lives in plantation slavery. This was facilitated by the planters' lack of interest in influencing "their ideas about life and the universe".[4] Says Philip Curtin,

> Since the whites were not anxious to force Europeanization any further than was necessary for plantation work, the slaves were left to educate their own children. Consequently there developed a new culture, compounded of the diverse elements of the African heritage and some European elements. . . . By the 1830's the Afro-Jamaican culture was solidly established, and it was passed on to each new generation as it had long been passed by a process of assimilation to new arrivals from Africa.[5]

This new Afro-creole culture embodied many elements of West African cosmology that were considered by the missionaries as antithetical to their Christian culture. According to Stewart,

> In that world, moral value was not so much derived from an individualistic relationship with a Supreme Being, who was generally regarded by Africans as aloof and remote from human daily concerns, but was rather a function of community. Acts were "good" or "bad" depending on their effect on the equilibrium of the family or village. There was no eschatological tension. Ultimate reality was distinctly worldly and temporal – not mechanistically, but through a primal unity of material and spiritual, represented, for example, in the land as the here-and-now medium of the community of the living and the dead. In the matrix of family, clan, and nation, communication with departed family and ancestors was essential in the maintenance of social well-being, order, and peace.[6]

This cosmology of "interpenetrating worlds of the physically living and of gods, ancestors, and spirits baffled the rationalistic distinction of sacred and secular that had split Western consciousness". Accordingly, the missionary response was to seek to eliminate it, by implanting "new ideas about the nature of the spirit world and the nature of God".[7] Stewart argues that their evangelical form of Christianity

> emphasized preaching, instruction, and observable response in word, moral behaviour, and church adherence. . . . [They] preached the inherent depravity of humankind, a disease of heart and soul inherited from Adam's fall, which humanity could do nothing on its own to repair. To believe that any righteous act aside from the acceptance of God's forgiveness could undo that state of sin was itself the sin of pride.[8]

But, as Turner observes, nothing in the slaves' theology prepared them for the idea of God the lawgiver. They admitted to sin only when they had grasped that to acknowledge their sinfulness was to acknowledge, as Christians, their individual spiritual value. Hence,

> The main thrust of mission teaching . . . directly conflicted with both the slaves' religious ideas and their established social mores. The salvation of the individual's soul, and the achievement of rewards in heaven, demanded that converts adhere to the pattern of social and moral conduct that mission teaching dictated. Religious practices, the missionaries emphasized, could not in themselves secure salvation; an internal or spiritual revolution was not enough. Christian conviction had to have social consequences. Here the missionaries were breaking completely new ground.

> This key Christian concept, that there was a vital connection between conduct in this world and fate in the world to come, was completely novel to the slaves. In the slaves' traditional religion nothing that happened on earth affected their prospect of feasting with the ancestors in the afterlife. The spirits had no power to trick or punish beyond the grave.9

Diane Austin-Broos observes that "the ethical rationalism that the Baptists brought was also a rationalism infused with white European moral practice assumed as the measure of civilization and of Christian spiritual worth". At the heart of this complex was the ordering and sanctification of life through the practice of Christian marriage and Christian forms of sexual restraint. In Jamaica these mores would become not only marks of civilization but also marks of assimilation to an orthodox Christian faith.10

From the very outset, therefore, the missionary goal was to eradicate this "debased" black culture, which they saw as the product of the heathenism of Africa and the depravity of the slave system. The "sexual looseness" of plantation life became a primary target of their efforts as they promoted monogamous marriage. As Turner notes, "The only alternative to monogamy countenanced by the missionaries was chastity." Both, however, went against the norm of plantation life and culture. The missionaries also attacked Afro-creole drumming, music and dancing:

> [D]ancing and drumming and the drinking that accompanied them were condemned as heathen practices. European as well as African dancing was indicted, though the latter was instinctively recognized as the greater enemy; it was connected with the slaves' traditional religion, and the alien drum rhythms suggested pits of sexual iniquity more fearful than scraping fiddles could evoke.

But they encountered firm resistance from the slaves at every turn.11 Not only was there an entire cosmology and world view that pre-dated these missionary incursions, there was a whole set of cultural values and practices reflecting those beliefs. In the dehumanizing system of slavery, the contortions and negotiations that had resulted in a distinct creole culture had also created a space in which Afro-creole ideas about the sacred and the profane (insofar as those were even separable) helped to make survival possible. As demonstrated earlier, the creativity of the Afro-creole spiritual world had served the slaves (and their descendants) well, and they were not about to abandon that world for one which was, at once, less real and more judgemental.

Curtin, Turner, Schuler and Stewart all note that the missionaries were not only fighting against an existing and functional Afro-creole culture that they regarded as heathen, but also against Afro-Christian Myal/Revival sects that actively competed against them. As shown in chapter 3, there were major outbreaks of Myal fervour during the 1840s and again between 1860 and 1862, which not only invaded the orthodox churches but even co-opted what had begun as genuine Christian revivals. By 1862 the missionaries were denouncing the Afro-Christian Revival movement.

Therefore, by the time of the Morant Bay outbreak, the missionary endeavour to civilize the Jamaican people seemed to be in a shambles. The Myal "takeover" of the Revival suggested that, despite the missionaries' best efforts, religion and morality, as defined by them, were in decline; the "savagery" of the rebellion suggested that civilization itself was in decline – that black Jamaicans were in fact "regressing into barbarism". The missionaries were shocked and disillusioned. Both Curtin and Stewart argue that the old relationship between missionary and ex-slave was significantly transformed thereafter. The missionaries were no longer aligned with the blacks in the struggle against white hegemony; now they sought to identify more closely with the authorities. They all distanced themselves from the outbreak at Morant Bay, and lined up behind Governor Eyre in his condemnation of the perpetrators.[12]

A cultural gulf seemed to open after 1865, with the foreign missionaries on one side and the Afro-creole majority on the other. The only way (it was believed) to bridge the gulf was to *intensify* the process of anglicizing and christianizing the latter. There could be no more toleration of religious unorthodoxy or wider Afro-creole cultural "deviance". Far from dashing "any lingering hopes that the Jamaican blacks could be reclaimed totally from 'heathenism' ", as Stewart claims,[13] there was a new resolve to civilize Jamaica, to drag it, if need be, out of its darkness towards the light. The civilizing mission had to continue, in part using new methods, but very importantly with a close alliance among the churches themselves, and in collaboration with the colonial authorities and elite society. New methods of social and cultural control were sought, partly because the show of force in 1865 had been distasteful to a nation (Britain) promoting itself as the harbinger of gentility and civilization. The mass executions after the uprisings in St Thomas-in-the-East convinced many that the better path was to curb, influence and change fundamental aspects of Jamaica's culture so that the people, as true British subjects, loyal to God and Queen, would not be left any cultural space for the kind of resistance that Morant Bay symbolized. The year 1865 was thus a critical watershed in the changing cultural landscape of Jamaican society.

A number of significant new configurations developed after 1865, aimed at achieving the goal of civilization. First, there was a growing distance between the mainstream churches and the native congregations. There was also increased hostility towards the latter, which replaced the old enmity between the planters and the nonconformist missionaries. Second, as the missionaries became more respectable in elite society, there was a closing of the divide between them and the mainstream churches, with whom they now shared a common objective: to christianize and civilize Jamaica. And third, most notably among the Baptists where there had been a very loose church organization, attempts were made through the Jamaica Baptist Union (formed in 1849) to bring independent congregations under one umbrella, aimed at speaking with one voice for one central purpose – civilization.[14] After 1865, then, the forces of civilization gathered to rescue Jamaica from the "savagery" that Morant Bay seemed to manifest.

But there were other changes as well. After intense petitioning by the nonconformist churches, especially the Baptists, a law was passed in 1870 to disestablish the Church of England.[15] While the loss of budgetary support did not eliminate the Anglican Church's position as the religious arm of the colonial state, it released scarce funds to the government for educational purposes, which became a key area in which the civilizing mission was pursued after 1865 (see chapter 7). The Anglican Church also lost its missionary arms: the Church Missionary Society began to wind down its Jamaican operations in the 1840s, while the Society for the Propagation of the Gospel ceased to operate in Jamaica in 1866. The critical issue for the latter was the failure of the parent church to indigenize its clergy; even when it belatedly began to recruit locals in the 1870s, it looked mainly to the upper classes. It was not until after 1880, when Enos Nuttall became bishop of Jamaica, that the Anglican Church added an evangelical posture to its image.[16] Thereafter it began to reach out more aggressively to working-class black Jamaicans in competition with, and complementing, the nonconformist churches. All of the important sociocultural institutions then, from the elite-centred Church of England to the (previously) ex-slave–centred Baptists, joined by the official colonial establishment, were united in the quest to bring the Jamaican people up to the standards of correct behaviour that the Christian Victorian ethic was deemed to capture so precisely and well.

The indigenization of the churches, however, was one of the principal ways in which the nonconformist missionary organizations sought to spread the

Word and to civilize after 1865. The Methodists and Baptists had begun this process through their ticket-and-class-leader systems even during slavery,[17] and the Baptist Missionary Society had gone further, establishing Calabar College in 1842 as a theological college to train local ministers. The Methodists later did likewise in establishing York Castle Theological College in 1874. The London Missionary Society, also, pushed its localization programme and formed the Jamaica Congregational Union in 1876. Although some of the white missionaries argued against this indigenization process on the grounds that the native clergy were morally lax, these denominations were more or less independent of their parent societies by the mid-1880s.[18] What this meant was that by the late nineteenth century, much of the work to "civilize" the working people was being carried on by *brown and black Jamaicans* who had been carefully selected and trained in local theological colleges, and had fully imbibed the ideas and values (religious and secular) of their British mentors. Bryan notes, "The torch of civilisation and of Christianity was to be carried, eventually, not only by the white Christian but by the black convert thoroughly trained in Christian religion and western life, an agent for the spread of western civilisation." As Stewart observes, "Native pastors in the Baptist Union, as well as in other Protestant churches, accepted the hegemony of white ministers and came to cherish their British ties as fondly as did the whites."[19]

Indeed, it was their selection and training that gave them an elevated status within standards prescribed by the dominant culture. They were fully convinced of, and perhaps just as importantly, ashamed of, the inferiority of the culture of their forebears; they believed that if they and their people were to make "progress" it was imperative that they leave behind the "base" beliefs and "dark" practices that marked them as un-English. Therefore, under the guidance and admonition of their British mentors, they set about rooting out the traditions and anchors of the past, as convinced as their benefactors that the only proper way was the British way. Significantly, some of these black and brown Christian Jamaican "Britons" were also recruited for missionary service in Africa.[20] A similar process took place in the post-bellum American South where, according to Evelyn Higginbotham, black Baptist missionaries emulated their northern white peers and "spoke of their work as if they had embarked upon a foreign mission field, and frequently referred to the 'heathenism' in both Atlanta and Africa. They strove to rid black worship of emotionalism."[21]

One other important change took place on the religious canvas after 1865, aimed at promoting civilization in Jamaica. Although some of the British Protestant missions were slowly withdrawing, the persistent manifestations of non- or quasi-Christian religious practices and Afro-creole beliefs and customs (such as Revivalism and Kumina, "concubinage" and bastardy, obeah and other "dark superstitions") meant that Jamaica continued to be perceived as a potentially fertile missionary field. This was further enhanced by the fact that in 1881, 45.6 per cent of the population professed no religious affiliation whatever (perhaps some were Revivalists); although that figure dropped significantly to 12.5 per cent by 1921,[22] it served to attract new evangelical groups not only from Britain but also from the United States. These included the Plymouth Brethren, the Society of Friends Iowa (Quakers), the Salvation Army, the Seventh Day Adventists, the Church of God (Pentecostal), and the Millennial Dawnists. According to one estimate in 1916, there were "something like fifteen" Christian religious organizations at work in the island, "not including the various strange sects that find their way from America".[23] There was no letting up in the mission to civilize Jamaica until and beyond the First World War.

Purifying Jamaica

The period after 1865 witnessed a concerted and intensified effort by the missions to cleanse and purify the "ungodliness" of Afro-creole culture and the abominations of Afro-Christianity. The missionaries came away from the subversion of the Great Revival and the outbreak of violence at Morant Bay convinced that only an intensification of their efforts to rid Jamaica of its immorality could prevent such occurrences in the future. In their anxiety to disassociate their congregations from the tragic events at Morant Bay, the missionaries spoke almost with one voice. Baptist Missionary Society secretary Edward Underhill argued that it was not religion, but its absence, that led to the outbreak, for, according to him, four-fifths of the people of St Thomas-in-the-East were without religious instruction. His colleague, James Phillippo, claimed that the majority of the rebels were not connected with any denomination; they were mainly "Africans as ignorant and debased as in their native wilds". Further away from the centre of violence, the Moravians stated that their church members had not been involved in the 1865 disturbances and their conduct had been very good. The Methodists went a step further, claiming that because of the detached conduct of some of their members towards the Underhill meetings, and their alleged support of Governor Eyre's conduct at Morant Bay, they had actually been ridiculed by some of those who were sympathetic to the sentiments of the rioters.[24]

The solution, therefore, was more religion. Even Governor Eyre had seemed to recognize the benefits of missionary efforts before he had reason to reappraise his position in the wake of the rebellion. In 1864 he praised the numerous "Dissenting Bodies" and their "zealous exertions" which were largely responsible for "the orderly and peaceful demeanour of the peasantry, and . . . their general obedience to the laws".[25] Although he changed his opinion the next year, from the missionary point of view it did not mean he had been wrong. In fact, the need for renewed and intensified efforts was highlighted by Reverend James Watson, the oldest Scottish missionary in the island; in 1866, while acknowledging that about one hundred thousand Jamaicans had been "brought forward" under Christian instruction, he warned that three hundred thousand yet remained "in unbroken heathenism". Perhaps many were practising Revivalists.

> It is not the fact that the religious portion of the community are retrograding or deteriorating; but the vicious, the criminal, and the ignorant, being more numerous, neutralise the good that has already been done, cast it into the background, and, in fact, give character to the whole population; and that character, as a whole and in bulk, [is] one of disorder, criminality, and irreligion. The good that has been done maintains its place and its standing in the locality where it exists. There it is palpable in the pure and blameless lives of thousands who have been redeemed from vice and ignorance through the instrumentality of missions. There is triumphant vindication that our labours have not been in vain. There, amid the present difficulties and hardships which the people have to endure, it may be seen in patient forbearance, in unmurmuring submission, and in quiet industrious prosecution of the toils by which they and their families are maintained, and in the peaceable unostentatious maintenance of the ordinances of the Gospel, and the walk and conversation which it upholds and enjoins. But beyond the pale of this life-giving influence there are thefts and robberies, drunkenness, vice and crime.[26]

The Society for the Propagation of the Gospel, which conducted an investigation into the "state of the Negro" after the Morant Bay uprising, was even more pessimistic: "At the end of twenty-five years, it is the opinion of many competent judges that the social and religious condition of the negro population, numbering more than 400,000 is below what it was at the time of emancipation."[27]

Thus commenced a period of determined and zealous proselytization to purify the Jamaican people. United in purpose although not in structure and organization, and now enlisting the support of trained native Jamaican pastors, the press, the social elite including the planters, and the state authorities, the churches embarked on a prolonged and intense campaign to civilize Jamaica. A very important addition to their armoury was the extension of the school system under their control through the financial support of the state (see chapter 7). The methods of spreading the message of Christianity took various forms, including warning, reproving, correcting and instructing the people.[28] In this new drive, the missionaries renewed war on most aspects of Afro-creole culture and attacked the basic way of life of the people: their mating patterns and family life, child-rearing, housing and work habits, attitudes towards saving, folk beliefs and religions, customs and rituals related to various stages of the life cycle, their music and dance, even their Christmas celebrations. They confronted and meant to overturn the people's cultural heritage; their objective was to purge these "unsavoury" and "ungodly" cultural features and replace them with a puritanical Christian Victorian morality.

The religious bodies went about this in a relentless manner. They built churches, chapels and schools wherever the people went and transformed these into community centres for both religious and secular activities. Very late in the nineteenth century, Jamaican peasants were still moving deeper into the mountainous hinterland in search of productive land, and the churches, fearing that this migration was taking the people outside of their influence and exposing them to "temptations of every kind and . . . the seductive power of sin" and "habits alien to an advancing civilization", followed them to maintain their control.[29]

The missionaries were able to call on the people themselves to provide "free labour" for the construction of edifices of Christian culture.[30] That in itself might be interpreted as an indication of the success they had in reasserting their influence over the people. Free labour was a part of the people's culture, a means by which they cooperated to accomplish tasks within their limited resources. They had used this means to help one another to clear grounds, to reap crops, and to engage in any effort that required more than one individual (termed "gi'e a day" or "len' hand"). Free labour in church construction represented the employment of one culture to facilitate and perhaps even to establish another. Where, as in this case, the people's cultural practice either benefited the churches or encouraged behaviour with which the missionaries agreed, it was left undisturbed. It was when the local culture challenged the Victorian moral code that it was confronted, and attempts were made to overturn it.

In 1885 the United Presbyterian Church at Pondside was built on a hill where a slave owner's house used to be:

> We have to carry all the dressed stones for the front up the hill, which is rather difficult work. I was puzzled how this could be done, but on appealing to the strong men all around to come and assist, they did so joyfully, some walking as far as nine miles. It was a sight to see fifty men, as busy as could possibly be, in a state of joyful excitement, drenched with perspiration, beneath a burning sun, lifting up the big stones and carrying them up the hill.[31]

The effort represented more than church building, however, because it gave the community a chance to socialize. The construction of a United Free Church of Scotland church in 1907 gives a good example of the people's culture employed for the church's benefit:

> The women provide the food for the breakfast. Some will bring a few yams; others a few breadfruits; another a few sweet potatoes, etc. Then a subscription is raised among the members to provide a little salt-fish and corned pork. While a few women are cooking the food, all the men and women, boys and girls, are at work, carrying stones, building lime-kilns, all as busy as possible at whatever work is on hand. Without free labour it would almost be an impossibility to attempt to build a church at the present time. . . . About 12 o'clock all hands are called together for breakfast, and, as a rule, they have a glorious feast. . . . There is another feature about a free labour day . . . and that is the harmony that exists between members of different denominations, and their willingness to help one another in building their churches. At our last free labour day at Happy Grove we had members from the Church of England, Baptists, Moravians and Wesleyans, all working side by side with our own members. . . . So far as the people of Jamaica are concerned, there is one Church – the Church of Christ, and all are working for the same end – the salvation of souls.[32]

The communal atmosphere of the construction made it much more than work. It was an opportunity for the community to cooperate, to share, to commune regardless of denomination. Thus, in their very construction these churches were regarded as community property; it did not matter what denomination the church purported to be. If the people did, in fact, believe that there was "one Church" and that faith was more important than doctrine, then therein might lie a partial explanation for the willingness to embrace Christ but to question and perhaps ignore or reject aspects of Christianity. This notion was supported by the Roman Catholics:

> The difficulty here is to find out who is Catholic and who is not. The bulk of the Jamaicans, and especially the negroes, seem to wish to belong to all Churches simultaneously. This is no figure of speech, but the simple fact. In their case the idea is not so absurd as it seems at first sight. They evidently think that religion is good, and they are far too ignorant to notice but the external differences between the different Churches. In their large-hearted tolerance, they desire to embrace all creeds alike. I do not know whether they attend the synagogue. I think the black people draw the line there.[33]

Perhaps the people were not ignorant; they adopted the beliefs that were the basis of Christianity and were tolerant of all creeds.

The people appeared to embrace the tenets of Christian salvation, along with their pre-existing ideas about God and the determination of right and wrong. In an ecumenical spirit, they refused to take too seriously the doctrinal differences that the churches and missionaries emphasized. In the spiritual flow that characterized their own belief system, one sort of church or another was simply a matter of preference for one sort of ritual or another. Anglicans, Catholics, Baptists, Moravians, Wesleyans, Presbyterians, Congregationalists and Quakers worked together and visited each other without any sense of violation. They were simply Christians; while the churches might not have agreed with their spiritual "looseness", it served the people well, and they were wary of attempts to change those beliefs and practices.

Church services were a central element in seeking to influence the lives of people in the community. Regular attendance at church was thus vital, and the clergy used every means at their disposal to encourage this. All the churches kept a close account of attendance and noted changes in their annual reports. Services were routinely held on Sundays, and several churches also held prayer and Bible study meetings on some evenings during the week. Most churches also had Sunday schools for children. From time to time some held special "days of prayer". For instance, in 1867 the Wesleyans organized ecumenical services where Wesleyans, Baptists and Congregationalists assembled at the Wesleyan chapel in Lucea.[34] This was probably part of an effort to promote cooperation among the rival denominations in the common drive to civilize Jamaica. In addition, all churches held special services for the major Christian festivals of Good Friday–Easter and Christmas–New Year.

Figure 16. Church congregation after Sunday service
Source: Francis Dodsworth, *The Book of Jamaica* (Kingston: Sollas and Cocking, 1904). Courtesy of the National Library of Jamaica.

By the end of the nineteenth century, midnight watch services had become a standard way of welcoming the new year, climaxing with the pealing of church bells. Worship at Roman Catholic churches was made more colourful by their observance, with special "High Masses", of feast and saint days – for example, the feasts of Corpus Christi, the Sacred Heart, All Saints, the Seven Dolours (or Sonocos) of the Virgin Mary, the Rosary, and Pentecost. Special masses were also held to celebrate the jubilee of Pope Leo XIII in 1888.[35] These festivals, feasts and services were often very entertaining; they provided one means of attracting the people into the churches' space, in order to deliver the message of civilized Christianity.

Of special importance were the harvest services. Not many were as impressive as that held at the Kingston Parish Church in 1891, when three services – morning, afternoon and evening – were held on harvest day:

> The Church was decorated with fruits, vegetables and flowers. A magnificent cross of grapes stood at the rear of the Altar, while on a table to the north, and on the Credence table to the south, were placed large loaves of the bread offering of many among the congregation. The first of the choir stalls and the capitals of the columns were decorated with fruit and vegetables of every description whilst around each column was entwined beautiful soft moss from the not distant hills.

The musical portion of the programme was pleasant and the offertory of the day was forty pounds, two-thirds of which was to be used to provide iron railings around the Kingston Parish Church.[36]

Across the island, especially in the rural areas, members brought what were often their best provisions to the church; the gifts were blessed and then sold for the benefit of the church. At the harvest service at Bethel Town Baptist Church in Westmoreland in 1899, "there was a special yam on the platform, which it is said, weighed 50 lbs. and among the other presents were poultry, rabbits, cakes, vegetables, fruit and plenty of ground provision". At the end of the service there was a gramophone exhibition in the chapel, and many popular and sentimental airs were rendered.[37]

As did the Bethel Town Baptist Church, many churches included other activities or entertainments with the harvest service in an attempt to make it even more attractive. In 1903, at Wallingford Baptist Church, there was an "exhibition of Native Arts and sale of fancy and useful articles" at the harvest service. The popularity of the harvest services was indicated across the period, and often the churches could not accommodate the large congregations which gathered; this was the case, for instance, in April 1909 at St Peter's Anglican Church in Wait-a-Bit, Trelawny. Some of the reports on these services made specific reference to the role that women played in the preparations, as, for example, at the St Ann's Bay Parish Church in 1893: "Too much praise cannot be given to the ladies who transformed the altar, Communion rails, and the pulpit from wood to pretty wreaths and nosegays."[38]

Throughout the period the harvest services or festivals occurred at different times in the year, and were not tied to crop-over (the end of the sugar crop), as sugar was in decline for most of the post-emancipation nineteenth century, and faced competition from new, peasant-grown agricultural products. Harvest services were often a high point of the congregation's socio-religious calender.[39] As the church delivered its blessings on the agricultural efforts of the people, reinforcing the adage that "only the best is good enough", the promotion of that sector was by no means hidden. Whatever their origins, in the Jamaican post-emancipation context these services promoted the virtue of agricultural labour, and reinforced the message that the people should continue to work on the land.

The churches also held special services for secular events. Most churches, particularly the nonconformist denominations, commemorated Emancipation Day as part of their effort to identify with the struggles of the black people whom they were seeking to civilize; this also served to remind those people of the churches' role in winning their freedom, thus ensuring their eternal gratitude. Indeed, there was a direct link between emancipation (salvation from slavery) and Christian conversion (salvation from sin) in the missionary mind. As Catherine Hall has argued, "Emancipation gave men and women their political, social and economic freedom. But only conversion gave them a new life in Christ, the possibility to be born anew, to be new black subjects, washed clean of the old ways – new black men and women."[40] So emancipation was appropriately celebrated by thanksgiving services in church, although towards the end of the century there appeared to be a decline in the observance of the great event.[41] Perhaps those who had expressed lifelong loyalty to the Knibbs and Phillippos of the past[42] were no longer in the majority, and interest in the celebration (and the churches' involvement) waned. There was, however, a corresponding growth in the importance attached by the churches to the celebration of the monarch's birthday and, after the turn of the century, of Empire Day as well. The churches also played a major role in the orgy of extravagance associated with the celebration of Victoria's jubilees in 1887 and 1897; the buildings were specially decorated for these events, and clergy and church members participated in public processions in various towns and villages (see chapter 9). This shift in emphasis from Emancipation Day to imperial festivities signified the growing link that all the British denominations made between service of God and service to the empire. In addition, it symbolized a move away from cultural items that could be specifically identified with the black Jamaican, and towards a more widely embraced "British" culture.

Thus, during the Boer War, which Jamaica followed very closely through newspaper reports, Reverend Caleb Reynolds of Little London preached a sermon entitled "Fight the Good Fight", which "spoke in glowing terms of the British Flag, the spirit of unity among England's soldiers, and the reliability of her Generals, with special reference to Roberts and Kitchener".[43] Likewise in 1916, at the height of the First World War, the pastor at the Ebenezer Church of the United Free Church of Scotland declared, "We are quite patriotic here in Jamaica – not a bit behind you in Britain. Last Sunday we had a 'Flag Day' ", for which this church was appropriately decorated, and the ideology of God and empire delivered within this hallowed sanctuary:

> As you enter the northern door of the church, gaze down the isle [*sic*], and in the centre, and at the back of the church [you] see the platform. It is beautifully decorated with Union Jacks and Royal ensigns. . . . At the north end of the church is the choir, and above them is another large Union Jack. The address was on the

flag. Mr. Noble spoke of its origin, what it means, what it demands, and last of all he referred to the Royal Ensign, and urged all to have the ensign of God our King flying over our lives. The choir sang . . . "The Lord is my shepherd". . . . The children recited all patriotic pieces: "The Charge of the Light Brigade", "England, my England," &c. I assure you it was a day to be proud of.44

The message, the messenger and the site of delivery were intended to impress upon the Jamaican people that a combined belief in all would transport them to the lofty position of "civilized British Christians". And there was every likelihood that if they followed the middle-class Victorian value system, which was Christian in its foundation, they would also be transported to heavenly rewards "in the sweet bye and bye". Where Victorian morality stopped and Christianity started was increasingly difficult to discern.

In their drive to purify and civilize Jamaicans, the missionaries supplemented church services with other activities. For instance, in 1887 in Savanna-la-Mar, an open-air meeting held in the evening drew nearly one thousand persons to hear the message: "We easily collected the masses by singing in the street and giving a[n] . . . invitation to all to come."45 Further,

> [we] carry on house-to-house visitation to the extent allowed by other duties, where we seek every opportunity to scatter the seed of divine truth; we regularly distribute tracts; we keep village meetings in which the precious seed is sown; and we try in every possible way to reach our fellow-men in order to lay before them the truth as it is in Christ.46

These house visits not only spread the Word, but also put the missionaries in a position to try to influence the people's private lives. A close relationship thus developed between parson and people, with the preachers offering "paternal" advice on every private domestic matter. As one member of the London Missionary Society put it, "The reserve of English people, the seclusion of their domestic life is quite different to the habits of the people here; they talk freely, they live much . . . in the open air, and if excited they give free utterance to their feelings. A pastor in consequence knows very much of the private life of his members which in England would be concealed." According to Baptist T.S. Penny, "They have not yet learned to think and act for themselves, nor have they the full confidence in each other which men with a more advantageous past have. Hence they continually look to their pastors, and do not look in vain, for counsel and for leadership."47 Just as Stewart has observed, therefore, after 1865 the relationship between pastor and people became increasingly paternalistic: "Missionaries became less and less *with* the working class, more and more *for* them, in a paternalistic sense."[48]

The extent of the missionary's involvement in the private lives of, and his paternalistic attitude towards, the people is revealed by a glance at the diary of Roman Catholic Father James Splaine in 1872. For instance, on 3 February he ordered one of his brown members (named Murray) out of a tavern where the man was drinking, to attend to his sick wife at home; on his visit to Roderick Forrester on the seventh he had to endure the latter's complaints about the dishonesty of thieving neighbours; on the thirteenth he attended to Chamberlain, "a protestant nigger" who was sick, and found him and all his children lying on the board floor while the large bed was empty; and on 14 March he visited Mrs Lindo who was "nursing a waif", abandoned by its natural mother, as if it were her own child.

But Splaine's visit on 26 February to the Robertsons at St Helen's to minister to a sick girl is reflective of the critical attitude of the clergy towards the lifestyle of the people they served, and of the latter's response. There he found two brown girls "living in sin": "The mother of the boys was there too, a regular hardened old prostitute (her sons being bastards)." He evidently refused to minister to the sick girl until the "abominable sinfulness" of the occupants was rectified. Returning the next day, he immediately asked the boys' mother when the scandal would stop:

> Soon as me able, was the reply, which means never in Jamaican phraseology. . . . I looked into the room where the boy was lying; his mother and his lady love were there. He said good morning, and there was no sign of shame or confusion anywhere; nor any sign of a moral change, so I left again.

Evidently Splaine was not prepared to perform priestly services if this open and unabashed display of "immorality" continued.[49]

Church attendance was important to the missionaries not only because it was used as a gauge of the success of their religious tasks, but also out of self-interest: they depended on the offerings collected for their own subsistence as well as the upkeep of their churches. According to one missionary, the financial department was "sometimes as good an index as we can find of the spiritual condition of a people". Subscriptions and, in some cases, tithes were an important part of this.[50]

Church contributions were expected even against a background of severe poverty among the majority of members of every denomination. Again and again there were references to periods of commercial depression and to the majority of the people being in deep despair.[51] Church attendance was affected by economic distress, as many could not afford the "decent clothes" that church attendance required. Attempts to encourage the people to attend church in their everyday clothes, however, were unsuccessful, because it was enshrined in their minds that churchgoing was a special event which they felt required expensive clothing. Some of the missionaries believed that this sometimes served as an excuse for nonattendance and that some persons took this business of clothes too far, because "[t]he love of finery, a desire for personal adornment, and a rivalry in dress lead to serious evils especially amongst the young female members of some churches".[52]

Some missionaries expressed consternation at the chronic poverty and lamented the effects on the church: "It is not the want of disposition, but the want of ability, that prevents our people giving more liberally." Nevertheless, the majority of reports made constant and even admiring reference to the fact that, in spite of the grinding poverty, many people continued to be patient and loyal to the church. Still, there was "a determination on the part of others not to give at all, or to contribute as little as possible. They are reported to have said that they can now read the Bible for themselves, and need no minister."[53]

This concern about the inability or unwillingness of some members to support the church and clergy increased as the churches became independent of their parent bodies overseas and those sources of funding gradually dried up. Indeed, according to the Moravians, their church was self-sustained only in theory, "[o]wing to the ever-recurring adverse conditions occasioned by storm, earthquake, drought, small price for produce, lack of employment, over-crowded villages, and many other circumstances, over which we have no control". Such distress was compounded by periodic epidemics – influenza, whooping cough and measles. At the end of the period, the situation had only worsened. Between 1915 and 1920 times were exceedingly bad due to the war, three successive hurricane years, and the fact that many members had to go abroad or move to other parts of the island. Still, whenever there was a temporary return to relative prosperity church attendance improved, and the "spirit of piety" appeared to revive along with the people's liberality.[54]

The churches argued that the chronically severe conditions were not only bad for them financially, but also for the spiritual welfare of their members:

> Extreme poverty is as unfavourable to the progress of the Gospel as luxury is fatal to the piety of its professors. Every day brings the fact more clearly before the minds of the friends of the evangelised peasantry of Jamaica that a certain measure of temporal prosperity is essential to the moral and spiritual elevation of the people.

... The people, from want of clothing and food, have been unable to sustain their ministers in their usual comfort, or to avail themselves of the means of education for their children.55

The prevailing conditions also caused consternation about the morality of the people since, in the face of severe economic pressures, there was widespread praedial larceny: "It seems as though half the population were banded together in an association of thieves."56 All over the island, farmers had to buy flour and rice, and were in debt. Still, the opinion was expressed that "[i]f these difficulties should teach our people to be more provident and thrifty, they would prove blessings in disguise". To this end, several churches established penny savings banks to encourage their members to save for the rainy day.57 For many missionaries, indications of the importance of the church to the people were to be found in the fact that the very poorest among them, in order to make their contributions, "consecrated" something. Some persons planted a few yams, a handful of corn or peas, while others consecrated a fowl or pig and cared for it until the harvest festival, when the proceeds were presented as an offering to God.58

In their drive to purify and civilize the island, the churches also published the tempering message of Christianity, notwithstanding the fact that the literacy rate was not high. Stewart observes that during the 1870s two nonsectarian newspapers were published – the (appropriately titled) *Queen's Newsman* and the *Jamaica Instructor* – which were both aimed at "inculcating a spirit of subordination among the black peasantry, and . . . teaching the peasantry their religious and civic duties and devotion to government". The connection between earthly and heavenly kingdoms was clear. Similarly in 1886 the vicar apostolic, the acting Roman Catholic bishop, announced his intention to publish the *Catholic News,* a "non-political but thoroughly Catholic" review, while the Presbyterians put out the *Christian Witness.* Then, in 1900 the *Daily Gleaner* started to print a series of sermons in its Saturday supplement under the banner "The Jamaican Pulpit", with a view to giving preachers and their messages a wider audience.59

These publications were joined by the Bible itself, which the churches successfully encouraged their members to purchase. By the end of the century it was one of the bestsellers of Kingston bookstores.60 The churches also circulated vast numbers of religious tracts among the people. In 1876, for instance, the tract distributors associated with the Presbyterian church in Lucea alone passed out twelve thousand religious booklets and were able to sell various religious publications. The works, primarily from the Religious Tract Society of London and the National Bible Society of Scotland, included *British Workman, Band of Hope Review,* and *British Messenger.* The church's library drew more than a hundred readers weekly, who paid a small sum for the privilege.[61] That the people of Lucea should support these efforts gives a clue about the sense of connectedness to the mission at hand; a sense of attachment to Britain, whence emanated the tracts, was also furthered. Since these religious tracts, newspapers and books were often the only reading material available in some areas, some of the apparent interest in them might be attributable to that fact. However, because of this, the missionaries were able to control the influences to which their congregations were exposed, and to reinforce their messages through these means.

Public Rituals

Apart from preaching, praying and singing, the churches served the community by the public performance of rituals. For some congregations, notably the Baptists, the act of adult baptism was central to the public declaration of conversion and acceptance of the Christian path. As with other church-related activities, the ritual of baptism sometimes became an occasion for gathering the community. At a baptism service at the Mandeville Baptist Church in 1886, for instance, according to custom they stayed up all of the previous night, singing, reading and praying. The church was crammed with people from as early as four thirty in the morning, when a congregation of between 500 and 600 assembled for the ceremony, which went on until seven o'clock in the morning. Another baptism took place in 1891 at a river called "Baptism Fording" in Clarendon, less than two miles from Porus. By six in the morning between 250 and 300 people had gathered, "decently attired" in various colours, while Reverend Washington, his chief deacon and the converts were dressed in special apparel. In the midst of singing and prayer the pastor descended into the water, followed by the deacon and the twenty-one converts, who were baptized in pairs. After being plunged into the water and emerging wet, they were sent out to dress in a booth.[62]

Although not nearly as public as the baptisms, among the Moravians and Wesleyans there were regular "love feasts", such as the one held in Fyffe's Pen in 1881 to commemorate the hundredth anniversary of the beginning of Sunday schools. These provided an opportunity for testimonies to be given regarding the conversion experience and the goodness of God:

It is true that the manner in which some few expressed themselves was such that may perhaps have caused a smile upon the face of those who are not accustomed to their way of speaking, but their earnestness and evident sincerity made up for all the peculiarities. . . . These simple hearted people [stand] up and with tears rolling down their black faces tell of the great things God had done for their souls.[63]

Baptisms and love feasts were but part of the communal side of the Christian experience for some Jamaicans. As part of a culture which was as public as it was exuberant, the water ritual of baptism (washing away of sins, emergence into a new life) and the emotional testimonies of the converted served to include family, friends and neighbours in what, in other societies, would have been a personal, private experience. However, this was the Jamaican creole culture, and the missionaries, despite themselves, had to negotiate with it and in some cases accommodate it.

Religious Associations

The churches used various organizations to maintain their hold on the people, and to ensure growth in things spiritual and cultural. There was a flowering of associations, clubs and societies, patterned on contemporary British models that were used to "civilize" the working classes there, which had as their primary focus the maintenance of Christian doctrine and the dissemination of Victorian culture. The Religious Tract and Book Association, the Jamaica Bible Reading Association, and the various Bible societies were just some of the organizations formed to keep the people focused on the "Book". In 1872 several denominations participated in a meeting of the Kingston Auxiliary Bible Society, where a collection for the parent society in Britain was taken.[64] There were also groups, such as the British and Foreign Bible Society, which were headquartered in Britain. At one meeting in 1888 they discussed a report on Bible circulation in India. That Jamaican Christians should meet to express concerns about the Indian "heathen" in their imperial midst reinforced the idea of an expansive political entity, and elevated the Jamaican (Christian) population above at least one other in Her Majesty's empire. There was also a lively interest in religious activities in Africa where, in fact, some Jamaicans went as missionaries; many churches, even in the midst of their own dreadful poverty, set up special mission funds to help the effort in the "dark continent".[65] The Jamaicans who participated in these associations with British connections no doubt developed a sense of belonging to the larger, wider entity of an empire within an empire – the Christian community across the British Empire (also, the British Empire in the wider universe of Christendom).

Another important and vibrant church organization was the Christian Endeavour that was a part of almost every nonconformist denomination. Its focus was on young people, who were deemed prone to stray from the teachings and directives of doctrine. Within each church there were also groups with exclusively male membership like the Moravian Men's Guild and the Church of Scotland's Young Men's Guild, whose activities included savings clubs. The Young Men's Guild, which had a membership of one hundred in 1904, distributed thousands of tracts to policemen, car conductors and drivers, and had among its facilities gymnastics, music and reading rooms.[66] The use of (Victorian) cultural activities to bring men into the associations, there to shape them into good, Christian, British colonials, was an important means of acculturation.

Several church organizations also focused on women and girls. Various churches had versions of mother's unions, mother's prayer meetings, and young women's classes that, often led by the missionaries' wives, had a spiritual focus and also presented an opportunity for women's issues to be addressed. It was here that directives about parenting and wifely responsibilities, the importance of chastity, and the goal of marriage were stressed – the elements of so-called social purity. Many churches also had social purity societies, which focused on the evils that resulted from intemperance and the three great "blots" on Jamaican society: promiscuity, concubinage and illegitimacy. The Upward and Onward Society, one of the most popular women's organizations, likewise found its most fertile home in the churches. Its purpose was "to unite as many as possible of the women of Jamaica in the promotion of womanly virtue, pure family life, and a healthy public opinion on moral questions, these ends being essential to individual happiness and the welfare of the state". The Moravian Church also sponsored the Anna Nitschmann Guild for Girls, which taught young women to sew and placed them in mentoring relationships with elite ladies in the community.[67] This work was intended to "lift them up" and to teach them the tenets of the cult of true womanhood that was fundamental to the Victorian middle-class culture being emulated.

Most church societies were in fact dominated by women: "We seem to have but few men of influence and weight of character. . . . We sometimes call them female societies for whether numerically, intellectually or influentially they belong to that sex, and many of them are women of no ordinary petty perseverance, and unwearied toil for Jesus." Although most of these women

Figure 17. Sunday Wesleyan procession, Savanna-la-Mar
© Trustees for Methodist Church Purposes; used by permission of Methodist Publishing House.

were "entirely dependent on their own scant earnings for subsistence . . . in the spirit of self sacrifice they endeavour[ed] to contribute of their means for the maintenance of the work".[68] What is significant, however, is that the members of these church societies, clubs and so on helped to support the means by which the joint messages of Christianity and civilization were spread. In other words, they facilitated their own indoctrination.

That women should become the backbones of these organizations and also be the targets of the missions gave the church another avenue along which to move. Given women's central role as mothers (and mates/wives) and the primary parents in many Jamaican homes, the church could hope that, once convinced of the superiority of Christian Victorian doctrines and values, they would pass on the tenets of civilization to their offspring and partners. Through the various societies, clubs and associations, then, the church could hope to reinforce Christian morality and to effect change in outlook, expectations and behaviour. No doubt, there was great hope that the next generation would benefit from an "enlightened" parent who would do her best to keep them on the straight and narrow path.

Charity

Apart from establishing penny savings banks and encouraging their members to save, the churches extended their influence among the people by seeking to relieve the "deserving poor"[69] through acts of charity. Primary among the churches that concentrated on charity was the Salvation Army, which had gained respectability by the early twentieth century. Although a latecomer, the Army rapidly became renowned for its focus on the "submerged tenth" of the community. Its work in Kingston was especially important after it opened a night shelter and soup kitchen for the city's destitute.[70]

The Roman Catholics were also quite active in charity for the poor, primarily through the efforts of the Kingston Catholic Association of Ladies of Charity, and the Brothers of the Poor of the St Vincent de Paul Society.[71] But all denominations were involved in charity of one sort or another. Time and again they were called upon to provide urgent relief to the poor, such as in 1881 during the opening of the United Brethren church at Mizpah, when the missionary was approached by several suffering people: "Minister, me hungry, me have nothing to eat." Many poor Jamaicans, especially in times of economic distress, became dependent on the churches, "without which assistance, perhaps some would actually die of starvation". A great deal of church charity was focused around the festive Christmas season; in both urban and rural areas, "the gift of clothing from the church, and beef and bread" from other members of the congregation was greatly appreciated.[72]

The role of the churches through their charity organizations served to reinforce the paternalistic relationship of this cultural institution to the people. Rather than working for an overall change in the condition of the masses (which would have meant fundamental changes in official policies, among other things) the churches alleviated the immediate distress of some. And even in dispensing charity they kept elite expectations in view, as those who were deemed undeserving (so labelled because they did not follow the tenets of Victorian middle-class culture) had a more difficult time gaining access to the scarce resources that were so desperately needed.

Religious and Social Entertainment

A considerable amount of entertainment for ordinary people took place in connection with the churches, which increasingly used cultural activities to attract into their sphere of influence persons who were not usually a part of their congregations. Indeed, particularly in the rural areas, the church, together with the school which was attached to it, was literally the community centre where religious observance and secular celebration took place. The churches were therefore the main sponsors of social entertainment. This gave them enormous influence on the form such entertainment took, and every effort was made to promote events that were considered morally uplifting and civilizing. Much church entertainment was thus oriented around promoting certain moral, religious and family values, and promoting a love of monarch and country. In addition, most events were designed to raise funds for the host church or denomination to further propagate its mission.

Among the faithful of some nonconformist churches, particularly the Baptists and Methodists, the "rally of the 12 tribes" was a popular pastime. The rally included a procession with banners, headed by the pastor. On the banners were inscribed the names of the heads of "tribes" (for example, Reuben, Simeon, Judah, Levi, Zebulum, Issachai, Dan, Gad, Asher, Naphtali, Joseph and Benjamin). These groups sang rally songs, collected contributions and listened to addresses by their leaders. Such events were usually brought to a close with the national anthem, the doxology and the benediction – reinforcing in the minds of those gathered the symbolic relationship between God and the imperial state.[73]

More popular perhaps were the variety of public cultural events sponsored by or associated with the churches: social meetings, fancy fairs, garden parties, bazaars, tea meetings, sacred concerts and theatricals, magic-lantern shows illustrating biblical and imperial events, excursions and picnics, and sports.[74] Through these entertainments the churches introduced many art forms and other aspects of British culture (especially dress and etiquette) to the Jamaican people in order to "improve" their tastes and behaviour. Indeed, in this role the churches functioned as a conduit for the transmission of middle-class Victorian culture to the masses. These entertainments also offered the people an opportunity to practise what they had learned from the pulpits of, particularly, the nonconformist mission churches, especially concerning appreciation of "good healthy decent" family recreation, decorum, teetotalism, and non-gambling (although the employment of raffles and other games of chance as fundraisers at the fairs of some churches casts doubt on the last).

"Positive" Assessments of Church Influence

Even among the clergy, and certainly in the wider society, there were divergent views about the success of the church in its renewed efforts after 1865 to civilize Jamaica. Many thought that progress was being made. They pointed out that not only were there large numbers of well-attended churches, but the very nature of the people had been affected:

> The Jamaica darkey is nothing if not religious, and the churches are well attended on Sunday. These simple people walk for miles to go to the service, often carrying their Sunday clothing on their heads and going to the hut of a friend in the town to change. Others carry their shoes on their heads, sitting on the grass near the church to put them on before going inside.[75]

The congregations were large and attentive, and the classes which prepared candidates for inclusion in the church membership grew every week. The people were said to be "earnest seekers of salvation". There were repeated observations of "more enlightened views" of Christian duty and "more scriptural conformity to the divine". Improved decorum and enhanced manifestations of "correct" culture were also in evidence. The people seemed pious and sincere in their faith, respectful and supportive of those who ministered to them, and embracing of the symbols and expectations of the community of which they had become a part:[76]

> As respects attendance or ordinance, the observance of family prayer, the performance of the duties of relational life, the formation of habit and character, the cultivation of domestic and public virtues, our observations of them . . . have seldom failed to gratify our hearts and stimulate our energies.[77]

The missions spoke in glowing terms of the influence of their work in transforming these "ignorant heathen" into a far more acceptable state through "mission . . . the power of the gospel". They claimed that the tone of the people's daily lives had changed significantly. Brompton, for example, which was once so noted for its "degradation and wickedness that it was called Sodom", had been transformed and was under the influence of the church. At Mulgrave, a district seventeen miles from Black River in St Elizabeth, the people had been scattered and "living in darkness" until the establishment of a Wesleyan chapel and day school. They were subsequently "full of earnestness", had completely changed, and the "orderly, intelligent (for Jamaican peasants), and appreciative congregation, is a living proof of the good results of Christian teaching in this land".[78] For many missionaries, Jamaica was an "object-lesson" of what the "quiet, systematic, persistent mission work" could achieve in "uplifting and steadying the negro race" and solving the problems associated with their development:

> There are few more peaceable, loyal, and happy citizens in the Empire.... When Americans visit the island they are amazed at the orderly social conditions, the absence of a colour line, and the independent and industrious character of the people. "How do you manage it?" they ask. If the question were put on a Sunday – or on an ordinary day, for that matter – one would only need to tell them to listen to the "clinkum clank" of the church bells as they ring out their persuasive appeal from hill-top to hill-top throughout the island.[79]

That the church should take responsibility for the creation of a "peaceable, loyal and happy" citizenry, who were behaving in an orderly way within the boundaries of the empire, is especially poignant. The church's "persuasive appeal" to the people to change their beliefs, world views and cultures seemed to have had great impact, and the satisfied tone of the missionaries' reports spoke volumes to the apparent success of the civilizing mission.

Allied to the display of increasing religiosity was an increase in material prosperity and "bright intelligence and manly self-respect which are the unmistakable indications of an advancing civilization". Stewart comments on this link that the missionaries made between material progress and civilization:

> The idea was that Jamaica could achieve civilization only as a result of the desire of laborers for material goods; the black's [stereotypical] laziness could only be overcome if he wanted more luxuries. These artificial wants were necessary for progress, for they created a need for useful crafts and skills. The more man wants beyond subsistence, the more skills of production are required, and the goal of civilization becomes closer. Moreover, the demand for luxuries leads to raising of the standard of living of the working class in that the workers share in the general prosperity of a society that thrives on artificial wants.[80]

This perception of progress continued into the twentieth century. According to the Quakers at Prospect, "In times past, quarreling and fighting with all manner of evils were so prevalent, that law abiding people were afraid to walk the streets after six in the evening. With no church or school, there was no restraining influence" until they established a mission in 1913. The desire that many had to be "morally right in the sight of God and the law of the land" was consequently in evidence, and some tried to remedy their situation by marrying legally, following "definite conversions":[81]

> Indeed concubinage [is] our great difficulty and grand obstacle in the ingathering of our hearers, as appears from the fact that almost every new marriage brings us two new members, thus making it evident that many are kept out of the Church by these unhallowed and unsanctified connexions, it being considered more disreputable to be married in a humble way than to live in concubinage. We have set our face against these evils and are endeavouring to instruct the people in the right appreciation of the true dignity and blessedness of the married state, and their solemn duty and obligation in this matter, both to God and man, and some, we are aware, are now making preparations for marriage.[82]

The idea that conversion led to a recognition of "inappropriate behaviour" and sometimes resulted in an attempt to correct that situation (in this case, through marriage), or alternatively that a change in behaviour (the decision to marry) could lead to conversion, brings home forcefully the connection between Christian morality and Victorian culture. It was possible for the one (Christianity) to induce the other (the Victorian culture), and vice versa; and insofar as they were tracks that ran alongside each other, sometimes intersecting, sometimes diverging slightly, Victorian culture and Christian doctrine could be, and often were, delivered by the same persons.

The missionaries also credited themselves with being able to supplant Afro-creole cultural practices with Christian ones. So, for instance, the Quakers claimed that in Port Antonio they had "taken over the old shop which was used for low vile African dances" and were converting it into "a hall for mission purposes": "We felt when we made the request that the dance be stopped that we must give the people more than our little mission home was able to give. Even before we took over the building we moved our house organ in and had our morning prayers there."[83] The direct trade of dances for religious songs and prayers was more than symbolic, and the people in Port Antonio who observed the transfer of cultural power must have wondered at the ascension of the church (even as they packed away their dance clothes and prepared to sing and pray).

Another area where the missionaries seemed successful in changing pre-existing Afro-creole practices was in the celebration of Christmas, where the colourful community-oriented street carnivals of Set Girls and Jonkunnu were gradually replaced by the end of the century with more quiet observances centred around the church (services) and the home (family, children and the Christmas tree).[84] The effort to replace one culture with another was deliberate, part of the ongoing war against "low, vile" non-European cultural manifestations. The substitution of Christianity for a pre-existing cultural activity pointed to the strategic employment of Christianity as a civilizing force, ridding the country of the darkness of Africa and putting in its place the lightness/whiteness of Christianity. After all, said the *Daily Gleaner*, "[i]n Jamaica we well know how important is the part played by the missionary in civilizing as well as Christianizing a country".[85]

If for many Jamaicans the church served as a centre for the transmission of Victorian Christian culture, then, corresponding to many indicators, its mission was extremely effective. According to Baptist T.S. Penny in 1910, Jamaican congregations arrived at church mostly on time and read the psalm along with the pastor. They sang heartily, if slowly, and the choirs dressed in similar costumes that included hats. The congregations liked long sermons, and their behaviour throughout was decorous:

> To members themselves the chapel is much more than the place where they worship. It is their intellectual and spiritual home; the only place, to very many of them, where they meet with uplifting and enlightening influences, where a banner is lifted for them against the allurements of the rum-shop, the obeahman (witchcraft doctor) and the sins of the flesh. The love of the older black people for God's house is beautiful and touching.[86]

The church was thus a vital source of "appropriate" culture, and it provided doctrines intended to guide the people along paths of righteousness.[87] Its place in the community was one of prime importance to the civilizing mission. It was often the only place where there was any organized social activity, and certainly it was, for many, the only source of entertainment and charity. As the bastion of Christian Victorian culture and morality, it was used to combat the Afro-creole belief systems and practices that were considered a threat to the moral fibre of a modern, civilized British colonial society.

Satan's Curse

Amidst the glad tidings and self-congratulatory celebrations about the advance of Christianity and civilization in Jamaica, there were ominous signs of the "devil's work" among the people. There were many outside (and even *within*) the influence of the churches who displayed great bouts of temper and uncontrolled anger that demolished the comforts of home, a propensity for drunkenness, and a mania for gambling, quarrelsomeness and spitefulness, superstition and a fear of ghosts.[88] The churches were thus in a constant struggle against the "evil" that was supposedly pervasive throughout Jamaican society, from top to bottom. Whereas in England, said Reverend James Watson, Christianity and civilization were "growing together and mutually influencing each other", in Jamaica the Bible "coexists and competes with ungodliness". This was attributed largely to the example of low morality prevalent among those who were looked up to "because of their social position". He continued, "Jamaican society is in a sad condition. The so-called upper classes are often tyrannical, oppressive, and arrogant, and to some of them is to be [a]scribed the backward state of morals and religion."[89]

Nowhere was this immorality more prevalent than in the area of conjugality.[90] The Baptists appealed to those "at home" (in England),

> Pray for us, on behalf of our work in this island. It is a lovely one, but sin, ignorance and superstition abound, and at times, we feel it hard work to battle with these. Immorality prevails to an alarming extent, and is one of the chief evils against which we have to combat. Most of those excluded have been so dealt with on account of them yielding to the pernicious influences emanating from the loose habits of those with whom they come in daily contact.[91]

In almost every report from every denomination, there were references to several members who had been placed under discipline for "gross immorality". In 1866 ten members of the New Bethlehem Moravian Church were excluded for immorality. Sins of the flesh were evident in the congregations at the Carmel, New Eden, New Fulneck, Nazareth, Beaufort and Bethany Moravian churches, especially among, but not confined to, young people.[92] Directly related to this "gross immorality" were the low rates of marriage across the island (see chapter 4). Confronted by the church about their "lives of sin", the people simply pleaded "hard times".[93] It was clear that the people had their *own* ideas about how to live their lives, and many ignored the admonitions of church, press or state, for that matter.

If the white missionaries did not subscribe to the racist stereotypes about the uncontrolled libido of black people that were so prevalent in the nineteenth century, they certainly seemed to be obsessed with the alleged sexual proclivities of Afro-Jamaicans, and did their utmost to restrain them. Sex was at the very centre of their drive to civilize. Very often they appealed to those "living in sin" to stop "fornicating". When that failed, they either suspended or excluded the guilty parties from church membership.[94] Social purity societies were formed, and sometimes there were other missionary meetings directed at this "scourge". Success was intermittent but occasionally dramatic, as, for instance, in 1879 when an English evangelist, Reverend E.W. Tayloe, arrived in Jamaica to work in the Moravian churches. In his travels around the island, he stopped at the various churches and directed his efforts at this phenomenon. He had some success, for in Fairfield he conducted ninety-six marriages on one day, and did sixty more in Patrick Town and Bethabara.[95] But these were a drop in the ocean, and well beyond the First World War the churches were still unable to make any significant inroads into this "problem". This was one vital area where they clearly failed in their civilizing mission, and since the family was and is regarded as the foundation of society, this was a major disaster. It was also a source of embarrassment when church members "fell into sin", because it was very hard for the clergy to bear the sneers and malice of the "worldly men . . . who look upon it as a triumph over [our] absurd ideas of civilizing and converting them".[96]

But they encountered other important setbacks as well. As shown in chapter 2, they met strong resistance in their war against obeah; all indications are that the belief and practice of this "black art" increased towards the end of the nineteenth century, notwithstanding the admonitions of the churches and draconian legal penalties of the state. The same goes for drinking and gambling. In the 1860s there were claims that the Jamaican people displayed great sobriety, and favourable comparisons were even drawn with the lower classes in England, the standard against which they were measured. By the end of the nineteenth century, however, distress about growing intemperance in the community was being expressed. The rum shops that emerged in many communities were seen as sources of evil. Since these were community enterprises, the shops were in easy walking distance of the people and were "the hotbeds of idleness and dissipation, and [went] far to account for the numerous defections from the church which have taken place in the course of years".[97]

At New Carmel in 1870, for instance, a rum shop opened on land near where the races were held on Emancipation Day, and at the end of the year the shop *and* the races were portrayed as twin evils. The same problem was highlighted for Ballard's Valley in 1905: "The rum shop and the race course, the favourite places of resort, exercise a demoralising influence on our people, and draw the minds of all interested in them from the church and from spiritual things"; while by 1913 at Broadleaf the rum shop had been in the district for some time and was "breeding many a vice, for drunkenness and gambling [were] both on the increase". In Port Antonio, said one of the Quakers, "[t]he rum shops are so largely patronized that I felt that they should pay our rent as they rob the people, so I started out to solicit, going to two wholesale men first and they each . . . subscribed a month's rent".[98]

By the end of the period, the missionaries complained that the significant increase in the number of rum shops was accompanied by an increase in drunkenness among women as well as men. According to the Baptists, "Drunkenness, uncleanness, and many other gross vices are indulged in, degrading to society and offensive to a holy God. These vices can only be eradicated by 'the blessing from on high' upon the faithful testimony, the holy activity and the constant example of the Lord's people."[99]

Often allied with the drinking was gambling, which increased with the opening of Chinese "drop-pan" lottery shops, mainly in Kingston, at the turn of the century.[100] But the "evil" of gambling was rampant throughout the island. According to the Moravians, in Carisbrook gambling was very common, especially among the young men, who squandered their money; at Nazareth the activity was linked to the extension of the railroad in 1890, which brought in "groups of strangers who are in a great proportion the scum of the Island – gambling and riotous living is carried on there all Sunday". By 1912 there was a great anxiety about the increase in the drinking and gambling habits of people across the island, and the churches' efforts were being directed at these evils and at strengthening the legal regulation and restriction of the liquor traffic. In both areas, however, the church recorded dismal failures (notwithstanding draconian legislation against gambling),[101] partly because the social elites were themselves guilty of these practices and were thus unprepared to see them stamped out.

The churches also faced the problems of "worldliness and indifference on the one hand, and fanatics and superstition on the other, [which] are hindering God's work". As already pointed out, chronically harsh economic and environmental conditions made it difficult for many people to attend church during the week and on Sundays. The missionaries, however, regarded this as a growing spirit of indifference. Many people explained their "carelessness" by claiming that they did not have clothing "suitable for public wear", and because they had lost contact with the church, they lapsed into indifference and were "living lives of sin and shame".[102] At the end of the period the lament was almost identical except that a new factor had been introduced – the First World War:

> Our Churches have felt the effects of that spirit of indifference and careless neglect of religion that seems to be one of the wide-spread after-results of the war – the war that was supposed to draw multitudes to the altar of Christ – but so signally failed, in fact has greatly hindered all religious activity. . . . Deadening effect on morals and all finer sensibilities brought on by the war, the unprecedented hardship occasioned by the unbearable prices of living necessities, the labour unrest, and the utter indifference of the upper class (ruling) to the grinding needs of the masses, all mitigate against the religious activity of all churches. Very few returned soldiers ever darken a church door. Their view of the outside world has bred independence and the lure of the dollar has taken most of them away from poor Jamaica. The sanctity of the Sabbath is being lost to an alarming degree.[103]

Indeed, as in Europe and the United States, after the turn of the century more people were treating Sunday as a holiday and indulging in secular leisure activities: picnics, sports, cinema and so on. Thus, the desecration of the sabbath became a major concern for the churches, but to little avail. Perhaps worse still, the connection between some people and the church seemed to be waning and, according to the Quakers, "some openly reject the gospel, while much indifference and hardness prevails among others".[104]

This apparent growth in indifference was said to be especially marked among the upcoming generation: "there is great lightness and a strong hankering after the lowest pleasures that are in vogue". The problem was blamed on "proper Christian family discipline [which was], alas! seldom practised, and consequently love and respect for parents, and attachment to the parental house, were very rare qualities in children". As a result, many young people reputedly neglected their parents and grandparents and were idle and immoral, "few of them marrying in an honourable way". At Cheapside the problem was supposedly worse among young women, who were more affected by the negative effects of home influence "as regards development of female mind and character".[105]

Thus, "scoffing at religion" and scepticism were said to be on the increase in some parts of the island. While it was acknowledged that a large proportion of people did come within the influence of the churches, "there is a very considerable number of the people who exist outside the area occupied by the religious forces, and are not, even indirectly, affected by their presence". At places like Porus where railway construction brought in workers from outside the district, the locals mingled day by day with "a number of lawless, Godless, characters from various parts of the country", and when they were not "consistently firm in their profession and without moral courage, and religious fortitude to resist temptation . . . [they] yield to vice, become careless, and so disqualify themselves almost from their Church connections".[106]

Against the litany of complaints and shows of consternation, the claims of Christian "progress" among the people had to be tempered. While more people seemed to be attending church and living within the prescribed admonitions than earlier in the century (attendance had fallen off after the 1840s, until the Revival of 1860), another large group was not. Some of those attended church but lived outside of the churches' rules of morality, some obeyed aspects of the code but ignored the rest of it, and still others rejected the ideology which surrounded Victorian Christianity.

The people did, however, seem to turn to God whenever natural disaster struck. A good example was the aftermath of the 1907 earthquake, when "there were nationally signs of much concern on the part of many who had been careless and also on the part of some who had long neglected the House of God. In some instances this concern gradually passed away but generally speaking it has so far borne fruit." However, once it became clear that the Second Coming was not imminent, people drifted back into normalcy. Thus, according to the United Free Church of Scotland, by 1910 many who had joined during that spiritual "awakening" had gone back into the "world".[107]

Concerns about indifference and carelessness were by no means restricted to the black lower classes. According to Jesuit Father Woollett, in one round-the-island journey he came across an Irishman who had not seen a priest in twenty-two years and who was not enthusiastic about the prospect either. The upper class also participated in the "culture of indifference" that caused the *Gleaner* in 1901 to wonder, "Why are the Churches not better attended?"[108]

The missionaries found it quite puzzling that many persons who claimed church affiliation often displayed un-Christian, antisocial behaviour which embarrassed and challenged the claim of moral authority. Church members were, for instance, frequently involved in quarrels, which sometimes necessitated the intervention of the missionaries:

> Our people are bound by Church-rules to bring these disputes to the minister for settlement, in order to avoid the evils which arise from their going to law for every trifle. The settling of these quarrels sometimes affords a sad insight into those feelings which the people otherwise contrive to hide. Vindictiveness, passion, bad language and a most shocking perversion of right and wrong are . . . often prominent features.[109]

The kindness and gentleness that were supposed to define middle-class Christian/Victorian life were not apparent in these disagreements and, despite the admonitions of the church, the people often sought remedy in the courts. Sometimes these quarrels were sources of distress for the church. At Dober, in more than one case, members and even office bearers left the church "because they had some disagreement with an opposite party, and would not like to be in the same church any more to see the face of the other".[110]

Some church members were also unruly, and "generally exhaust our idea of what a spiritual character should be. And we mournfully wonder at the intractableness of sinful human nature which keeps men low under means divinely powerful to lift them high." Again, "It would be trying if it were only out of the pale of the Church we saw so much that is vile and repulsive in character and conduct; but when among our church members and in their families, we, after all we have said to them and done for them, find a continuance of so many evils, our faith and patience are pretty well tried." This problem was clearly demonstrated at a baptism at the Mandeville Baptist Church in 1886 (also cited above). The *Gleaner*'s correspondent went to the church at four thirty in the morning, stood by a window, and reported that he had to retreat due to the rowdy behaviour of some people. The "rowdies" went to the pond where the baptism was to take place and elders, sticks in hand, had to use all their muscular force to open a way for the minister and candidates: "Rowdyism was carried to its fullest extent and . . . the juniors were the very worst of the lot."[111]

Within the church and without, the Jamaican people behaved in ways that some members of the cultural elite (especially the missionaries) found difficult to understand and, in some cases, appalling. In spite of their declarations, apparently genuine conversions, and ritualized entry into the body of Christ, the people were still influenced by a culture that was decidedly different from the Victorian model which they were expected to embrace.

Victorian Culture, Jamaican Christianity

One of the strongest themes running through the evidence of the religious life of the Jamaican people seems to be the emergence of a Jamaican Christianity. The apparently mutually opposing pictures – of a pious, sincere, Christian people, and of a people bent on maintaining Afro-creole belief systems (see chapters 2 and 3), often contained in the same individuals – bear further examination. The mantra of the missionaries' reports ran in two directions to the same conclusion: that progress was being made in the acceptance among the people of the Christian ethic, and inasmuch as that ethic was defined by Victorian culture, it also embraced a mission to civilize. However, running in a parallel stream, whether above or below the other, was another set of beliefs and behaviours which fit neither the Christian ethic nor the demands of Victorian culture. This distinction was captured in the assessment of Quaker missionary Gilbert Farr:

> The people are in many ways less like heathen than I expected – and on the other hand sunk lower in the *vices* of heathenism than I could have thought. Many a time I have thought it would be a relief to work with a people who were heathen, and knew it and acknowledged it; rather than with those who, almost to a man, if you ask them if they are Christians will answer "yes", while their moral life would shame a coolie.[112]

The people, then, having embraced the doctrines and ideologies of Christianity, were certainly not "heathen", but the behaviours and standards prescribed by the church and the dominant Victorian culture were not always observed, even by those who accepted those doctrines. They continued to have at their disposal an alternative set of beliefs, called "superstition" by the authorities and churches, which seemed to answer concerns or to explain aspects of life where the doctrinal offerings of the church were inadequate. Except for the slur about "coolies", the statement by Gilbert Farr provides a clue about the particular strain of Christianity practised by many of the people. They would receive the creed, submit to ritual and ceremony and observe ordinances, but otherwise would not behave "properly". They imposed limits on how much of the "superior" moral code they would adopt. These Jamaicans, from the churches' perspective, were Christians "only in name".[113]

The missionaries were able to speak with what they believed was some authority about the type of Christianity that the people practised because they lived among them and thought they knew them. But "One is often surprised by the strange combinations of opposite features in the same character. Earnestness, liberality apparent, and as I think real devotion exhibited for years, and then in a moment of temptation or excitement actions are committed, and words are spoken, which one finds hard to reconcile with a heart sanctified by Divine Grace." It was difficult for the missionaries to understand what they saw, to appreciate the Jamaican version of Christianity where acceptance of faith did not necessarily mean wholly embracing the culture which accompanied it: "To outward appearance they can serve [both] God and Mammon with a zest which is most unaccountable." The fact that "the vast bulk of the people" came under the direct influence of Christianity did not mean that they were "truly christianized" in accordance with European ideas.[114]

Nevertheless, the proselytization of Christianity in Jamaica could by 1920, all things considered, be called a success. The majority of the people had been exposed to the basic doctrines and many did genuinely accept the philosophies and creeds of the faith. However, the spread of the gospel was not the only mission of the churches. They sought to "uplift", to "improve", and to "civilize" the people. This is where they oft-times came into conflict with the people's culture. As Austin-Broos puts it, "The orthodox missions' regime sought to use moral discipline as their means to articulate [the] world. Their project was undermined by continuing cultural differences between Europeans and those of African descent."[115] Even if, like Methodist Joseph Prior, the missionaries could conceive of the people as having minds of their own and as capable of making their own decisions on matters of personal status, they nevertheless wore a haughty paternalistic demeanour: "The people may be led but *will not be driven.*"[116] The reality, however, was that the people wanted to be neither led nor driven. They wanted to decide *for themselves* what was suitable and meaningful for them, in accordance with their own world view and moral system. They sought cultural self-determination, not cultural paternalism. Hence, they were selective in their adoption of the moral precepts of Christianity.

This is vividly demonstrated in the Quaker complaint (from 1920) that "There has been much to fight against in the way of picnics at night, races, etc., which so many do not see the evil in." The churches preferred that their members participate in "appropriate" forms of entertainment: "[day] picnics, concerts, services of song, C.E. [Christian Endeavour] rallies and [in the season] Christmas trees".[117] The people, however, clearly had their own views about entertaining themselves. But when they did not adhere to the prescribed *Victorian* moral code, the missionaries and their supporters regarded that as a lapse in *Christian* behaviour. For many, therefore, the people were marked by their ability to claim Christ, and at the same time to be notably "out of order". They were not the sort of *Victorian Christians* that the church would have liked to see. Perhaps not, but they were nevertheless Christians – Jamaican creole Christians.

Chapter 7

Schooling for God and Empire
The Ideology of Colonial Education

VITAL TO THE RENEWED EFFORTS TO civilize Jamaica and influence the minds of the black majority in the later nineteenth century was the schooling process. Elementary education, so called, was intended to provide the lower classes in particular with the ideological tenets to become civilized, loyal British colonial subjects, and to equip them with basic skills of literacy and numeracy to function at the bottom of society in their presumed role of dependent agricultural labourers. It was designed to reinforce their subordination within the white hegemonic sociopolitical system, and their dependence on a plantation system that was supposed to remain the primary engine of economic development in the West India colonies. Furthermore, as Ruby King has argued, particularly after the events of 1865, "the belief was reinforced that the safety of the upper classes and the prosperity and stability of the country would depend on the extent to which they could successfully promote 'the enlightenment and the moral and social elevation of the people', through education".[1]

Schooling at all levels was also supposed to bolster the new, middle-class Victorian religio-moral order that the churches were seeking to build, as well as a more "rational scientific" approach to life, in sharp contrast to the maligned "superstitious spiritism" of the Afro-creole belief system. Education and Christianity were thus to go hand in hand to create a new Jamaican society in the wake of the "barbarism" of Morant Bay, and it is not surprising that the missionaries who were largely responsible for the propagation of the

Christian gospel were also entrusted with the task of educating the children of slaves into "civilized" ways.

The "Mission Statement"

From the birth of free Jamaica in 1838, therefore, the missionary societies and churches undertook the task of setting up elementary schools for the ex-slaves, and remained more or less in sole charge of education until crown colony government was inaugurated in 1866. Thereafter, in the new thrust to civilize the black majority, the colonial state also became involved, setting up its own schools and granting financial assistance to the church schools. But even then, unlike Trinidad where (particularly after 1870) the government played a major role in providing primary/elementary education,[2] in Jamaica the government played only a supplementary role. As late as 1910 there were only 68 government schools (9.8 per cent) out of a total of 693 elementary schools.[3] The churches were thus permitted dominance in this sphere, and the ramifications of this were difficult to ignore. Christian colonial education was designed to mould a new type of Jamaican who would step out of the ignorance that slavery had encouraged into "civilized citizenship". As the Wesleyan Missionary Society pointed out, "It was forgotten that slavery had left behind a legacy of social and moral degradation." Thus, even until the late nineteenth century, the annual *Handbook of Jamaica* stated, "Knowing the sad state of ignorance that prevailed among the prædial classes of the West Indies during the last days of slavery one of the first subjects to which the friends of emancipation turned their attention after the abolition of slavery, was the education of the working classes."[4] The churches thus used their other main entrée into the community, the church-controlled schools, to deliver the message of correct (Victorian) standards.

The Negro Education Grant[5] was intended primarily for the establishment of schools to provide elementary and basic education for the people. The government's decision to leave the education of the people in the hands of the clergy created the conditions for a "moral education". From the outset, the churches saw the possibility of instilling "correct" ideologies in the youngest colonial subjects. If the peasantry could be encouraged to believe that their children's social and economic advancement could be attained through education, then the churches would have in their clutches even those who were not a part of the church congregations that had sprung up in many communities. Alongside the church, therefore, grew the school, supervised by the clergy and sometimes even instructed by them. The hiring of staff was controlled by them, and they also had enormous input in the schools' curricula.

It was agreed that given the state of the Jamaican people, there was a "need for continued missionary work . . . in reclaiming the grossness and immorality of the neglected. Such vice as prevails in Jamaica, poisoning the very basis of society, is not to be conquered in a day", and could be partially overturned by Christian-based schooling. With such an education, not only would Jamaica herself be uplifted but she might yet become a great source of light, especially for Cuba, the Dominican Republic and Africa. And if the Presbyterians are to be believed, this mission to civilize was not questioned by the recipients: "The people understand that it is the purpose of the mission to seek their salvation, the education of their children, and to promote their social and domestic happiness."[6]

The place that religion had in the curriculum cannot be overemphasized. As in Trinidad, government education officials and the clergy shared the view that religious instruction was an absolute necessity in education. According to Carl Campbell, "Both clerics and government officials believed that morality and character in children could best be founded on religious instruction, and that the preservation of social order and well-being depended on the diffusion of religious morality." Religious instruction had three objectives: the teaching of scripture with a view to conversion; character training and morality designed to preserve the social order; and congregational activities to promote denominational loyalties.[7]

Hence, a part of the daily ritual in school always involved prayer and catechism. The church did not mean simply to deliver a secular education to the people: "Christian education is an absolute necessity for the future well-being of this country. Our people must be raised thereby. It is the best lever for the uplifting of poor humanity from the mire of superstitious ignorance and corruption."[8] Further, the education was not only Christian in direction, it was English (Victorian) in focus. At the Ebenezer Academy, run by the Presbyterians in the 1870s to train young men for the mission field, the intentions were clear. The students received lessons in "classics and mathematics, in English composition, in history, and natural philosophy. . . . A good English education is kept prominently in view, and due space and time are given to increase the religious knowledge of the young men, and their acquaintance with geography . . . Latin and Greek." While it was the belief that the "negro mind finds Euclid rather tough work", there was praise for the "fine specimens of calligraphy and of map-drawing, for in the imitative arts the negroes make great attainments".[9]

The relationship between the government of the island and the churches where the education of the people was conducted was one of mutual dependence. After 1867 the churches relied on the government to support their efforts, and the government depended heavily on the churches to deliver education to the people. By the 1870s, according to the Presbyterians, the educational process had improved and the standards were higher than ever before, mainly due to "the enlightened policy initiated by Sir John Peter Grant".

> That Governor opened the way of the missionaries and their schoolmasters, whose work it was to ply their pupils with christian education, at the instance and expense of the churches and societies to which they and their schools properly belonged. The larger proportion of the teachers' salaries has been provided by the Government, while the missionaries have chosen the teachers, and paid them for their *religious* teaching, the Government paying them for the secular education they imparted.[10]

However, in their zeal to school, christianize and civilize the island's children, the churches were fiercely competitive with one another. This was by no means unique to Jamaica, for it occurred in Trinidad and elsewhere in the region. This fostered denominational jealousy and rivalry for, as Campbell observes, "The church schools were expected to boost church membership through religious instruction."[11] It also tended to multiply schools unnecessarily in a district, often under poor teachers, where one school with a first-class teacher would frequently have sufficed. Moreover, some churches refused to take children into their schools if their families were members of another denomination. In 1890, for instance, two *Gleaner* reporters encountered a nine-year-old girl near Hopeton (near Bull Head) in Manchester who "walks eight miles to school, that is sixteen miles every day, she plods over the rough roads. There is a school within a mile of her home but it is an Episcopal school and she is a Presbyterian, so [the] 'minister told her go to Presbyterian school' which she courageously does."[12] No doubt to put an end to that egregious practice, the education laws after 1892 threatened to withhold government grants from schools that refused admission to any child on such grounds, and also permitted parents to withdraw their children from any religious instruction or observance in a school of a different denomination.

But such legislation was neither practically enforceable nor, indeed, enforced, in a society in which the church was in active partnership with the state in delivering civilization; not even the growing presence of a small body of non-Christians, referred to loosely by Governor Swettenham in 1906 as "Jews, Muslims, and Chinese Taoists", tempered the churches' excessive zeal. Thus even that governor was obliged to remark, "I know of no common measure of religion applicable with equal fairness in all those indicated."[13] But since the government was not about to take full responsibility for education, the task was not to remove the churches from the schools, but rather to control their religious excesses. For all practical purposes, however, it was business as usual, and the alliance between church and state remained a *fait accompli* until well after the First World War. The church-controlled school, with its delivery of a British-based secular education that was inextricably linked to the Victorian Christian ethic, continued to be an important site for the transmission of moral culture: "The week-day schools are a valuable auxiliary to the missionary. The influence of the schools connected with the congregation is seen in a large increase of intelligence among the rising generation. I am often surprised and delighted when examining them on the sermons which they have heard at church to get such an accurate account from them."[14]

By the turn of the century, the school was also a major agency for promoting loyalty to king and empire. As will be shown in chapter 9, Empire Day was strongly promoted and observed in the schools after 1904; in 1905, when a "national"/imperial catechism was being prepared for use in the public schools, it was overseen by Enos Nuttall, the Anglican archbishop, who wanted a document that was open enough "for the sake of securing unity with all the protestant bodies". This catechism was entitled "One King, One Flag, One Fleet, One Empire".[15] The links between church, school and empire could not be clearer.

In practical terms, the main thrust of the education system in the period was in the area of primary or elementary schooling. There was a general belief that the population needed most to be introduced to the basic skills of literacy and numeracy; beyond this little was done. In common with other European imperialisms all over the world, British colonial schooling in Jamaica at the primary level was intended to provide the people with just enough education to function in a modern Western society (that is, basic functional literacy and numeracy), but not enough for them to become ambitious. Most importantly, schooling was not intended to pull them away from the land. If anything, it

Figure 18. Elementary schoolroom
Source: Library of Congress, Prints and Photographs Division, LC-USZ62-65573.

was designed to transform them into an intelligent class of agricultural workers or yeoman farmers who could make use of new agricultural technologies to become more productive. As Campbell puts it,

> Whatever was done for the welfare of the lower classes was done as cheaply as possible. Education for them was not to be overambitious; something was done, but not too much. These attitudes conformed to the essentially conservative function assigned to popular education. The purpose was to spread Christianity, literacy and, as always in education, social discipline preferably without social change. The maintenance of the colonial social structure and the labour requirements of the sugar plantations and sugar companies were compatible with an oversupply of illiterate or barely literate youths.[16]

Religious schooling was to transmit the civilizing moral code, while physical drills were intended to promote healthy bodies, to instil discipline, and to socialize the children to take and follow orders from people in authority. Ruby King has commented on the list of morals that, according to the Jamaican Codes of Regulations (1867, 1900 and 1902), were to be inculcated at school:

> During eight years of schooling the future citizens of the empire learned, among other things, obedience to persons in authority, love of country, patriotism, the duties of the citizen, fidelity to official trust, industry, temperance, honesty, and gentleness. Colonial officials seemed to regard these qualities as of greatest benefit to the well-being of the empire. They were able to show eventually how the entire curriculum could be directed to train desirable citizens. The qualities that marked the successful agriculturist were felt to be mainly moral qualities such as industry, patience, and the realization of responsibility – and conversely, agriculture, manual training, drill, and needlework were regarded as ideal instruments for moral training.[17]

Schools and Attendance

Before the installation of crown rule in 1866, education was hardly a priority for the planter-dominated assembly. According to the *Missionary Herald*, the government seldom spent more than £1,200 a year (in reality it was £3,000) on the maintenance of schools, "while it lavished £50,000 annually in stipends to the Anglican clergy". The greater part of the cost of primary education in the island was met out of the funds secured from voluntary sources by the religious bodies; and the active work of maintaining, directing and managing the schools, and creating public interest in education devolved almost entirely on the churches.[18] In 1867, however, the crown administration of Sir John Peter Grant implemented a system of state support for elementary education through grants-in-aid to the denominations. Based partly on the number of children in average attendance at a school, and partly on the classified results of the teaching as tested by an annual examination, these grants were purportedly "more liberal and uniform, and more in keeping with the growing interest in education and the needs of the country than anything before attempted".[19]

By no means, however, did these grants cover the entire amount spent on elementary education, so parents were required to pay fees for their children to attend school. In 1874 school fees amounted to £6,087, while another

£5,000 was contributed by private persons and religious societies. Endowed schools, normal schools (where elementary-level teachers were trained) and private schools which were entirely independent of the government were estimated to cost £15,727, which was met without government assistance.[20] The government also built new school buildings and assisted in training teachers at the Mico Institution, while some religious bodies (Baptists, Moravians and Roman Catholics) provided separate training facilities for the teachers who would operate in their schools (see below).

According to the *Blue Book of Statistics* (see appendix 5, table 1), in 1867 when this new system was started the Anglican Church controlled the largest number of schools and scholars (26.1 per cent of those "on the books" – that is, registered – and 25.4 per cent of those who attended school). No doubt using the official support which it enjoyed until 1870, when it was disestablished, the Church of England had more than a quarter of the island's children attending school under its wing. The schools run by the Baptists, the Wesleyan Methodists and the Presbyterians came next in terms of attendance, with the American Mission and the Jewish school having the smallest numbers.

The new system may have put elementary education on a more secure footing and facilitated its expansion. As appendix 5, table 2 shows, the number of elementary schools increased significantly: from 394 in 1867 to 962 in 1894–95. Thereafter, as a result of a series of amalgamations and closures on account of small student numbers, the number of schools fell to 690 in 1908–9 and fluctuated after that, ending the period with 693 schools.

But, as in other West Indian colonies, attendance at school was considered by the officialdom to be unsatisfactory.[21] Up to and beyond the First World War, just a little over one-quarter of Jamaican children of school age were taking part in the school system. As that system was one of the principal agencies for conveying the tenets of civilization, this was a matter of official concern. Officials pointed to the significant gap between those who were registered and those who actually attended, but perhaps they should have been more concerned with the large number of children of school age (five to fifteen years) who were not even registered. Although registrations for the period increased, with some fluctuations, up to a high point of 101,149 registered students in 1894–95, this represented less than 40 per cent of school-age children. Thereafter the number of registered students fell steadily, reaching 81,857 in 1905–6; between 1907–8 and 1920 the numbers ranged between 85,470 and 99,910, ending the period with 92,176 students registered. But even then, this was just about 40 per cent of school-age children.[22]

Much worse than the low registration, however, was the actual attendance. Between 1867 and 1893–94 the percentage of registered children who actually attended school never reached 60 per cent; even more alarming, less than 30 per cent of the total number of school-age children did so. In 1893–94 the percentage attendance of registered students jumped to 66.38, and except for small dips below 60 per cent between 1895 and 1897, the attendance remained above that mark, reaching a high point of 66.56 per cent in 1919–20. But these statistics must be taken in context, since these higher attendance rates came against a background of fluctuating figures which remained below the registration high point of 101,149 in 1894–95. In reality the percentage of school-age children attending school in 1920–21 was just 26.5.[23]

As in Trinidad and Guyana, the most common reason that children did not attend school at all, or attended irregularly, was the cost. In addition to the weekly school fees, writing and reading materials and acceptable clothes had to be provided.[24] But even after the fees were abolished in 1892, after a brief upward spurt attendance continued to decline. While many were willing to go without shoes, a meal of some sort, which was needed during the school day, was difficult for many families to provide. At home a child could eat of the meagre provisions in the household, but to take that "poor food" into a public space was embarrassing for many: "[T]he common excuse of the parents is, that they have no food to give the children to take with them."[25] But as far as the Quakers were concerned,

> If the fault lay with the children, it would be corrected easily, but the chief blame rests upon the parents. Some are too poor to keep the children in suitable clothing and many are too careless and indifferent. Very few have any proper conception of the importance of regular attendance as a means of education, so if there is some errand to be done or work at home or field, or a baby to mind while the others go out, the school must be sacrificed as being less important than the other things.[26]

Indeed, like those in Guyana, Trinidad and Barbados, many Jamaican parents relied on children's assistance in farming to ensure their family's survival: "[T]hese little workers are of great use and the parents could in most cases ill afford to do without them." Those who did attend school did so irregularly, especially in the rural areas, where it was the "custom of even respectable families to send their children only in rotation".[27] Then there were periodic weather factors – drought, flood, hurricane – and other disasters such as, for instance, a calamitous fire in Kingston in 1882, and the 1907 earthquake.[28] Sudden declines in school attendance were also occasionally caused by the outbreak of epidemic diseases: measles in Kingston, Manchester and Trelawny in 1882 and 1920, and influenza in 1918.[29] Other reasons such as the "[poor] character of the schools in the neighbourhood" also affected school attendance. In addition, some parents believed that they were being pressured by teachers and school managers to send their children to school because of "selfish motives"[30] – on account of the government grants-in-aid, which were partly determined by school attendance statistics.

Lateness was also a chronic problem in Jamaican schools, not least among the teachers. Clocks were almost universally absent from schoolrooms, and indeed from many homes. Rural life had its own rhythm of natural timetables, and the people their own concepts of time and punctuality, that did not correspond with the precision of Western notions of clock time. Hence,

> It is not uncommon, in a considerable number of schools, to find scholars dropping in for two hours or more after school has nominally begun; and too often the Teacher sets a bad example by being himself half-an-hour or more late. With irregular and unpunctual attendance it would be strange if any great results were attained.[31]

The twin evils of truancy and tardiness were thus held responsible for the failure of the education system to produce the desired results of enlightenment and civilization. Of course for some, like the Quakers, there were other contributing factors such as the enervating climate and, not least of all, the quality of the students themselves:

> [T]he teacher in Jamaica does not have just the same material to work upon as the schools in more enlightened countries are able to furnish. While some of the children here are remarkably bright others are just as remarkably stupid. Few have any means of education outside of the school-room. Some of the parents are utterly illiterate, and the habits of the home and social life especially in the use of the vernacular dialect as opposed to English as taught by the Grammarians – make the reception of knowledge in the school-room necessarily a much slower process than it otherwise would be.[32]

All of this meant that the progress of civilization through education was being severely handicapped. Even the black-owned newspaper, the *Jamaica Advocate*, complained that

> both parents and children regard the schoolroom only as a convenient place in which to spend a few idle moments. . . . Thus the important duty of training our

youths in the way of civilized citizenship, is relegated to the undisciplined occupation in the coffee fields and pimento walks or deputed to the driver of a small gang on the common pasture whose coarse habits and foul language become the elements from which ideas pertaining to the social and moral duties of . . . life are drawn.[33]

Such misguided truancy was liable to create "ignorant indolence" and encouraged an evil which would "increase and multiply indefinitely" and result in "a menace to the good order of society". Not surprisingly, the *Advocate* demanded that the state "should do its utmost to prevent and counteract both the generation and the multiplication of the evil"; while the missionaries lamented that "our schools, which might be a means of elevating the people, scarcely suffice to prevent the next generation from lapsing into barbarism".[34] The civilizing mission seemed to be failing.

One might have thought that in the face of such fears the colonial authorities would ensure that every effort was made to compel children to remain in school for as long as possible. Instead, by Law 31 of 1892, beginning in 1894 the *maximum* age of attendance was lowered from sixteen to fifteen years of age, and in the following year still further to fourteen. Law 23 of 1899 then raised the *minimum* age from five to six. The restriction of the school age from six to fourteen years was expected to save approximately forty-five hundred pounds per annum.[35] At the same time, however, where higher education was not available, the laws permitted the inspector of schools to establish a seventh standard or grade in some schools, at which selected pupils could stay to age sixteen, but only if they were of the same sex as the teacher.[36]

A major concern, then, was the potential for sexual impropriety between the predominantly male teachers and their female pupils. This meant, however, that it was mainly girls who were required to leave school early, thus robbing them of time there. This was especially problematic as there were fewer girls than boys in school to start with (see appendix 5, table 3). However, financial considerations and a "higher" moral imperative (the need to protect the virtue of young girls) combined in this context to curtail the exposure of at least some children to the broader civilizing influences of a Christian education. It was a fine balancing act.

The gender inequity could be justified, presumably, by the Victorian precept that education was not as important for girls as for boys. The Quakers, however, saw it differently, albeit again on moral grounds. When girls had to leave school at fourteen, "They do not know but little at that age", and since they were left in their homes and their fields, "the chances multiply every year that they will fall into lives of sin". This was especially so because many children began school quite late, and were just beginning to learn when the law required that they withdraw. Further, those who had a desire to pursue their education beyond age fourteen could not do so because of this law "which has its existence for moral reasons". The Jamaica Union of Teachers also claimed that by being forced to stay home, "a large *vagrant* class" would be created, or else the children would develop "vicious habits". But Governor Swettenham cynically countered, "If their home influences are of such a nature as to develop these, then attendance at school for a few hours daily would hardly save them."[37]

Compulsory Education

More puzzling was the attitude of the colonial authorities to compulsory education. To people who were so concerned about civilizing the Jamaican masses, compulsion should have recommended itself. But from the time this idea was first mooted in 1880, a variety of reasons were advanced in opposition. The inspector of schools cited the following: the habits and customs of the lower classes, especially the country peasantry; the great difficulty in obtaining reliable information as to the state of the population in the numerous settlements scattered throughout the interior of the country, and in influencing the people by means other than the religious institutions; the mountainous terrain and poor roads, and the way the people were scattered in isolated spots along the ravines and hillsides, which ostensibly presented "most formidable" difficulties in enforcing compulsory education; the "extreme sensitiveness" of the people to any interference between them and their children, and their resentment of the slightest attempt to control them in domestic matters. To enforce attendance of their children at school by the arm of the law would produce immense irritability, which might lead to disastrous consequences. The inspector also pointed to strong denominational preferences among parents, which would be inconvenient under the compulsory system and would probably frustrate the whole design of such a measure. Besides, like the officials in Trinidad, he cited the cost of implementing compulsory education as a major deterrent. The machinery that would be necessary to run the compulsory system would be enormous and beyond the power of the government to provide, while the expense of such a system would be very great and probably far beyond what could be legitimately appropriated to education. Therefore, a special tax would be needed to raise revenue; this would prove to be obnoxious to the people, who would rather pay fees as they were already doing.[38]

The idea of a tax to support compulsory education was bound to turn people off, but that was precisely how it was sold to the public; not surprisingly, even organizations long associated with education, like the London Missionary Society, opposed it on those grounds.[39] Unquestionably the parlous state of Jamaica's economy did make it inconceivable to its colonial officials that the costs of compulsory education could be met out of the colony's shrunken public revenues. Indeed, when Law 31 of 1892 made provision to introduce compulsory education (from January 1895) to "a limited extent" and in "a tentative manner", it also proposed to fund it by a school tax on houses that was expected to yield ten thousand pounds per annum.[40] Nothing came of that, however, and despite the recommendation of the 1898 Education Commission that compulsory education should be instituted in 1900, Governor Hemming baulked at the idea, partially on account of the high cost of implementation.[41]

But there might have been other, sinister motives for the official reluctance to introduce compulsory education. Apart from taking a "highly principled" position on the issue by arguing that education was a matter of faith and conscience for black Jamaicans and thus could not be enforced by law, Governor Musgrave thought that

> Compulsory education is . . . far too much advanced treatment for the lower strata of population which fifty years ago had not emerged from a debasing state of slavery in which any education at all was forbidden and even marriage was discouraged. What these people first need is all the help that can be afforded to them in moral training, in improving the character of their homes, and their standards of domestic and social life. When these are sufficiently raised there is ample evidence that they will be keenly alive to the advantages of secular education. To stimulate that now by artificial pressure can I fear only produce a distorted development, and more of a class of which there are already too many[:] the half educated vagabonds who are too proud of their smattering of knowledge to be able to dig, but to beg are not ashamed.[42]

How far these views were shared by other officials, or indeed by the local elites, is difficult to ascertain. But embedded in them is the apprehension that education was encouraging some people to leave agriculture – especially plantation agriculture, the core of the colonial economy – and threatening social unrest among those who could not find jobs that they thought "their smattering of knowledge" entitled them to. So while education might have been considered desirable to "improve" the character of the people, care also had to be taken not to embark on any measure that might cause them to forget their place and primary function in society: to provide labour. Robert Stewart notes that "the education of the peasantry and estate laborers in proper attitudes of industry" became a major preoccupation of the churches after 1865, for which purpose they published two newspapers, the *Queen's Newsman* and the *Jamaica Instructor*.[43] The duty to work was just as important to the construction of a civilized society as the character of its people. It was, once more, a fine balancing act.

There were some, however, both locally and abroad, who were not happy with the way the pendulum was swinging. I. Hales of the Colonial Office thought that Musgrave's expectations of raising the moral standards of the domestic and social life of black parents were not likely to be realized, and that it was clearly to the upcoming generation – through the agency of education, compulsory or otherwise – that they must look for this improvement. His superior, Edward Wingfield, asserted that he hardly thought the "negroes" would entertain a conscientious objection to being compelled to educate their children and that if they did, it was not one which should be indulged. Although compulsion would probably set the people against education *per se*, the risk was preferable to leaving so large a proportion of the juvenile population to "run wild". The secretary of state, the Earl of Kimberley, also felt that for the sake of the children and the general good of the community, some measures were urgently needed, perhaps beginning with compulsory education in Kingston.[44] Yet they did not insist on it.

Likewise the *Gleaner*, comparing the situation in Jamaica with that in Germany, France and "all over progressive Europe", argued that "compulsory education is considered vitally necessary". The section of the community that was being educated was being "kept back" by the section that was not: "The children that are not sent to school are drags on the wheels of public progress." Since the 1880s, it noted, "opinion in Jamaica has been that compulsion would be needed and must come; but we pause and stop in the action needed to give effect to it".[45] This was the fundamental dilemma that persistently dogged the local elites: how could they claim themselves to be members of an enlightened and civilized society if the vast majority of their fellow citizens were ignorant and superstitious? Oddly, no one referred to the experience of Guyana, where compulsory education had in fact been implemented in 1876, more or less simultaneously with the mother country itself, where it was gradually implemented between 1870 and 1880.[46]

Continued prodding by various sections of the society eventually led in 1910 to another law sanctioning compulsory education, but it was not until 1912 that it was finally implemented, and then only in Kingston (including Port Royal), Falmouth and Lucea. The initial impact was not great. Despite the fact that parents and guardians were liable to be fined if their children did not attend school, and imprisoned if they did not pay those fines, attendance in Kingston in 1912 increased only by 24 per cent, from 4,426 to 5,480, while in Falmouth the numbers rose from 155 to just 199 and in Lucea from 205 to 223. Hence, further action seemed necessary, and the legislature moved from one extreme to the other – from utter inaction to draconian action. Laws 6 of 1913 and 35 of 1914 empowered the school boards to declare any child "an incorrigible truant" if he or she were "persistently absent" from school; sanctioned the whipping – up to twelve strokes with a strap or a cane – of any male child declared an incorrigible truant, under the order of a resident magistrate or a court of petty sessions; and allowed attendance officers to "seize and arrest" such a child during school hours and take him or her to any school in the district. The laws also provided that when a parent was prosecuted for not sending a child to school, the offence was automatically "proven" and the defendant had to prove her or his defence.[47]

These laws were harsh in both their conceptualization and their application, and were not supported by the governor, the attorney general or the Colonial Office; but the Kingston School Board insisted on them and was allowed to have its way. A number of parents were summoned before the attendance committee of the board due to their children's nonattendance at school. Governor Manning observed that while there were some cases of negligence on the part of parents, it was found that in a large number of cases, parents who had to leave their homes for work early in the morning, and had first supplied their children with all the necessities for going to school, were nevertheless summoned if the children had instead gone to play in the streets. It was patently unjust for such parents to be punished when the fault was not theirs. In 1913 six children were declared "incorrigible truants", and in February 1914 one boy was whipped in Kingston, but there were no whippings in either Falmouth or Lucea.[48]

The Colonial Office was none too impressed by this law. C.T. Davis argued that sections of the law were unjust, while George Grindle opined that the whole law seemed oppressive and open to abuse. C.A. Harris observed that although the strap was "hallowed" by ancient use in many parts of the United Kingdom, he had never heard of it being legalized anywhere. All in all, he found the law to be "a most unsatisfactory piece of legislation". Yet they allowed it to stand, for the greater good of "civilization" in the colony. The Colonial Office, advised Grindle, must trust the school boards and magistrates to mitigate the rigours of the law.[49]

Curricular and Extra-Curricular Activity

The role of the elementary schools in the period was not simply to impart the rudiments of knowledge for social functioning.[50] They played a crucial role in attempting to mould Jamaican children into civilized Christians and model British colonials, proud of the heritage of the supposed motherland and delighted to share in the glory, protection and civilization that the British Empire bestowed. In order to achieve this, the content of the curriculum was simply imported, without regard for its (un)suitability. According to the *Semi-Weekly Gleaner* in the 1870s, the conservative European believed that

> having changed climate, habits, duties, responsibilities, surroundings &c.,&c. for others totally different . . . the systems carried out by his fathers, in the old home, will necessarily suit the peculiarities of the new. . . . Because a school system has worked tolerably well in turning out English boys, for instance, into the world fit for its responsibilities and its cares, an almost exact copy of it must be equally suited for the little Darkey.

But the newspaper was eager to point out the error of this assumption, upon which the entire elementary system was based:

> The Negro child comes of a race of slaves, the English child of a race of free men. They are equal now in theory. We hope, in time, to make them equal in reality; not certainly, by lowering the standards of the latter but by improving that of the former. It will not do, however, to apply the system used for checking the bold, daring rule-breaking little Briton to the comparatively listless and obedient Negro child.[51]

What was at issue was not just the content of the curriculum but its thrust, which was likely to produce a markedly different end-product in black Jamaica than in white Britain.

Although the educational authorities did recognize that the foreign content of the curriculum, especially the lessons from the Royal Star Readers or the

Longman's series of readers, was unfamiliar to Jamaican children and placed them at a disadvantage, it was nevertheless retained. According to the education report of 1882–83,

> School children in Jamaica are greatly at a disadvantage in the matter of suitable school songs. A large proportion of the best songs in the singing books are wholly lacking in adaptation to them. The marvellous change from winter to spring, the fruitage of autumn, the experiences in the wheat fields and hay fields, the varied occupations in vineyards, mills and mines, the peculiar delights of winter, the glowing fire, the piercing cold, the snow and ice, – which form the texture or are woven into so many delightful school songs in other lands, – are here unknown. The range of selection is therefore much restricted; but certainly it is wise to keep within those limitations than to select songs which are as foreign to the children as if written in a different language. I believe, however, that "Snow! Snow! Beautiful Snow!" is a favourite song in our schools and "See How Merrily the Skaters Go!" is hardly less known.[52]

Nevertheless, the focus of a good education had to remain British. It might be lamentable that there was a "want of a good Geography and History of Jamaica for the use of schools", and that some schools had no map of Jamaica, but it was even worse that a larger number had none of Europe or England.[53] How then were the children of the empire supposed to know and appreciate the larger, glorious whole of which they and Jamaica were a part?

Ruby King notes that even after the turn of the twentieth century, when some attempt was made to introduce local materials into the curriculum, according to the revised Code of Regulations a child who had completed eight years of elementary schooling was expected to be able to read from a Standard Six reader containing "choice selections from Shakespeare, Tennyson, Longfellow and other standard authors", or from a current newspaper, the *Journal of Agriculture,* or the second *Tropical Reader.* She continues,

> In geography (with incidental history) pupils studied the world in broad outline and spent rather more time on Britain and the Empire. In the attempt to include Jamaican studies, the Code included the study of the location of parishes and parish capitals of Jamaica, prominent events in Jamaican history, and six leading persons "prominently connected with the history of England or Jamaica". The persons suggested were Alfred The Great, Henry V, Columbus, Queen Elizabeth [I], Cromwell, Rodney, Nelson, Wilberforce, Wellington, and General Gordon [of Khartoum fame]. Up to then apparently no Jamaican was considered prominently connected with Jamaican history.[54]

If, therefore, there was any generally recognized deficiency in the curriculum according to elite contemporaries, it was not in its British bias, but rather in its failure to teach the swarthy descendants of slaves an appreciation for the noble virtues and skills of agricultural work. By 1890 there was almost a universal call for agricultural and industrial education. The existing education programme, it was feared, was encouraging children to spurn manual labour. Said the *Colonial Standard* in 1893,

> In this country there unfortunately exists a strong antipathy to manual labour. An industrious, respectable yeoman or small settler in Manchester or St. Elizabeth sends his sons to school and the youngster, having received a smattering of learning, looks down with scorn on any employment involving manual labour, and leads the life of idleness which is too often the dismal prelude to a career of criminality and vice.[55]

What was required, therefore, was "the education of the hand as well as the head – an education adapted to the physical, intellectual and moral departments of our nature". This view was fully endorsed by the 1898 Education Commission, which stated that, among other things, the education system should aim to give fundamental manual and agricultural instruction in order that scholars could earn their living and discharge their duties as citizens. Further, argued the *Colonial Standard,* "If agricultural or industrial instruction formed a portion of the regular teaching at the elementary school, the probability is that the rising generation would acquire, unconsciously it may be, but effectually, a correct perception of the dignity, the duty, and the independence associated with honest labour of every description."[56]

This view became official education policy after Colonial Secretary Joseph Chamberlain issued orders in 1899 to the West Indian governments to institute agricultural education, and to transfer a considerable portion of the funds allocated for general education to agricultural education. This move, however, was strongly resisted by the Jamaica Union of Teachers, formed in 1895 and composed largely of the rising black and coloured middle-class intelligentsia, who viewed it as a deliberate step to hold back the social progress of black Jamaicans. According to Harry Goulbourne, they argued that elementary schools were not places to equip children with the training for a career, or to provide specialized knowledge at a basic level.[57] Ruby King notes that black and coloured parents also opposed agricultural training:

> Whereas colonial educators perceived schooling as a means of preparing black children for a life of toil in the field and in their homes or the homes of their betters,

black Jamaicans saw schooling as an escape route from agriculture to more socially respectable occupations such as school teaching. To these persons a more literary curriculum was more attractive, and many withdrew their children from school during sessions when practical agriculture was taught.[58]

Nevertheless, colonial officials continued to believe that education, if "properly conducted", would solve many of society's ills. Not only would it reform "the habits and character of our people", but it would also eradicate "the increasing crowds of social pariahs of every class, from the big, lazy, hulking loafer to the idle imp whose wits have been prematurely sharpened in every form and practice of wickedness".[59] It would instil the discipline and duty of honest work, considered so vital not just to economic growth, but to civilization itself. The work ethic, a critical characteristic of a civilized being, needed to be inculcated through education.

The schools' curriculum was also intended to train children to become good, worthy, civic-minded citizens. Reverend William Simms (acting inspector of schools in the 1880s, later a canon in the Anglican Church and headmaster of Jamaica College) argued, "The future of the country depended on the intelligent use of the franchise by the people who have it, and therefore the future of Jamaica depended largely on the education of the people." Since "ignorant people" tended to resist "improvement", education was necessary for there to be real progress.[60]

Thus, the "moral improvement" of the children was given no small amount of importance in the schools. As a leading Anglican cleric himself, Simms was fully supportive of religious education in the denominational schools, and urged "that there should be constant striving to train up the children to know the eternal principles of right and wrong". Hence, apart from scripture lessons, the children were taught aspects of civics. In 1907–8, for instance, "much prominence [was] given to the subject of Kindness – kind feeling and kind action towards animals generally, and loving care of little brothers and sisters in the home".[61]

Another means by which the schools tried to pass on civic lessons was through physical drills. While these were used in part to promote the pupil's health and "giv[e] him full possession of his physical powers", there was a higher purpose: to "build up the moral and intellectual nature, and so stand truly related to the whole life of the child or the man". Thus, the drills could assist in "the development of strength, speed, skill, self-control, accuracy, grace, endurance, courage, moral fibre, mental power, will power, *character*". No less importantly, they were believed to have a positive effect on "school discipline, in improving the alertness of the children's obedience".[62] Discipline and obedience to people in authority were very important lessons for later life in colonial society.

The authorities hoped that the penny savings banks that were established in many schools (and churches) would encourage the children in "habits of thrift" that they were likely to retain in their lives after school – "and if such habits become general, the effect upon the prosperity of the Island may be expected to be very marked". Thriftiness was considered an important characteristic of a civilized person because it reinforced the work ethic (by placing a value on earning and accumulating money and material possessions), and lessened the individual's dependence on the community and his or her likelihood of becoming indigent and a burden on the state or, alternatively, a criminal. Inculcating the habit of thrift and frugality, itself regarded as a virtue of civilization, in order to accumulate savings with which to acquire material goods (*in moderation,* of course) was central to this social philosophy.[63]

Teachers

That the school system was as much a means of "moral upliftment" as it was a system of instruction was clear not only in the lessons that were taught (which gave a primary place to religious knowledge, character training and civic education), but also in the careful attention given to the morality of the teachers themselves. According to the 1867 regulations, "the respectability or moral character of Teachers" was a key part of what determined their status within the system. As in Trinidad, it was expected that the lives of classroom teachers should exemplify the influence of religion. They were, after all, "the main cogs" in the dissemination of religious instruction to the younger generations of the colony.[64]

The role of the teacher, as leader and trainer of the end-product of the civilizing process, was held under fairly strict scrutiny, and teachers could be and were dismissed for morally questionable behaviour. The most common offence that warranted teachers being placed on the significantly titled "Black List" was "immorality" – that is, illicit sexual relations. In 1893–94 alone as many as "twenty-eight fresh names" were added to the list, mainly because "of the common immorality of the country as heretofore".[65] What the education reports do not make clear is whether these "immoral acts" occurred within the schoolroom (between teachers or with students) or referred to the teachers' private lives, which, in the scheme of the nineteenth century, did not really exist. The difficulty, however, was to prove allegations of immorality against the teachers:

> From the nature of case[s] most of the offences committed remained undiscovered and uninvestigated, and it is to be feared that the moral tone of many teachers is so little above that of the community in general, confessedly and deplorably low as that is, that it can have little of the elevating effect which we ought to [be] able to expect.[66]

Notwithstanding the intense scrutiny to which the teachers were subjected, it was claimed that the low salaries often discouraged people of the highest character and calibre from seeking those jobs. The education authorities, however, argued that it was not that teachers were not properly paid (the better class of teachers ostensibly being able to earn as much as or more than their peers in Germany), but that, because of their superior intelligence compared with the rest of the community, such people could earn even more "as a shopkeeper or planter, and as a consequence, the profession of teaching is left, for the most part, to men of low calibre". Since the government did not pay the whole salary of the teacher, that person was obliged to subsidize his or her income by other means. Hence, a significant number of the teachers did "catechetical duties on Sundays for which they receive distinct remuneration", while others made substantial supplemental incomes through agriculture.[67] This probably accounts, too, for why so many of them were late or spent too little time in the classroom.

The character issue was brought into sharp focus whenever teachers tried less honourable ways to boost their earnings. In too many cases, it seems, they resorted to falsification of registers and claimed to have taught more children than they actually did, in order to get more than their due in grants. As in Trinidad, the salary of the headteacher depended on the class of his or her certificate, the number of children who attended school regularly over the year, and the number who passed the annual examination. According to Campbell, "This system put a premium on the size of the school, hence the temptation – to which several headteachers succumbed – of dishonestly inflating the attendance registers."[68] This was a perennial problem in Jamaica where, as Inspector Thomas Capper reported in 1880–81, "the cases of fraudulent registration . . . are most gross and flagrant", and in nearly every case "systematic fraud" had been carried out. Although, after due investigation, some of the cases were proven without doubt, in no case did the teachers in question confess to the fraud. That in itself must have been of grave concern to the authorities, given the teachers' positions as role models and community leaders. The problem was compounded by the fact that, on occasion, school managers gave good character references to teachers who had been convicted of gross falsification of registers (even on the managers' own admission) when they sought employment elsewhere. This not only kept corrupt teachers in the school system but cast doubt on the character of the managers themselves, who were sometimes clergymen. An exasperated Capper naturally found "the laxity of opinion prevailing on the subject" to be "astonishing and almost incredible". Yet, despite his Victorian outrage, he decided for that year not to publish the names of the teachers who were found to be in violation, hoping to provide them with an opportunity to re-examine their behaviour. Perhaps this had some positive effect, since later in the period Capper reported that the number of cases of fraudulent registration was proportionately smaller than it had been.[69] The fundamental problem for the authorities was that the teachers, and some managers, were themselves moulded by the same "morally flawed" creole society that the social leaders were seeking to transform.

This clash between imported Victorian morality and creole convention occasionally brought local communities in conflict with the school authorities. For instance, in 1913 at the Moravian school at Eden (possibly in St Mary), a teacher was dismissed "owing to the refractory and insubordinate spirit evinced in his dealings with the manager". The teacher "took umbrage" at his notice of dismissal and called in the people to help him oppose the manager and to subvert his authority: "Accordingly some of the people, especially those of one district, mistakenly and readily fell in with the teacher's move and positively and fearlessly stated that if the teacher should be sent away they would withhold their subscription." The teacher's dismissal was indeed upheld, but all the protesters, except for one family, refused to pay their subscriptions. Further, they largely or entirely withdrew from divine service.[70] The challenge to the authority of the church was clear.

The expected role of the teacher was clearly enunciated by Reverend William Simms, acting inspector of schools, at a meeting of the Manchester Educational Association in December 1889. He informed those gathered that teachers were members of a noble profession and that they operated as "missionaries" in the schools. They could get great results from their students if they were "efficient teachers"; after all, he said, "An earnest, unselfish, high-minded man cannot fail to exert a great influence on his school." The teacher, in other words, was to be a moral leader, mentor and exemplar to his or her young, impressionable pupils. There was no gainsaying the fact that, as in other parts of the Caribbean and in the American South, the teacher's was a dual role: that of secular teacher *and* auxiliary Christian missionary.[71]

Teacher Training Colleges

As the need for competent and morally upright teachers became apparent if the elementary school system was to deliver a civilized product, both the government and the churches turned their attention to setting up training institutions. The earliest of these, the Mico Institution, was set up under Lady Mico's Charity in 1834. In 1870, as more and better-trained teachers were required, the government began to subsidize Mico, and it also established a training college at Stony Hill. Although the latter was closed in 1890, a female college (later named Shortwood) was set up in 1885. Of the churches, while the Wesleyan Methodists had it in mind that York Castle (see below) should train teachers for their schools, that goal was never quite realized. The Moravians established two teacher training schools: one for males at Fairfield, Manchester, in 1840, and the other for females at Bethabara in 1861, which was later relocated to Bethlehem in the Santa Cruz mountains. Likewise, the Baptists established the Calabar Institution in 1842 to train teachers and ministers; in 1897 the Roman Catholics established St Joseph's College in Kingston, with half a dozen female students.[72]

These voluntary denominational training colleges, as they were called, received grants-in-aid from the government,[73] which consequently prescribed the basic course of study that lasted two years. This focused on sharpening the teachers' skills in the principal subject areas of elementary education – reading, writing, arithmetic and religious knowledge – and also on practice teaching and class management. But if Bethlehem can be used as a guide, greater demands were placed on the female pupil teachers, who, in addition to the course prescribed by the government, also did Euclid, algebra, French, harmonium playing, and "considerable [amounts] of housework".[74]

Although the Mico and government schools were nonsectarian, all the teacher training colleges subjected their students to heavy doses of religious instruction as part of the required training to teach in elementary schools; enormous attention was also paid to character development. This was very similar to what Campbell found at the denominational training colleges in Trinidad, where pupil teachers were encouraged to live in so as to be wholly immersed in religious doctrine, and also what Higginbotham found at Spelman (Baptist) Seminary in Atlanta in the United States, where the tutors "sought to surround their students with refined manners, 'correct' Baptist doctrine, and 'proper' religious and social deportment". Hence, they were required to attend devotional exercises daily, as well as a class in the systematic study of the Bible. Once graduated, these teachers were more or less intended to be lay "missionaries" and several, as already noted, served as catechists on Sunday. As has been shown above, the products of the teacher training colleges were to be moral messengers, even if some fell short of the ideal. They were received into the communities where they worked as second-tier missionaries and highly respected leaders of community organizations. Yet, as in other Caribbean territories and the United States, they formed part of a black and coloured middle-class whose status relied heavily on their adherence to the "superior" white culture, and oft-times found themselves at odds with the "uncultured" people from whom many of them came, among whom they worked, and whom they sought to "elevate".[75]

Secondary Education

While for both the missionary societies and the colonial authorities the main thrust of schooling was at the elementary level, there was also a recognition that a limited measure of higher education was necessary to provide a small body of middle-class native leaders, steeped in British culture, to carry forward the civilizing process, and also to provide a cadre of suitable persons, imbued with sentiments of imperial loyalty, who could function efficiently and intelligently in middle and lower administrative positions. "Secondary Education" was defined by law to be

> a course of Education which does not consist chiefly of elementary instruction in reading, writing and arithmetic, but which includes instruction in Latin, the English language and literature, modern languages, mathematics, natural and applied science, commercial arithmetic, the principles of agriculture, commercial geography, book-keeping, shorthand, drawing . . . and generally in the higher branches of knowledge.

Religious knowledge formed an essential part of the secondary curriculum for, as stipulated in the government regulations, "The leading facts of the Old and New Testaments, especially the history and teaching of the Lord Jesus Christ, and the essential truths of the Gospel [should be] familiarly known."[76]

By the "secular" definition, there were very few schools in the late 1860s that could be classified as secondary, and those that could were generally out of the financial reach of most Jamaicans, including many whites. As they were all small, private schools, their fees were high. According to London missionary W.J. Gardner, in 1869 the Church of Scotland's Collegiate School, for instance, charged twelve pounds a year, along with heavy "extras". When it was amalgamated with the Church of England High School in 1881, the charges for board, washing and repairing of pupils' clothing amounted to ten pounds three shillings *per term*. Basic tuition was separate: two and three pounds per term in the junior and senior departments respectively. Instruction in drawing and modern languages attracted additional charges of seven shillings and sixpence per course per term. Clearly only the very wealthy could afford these high fees; in 1883 the upper-class parents of 150 children did.77

Likewise, when in 1871 James D. Ford decided to open a "Classical and Commercial Academy . . . for the instruction of Youth of both sexes, in association with the members of his own Family", only the well-to-do could afford the fees of twelve pounds per annum for day scholars and forty-eight pounds per annum for boarders. At this Kingston University School, Ford offered "the usual English course", including mental and commercial arithmetic, geometry, history and geography, with drawing and music as extras, in addition to Greek, Latin, Hebrew, French, German, Spanish and Italian. These subjects, spanning both the "modern" and "classical" branches of knowledge, were not only designed "to fit a boy either for business or for professional life", but also to provide "a sound, practical [and] liberal Education, based upon high moral and intellectual principles".78

The inability of children from less privileged families to access such schools motivated Gardner to propose the establishment of a "middle class school" in Kingston, not simply because he felt that the socially mobile black and coloured people needed "a higher class" of education, but also to attract a class from which a suitable "Native Agency" of brown and black Jamaicans could be obtained to advance the civilizing missionary effort. White children, he recognized, as products of a society which he and his British peers thought morally deficient, also needed to be brought early under "proper Christian influence", which a good, affordable high school would provide. Although the London Missionary Society directors in London did not support Gardner's scheme, his idea was evidently shared by the Presbyterians who, according to him, had established a middle-class school (probably the Collegiate School) "on the north side" of the city, and by the Jesuits who in 1868 resuscitated St

George's College in Kingston. Another effort was subsequently undertaken by Jesuit Father Jaeckel who in 1877 opened a "Classical School" called Mary Villa College in Duke Street with 104 students. The syllabus of English, French, Latin, Greek and most of the sciences was designed to fit "the college boys for respectable lucrative places in their after life".[79]

The Wesleyan Methodists were not far behind. A trained core of anglicized native leaders was required to carry forward their civilizing work:

> We are especially anxious for the education of youths of the purely African race. It is to this class that our Mission is specially sent, as they form the majority of the population. Much painful remark in connexion with the chronic decrease in our West Indian Societies, has been made in England on the fact that after three quarters of a century our ministry in the West Indies is confined to Europeans, or persons of European descent, the inference being that the African population have not had their fair share of attention, especially as regards their Educational necessities. We are aware of the peculiar difficulties which have stood in the way but are nevertheless not less anxious that these should be grappled with and overcome. If our Baptist Brethren have succeeded in raising up a purely African Ministry, why should this be beyond our ability?[80]

Thus, in 1874 the Wesleyans acquired a "suitable property" at Brown's Town where the York Castle High School was established and a theological college attached. Then they set about working on the students. "Family worship" was conducted every morning and evening: "The school is opened and closed with prayer and the reading of Scripture is part of the daily work." In addition, two "Society" meetings (that is, amongst themselves) and two public prayer meetings were held every week, public worship on Sundays, Bible and catechism classes for the pupils, and a Bible class for the servants (so that even the "dependent" helpers of the institution's community were not exempt from the influence of Christian education and doctrine). Soon "the discipline and moral and religious influence imposed on the boys was very satisfactory"; indeed some had experienced a "change of heart". The first principal, Andrew Kesson, was thus sanguine that "the School may expect . . . a long and useful career and the whole Establishment – a little city on a hill – will spread its influences far and wide". By all accounts this expectation was borne out, as the *Gleaner* described York Castle in 1885 as "perhaps the foremost educational establishment in Jamaica". Indeed, in the first fifteen years after the prestigious Jamaica Scholarship was established in 1881, York Castle scholars won it on eight occasions. The school not only featured "well kept promenades, recreation grounds, [and] a large cricket ground", among other things, but the principal, Reverend W.C. Murray, and his able staff had been quite successful at adopting "the system of English and Classical Education".[81]

The Calabar Institution, established by the Baptists near Rio Bueno in 1842, was designed as a theological training college for their African and local missions. It was moved to Kingston in 1869, and after the Baptist Missionary Society withdrew from Jamaica and the West Indies in 1892, Calabar remained its only interest in the Caribbean. In the mid-1880s, Calabar had a high school for those who sought "a more advanced education than the elementary schools usually supply", but it did not last. In September 1912, however, a new high school was established with sixteen boarders and thirteen day boys. It quickly established an excellent reputation, and by 1915 it had eighty students.[82] Again, the juxtaposition of a denominational high school with a theological college is clearly suggestive of the programme of religious indoctrination to which the students were subjected and the high emphasis placed on "character" training.

In Spanish Town a "Graded Middle Class School" was established in 1876 with monies from the Beckford and Smith charity. The curriculum of the secondary grade was standard (languages, mathematics and bookkeeping) with a heavy dose of religious knowledge thrown in. Indeed, the provisions of the trust required that the principal should be an Anglican and that the "distinctive Church of England teaching . . . will be given daily throughout the school". There could be no clearer statement of the social intention of the school's management. The fees were nine pounds per annum, excluding books and stationery.[83]

All this meant, as King notes, that lower-class children had no access to secondary education, since they could not meet the entry requirements of either paying fees, belonging to a higher social class, or having had previous exposure to secondary education. For this reason, King labels secondary education "middle class education", and she quotes Frank Cundall as saying that secondary education was of a high grade, intended for "those classes of the community who would value it, if placed within their reach but whose means do not enable them to send their children to Europe for the purpose of receiving it" (as the upper classes did). Thus, for King, this "middle class secondary" education was sharply different and distinct from the "lower class elementary" system:

> The two systems were designed to be separate from each other. It was not intended for working class children to attend secondary schools; the superior secondary schools were intended specifically for middle class children. . . . The

two systems operated like parallel lines which never met. "Inferior" elementary education for the many, "superior" secondary education for the few became the norm.[84]

But by the late 1870s it had become patently obvious that neither the churches nor private individuals could meet the growing need for secondary-level institutions in the island. The government, which had until then been content to do nothing, finally emerged from its inertia and set up the Jamaica Schools Commission. Law 34 of 1879 authorized the commission to establish a national grammar school, to be called Jamaica High School. It also empowered the commission to visit the endowed schools across the island and if necessary prepare plans for the efficient utilization of their trust funds. Accordingly, schemes were prepared to manage the trusts of Manning's Free School in Westmoreland, Rusea's in Hanover, Titchfield in Portland, the Munro and Dickenson's in St Elizabeth and several free schools in Vere and Manchester. The management of these trusts was put on a sound financial basis, the schools were upgraded, and surplus monies were utilized to finance scholarships tenable at Jamaica High School. Over time each of these "free schools" was transformed into a high school, including Potsdam (established in 1856 for boys) and Hampton (for girls) which were funded by the Munro and Dickenson charity.[85]

The government further attempted to facilitate the expansion of secondary education by Law 32 of 1892, which laid down the procedures for establishing and maintaining new high schools in areas where they were deemed necessary. These were to be entirely government schools, funded out of public revenues, and they were to enable students to pass the Junior Oxford and Cambridge Local Examinations. Fees would range between three and eight pounds per annum, thus making them affordable for middle-class Jamaicans; the amount to be spent on any one school was limited to five hundred pounds for the establishment of a school, and two hundred pounds a year for its maintenance. Teachers were to be appointed by the governor on the recommendation of the board and superintending inspector of schools, and scholarships were to be provided, tenable at any efficient school within or outside of the island. In 1895 the Montego Bay High School was established under this law.[86]

The flagship of the secondary education system, however, was the Jamaica High School. Formerly the Jamaica Free School at Walton, St Ann, it was transformed by Law 34 of 1879 into an elite grammar school modelled along the lines of those in Britain, and relocated to Kingston in 1885. Jamaica High School enjoyed similar status and had similar objectives to elite boys' schools

Figure 19. Montego Bay High School
Source: Alfred Leader, *Through Jamaica with a Kodak* (Bristol: John Wright, 1907). Courtesy of the National Library of Jamaica.

in other West Indian colonies, such as The Queen's College in Guyana, The Queen's Collegiate School (later Queen's Royal College) and the College of the Immaculate Conception (later St Mary's) in Trinidad, and Harrison and Lodge in Barbados. As Governor Norman indicated, one of the primary objectives of this school was to provide a high-quality education to train "a proper number of qualified candidates for the public service". The school, in other words, would groom a cadre of young men for positions of leadership in the service of king and country; and the inclusion of religious instruction in the curriculum would ensure that the "correct" religious, moral and civic character-building qualities were inculcated in the boys. This school thus epitomized the ideal of education for God and empire by providing "a good classical, mathematical and general education" along with religious education, which was "given generally throughout the school". The curriculum more or less aped what was offered at the grammar schools in Britain: English, Latin, Greek, German and French; mathematics, chemistry and science; geography, history and political economy. The presence of a playing field indicates that, as for its British models, sports and games, especially cricket, formed a prominent part of the curriculum. While students could gain entry as "paying term boarders" or "paying weekly boarders", the fees were high: sixteen to twenty pounds per term for the former, according to age, and thirteen to

Figure 20. Jamaica High School

sixteen pounds for the latter. However, the award of full and partial scholarships made places available to bright children from both town and country.[87]

By 1912, when it was renamed Jamaica College, the school could be considered a successful clone of the British grammar school. According to H.H. Piggott, visiting inspector of the English Board of Education, in his report on the condition of public secondary education in Jamaica, "In its general standard of work the school compares favourably with the better English Grammar schools of a similar size. Games and school societies are well organized and the boys are trained in self-government much on the lines of a good English Boarding School." There could be no higher praise offered for an institution modelled on the British standard and doing its utmost to turn out good, loyal, Christian British colonials. Several of these lads volunteered to fight (and died) for king and country in the First World War.[88]

Secondary Education of Girls

The focus of secondary education was markedly skewed in favour of boys. This is not surprising since, according to Victorian tenets, the woman's place was in the home. Insofar as girls were to be educated, it was to provide them with the necessary attributes to become good wives and mothers. An education to provide them with "accomplished gentility" by enabling them to read for entertainment, to converse intelligently, to sing and play a musical instrument, and to sew and knit, was considered sufficient for upper-class girls to qualify as prospective wives for eligible suitors who might come knocking.[89] Because they were expected to have and supervise an army of domestic servants, they were not required to learn to do too many onerous household chores like cooking, cleaning or washing, although they still needed to know how to perform them. Education was also designed to instil in them good Christian values for a wholesome family life and for transmission to their offspring. The foundation of civilized society, after all, began in the home with the family, and women as good nurturing wives and mothers were vital to that institution. Women were in fact expected to be the moral guardians of society and, as they were also considered the "weaker" sex (evidenced by their periodic "sickness" of menstruation), their education reflected that expectation. As Marion Amies put it, "a high moral tone was considered paramount to intellectual development; training in practical housewifery gave way to the acquisition of accomplishments and ornamental handicrafts; initiative and confidence were subdued to submissive dependency".[90]

By the late nineteenth century, however, secondary education for girls was increasingly seen as important for the enhancement of womanly qualities and virtues. It would provide the finish to turn unsophisticated girls into refined young ladies. Thus in 1875, for instance, Methodist Reverend W.C. Murray lamented "the defectiveness of the machinery that exists for the education and training of our girls". The *Morning Journal* added its own voice: "They say that woman's proper place is in the domestic circle. We grant all that. But is it a fact that a woman is less qualified to be a good wife, a careful housewife, an affectionate and discreet trainer of her children, because she is a very highly educated person?" As in Trinidad, then, secondary education for girls in late-nineteenth-century Jamaica was designed to make them more accomplished and refined wives and mothers of professional men. As Campbell states, it "could increase the respectability and marriageability of daughters" to upper-class men.[91]

In response to this perceived need, various schools were gradually established for young ladies, and their offerings were in absolute concord with the gender values of Victorian culture. According to the *Gleaner* in 1875, the Roman Catholic Church was among the earliest to speak to this particular need, as it established a seminary for young ladies which operated without regard to colour.92 This aroused sectarian jealousy among Protestant missionaries. Methodist George Sargeant expressed a concern that the needs of the increasing numbers of blacks and coloureds in the middle class who had no suitable schools in the country were being answered by the Catholics. His colleague, S. Goodyer, complained, "Some of the brilliant girls of this Island are obliged to go either to some Ritualistic Parson or else *direct* and *straight* into the influence of Popery to be educated by Jesuits."93

Notwithstanding those jealousies, the Roman Catholics continued to reach out to Jamaica's girls. By the early twentieth century, the Alpha Convent High School comprised both boarding and day school facilities "in which a high class English education [was] imparted" to girls. The Sisters of St Francis at the Convent of the Immaculate Conception also operated boarding and day schools where English and French, the catechism, geography, history, arithmetic, algebra, bookkeeping, astronomy, typewriting, shorthand, chronology, plain and ornamental writing, needlework, and embroidery were taught to girls.94

To counteract this growing influence of "popery", Sargeant called for an increased number of nonconformist high schools that would help to take forward the work of "higher Christian civilization" by giving a Christian character to the domestic life of the country. By 1878 he had devised a plan to found a high school for the education of middle-class girls and he wrote to England, asking that two ladies be found to run the school.95 The establishment in 1881 of the Barbican School for Girls, located in Liguanea (St Andrew) and headed by Susan Skinner, was the result. At the school, "Religion, as the divinely formative and sustaining force in a noble character and a pure womanhood, will be carefully taught [free] from Sectarian tendencies. The course of instruction comprises all branches of a thorough English Education – English Language and Composition, Arithmetic, Geography, History and Literature, Religious Knowledge, French, Algebra, Euclid, Political Economy, Botany and Geology, Calisthenics and Needlework." Music, singing, drawing, theory and harmony class, washing and special medical attendance were available as "extras".96

The Baptists were not far behind when Reverend William M. Webb established the Trelawny Girls' School near Stewart Town in 1884. Relocated to more spacious quarters in 1895 and renamed Westwood High School for Girls, by 1913 it had seventy pupils, a library of three hundred volumes, a tennis court and recreation ground.97 In 1890 two *Gleaner* reporters were

Figure 21. Barbican School for Girls
© Trustees for Methodist Church Purposes; used by permission of Methodist Publishing House.

impressed with the curriculum and management of the school, which prepared the girls for the lives they were expected to lead afterwards:

> The course of instruction embraces all the branches of a thorough English education, together with French, drawing, painting, music and singing, calisthenics, needle and fancy work. In addition to this the girls are taught to sew, cut out and make dresses, plain work, and all details of household work. They assist in the laundry, in washing and ironing, in caring for their rooms and in cooking the meals. All this class of work is done under proper superintendence and with the help of proper hired servants, the idea being to give the girls thorough instruction in all matters pertaining to household management.[98]

The "civilizing" objective of the programme, too, was considered laudable:

> Every effort is made to cultivate in the girls a high moral and religious standard of feeling and character and to fit them for any position at all as useful women. . . . We were quite surprised at what we saw there of the progress made by the black and colored girls, and the high plane of education they had reached. The girls who go from such a school, with a liberal education and good attainment, must spread around them in their homes and localities an influence for good and for the uplifting of the people that cannot be too highly considered.[99]

The Church of England, too, answered the call for middle-class girls' high schools when they established St Mary's College, close to the border of Manchester and St Elizabeth: "It is designed as a High School for Girls in which is formed a class for preparing Teachers in private families or High Schools", and it provided instruction in English and foreign languages, science, vocal and instrumental music, and drawing. The costs of boarding and tuition amounted to ten pounds and five shillings per quarterly term. A similar course of education could be obtained from the Diocesan High School, formed in 1907 in Brown's Town: "The object of the school is to afford a liberal and thorough education for girls combined with moral and religious training in the doctrines of the Church of England."[100]

Some of the endowed trusts also provided secondary education facilities for girls. These included Wolmer's, Hampton, Manning's, Titchfield and Rusea's. But the number of girls who benefited was small.[101] Private educators also set up high schools for girls. In 1875, a "middle-class boarding and day school" at Mt Moses, five miles from Stony Hill, was advertised in the *Gleaner*. The prospectus promised "all the advantages of a fair English education, residence in England only excepted, with a climate quite as salubrious". English history, elocution, botany, zoology were some of the subjects tackled under the supervision of J.J. Wood, a former assistant government inspector of thirty years' experience.[102] Also, in 1876 Mrs Palmer, wife of a Kingston clergyman, started a seminary for the education of young ladies. She was even more explicit in her search for middle-class students, promising to receive girls of any colour so long as their character was "as good as their neighbour". According to the *Gleaner*,

> The want of such an Institution in this Island had hitherto been severely felt by the genuine Negro; for, say what you may, at present, the black girl of rich parents is as far from being received into the best Jamaican Schools as she was thirty years ago. Now that a liberal education . . . is fairly within the reach of Quashie's daughters, it remains to be seen, whether he intends to elevate his off-spring, by laying hold of the opportunities which this new Institution will afford him.[103]

Whether or not "Quashie" could indeed avail himself of such opportunities for his daughters is debatable, but the demand for higher education for girls was certainly growing towards the end of the nineteenth century. When in 1891, for instance, the Kingston High School for Girls was opened in Duke Street, the number of girls increased so quickly that by April 1892 the school had to seek new premises on Elletson Road.[104] But perhaps many of those whose parents could afford to pay for their education already knew that their future did not depend on how well they performed. The Girls' High School in East Street, Kingston, according to its headmistress Annie Johnstone, attracted girls from "the best class of people in the island . . . [who] will not have to earn their own living, but will be supported by their parents, if necessary to the end of their lives". Hence, there was a clear impression that although possibly intelligent, the girls were not especially studious, and had a tendency to gravitate towards "showy" subjects such as "elocution". While many had fairly good characters, they were reputedly quite self-willed with less than ideal ideas of morality, having been pampered by their parents and influenced by their servants. The tendency to pursue "softer" subjects was also in evidence at Miss Harris's High School for Girls, where a prize giving ceremony in December 1894 showed off skills in piano playing, essay writing, elocution, scripture, music, drawing, drill, botany and needlework.[105]

At many of these schools, therefore, "It [was] not uncommon to see black girls taking lessons in music, languages and other branches of knowledge, from white instructors, preparatory to marriage with respectable negroes." Not only did the education prepare these girls for Victorian marriage to appropriate persons, but when delivered well "the ideals of European civilization [could not be] more pure and honest".[106]

But not all female educators favoured this type of "genteel" curriculum for girls. Both Miss M.M. Barrows, headmistress of Wolmer's (Girls'), and Miss Long, principal of the Kingston High School for Girls, felt that their charges should be exposed to a more worthwhile education, aimed at making them independent, self-sufficient women on par with men. Miss Barrows argued that mathematics, biological science, literature, language and history were some of the important areas of study that young ladies should pursue. She believed that mental needs should be balanced with moral and spiritual ones, and physical exercise should also be encouraged by games and nontrivial pursuits.[107]

Miss Long believed that her institution was training the girls to be "honourable women, self-respecting, and respecting the rights of others, appreciating public as well as private virtues, loving learning for its own sake, and regarding moral qualities and intellectual gifts more than position, wealth or dress". As was the case at Westwood, the Kingston High School offered a course of study that included mathematics, science, modern languages, history, and English language and literature, aimed at preparing the girls for the future, "whatever their lot in life".[108]

By 1912 secondary education for girls had become so well developed that they were offered a Jamaica Scholarship worth one hundred and fifty pounds (fifty pounds less than the boys' scholarship), tenable for three years at an English university. However, the selection criteria occasioned considerable controversy. Whereas the boys' scholarship was based entirely on academic achievement in examinations, the girls were to be subject to evaluation by a selection committee, confidential reports from their headmistresses, and a bias towards those who were "devoted" to "games". The unevenness of the selection process and its apparent attempt to exclude some girls who might excel academically, allegedly because of "their class and colour", were rejected out of hand by some. However, the director of education, J.R. Williams, claimed that 75 per cent of the marks towards the scholarship were awarded for "scholastic proficiency", while the selection committee awarded the other 25 per cent for three main areas of accomplishment: achievements in art or music; personal qualities of truth, courage, devotion to duty, unselfishness, kindliness, sympathy and morality, as attested to by the headmistress; and devotion to games, also attested to by the candidate's headmistress and school records. Nevertheless, the charge of bias against the brilliant girls of the lower classes continued to be levelled, and a demand was made that the girls be awarded the scholarship on the same basis of merit on which the boys earned theirs.[109]

Tertiary Education

Throughout the period under study, tertiary-level education hardly featured significantly on the agenda of either the churches or the state. The nearest attempt to establishing a tertiary-level college in the island was a half-hearted and ill-conceived plan by William Chadwick, M.A., and Grant Allen, B.A., who (apparently with the support of Governor Grant) in August 1873 announced their intention to set up Queen's College in Spanish Town under the auspices of the government. They solicited letters of application and invited prospective entrants to an examination. Only four candidates, however, presented themselves for the entrance examination. Realizing their isolation, "[t]hey were 'plucked', and 'made tracks' for home". This attempt was an abysmal failure. Said the *Morning Journal*, "We are not among those who would rejoice at the idea of the failure of this thing. It is something full of good to the country and deserved to succeed, and we hope it will." But, it claimed, the effort failed because public expectations of the institution were too low. The college was perceived as little more than a glorified elementary school.¹¹⁰

The *Handbook of Jamaica*, however, saw it quite differently. It argued that education was not sufficiently developed in Jamaica to supply the college with enough qualified applicants:

> In short, too great a distance intervened between the common schools of the country and the Queen's College, and to bridge over this interval good grammar schools are needed, and as these are for the most part wanting it must take some years of educational progress before such an establishment as an island college can hope for success.¹¹¹

Insofar, therefore, as tertiary education was facilitated, it was by way of providing *individuals* (as opposed to the society at large) with the opportunity to access British educational institutions. This was done in two ways: by enabling individuals to write the examinations of certain British universities locally, and by financing via scholarship the university education abroad of a few outstandingly bright persons. With respect to the first, following the Queen's College debacle, it was not until 1889 that an alternative to establishing a local college or university was tried. The Schools Commission proposed to extend university teaching and the procuring of degrees to Jamaica by setting up a university college in 1890, on the grounds of the Jamaica High School, where suitably qualified Jamaicans could be tutored for the Bachelor of Arts (except in modern languages), the Master of Arts, and the Bachelor of Theology degrees awarded by the University of London. These examinations were thus sat locally. However, very few persons seemed able to capitalize on this opportunity, and up to the end of the First World War only ten had successfully completed this programme of study locally.¹¹²

In 1882 the Institute of Jamaica arranged for the island to be one of the centres for the University of Cambridge Local Examinations, which served as matriculation for entry into British universities. Those examinations were held in December each year. There were two levels of examination: one for juniors up to age sixteen, the other for seniors up to age eighteen. Those subjects done in high school were tested, and to qualify for consideration for a scholarship, candidates were required to pass all subjects. However,

> a pass can be obtained by any boy who has made proper use of the opportunities afforded him in any school giving sound teaching even in English subjects. It is only fair to add that in the large majority of cases even a pass implies more than

this, and that the majority of those who "satisfy the Examiners" do so in Latin, Mathematics, or some modern language.[113]

The Institute of Jamaica also arranged for the music examinations of the Associated Board of the Royal Academy of Music and Royal College of Music to be written locally. This was started in 1908, and by 1919 fifteen Jamaicans, all women, had been awarded licentiate certificates of the Associated Board. This was in keeping with the concept of the "finished" girl, and would have reinforced the idea that these were womanly activities. After the war, provision was also made for sitting the examinations of the Royal Drawing Society locally.[114]

The second method of facilitating access to tertiary education was by scholarship to British universities overseas. In 1881 Governor Anthony Musgrave inaugurated the award of the Jamaica Scholarship. With an annual value of two hundred pounds (by 1920 it was worth two hundred and fifty pounds), this scholarship was awarded to one boy each year, aged between seventeen and nineteen years, who earned the best results in an examination of the same standard as that required for matriculation at London University. This was subsequently changed to the best results attained in the Local Examination of the University of Cambridge for Senior Students (later called the University of Cambridge Higher School Certificate Examination). The scholarship was tenable for three years at any recognized tertiary institution in the British Empire. As shown above, from 1912 Jamaican girls were also eligible for one similar Jamaica Scholarship which, valued in 1920 at two hundred pounds per year for three years, was fifty pounds less than the boys'.[115]

Jamaican boys also benefited from the Gilchrist Scholarship awarded by the Gilchrist Educational Trust that had been established in 1869. This, valued at one hundred pounds per annum for three years, was open to candidates from the entire British Caribbean, and was tenable at either the University of Edinburgh or the University of London. The award was based on the results of the annual matriculation examination, and candidates could not be more than twenty-two years old. The award of these scholarships, however, was terminated after 1885.[116]

The most prestigious award, however, was the Rhodes Scholarship, which was first won by a Jamaican in 1904. It enabled the recipient to study at one of the Oxford University colleges, and was valued at three hundred pounds per annum for three years. The scholar was to be male and no older than twenty-five. In addition to his scholastic achievements, he had to demonstrate "his fondness and success in manly out-door sports, such as cricket, football [and so forth] . . . his qualities of manhood, truth, courage, devotion to duty, sympathy for and protection of the weak, kindliness, unselfishness and fellowship . . . [and] an interest in his schoolmates".[117] In many respects, the Rhodes scholar epitomized the quintessentially ideal end-product of the elite high-school system: a well-rounded young man honed intellectually, morally and physically to provide leadership in the service of God, country and the British Empire. He symbolized the success of, and validated, the colonial clones of the British grammar school.

Conclusion

As a vital part of the civilizing mission, the schooling of the children of Jamaica had very clearly defined objectives. Through the island's schools, whether established by trusts, privately, or by government funding, children were to be exposed to a Christian "moral" education which, while teaching the basics of literacy and numeracy, included a heavy dose of religious indoctrination. Patrick Bryan gives the impression that from 1895 religious education was de-emphasized, as "the Churches accepted the secularisation of syllabuses". This, however, is misleading. Religion continued to form an essential part of the curricula at *all* levels of the education system up to and beyond the First World War. According to Ruby King, the Code of Regulations (1900 and 1902) still required senior children in elementary schools to be taught the main facts of Old Testament history, the lives of the apostles, and the life and teaching of Christ.[118]

Primary education was designed essentially for lower-class children in order to create good, Christian, British colonial subjects, functionally literate but not so well educated that they would be attracted away from the agricultural sector that was believed to be the cornerstone of the economy and society. As Campbell observes, "The intention was not to promote upward social mobility since the colony needed a plantation labour force."[119] The education system was therefore pyramidal, since very few lower-class children were able to move beyond the primary level to the high schools that had the creation of a "native" educated middle class as their objective. These were the men (since few of the even smaller number of educated women were expected to have career aspirations) who would form a cadre of loyal British colonials, just sufficient to fill middle-level positions in government and business, and loyally execute the policies and decisions of their employers, whether public government officials or private planters and entrepreneurs. At the same time there were not sufficient high schools to generate an oversupply of highly educated persons who might constitute a nationalist opposition to British rule.

Moulded by a British curriculum, no matter its inappropriateness, the children were integrated into a wider imperial whole, sharing with others around the world the belief that the British culture to which they were exposed every day was superior and ought to be aspired to. Amidst reading, writing and arithmetic, the children prayed, learned about their civic responsibilities (and far less, if anything, about their civic rights) and sang about the glory of the empire (which was mighty enough to quell any thoughts of rebellion that they might entertain). Controlled by the churches in the majority of cases, the schools operated as conduits for church membership; they also allied with the colonial and imperial state to impart, through formal and informal lessons, the ideologies on which the colony and the empire turned. Ultimately, then, they intended to and did pass on the important lessons by which they hoped to shape Jamaica's children: ideas about God, duty and empire. Yet the fact that for most of the period surveyed less than a quarter of the children of school age actually went to school means that the civilizing ideology was not reaching the vast majority of young Jamaicans via this medium, and it goes a long way towards explaining why the mission was broadly ignored by many of the people.

Chapter 8

Proselytizing the Asian Immigrants

THE CIVILIZING MISSION WAS ALL EMBRACING. It was intended to transform the culture and character of all persons and groups with whom it came into contact. No ethnic group, so long as they intended to settle permanently in British Jamaica, could hope to escape its clutches for, since British culture was considered to be the foundation of colonial civilization, and all others were relegated to the ranks of the uncivilized, it was incumbent on the bearers of this "superior" way of life to uplift those who were not so blessed. Besides, as far as the cultural elites were concerned, the colony was judged by the extent to which British culture pervaded the society. If Jamaica were to qualify for classification as a civilized territory, then it was imperative that all resident groups should embrace the standards, ways, beliefs and mores of the imported Victorian ethos. There could be no segment of the population that was allowed to retain its "pagan" or "heathen" beliefs and customs.

Of the new immigrants who entered Jamaica in the nineteenth and early twentieth centuries, only the Indians were of any numerical significance. They were first introduced into Jamaica in 1845 as contract labourers for the plantations, which were experiencing a mass exodus of ex-slaves. But although the British government made a massive loan of five hundred thousand pounds available to the West Indian planters to fund large-scale immigration, the Jamaican planters could not afford to draw down on this loan fund. As a result, only about 37,027 Indians had been imported into the island up to 1917 when the immigration ended. However, due to repatriation and mortality, the Indian population rose slowly to 11,016 in 1881, and by 1921 it had risen a further 68 per cent to 18,610. Chinese imported labourers were even fewer than Indians. Although they were first introduced into Jamaica in 1854, by 1921 there were only 3,696 Chinese residents in the island, comprising less than 0.5 per cent of the total population.[1]

These Asian immigrants were markedly different in appearance and culture from the Afro-creole population of Jamaica. They looked and "smelled" different, dressed and behaved "peculiarly", spoke an unintelligible "gibberish", ate "strange" foods using their fingers (Indians) or "sticks" (Chinese), had "queer" customs and worshipped "weird" gods. They were, in a nutshell, "pagan" and "uncivilized". But until the 1880s they were relatively sparse, too few to matter. They posed no serious contaminating threat to the Afro-Jamaican people who, in any event, generally looked down on them as inferior aliens, both on account of their coming to do work that was considered menial and degrading, which the Afro-creoles were seeking to leave, and because of their "inferior" customs. Moreover, they were intended to remain only for a short time, and so were not likely to be a permanent problem for the colony. For all these reasons, it was not considered worthwhile to stretch already limited human and financial resources to "civilize" them. They were someone else's problems: India's and China's.

But, particularly as the number of Indians increased in the late nineteenth and early twentieth centuries, and as some began to settle and become integral constituents of the society, there was a new urgency to civilize these groups. They were fast becoming Jamaica's problem, who might indeed contaminate the Afro-creole population if not themselves reformed. In particular reference to the Indians, Reverend Carlile, a Scottish Presbyterian priest, complained in 1884 that

> Their mode of dress is extremely indecent, and they cannot be induced to wear almost any covering but a small piece of cloth round their loins. Some of them are Mohammedans, but the greater part are idolaters, and sometimes make great parade of their image-worship. I need not say how extremely dangerous it is to our poor negroes, who are just emerging from darkness, and whose minds are generally to a considerable extent under the influence of superstition, to be called upon constantly to mingle with a people so debased in all their habits as the coolies.[2]

Both groups of Asian immigrants were also considered to present serious moral challenges to Jamaican society by their excessive use of narcotics (ganja and opium) which began to be taken up by the black creoles, and especially by the opening of Chinese gambling dens, which became very popular among Afro-Jamaicans. The spread of these baneful influences had to be checked. The civilizing mission, therefore, had to be extended to the Asian immigrants as well.

Belief Systems of the Asian Immigrants

Both the Indians and the Chinese arrived in Jamaica with belief systems markedly different from those already extant in the host society. They were heavily influenced by the religious tenets mainly of Hinduism, Islam and Confucianism. The documentary sources, however, reveal very little about these religious beliefs and practices. This is no doubt explained by the fact that the Indians and Chinese were small, dispersed, foreign ethnic groups who until the late nineteenth century attracted very little attention from mainstream Jamaican society. So hardly anyone bothered to pay close attention to their religious activities except to label them as heathen and, in the case of the Western missionaries, to attempt to convert them to Christianity. It simply did not matter what, if anything, they believed in or practised.

Although it is unknown whether the majority of Indian immigrants to Jamaica adhered to the Shivite, Vaishavite or Shakti forms of Hinduism, it is probable that, as in the southern Caribbean, the *bhakti* movement was the most popular manifestation of the religion in the island. Because this was tied to neither shrine nor holy place, it could survive anywhere. This obviated the need for temples and places of worship to preserve Hinduism in the alien environment. The absence of those structures in Jamaica, therefore, did not mean that the immigrants ceased to adhere to traditional Hindu beliefs. Sacrifice and prayer, which form an essential part of Hindu worship, could have taken place mainly in the home in Jamaica as elsewhere. In addition, their spiritual needs were serviced by Brahmin priests who formed part of the immigrant population.[3]

Although Muslims were considerably smaller in number, they too could preserve their religious beliefs. Gillion argues that regardless of the variant (Sunni or Shiite), Islam does not suffer much disruption when transplanted overseas, again because it does not require formal places of worship. Besides, Muslim imams who migrated were able to attend to the spiritual needs of their people. Presumably, therefore, in Jamaica as in the southern Caribbean and Fiji, "most of the religious duties and festivals were maintained, except for the *namaz* (prayers five times a day), *pardah* (the seclusion of women), and the full observance of the fast of Ramazan"[4] – none of which would have been permitted by the plantations.

Notwithstanding the documentary silence on the religious beliefs and practices of the immigrants, one might nevertheless reasonably conclude that both Hinduism and Islam survived the crossing and were installed in Jamaica, especially as to the religious principles and tenets that the adherents carried in their heads. But from time to time there were references to some outward manifestations of Indian religious practices in Jamaica, most notably the *Hosay* or *Tadja/Tadjeah* street festival. This annual festivity was supposedly related to the Islamic *Mohurrum* festival to commemorate the martyrdom of Hassan and Hosein, the two sons of the prophet Mohammed (Ali) in the forty-sixth year of the *Hirjah* (the flight of the prophet). The festival is supposed to be observed by devout fasting for thirteen days during which Muslims, especially Shiites, are required to abstain from all work. In several parts of Jamaica, notably Kingston, Port Antonio, Annotto Bay, Port Maria, Savanna-la-Mar and Vere, there were grand processions through the streets, with men carrying large "Hussays" (described as miniature "temples" made of wood or bamboo and decorated with coloured paper and gold and silver tinsel) and accompanied by loud music, drumming, flag waving and mock fights. These Hussays contained the coffins of the two martyrs (Hassan and Hosein), whose names the devotees shouted as they processed. The climax of the processions was the ritual casting of the Hussays into the sea or river just before sunset.[5] The growing participation of creole Jamaicans in these "idolatrous" festivities aroused concern among the cultural elites and intensified the desire to christianize the "heathen" Indians.

That desire was reinforced by evidence of the Indians apparently cultivating a belief in the power and efficacy of obeah. This can be interpreted as an indication of creolization, but it is also highly probable that, as in Guyana, the Indians brought their own beliefs and practices that resembled obeah.[6] When one adds to this their penchant for smoking the narcotic "weed", ganja, which was rapidly being adopted by sections of the creole lower classes, and their growing love of rum, which oft-times induced intoxication, there was clearly a pressing need to "civilize" these immigrants.

Documentary data about the belief system(s) of the Chinese are even more sparse. There are many references to the existence of a Confucian temple compound, built in 1895 at Barry Street and Matthew's Lane in Kingston, where Chinese immigrants gathered, worshiped and socialized; but far more attention was paid to the gambling and opium smoking that were done on the compound. The lack of information about the religious beliefs and practices of the Chinese, however, was augmented by the fact that outsiders were not allowed to enter their temple.7 But that they were decidedly not Christian, and furthermore indulged in morally dubious practices that were spreading to the creole population, were sufficient to draw hostile attention to the Chinese by the end of the nineteenth century. They too became targets of the civilizing process.

Converting the Indians to Christianity

From quite early on there were a few individuals, both lay and clerical, who tried to encourage the churches to evangelize the Indians. In 1860 Stipendiary Magistrate Bell called for missionaries knowledgeable in Eastern languages to christianize the immigrants "and so do away with the influence that results from their example in heathenism, bad customs, etc. as well as to carry out the great work looked forward to by all Christians". Yet, although recognizing the necessity of something sustained being done for the spiritual "benefit" of the immigrants,8 the churches were slow to act. In 1887 Wesleyan priest C.T. Boyd (in Morant Bay) lamented the fact that after forty years of Indian immigration he had not seen or heard of a single organized Christian mission to them. Hundreds, he complained, had returned to India and died without knowledge of the gospel. While the government was concerned only with their temporal welfare, "The majority of the managers on the Sugar Estates, are men leading immoral and inconsistent lives; men, the mass of whom do not attend Divine Worship and I am sorry to say a goodly number are Europeans." These men, as we have shown, adhered to the old plantocratic cultural tradition which competed against the new Victorian morality introduced primarily by the missionaries, and were consequently seen as setting a bad example to those below them. Hence, "If you had only seen [the Indians] as I have, washing clothes on Sundays – travelling from place to place trafficking among themselves and violating the Sabbath in various ways you [would] agree with me that a Mission to them is as requisite as anywhere."9

Some clerics, however, took the initiative on their own. In 1868 Methodist minister John Duff was working among Indians in Port Antonio. A decade later his co-religionists S. Goodyer and William Westlake were doing likewise at Lucea and Annotto Bay, respectively. In 1871 Reverend Dr H. Croskery of the London Missionary Society, who was also a government medical officer, was working quietly among the Indians in Chapelton. And Scottish Presbyterians J. Hendrie at Vere and R. Drummond in the west were active in the early 1880s, as was Baptist pastor S.V. Robinson at Port Maria.[10]

These small beginnings slowly spurred the churches into action. In response to Hendrie's evangelical work in Vere, the Foreign Mission Committee of the United Presbyterian Church of Scotland agreed in 1880 to collaborate with the Church of England (which had laid aside eighty pounds a year for such work in Jamaica) by transferring Hendrie to the Anglicans and contributing to his salary. But by 1883 that work was already in abeyance, and the only missionary activity among the Indians was being done by Reverend S.V. Robinson, who in 1881 had started the Baptist Association Coolie Mission in Port Maria. In that same year, however, the United Presbyterian Church agreed to recruit Reverend T.M. Christie, who had worked in Trinidad, to proselytize the Indians in Clarendon and St Catherine at a salary of no less than two hundred and fifty pounds per annum. But neither the Jamaica Executive Committee nor the Foreign Mission Committee in Scotland provided the necessary funding for this work, and in 1887 the former claimed that a reduction in the number of immigrants had, in fact, lessened the importance of a "coolie mission".[11]

Funding was just one problem that affected missionary work among the Indians. As early as 1860 Methodist priest Henry B. Foster pointed to the difficulty of obtaining access to them on the plantations; half a century later Quaker Lora P. Arms noted that the transference of indentured Indians from one property to another further hampered missionary work. Another major problem was the language differences, which made communication, especially of abstract religious ideas, very difficult. Despite the recruitment over the years of missionaries and catechists who could speak Hindi, Urdu, Telegu and other Indian languages, this remained a serious problem for the evangelizing process since the Indians spoke several languages and dialects. Arms also pointed to other problems that faced missionary work: disease and poverty (lack of clothing and nourishing food), which prevented the Indians from attending church and school (perhaps these were mere excuses); "sin and degradation, immorality and vice of every kind"; caste; "ignorance"; and, not least of all, the powerful influence of their own traditional religions, Hinduism and Islam.[12]

In the face of such difficulties, it was only when the number of Indians imported increased during the 1890s that the churches began to scramble to organize Indian missions. To some extent they were encouraged by evidence that some Indians, who may perhaps have arrived as Christians, had long appeared to exhibit an interest in going to church and sending their children to Sunday school. So in 1894 the Scottish Presbyterian church resolved to start a regular mission to the Indians. The language problem was overcome by the Canadian Presbyterian Church in Trinidad sending two Indian catechists – one located at White Marl (Ewing's Caymanas estate), St Catherine, the other at Paul Island, Westmoreland.[13]

These were followed by missions in Wakefield, Linstead (1895); Aleppo, St Mary (1897); Smith's Village and Hope in Kingston, Vere, and Burlington, Port Antonio (1899); Great Salt Ponds, Spanish Town (1900; this was in fact transferred by the Quakers: see below); and Fellowship, Annotto Bay (1901). All of these stations were run by Indian catechists who worked under the superintendents of the Presbyterian East Indian Mission, the first of whom was Reverend William F. Martin (1897).[14] He was succeeded by Reverend John P. Gartshore (1908). In 1898 the mission was strengthened by the addition of *zenana* missionary Martha B. Croll who worked among the Indian *women*, principally in and around Kingston (mainly Smith's Village and Hope), and at Great Salt Ponds. By 1911, however, the Burlington and Fellowship stations had ceased to grow, and in the following year the synod decided to turn them over to the Quakers, who had a much stronger presence on the north side of the island.[15]

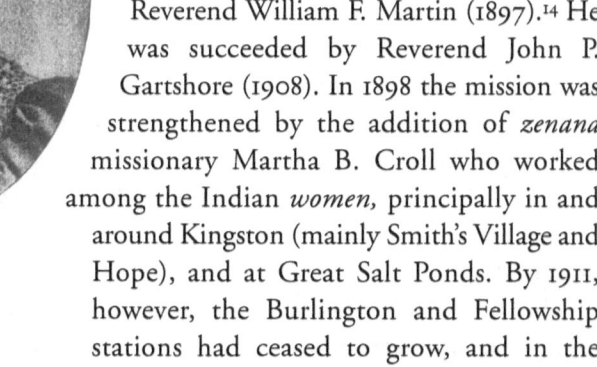

Figure 22. Martha B. Croll
Source: *Women's Missionary Magazine* 6 (1906).

The growing number of Indian immigrants in Jamaica also reawakened the Church of England in 1892 to the "need" to pay serious attention to them. The following year a committee was formed at Port Antonio to organize a mission to the Indians, and hired the services of Arthur A. Hallam to work for three months. His laborious efforts in several parishes were so impressive that in 1895 the Jamaica Home and Foreign Missionary Society made arrangements to procure his services for one year as lay superintendent of missionary work among the Indians. In that same year Archbishop Enos Nuttall appointed S.R. Mitchell, who was visiting from Guyana, as an evangelist to the Plantain Garden River district in St Thomas. In 1896 O.H.

Williams solicited help to build a chapel for Indians at Serge Island, St Thomas, and the Anglican Church made a grant of one hundred and fifty pounds for missionary work there. By 1901 that body had three East Indian missions: at Golden Grove and Morant Bay in St Thomas, and at George's Plain in Westmoreland. They later expanded their work among the Indians to Kingston, St Andrew (mainly Constant Spring), Spanish Town, Vere, and Annotto Bay.[16]

Perhaps the most active of the Christian bodies in the missionary field among the Indians was the Society of Friends, Iowa (the Quakers).[17] In 1891 Reverend Arthur Swift took up residence at Bowden, St Thomas, and began his work. Four years later, he and Captain L.D. Baker, manager of the United Fruit Company, erected the first church for the Indians at Golden Grove, St Thomas. This was followed by another Indian church at Salt Pond, St Catherine, but that (as we have seen) was later turned over to the Presbyterians, who were stronger in that area. Quaker missions were also started at Amity Hall, St Thomas; Happy Grove (Hector's River), Seaside (Manchioneal), Orange Bay and Glen Haven in Portland; Orange Hill, Albany, Trinity and Highgate in St Mary; as we have already noted, in 1912 the Presbyterians transferred their mission stations in Portland (Burlington and Fellowship) to the Quakers, which conferred on the latter denominational dominance among the Indians in the north of the island. Hence, according to Mary White in 1917, "all along the north coast each Sabbath day religious services are being held, not only where the schools are kept but other places as well".[18]

The Wesleyan Methodists were far less prominent among the Indians. In urging his church to start missionary work at minimum expense, Reverend C.T. Boyd had argued in 1887 that there was no need for special churches for them – they could worship with "the natives". However, the experiences of the Quakers did not bear out such optimism. Wherever Afro-creole catechists were employed, the attendance of the Indians dropped dramatically, ostensibly because of race prejudice;[19] this was reflected in their attitude towards schooling as well (see below). Not surprisingly, therefore, when in 1894 the Wesleyan annual conference finally recognized the need to start proselytization, like the other denominations they sought to engage two *Indian* evangelists to assist.[20]

The Christian missionaries had mixed fortunes among the Indians, although overall they maintained a positive and optimistic attitude. Verene Shepherd asserts that the earliest attempt to convert Indians to Christianity was probably made in 1869 by the Anglicans, but at least thirteen Indians were baptized by Methodist missionary John Duff in Port Antonio in the previous year,[21] and there might well have been a few even earlier. Although individual clergymen continued to make occasional converts of Indians,[22] given the lack of any concerted evangelical effort by the churches and the absence of missionaries knowledgeable in Indian languages, it was not until after the mid-1890s that some progress began to be reported.

After the establishment of the first Presbyterian Indian mission at Ewing's estate, Caymanas, in 1894, Reverend James Robertson reported that the church was doing well, and on 4 November the first two converts (males) were baptized, while others were being instructed. By 1896 the Presbyterians were very encouraged by the growing Indian membership of their missions, and boasted of a Christian community of over one hundred in just two years. They reported that attendance at public worship was very satisfactory, and the spirit of devotion was not confined to church. "They meet in each other's houses for worship", and were also reportedly active in seeking to bring others into the fold, while making substantial financial contributions to the missions' coffers. "Some of these converts have yielded themselves to the truth after a long struggle against it. In Kingston, for example, a leading Brahmin, who had long been a bitter opponent, has accepted Christ and now seeks to build up that which he formerly destroyed."[23]

The Quakers, who were the other major Christian denomination working among the Indians, were likewise encouraged by what appeared to be good results of their missionary efforts. An 1899 report stated, "Such an improvement in personal appearance as is seen each year, speaks well for the instruction that is imparted and the influence of the work." The following year Mary White observed, "The questions to bring out argument and the large amount of chatting among the people about what is being told them are becoming things of the past. A reverential attitude with a feeling of respect [is exhibited] while they quietly sit and listen to the words that are being spoken to them." This optimism, however, was tempered with cautious realism: "We see signs of the breaking up of the strong prejudice against Christianity among that people, but we find it takes a long time to gain converts."[24]

Still, there was a growing feeling that "[a]way from home the Indians seem more accessible to the gospel". In 1906 the synod of the Presbyterian Church was ecstatic about the "wonderful results which, under Divine blessing, have been achieved [after ten years] both in the agents raised up and the number of converts gathered in". Another decade witnessed even further signs of success. Quaker Lora Arms stated that a number of Indians on estates in Portland wanted to be Christians and were asking to be taught to read so that "they may know more about the way", while Mary White reported that the missionaries "have a welcome in every Indian home". Likewise Alice Kennedy asserted, "The bitter opposition that we used to meet from those of high caste is giving way to attentive listening to the Gospel truths." These assertions were corroborated by independent reports of the Presbyterians from other parts of the island. By 1920 the two major missionary organizations were reporting perceptible growth and success among the Indians.25 The Indians were, it seems, slowly joining the ranks of the converted "civilized" in Jamaica.

Evangelical work was greatly facilitated by estate owners and managers, who not only granted the missionaries access to the Indian workers on their estates, but in some cases provided physical facilities for them. The best-known example was A. Crum Ewing's grant of land to the Scottish Presbyterian Church for the construction of the Susamachar Church at White Marl, Caymanas (1894). In 1910 Crum Ewing also made a large donation towards the erection of a new Indian Presbyterian church on his Caymanas estate in memory of missionary Martha Croll, who died in 1906. Another example of this kind of philanthropy occurred in 1900 when two United Fruit Company managers, Captain Baker and Mr Hopkins, provided a building and undertook to support a catechist on one of the company's properties at Great Salt Ponds. Also, Sir John Pringle leased a small site at a nominal rent to the Quakers for a church on his Hopewell estate in St Mary. The government too assisted when in 1901 it leased land at Hope near Kingston to the Presbyterian Church at a nominal rent, and also sold them a plot of land in Smith's Village at a reduced price.26

Most of the apparent success of the Indian missions was due to the work of catechists who were converted Indians. All the churches that undertook to proselytize the Indian immigrants found it advantageous to employ Indian catechists. The most obvious benefit was their knowledge of one or more of the Indian languages. But they also shared the same cultural background as their compatriots and intimately understood their values, beliefs, ideas and prejudices. It was believed that these attributes made them more readily acceptable to most Indians. Of course, as we shall see, this could also militate against them because they were viewed as traitors. The Presbyterians in particular were heavily dependent on Indian catechists. All their mission stations were run by them under the general supervision of regular ministers in the presbyteries and the superintendent of the East Indian Mission. Some,

Figure 23. Indian catechist Kangaloo and two converts
Source: *Women's Missionary Magazine* 4 (1904).

like Jonathan Rajkumar Lall, Simon Siboo, Samuel and Henry Kangaloo, F.W. Tar Mohammed and John Jones Subaran, were imported from the Canadian Presbyterians in Trinidad; a few, like Lal Behari Singh, Pahar Singh and Samuel Joseph Rupert, were sent to Trinidad for training; while others, like Moti, Joseph Shivdayal and Phul Singh, were local converts who were then employed as catechists.[27] So, just as it was with the creole population, the civilizing mission was not exclusively a white (wo)man's burden but, among the Indians, was shared with select Indian converts.

Indian converts to Christianity were reportedly steadfast in their new religion: "They are steadily growing in Christian knowledge and character. They appreciate some point of Christian teaching and practice in a remarkable degree, for example, Christian brotherhood and forgiveness. Many of them give themselves in personal effort for the cause of Christ." A few examples of conversions should suffice. In July 1904 convicted wife murderer, Bessambra, was ministered to by the Presbyterians while on death row, and "The unfortunate man accepted the ministrations cheerfully, and expressed his belief in the Christian faith. He prayed himself and was prayed for, and he

Figure 24. First Indian converts of Scottish Presbyterians in Kingston
Source: *Women's Missionary Magazine* 6 (1906).

died expressing hope in a newly found saviour." In 1913 an indigent man at the almshouse "confessed Christ, renouncing his heathen gods, and was baptized into the three fold Name". At Fellowship in 1916, an Indian boy named Pooran was reportedly pushed into a fire by some Indian men for refusing "to bow down to their stone god" and to eat the same food offered to the Hindu god. Seeking refuge in the Quaker mission, he feared returning home. His parents said that they did not want him to convert because it would cause trouble when they returned to India. They went to the mission and drove him back home, whipping and threatening him all the way; once there, he was tied in the house for two days. Although his parents seemed to relent, allowing him to attend church and Sunday school, they never gave up, and so fervent was he in his new faith that he was eventually obliged to leave home altogether and live in the mission home.[28] The prospects for influencing the Indians in the ways and beliefs of civilization looked promising.

But, as the last case indicates, conversion to Christianity often met with persecution and ostracism from the rest of the Indian community: "Those who have embraced Christianity have suffered great persecution from those

Figure 25. Indian congregation at Paul Island, Westmoreland
Source: *Women's Missionary Magazine* 6 (1906)

who still remain heathen in heart and life. They have been literally cut off, and are regarded as unfit to associate with." Because Christian converts were required to refuse to partake of any food or drink offered by their Hindu friends to their gods, "This brings upon them fully much reproach. The religion of that people enters into the life of nearly every one, and when one turns to the Christian religion there are hundreds who do not have a grain of sympathy with him. He is alone, against an overwhelming majority: he must serve God, refuse to follow former customs and truly separate himself." According to Reverend P. Stubbs, "Many men and women who feel the attraction of the Christian Gospel are hindered from open confession by fear of their non-Christian relatives and friends." In short, life for the Christian Indian could be well-nigh unbearable, and consequently "backsliding" among converts was a serious problem for the missionaries.[29]

The Indians, therefore, could not and did not relinquish Hinduism and Islam easily. It is true that the missionaries did experience a fair degree of success: up to 1921 some 6,007 Indians (32.3 per cent of that population) claimed to be Christians. This is quite high by comparison to Trinidad and

Guyana, where the rates were less than 12 per cent.[30] Still, approximately two-thirds remained loyal to their old religious beliefs and practices and, moreover, were prepared to defend them vigorously if necessary. Resistance was strongest where Indians were relatively large in number and the missionary presence comparatively weak, but opposition was manifested everywhere and took many forms, at both an individual and a communal level. A few examples will suffice.

From very early in the missionary efforts at proselytization, they encountered problems that went beyond their failure to communicate in Indian languages. Methodist John Duff employed an Indian as interpreter, "but it was not very encouraging to know that shortly after I left, this same Interpreter, would be leading them in the rites of their own native superstitions; and what guarantee had I that the man had faithfully conveyed what I had sought to teach". Quaker Mary White discovered that after several months of work she had ready listeners, but very few sought the church. She was welcomed into the homes of the Indians, but that was as far as it went. Progress was slow.[31]

Hindu and Muslim priests presented formidable obstacles to missionary work. According to Martha Croll,

> Just at the commencement of my work in Smith Village, I was sorely tried by two men – East Indians – who persisted in following me about the yards and interrupting me when I talked to the women. I tried many devices to send them away, but to no purpose. Ultimately, I decided that I had better accept their presence with as good a grace as possible. . . . It transpired afterwards that I had been the recipient of the well-planned attentions of two Hindu priests.[32]

Hindu priests remained "active in their persecution, and all sorts of heathen worship was rampant in Smith's Village. Although some East Indians listened eagerly to the Christ teaching, many jeered and mocked, and saddest of all, so-called Christian East Indians were living as utter heathen, literally 'bowing down to gods of wood and stone!' " And as soon as the Presbyterians opened their church there, "the Brahmin priests . . . flocked from all parts of the Island, and banded themselves together to stop the onward movement of the Holy Spirit's work. Their persecution was bitter before, but it is ten times more so now." In Portland in 1901, a "Maraj" rallied his people, threatened to beat Quaker Indian catechist Rufus King with clubs, and forced him to stop preaching.[33]

Likewise, in Vere, the Presbyterians encountered "strenuous opposition as the Brahmins are strong in the neighbourhood and they have a priest of their own who wields considerable influence". In that district "the old religion has a very strong hold upon the people and the heathen teachers keep careful watch that the flock does not stray". It was the same in St Thomas, where the Hindu and Muslim priests "became as fierce as hungry lions. They feared for their livelihood if [the Anglican missionary, S.R. Mitchell] had stayed very long in the district. The respect they obtained from their followers would be cut away. They spoke all manner of evil words against him, and instructed one and all not to receive him nor to pay heed to his instruction. If anyone were found doing so he would be put away from their society." In the early 1920s, just when the churches were beginning to think that they were making significant inroads among the Indians, they encountered "[a] new line of teaching by the Indians, [and] an increased number of Priests with instructions from India not to give up the faith", which created an impression that there was a revival of Hinduism in the island.[34]

Rank-and-file Muslims and Hindus expressed vehement opposition to missionary intrusion in their lives. In 1912, for instance, when Christian Indians who were invited to a traditional Indian wedding in Kingston were warned against attending by the Indian Presbyterian catechist, "This incensed the heathen who marched past the Church shouting: 'We are heathen'."[35] Anglican S.R. Mitchell encountered enormous hostility in St Thomas. The Indians refused to listen to him:

> They counted him a fool and mad; and did laugh at him. They dishonoured him with childish jeering, and rejected him from their presence altogether. Instead of receiving him in their houses they hated him saying he came to deceive them. One in a rage cried he would be glad if (Mr. Mitchell) died of hunger and thirst, but not at his door, as he would rather bury a dead dog and not a Christian. This same person asked him why he became a Christian and thereby defected his caste. He then remarked that Mr. Mitchell became a Christian to eat beef, pork, fish, and worms. As time passed they grew worse and worse and did all they could to accuse and persecute him.

Mitchell became so distraught that he "felt every minute like leaving for British Guiana and in a hurry too". Archbishop Nuttall, however, persuaded him to persevere.[36] That the small number of Indians in St Thomas should have made life so very difficult for Mitchell, who had had previous mission experience among substantially larger numbers of them in Guyana, speaks volumes about their determination to resist Christian proselytization.

The Quakers too complained about being "unable to meet the arguments of the Hindu and the Mohammedan. If defeated he would not admit it, much less accept our doctrine if he found his own was gone."[37] In 1897, for instance, Arthur H. Swift found himself locked in an animated argument with a Muslim man:

> He was very much wrought up because Mr. Swift told him that our Bible was of higher authority and a purer standard of morality than the Koran. He said that in India he could prove that our Bible was false by putting it and the Koran into water, [and] ours would dissolve first. He said God made him but only Jesus Christ made Mr. Swift and that he [Swift] could never go to Heaven because he had spoken against the Koran. There would an occasional sound come from indoors – a woman took sides with the Mohammedan. . . . Eventually the man said, "Me gone now" and shook hands very kindly.[38]

Fellow Quaker Lora Arms declared, "Many times the [Hindu] Indians have told me that their god Ram and my God were the same god. It takes time to convince them of the difference." And when she tried to convert one, "he said his father and mother in India were not Christians and what was good enough for them was good enough for him. He observed that coconut tree bears coconuts not oranges . . . [and] insisted that his religion was good enough for him, that if he became a Christian all his friends would curse him and his mother." In 1915 Presbyterian priest R.C. Young reported that many of the newly arrived Indians in Westmoreland were opposed to Christianity, and held to their own rites as far as circumstances permitted.[39]

Ironically, the process of creolization also hampered missionary work. The Indians rapidly acquired a taste for rum, which was manufactured on some of the estates where they worked, and drunkenness became a major problem for some. Still others kept up the practice of heavy ganja smoking that they had brought to Jamaica. The churches' outlawing of both did not endear them to many Indians: "The rule of membership is that no rum or ganja is to be used. This is naturally resented by rum store keepers and users of rum. The Catechist [at Salt Ponds] has been threatened more than once because of his pronounced attitude in reference to the use of rum." A Christian Indian complained about the sale of rum to Indians on Sundays, and cited one meeting at a chapel in Port Antonio at which many Indians were so intoxicated and ill-behaved that the preacher had to terminate the service prematurely. In addition, those Indians who lived and worked in Kingston were reputedly influenced by many of the "vices" of the creole population with whom they interacted. There, too, "[t]he love of Rum wrought havoc with some members in recent years".⁴⁰ These factors compounded the difficulties of the missionaries in winning Indian converts.

Sada Stanley, among others, believed that it was more rewarding to work among Indian children than the adults:

> The Coolie's heart and conscience is not easily reached. They have but little respect for a statement or theory unless they see its practical demonstration, and one must always be prepared to give a reason for the hope that is within. . . . The hope of the Hindu is in the children, for the Coolie adult is so intrenched [*sic*] in his heathen customs and beliefs, that he despises the truth, literally loving darkness better than light.⁴¹

But while the children were indeed more impressionable and susceptible to missionary indoctrination, they were not pushovers. In 1897, for instance, a little Indian boy flatly denied any truth in the story of the Crucifixion: "He still remains a staunch heathen despite influences being used to save him." One day in Sunday school the children were required to put their hands to their faces with heads bowed and eyes closed, saying the Lord's Prayer. "When he thought no one was observing he straightened himself up and took the hands of his little brother away from his face. We are especially surprised when we consider how very young he is."⁴²

Indian resistance to Christianity was not always peaceful. All missionaries were vulnerable to threats of physical assault. Several times the Indians of St Thomas attempted to beat Anglican evangelist S.R. Mitchell: "If they had had the power to kill him they would have done so and left him in some corner of a road or so." But Indian catechists were especially singled out for the ire of others, perhaps because they were regarded as turncoats. They thus encountered considerable hostility, and a few certainly wilted under the pressure. In 1901, for instance, a catechist drew so much opposition from his Indian compatriots, who threatened him with violence, that he broke and began to curse and swear! After being similarly threatened, Quaker catechist Rufus King became so frustrated with the Indians of one village in Portland that he vowed never to return, because "they think so lightly of the Christian religion". In Kingston, Salt Ponds and Vere the Presbyterian catechists were repeatedly threatened. For instance, at Vere in 1912 a meeting held on an estate was broken up, and the catechists had to flee for their lives after being stoned for several miles.⁴³ The civilizing mission was not just being resisted but was under attack by some of the Indian immigrants.

Thus, evangelical work among the Indians was very difficult and progress quite slow up to 1920. When, for instance, Quaker catechist J. Kissoon visited one Vere community in 1918 with a view to starting work there, he encountered "rather strong opposition to his message from the people. Only two avowed Christians were found amongst about 600 people." Indeed, so consistently hostile were the Indians of Vere that despite the presence of the Presbyterians in that district since 1899, their first convert was not made until 1920. Likewise, in Port Antonio there were reportedly only two or three Christian Indians in 1918, despite missionary work there from at least 1868![44] This certainly raises questions about the reliability of the census figure of 6,007 Indian Christians in 1921. If accurate, perhaps it suggests that the greatest success in proselytization occurred where sizable bodies of Indians were not located and resistance was thus weakest.

Certainly up to and just beyond the First World War, therefore, christianization did not play a dominant role in "civilizing" the Indians. Despite their small numbers (just about 2 per cent of the total population in 1921) and general dispersal over the island, two-thirds were able to resist attempts to convert them to Christianity, and to retain their distinctive Hindu and Islamic religious identities. The civilizing mission was thus only partially successful among the Indians.

Arriving in Jamaica with their cultures very much intact, the Indian immigrants were hostile to the idea of relinquishing the beliefs that had sustained their people for centuries. Unlike their black Jamaican counterparts in the period, they did not have to struggle to retain their cultural memories; these were current experiences with which they had travelled. Further, viewed as a temporary population and therefore largely ignored by the "civilizers", they were able to re-establish their beliefs in their new residence and, supported by their priests (who had everything to lose by their conversion), were able in large measure to resist (for the time being anyway)[45] the attempt to bring them into Christendom.

Schooling the "Coolies"

As was the case with the creole population, the schooling of the immigrants was left largely to the churches, with financial support from the state in some cases. This meant that the education on offer, apart from teaching literacy and numeracy, embodied a considerable amount of Christian dogma. The missionaries believed that the best way to convert and civilize the Indians was through the children, and they made no bones about utilizing the schools to achieve that objective. Quakers Sada Stanley and Jennie Hoover admitted that school provided a good opportunity to teach scripture, and claimed that the results on young Indian minds were good. The fourteen boys at their Orange Hill school in 1915 were not only learning to read and write in English and do a little arithmetic, they were also learning to read the First Psalm. Six of them had sought pardon for their sins at Sunday night services, and formed the backbone of the Sunday school.[46] Eleven-year-old Harold Balisingh was exceptionally bright, and "drinks in the Gospel". He even sought to stop his mother from making sacrifices at the annual Hosay (Mohurrum) festival. Louise, a nine-year-old Indian girl who lived at Stanley's home, refused to go with her mother to attend the Hosay festival: "They came after me, but they are not going to get me."[47] Incidents like these did not encourage Indian parents to send their children to school. Christian indoctrination was an especially troubling issue for those who planned to return to India.

Indians were also reluctant to send their children to school on account of both caste and race prejudices: they did not want theirs to mix with Afro-creole children. Government and public denominational schools made no distinction between Indians and Afro-creoles, and as a result the Indians refused to send their children to elementary schools even if within easy reach. They also did not want their children taught and disciplined by Afro-creole teachers. Quaker Mary White stated in 1915, "These children even though we wished them to would not go to a Native teacher." Her colleague Sada Stanley even more perceptively observed that "the Indians will not trust their children to anyone unless they have great confidence in them and prefer to have them with them rather than see them getting an education".[48]

Parents also felt that they could get greater benefit from their children if the children worked rather than spending their time in school. As early as 1880 the protector of immigrants, A.H. Alexander, observed that "there is a decided disinclination on the part of the parents to allow any of their children, who are able to do any work, to attend school". According to Quaker Alice Kennedy, "In some instances they are wanted to work to help maintain the family, while some (especially the girls) are kept back to care for the smaller children." Generally speaking, the Indians were far less enthusiastic about girls going to school than boys. Jennie Hoover lamented, "While we have put in our best efforts to get Indian girls in our school [at Orange Hill, St Mary], there are only three on the roll at present . . . there are numbers of Indian girls within reach of the school who should be there. This is the most distressing problem we have." The simple fact, as Mary Allen discerned, was that "the Indians think the girls ought not to be educated and will hardly ever send them to school". She observed, "The girls are kept at home until about 10 yrs old then are married according to the Indian rule." Allen, however, had a Victorian view of the purpose of female education: "the greatest hindrance to school was that no girls are allowed to come for very long. Indian boys attend regularly and learn well, but it seems too bad that there are no girls who can make their homes what they will look for when that time comes. There is such a need of better homes and more intelligent women among the Indians."[49] In the absence of parental encouragement, the girls thus tended to be quite lackadaisical about school. They "preferred to run and play at the riverside or in the banana-walks, only coming to school with their towsled hair and dirty little faces long enough to tell Mrs. Hoover 'Salaam' ". As a result of all these factors, therefore, the general attendance of Indian children at schools up to 1920 was poor, and in some instances not even legal prosecution could press the Indians to educate their children.[50]

Recognizing that "education" was largely a means of persuading their children away from the beliefs, culture and heritage of their ancestors, the Indian parents cut off the missionaries' access to their offspring. For those who intended to return to India (although the fulfilment of that intention was entirely another matter), the indicators of status in Jamaican society (such as education) meant little; they had their own priorities, determined by their own belief systems, regarding what was important for their children. The frustration of the cultural elite and the main bearers of the civilizing mission was understandable: their contact with Indian adults did not encourage them, and their contact with Indian children (whether through the Sunday schools or through day schools) was, at best, limited.[51]

This situation induced Inspector of Immigrants Ripoll as early as 1880 to propose the establishment of separate schools for Indian children, run on strictly nonsectarian principles, with Indians as teachers to instruct the children in both English and Hindi. He also urged that attendance should be compulsory. A "School Manager" echoed this call in 1896, arguing that the establishment of separate schools for Indians was the only way to circumvent the prejudice against sending their children to school. He called on the Board of Education to provide help to a few schools in which Indians could be taught alone: "Something would then be done for their Education and there would be intimate association with the Creole teacher; more or less frequent association with the Manager and a gradual assimilation of ideas with those of the people of the country seeing that the books used and lessons given in *all* Schools would be the same."[52] The attempt to assimilate and anglicize these, and all the children in the island, into a community of "British colonial children" embracing the ideals, behaviours and expectations of good and loyal subjects of the empire, was clear.

It was the Quakers who first began to push schooling for Indian children, in Portland and St Mary. Their first Indian school was established at Golden Grove in 1896, and in 1898 they reached an agreement with the government to take Indian orphan girls into their Happy Grove School at Hector's River. Their schools at Orange Hill and Trinity (near Port Maria) were established in 1907, and other Quaker schools were subsequently set up at Highgate in St Mary, and Prospect (near Port Antonio), Burlington and Stanton in Portland. Largely through the efforts of Henry Kangaloo, an Indian catechist recruited from Trinidad, the Scottish Presbyterians also started an Indian school at Smith's Village in 1904 but another, established at White Marl near Spanish Town, closed in 1910 after just one year. Likewise, the Anglican Church later set up schools for Indian children at Golden Grove, Annotto Bay, Vere and Spanish Town.[53]

It was not until 1910, however, that the government began to take active measures to promote schooling among the Indian population. The protector of immigrants, Charles Doorly, persuaded the government to fund three experimental schools exclusively for Indian children, initially for two years, in conjunction with two churches that would provide the teachers. These schools were at Fellowship in Portland, Orange Hill in St Mary (both administered by the Quakers) and Smith's Village in Kingston (administered by the Presbyterians). In 1915 another government-funded Indian school, administered by Anglican Canon Wortley, was established at Constant Spring, St Andrew.[54] The government also ran five industrial schools (at Happy Grove, Kingston [Alpha Cottage], Stony Hill, Belmont and Broughton) which, between 1915 and 1920, about twenty-five Indian children and orphans attended. And notwithstanding a broad communal reluctance, some Indian children also attended general government schools in their communities. Thus, altogether, attendance of Indian children at government-supported schools rose by 36 per cent from about 800 in 1914–15 to a peak of 1,089 in 1919–20. But this represented only 19.9 per cent of Indian children of school age.[55] As among the creole population, therefore, schooling had very limited impact in "civilizing" the Indians up to 1920.

Nevertheless, by the outbreak of the First World War, some Indians were beginning to see the possible benefits of schooling. Indeed, by then a few were reportedly quite keen to have their children educated, despite the risk of conversion to Christianity. They apparently made a distinction between "day school" and Sunday school, opting to take a calculated risk to send their children to the former in the hope of minimizing exposure to Christian dogma, but not to the latter. Perhaps most of these people had decided to settle in Jamaica permanently and were thus seeking social advancement for their children. In 1916 Jennie Hoover spoke about a greater interest and cooperation among some Indian parents in their children's schooling. They would call at the school and enquire about their children's progress; further, "One day some of the boys played 'hookey' and they received from the parents a just reward for their actions."[56] By 1918 Lora Arms had detected a growing eagerness in some parents for their *boys* to have an education:

> It is not unusual for a father to call and enquire how his boy is doing in his school work and to urge us to "beat him hard if he does not learn". After the Annual Government Inspection they question the teacher closely as to whether their child passed and if he is to be promoted into a higher standard. If told that their child got every one of his sums correct or that they read very nicely they look very proud and contented.

Arms also made particular mention of a Muslim man who sent his daughter to school from age two, and during her first year she completed two years' work. However, when he went to Cuba the child's mother kept her at home to help with the chores. On his return to Jamaica for a visit, the father was incensed about this, and made arrangements for her to attend school each day.[57]

Increasingly a part of the Jamaican community, the Indians began to relent in their insistence that their children be kept away from the influences of the local (Christian-based) educational system. Once they decided to remain in the island, they became determined that their succeeding generations should have the advantages which would, perhaps, take them into non-agricultural professions, and thereby help to lift the family and community into new social spaces. Having decided to recognize the rules of the local system of hierarchy, some of them became anxious that their children do well in that system; since education seemed to be one means by which access might be had, they began to encourage their children's attendance at school.

The teaching of Hindi in some schools helped to make schooling more acceptable to the Indians. For instance, starting in 1915 the Quakers used a Hindi-speaking teacher to give lessons in that language as a means of promoting their programme of elementary education, especially for girls. In 1915 the Indians at the nearby barracks were so impressed to hear the young girls of the Happy Grove orphanage read and sing in Hindi that one man took his three-year-old girl to the missionaries and said, "Mama, take bhachwa and teach 'im good; like fe dem pickny."[58]

Still, as late as 1920 only a relatively small percentage of Indian children were attending elementary schools, and the majority of parents were still opposed, or at best lukewarm, to the process. Shepherd asserts that during the 1920s and 1930s opposition waned, and they began to send their children to school more regularly. But as an agent of civilization, schooling was not by 1920 reaching sufficient Indians to have a significant impact.

Christianizing the Chinese

Not nearly the same degree of attention was paid to converting the Chinese to Christianity as was paid to the Indians. This no doubt relates to the fact that they were very few in number and scattered throughout the island. In addition, as with the Indians, it would have required missionaries and catechists fluent in their native languages to be effective. Thus, as late as 1887 Methodist missionary C.J. Boyd, commenting on what he thought was a penchant of the Chinese to decapitate their countrymen, urged his Society to do something: "under Heaven there is no means of saving man, and restraining them from such atrocious actions, but by scattering Gospel, light and liberty among Mankind".[59]

The Anglicans seemed to take the initiative, and soon reported some measure of success. Speaking at the Provincial Synod in Georgetown, Guyana, in March 1895, Anglican Primate of the West Indies Enos Nuttall observed that in Jamaica, "among the smaller number of Chinese in our midst we have had a kind and degree of success answering to what you [Guyana] report; and some of these converts are bright, intelligent, liberal-minded, self-denying Christians". If that was indeed so then most of the Chinese must have converted to Christianity, as they had done in Guyana.[60] But it was not only the Anglicans who were making great claims; the Church of Scotland was, too. In 1900 they reported that the Chinese congregations in Kingston were active and prosperous, and they proposed to start a Sunday school for the Chinese. In particular, they were targeting the young women between sixteen and twenty-five years, "a class largely neglected, to the great loss of the Church and the social hurt of the community". They also reported good progress at mission stations in the rural areas, where the numbers were increasing. By 1912 the Roman Catholics, the Quakers and (belatedly) the Methodists were also reportedly active among the Chinese.[61]

But the Christian churches had to compete with the presence of a vibrant Confucian temple in Kingston. And when a new Chinese cemetery was opened at Leaders Lane in 1911, the Roman Catholics and Anglicans had separate sections for their members, alongside the Confucians. This is not to suggest that the Chinese were either Christians or Confucians; more probably they were both simultaneously, having grafted elements of Christianity to their traditional Confucian belief system. So the presence of large numbers of Chinese at the consecration of both the Catholic and Anglican sections of the Chinese cemetery,[62] while suggesting that the Chinese Christian community was growing, does not mean that this was at the expense of Confucianism.

As further evidence of a growing desire among the Chinese to identify with the salient features of the dominant cultural system, some sent their children to a Sunday school organized by the Kingston Parish Church for Chinese (by 1918 attendance totalled over forty students). This further encouraged this church to establish a reading room for young Chinese between the ages of eleven and seventeen: "These young people are highly intelligent, are well prepared to appreciate reading opportunities as of course they all know English." But while noting that a large number of Chinese children were baptized at that church (and took English names), Rector R.J. Ripley acknowledged that they were not being brought up as Christians. This reinforces the point that they continued to adhere to Confucian principles of life even as they appeared to adopt Christianity.[63]

As was the case in Guyana and Trinidad, therefore, Chinese immigrants in Jamaica seemed to recognize what was required to make socioeconomic progress in a nominally Christian society, and were prepared to play the game while continuing to adhere to aspects of their traditional religion.[64] As petty entrepreneurs in a hostile alien environment that brought them into daily contact with members of the host society, the Chinese very early seemed to recognize the importance of doing in Rome what the Romans did. Besides, unlike the Indians who were encouraged, by a guaranteed passage back home, to see their sojourn in Jamaica as temporary, the Chinese immigrants were perhaps more inclined to view Jamaica as a place of permanent settlement, or else to pay their own passages back home or elsewhere. So there might have

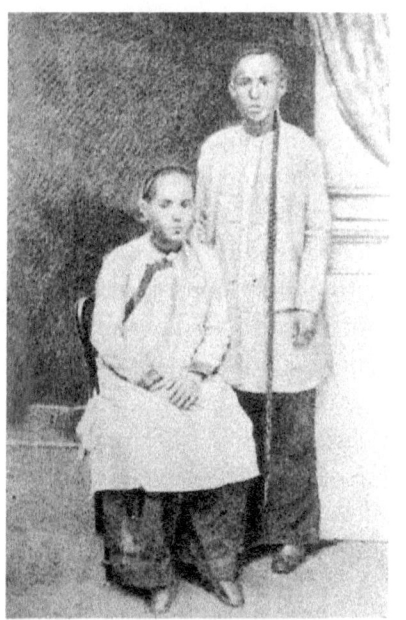

Figure 26. Chinese immigrants
Source: Henry Kirke, *Twenty-five Years in British Guiana* (London: Sampson Low and Co. 1898).

Figure 27. A westernized Chinese gentleman
Courtesy of the National Library of Jamaica.

been a greater, and earlier, willingness among them than among the Indians to adapt to local customs. Moreover, there were no binding doctrinal proscriptions in traditional Chinese religions against embracing other religious ideas, unlike the cases of Hinduism and Islam. All these factors made it possible for the Chinese to be selective in adopting aspects of the local culture, including Christianity, without losing their fundamental "Chineseness".

Conclusion

Because the Indian and Chinese populations in Jamaica were quite small, and for a long time were regarded as transient, hardly any effort was initially made to "civilize" them. It was only very slowly and belatedly that some Christian denominations, and to a far lesser extent the government, made serious attempts to expose them to the agencies of civilization. Indeed, it was only when the number of Indian immigrants began to rise perceptibly in the late nineteenth and early twentieth centuries that some missionaries expressed concern that Indian "idolatry" might have a baneful effect on the Afro-creole population, and undo the work that they had so sedulously attempted over so long a period. Similar concerns began to be expressed about the malign influences of Indian ganja smoking, Chinese opium smoking and gambling. Hence, the churches belatedly began to scramble around to set up missions to proselytize the Asians. Even then, however, not many resources were made available for this purpose, and pockets of determined Indian resistance to Christian proselytization in both church and school slowed the civilizing mission among them to some degree. Still, it must be recognized that significant inroads were made in less than thirty years of active proselytization, and the pace of this was to increase in the next two decades.

The attitude of the Chinese was altogether different from that of the Indians. Their smaller numbers – scattered over the island, mainly as shopkeepers and gambling-den operators in daily contact with the Afro-creole population – would, in any event, probably have made it difficult for them to withstand a concerted onslaught of Christian proselytization and the process of creolization. But not being assured a free return passage to their homeland, most of them were soon reconciled to the reality that Jamaica was likely to be their permanent place of residence. Further, without any strong religious or other cultural prohibitions, they were quite willing to adopt selected elements of the local culture, including Christianity, if those would promote their economic interests in Jamaica. Their embrace of Christianity and Western education was thus largely strategic and self-serving, and effected without much resistance or opposition, although they persisted in the practices of opium consumption and gambling. On the whole, however, by 1920 the agents of civilization in Jamaican society could be pleased with the progress being made among the Asian immigrants.

Chapter 9

The Cult of Monarchy and Empire
Moulding British Colonial Subjects

THE FINAL LINK IN THE CHAIN OF "civilization" was to mould the Jamaican people, of all races and classes, into good, loyal British colonial subjects. This entailed promoting the British monarchy and empire almost as a cult, fashionable symbols of Britishness and imperial unity that were virtually deified and worshipped for the benefits they bestowed on all who lived under their "protection". Indeed, a very close linkage was fostered between loyalty to God and to queen or king, between Christianity and empire. The British monarch, already head of the Church of England (which was considered the "state church" even after its disestablishment in Jamaica in 1870), was portrayed almost as God's representative on earth, and the British Empire "on which the sun never set" as God's earthly kingdom. To be one of Her or His Majesty's loyal, civilized subjects, Britons overseas, was tantamount to being certified for entry into heaven. It was an extraordinary privilege to be British.

These sentiments were not a new development after 1865. Since emancipation in 1838 Jamaica and the British West Indies had been characterized by great social uncertainty, especially for whites, who lived in the long shadow of the aftermath of slavery and were very apprehensive of possible retaliation by disaffected ex-slaves and their descendants. From Guyana to Jamaica every disturbance, no matter how small, was regarded as a potential rebellion aimed at overturning the established social order and, perhaps, even annihilating the whites. Morant Bay served as a keen reminder of that. Social and physical security were, therefore, uppermost in the minds of the social elites, and they felt an ever stronger psychological need to attach themselves as closely as possible to the mother country, Britain, and to its sovereign. The long reign of Queen Victoria made this identification easier and, as the century wore on, she came to be regarded as the embodiment of the majesty, greatness and virtues of British rule. She was the mucilage that bonded the British "race", nation and empire together, the symbolic mother of the British people, and of her subjects in the colonies overseas.[1] But tiny Jamaica occupied a very special place in Britain's vast empire. Amidst all of the British monarch's pompous titles, he or she was *separately* titled "Lord of Jamaica", and so Jamaicans had even more reason to be proud of their link with the monarch.

Throughout the British Empire, but nowhere more so than in the West India colonies, loyalty to the queen and the royal family assumed enormous importance long before it did in metropolitan Britain itself.[2] David Cannadine has shown how uninterested, indeed even hostile, the mid-Victorian Britons were towards their monarchy until the 1870s. Hence, there were few public ceremonies centring on royalty, and very little public pageantry. It was only during the last quarter of the century, particularly following Victoria's entitling as "Empress of India" and the acquisition of new colonies, that the monarchy was transformed into a grand national and imperial institution, and every royal occasion became an imperial one – a development which reached its climax in Victoria's jubilees (1887 and 1897) and the coronations of Edward VII and George V.[3]

In the Caribbean this identification with crown and empire by the social elites was not just on account of a sense of nostalgia engendered by their exile in far-off colonies, but also largely due to the uneasy social situation in which they were a small minority. Notwithstanding their anger and disgust at the way British governments had treated them over the ending of slavery and the movement towards free trade, which they blamed for their economic woes after 1838, white West Indians could not afford to adopt the rebellious course of their North American cousins, because they were a very tiny minority in the colonies. Instead, they felt the need to emphasize their racial, national and cultural connection with Britain, and their intense loyalty to the queen. This, they thought, would guarantee their security and physical wellbeing, and every suppressed riot served as a tangible reminder of the benefits of this connection. But nothing reinforced this feeling more than the calamitous outbreak at Morant Bay in Jamaica in October 1865. It brought all their racial fears to the fore, and their support of the brutal repression orchestrated by Governor Eyre bore testimony to this.[4]

Morant Bay also served to emphasize another important issue that had remained largely unresolved since emancipation: the survival of white civilization in the West India colonies. Although not blessed with any serious claims to possessing a "higher" form of civilization (except on purely racial grounds) than the ex-slaves, the white elites had long asserted that one of the sad consequences of emancipation was the demise of civilization itself; that the decline of the plantation system and rise of independent peasantries in some of the territories, especially Jamaica, was accompanied by a corresponding decline in civilization; and that there were, in some remote areas, even "relapses into barbarism" – that is, a resurgence of African cultural practices.

Notwithstanding the significant advances made in the spread of Christianity through missionary work (see chapter 6), white Jamaicans felt trapped in a cultural morass of African fetishism and superstition, which they feared would taint their own claims to being considered British at a time when they most needed to assert those claims. They were highly sensitive to being seen as the degenerate cousins of their fellow Britons "at home". This may in part have prompted the wealthy Scottish businessman, James Gall, to start a monthly illustrated newspaper in 1871 called the *Queen's Newsman*, as "an attempt to instruct the peasantry of Jamaica in loyalty and obedience, and lead them to works of industry and social advancement". Very significantly, Gall placed the paper under the direction of a committee of ministers of religion,[5] thus clearly making a link between Christianity and imperial patriotism. This hand-in-glove alliance among church, state and private enterprise (in particular the local press), and the intricately interwoven linkage between the spread of Christianity and the spread of imperial ideology, became vital aspects of a concerted and coherent agenda after 1865, designed to civilize the Jamaican people and to transform them into good, loyal, Christian black and brown colonial subjects. Imperial ideology, symbols and rituals were thus to assume enormous importance in the civilizing mission in late-nineteenth- and early-twentieth-century Jamaica.

Ironically, by then the Jamaican peasantry did not seem to require much to stimulate their warm sentiments towards the queen. For the most part they felt a *personal* sense of loyalty to, and connection with, Victoria, because many attributed their freedom from slavery directly to her.[6] This was one reason that, when they were suffering from the economic desperation and destitution that marked the early 1860s, they petitioned *her* for relief. And although many may have empathized with the rebels in St Thomas-in-the-East, they did not condone their action, which spelt disloyalty. So while the events at Morant Bay generated fear and consternation among the social elites, they also evoked shame and embarrassment among large groups of the black and coloured population who, with the assistance of the missionaries, went to great lengths to distance themselves from and denounce the "disgrace", and pledge their loyalty to the queen. Most of these were members of Baptist and other nonconformist congregations all over the island, many of whom had been accused of being involved in or instigating the unrest. From Salter's Hill, Maldon, St Ann, Trelawny, St James, Clarendon, Westmoreland, Hanover, St Catherine, North Cornwall, St Elizabeth and Kingston, missionaries (often claiming to speak on behalf of their congregations) rushed forward with protestations to the contrary.[7] The period after 1865 thus witnessed an immense keenness by Jamaicans of all classes to demonstrate their loyalty to the queen and royal family, and an intensified desire, especially among many upper- and middle-class Jamaicans (although not all), to acquire the cultural attributes of Britishness.

Royal Celebrations

One of the means by which Jamaica's British subjects kept alive their connection with the wider empire, and especially the metropolis, was by the marked curiosity that they expressed in all things royal. Loyal Jamaicans closely followed news of the activities of the imperial celebrities, as fairly detailed accounts of developments in their personal lives were regularly reported in the local press.[8] This coverage included royal birthdays, although tangible demonstrations of loyalty around these events were reserved for those closely related to the queen. For instance, the military and naval personnel at Up Park Camp and at Port Royal usually marked the birthday of the Prince of Wales by hoisting the Royal Standard.[9]

But pride of place in such celebrations was accorded the sovereign, and none more so than Queen Victoria. That she was a dowdy, uncharismatic person in real life was generally unknown to ordinary Jamaicans who honoured her.[10] So her official birthday was a red-letter day in Jamaica, as it was in Guyana, Barbados, Australia, the Cape and all over the empire; it was celebrated as a public holiday every year on 24 May with great pomp and pageantry. Given the fact that this event was not celebrated in Britain itself until the late nineteenth century, it represented an invented tradition[11] in the colonies aimed at promoting imperial loyalty. It was a symbol around which a consensus of ideological values could be cultivated to unite rulers and ruled, based, however, on the latter's "voluntary" subordination to the crown/constituted authority (and to whites in general).[12]

Hence, local and visiting "Britons" decorated public buildings and ships in the harbours with flags, buntings and illuminations; the military and volunteer militia all over the island conducted parades and reviews where *feux de joie* (gun salutes) were fired, and there was much flag and banner waving by people of all classes. As in Australia, Guyana and elsewhere,[13] the governor hosted levees to which public officials, high-ranking military officers, the clergy, doctors, solicitors, justices of the peace and elite private individuals were invited. In the evening the governor hosted a dinner and ball at King's House, which were normally elite social events to which only the *crème de la crème* of Jamaican society was invited; in the parishes the custodes did the same at the parochial courthouses. Private associations and social clubs also organized their own celebrations: for instance, the Royal Jamaica Yacht Club usually held an annual regatta; churches all over the island conducted special services; there were concerts, picnics and dinners for the poor; and sports clubs organized a day of fun and games including cricket matches, athletic events and horse-racing meetings. From time to time private individuals also put on fireworks displays at night. All Jamaica participated in these events at one level or another, if only as spectators. The celebrations of the birthdays of Kings Edward VII on 9 November and George V on 3 June followed the same pattern. At all these events the strains of the national anthem "God Save the Queen/King" could be heard, and the celebrants made loyal toasts and cheers to the monarch, the governor, magistrates and in some instances to ministers of the gospel as well.[14] The celebration of a mighty empire, endorsed and acclaimed by the church, was clear.

An essential ingredient in these and other imperial celebrations was the use of rituals and pompous pageantry. P.J. Rich argues that ritual was much more important to British imperial rule than arms or money: "These rituals kept millions of people in their place. To orchestrate them, the British Imperialists became impresarios, directing a great worldwide extravaganza." They "used ceremonies as a substitute for gunboats" in order to create an impression of imperial magnificence. In this context, ornate gubernatorial and military costumes/uniforms (complete with plumed helmet in the case of the governor, glittering medals, ceremonial swords, and other regalia and accoutrements),[15] together with pompous honorific titles, conveyed the image of imperial glory, might and power. The British used all of these in Jamaica with a view to reinforcing the deep sense of loyalty of the people, and the latter's genuine love and respect for the monarch and empire were never more on display than during royal jubilees, coronations and visits. Although Victoria's coronation day (28 June) was an annual holiday for the military establishments in the colony, it was generally observed in a relatively low-key manner by decorating the vessels of war and buildings at Port Royal and Up Park Camp, and by firing royal salutes of twenty-one guns at noon.[16] By contrast her two accession jubilees, golden in 1887 and diamond in 1897, were the high-water marks of her reign. Jamaicans joined the rest of the empire in lavish public celebration of these landmarks for their lord, queen and empress.[17]

In preparation for the celebrations of the golden jubilee in June 1887, the Legislative Council began to make plans from October 1886.[18] In response to the governor's proposal to commemorate the jubilee by establishing a hospital for training nurses to attend women in childbirth, churches and communities in all parishes across the island held public meetings from early 1887 to consider this and determine how to celebrate the great event.[19] In April a select committee of the Legislative Council recommended the establishment of a permanent institution to benefit all classes and adopted the governor's proposal of a hospital. Not only would Victoria's name live on, but her symbolism as "great mother" would survive in the birthing centre dedicated to her.

The council also recommended that 28 and 29 June should be declared public holidays for the celebrations. At the same time, the spirit of charity should be a feature of the observances, and the poor were to be given special consideration. "Outdoor paupers" were to be provided with some addition in their weekly allowances of money, clothing or otherwise, while all "indoor paupers" were to be served with a good dinner on Coronation Day.[20]

At the end of May the official programme of celebrations was published in a *Gazette Extraordinary*, and preparations began in earnest. Large numbers of bamboos were brought into Kingston from the parish of St Mary to serve as flagstaffs at public buildings and celebration venues such as the town hall, where flags of many nations were displayed for the governor's levee. That building itself was transformed: its walls and pillars were draped with flags and trophies formed of swords, pistols and bayonets, symbolic of British military might.[21] While "the good Victoria" might have been the focus of the celebrations, the empire over which she ruled was never far out of the frame.

Merchants and house owners in Kingston and in rural towns decorated and illuminated their buildings without regard to expense, time or trouble. The *Gleaner* commented, "The illumination of the City on Tuesday night [28 June] exceeded in character and extent the most sanguine expectations. . . . The whole question of decorations and illumination was taken up in a spirit of hearty liberality that proves that the business men of Kingston, depressed as they may be by bad times, are ready to throw off the cares and anxieties of business to do honor to their Sovereign and display their loyalty." Likewise the square in Spanish Town was decorated and illuminated, and decorations were to be found in towns all over the island: Old Harbour, Porus, Mandeville, Black River, Savanna-la-Mar, Lucea, St Ann's Bay, Port Antonio, Hope Bay and Linstead, to list just a few.[22]

Although preparations were still in progress, Accession Day (20 June) which marked the fiftieth anniversary of Victoria's accession to the throne, signalled the commencement of festivities with a royal salute at noon from HMS *Urgent*, followed by a grand concert on 22 June at the town hall in Spanish Town, which terminated with a tableau entitled "Britannia". The night of 27 June resembled Christmas Eve in Kingston, with large crowds of people promenading the brilliantly illuminated streets. The Coronation Day (28 June) activities commenced with a royal salute at six in the morning from HMS *Tourmaline*, and the ringing of "Joy Bells" from churches all over the island for fifteen minutes. That the churches should play such a role in the celebrations spoke not only to their willing participation in a national festival but also to their identification with the ideologies (and even the cult) of empire. Then followed the gathering of people at Victoria Market. By six o'clock in the morning, an estimated eight to ten thousand people had already assembled there to witness the inspection of the market by the governor and the custos, while being treated by the popular Watson's Band to a programme of music that included marches, polkas, waltzes, galops, and Spanish and Cuban dances. On an occasion like this no programme could omit some stirring patriotic songs like "Britannia the Pride of the Ocean", "God Bless the Prince of Wales" and, of course, the national anthem when the governor arrived on the scene.[23]

As if the ringing of church bells was not enough, the invocation of the cult of empire was highlighted by special religious services from eleven in the morning at all churches and synagogues across the island, followed by a pompous state service of thanksgiving at the Kingston Parish Church at four in the afternoon. This was attended by the governor, judges and officials, army and navy officers – all resplendent in their colourful wigs, robes, bands, uniforms and other paraphernalia of office – as well as by the clergy of all denominations.[24] This congregation of officers of empire and competing churches in a colourful ritualistic display, for the common purpose of honouring the sovereign before God, was symbolically very significant. As the *Gleaner* put it,

> Nothing can so firmly impress respect and affection for true religion, upon the heart of the people, than such a service . . . where the Ministers of the various religious bodies, some of them differing most widely upon important religious points, joined in friendship and brotherhood in rendering thanks to the one God for his prolongation and protection of Her Majesty's life, and the grand developments of social and religious liberty and scientific progress that mark the Victorian era.[25]

The mighty British Empire, symbolized in the person of Victoria and blessed by God, was represented in other ways, not least of all through a rich use of rituals. Detachments of the military and the volunteer militia, in full dress, were on parade outside the church, which was decorated inside with rich plant and floral arrangements representing both the cross and the crown.[26] The service began with the national anthem, which included two new stanzas, specifically written for the jubilee, that invoked divine blessing for the queen.[27] A special prayer for her by the bishop of Jamaica thanked God that

> the increase and extension of the Empire, have been made a blessing to the manifold peoples brought under the sway of the Sceptre of our Queen; and that our nation has been used by Thy providence to spread abroad in the earth the principle of Truth, Justice and Liberty, and above all the knowledge of Thee our Father, and of Thy Son Jesus Christ, and of the Holy Spirit the Comforter – one only Triune God.[28]

No clearer statement tying God with the blessed queen and her empire could be enunciated.

Following the service there was a procession up Duke Street to the race course of school children carrying flags and banners and singing the national anthem, "Rule Britannia" and other patriotic songs. Similar children's processions took place in other parts of the island – Spanish Town, Old Harbour, Porus, Mandeville, Black River, Spettlewood Pen (Hanover), St Ann's Bay, Port Antonio, Hope Bay and Linstead, for example – after which they were treated to buns, cakes and lemonade. Special commemorative medals, personal keepsakes of imperial glory, were also imported for distribution to those children who participated in the jubilee demonstrations. In Kingston the first day's celebration came to an end with the illumination of the streets and buildings, and a display of electric light by HMS *Tourmaline*.[29]

Day two in Kingston began with the grand reopening of the Sollas Market (severely damaged by hurricane in the previous year) by the governor at eleven in the morning; it was renamed Jubilee Market, and would thus remain an enduring monument in remembrance of this great event. The market was opened free of charge to stall holders for the first two days, and was illuminated and kept open from two to ten in the morning, as on Christmas Day.[30] This was possibly an attempt to associate the festivities of Christmas (centred around religion), the most widely celebrated annual "carnival" in the island, with those of the jubilee (centred around queen and empire) in the minds of the people.

The reopening ceremony was followed by the governor's levee at the town hall, where officials and other elite persons conducted a tedious but nevertheless symbolically important ritual of presenting to the governor formal addresses paying homage to the queen. At five in the afternoon there was a review of the imperial troops (both army and navy) and the Kingston Volunteer Militia by the governor at Up Park Camp. As a ritualistic exhibition of British military – especially naval – prowess, it seemed to offer exemplary proof of why Britannia *did* rule the waves:

> The people . . . were able to see of what stuff Jack Tar [the British sailor] is when he takes to *terra firma*, and after seeing the business-like appearance of the Naval Brigade, none will wonder that where there is fighting or work to be done Jack is always to the fore. Our hearts went out to the gallant Blue Jackets as they stepped by with their guns.[31]

For some in the crowd, the fact that those guns might be used to quell any uprising they might attempt was not an aspect of the great display that was lost on them.

In addition to the ritualism and pageantry, in several parts of the country the jubilee celebrations took on various forms: athletic sports at Heathfield in Vere, Mandeville, Lucea, St Ann's Bay and Linstead; a regatta at Black River; and picnics at Lower Works Pen near Black River and Caenwood near Hope Bay. The grand finale to the jubilee extravaganza came in the form of fireworks: in Kingston, Spanish Town, Mandeville, Black River, Lucea, St Ann's Bay and Linstead. The display in Kingston, held at the race course, was by far the most elaborate. To accommodate the social elites, the governor had two large stands built on either side of the grandstand, to seat about one thousand people. Admission to the grandstand cost two shillings, making sure that whatever the aspirations of equality held by some of Britain's newest additions to the empire, they were to be unrealized on this occasion. In keeping with the theme of the celebrations, the fireworks show included the words "God Bless Our Queen" worked out in large block letters surrounded by a fringe of silver fires marooned, and a colossal portrait of the queen in lines of fire. The spectacle of the queen emblazoned on the evening skies could not but leave most in awe and reverence, and serve as reassurance about their mighty queen and the sprawling empire that she led. The curtains came down on the festivities with a grand ball hosted by the governor at King's House on 30 July.[32]

If any proof were needed of the reverence in which the people held *their* queen, it was most adequately provided by their attendance at events all over the island and by their exemplary behaviour throughout the celebrations. They were

> quiet, orderly, good humoured, courteous. . . . [Wherever they congregated,] the same good order, sobriety and kindly feeling for one another prevailed throughout. We do not remember to have seen a single case of drunkenness among the people, certainly there were no rows or street fights. No robberies from the persons, or assaults have been reported, and we do not think half a dozen arrests have been made during the whole period of the festivities. Nothing could speak in higher praise of the good humour, good order and good taste of our people. Volumes could not say more of their loyalty to their Sovereign and the law.[33]

That "good behaviour" should have caused comment and should have been used as a marker of loyalty gives an excellent clue to the concerns about bringing the Jamaican people "up to scratch" within the empire (see chapter 5). Inherent in the comment was a concern about "good behaviour", and perhaps even an admission that it had not been expected. But, on this occasion, those who sought to "civilize the natives" and to mould them into good British subjects could see the fruits of their hard work on display, and must have felt great pride in the midst of their apprehension. Her Majesty's Jamaican subjects seemed to be responding positively to the lessons of appropriate Victorian etiquette, and the jubilee of their beloved queen was one occasion on which they responded to the regular admonitions to "behave".

Jamaicans also found other ways to express their loyalty. The Women's Self-Help Society of Kingston sent several articles of their fancywork as a jubilee offering to the queen. Charles William Chapman and William Titley Malabre, both of Kingston, wrote jubilee odes for Her Majesty. As a general rule, Jamaicans of all classes felt proud of their grand display of loyalty. The *Gleaner* observed: "From the capital of the island to the smallest of negro huts, the same feelings of love and loyalty have been shewn. From the white sands of our shores . . . to the towering peak of the Blue Mountains . . . there has been but one heart, one mind, one desire; to do honor and show love and affection to the Queen on the occasion of the celebration of the Jubilee year." The *Colonial Standard* concurred: "The sentiment which we entertain towards Her Majesty is one of loyal reverence in so far as she is to be regarded as the embodiment of the national sentiment – the type and pattern of all that we reckon worthy and worshipful. In giving expression to this loyal sentiment, we feel that we are taking common part with our fellow-subjects throughout the wide extent of the common Empire; and this sense of loyal combination is to be regarded not only as a sign of national identity but as a source of Imperial strength and security."[34] British Jamaican subjects were encouraged to remember that they were a part of a mighty whole, at the centre of which was a power so distant yet so omnipotent and worthy that only displays of adoration were deemed appropriate.

Victoria's diamond jubilee was celebrated in similarly pompous vein with public holidays on 22 and 24 June 1897, and with perhaps even greater enthusiasm among the ordinary people. On Sunday 20 June, every church in the island held special services in honour of the queen, and "sermons, patriotic in spirit and exhorting the people to loyalty, exhibiting Her Majesty as an example and a pattern to maidens and to womanhood, were delivered". Even as lower-class Jamaican "maidens" behaved in "deplorable" ways which caused only consternation to the cultural elites of the upper and middle classes (see chapter 5), Victoria, the ultimate "true woman", was held up as the standard for which they should strive. Wife and mother, virtuous and pious, Victoria embodied the ideal woman, and based at least in part on the tenets of the "cult of true womanhood",[35] this age was named in her honour.

The official celebrations followed the pattern of 1887, with similar imperial ritualism: a gathering of children and unveiling of a statue of the queen at the Parade, a state service at the Kingston Parish Church, the governor's levee, his review of the military, and a grand display of fireworks. Unofficially, the celebrations continued for over a week, with a horseracing carnival and cycle processions on 23 and 24 June, and a concert by the Institute of Jamaica in the following week.36

Commercial and public buildings, and private houses in Kingston and other towns around the country, were "lavishly and profusely decorated" and illuminated; every village and hamlet, even in the most remote mountain glens, had its local celebration, "the people contributing most cheerfully for the decorations". This was perhaps the most striking difference from the 1887 celebrations. The *Gleaner* observed that "never before have the people themselves done so much. One could observe this by walking through the bye-ways and lanes. Little flags, bannerettes, and streamers brightened the poorest and most dingy localities." In 1959 Ethel Scott recalled these joyful scenes: "there was great rejoicing, everyone gaily dressed with the Red, White and Blue satches [sic], rosettes, and streamers hanging from their hats".37 The rituals of the cult of monarchy and empire were increasingly in place, and the people not only accepted, in large measure, the symbols of British imperial might, but were willing and enthusiastic participants in the celebration of that might, although it could be used to keep them in check.

About thirty thousand persons witnessed the unveiling of the queen's statue by Lady Blake (the governor's wife), including seven thousand children with banners and pennants who, after their demonstration which included the singing of "Rule Britannia" and other "patriotic" songs, were shepherded to a reserved spot to view the proceedings. Similar children's demonstrations took place in the rural areas. Children, as an important part of Victorian middle-class culture, were central to the task of empire building. No doubt it was believed that there was a real chance of creating black British colonials if one started early and worked at it consistently. In keeping with that thrust, commemorative medals were distributed to all school children. The celebrations continued with the poor being fed, and at night bonfires blazed on "every hill top". Many thousands of people viewed the grand fireworks display that brought the celebrations to a close.38

Once more the reverence with which the queen was regarded by "her people" was evidenced in their exemplary behaviour throughout the celebrations: "orderliness and good behaviour were everywhere recorded", and "Throughout the [final] day our eyes were never offended by a single unpleasant sight in the way of drunkenness, or debauchery or brutality, and our ears only very occasionally by a few coarse expressions. Nowhere in the wide realms of Her Majesty's empire could the behaviour have been more creditable." Jamaicans were as proudly loyal to "Missus Queen" in 1897 as they

The Cult of Monarchy and Empire — 283

Figure 28. Statue of Queen Victoria, "Lord of Jamaica" (photographed after the 1907 earthquake)
Source: Sir Frederick Treves, *The Cradle of the Deep* (London: Smith, Elder and Co., 1913).

had been ten years before. One loyal son, Dennis Montague James of Montego Bay, even composed a poem and sent it to the queen. The *Jamaica Post* observed: "Our people of every grade and every section, are loyal to the heart's core. The name of the Queen is a talisman that weaves a magic spell around the hearts of Jamaicans whenever uttered; and if occasion demanded there are thousands among us that would be as ready to die in Her Majesty's defence as they would be to live in her service."[39]

Another of the focal events which helped to bridge the geographical gap between mother country and colony was the installation of a new monarch. Edward's proclamation as king on 25 January 1901, however, was solemn, coming when the people were in the height of mourning for their beloved and revered Victoria. So while it was hoped that

> the mourning city would rise from her sorrow for an hour or two . . . that the vast multitude should have been in holiday garbs . . . the people's sorrow was too overmastering to allow any such thing, and apart from the flash and glitter of the soldiers . . . few indeed were to be seen arrayed in anything other than black or black and white.

Flags were flown and bugles sounded, but "the heart of the people was with the Queen that had passed".[40] The extraordinarily long hiatus of nineteen months between the proclamation and the actual coronation, however, provided sufficient time for healing to take place.

The coronation of Edward VII was a remarkably joyful gala affair. Preparations for the coronation, set for 26 June 1902, began in April; despite a scarcity of money, Jamaicans rich and poor found the means to decorate their surroundings to such an extent that they reportedly surpassed any previous display. The *Jamaica Times* noted, "The store windows are bright with Union Jacks, and portraits of the King and Queen are thicker than leaves when the Almond is changing its foliage. Private residences are already taking unto themselves decorations, and even the humble vendor before the Sollas [Jubilee] Market has his little flag surmounting his pile of Jackass Rope Tobacco." The *Gleaner* observed, "Even the poorest houses in and around Kingston were prettily decorated with flags, and in nearly every street one saw decorated dwellings. This shows the loyalty of the people, though poor, and hampered with taxes." All over the island the forthcoming coronation was the talk: "everybody is going to 'coronate' ". At Petersfield many believed that the king would be crowned *in person* at Savanna-la-Mar, and that the law demanded that all the men should go in khaki suits and the women in khaki skirts.[41]

Imagine the disappointment when news arrived that the king had fallen ill and the coronation had to be postponed! But recognizing the raised expectations, and the great expense incurred all over the empire, the king requested that the festivities should still go on. Retitled "Thanksgiving Festivities", in Jamaica these were set for 10–11 July. This, however, struck some people as odd. One country woman bemusedly exclaimed, "Lard! eberyting very fine, but it's de fust time I hyar a king have two crownations. Dem have one now, and dem mek anodder one nex mont wen him be betta."[42]

Nevertheless, on those two days in July Jamaicans indulged in a carnival of celebration. Kingston and other major towns were brilliantly illuminated, and huge crowds gathered in the streets in their best clothes to view the decorations and participate in the events. In Kingston these included an assembly at Victoria Market with the Kingston Infantry Militia Band providing music; a procession of decorated buses and drays through the streets; a "Trades Procession", featuring floats and costumes of Chinese, clowns, the military (the "Roughriders"), "Peace" (commemorating the end of the Boer War), "jippi-jappa" (Panama) hat-making, the sugar industry, and so on; a costume cricket match at Sabina Park; a horserace meeting at the race course; a water pageant at Rockfort Gardens, which included an illuminated flotilla and a display of illuminated models of animals floating on the water; a magnificent fireworks display at the Myrtle Bank Hotel; and a massive bonfire at the race course. In addition, in a joint promotion, the Montpelier Cigar Store (also known as the Golofina) gave away free cigars with the purchase of a *Gleaner* newspaper; the Salvation Army fed the poor at its home on Orange Street. Again, the newspapers commented that, throughout, the people "behaved themselves".[43]

The 1902 thanksgiving festivities were an important litmus test of the extent of the loyalty of the people. The occasion clearly demonstrated that despite the sense of *personal* loyalty felt towards Victoria, it was not limited to her but extended to her heirs and successors, and to the empire at large. As the *Gleaner* put it, the celebrations revealed

> the intense reverence and affection cherished by the people towards the [new] King and Queen, and the glorious institution of the British Crown and Empire. The people did not merely seize the occasion of a holiday to make merry. They embraced an opportunity of demonstrating their loyalty and their joy at the recovery of their monarch from an illness which threatened to prove fatal. We may say of the festivities that they were indeed the voice of the people proclaiming their loyalty and love.

Significantly, for the first time it was observed that some of the new immigrant groups, particularly the naturalized Lebanese/Syrians and the Cubans, made significant contributions to and participated in the celebrations; the Chinese displayed much less enthusiasm, being for the most part passive observers.[44] There was no mention of any Indian involvement.

The actual coronation celebrations on 11 August were an anticlimax, however. The people had already exhausted their money, energies and enthusiasm on the thanksgiving extravaganza, and the rains dampened their spirits even more. Although the newspapers did their part by printing special coronation issues with full-page pictures of the king and queen, the decorations were not as lavish as the previous month's, and several events were spoiled by rain. There was the ritualistic military trooping of the colours and military review at the race course. But even the acting governor's levee at the town hall was poorly attended, while a decorated bus and dray procession failed for want of sufficient entries, and the fireworks exhibition at Myrtle Bank had to be postponed because of inclement weather. The poor did enjoy another good dinner, and there was a fine horserace meeting at the race course. Altogether, however, the celebration was a "very dull and flat" affair.[45]

Nevertheless the state and churches rallied in full force to the cause. Special church services were held, including a pompous state ceremony at the Kingston Parish Church, attended by the usual dignitaries. At the East Queen Street Baptist Church, for instance, Reverend W. Pratt preached a sermon on "Christian Imperialism", and argued that the British Empire could not rely entirely on its army and navy to save it:

> The saviour of the British Empire must come from the spreading of justice and righteousness and true light to its people. Let them pray that their ruler might strive to put down all evil and to encourage and support all that was good; that those who made laws should make such laws as would render it more difficult to do wrong and more easy to do right. That was the right kind of Imperialism; that was the true Christian Imperialism. They should make the British Empire to be as the Garden of Eden in which the fruits of prosperity and justice should flourish not only for their own advantage but for the advantage of the whole world.[46]

The coronation of George V in 1911 was once more a time of enthusiastic celebration. Again, a long period of thirteen months was allowed to elapse between the death of Edward VII and the crowning of his successor, which gave the empire an opportunity to get over its collective grief. The dates 22 and 23 June were declared public holidays for the celebration, and the leading newspapers published special issues for the occasion, featuring large pictures of the king and his wife, Mary.[47] Kingston and other major towns were ablaze in the colour of their lavish decorations and illuminations; very strikingly, amidst all this the Chinese temple on Barry Street stood out. It "was magnificently decorated. It stood in a class by itself and attracted enormous

Figure 29. God, King and Empire: the trooping of the colours
Source: *Handbook of Jamaica* (1921). Courtesy of the National Library of Jamaica.

crowds who were not only content to behold the beautiful exterior, but who invaded the inside which was also decorated with true oriental gorgeousness." Huge crowds gathered at every venue. "Never before has there been a more loyal enthusiastic assemblage of people and the celebrations will always stand unrivalled for the orderly and successful manner in which everything was carried through."48

There were the usual ritualistic ceremonies: special services in all churches and a state service at the Kingston Parish Church; governor's levee at Headquarter House; the trooping of the colours and military review at Up Park Camp, and military parades in other town centres; an "At Home"49 and a brilliant ball at King's House. There were horseraces at Maverly, yacht races in Kingston Harbour, and sporting events throughout the island. Children's processions with flags and banners were held all over the island, and featured the singing of "patriotic" songs and addresses pointing out their duty to their sovereign and their country. Theophilus Wright considered this "the best day I ever seen in my boy hood". A magnificent fireworks display at the race course provided the climax to the celebrations; it was reputedly the best of

Figure 30. Coronation Day in Mandeville
© Trustees for Methodist Church Purposes; used by permission of Methodist Publishing House.

Figure 31. Coronation Day military parade (George V, 1910)
Courtesy of the National Library of Jamaica.

its kind since the 1887 jubilee, and could be seen for miles around. The high point of the display was a device that portrayed the late Edward VII and wife, Alexandra: "The mighty crowd cheered heartily the appearance of this device"; and although a spark scorched a new and expensive hat that Miss S.H. Brydson had worn for the occasion, "I didn't care though it cost me a fair sum. What I saw far out valued what I lost in the hat"[50] – such was her loyalty to her king and empire.

To a far-flung outpost of empire like Jamaica, seeking to maintain a close identity with the so-called motherland, visits by members of the royal family, although few, were occasions for great rejoicing and exhibitions of loyalty. In 1861 Prince Alfred, one of Victoria's sons, visited the island and received "red carpet" hospitality. People from all walks of life congregated at various points along the streets to get a glimpse of him. But most striking, according to Governor Darling, was what happened when the prince was obliged to cut short his visit on receiving the news of the Duchess of Kent's death. A respectful silence was observed, and the people withdrew from the streets as he made his way back to the Kingston harbour for a hasty departure:

> The contrast which the state of the City presented on that occasion, with the joyous and exultant scenes of the preceding day, when His Royal Highness made a public entry from Spanish Town into Kingston constitute in my mind the most convincing proof of the affectionate and sympathizing character of the loyalty which animates Her Majesty's Subjects in this Colony.[51]

It was not until 1880, nineteen years later, that another royal visit would take place, in the form of the two sons of Albert Edward, the Prince of Wales (heir to the throne): Princes Albert Victor (aged sixteen) and George Frederick (aged fifteen). Great concern was displayed over the dirty condition of the streets of Kingston, which, it was feared, might oblige the authorities to confine the royal visitors to Spanish Town and the north side. As a result, a Reception Street Sweeping Fund was hastily launched to raise voluntary subscriptions to pay gangs of labourers, provided with brooms, dust carts and bottles of Florida water (a perfumed water resembling eau-de-Cologne) to "purify the streets" twice a day. The post office building was entirely cleared, repaired and cleaned to prepare a ballroom, and King's House was provided with gas lighting. An attempt was also made to illuminate Port Royal on the evening of the princes' arrival. These urgent infrastructural improvements ensured that the visit was a success, and large numbers of people gathered eagerly at various vantage points to see the two boys. Houses along the railway line from Kingston to Spanish Town were decorated with flags and arches of coconut boughs[52] in a sort of show of "tropical loyalty".

When Prince George returned eleven years later to open the Jamaica Exhibition in January 1891, four triumphal arches were erected along the route that he took after landing at Kingston. Steamers brought people from the coastal countryside to see the prince when he disembarked, and a great show of loyalty was displayed. The *Jamaica Post* thought it was a wise thing to invite a royal personage to open the exhibition, "For, however Radical and Democratic we may be in Jamaica, we certainly fall behind no British colony in our loyalty to Queen Victoria."[53]

Twenty-two years later, on 22 March 1913, Prince Albert, son of George V, stopped in Kingston Harbour while on a training course with the British fleet. Although advised that this was not an official visit, Kingston buzzed with excitement. The *Jamaica Times* banner headline read, "Loyal Welcome to the Prince, Son of King George V, Great-Grandson of Queen Victoria" (which was, perhaps, his real claim to fame among the people of Jamaica); this was accompanied by a large picture of the prince and a biographical sketch.[54] Large numbers of people assembled near Victoria Pier in anticipation that the prince might come ashore, while business establishments decided to decorate their buildings, just in case. Although there were several reported "sightings" of the prince shopping in Kingston stores, it was not until 26 March that he made a formal landing in ordinary cadet uniform, was met by the mayor, and then proceeded unescorted to King's House while the governor was busy presiding at the Legislative Council. As he drove slowly along the city streets word quickly spread, and hundreds of curious well-wishers gathered, cheering enthusiastically and waving flags, hats and handkerchiefs. After leaving King's House the prince attended a regatta at the Royal Jamaica Yacht Club. In the course of his training he also visited the old King's House in Spanish Town.[55] These spontaneous, enthusiastic outbursts of loyalty spoke of support for the monarchy and the empire which it ruled.

In January 1914 Princess Louise of Schleswig-Holstein, Victoria's granddaughter, visited Jamaica. Although she was greeted less effusively than Albert, her welcome was nevertheless decidedly hearty, as Kingston once more exhibited its hospitality to royalty with lavish decorations.[56] The final royal heartbeat during this period came with the announced visit of Edward, Prince of Wales, in September 1920. An elaborate programme of activities was planned for two public holidays on 15 and 16 September. These included the decoration of the streets and public buildings, the erection of arches on King

Figure 32. Royal arch of welcome for Princess Louise, 1914
Courtesy of the National Library of Jamaica.

Street and at the Victoria statue in the Parade, a military parade and review, a civic reception at the Ward Theatre, a gymkhana at Knutsford Park, an officers' ball at the Constant Spring Hotel, an address by the prince to school children on the Mico grounds, and a treat for the poor and the school children. Great was the disappointment when the outbreak of Alastrim or "Kaffir Pox" caused the prince to bypass Jamaica on his West Indian tour.[57]

The apparently strong identification of the people with the cult of monarchy was also displayed in keen interest in the personal lives of the royals. The social privilege that was accorded to the monarchy was enhanced by a sort of prototype "celebrity status" that was given to members of the royal family. A particular point of interest was the royal marriages, which were sometimes occasions for public celebration in Jamaica, as in other colonies.[58]

For the marriage of the Prince of Wales and Princess Alexandra of Denmark in 1863 a public holiday was observed. Public buildings throughout the island and ships in the Kingston harbour were decorated with flags. At the chief military garrisons and in the major town centres, there were parades and *feux de joie* were fired, followed later in the day by sumptuous dinners at which the queen and the royal couple were toasted. In Lucea Captain Browne of the Hanover Volunteer Rifle Corps alluded, "in happy terms, to the character of our beloved Queen, who, in every relation of life, as daughter, wife, mother and sovereign had won the love and esteem, not only of her subjects, but of all the civilized inhabitants of the Earth". As if to prove this, twelve thousand Jamaicans "of all ranks and classes" signed an address of congratulation to the queen[59] rather than to the newly married couple. Likewise the marriage of the Duke of York, George Frederick, Victoria's grandson (later George V), to Princess Victoria Mary in July 1893 was marked by gaudy decorations on public buildings, hotels and ships, and by the firing of royal salutes.[60]

Mourning Royalty

Where coronations, visits and marriages were the apparent sources of great celebration, royal deaths were by contrast occasions of immense sorrow and solemnity. The newspapers generally commemorated these by printing thick black borders on their columns. Following the death of the queen's husband, the Prince Consort (Albert), in 1861, numerous messages of condolence from all over the island were sent to Victoria. In addition, public meetings were held in every parish to solicit funds to erect a memorial at the Kingston Parade gardens in his honour.[61] When the queen's fourth son, Prince Leopold, died in March 1884, the Half-Way Tree Church was draped in mourning, and minute guns were fired at Port Royal at the precise hour of his burial. Similar reverence attended the death of Prince Albert Victor, Duke of Clarence and Avondale (son of the Prince of Wales) in January 1892, when a series of memorial services was held throughout the island.[62] On each of these occasions, public entertainments that had been previously scheduled were postponed.

But no occasion was more solemn than the death of a British monarch, and none more so than Victoria's in January 1901. After a reign of sixty-three years, she was loved and revered by Jamaicans, elites and masses alike. The news of her death brought everything literally to a standstill in the island. In addition to the usual newspaper columns with bold black borders, the front page of the *Jamaica Times* carried a large portrait of Victoria under the headline "Queen Victoria Dies", and it featured an article entitled "The Dead Queen – The Story of Her Life". From all over the island, even the deepest rural districts, the reports were the same. For example, from Gayle: "A deep gloom was cast here by the sad news of the death of our beloved Queen. Merchants as well as labourers, the wealthy as well as the unlettered, seem all bowed with grief. The Queen is dead. We can hardly realize it"; and from Ewarton:

> The death of our beloved Queen cast quite a gloom over the district. When the bells began to toll many persons were at a loss to know what they meant, but as they got to know the disaster that had fallen on the Empire, the hearts of all sank low, and were only lifted by the belief that instead of the earthly crown, she wears the heavenly. The leading stores here, although not closed on Wednesday, were draped in black.[63]

Almost sixty years later (in 1959), Henry Avis recalled that on hearing the sad news, "People put their hands on their heads and bawl. The churches were dress with black and members wear black as a symbol of morning [sic] on their hands for six months." This reaction was reflected in the lamentation of Bahamian-born black journalist and politician, Robert Love, and his People's Convention, who stated that the nation had been deprived of the guardian care and exemplary life of its great sovereign.[64] Robert Messias Bennett, a black small settler from St Catherine, wrote in a letter to the editor of the *Daily Gleaner*,

> all feel the loss which the British Empire and the world has sustained by the death of the best, the greatest and the noblest Ruler that England and the world have seen – whose first act gave to the Negroes of the West Indies a full, and unconditional Freedom; by whose generous acts and humane laws all the nations of her world empire . . . have been brought together under one Flag, one Queen, one common Destiny; the civilizing and beneficial influence of whose laws has knitted together the hearts of all her subjects throughout her world empire in one common bond of unity – the power of whose arm . . . has been felt by the nations of Europe and the world, and kept the balance even, and made even her enemies *feel* that to *her*, and the Anglo Saxon race, God has bequeathed the destinies of the world.[65]

Sydney Olivier, the acting governor, was thus a trifle overzealous in ordering all public officers to wear mourning and inviting the public to do the same. They would have done so anyway, albeit for their own reasons. He was obliged to observe,

> The general feeling of sorrow which pervades and is exhibited by all classes in this loyal Colony can hardly be exaggerated. The shops in Kingston and through out the Island have been closed, all kinds of ceremonies, meetings, and entertainments have been abandoned, and almost every person, from the highest to the lowest, has donned some mark of mournful respect for the Queen who was universally beloved and reverenced, and is now greatly and sincerely mourned.[66]

Constructing a further link to Britain, 2 February 1901 was declared a special day of mourning, to coincide with the actual funeral of Victoria in London. Even in death there was imperial ritualism: a state service was held at the Kingston Parish Church, attended by public officers, high-ranking military officers, and detachments of the military stationed in the colony. Special services were also held at other churches and Jewish synagogues throughout the island, and "the day was everywhere observed with decorum and solemnity by all classes". A similar pattern of solemn observance and ritualistic ceremony was occasioned by the death of King Edward VII in 1910, although the sense of *personal* loss among ordinary Jamaicans was, understandably, less.[67]

Special Imperial Holidays

Although the Jamaican people celebrated the succession of Edward VII to the throne, they could not abandon the memory of Victoria, and in the months following her death there was a groundswell of support for continuing to celebrate her birthday. Jamaica was not unique in this regard: Barbados and Canada also proposed to establish 24 May as a public holiday, and the Jamaican legislature passed a resolution to that effect. Without committing himself in perpetuity, Governor Hemming proclaimed the holiday for the year 1901; in 1902 the legislature passed two laws making 24 May an annual public holiday. In the following year the governor approved the Board of Education's recommendation that Victoria Day should be observed as a school holiday in public elementary schools when it fell on a school day, and that the preceding day should be used to instruct the children in their duties and privileges as members of a great empire.[68] The desire to instruct the empire's "dark"[69] children about the might of the empire served to reinforce the sense of a larger whole, in which they ought to have been proud to take part.

This local sentiment coincided with a broader "Empire Day" movement started by the Earl of Meath in Britain, which had as its objective the training of young people all over the empire in the virtues of loyalty and patriotism, and in the duties attached to British citizenship. Meath proposed that 24 May should be observed throughout the empire, particularly in schools, so that by its observance children might be reminded of their privileges and responsibilities as British subjects. This proposal was readily adopted in Jamaica, and from 1904 Empire Day replaced Victoria Day; on that day children all over the island (and empire) would gather in public places, listen to "patriotic" speeches and sing "patriotic" songs. This celebration was married to "Arbor Day", borrowed from the United States, for the purpose of planting trees. In this way, imperial patriotism was twinned with environmentalism:[70] the act of planting a tree served to tie a practical, physical activity to the cult of empire, and made for a more memorable occasion than it might otherwise have been. So, as those trees grew, the children who grew alongside them were to be reminded of the ideas that accompanied the ceremonies: the privilege, loyalty, duty and responsibility inherent in the support for monarch and empire.

Empire Day was celebrated with great fervour in Jamaica, and, more than anything that had preceded it, was a key instrument for implanting the ideology of British imperialism in the minds of young children. Every year children all over the island gathered to hear the message and absorb the symbols of empire. For instance, in 1905 at the Titchfield School in Port Antonio, the children were made to stand with rosettes of red, white and blue, and miniature Union Jacks, on ground overlooking the Caribbean Sea, while singing the words "Britannia rules the waves". The powerful conflation of symbol and ideology could not have been lost on the little children of Portland. Likewise, those of the White Hall Roman Catholic School, similarly attired, marched around the grounds with banners bearing such inscriptions as "God Save the King" while singing "Rule Britannia". After planting trees, they closed with the national anthem. Similar scenes were replicated in every parish, every year.[71]

The celebration of Empire Day assumed an even more insidious character (in relation to the mainstream creole culture system) in 1907, when the Board of Education adopted a catechism for schools modelled on one circulated to the colonies by the Earl of Meath. Designed to indoctrinate children in the ideology of British imperialism, it was to be read at all Empire Day celebrations. Prepared by A.B. McFarlane of Mico Training College, and entitled "One King, One Flag, One Fleet, One Empire", the catechism attempted to locate Jamaica within the mighty British Empire while extolling the greatness and virtues of the latter: its sheer size ("the sun never sets on the King's dominions"); its vast, cosmopolitan composition (one in every five persons on earth lived in the empire, and it comprised people of all races, languages and religions); its immense commerce (the empire held first place in the world's commerce, and British ships could be found on every sea); and its overwhelming naval might (the Royal Navy was the most powerful in the world).

But, intoned the catechism, the empire's real strength and greatness resided "in the love and esteem which the various colonies and dependencies feel towards the Mother Country, which bind them to her with a strong tie and make them ready to come to her assistance in time of need". It was a grand privilege to be a British subject, and as such everyone should do his or her very best to be worthy of the honour. British citizenship guaranteed personal liberty and freedom unsurpassed anywhere else, while the army and navy protected British subjects, wherever in the world they might be. It was thus their duty to honour and obey the king and his representative, the governor, and all in authority under him. Not only should they be proud of the empire, but they should try to make it proud of them, and promote its best interests at whatever cost. The catechism concluded thus:

> On Empire Day our national flag, the "Union Jack", should be flown on all public buildings, reminding us of the glorious traditions of the past and of our duty to the Empire in the present and the future; and whilst we reverently salute the dear old flag we should sing with all our hearts our "National Anthem".72

This was the doctrine that generations of Jamaican children were exposed to, and it served to underscore all the symbols, rituals and sermons on British imperialism to which they were exposed on a regular basis in school, church and the press. This systematic indoctrination was designed to foster a widespread sentiment that assigned preference to things British and elevated British institutions, customs, values and morality into ideals to aspire to and emulate.

While the invention of Victoria Day (later Empire Day) as "tradition" was based on the widely popular sentiment of keeping alive the memory of Victoria, it was by no means the only such commemoration. Following the death of Edward VII there was considerable demand both inside and outside the Jamaican legislature to set aside a day in his memory as well. Although the Colonial Office was not keen to sanction this new holiday, the king himself, George V, bowed to the wishes of his Jamaican subjects and approved it. Accordingly the governor proclaimed 9 November "King Edward the Seventh Day", later labelled "Peacemaker's Day".73 Jamaica, then, even more than Britain, displayed a keen need for and interest in identifying with the crown and all that it symbolized. In the (geographical and perhaps cultural) hinterlands, conscious of their vulnerability before the numerical dominance of the descendants of slaves (as Morant Bay had made clear), the social elites clung even more tightly to the supposed motherland, extremely anxious that their loyalty be held above reproach, in case they might need to be rescued from the "barbarous" mass.

Imperial Institutions and Symbols

The high esteem that was accorded to the crown was also extended to the sovereign's representatives in the colony. The governor was tantamount to a local potentate in status and in the execution of his duties as the representative of the sovereign. He was *in loco regis,* the commander-in-chief of the armed forces stationed in the colony, and as the chief executive officer of the civil administration in a crown colony, he exercised even more power locally than the monarch did at home. It is not surprising, therefore, that he behaved and was treated as if he were king, complete with a full display of imperial ritualism. The arrival of a new governor in the colony was almost a royal occasion. As his ship entered the Kingston harbour, the guns of Port Royal would fire a salute. On disembarking in full ceremonial dress, complete with plumes, sword and medals, he would be met by the heads of department of the civil government, military officers, the clergy, members of the legislature, the mayor, the bar, and prominent citizens. Then he would review the guard of honour of the West India Regiment, and the national anthem would be played. He would thereafter proceed to Headquarter House, home of the legislature, where, after being met by another guard of honour, he would be formally sworn in before moving on to his official residence, King's House.74

Large enthusiastic crowds usually greeted the new governor when he arrived in the colony, and also when he undertook familiarization tours of the island. Successive governors commented on the great warmth and respect with which the people received them, as the representatives of the sovereign. Wherever the governors went the day was treated like a holiday: the towns were gaily decorated, triumphal arches with banners ("God Bless the Governor" and so on) had been erected, school children sang "patriotic" songs, and large numbers of working people travelled long distances with their flags and flowers to pay homage. The governors were royally regaled by the custodes, parochial officials, clergy and prominent citizens: there were levees, church services, public and private banquets, balls, and other entertainments.75 Governor Eyre put it most succinctly in 1864:

> The loyalty and good feeling which accompanied my receptions in the different Parishes were most gratifying to me; nor were these feelings confined to any classes

or parties. All seemed to vie with each other in welcoming and doing honor to their Governor. The gatherings of the people were often very large. In some cases many thousands were congregated, amongst whom were pointed out to me many who had come 10, 15, 20 and even 25 miles for the occasion. Everywhere I met with the most enthusiastic loyalty. In most of the Parishes Arches of welcome and congratulations gaily decorated with flags, flowers and fruits, were erected across the roads or the entrances to different cottages. . . . Bouquets of flowers were occasionally thrown literally into the carriage as it passed along and wherever I halted for the day, Public Addresses were presented to me by the Inhabitants of all classes and denominations.[76]

Clearly, then, before the Morant Bay Rebellion caused him to revise his assessment and to question the loyalty of several hundred citizens before having them hanged, Eyre was convinced that the symbols and meanings of British patriotism had been inculcated. That some of these people would challenge the authority of the local representatives of imperial power does not, however, mean he was wrong. For as Abigail Bakan has observed, as in pre-industrial Europe, the Jamaican people made a clear distinction between the distant and remote "benevolently despotic" monarchy which they assumed protected their interests, and the ruling colonial authorities whom they held accountable for the racial oppression and economic exploitation from which they suffered; they believed, moreover, that the former sympathized with their challenges to the injustices perpetrated by the latter.[77]

What is very evident from the foregoing is the extensive use made of symbols in fostering loyalty to the monarch and to the empire: flags, banners, the national anthem, "patriotic" songs, firework images and published pictures of royalty, statues and other memorials. Very serious attention was paid to such emblems of empire by the colonial officialdom. But perhaps the most impressive symbols used to instil loyalty in the people were the armed forces. Enormous use was made of the army, the navy and the local militias in ritualistic parades on all official occasions: the ceremonial opening of the legislature, the annual birthday parades of the monarch, jubilee and coronation parades, arrivals of royal visitors and governors, and even religious state services. Resplendent in their colourful uniforms and regalia, these units were always awe-inspiring in their pageantry and precision drills.[78] The Jamaican case amply bears out P.J. Rich's point about the importance of imperial rituals in colonial governance.[79]

But pride of place went to "the Fleet", the British North American and West Indian Squadron, which visited the island every spring and remained for about one month, moving from one Jamaican port to the next. Whenever the fleet came there was a stir in Kingston and the other major coastal towns, and several entertainments were organized for the officers and men: regattas, cricket matches and other sporting events, balls, banquets, and concerts. But the presence of the fleet signified much more than fun: Jamaicans were entirely overawed by this grand display of British naval power. It was "suggestive of the vast naval armaments and colossal maritime power by means of which the mother country maintains around 'the broad belt of the world', the supremacy and security of an Empire greater than that of ancient Rome".[80]

> [It] never fails to thrill the landsman and fill him with a sense of the power and the grandeur of the great nation which has for centuries been dominant on the sea. . . . To the loyal it is a means of fanning the flame of patriotism. . . . That inhabitant of Jamaica is to be pitied who amid scenes recalling historic naval victories and in the presence of these successors of the ancient "wooden walls" does not feel prouder of his country [Britain] which has accomplished so much for the civilizing of humanity in every portion of the globe.[81]

But every inhabitant of Jamaica who felt proud of the civilizing mission that *his country* had pursued would also have been aware of the implication of the annual arrival of the fleet – no disorder would be allowed to mar this corner of the empire.[82]

It is important to note that what was happening in Jamaica with the fostering of the imperial ethic was by no means peculiar to the colony. In the late nineteenth century there was an upsurge in imperialist sentiments both in Britain and in its colonies. Referred to as the age of the "new imperialism" by some writers, this period was generally characterized by the rapid territorial expansion of Britain, France, Germany, Belgium and the United States overseas. A school of "new British imperialists", including Lord Rosebery, Joseph Chamberlain and the Earl of Meath, rose to prominence and articulated "extremist" positions in favour of imperial expansion and closer imperial unity. Chamberlain was the architect of the idea of imperial federation. For these people the empire ought to be the centre of Britain's worldwide interests, and the fostering of strong imperial sentiments within it was critical to its unity and strength in a world that was increasingly regarded as hostile at the turn of the century and beyond. So, even as the imperial agenda crystallized in the late nineteenth century and imperial sentiments ran high in Britain and its colonies, institutions and organizations were created to promote the cult of monarchy and empire.

Promoters of the cult of empire did not take it for granted that British imperial subjects would become a unified force, aware of and loyal to the monarch and the kingdom; so various means, institutions and organizations were created expressly for that purpose. Meath's Empire Day movement was just one of several which sprang up across the empire. The Victoria League was another, founded in Britain in 1901 by patriotic men and women who, according to J.G. Greenlee, were bent on combating the moral challenge to imperialism raised during the South African war.[83] Its aim was to encourage and develop relations of closer sympathy between Britons at home and overseas, to spread knowledge of the different parts of the empire, to organize mutual hospitality, and to secure a welcome for British subjects throughout the world. It was established all over the empire, although in Jamaica its membership was small, just 110 by 1914. Yet its influence was considerable since several elementary and secondary schools, and working men's clubs, were affiliated. The league sought to ensure that Victoria/Empire Day was properly observed, especially with respect to how the Union Jack was displayed on public buildings; it urged all citizens who owned flags to hoist them on that day and show publicly their loyalty to the empire. It also distributed to schools flags and other imperial emblems, including an "Empire Calendar" that provided information about notable events, and great personages who built the British Empire. The league also advocated that children should salute the flag every Monday morning and sing a verse of a patriotic song.[84]

The Overseas Club was similar, primarily designed to establish a conscious relation among emigrants from Britain, colonial-born Britons, and the people at home. It also aimed to create "a sentiment of Empire in the hearts of all the subjects of His Majesty the King – to establish a Brotherhood of Empire all over the world, including people of all races, creeds, colour and social rank". This organization took root in Jamaica in 1912, first in Ocho Rios and later in Kingston, mainly through the efforts of Reverend G. Nutt (again emphasizing the link between church and empire), and soon had a growing membership, including women. They pledged four things: to help one another when necessary; to emphasize the necessity of every able-bodied man to bear arms in defence of his country and the empire; to insist on the maintenance of Great Britain's supremacy on the sea; and to assist as far as possible in creating a bond of comradeship among all the peoples who lived under the Union Jack.[85]

Women and children were very much a part of this broad empire movement. In 1901, for instance, J. Smallpage established a local branch of the League of the Children of the Empire. This was aimed at developing loyalty and patriotism in children, and promoting friendly intercourse between children in Britain and the colonies. One clear objective was to encourage boys to join Cadet Corps and thus place themselves in training to fight for the empire when called upon. The league also introduced boys to "manly exercises" such as riding, saddling, grooming and shoeing horses, and sought to help every boy to learn a useful handicraft or technical skill. To entice children to join, it organized entertainments in which historical tableaux, magic-lantern illustrations of colonial life, and patriotic songs were leading features. Children were also encouraged to write patriotic essays and poems, for which they were awarded prizes.[86]

Lads'/Boys' Brigades were formed by churches all over the island at the turn of the century, and held sway for a decade until eclipsed by the Boy Scout movement.[87] Although the spread of Christian values was the primary focus of these brigades, in the heyday of British imperialism little distinction was made between Christian principles and imperial ideology. This was also reflected in The Boys' Social League, a branch of which was established in Jamaica by W. Logan and R.H. Kelly during the First World War (December 1915). Its aims were, among other things, to foster a true spirit of comradeship among young people; to encourage "clean, useful and upright living"; to promote all useful recreations, sports and hobbies; and to establish links between young people of the "Homeland and our Empire beyond the seas".[88]

By far the most important boys' organization, however, was the Boy Scouts Association. Founded by Lieutenant-General Sir Robert Baden-Powell in 1908, the scout movement epitomized the conjunction of God, king and empire. The organization was explicitly designed to foster loyalty to king and country among boys aged fourteen to eighteen, to disseminate knowledge about the history of the empire, and to instil pride in the flag. Scouts were bound on their honour to keep three rules: to be loyal to God and the king, to help other people at all times, and to obey scout law. The potential social value of this organization was so widely recognized that it rapidly took root all over the British Empire and beyond. The activities that it sponsored (camping and other sorts of "manly exercise") were great attractions for the boys whom it hoped to influence; once they came within the fold, they were sure to face a veritable onslaught of ideological manipulation, promoting the causes of God, monarch and empire.

Jamaica was very quick to embrace the movement, forming the first troop in Kingston in 1911, and Baden-Powell himself visited the island to promote his idea. As every scout was required to belong to a Christian denomination, the movement appealed to the churches. It also received official support, particularly after Governor Manning assumed office. The outbreak of the First World War pushed the movement into greater prominence, as the scouts were used to provide ancillary nonmilitary services for the defence forces. Hence, in that year (1914) the Boy Scouts Association of Jamaica was incorporated by royal charter, with the governor as chief scout.[89] Now these young boys, already church members, were the king's representatives who were being programmed to believe that in assisting to defend the empire they were being good Christians.

The female counterpart of the Boy Scout movement was the Girl Guides Association, which was also started in Jamaica in 1911. It aimed to develop "womanliness" among girls between eleven and eighteen years old, not only through encouraging physical fitness and good health by means of exercise (picnicking and hiking) and cleanliness, but also by training the girls in needlework, swimming, physical culture, a knowledge of the human body and moral lessons. Of course, loyalty to God, king and country was central to the movement.[90] Established at a time when feminists in Britain were struggling for the vote, this organization's emphasis on physical fitness for adolescent girls appeared to be progressive and represented a mild challenge to the tenets of Victorian gender ideology, which held women to be helpless and restricted to the home. Its ready and early adoption in Jamaica, therefore, is significant of a gradual, perhaps as yet imperceptible, realignment of gender relations, while at the same time emphasizing the importance and place of colonial women in the construction of the wider empire upon which the sun never set.

Another female organization that took root in Jamaica was the Imperial Order of the Daughters of the Empire. Allied with the Victoria League, it had branches all over the empire. Membership was open to all women who were loyal subjects, and its motto was "One Flag, One Throne, One Empire". In 1906 chapters were established in Montego Bay and Port Antonio. Its aims were to stimulate and give expression to the sentiment of patriotism which bound women of the empire around the throne and the person of the sovereign; to supply and foster a bond of union among the daughters of the empire; to bring home to the rising generation the greatness of the empire, the glory of its past, and their duty to its future; and to cultivate respect for those who had served the king and flag. There was also a children's chapter that met in schools, churches and private houses, and they were required, among other things, to salute the flag and sing the national anthem.[91]

The Imperial Order of the Children of Empire was formed in 1906 by Miss A.P. Thomson, principal of the Church High School in Montego Bay, who "[was] well known for her living patriotism". Although given a male nomenclature, the "Prince David" chapter, it was all female and sought "to foster patriotism in a sound thorough way, stimulating its members to take pride and an interest in their own bit of the Empire and in the Empire as a whole".[92]

War and Patriotism

If royal celebrations brought out the joyful side of the people's loyalty to their sovereign and empire, war called upon their sense of duty, obligation and sacrifice as British subjects, and Jamaicans were as eager to prove their readiness to defend "their empire" in time of war as they were to enjoy the "benefits" it bestowed in peacetime. Although the Boer War was remote and the existence of the empire not threatened, Jamaicans provided material and moral support to the British troops fighting in South Africa. Blow-by-blow accounts of the war were printed in the daily press, and the *Gleaner* launched a war fund to compensate the widows and orphans of fallen soldiers, which was well supported by all classes. A Kingston tavern keeper even refused to serve any Boer sympathizers in his bar. Every British victory was greeted with a celebration (bonfires, torchlight processions, and so forth); when news arrived of the final victory in 1902, Jamaica burst into spontaneous celebration: joy bells rang from every church, flags fluttered from buildings in Harbour and King Streets, people sang the national anthem, and effigies of General Kruger were burnt.[93]

The supreme test of their loyalty, however, came during the First World War. As with the Boer War, Jamaicans were able to follow the course of this war in the press, but no one expected that the mighty British Empire would find it so difficult to defeat Germany and its allies. That reality, the ensuing economic hardships – especially the scarcity of imported saltfish and flour[94] – compulsory military service, enforced lights-out from 1917, and three hurricanes in consecutive years (1915–17), tested Jamaica's loyalty. Yet the people remained steadfast in support of the empire and the war effort, as typified by the proto-nationalist leader Marcus Mosiah Garvey and his Universal Negro Improvement and Conservation Association and African Communities League. This organization transmitted a letter and resolution to the king indicating that their "love for, and devotion to, His Majesty and the Empire, stands unrivalled and from the depths of our hearts we pray for the crowning victory of the British Soldiers now at war". The resolution stated that,

> being mindful of the great protecting and civilizing influence of the English nation and people, of whom we are subjects, and their justice to all men, and especially to their Negro Subjects scattered all over the world, [we] hereby beg to express our loyalty and devotion to His Majesty the King, and Empire and our sympathy with those of the people who are in any way grieved and in difficulty in this time of National trouble. . . . We rejoice in British Victories and the suppression of foreign foes. Thrice we hail God save the King! Long live the King and Empire.[95]

Another loyal son, Z.E. McFarlane, said that his heart, "as that of every true Britisher", went out for the bereaved ones of England, and called on his fellow Jamaicans to support the *Jamaica Times*' Shilling War Fund, aimed at raising money for those who suffered from the war, including the relatives of the fighting men.[96]

The war provided a golden opportunity for elite women to extend their traditional role as charity organizers to include raising money for the war effort. In keeping with the reforming impulse and social activism which had so marked elite women's activities in the late nineteenth and early twentieth centuries, in 1915 the wives of Michael de Cordova, Sydney Couper and William Wilson (who were not referred to by their own first names since, presumably, middle- and upper-class women were not regarded as possessing social identities independent of their husbands) formed a committee to plan "Flag Day" on 27 July. The idea was to sell Union Jacks all over the island, the proceeds from which would go to the War Contingent Fund. The plan was also aimed at raising the patriotic spirit of the people, who were asked not just to buy flags, but to cheer the flag: "it is the flag we have to keep flying, the flag of the triple Cross. The flag of freedom and liberty, the like of which is unknown in the whole wide world."[97] Flag Day was a glorious success: "Thousands upon thousands of flags, big and little, were sold." All the major towns of Jamaica were dressed in flags, bunting and palms. In Kingston there was a motorcade in which

> A land "dreadnought" – a motor car made up to resemble a warship – with a formidable gun "forward", came round the bend and started down King Street, and behind this powerful looking craft came a long string of gaily bedecked motor cars, bringing the invaders – scores of ladies in white, wearing white red and blue ribbon

Figure 33. Concert performers draped in the Union Jack: Flag Day 1915
Courtesy of the National Library of Jamaica.

on their dresses and hats. Every member of the attacking force was lavishly supplied with "ammunition" – flags – and at once they started their campaign against the citizens.

From all over the island the reports were the same: virtually all the flags were sold out. People from all walks of life, including the governor, willingly bought flags to demonstrate their loyalty to the imperial cause. In fact, not to do so could prove dangerous, as an Indian vegetable vendor discovered when he was attacked by a group of women and told that unless he had a flag he could not do business. Flag Day netted over fifteen hundred pounds,[98] and sentiments of loyalty, patriotism and duty were promoted.

In 1916 the ladies were again quite active in the organization of "Our Day", celebrated throughout the empire on 19 October to raise funds for the Red Cross Society. Fifty thousand buttons with the image of Florence Nightingale were made locally for sale. This turned into another red-letter day in Kingston, as people donned holiday garb and turned out in large numbers to buy their badges and to witness a procession composed of the Salvation Army, the Alpha Cottage band, the Boy Scouts and Girl Guides. Similar parades were staged in Spanish Town, Old Harbour, Port Maria and other rural towns. During the afternoon there was an open-air concert by the West India Regiment band in front of the public buildings in Kingston, and a gymkhana in Spanish Town. Like Flag Day, this was an outstanding success, and almost twenty-two hundred pounds were raised.[99]

As the war ground on in a seemingly interminable manner, elite women remained in the vanguard of the patriotic movement, taking a lead in the drive to encourage the men of Jamaica to volunteer and thus avoid the introduction of conscription. With the active support of Governor Manning, on 23 May 1917 they held a great demonstration in front of the statue of Queen Victoria in the Parade, which the Gleaner described as the finest pageant ever witnessed in the island. Participants included the West India Regiment band, the Boy Scouts, Girl Guides, a detachment of the Sixth Jamaica War Contingent, a police squad, small children carrying flags, and an array of huge lorries and motor cars festooned with flags, bunting, flowers and foliage, conveying young ladies costumed to represent the Entente Allies: "It was a living kinetoscope of colour." The entire pageant moved in procession from the sugar wharf to the south Parade, where the huge assembled crowd was addressed by the governor and several ladies, before terminating with the stirring strains of the national anthem.[100] On public issues such as the promotion of the empire during this devastating war, elite Jamaican women stepped outside of the prescribed "privacy" that was to have marked their concerns and activities. As in Britain, the cause allowed for the usual opposition to women's public speaking to be suspended, as both king and empire benefited.

The ending of the war in November 1918 was greeted with great joy and thankfulness by Jamaicans, but the Peace Day celebrations on 19 July 1919 to mark the formal signing of the peace treaties with Germany were rapturous throughout the island. Kingston was decorated and illuminated, church bells pealed, thanksgiving services were held, and there was a "peace carnival" at the (coloured) Melbourne Cricket Club.[101] Loyal, patriotic Jamaicans rejoiced in the hard-won victory of *their* empire over "the forces of evil".

There is no gainsaying the fact that Jamaicans of all classes shared a common sense of loyalty to the sovereign, Britain and the empire. In 1897 Margaret Newton thought that no British colony was more loyal than Jamaica, not even Barbados! In 1959 Etheline Nugent of Stony Hill, recalling life at the turn of the century, said, "My first real impression was to hear my elders talk of 'Missus Queen' and sing 'God save the Queen'." Likewise, Gladstone Burke of Kingston asserted that "We, in Jamaica have always been loyal Britishers, showing interest in the lives, visits, fortunes of Royalty, taking part in whatever war took place."[102]

But there were some who questioned the seemingly blind nature of this loyalty. *Gleaner* editor W.P. Livingston noted in 1899 that Britain was so far away that "to the negroes who are able to conceive of it at all it is a confused dream of greatness. To all others it is simply the person of a good and powerful Queen."[103] But perhaps it was its very distance which made its greatness apparent. The myth of the indefeasible imperial will, the stories of wealth, might and grandeur, helped only to assure the continued loyalty of the people.

"Climaticus" (1904) too thought that the loyalty of Jamaicans was limited – exhibited only towards the British crown – and complained, "The present generation of my countrymen are neither loyal to their island or to themselves."[104] Perhaps it was the effusiveness of the celebrations of Victoria's diamond jubilee that caused some people to be more introspective and to wonder where *Jamaica* stood amidst the carnival.

William Morrison, the white associate editor of the *Jamaica Daily Telegraph and Anglo-American Herald,* began to question publicly these one-sided expressions of patriotism. He was by no means anti-imperialist: on the contrary, he commended the "genuine loyalty [of Jamaicans], not only to the person and rule of our beloved Queen, but to the instinctive sentiment or rather sense of a common nationality". But he argued that this sentiment of imperial loyalty was quite consistent with a *stronger* feeling of devotion to Jamaica, the colonial home: "It cannot be denied that their own colonial homes have a foremost place in the affections of the inhabitants of the Greater Britain. It is not that they love the mother country less, but that they love [Jamaica,] Canada, Australia, or New Zealand more. And this surely is very natural and very proper." He thought that Jamaicans ought to be very fond and proud of their country, and consequently criticized those who called Britain "home". Morrison urged the people to "be steadfast in your devoted fealty to your beloved Queen but . . . above all to your own country be leal and true, bearing in mind the gospel of genuine orthodox patriotism:– 'That man's the true cosmopolite / Who loves his native country best.'"[105]

In this vein, the *Daily Telegraph* welcomed Australia's first cricket test series victory over England in 1899:

> In Jamaica we are all loyal imperialists, but we are also sufficiently "Colonial" to rejoice in the splendid triumphs of our Australian fellow-colonists. It is not that we love England less, but we love the colonies more. . . . It is a good thing for the

mother country that she can boast of colonial offsprings capable of performing exploits worthy of the best traditions of the parent stock.[106]

Morrison and others who thought as he did were taking a slant which threatened to invert the whole purpose of the cult of monarchy and empire, but which may have succeeded in strengthening it. Inasmuch as the "colonials" loved their countries, and loved Britain, they were more likely to see a relationship of partnership which they would want to keep for the mutual benefits it provided. Local patriotism could be used as a way of strengthening the empire by constructing a *British* Jamaica, rather than a Jamaica chafing under the pressures of colonialism, and straining to break the hold of a domineering "mother".

This sentiment began to manifest itself in some of the most imperialist movements in the colony soon after the turn of the century. The Children of Empire order, for instance, took special care to instil a sense of pride in Jamaica, although that was secondary to Britain and the empire, and Meath's Empire Day catechism for schools was specifically revised by the Board of Education to focus more on Jamaica.

But it was not until 1914 that a wholly home-grown Jamaican organization was established which specifically sought to foster a sense of *colonial Jamaican* patriotism. This was the Jamaican Patriotic League, founded by coloured musician Astley Clerk. Its stated object was "to promote amongst Jamaicans the spirit of patriotism, unity, mutual love, comradeship and citizenship", and its motto was "Jamaica's Welfare first". Its coat of arms incorporated the existing Jamaican one, but draped with the British flag. Membership was extended to men, women and children born in Jamaica, or whose parents were born in Jamaica, or who spent their working lives in Jamaica. Each chapter was named after a deceased patriotic Jamaican or a well-known patriot of the British Empire. At meetings "Jamaica" and other Jamaican patriotic songs or poems were sung and recited.[107]

Likewise, A.W. Farquharson's Jamaica Imperial Association, founded in December 1917, seemed to put Jamaica's interests first within the context of the British Empire. Its members comprised mainly planters, merchants and professional men, and it aimed to focus influential attention locally on Jamaica's own economic situation and on promoting Jamaica's economic interests within the wider empire. It also sought to support institutions like the West India Committee, the Royal Colonial Institute, and the British Empire Producers' Organization to ensure that Jamaica played its part in consolidating and developing the British Empire.[108] These organizations would have satisfied William Morrison's idea of placing Jamaica first while pledging loyalty to the sovereign, Britain and the empire. They signified that Jamaicans were beginning to see themselves and their country as separate from Mother England but, at the same time, as part of a greater and more powerful imperial whole.

Conclusion

The promotion of the cult of monarchy and empire was born largely out of a perceived need among the white upper and middle classes to bolster their connection with "Mother England" in order to give them a sense of security in the uncertain times that followed the emancipation of slavery, which had unleashed the mass of "illiterate", "ignorant, semi-savage" blacks on society. As a small minority "in a sea of blackness", and stripped of their absolute power over the ex-slaves, they had a psychological need to rely more heavily than ever on the military and naval support of the mother country. The Morant Bay outbreak seemed to prove this beyond the shadow of a doubt. One way to ensure this was to pledge loyalty to the monarch and the empire. Hence, the later nineteenth and early twentieth centuries witnessed an intensification of the efforts to promote the cult of monarchy and empire.

As part of these efforts, the upper and middle classes not only invented and embraced royal traditions and symbols, but enshrined them within ceremonial rituals and pompous pageantry designed to convince the mass of ex-slaves and their descendants of the might, majesty and magnificence of the British Empire; this was further reinforced after the turn of the century by a proliferation of imperial organizations. As Bryan asserts, "The symbolic universe of empire crowned the legitimation of white authority. Jamaicans belonged, perhaps, to the 'slums of empire' but their presence in the slums could not conceal the imperial glitter which shone across race and class lines."[109]

Yet, however important the imperial symbols, rituals and organizations were in extolling the greatness of the British monarch and empire, the receptivity of the people to this cult was to a large extent determined by their own sense of personal loyalty to Victoria as liberator.[110] Much of the success of the royal/imperial cult in Jamaica, therefore, was due not only to the methods of its propagation, but no less importantly to the *voluntary disposition* of the people themselves to identify with it. It was thus to a significant degree self-determined (albeit certainly reinforced by the symbols from above), because it had deep meaning and significance to *them* quite separate from what it meant to the social elites. The monarchy and empire were thus among the strongest bonds that united the different social classes in Jamaica after emancipation. By the outbreak of the First World War, Jamaicans of all classes were so fiercely loyal to Britain's cause that they were queuing up to defend *their* empire because it was closely linked in their minds to their personal freedom.

Chapter 10

Britannica versus "Africana"
Contestation and Negotiation

THE PRINCIPAL CONCERNS OF THIS BOOK have been, first, to demonstrate that during and after the nineteenth century, Jamaicans possessed a coherent, functional and self-determined body of cultural beliefs, values and practices that, although labelled "inferior" because they were rooted in "darkest Africa" and the slave plantation complex of old, constituted the *mainstream* (creole) culture of the island; second, to examine the methods that the British rulers employed, in the name of "civilization", to uproot this indigenous creole cultural matrix and supplant it with their own *alternative* (self-styled "superior") brand of culture, "made in England", and fashioned from the prevailing middle-class Victorian system of beliefs and values; third, to assess the responses of the people, mainly Afro-Jamaicans but also including small numbers of Asian, African and other immigrants, and the old planter elite, to the new British "cultural imperialism", as well as their self-determined efforts to advance their own independent cultural agenda; and fourth, to analyse the interplay or contestation among these several competing cultural forces just beyond the end of the First World War.

The years 1860–65 represented a tumultuous turning point in Jamaica's history. The Great Revival and the Morant Bay Rebellion forced colonial officials, missionaries and the social elites to take stock of the "progress" that the emancipated people had made since their release from slavery in August 1838. Their assessment, however, was almost universally negative. Both cataclysmic events seemed to offer clear and tangible proof that the black people of Jamaica were fast "regressing into barbarism". Instead of adopting the mantle of pure Christianity and civilized British ways, they seemed to have chosen the path to heathenism, "dark" superstition and savagery. The work aimed at improving the behaviour of the "decadent" plantocrats and "uplifting" the people of African and Asian origin from the "darkness" of their cultural pasts – so sedulously pursued, especially by missionaries, for more than two generations in some cases – now seemed in tatters. The civilizing mission was deemed by some a failure. The big challenge after 1865, therefore, was to try to save Jamaica, once the pearl of the British West Indies, from becoming the shambles of another Haiti.[1]

Britain had recently faced a similar disaster in India, when the "Mutiny" of 1857–58 cast doubt on what they were doing there, too. Their response in Jamaica was not too dissimilar from what they did in India. There the rule of the East India Company was terminated and the British government took full responsibility for governing India. Likewise, in Jamaica, the oligarchy of wealthy planters and merchants was ended when the assembly was cajoled to abolish itself, and the British government assumed direct responsibility for governance – full crown rule (also known as crown colony government). Although severely shaken in both cases, the British emerged from these crises, first, convinced that neither the Jamaican nor the Indian people were capable of governing themselves and that enlightened white (British) rule was essential to their political wellbeing, and second, with a greater resolve to inject more vigour into the civilizing process, which was deemed absolutely essential for progress.[2] Where previously in Jamaica that effort had more or less been left exclusively to the churches and missionary organizations, which lacked the confidence and support of the planter-dominated assembly, after 1865 the colonial state under the control of the crown aligned itself more closely with the religious bodies and underwrote their efforts in a new partnership for civilization.

It was also recognized that the old coercive methods of maintaining law and order were no longer effective on their own. Vagrancy laws had not stopped the movement of ex-slaves away from plantation employment; taxation of items of common consumption, and the imposition of licences on shops, carts, draught animals and so forth, had not prevented the people from seeking alternative, independent economic pursuits; they had also got around high land prices by squatting, on both private and government lands; and the show and use of military and police force did not deter them from taking to the streets periodically in their quest for "justice". On the other hand, the lethal force unleashed by the state at Morant Bay in 1865 alarmed and unnerved even some of those hawks who favoured a hard line to keep the blacks in check, for they now knew that it could only offer temporary respite. The Colonial Office and the British public themselves were no longer prepared to tolerate the wanton use of naked and brutal military power in their colonies to preserve privilege. New strategies thus had to be devised and tried, and the government itself had to play a more central role in this regard.

Devoid of local interests, or so they claimed, crown colony officials saw themselves as best suited to forge a new equilibrium between the vested landed and commercial elites and the largely illiterate and powerless lower-class majority. As all Jamaicans were, until 1884, shorn of their political rights and privileges, the crown had a free hand to embark on new programmes aimed at stabilizing Jamaica and civilizing the people. But its hands were fettered by its continued belief that economic and social progress was inextricably linked to the preservation of the plantation system. Both colonial officialdom and the local elites shared the view that a return to prosperity of the plantation sector was the best (probably the only) way to generate general economic growth, and that in turn was an essential base upon which civilization itself could be secured. For it would mean the continued presence of wealthy British whites in the colony, who would be the primary bearers and promoters of civilization. Tied to this was the concomitant obligation of black Jamaicans to work – as dependent labourers – to facilitate the resurgence of the plantation economy. Inculcating that peculiarly conceived "duty to work" was in itself regarded as key to civilizing the black labour force, who would also seek more material goods and acquire a taste for things British.

So the economic policies of the crown government after 1865 (certainly until the 1890s) continued to favour the stagnating plantation sector at the expense of others, especially the struggling black peasantry, which was equated with economic, social and cultural retardation. However, what differentiated the post- from the pre-1865 period in this area was the relaxation of the intense pressure on the peasants to *force* them to return to plantation labour. The peasants were still *encouraged* to provide labour to the plantations – at first sugar, later banana as well – but coercion was no longer a preferred option. There was now a certain resignation to the reality that the peasantry, however unwelcome, was there to stay. Towards the end of the nineteenth century, therefore, an uneasy and unequal relationship existed between the plantation and peasant sectors. This went a long way towards reducing social tension and the frequency and intensity of popular protest. Between 1865 and 1920 Jamaica was remarkably peaceful, especially in comparison with other British West Indian territories like Guyana and Trinidad; there were small outbreaks, however, most notably at Montego Bay in 1902, Kingston in 1912 and St Catherine in 1918.

This state of relative calm did not mean that the colonial authorities got rid of the forces of state violence. On the contrary, the Jamaica Constabulary Force was established in 1867, and was supported by a Rural Police Force. As a paramilitary organization, the constabulary was intended to deal with civil disorder in addition to its normal police duties; while the rank and file were black and brown, the officer corps was exclusively white.[3] Although the old conscript militias were disbanded after 1865, new volunteer militias were formed whose membership was restricted to the middle and upper classes. Behind them were the garrisons of two West India Regiments at Up Park Camp in Kingston (manned by blacks, but commanded by white officers); all-white British forces were stationed at Port Royal and Newcastle. While on paper this was a formidable array of military power at the disposal of the state, the reality was that, even supported by the mighty British "Fleet", they would have been hard pressed to put down an island-wide insurrection.

So, in addition to engendering economic growth, the long-term answer to Jamaica's social problems after 1865 was deemed to lie not so much in military/police repression, but increasingly in transforming the beliefs, values, customs, character and behaviour of the Jamaican people themselves, and in reinforcing their keen sense of loyalty to Britain and its monarch. In short, they needed to be civilized and anglicized in order to create both a consensus of values that would render British rule more palatable, and a stable environment for colonial economic growth. This book has shown that this process, which had begun just after emancipation (but appeared to be in jeopardy by the early 1860s), was intensified and expanded in the later nineteenth century. There were, however, four fundamental changes from the earlier attempt.

First, the church was not the only agency of civilization. It was now supported by the colonial state, and the press was enlisted to spread the message. Second, instead of relying mainly on white "Brits" to bear the brunt of the civilizing mission, carefully recruited brown and black Jamaicans were trained (mainly through the teacher training colleges and theological seminaries) to carry forward the work. Civilization, therefore, was no longer exclusively a white man's burden. It was hoped that the people would be more receptive to the message if it came from their own kind. Third, there was a massive importation of British cultural items, ideas and values, which formed essential ingredients of the civilizing process.4 Finally, images of British imperial might and glory, and the ideology that bolstered them, were systematically projected and promoted with a view to reinforcing loyalist sentiments among all classes of the Jamaican society.

In this thrust for civilization, Christian dogma and principles were inextricably intertwined with middle-class (bourgeois) British Victorian values and morality, and British imperial ideology, symbols and rituals. There was also a strong racial dimension to this thrust, aimed at fortifying the social pre-eminence of whites in Jamaican society. Hence, under the new, white-dominated crown colony regime, reverence of a white Christian god was associated with loyalty to the white British monarch and her or his white representatives in the colony. A conscious effort was thus made to bolster the white bias long extant in Jamaican society.

Even before 1865 the social elites, like their fellow colonists in other parts of the empire, had developed a strong attachment to the British monarchy and had invented the tradition of celebrating the queen's birthday annually. In Jamaica and the British Caribbean this sense of loyalty was reinforced by an acute feeling of insecurity following the emancipation of the slaves. But royal celebrations became much grander affairs in the late nineteenth century, full of pomp, splendour and colour, as loyalty to the British throne and empire intensified. Events in the lives of British royalty were closely monitored in the local press, and royal events (births, marriages and deaths) were appropriately commemorated in the island. As imperial fever was promoted throughout the empire at the turn of the twentieth century, the royal jubilees of Queen Victoria and the coronations of her heirs and successors, Edward VII and George V, were occasions for mammoth, island-wide celebration; these loyalist sentiments were further promoted by a proliferation of imperial associations, the churches, the schools and the newspapers.

Imperial rituals and symbols played a major role in all this festivity. All such celebrations were marked by magnificent parades involving military detachments, the police, militias, and later on the Boy Scout and Girl Guide organizations, all on show in "full dress", complete with eye-catching regalia and accoutrements (colourful sashes, glittering medals, ceremonial swords and rifles with gleaming bayonets). The monarch's chief representative, the governor, was the central figure in these colonial celebrations, bedecked in full gubernatorial uniform, complete with plumed helmet, an array of medals, and sword. These parades were accompanied by colourfully attired military bands playing familiar march tunes, regimental flags and horse-drawn cannon. The trooping of the colours, royal gun salutes and the playing of the (British) national anthem added to the pomp and magnificence of these parades. Major royal festivities were also marked by grand religious services in churches abundantly adorned for the occasion, fireworks displays, bonfires, and the decoration of public buildings and streets with flags, banners, bunting, arches and fancy lights; meanwhile, there were levees, sumptuous dinners and balls exclusively for the social elites. These were indeed gala "entertainments", designed to impress upon all who witnessed them the grandeur, glory, magnificence and, not least of all, omnipotence of the British monarchy and empire.

But ordinary black and brown Jamaicans had quite separate and very compelling reasons for identifying with the British monarchy and empire: they had fashioned a close personal loyalty to Queen Victoria, whom many regarded as their "liberator", *their* "imperial mother". Whether or not the social elites had staged their "orgies" of imperial festivity, these people would have been staunchly loyal to their queen, to her heirs and successors, and to the vast empire over which she reigned so "benignly". Their fealty, therefore, was largely self-determined and hardly needed to be instilled from above. The imperial rituals and symbols reinforced the people's own strong loyalist sentiments. This did not make Britons out of them; they were merely expressing their own personal gratitude to "Missus Queen" and her family who had, they strongly believed, freed them from bondage.

The cult of monarchy was further legitimated by the churches, who tied it to their christianizing mission. The two were by and large regarded as inseparable. The British monarch was, after all, the head of the Church of England, which – although under pressure from the nonconformist denominations after it was disestablished in Jamaica in 1870 – clearly remained the preferred church of the sociopolitical elite establishment. (Indeed, even after 1870 the Anglican bishop was still entitled to use "Jamaica" as his titular surname: hence, for instance, Enos Nuttall signed himself as "Enos Jamaica".) The British queen or king was projected as God's representative on earth, and the British Empire as a virtual extension of God's heavenly kingdom. Serving the British monarch was tantamount to serving God. The British-affiliated church bodies and their clergy, therefore, had no difficulty in fitting their religious work into a wider framework of duty to monarch, country and empire (even though the nonconformists did not necessarily see eye-to-eye with the Anglicans on several issues). Imperial celebrations, as we have seen, were commemorated by grand church services, while the virtues and benefits of being loyal British subjects were preached from time to time in Sunday sermons.

On the other side of the coin, notwithstanding the disestablishment of the Anglican Church, after 1865 the efforts of churches (as a collective body) to civilize the Jamaican people were more firmly supported by the officials of the state, and the churches were granted financial assistance to fund their elementary schools. This partnership may not have been as formal or close-knit as that between church and state in French, Portuguese and Belgian Africa, but it was no less pervasive. The primary goal of church and state in late-nineteenth- and early-twentieth-century Jamaica was to create a new moral order, based essentially on imported Victorian beliefs, values and ideas. Christianity was the foundation of this moral order, reinforced by secular, middle-class Victorian notions of propriety and etiquette. And so a systematic programme aimed at changing the religious beliefs, ideas, manners, behaviour and customs of Jamaicans, not only the black lower classes and new Asian immigrants, but also the "coarse" rural plantocracy, was embarked upon with increased vigour after 1865; church and chapel, schoolroom and the press played major roles in this endeavour.

This programme entailed an orchestrated assault, particularly on cultures that were considered pagan or heathen (African and Asian), or vulgar, uncouth and uncivilized (Euro- and Afro-creole). Myal/Revival, Kumina, Hinduism, Islam, obeah, duppies and other "dark superstitions", sexual promiscuity ("licentious fornication"), "concubinage" and "illegitimacy", noise, ribaldry and profanity, drinking and gambling, "bad" behaviour, aggression and "coarse" manners – all of which were considered integral aspects of the "debased" creole (both Afro- and Euro-) and "heathen" immigrant cultures – were attacked. In their place was to be substituted a new moral order that emphasized respectability, refinement and piety, "good breeding" and decorum, politeness and gentility, kindness and courteousness. The end products of this cultural transformation were expected to be soft-spoken and "well behaved", legally married and monogamous, as well as family-oriented. The unrestrained public exuberance that seemed to characterize the creole personality was to be curbed in favour of a more sober, quiet, self-controlled persona. This was an essential requirement for upward social mobility. While many among the middle and upper classes strove to conform to that image of respectability and civility in their everyday lives, some social elites actually resisted it, while many of the poor working classes simply ignored it and continued to behave as they always had. However, it is clear that they knew and understood the Victorian code and did, when it suited them (for example, in church or on royal occasions), behave "properly" and "respectably".

Missionary work among the subordinate population, both creole and immigrant, was continued in the schools, which for all intents and purposes were extensions of the churches. It was felt that the real hope of civilizing Jamaica lay in the children. Thus, heavy emphasis was placed at all levels of the school curricula on religious and civic indoctrination, and serious efforts were made to select and train morally erect teachers to transmit the message. Teachers, therefore, served as auxiliary missionaries.

The messengers of this imported moral order, however, not only found that the old plantocratic elites were unwilling to relinquish many of their time-honoured rural traditions, but also that the Afro-creole culture had an internal cosmology and functional order that were not easily eradicated and supplanted, certainly not as they related to matters of faith and family (that is, to personal status). Besides, neither category of people was willing to be dictated to by these new self-appointed bearers of "civilization". The planters were still sufficiently wealthy and socially powerful to preserve those aspects of their culture that they prized, regardless of reproach. Many were Christian in name only and hardly visited a church, and they maintained much of their rugged rural way of life, characterized by "coarse", "raucous" behaviour, feuding in defence of honour, brawling, heavy drinking and conspicuous consumption, and "licentious womanizing".

For their part, although Afro-Jamaicans did embrace the basic tenets of Christianity and the concept of salvation through Christ, they did not adopt the Euro-Christian notion that man was helpless before God and could only entreat him through prayer and await his forgiveness. Instead, they retained the African cosmology of interpenetrating worlds in which God (as a spirit) along with other spirits, good and bad, interacted with humanity and could be appealed to, and propitiated, in order to influence life. Thus Christ, who was grafted on to their pre-existing cosmology, was one of a pantheon of spirits that included those of their ancestors, the Christian divine trinity, the angels and archangels, and Jesus' disciples. The emphasis in their practice of Christianity was on spirituality, not on "rational" morality. For them the true Christian was one who experienced, or was possessed by, the spirits, not one who simply went to church, listened to the Word, and adhered to the moral teachings of the church. These people were sincere in their beliefs and pious, but they were not Euro-Christians; they were Afro-Jamaican Christians.

In matters of faith, they determined for themselves what they should believe and how best to put their religious beliefs into practice. This was in essence a powerful expression of cultural self-determination. They were not prepared to be led or driven in matters of belief.

But steeped in their ethical rationalism, the British and American missionaries could only conceive of Afro-Jamaican Christianity as blasphemy – a corruption or falsification of *their* true religion – nay, perhaps just a higher form of obeah. For while apparently embracing the Bible, God as Saviour, the Holy Spirit and the rite of baptism, the people still believed in the spirit world and obeah (even if they were digging it up), and they could not, it seems, in a perfectly "rational" manner differentiate between the sacred and the secular like "normal" people. This rendered missionary work very frustrating and ultimately unrewarding. Just when it seemed that progress was being made, some trusted convert(s) would backslide and have to be disciplined by suspension, or even exclusion or dismissal. Alternatively there might be another outbreak of (Afro-creole) Revival fervour that would undermine years of work by the missionaries in a community.

The Jamaican cultural landscape was further complicated by growing numbers of Indian and Chinese immigrants who, although small in number and scattered in different parts of the island, not only arrived with "heathen" religions (Hinduism, Islam and Confucianism) and with their own priests, but initially evinced no intention to settle (the Indians in particular). So there was initially no incentive for them to convert to Christianity, nor was there much effort exerted by the churches to convert them until the very end of the nineteenth century. However, despite pockets of relatively strong resistance to missionary efforts at proselytization, by 1920 both groups were beginning to succumb to the forces of Christianity, although whether their general behaviour was transformed "for the better" is debatable.

At the heart of the new Christian, Victorian moral order that the missionaries and the colonial authorities sought to construct was the curbing of what they regarded as the lascivious, licentious sexual behaviour of Jamaicans of all classes, whose libido was stereotypically portrayed as being out of control. The missionaries, in particular, were obsessed with black sexuality. The alleged freedom with which lower-class Jamaicans changed partners ran directly counter to the Victorian emphasis on sexual purity, the sanctity of legal, Christian, monogamous marriage and the resulting nuclear family. The failure or refusal of the majority of Jamaicans to marry legally, notwithstanding the fact that their children were branded "illegitimate" or "bastards", was thus taken as a sure sign that they had failed to grasp the fundamental concepts of Christian morality that underlay Victorian civilization. What was worse, so far as the cultural elites were concerned, was the idea that conjugal unions not sanctioned by law (the state) or by God (the church) brought no shame to the participants. As in faith, so too in family life: the people clearly indicated that they intended to determine for themselves what was appropriate for them, and would not be led or driven to adopt a model of marriage and family imposed from above. Cultural self-determination, not cultural imposition/imperialism, was the operative condition in this sphere of life.

But no less troubling for the bearers of this imported morality was the realization that "sexual promiscuity" was not confined to the lower orders, but was practised by some of the most respectable members of Jamaican society who, although legally married in church, had "illicit" extramarital partners (concubines in the proper definition of the word) and even fathered children out of wedlock. These were the people who used their influence to block all efforts to have their identities revealed by compulsory registration of paternity. On the issue of marriage and family, therefore, the civilizing mission was thwarted as much by the persistence of elite "concubinage" within the old plantocratic cultural tradition as by the refusal of the ordinary people to be dictated to on this matter.

In the contestation and negotiation between anglicization and creolization that characterized the period under review, it is clear that the former was to a large extent successful in not so much instilling, but reinforcing, a sense of intense loyalty to the British monarchy and the empire that transcended all classes of society; the anglicizing forces also significantly succeeded in transforming the ideas, beliefs, attitudes, values and behaviours of those Jamaicans who sought upward social mobility. Although the British state, unlike the French or Portuguese, did not offer social equality as a reward for full assimilation (in this case, anglicization), it made it abundantly clear that social advancement in colonial society was largely dependent on the adoption and inculcation of British culture and morality. Many educated, upwardly mobile middle-class browns and blacks, including Robert Love and Marcus Garvey, therefore, embraced the imported Victorian culture and its symbols in their quest for social elevation and respectability; they not only felt ashamed of the "uncivilized" beliefs and customs and the "coarse" behaviour of fellow blacks, but openly deplored them as being unfit for "cultured" society. But many among the middle and upper classes themselves still bore the traits of the very creole culture they deplored, oft-times secretly (for example, their belief in obeah and their "illicit" concubinary relationships), while seeking to distance themselves from it. These double standards generated considerable ambivalence, and in some cases even cultural schizophrenia, for these people were caught in two opposing cultural worlds.[5] This ambivalence further hampered the civilizing mission, because the very people who were expected to carry the mission forward were themselves some of the principal transgressors of the Victorian moral code, and so could not afford to see the mission reach its logical conclusion.

At the lowest levels of society, the reality of everyday life was Afro-creole, although the keenness to attain some social respectability within the colonial context made some working-class Afro-Jamaicans receptive to the dominant Anglo-creole culture. Many of these people thus developed the tendency to look down on their own Afro-creole cultural heritage, even though their day-to-day behaviour and practices, nurtured in the yards and streets of poor rural villages and squalid urban slums[6] and informed by their traditional African world view, manifested many aspects of that tradition. Not surprisingly, these people too were culturally ambivalent, despising some of the very things that could give them a sense of self-esteem, dignity and identity in the face of the opposing Euro-Christian tradition that continually derided their claims to a viable culture of their own.

But not all working-class Afro-Jamaicans were ambivalent. There were many others who were largely unimpressed with the cultural influences emanating from above, and instead chose to adhere to their Afro-creole traditions, with all the negative implications that this held for their chances of social mobility. It was among these people that the process of creolization garnered its real potency. Although under varying degrees of pressure to "improve" their way of life – that is, to anglicize themselves – the lives of these people were influenced by a belief system and world view, derived from Africa, that were reshaped but never eradicated on the slave plantation. To these they held steadfastly, even while appropriating and creolizing elements of the Christian British culture to form a seamlessly integrated continuum of creolity. So while Afro-creole Jamaican culture was continuously being renewed, reformed and revitalized by fresh inclusions – mainly from Britain, but also from India, China and elsewhere, as immigrants from those sources entered the society – it never lost its fundamental African world view and the core beliefs that were integral to that.[7]

This was the basis of the "cultural power" of the Afro-Jamaican people that facilitated their exercise of self-determination in cultural matters, both secular and religious – although they themselves made very little distinction between the two. This exercise of cultural self-determination emerges as the single most important characteristic that influenced Afro-Jamaican cultural life in the period under review. Where it coincided with the objectives of the cultural elites – as, for instance, in the promotion of the cult of monarchy and empire – there was synergy, and a process of negotiation took place that sometimes created the impression (perhaps even the illusion) that anglicization was in fact advancing. Where, however, it clashed with the objectives of the upper- and middle-class reformers – as, for instance, in the spheres of faith and family – there was a contestation that retarded the process of anglicization and rendered it largely irrelevant and even impotent. This is notwithstanding the fact that transgressors of the dominant behavioural code, its prescriptions and proscriptions, could be jailed and flogged for practising obeah, or excluded from church and "polite" society in general for not adhering to the "accepted" conventions of Victorian morality. As Gramsci recognized, there were clear limits to which the cultural elites were prepared to negotiate with the subordinate population; beyond those limits they were quite prepared to resort to the coercive power of the state. Such legal and social sanctions, however, ultimately had very little, if any, real impact on the people's behaviour, because they had constructed a cultural system that had its own inherent integrity and logic, based on a coherent body of functional beliefs and values.

This Afro-creole cultural system, effectively (by sheer force of numbers) the *mainstream* culture of post-emancipation Jamaica, was the cornerstone of the process of creolization that in some aspects of life pushed back the countervailing process of anglicization, and in others subsumed it. But there was no conscious design or intention to overthrow the *alternative,* but yet (by virtue of the pre-eminent social status of its principal bearers) *dominant,* British cultural system. For the latter had the apparatus of the state (including the laws, police, courts and prisons), the churches, schools, press and other cultural elite institutions behind it.

Nevertheless, a very substantial proportion of the Jamaican people were highly effective in nullifying the punitive impact of the legal system, as well as the exhortations, cajolements, admonitions and denunciations of, in Gramscian terms, the "organic intellectuals" (missionaries, teachers, journalists and other elite opinion makers), by simply ignoring them and continuing to live according to their own Afro-creole tenets, ideas, beliefs and values. This was a remarkable achievement, representing the successful exercise of *their own cultural power* that emanated not only from their deeply held conviction in their own belief system and the tenacity of their own world view, but also from their physical numbers, which were continuously expanding and moving into spaces (the mountainous interior of the island) where the agencies of "civilization" were weak. This fact made the process of creolization expansionist, continuous and silently relentless. Not only did it effectively retard the spread of anglicization, but by the sheer force of numbers, its own influence became increasingly pervasive, to the point where, by the turn of the century, many elite observers expressed the fear that the civilizing mission was in danger of failing.

There is no doubt that the cultural elites, in particular the organic intellectuals, attempted to lead Jamaican society and to set its cultural and ideological agenda. A process of negotiation did take place between the dominant and subordinate classes that promoted a core of shared ideas and values, leading to a modicum of societal consensus and social stability. But, as we have seen, the cultural elites were not homogeneous in their embrace of the imported Victorian culture. Many were quite uncomfortable with, and ambivalent towards, several aspects of it. Within the very powerful plantocracy itself there was in fact a strong strain of resistance to much of this new cultural agenda. No less importantly, Afro-Jamaicans were not by any means wholly co-opted into the new moral order, nor did they subscribe in entirety to its values and ideals. Instead, they contested important aspects of it, and were able to preserve a high degree of cultural autonomy. Effectively, therefore, the "dominant cultural system" was less than "hegemonic". Nevertheless, the organic intellectuals were able to set clear limits on the extent to which they were prepared to negotiate with, and make concessions to, the people; thereafter the punitive apparatus of the state was brought into play.

This brings us to consider Richard D.E. Burton's typology of "resistance" and "opposition". Burton argues that Afro-creole culture is essentially oppositional because it not only makes use of British cultural items to contest British domination, but it does so on the dominant order's own ground. Following Michel de Certeau's categorization,[8] he defines opposition as a form of contestation of a system that is conducted from *within* that system, using weapons and concepts derived from the system itself. This, in his view, is significantly different from resistance, which must utilize cultural items from *outside* the dominant system, and should lead to a fundamental change or overthrow of the dominant system. Hence, he classifies all of Afro-creole culture in the post-emancipation period as opposition rather than resistance.

Burton himself admits that his definition of resistance is "circumscribed",[9] and certainly his distinction between that and opposition, while thought-provoking and in some ways interesting, is highly semantic. Resistance can take many shapes and forms, not least of all that of rendering the dominant system irrelevant and impotent. Indeed, Michel Foucault, from whom Burton himself draws some of his intellectual inspiration, speaks of "a plurality of resistances" that differ in shape and form, but all form part of a network of power relations.[10]

What the data analysed in this book demonstrate is that Afro-Jamaican creole culture, while utilizing several cultural items from the dominant British system, was centred around a belief system and world view derived from an African past that was certainly external to the dominant system. So even by Burton's own circumscribed definition, many aspects of that culture would qualify as resistance. But even if that were not so, to argue that the utilization of the cultural items of the dominant system by definition precludes resistance is too artificially constricting. To further add the requirement of overthrowing or fundamentally changing the dominant system as a qualification for resistance renders the concept virtually useless in the Caribbean context. For Afro-Jamaicans certainly did not overthrow or fundamentally change the dominant cultural system (and the evidence indicates the same for Afro-Guyanese and Afro-Barbadians).[11] So there is no disputing that fact. *But that was never their intention; nor was it necessary for them to have done so in order for Afro-creole culture to qualify as resistance to British cultural dominance. Afro-creole was, after all, the mainstream culture.*

The material in this book seems to highlight not only the untenable narrowness of Burton's definitions, but also the limitations of his typology of opposition and resistance for analysing post-emancipation West Indian society. In *addition to* opposition and resistance, many Afro-Jamaicans effectively rendered the dominant system largely irrelevant and impotent *as it related to the core of their culture,* by simply *refusing to engage* it directly. This was a very powerful tool in their quest for cultural self-determination. At the same time, some negotiated with the dominant system, and still others sought accommodation within it. The reality is that their cultural development in colonial Jamaica depended on their use of several strategies. No viable strategy could be excluded from their armoury.

What is quite clear, however, is that they determined for themselves which cultural elements they would appropriate from the dominant system and, moreover, immediately set about *creolizing* those items to suit their own Afro-creole world view and way of life. Beyond that, the dominant cultural system seemed to have very little impact on their day-to-day lives because they simply ignored it. They consequently made very little effort to alter their lifestyles to meet the lofty expectations of their "moral superiors". That was what so many bearers of Victorian civilization found frustrating, and why they frequently despaired that their efforts had been in vain, had fallen on barren ground, and that they had failed in their mission. So while Afro-creole culture may not have sought to overthrow the dominant system, it certainly impeded the anglicization and "civilization" process, and in many respects threatened to engulf it. This, therefore, could be construed as one of the "plurality of resistances" that Foucault speaks of, although this analysis prefers to treat it as more than simply "opposition" or "resistance".

The data and analysis in this book have further clearly demonstrated that "cultural power" was not the monopoly of the elites and their metropolitan backers, as Burton seems to imply.[12] Afro-Jamaicans possessed their own cultural power; even though it was not organized or buttressed in the same way as that of the cultural elites, it was resilient, irrepressible and, at the end of the day, no less potent or dynamic than that of the dominant system. While Afro-Jamaicans might have been under varying degrees of pressure to adopt more and more British cultural elements to attain "civilization", the dominant system was itself also under intense pressure to resist or contain the pervasive expansion and encroachment of the "debased" Afro-creole mainstream culture (spread by the power of numbers) by which it was being continuously undermined, creolized and transformed. If anything, therefore, it was the Victorian culture that was oppositional, as it struggled to resist the "dissolute" forces of Afro-creolity. To invert Burton, the cultural elites *did* try to fundamentally change Afro-creole culture, but either failed or were only partially successful, depending on which contemporary observers one listens to. This contestation and negotiation between the forces of anglicization and creolization, however, was far from achieving a final resolution by the end of the First World War: rather, it lay at the heart of a continuous struggle for the cultural soul of Jamaica that persisted throughout the twentieth century.

Appendix 1

Governors of Jamaica, 1864–1920

1864	Edward John Eyre
1865	Lieutenant General Sir H.K. Storks
1866	Sir John P. Grant
1874	Sir William Grey
1877	Sir Anthony Musgrave
1883	General Sir Henry W. Norman
1888	Sir Henry Arthur Blake
1898	Sir Augustus W.L. Hemming
1904	Sir James A. Swettenham
1907	Sir Sydney Olivier
1913	Sir W.H. Manning
1918	Sir Leslie Probyn

Appendix 2
Population Statistics, 1861–1920

Category	Sex	1861[a]	1871[a]	1881	1891	1911	1921
Whites	Male	7,295	6,909	7,637	7,824	8,188	7,322
	Female	6,521	6,192	6,795	6,868	7,417	7,154
	Total	13,816	13,101	14,432	14,692	15,605	14,476
	%	3.1	2.6	2.5	2.3	1.9	1.7
Coloureds	Male	38,223	48,048	51,293	54,208	74,423	69,818
	Female	42,842	52,298	58,653	67,747	88,778	87,405
	Total	81,065	100,346	109,946	121,955	163,201	157,223
	%	18.4	19.8	18.9	19.1	19.6	18.3
Blacks	Male	167,277	191,498	216,452	236,225	301,708	309,994
	Female	179,097	201,209	227,734	252,399	328,473	350,426
	Total	346,374	392,707	444,186	488,624	630,181	660,420
	%	78.5	77.6	76.5	76.4	75.8	77.0
Indians	Male	n/a	5,339	6,941	5,774	9,928	10,203
	Female	n/a	2,454	4,075	4,342	7,452	8,407
	Total	2,260	7,793	11,016	10,116	17,380	18,610
	%	0.5	1.5	1.9	1.6	2.1	2.2

Table continues

Category	Sex	1861[a]	1871[a]	1881	1891	1911	1921
Chinese	Male	n/a	131	80	373	1,783	2,817
	Female	n/a	10	19	108	328	879
	Total	239	141	99	481	2,111	3,696
	%	0.1	0.0	0.0	0.1	0.3	0.4
Not Specified	Male	n/a	–	554	1,544	1,409	1,819
	Female	n/a	–	571	2,079	1,496	1,874
	Total	9	–	1,125	3,623	2,905	3,693
	%	0.0		0.2	0.6	0.4	0.4
Total	Male	212,795	246,455	282,957	305,948	397,439	401,973
	Female	228,460	259,699	297,847	333,543	433,944	456,145
Grand Total		441,264[b]	506,154	580,804	639,491	831,383	858,118

Source: Decennial censuses 1861–1921. There was no census taken in 1901.

[a] In the 1861 and 1871 censuses, the Indian and Chinese immigrants were added to the coloured and black population statistics based purely on their skin colour. So although listed separately in the table above, their number is already included in the coloured and black figures for those two years.

[b] The grand total is nine more than the totals listed for males and females on account of persons who apparently did not identify themselves by colour. See B.W. Higman, ed., *The Jamaican Censuses of 1844 and 1861* (1980; reprint, Kingston: Social History Project, Department of History, University of the West Indies, 1995), vii.

Appendix 3

Legal Marriages, 1879–1920

Year	Number	Rate per thousand
1879–1880	2,101	3.7
1880–1881	2,178	3.7
1881–1882	2,368/*2,026*	4.0/*3.4*
1882–1883	2,869/*2,631*	4.9/*4.4*
1883–1884	2,953/*2,936*	5.0/*4.9*
1884–1885	2,995/*2,984*	5.0/*4.5*
1885–1886	2,390/*2,729*	3.9/*4.5*
1886–1887	2,551	4.2
1887–1888	3,353/*2,951*	5.4/*4.8*
1888–1889	3,387	5.4
1889–1890	3,397	5.3
1890–1891	3,560	5.5
1891–1892	3,405	5.2
1892–1893	3,349	5.1
1893–1894	3,734	5.5
1894–1895	3,629	5.3
1895–1896	3,242	5.6
1896–1897	3,026	4.3
1897–1898	2,661	3.7
1898–1899	3,362	4.6
1899–1900	3,767	5.0
1900–1901	3,221	4.2
1901–1902	3,202	4.1

Table continues

Year	Number	Rate per thousand
1902–1903	3,601	4.6
1903–1904	3,576	4.5
1904–1905	2,880	3.6
1905–1906	3,116	3.8
1906–1907	5,507	6.6
1907–1908	6,251	7.4
1908–1909	3,526	4.1
1909–1910	3,543	4.1
1910–1911	3,340	4.0
1911–1912	3,607	4.2
1912–1913	3,218	3.7
1913–1914	2,683	3.1
1914–1915	2,721	3.0
1915–1916	2,677	3.0
1916	2,964	3.3
1917	2,966	3.3
1918	2,776	3.1
1919	3,305	3.7
1920	4,124	4.8

Source: Annual Reports of the Registrar General, printed in annual *Department Reports*, University of the West Indies (Mona) Library, Kingston.

[a]The italicized figures for the years 1881–88 were provided in the 1890–91 report, and may have been revised for accuracy.

Appendix 4
"Illegitimate" Births, 1878–1920

Year	Kingston	St Andrew	St Thomas	Portland	St Mary	St Ann	Trelawny	St James	Hanover	Westmoreland	St Elizabeth	Manchester	Clarendon	St Catherine	Whole Island
1878–1879	65.5	53.4	71.0	67.1	65.6	58.7	59.7	64.8	61.7	51.9	45.9	43.7	69.2	67.6	59.3
1879–1880	63.7	50.6	70.7	62.3	64.0	56.4	58.9	61.1	59.5	57.1	50.6	45.2	66.5	68.6	58.9
1880–1881	61.8	51.0	67.8	60.9	60.2	57.9	58.2	57.8	60.3	56.6	47.9	44.7	63.6	67.6	57.7
1881–1882	59.8	48.7	66.2	63.0	62.7	52.1	59.8	64.3	63.4	57.4	50.5	46.4	65.2	66.6	58.2
1882–1883	63.3	54.3	72.0	63.8	62.7	58.9	61.7	58.6	62.6	56.3	53.9	51.0	65.2	65.5	60.9
1883–1884	62.0	52.6	69.9	58.1	60.4	54.5	62.7	62.2	64.1	57.9	52.6	48.2	61.8	67.6	58.9
1884–1885	62.1	52.8	71.5	59.0	60.1	58.8	65.0	62.3	64.4	59.7	54.3	49.1	62.0	68.4	59.9
1885–1886	61.8	50.2	71.9	64.1	62.5	57.0	61.3	62.8	62.4	59.3	54.7	47.7	62.3	67.3	59.6
1886–1887	59.7	53.3	71.7	61.1	61.7	55.0	65.6	63.9	62.9	59.6	55.8	50.3	61.1	67.6	59.8
1887–1888	60.1	53.7	72.6	61.5	63.9	57.6	66.1	65.6	64.8	62.1	55.6	50.3	61.6	66.7	60.6
1888–1889	58.7	51.4	74.3	59.2	64.6	57.5	61.4	65.7	60.5	62.7	56.3	52.1	68.4	66.6	60.5
1889–1890	62.3	51.3	75.8	62.1	65.1	56.8	61.6	68.6	69.1	62.0	57.3	51.3	63.5	68.8	61.7
1890–1891	60.8	49.9	70.8	58.5	64.5	54.9	64.8	65.5	68.3	62.5	56.0	52.5	62.8	67.3	60.7
1891–1892	62.0	53.3	73.2	59.8	63.5	53.9	62.8	65.6	68.8	60.8	55.5	53.2	61.6	66.2	60.6
1892–1893	62.1	49.6	69.4	58.9	66.7	55.7	62.4	62.9	66.9	60.4	55.2	50.2	62.6	66.5	60.1

Table continues

Year	Kingston	St Andrew	St Thomas	Portland	St Mary	St Ann	Trelawny	St James	Hanover	West-moreland	St Elizabeth	Man-chester	Clarendon	St Catherine	Whole Island
1893–1894	61.1	50.7	71.2	61.2	65.3	54.7	61.3	67.3	67.1	59.9	55.3	51.9	62.9	67.0	60.6
1894–1895	60.7	49.8	70.0	62.7	66.4	53.9	63.7	64.4	67.4	61.3	53.8	52.2	65.2	69.5	60.8
1895–1896	60.1	53.8	73.7	62.4	65.6	57.4	61.7	63.0	67.2	61.6	53.1	53.0	63.0	65.9	60.8
1896–1897	62.5	51.2	72.5	60.7	65.5	56.3	63.4	62.9	68.4	60.4	53.7	52.8	65.7	67.0	61.1
1897–1898	59.3	52.0	73.7	62.5	66.4	58.7	65.6	66.2	66.0	60.8	55.7	55.8	66.0	68.8	62.3
1898–1899	64.3	53.4	73.3	62.7	66.9	58.8	64.8	64.2	68.0	61.8	56.1	56.4	70.4	70.2	63.4
1899–1900	64.2	53.7	73.7	62.0	65.7	61.2	66.2	65.9	68.8	61.3	58.0	57.1	68.0	0.4	63.7
1900–1901	62.6	51.6	71.1	61.2	65.0	58.6	64.1	64.0	65.8	60.0	58.7	56.9	67.9	68.7	62.4
1901–1902	64.0	54.3	75.7	60.1	66.9	59.9	68.6	65.5	68.0	61.1	59.2	58.1	69.3	69.1	64.0
1902–1903	65.2	54.0	73.8	64.4	67.7	60.9	67.0	67.1	67.9	63.3	60.6	58.8	70.2	68.5	64.5
1903–1904	65.4	54.6	73.6	61.4	66.0	62.0	69.8	67.1	69.6	63.6	62.2	59.6	70.9	69.1	65.1
1904–1905	63.9	52.2	69.4	58.1	64.3	59.5	68.7	65.9	69.2	61.7	60.8	58.3	69.1	68.1	63.2
1905–1906	65.3	53.7	71.6	61.3	66.5	62.7	68.7	70.0	68.1	64.1	62.0	59.9	71.6	69.0	65.2
1906–1907	62.9	53.3	72.6	61.0	65.4	62.1	71.7	71.2	69.8	66.2	61.8	59.1	70.6	69.3	65.2
1907–1908	60.5	48.8	70.5	56.2	57.8	53.4	69.0	66.7	65.7	66.0	62.7	61.0	67.4	62.7	61.7
1908–1909	60.1	46.8	62.4	57.4	58.0	53.8	66.5	68.7	70.5	63.4	62.0	56.9	65.4	61.0	60.5
1909–1910	62.2	48.1	68.0	56.6	58.8	55.6	67.9	65.0	69.6	64.9	63.4	58.7	68.2	65.2	62.0

Table continues

Year	Kingston	St Andrew	St Thomas	Portland	St Mary	St Ann	Trelawny	St James	Hanover	West-moreland	St Elizabeth	Man-chester	Clarendon	St Catherine	Whole Island
1910–1911	62.4	50.4	69.9	57.0	60.0	55.8	65.6	69.8	66.8	62.7	64.9	60.5	65.7	65.6	62.4
1911–1912	64.9	48.1	71.5	59.4	63.3	58.4	70.1	70.9	67.5	65.5	63.9	59.7	69.0	67.6	64.1
1912–1913	66.6	50.7	71.1	61.2	63.9	58.2	69.1	71.1	71.1	65.2	64.5	59.5	64.9	67.8	64.2
1913–1914	63.6	51.8	72.1	58.9	65.2	59.8	69.8	68.6	71.7	65.0	63.1	58.2	67.7	69.2	64.5
1914–1915	68.4	54.9	72.1	64.8	67.9	60.5	71.3	70.2	71.7	65.4	67.6	62.4	69.8	70.8	66.8
1915–1916	68.3	54.9	73.5	64.0	67.8	61.5	69.8	73.4	72.4	64.9	66.4	62.9	69.7	70.4	66.9
1916	66.8	54.6	74.0	64.2	69.2	62.0	71.0	71.1	71.6	67.5	67.3	63.9	69.6	72.6	67.5
1917	64.8	57.6	75.5	66.9	69.0	61.7	68.9	74.9	75.0	65.3	67.3	62.0	71.2	71.7	67.7
1918	67.1	60.1	77.8	67.9	69.5	62.3	72.2	73.7	75.2	65.0	67.8	62.9	70.3	73.0	68.5
1919	69.27	67.03	76.83	67.14	72.50	61.36	73.03	77.41	76.12	67.18	69.23	65.27	71.22	74.59	70.07
1920	68.62	68.19	81.50	70.83	75.37	63.52	76.27	76.42	75.95	71.84	71.47	66.38	73.76	75.74	72.14

Source: Annual Reports of the Registrar General, printed in annual *Department Reports*, University of the West Indies (Mona) Library, Kingston.
Note: Figures in the table represent "illegitimate" births as a percentage of total births.

Appendix 5
Education Statistics

Table 1 Schools by Denomination, 1867

Denomination	Number of Schools	Pupils on Books	Attendance
Anglican	104	6,446	3,613
Wesleyan Methodist	39	3,213	1,537
Moravian	50	2,926	1,558
Presbyterian	43	3,114	1,865
Baptist	95	5,732	3,500
London Missionary Society	16	1,106	817
American Mission	5	205	117
United Free Methodist	7	367	168
American Christian Mission	6	204	123
Roman Catholic	6	138	99
Jewish	1	25	19
Non-denominational	22	1,172	772
Total male scholars		15,088	8,796
Total female scholars		9,578	5,422
Grand Total	394	24,666	14,218

Source: Blue Book of Statistics 1867, CO 142/81, Colonial Office Papers, Public Record Office, London.

Table 2 Registration and Attendance at Schools, 1867–1920

Year	Number of schools	Children of school age (5–15 years)[a]	Students registered	Actual average attendance	Percentage of registered students attending	Percentage of school-age children attending
1867	394	110,518[b]	24,666	14,218	57.64	12.86
1868–1869	397		33,453	16,521	49.38	
1869–1870	447		33,128	18,805	56.76	
1870–1871	455		35,570	21,050	59.17	
1871–1872	485		40,275	23,886	59.30	
1872–1873	492		38,917	22,955	58.98	
1873–1874	595		43,714	25,542	58.42	
1875–1876	569		46,654	27,270	58.45	
1876–1877	586		50,575	29,333	57.99	
1877–1878	617		51,488	29,679	57.64	
1878–1879	646		52,243	28,661	54.86	
1880–1881	687	146,934[c]	48,960	26,649	54.43	18.14
1882–1883	668		56,312	32,203	57.19	
1883–1884	703		57,289	33,215	57.90	
1884–1885	728		62,106	36,079	58.00	
1886–1887	725		62,424	35,613	57.00	
1887–1888	771		71,643	41,920	58.50	
1891–1892	888	164,452[d]	84,119	46,161	54.48	28.07
1892–1893	912		92,135	52,983	57.50	
1893–1894	957		97,456	64,695	66.38	
1894–1895	962		101,149	62,587	61.87	
1895–1896	932		99,790	58,650	58.77	
1896–1897	924		98,559	58,411	59.26	
1897–1898	913		98,205	57,983	59.04	
1901–1902	728		84,799	52,156	61.51	
1902–1903	717		84,652	54,448	64.31	
1903–1904	711		88,474	56,274	63.30	
1904–1905	706		83,994	51,551	60.30	

Table continues

Table 2 Registration and Attendance at Schools, 1867–1920 (*cont'd*)

Year	Number of schools	Children of school age (5–15 years)[a]	Students registered	Actual average attendance	Percentage of registered students attending	Percentage of school-age children attending
1905–1906	692		81,857	51,931	63.40	
1907–1908	690		88,862	53,691	60.55	
1908–1909	690		85,470	54,555	62.32	
1909–1910	693		89,902	57,849	64.34	
1910–1911	698	216,356[e]	94,923	59,256	62.40	27.28
1915–1916	696		97,290	54,028	66.85	
1916–1917	696		97,467	53,447	64.07	
1917–1918	696		99,910	50,730	63.22	
1918–1919	693		94,169	45,941	63.98	
1919–1920	694		90,136	53,759	66.56	
1920	693	226,010[f]	92,176	59,915	65.00	26.51

Sources: Blue Books of Statistics 1867–81, 1891–98, 1901–5; Manning to Long, 25 August 1917, No. 326, CO 137/722; Probyn to Long, 11 October 1918, No. 382, CO 137/727; H. Bryan to Milner, 8 November 1919, No. 572, CO 137/734; all in Colonial Office Papers, Public Record Office, London. Also, *Department Reports* 1882–88, 1893–94, 1905–11, 1919–20, and decennial censuses 1871–1921, in the University of the West Indies (Mona) Library, Kingston.

[a]No data presented for non-census years.
[b]This is the number of children of school age (5–15 years) according to the 1861 census.
[c]Per 1881 census.
[d]Per 1891 census.
[e]Per 1911 census.
[f]Per 1921 census.

Table 3 School Registration and Attendance by Sex, 1868–1905

Year	Boys Registered	Girls Registered	Boys Attending	Girls Attending
1868–1869	20,439	13,014	11,660	4,861
1894–1895	53,177	50,972	31,953	30,634
1895–1896	50,952	48,838	29,943	28,707
1896–1897	50,856	47,703	30,137	28,274
1897–1898	49,488	48,717	29,257	28,726
1901–1902	42,756	42,043	26,335	25,821
1902–1903	42,592	42,060	27,463	26,985
1903–1904	44,407	44,067	28,321	29,953
1904–1905	42,087	41,907	26,057	25,494

Source: *Blue Books of Statistics* 1867–81, 1891–98, 1901–5, all in Colonial Office Papers, Public Record Office, London.

Table 4 Indians: School Attendance

Year	1914–1915	1915–1916	1916–1917	1917–1918	1918–1919	1919–1920	1920–1921
Boys	n/a	601	577	619	602	641	552
Girls	n/a	322	382	425	407	448	357
Total	800[a]	923	959	1,044	1,009	1,089	909

Source: Reports of the Immigration Department, printed in annual *Department Reports*, in the University of the West Indies (Mona) Library, Kingston.
Note: Although the attendance fluctuated, the percentages remained more or less steady, with boys constituting about 60 per cent. Textual data indicate that boys attended more regularly than girls and for longer periods.

[a] Estimate – no precise figures available.

Appendix 6

Conversion Statistics of Indian Immigrants

Table 1 Presbyterian East Indian Mission

Year	Baptisms	Baptisms since 1894	Communicants	Receipts
1899	132	339	113	40
1900	147	486	125	52
1901	114	600	192	80
1902	124	724	176	75
1903	135	859	226	93
1904	113	972	195	71
1905	97	1,069	215	n/a
1906	47	1,116	n/a	n/a
1907	94	1,210	264	n/a
1908	63	1,273	253	101
1909	61	1,334	257	94
1910	60	1,394	261	117
1911	28	1,422	254	116
1912	51	1,473	227	117
1913	65	1,538	215	102
1914	50	1,588	206	108
1915	85	1,673	230	117
1916	55	1,728	256	113
1917	38	1,766	280	124
1918	43	1,809	290	114
1919	31	1,840	272	108
1920	74	1,914	286	171

Sources: United Presbyterian Church, Report on Foreign Missions 1899, New College Library, Edinburgh; United Free Church, Report on Foreign Missions 1900–1905, New College Library, Edinburgh; Minutes of the Synod of the Presbyterian Church in Jamaica 1901–21, National Library of Jamaica, Kingston.

Note: The aggregates of baptisms since 1894 have been recalculated to correct errors made in the original documents. Shepherd, however, replicated the original error by citing 1,927 Presbyterian baptisms up to 1920. See Shepherd, *Transients to Settlers*, 163, table 13.

Table 2 Baptisms at Presbyterian Mission Stations, 1894–1920

White Marl	382
Paul Island & Cornwall	669
Linstead	105
Kingston	188
Great Salt Ponds	352
Annotto Bay/Aleppo	59
Vere	1
Port Antonio	158
Total	1,914

Source: Minutes of the Synod of the Presbyterian Church in Jamaica 1921, National Library of Jamaica, Kingston.

Notes

Introduction

1. Roy Augier, "Before and After 1865", *New World Quarterly* 2 (1966); H.A. Will, *Constitutional Change in the British West Indies, 1880–1903, with Special Reference to Jamaica, British Guiana and Trinidad* (Oxford: Clarendon, 1970); Graham Knox, "Political Change in Jamaica (1866–1906) and the Local Reaction to the Policies of the Crown Colony Government", in *The Caribbean in Transition: Papers on Social, Political and Economic Development*, ed. F.M. Andic and T.G. Matthews (Río Piedras: Institute of Caribbean Studies, University of Puerto Rico, 1965); James Carnegie, *Some Aspects of Jamaica's Politics, 1918–1938* (Kingston: Institute of Jamaica, 1973).
2. See Rupert Lewis and Patrick Bryan, eds., *Garvey, His Work and Impact* (Trenton, N.J.: Africa World Press, 1991); Rupert Lewis and Maureen Warner Lewis, *Garvey: Africa, Europe, the Americas* (Trenton, N.J.: Africa World Press, 1994); Tony Martin, *Race First: The Ideological and Organizational Struggles of Marcus Garvey and the Universal Negro Improvement Association* (Westport, Conn.: Greenwood, 1976); Robert Hill, ed., *The Marcus Garvey and Universal Negro Improvement Association Papers*, 10 vols. (Berkeley: University of California Press, 1983–); Rupert Lewis, "Garvey's Forerunners: Love and Bedward", *Race and Class* 28, no. 3 (1987): 29–40; Joyce Lumsden, "Robert Love and Jamaican Politics" (PhD diss., University of the West Indies, 1988; Rupert Lewis, "Claude McKay's Political Views", *Jamaica Journal* 19, no. 2 (1986); Winston James, *A Fierce Hatred of Injustice: Claude McKay's Jamaica and His Poetry of Rebellion* (Kingston: Ian Randle, 2001).
3. Patrick Bryan, "The White Minority in Jamaica at the End of the Nineteenth Century", in *The White Minority in the Caribbean*, ed. Howard Johnson and Karl Watson (Kingston: Ian Randle, 1998), 116–32; and Thomas G. August, "An Historical Profile of the Jewish Community of Jamaica", *Jewish Social Studies* 49, nos. 3–4 (1987).
4. Walton Look Lai, *Indentured Labor, Caribbean Sugar: Chinese and Indian Migrants to the British West Indies, 1838–1918* (Baltimore: Johns Hopkins University Press, 1993); Howard Johnson, "The Anti-Chinese Riots of 1918 in Jamaica", *Immigrants and Minorities* 2, no. 1 (1983); Jacqueline Levy, "The

Economic Role of the Chinese in Jamaica: The Grocery Retail Trade", *Jamaican Historical Review* 15 (1986): 31–49; Patrick Bryan, "The Creolization of the Chinese Community in Jamaica", in *Ethnic Minorities in Caribbean Society,* ed. Rhoda Reddock (St Augustine, Trinidad: Institute of Social and Economic Research, 1996); Verene Shepherd, *Transients to Settlers: The Experience of Indians in Jamaica, 1845–1950* (Leeds: Peepal Tree, 1994).

5. See, for instance, Brian L. Moore, *Cultural Power, Resistance and Pluralism: Guyana, 1838–1900* (Kingston: The Press, University of the West Indies, 1995); Hilary McD. Beckles, *The Development of West Indies Cricket,* 2 vols. (Kingston: University of the West Indies Press, 1999); Aviston DeC. Downes, "Barbados, 1880–1914: A Socio-Cultural History" (PhD diss., University of York, 1994).

6. Bill Schwarz, "Cultural History", in *Encyclopedia of Historians and Historical Writing,* ed. Kelly Boyd (London: Fitzroy Dearborn, 1999), 277.

7. Martha Warren Beckwith, *Black Roadways: A Study of Jamaican Folk Life* (Chapel Hill: University of North Carolina Press, 1929); Martha Warren Beckwith, *Jamaica Folklore* (New York: American Folklore Society, 1929); George Eaton Simpson, *Religious Cults of the Caribbean: Trinidad, Jamaica and Haiti* (Río Piedras: Institute of Caribbean Studies, University of Puerto Rico, 1980); Joseph John Williams, *Whisperings of the Caribbean: Reflections of a Missionary* (New York: Benziger Bros., 1925); Joseph John Williams, *Voodoos and Obeah* (New York: Dial, 1932); Joseph John Williams, *Psychic Phenomena of Jamaica* (New York: Dial, 1934); W.F. Elkins, *Street Preachers, Faith Healers and Herb Doctors in Jamaica, 1890–1925* (New York: Revisionist Press, 1977); Barry Chevannes, *Rastafari: Roots and Ideology* (Syracuse: Syracuse University Press, 1995); Diane J. Austin-Broos, *Jamaica Genesis: Religion and the Politics of Moral Orders* (Chicago: University of Chicago Press, 1997).

8. Philip Curtin, *Two Jamaicas: The Role of Ideas in a Tropical Colony, 1830–1865* (1955; reprint, New York: Atheneum, 1970); Mary Turner, *Slaves and Missionaries: The Disintegration of Jamaican Slave Society, 1787–1834* (Urbana: University of Illinois Press, 1982); Monica Schuler, *"Alas, Alas, Kongo": A Social History of Indentured African Immigration into Jamaica, 1841–1865* (Baltimore: Johns Hopkins University Press, 1980); Robert J. Stewart, *Religion and Society in Post-Emancipation Jamaica* (Knoxville: University of Tennessee Press, 1992); Catherine Hall, *Civilising Subjects: Metropole and Colony in the English Imagination, 1830–1867* (London: Polity, 2002).

9. Bryan, *Jamaican People,* ix–xi.

10. See in particular Edward Brathwaite, *The Development of Creole Society in Jamaica, 1770–1820* (Oxford: Clarendon, 1971).

11. Raymond Williams, *Keywords* (London: Fontana, 1983), 90.

12. For Arnold, only "high culture" counted as culture; everything else was a frightening threat from the masses which endangered social stability. See John

Storey, *An Introductory Guide to Cultural Theory and Popular Culture* (Athens: University of Georgia Press, 1993), 22.

13. Matthew Arnold, *Culture and Anarchy* (London: Cambridge University Press, 1960), 76.

14. Storey, *Introductory Guide*, 24. By no means was this only a nineteenth-century position. In the 1930s, F.R. Leavis took the conclusions and suggestions offered by Arnold and applied them to what he saw as "the cultural crisis" of the period. See Simon During, ed., *Cultural Studies Reader* (London: Routledge, 1993), 2.

15. For many scholars dealing with cultural studies, this might best be described as "popular culture". For a clear definition of popular culture, see Storey, *Introductory Guide*, 7–12. For some of the theoretical concerns influencing cultural studies, see Antonio Gramsci, *Selections from Prison Notebooks*, ed. and trans. Quintin Hoare and Geoffrey Nowell-Smith (London: Lawrence and Wishart, 1971); Theodor Adorno and Max Horkheimer, "The Culture Industry: Enlightenment as Mass Deception", in *Dialectic of Enlightenment*, trans. John Cumming (New York: Seabury, 1972); Raymond Williams, *Culture and Society* (Harmondsworth: Penguin, 1963); Richard Hoggart, *The Uses of Literacy* (Harmondsworth: Penguin, 1990); Ferdinand de Saussure, *Course in General Linguistics* (London: Duckworth, 1983); Jacques Derrida, *Writing and Difference*, trans. Alan Bass (Chicago: University of Chicago Press, 1978).

16. Storey, *Introductory Guide*, 124–25.

17. Edward Kamau Brathwaite, *Contradictory Omens: Cultural Diversity and Integration in the Caribbean* (Kingston: Savacou, 1974), 20–22, 50–64.

18. O. Nigel Bolland, "Creolisation and Creole Societies: A Cultural Nationalist View of Caribbean Social History", *Caribbean Quarterly* 44, nos. 1–2 (1998): 25.

19. Ibid.

20. "At its best, it will inspire greater appreciation for the internal evolution of island cultures without neglecting the importance of wider imperial relationships. At its worst, it will provide little more than the flip side of an older imperial history, ignoring global issues and blurring metropolitan distinctions while concentrating exclusively on indigenous colonial struggles." William A. Green, "The Creolisation of Caribbean History: The Emancipation Era and a Critique of Dialectical Analysis", *Journal of Imperial and Commonwealth History* 14, no. 3 (1986): 150.

21. Green, "Creolisation", 150–62.

22. Richard D.E. Burton, *Afro-Creole: Power, Opposition and Play in the Caribbean* (Ithaca: Cornell University Press, 1997), 6–12.

23. Bolland cites Michel de Certeau's *Practice of Everyday Life,* trans. Steven F. Rendall (Berkeley: University of California Press, 1984); Burton cites de Certeau's "On the Oppositional Practices of Everyday Life", *Social Text* 3 (1980): 3–43.

24. Burton, *Afro-Creole*, 6–12.

Chapter 1

1. The use of the phrase "two Jamaicas" does not imply that there were only two social groupings in the island. It is used here to signify the diametrically opposed interests of the two primary "race" groups: the dominant whites and the ex-slaves, who were mainly black.
2. Many studies have examined the growing conflict between white and black Jamaica in the first quarter century after slavery; for instance, Curtin, *Two Jamaicas*; Douglas Hall, *Free Jamaica 1838–1865: An Economic History* (New Haven: Yale University Press, 1959); Thomas C. Holt, *The Problem of Freedom: Race, Labor, and Politics in Jamaica and Britain, 1832–1938* (Baltimore: Johns Hopkins University Press, 1992); and William A. Green, *British Slave Emancipation: The Sugar Colonies and the Great Experiment, 1830–1865* (Oxford: Oxford University Press, 1976).
3. For a detailed analysis of the Morant Bay massacre, see Gad Heuman, *"The Killing Time": The Morant Bay Rebellion in Jamaica* (Knoxville: University of Tennessee Press, 1994); also Don Robotham, *"The Notorious Riot": The Socioeconomic and Political Bases of Paul Bogle's Revolt* (Kingston: Institute of Social and Economic Research, 1981).
4. See Augier, "Before and After 1865".
5. Holt, *Problem of Freedom*, 341.
6. Patrick Bryan, *The Jamaican People, 1880–1902* (London: Macmillan Caribbean, 1991), 15. The literacy test was implemented by Law 39 of 1893.
7. *Daily Gleaner,* 27 and 29 August 1918, 16 September 1918, and 16 May 1919.
8. For detailed information on Revival in Jamaica, see chapter 3.
9. Hall, *Civilising Subjects*.
10. See Sir Sibbald David Scott, *To Jamaica and back* (London: Chapman and Hall, 1876), 299; and Bessie Pullen-Burry, *Jamaica as It Is, 1903* (London: T. Fisher Unwin, 1903), 23.
11. Bryan, *Jamaican People*, 23.
12. Ibid., 79.
13. See Gad Heuman, *Between Black and White: Race, Politics, and the Free Coloureds in Jamaica, 1792–1865* (Westport, Conn: Greenwood, 1981); and Mavis Campbell, *The Dynamics of Change in a Slave Society: A Socio-political History of the Free Coloreds in Jamaica, 1800–1865* (Rutherford, N.J.: Fairleigh Dickinson University Press, 1976).
14. Censuses 1861–1921, University of the West Indies, Mona (UWI Mona) Library, Kingston. See appendix 2 for a breakdown of the number of women among the Indian and Chinese immigrants.
15. Bryan, *Jamaican People*, 67–68.

16. Veront M. Satchell, *From Plots to Plantations: Land Transactions in Jamaica, 1866–1900* (Kingston: Institute of Social and Economic Research, 1990), 140–41.
17. Bryan, *Jamaican People*, 71.
18. Ibid., 74–77.
19. Ibid., 93–94, 165.
20. Ibid., 77–81.
21. See Brian L. Moore, "Race, Class and Politics in Guyana, 1891–1928", in *Before and After 1865: Education, Politics and Regionalism in the Caribbean*, ed. Brian L. Moore and Swithin R. Wilmot (Kingston: Ian Randle, 1998), 123–35.
22. Bryan, *Jamaican People*, 81–82.
23. For a picture of the socioeconomic condition of the peasant class in rural Jamaica circa 1890, see Brian L. Moore and Michele A. Johnson, eds., *Land We Live In: Jamaica in 1890* (Kingston: Social History Project, Department of History, University of the West Indies, 2000); and for a vivid portrait of the plight of the urban poor, see Moore and Johnson, *"Squalid Kingston", 1890–1920: How the Poor Lived, Moved and Had Their Being* (Kingston: Social History Project, Department of History, University of the West Indies, 2000).
24. The major mountain ranges in Jamaica include the Dry Harbour Mountains, the Santa Cruz Mountains, the May Day Mountains, the Don Figuerero Mountains, the Mocho Mountains, the Bull Head Mountains, the John Crow Mountains, the Cockpit Country and the Blue Mountains.
25. Bryan, *Jamaican People*, 143.
26. Satchell, *Plots to Plantations*, 129–55.
27. Holt, *Problem of Freedom*, 345–79.
28. See Moore and Johnson, *"Squalid Kingston"*; also Moore and Johnson, " 'Fallen Sisters'? Attitudes to Female Prostitution in Jamaica at the Turn of the Twentieth Century", *Journal of Caribbean History* 34, nos. 1–2 (2000): 46–70. For an examination of domestic service in twentieth-century Jamaica, see B.W. Higman, "Domestic Service in Jamaica since 1750", in *Trade, Government and Society in Caribbean History, 1700–1920* (Kingston: Heinemann, 1983), 117–38; Michele A. Johnson, "Intimate Enmity: Control of Women in Domestic Service in Jamaica, 1920–1970", *Jamaican Historical Review* 18 (1993): 55–65; Johnson, "Decent and Fair: Aspects of Domestic Service in Jamaica, 1920–1970", *Journal of Caribbean History* 30, nos. 1–2 (1996): 83–106; Johnson, "Young Woman from the Country: A Profile of Domestic Service in Jamaica, 1920–1970", in *Working Slavery, Pricing Freedom: The Caribbean and the Atlantic World since the Seventeenth Century*, ed. Verene Shepherd (Kingston: Ian Randle, 2002), 396–415.
29. Bryan, *Jamaican People*, 80.
30. Bridget Brereton, *Race Relations in Colonial Trinidad, 1870–1900* (Cambridge: Cambridge University Press, 1979), 94.

Chapter 2

1. Moore, *Cultural Power*, 145.
2. Schuler, *"Alas, Alas, Kongo"*, 33, 36.
3. Turner, *Slaves and Missionaries*, 54–59. Turner made reference to John Shipman, "Thoughts on the present state of Religion among the Negroes in Jamaica. A plan for their moral and religious improvement suggested by which a knowledge of the Christian religion may be communicated to them with but (comparatively) little clerical assistance: and without teaching them to Read. And the propriety and necessity of their Instruction considered in a number of Arguments", 1820, 2 ms. vols., MMS Box 558.
4. "What Is Obeah?", *Daily Gleaner*, 14 October 1904; "Obeah and Myal", *Daily Gleaner*, 18 October 1904.
5. Williams, *Psychic Phenomena*, 59–65.
6. Beckwith, *Black Roadways*, 106–7. See also Villiers Stuart, *Adventures amidst the Equatorial Forests and Rivers of South America (and Jamaica Revisited)* (London: J. Murray, 1891), 178–82; Frank Cundall, "The West Indies Today, 1908", NLJ MS 934, p. 96.
7. Moore, *Cultural Power*, 143–44. In Guyana obeahmen were feared for their knowledge of the use of poisons, but they were also regarded by the elites as confidence tricksters.
8. Rev. R. Thomas Banbury, *Jamaica Superstitions or the Obeah Book* (Kingston: Mortimer C. DeSouza, 1894), 6; see also Pullen-Burry, *Jamaica as It Is*, 135. This was a trope used in nineteenth-century fiction set in the West Indies, where a visit to the (physically repulsive) obeahman was a mandatory scene.
9. Charles Rampini, *Letters from Jamaica* (Edinburgh: Edmonston and Douglas, 1873), 131–32. The focus on the alleged "strange" appearance of the obeahman fell very easily into a tradition that allied image and demeanour with character. In order to mark the practitioners of obeah as "different", observers claimed that they operated outside of the acceptable norms, that they dabbled in evil and that they even *looked* abnormal.
10. *Jamaica Times*, 15 December 1900.
11. According to North, the Africans expressed great contempt for the Jamaican creole people, describing them as "lazy brute nigger[s]" and advocating that the government send for some good, nice African girls since the creole white women were lazy brutes and the mulatto (half-black/white) women were lazy like the blacks and dishonest like the whites. Marianne North, *Recollections of a happy life* (London: Macmillan, 1892), 105. In Guyana, too, Africans were stereotyped as obeahmen. See Moore, *Cultural Power*, 144.
12. See sub-section on "Duppies", below.
13. "A Sensational Obeah Case", *Daily Gleaner*, 21 September 1893. See also "The St

Thomas Obeah Case", *Daily Gleaner*, 25 September 1893. There were reports of other "middle-class" obeahmen; see, for instance, *Daily Gleaner*, 30 October 1893 and 1 March 1895. For a full discussion of the obeah laws, see sub-section entitled "Controlling Obeah", below.

14. "The Black Art", *Jamaica Times*, 10 June 1899. According to Beckwith, the objects that were used in obeah included articles associated with the dead: little carved coffins, bones (especially of animals or infants), teeth, blood and grave dirt, feathers, birds' beaks, horns, hoofs and animal hair, animal bones, dried herbs and seeds, and dried parts of animals (Beckwith, *Black Roadways*, 109–10). Banbury's list of paraphernalia included pieces of broken bottles, cats' or serpents' teeth, nails and bones, pins, needles, vials, pieces of cloth, and belongings of the individual client or intended victim (Banbury, *Jamaica Superstitions*, 6). For Rampini the stock-in-trade consisted of lizards' bones, old eggshells, tufts of hair, cats' claws, ducks' skulls, an old pack of cards, rusty nails and so forth, as well as ground glass, arsenic and other poisons (Rampini, *Letters*, 132–33). See also *Jamaica Guardian*, 19 May 1865; *Daily Gleaner*, 27 October 1893; *Jamaica Times*, 20 December 1902. Also Pullen-Burry, *Jamaica as It Is*, 136; Emelia Gurney, *Letters of Emelia Russey Gurney* (London: James Nisbet, 1903), letter of 21 January 1866. Very similar paraphernalia were used in Guyana; Moore, *Cultural Power*, 144.

15. Banbury, *Jamaica Superstitions*, 10–11. Perhaps because the paraphernalia of obeah was to be found in everyday life, sometimes the cases against alleged practitioners were difficult to prove. Such was the situation in 1892, when George Evans was brought before the resident magistrate in the Half-Way Tree Court, charged with "practising as a doctor without the necessary qualifications" and the "dark art of obeahism". A number of bottles thought to be his stock-in-trade were sent for analysis by the government analyst, who found that they contained only coloured water, senna and salts. The case was dismissed (*Daily Gleaner*, 4 May 1892).

16. *Daily Gleaner*, 4 May 1893.

17. Beckwith, *Black Roadways*, 113; see also Banbury, *Jamaica Superstitions*, 10–11.

18. Several in the crowd were said to be brutally handled by the police, who were themselves pelted with stones. Eleven men were arrested and charged with stone throwing (*Daily Gleaner*, 30 March 1881). In 1897 another case of "duppy catching" was reported; at Top Road, Brown's Town, a young woman who was ill was said to be afflicted by spirits and an obeahman from Runaway Bay was brought in to consult on the case. In spite of his efforts, according to the *Gleaner*, the woman continued to rave, and she was finally taken to see a medical doctor. *Daily Gleaner*, 22 February 1897.

19. Beckwith, *Black Roadways*, 117, 137. Also District Medical Officer Gayle (St Mary), Report to Senior Medical Officer Dr Lecare, *Jamaica Times*, 9 December 1911. The district medical officer advocated that parents who preferred to seek the intervention of obeah(wo)men rather than medical assistance should be prosecuted.

20. Banbury, *Jamaica Superstitions*, 6 and 10.
21. When Beckford found her plait missing (Graham had entered her home at night) and the withes, she went to police, who arrested Leslie. He was sentenced to twelve months in the General Penitentiary, where he was to receive "12 lashes with the cat-o-nine tail [a whip of nine knotted cords] on his bare back". For his part, Graham was sentenced to twelve months for stealing £1 16s. in order to pay Leslie and for soliciting obeah, and three months for assaulting Beckford. Graham's sentences were to run concurrently. *Daily Gleaner*, 13 July 1899.
22. Banbury, *Jamaica Superstitions*, 7. Francis denied any knowledge of the package, while her lawyer intoned that it was hardly complimentary to him that she had found it necessary to supplement his efforts with those of an obeahman. The judge let her off with a warning. "Woman's Trick", *Daily Gleaner*, 5 October 1909.
23. Bessie Pullen-Burry, *Ethiopia in Exile: Jamaica Revisited* (London: T. Fisher Unwin, 1905), 140, 164–65; (Mrs) T.B. Butcher, *A Peep at Jamaica and Its People* (London: Charles E. Kelly, 1902), 31; also *Friends Jamaica Mission* 7, no. 11 (November 1899), JA 5/8/78/5936.
24. In 1906 Stephen Brown was charged with "duping" a man named Morgan by offering to give him "luck". Isaac Lindsay was accused of taking advantage of Isabella Richards and another girl, promising, upon being paid, to get them good jobs. *Daily Gleaner*, 17 February 1906.
25. "Superstition in Jamaica", *Jamaica Advocate*, 4 December 1897; *Colonial Standard*, 28 October 1891. Also Banbury, *Jamaica Superstitions*, 10; and C.G. Bailey, Spanish Town, 7 December 1959, Jamaica Memories, JA 7/12/160.
26. Pullen-Burry, *Jamaica as It Is*, 135; Warrand Carlile, "38 years' Mission Life in Jamaica", *United Presbyterian Church Missionary Record*, January 1861.
27. Beckwith, *Black Roadways*, 135–37; Banbury, *Jamaica Superstitions*, 8.
28. For the full "confession" in the tract see "The Late Obeahman! John Nugent's Roll Book Found At Last: All His Customers Fully Exposed", NLJ MST 1842, no. 1; also C.R.C., "The Full Confession of The Great Obeahman, Old George Elleth: A Native of Hampton Road in Porus", NLJ MST 1842, no. 2; "Obeah Literature", *Daily Gleaner*, 29 May 1894.
29. See J.H.W., "The Awful Death and Confession of Old Mother Austin", NLJ MST 1842, no. 3. The confessions also contained a long list of names and "workings" that the obeah(wo)men were alleged to have performed during their careers. See F.A. Symson, "Death and Confession of Daniel Hart: A Native of Long District, Portland", NLJ MST 1842, no. 4; Symson, "Balance of the Confession of Daniel Hart", NLJ MST 1842, no. 5; "Hannah Grant alias Mrs Bywater and Richard Daly of Grant's Pen and How He Killed Sarah DaCosta and Others", NLJ MST 1842, no. 7. See also Williams, *Psychic Phenomena*, 124–28, for an account of these confessions.
30. *Daily Gleaner*, 29 May 1894.

31. C.R.C., "Full Confession of Old George Elleth"; "Obeah Literature", *Daily Gleaner*, 29 May 1894.
32. David P. Mendes (Spanish Town) to the editor, *Daily Gleaner*, 31 May 1894; and *Daily Gleaner*, 11 June 1894. The case of Joseph M. Campbell, an herbalist who had displayed his wares at the 1891 Exhibition and who had gained fame for his herbal concoctions, was highlighted by the *Gleaner*. After his release Campbell stated his intention of proceeding against the government for false imprisonment. *Daily Gleaner*, 25 June 1894. See also "Interest in Obeah", *Daily Gleaner*, 14 October 1907.
33. Banbury, *Jamaica Superstitions*, 18. For the *Morning Journal*, the fact that whites might be involved was not surprising, since in England and Scotland they were involved in witchcraft; *Morning Journal*, 7 October 1872. Let it not be supposed, claimed "Climaticus", that those who patronized the obeah(wo)man/bush doctor or herbalist/balmist were to be found only in the illiterate class, or among the peasantry: "Oh no! they are also to be found among the members of the middle class, and alas, even among some of those whose names are to be found in the register books of the churches." "Climaticus", "Praedial Larceny and Obeahmen", *Jamaica Times*, 15 May 1909.
34. "Obeahism Extraordinary", *Daily Gleaner*, 5 May 1899; and Report of the Friends Jamaica Mission, 1920, JA 5/8/4/540.
35. S.H. Brown (Portland) to the editor, *Daily Gleaner*, 23 November 1898.
36. *Friends Jamaica Mission* 7, no. 11 (November 1899), JA 5/8/78/5936.
37. "Truth" to the editor, *Jamaica Times*, 4 April 1903. A Methodist priest, Rev. Dr Murray, asserted in 1901 that the church had its hands full with three categories of persons. First, those who practised obeah, he thought, should be excluded from church membership as receivers of money under false pretences. Second, those who believed in obeah and sought practitioners and, third, those who believed in it and feared it but who did not seek to engage with it deserved, he thought, more consideration. He did not approve of such persons being excluded from church membership. "They should not be allowed to have leading positions in the church, but for an intellectual weakness the cure they need is continued special teaching to bring them into clearer and fuller knowledge." Rev. Dr Murray's article in *Wesleyan Methodist*, November 1901, cited in "Obeah", *Jamaica Times*, 16 November 1901.
38. The belief in obeah was reputed to be very strong in the rural areas, especially on and near the sugar plantations. See "A Brief Report of the [Methodist] Societies in the Jamaica District 1907", Appendix A in: *Minutes of the District Synod of the Jamaica District 1908*, JA 5/6/7/2; *Periodical Accounts Relating to the Missions of the Church of the United Brethren established among the Heathen*, June 1867, June 1868, September 1869, and June 1871, Moravian Church Papers, all JA 5/5. Also *Report of the Wesleyan Methodist Missionary Society*, 1907, SOAS; Minutes of the Synod of

the Presbyterian Church of Jamaica [hereafter cited as Presbyterian Synod Minutes], Life and Work Committee, 1912 and 1913, NLJ MST 2089; H. Alma Swift, Report of the Friends Jamaica Mission, third quarter 1918, JA 5/8/4/524; Report of the Friends Jamaica Mission, second quarter 1919, JA 5/8/4/532; Report of the Friends Jamaica Mission, 1920, JA 5/8/4/540.

39. Annual Report of the Moravian Church in Jamaica, 1890, JA 5/5.
40. Matt. 12:28. This and all subsequent biblical quotations are taken from the King James version. According to James Strong, there are more than five hundred references to "spirits" in the Bible (some to the spirit of God, to restless spirits, to evil spirits, to demonic spirits, and so forth). James Strong, *Strong's Exhaustive Concordance* (Gordonville, Tex.: Dugan Publishers, n.d.), 967–69.
41. A multiplicity of obeah cases were reported from different parts of the island. Indeed, in 1915 Emerick had justifiable cause to declare that obeah "flourished" in Jamaica in spite of the most drastic laws against it. Abraham J. Emerick, "Obeah and Duppyism in Jamaica", from *Woodstock Letters* (Woodstock, Md., 1915), 191. Numerous cases were reported in Buff Bay, Chapelton, Frankfield, Gayle, Hope Bay, Hopefield, Hopewell Hill Gap, Juno Pen, Kingston, Linstead, Little London, Mandeville, May Pen, Mile Gully, Mocho, Morant Bay, Montego Bay, Mount Simple, Port Maria, Richmond, Roehampton, Sandy Bay, Savanna-la-Mar, Spanish Town, Temple Hall, Thompson Town, Walk's Wood, York Land, and even further afield in Costa Rica, to which many Jamaicans had migrated. See, for instance, *Jamaica Post*, 11 July 1891 and 18 February 1897; *Jamaica Daily Telegraph*, 20 October 1899; *Jamaica Times*, 24 November 1900 and 4 December 1915; *Jamaica Guardian*, 12 March 1909; *Daily Gleaner*, 5 May 1899 and 25 November 1918.
42. "Hypothesis" to the editor, *Daily Gleaner*, 24 January 1894; S.H. Brown (Portland) to the editor, *Daily Gleaner*, 23 November 1898; and "Our Social Health", *Jamaica Times*, 15 December 1900. Reports from Little London in 1899 spoke of a girl who was creating havoc in Broughton District with her claims that obeah was buried to prevent her hostess from getting married; she offered to remove the obeah, but no candles were available on the appointed evening. "The miserably superstitious girl" soon returned home to Hanover. *Jamaica Times*, 17 June 1899 and 1 July 1899.
43. *Morning Journal*, 20 February 1868.
44. "The Effects of Custom and Poverty", *Jamaica Advocate*, 12 and 19 August 1899.
45. Pullen-Burry, *Ethiopia*, 164; and William Pringle Livingstone, *Black Jamaica: A study in evolution* (London: Sampson Low, Marston and Co., 1899), 110. According to some church sources, places like Moore Town did not suffer from the prevalence of obeah "on the account of missionary work". Mr Kilburn in *The Jamaica Church Chronicle*, quoted in *The Mission Field: A Monthly Record of the Proceedings on the Society for the Propagation of the Gospel, at Home and Abroad*,

1877 (London: G. Bell and Sons, 1860–1920), Papers of the Society of the Propagation of the Gospel in Foreign Parts, Partnership House, London.

46. In Guyana a law was passed in 1855 outlawing obeah. As in Jamaica, however, the problem lay in legally defining obeah. In both colonies it was originally equated with witchcraft, fortune telling and confidence trickery, but in 1877 the Guyana court found the absence of a strict definition of obeah untenable. Consequently a new law was passed in 1877, which made anyone practising witchcraft, sorcery, enchantment, conjuration, fortune telling, and palmistry aimed at deceiving punishable as a rogue and a vagabond. In Guyana flogging with the cat-o'-nine tails was done in public in front of the Stabroek Market in Georgetown, with a view to sending a lesson to those who believed in and practised obeah. See Moore, *Cultural Power*, 146.

47. While the 1856 law spoke loosely of "dealers in obeah or myalism", the 1857 legislation stated that "any person who shall for false, crafty, or unlawful purposes pretend to the possession of supernatural power, or who, by threat, promise, persuasion, or action, shall induce, or attempt to induce, any other person to believe that he can, by the exercise of any such supernatural power, bring about or effect any object, or carry out any design of his own, or of any other person, or, for the purpose of carrying out any such design or object, shall falsely, cunningly, or unlawfully make use of omens, spells, charms, incantations, or other preternatural devices, shall be deemed and taken to be an obeah or myal man, or a dealer in obeah and myalism". This was amended by the Obeah and Myalism Acts Amendment Law, No. 28 of 1892. See Blake to Knutsford, 26 May 1892, no. 175, and encl., Attorney General's Report, 17 May 1892, CO 137/549; also appended minute of Edward Wingfield, 23 June 1892, CO 137/549; and Knutsford to Blake, 4 July 1892, no. 166, CO 137/549. It is significant that even when committing a "heinous" crime like practising obeah, women were protected by gender ideology (as the "weaker" sex) and exempted from the harshest punishment – flogging. See the Obeah and Myalism Acts Further Amendment Law, No. 1 of 1893. See Blake to Ripon, 28 September 1892, no. 329, CO 137/550; Blake to Ripon, 5 May 1893, no. 135, and encl., Attorney General's Report, 26 April 1893, CO 137/555; also appended minute of G.H. Wedgwood, 5 June 1893, CO 137/555. Flogging for other offences was regulated by Act 29 Vict. Sess 1 c. 7.

48. The Obeah Law, No. 5 of 1898. See Hemming to Chamberlain, 18 June 1898, no. 237, and encl., Attorney General's Report, 1 June 1898, CO 137/591; also minutes of H.B. Cox, 9 July 1898, and C.P. Lucas, 9 July 1898, CO 137/591. In 1900, after a resident magistrate directed that a convicted person should be whipped in the district where the offence had occurred, it was determined that whipping should take place in the prison where the convicted person was installed. See Hemming to Secretary of State, 4 April 1900, no. 135, re the Whipping Law Amendment Law 1900, No. 4 of 1900, and encl., Attorney General's Report, 17 March 1900,

CO 137/610. The law equated obeah and Myal (see chapter 3), and some people argued that the definition of obeah could be interpreted to include "palmistry" and "fortune telling". This was perhaps in answer to the concerns that, while obeah was vigorously prosecuted, "clairvoyance" was openly available to the public ("Hanover" to the editor, *Colonial Standard*, 2 September 1892). But since those were not specifically mentioned in the law, advertisements for clairvoyance, astrology, palmistry and phrenology still continued to be published in the local newspapers. "Is Clairvoyance, etc. Obeah?", *Jamaica Advocate*, 1 April 1905.

49. "Obeah", *Jamaica Advocate*, 27 May 1899; "Obeah and the Law", *Jamaica Advocate*, 8 July 1899.
50. The Obeah Law, No. 8 of 1903; Hemming to Chamberlain, 31 March 1903, no. 168, and encl., report of Attorney General, 19 March 1903, CO 137/633; appended minutes of J.S. Risley, 6 May 1903, H.B. Cox, 7 May 1903, and C.P. Lucas, 7 May 1903, CO 137/633; and Chamberlain to Hemming, 12 May 1903, no. 202, CO 137/633. See also Hemming to Chamberlain, 3 June 1903, no. 320, and appended minutes of T.C. Macnaghten, 23 June 1903, and J.S. Risley, 25 June 1903, CO 137/635; and Chamberlain to Hemming, 3 July 1903, no. 269, CO 137/635.
51. *Daily Gleaner*, 8 January 1894 and 25 October 1898; *Daily Telegraph & Anglo-American Herald*, 29 July 1899; *Jamaica Times*, 21 October 1899 and 6 December 1913. Earlier in the period Governor Musgrave argued that the increased number of convictions could be taken as a sign that "the evil practice is gradually losing its control over the minds of the people". See Governor's Report, *Department Reports*, 1879–80, UWI Mona Library, p. xx.
52. *Daily Gleaner*, 23 March 1901.
53. *Jamaica Times*, 19 October 1907.
54. *Falmouth Post*, 8 December 1865 and 14 February 1868; *Daily Gleaner*, 27 January 1892, 30 June 1893, 13 and 16 October 1893, and 1 December 1893.
55. *Daily Gleaner*, 8 and 9 December 1893; *Colonial Standard*, 7 December 1893. Also Acting Governor to Chamberlain, 22 September 1902, no. 537, JA 1B/5/18 vol. 56. Ephraim Campbell, on whose behalf and at whose instigation Murray "worked" the obeah, was sentenced to ninety days' imprisonment. *Jamaica Times*, 8 April 1899.
56. *Jamaica Times*, 29 April 1899, 2 September 1899 and 13 July 1901; *Daily Gleaner*, 17 February 1894, 12 January 1898 and 13 April 1909.
57. See E.H.B. Hartwell, Report of the Inspector General of Police, *Department Reports*, 1879–80, UWI Mona Library, p. 249; Livingstone, *Black Jamaica*, 198–99; and "A Good Licking – Its Place", *Daily Gleaner*, 9 March 1893.
58. S.C. Morris to the editor, *Daily Gleaner*, 7 July 1893; Emerick, *Obeah*, 191.
59. W.F. Jones to the editor, *Daily Gleaner*, 29 January 1909; and "Flagellomania", *Jamaica Times*, 17 November 1900. See also "A Friend of the Lash", *Jamaica Times*, 24 August 1901.

60. "Eighteen Lashes", *Daily Gleaner*, 26 January 1909.
61. Eyre to Newcastle, 23 September 1862, no. 83, and enclosures: report of the Attorney General, Alexander Heslop to Govt. Sect. Austin, 3 June 1862; Heslop to Austin, 12 June 1862; appended minute of Sir F. Rogers, 15 January 1863.
62. See minutes of Edward Wingfield, 23 June 1892, and Knutsford to Blake, 4 July 1892, no. 166, appended to governor's despatch no. 175, CO 137/549; also minutes of R.V. Vernon, 30 December 1901, W.D. Ellis, 3 November 1902, H.B. Cox, 3 November 1902, and Secretary of State J. Chamberlain, 7 November 1902, all appended to governor's despatch no. 684, 3 December 1901, CO 137/622.
63. Sir Fielding Clarke to C.P. Lucas (Colonial Office), 24 September 1901, CO 137/625.
64. Hemming to Chamberlain, 3 December 1901, no. 684, and encl.: minute of Attorney General, 20 November 1901; appended minutes of R.V. Vernon, 30 December 1901, W.D. Ellis, 3 November 1902, H.B. Cox, 3 November 1902, and J. Chamberlain, 7 November 1902; all CO 137/622.
65. Sir Charles F. Lumb, LLD, "How Obeahism May Be Killed", *Daily Gleaner*, 18 December 1909; Olivier to Crewe, 27 April 1909, no. 178, JA 1B/5/18 vol. 64.
66. The resident magistrates and inspectors of police were also asked to comment on the proposal to bring back the stocks. While the resident magistrate for Kingston said he thought the stocks would be a deterrent, others, like the resident magistrate for St Ann, thought that imprisonment in the stocks would engender pity and commiseration from the people and that flogging was the preferred punishment, as "obeah men dread flogging". Among the inspectors of police there was a definite preference for "a sound flogging". Précis of opinions of Resident Magistrates and Inspectors of Police, and minute of Acting Attorney General, 17 June 1909, encl. in Olivier to Crewe, 15 October 1909, no. 470, CO 137/673.
67. While some like "Justice" and "Black Jamaican" argued that there was "no doubt that the lash has acted as a deterrent" against the practise of obeah (especially poisoning), others like "First Principles" said that all that was being punished was ignorance and that many of the things that obeah workers were accused of were impossibilities. See "Justice" to the editor, *Daily Gleaner*, 18 February 1909; "First Principles" to the editor, *Daily Gleaner*, 22 February 1909; "Black Jamaican" to the editor, *Daily Gleaner*, 1 March 1909. Support for the lash also came from S. Percival Hendrick, archdeacon of Panama, who said that he believed that flogging would reduce the amount of obeah in the island; see S. Percival Hendrick, "The Lash", *Jamaica Times*, 21 September 1901.
68. Olivier to Crewe, 17 May 1910, no. 165, CO 137/678. George Grindle of the Colonial Office, however, thought the experiment was worthless, since once it was known that offenders would not be flogged, potential offenders would realize that they were safe from flogging for twelve months. Minute of George Grindle, 6 June 1910, appended to no. 165, CO 137/678.

69. Olivier to Harcourt, 16 March 1911, no. 90; and appended minutes of H.R. Cowell, 13 April 1911, E.A.W., 15 April 1911; T.C. Macnaghten, 18 April 1911, and H.B. Cox, 18 April 1911; all CO 137/683. Also Williams, *Psychic Phenomena*, 103. Obeah still remained on the statute books as a criminal offence beyond 1919.
70. Banbury, *Jamaica Superstitions*, 32–33; William James Makin, *Caribbean Nights* (London: Robert Hale, 1939), 163.
71. Beckwith, *Black Roadways*, 99. According to Nadel, the Nupe believe that when the witch attacks a person at night in his or her sleep, it is always the *rayi* (living state) or *anima* (life soul) she feeds on, thus causing the *naka* (body) to fall ill and waste away. But when the witch takes her victim to the gathering place where all other witches will feast on him or her, it is only the *fifingi* (shadow soul) that is brought along and devoured, not the person in the flesh, who remains asleep in the house. Likewise, when witches move around at night (flying), they do so not in body but in soul (their *fifingi*). Hence, it is a shadow feeding on a shadow. S.F. Nadel, *Nupe Religion* (London: Routledge and Kegan Paul, 1954), 168. But the belief in witchcraft was not unique to Africa. For instance, "witches" of seventeenth-century Salem, Massachusetts, were targets primarily because they were older women who had difficulties with the larger community. Stephen Foster, *The Long Argument: English Puritanism and the Shaping of New England Culture, 1570–1700* (Chapel Hill: Published for the Institute of Early American History and Culture, Williamsburg, Va., by the University of North Carolina Press, c.1991); Avihu Zakai, *Theocracy in Massachusetts: Reformation and Separation in Early Puritan New England* (Lewiston: Mellen University Press, c.1994).
72. Banbury, *Jamaica Superstitions*, 32–33.
73. Beckwith, *Black Roadways*, 99; Banbury, *Jamaica Superstitions*, 33. Pullen-Burry referred to the same phenomenon as "vampires" or "loogaroos"; Pullen-Burry, *Ethiopia*, 165. Another common method of capturing the witch in Guyana was to set an odd number of grains of corn near her skin, and since she could only count in pairs, she would have to count over and over until she was caught. Moore, *Cultural Power*, 151.
74. *Jamaica Times*, 20 September 1902. The same phenomenon of targeting old women as witches existed in Guyana; Moore, *Cultural Power*, 150.
75. Banbury, *Jamaica Superstitions*, 35.
76. Williams, *Psychic Phenomena*, 173.
77. Moore, *Cultural Power*, 138–39.
78. Banbury, *Jamaica Superstitions*, 35.
79. Ibid., 27. Banbury seemed to rely, almost exclusively, on previous *Gleaner* publications; see "The 'Superstitions' of Jamaica", *Daily Gleaner*, 10, 17 and 24 February 1912. See also Frank Cundall, "Jamaica in 1905", NLJ MST 9311, pp. 97–98.
80. Williams, *Psychic Phenomena*, 155.

81. Alice Spinner, "Duppies", *Daily Gleaner*, 30 September 1895, reprinted from the *National Review*.
82. Banbury, *Jamaica Superstitions*, 27–29; Emerick, *Obeah*, 339–41.
83. Rampini, *Letters*, 83; "Jamaican Ghosts", *Daily Gleaner*, 23 April 1884, reprinted from *All the Year Round*; and Spinner, "Duppies".
84. Rampini, *Letters*, 83; Emerick, *Obeah*, 341.
85. Rampini, *Letters*, 83; see also Williams, *Psychic Phenomena*, 153.
86. Beckwith, *Black Roadways*, 90, 98–99. According to Walter Jekyll, it was agreed that "the 'baddest' of all is Coolie Duppy". Walter Jekyll, *Jamaican Song and Story: Anancy Stories, Digging Songs, Ring Tunes, and Dancing Tunes* (London: David Nutt for the Folklore Society, 1907), 175. The "Long Bubbies" in Guyana are similar. They were supposed to be spirits of dead women which appeared with the right breast elongated or lengthened at pleasure, with which they threatened certain night walkers and flogged others. See Moore, *Cultural Power*, 148.
87. Moore, *Cultural Power*, 148; Rampini, *Letters*, 83; Pullen-Burry, *Jamaica as It Is*, 138; Makin, *Caribbean Nights*, 164; and Beckwith, *Black Roadways*, 100.
88. Banbury, *Jamaica Superstitions*, 24–25. Williams disagreed with Banbury's use of "roaring", suggesting that "rolling" referred to "wandering" or "roaming" and was the more appropriate term; Williams, *Psychic Phenomena*, 162. See also "The 'Superstitions' of Jamaica", *Daily Gleaner*, 17 February 1912; Rampini, *Letters*, 83; Spinner, "Duppies"; and "Jamaica Superstitions", *Jamaica Times*, 4 March 1899.
89. Charles H. Distin to the editor, *Jamaica Times*, 5 September 1903.
90. Banbury, *Jamaica Superstitions*, 29; Beckwith, *Black Roadways*, 90; Jekyll, *Jamaica Song*, 176.
91. The Salt Ponds were said to have been a resort of the buccaneers in the "brave old piratical days"; Rampini, *Letters*, 83. Also Banbury, *Jamaica Superstitions*, 19; Scott, *To Jamaica*, 237; and Beckwith, *Black Roadways*, 90.
92. Emerick, *Obeah*, 341; Makin, *Caribbean Nights*, 173–74. In her novel *Myal* (London: New Beacon, 1988), Erna Brodber describes incidents of mysterious stonings of a house (see pp. 28–31, 39–40). See also *Morning Journal*, 12 July 1873; *Daily Gleaner*, 18 February 1878, 11 July 1878 and 18 July 1900.
93. *Morning Journal*, 29 and 30 March 1875.
94. *Jamaica Times*, 11 April 1903.
95. *Daily Gleaner*, 17 July 1877 and 22 September 1879; *Colonial Standard*, 6 April 1881; *Jamaica Times*, 8 July 1899 and 19 August 1899. According to Jennie Hoover, it was the general belief that sickness came because of the interference of evil spirits; Jennie M. Hoover to Ross Hadley, 26 October 1917, Friends Jamaica Mission papers, JA 5/8/2/439. In another case in Darliston, Westmoreland, duppies were chased from a home by the use of "chalking", two fires and the burning of various sorts of things which caused "strange odours". "Duppy Catching", *Jamaica Times*, 4 March 1899; see also "Duppy-Catching at

Clarkesonville", *Jamaica Times*, 1 April 1899; "More Duppy-Catching", *Jamaica Times*, 11 March 1899.
96. "In the Shadow of Superstition", *Jamaica Times*, 6 April 1901.
97. The correspondent decided that these were the "workings of Satan"; *Jamaica Times*, 17 January 1903.
98. "Darkest Jamaica", *Jamaica Times*, 16 July 1904. "Guard" refers to some form of ornament that the person being protected was required to bear or wear.
99. "Shooting a Duppy", *Jamaica Times*, 30 January 1904.
100. Spinner, "Duppies".
101. Makin, *Caribbean Nights*, 175.
102. Banbury, *Jamaica Superstitions*, 29. "Pap" referred to an inexpensive porridge (usually made from cornmeal) which was a mainstay of the people. See also Pullen-Burry, *Ethiopia*, 152.
103. The idea was that the living baby was being "given" to the departed one, and then taken back; Pullen-Burry, *Ethiopia*, 152.
104. Isabel Cranstoun MacLean, *Children of Jamaica* (Edinburgh: Oliphant, Anderson and Ferrier, 1910), 32.
105. Banbury, *Jamaica Superstitions*, 29; Beckwith, *Black Roadways*, 92–94.
106. Rampini, *Letters*, 84.
107. Ibid., 84. According to Pullen-Burry, the killing of the Anancy spider would result in the breaking of plates; *Ethiopia*, 150. See also Ethel Maud Symmonett, *Jamaica: Queen of the Carib Sea* (Kingston: Mortimer C. DeSouza, 1895), 13.
108. Symmonett, *Jamaica*, 13. "San-pattern", commonly pronounced *sanpata* in Jamaica, is thought to be derived from the Spanish *zapata*. See *Jamaica Times*, 10 December 1898.
109. Pullen-Burry, *Ethiopia*, 151.
110. Ibid., 150.
111. Later Porter was sentenced to fourteen days' hard labour in the Falmouth District Prison for his involvement in the "practices" of the bible-and-key; *Falmouth Post*, 11 September 1860. In Guyana the bible-and-key was also employed as a method of investigation by obeahmen; Moore, *Cultural Power*, 145.
112. *Colonial Standard*, 2 October 1890.
113. Cundall, "West Indies", 95.
114. Banbury, *Jamaica Superstitions*, 36.
115. Ibid., 38.
116. "Obeahism in the Parish of Hanover", *Falmouth Post*, 22 January 1869.

Chapter 3

1. Curtin, *Two Jamaicas*, 33.
2. Turner, *Slaves and Missionaries*, 57–58; also Curtin, *Two Jamaicas*, 34.

3. Stewart, *Religion*, xviii, 143–44.
4. Monica Schuler, e-mail correspondence to Brian L. Moore, 3 April 2002; Schuler, *"Alas, Alas, Kongo"*, 32–36.
5. Curtin, *Two Jamaicas*, 34.
6. Austin-Broos, *Jamaica Genesis*, 53–54.
7. Ibid., 52–53.
8. Schuler further argues that Myalists recognized social enemies "within and without", and sought to control them. It "thus proved far more relevant to many Afro-Jamaicans than any missionary version of the Christian faith"; Schuler, *"Alas, Alas, Kongo"*, 36. Stewart too argues that Myal offered social cures to its adherents against a background of European political, economic and cultural oppression which was interpreted as a form of sorcery; Stewart, *Religion*, 144.
9. "Pickney" is a Jamaican Creole word meaning child or children; Curtin, *Two Jamaicas*.
10. Beckwith, *Black Roadways*, 158–59.
11. Schuler, *"Alas, Alas, Kongo"*, 41. The gender equality before God is worthy of note in a society that had long imported the patriarchal structures of the dominant culture. If each soul was as worthwhile as the other, the Revival faith was bound to be attractive to a community which had experienced more gender equality than the dominant culture had been able to accommodate comfortably. The claims to greater gender equality than occurred among the elite (and even to female dominance) were made by several contemporaries who saw the economic contributions and independence of working-class women as the source of their challenge to the more "acceptable" ideology of female subordination. See Moore and Johnson, *Land We Live In*; Bryan, *Jamaican People*, 97–100. Whether more equality meant *absolute* equality, however, is open to question, since the overarching gender ideology still gave men more power, even where women made their economic contributions. See Brian L. Moore and Michele A. Johnson, " 'Married but not Parsoned': Attitudes to Conjugality in Jamaica, 1865–1920", in *Control and Resistance in the Post-Emancipation Caribbean*, ed. Gad Heuman and David Trotman (London: Macmillan, 2004); Marietta Morrissey, "Explaining the Caribbean Family: Gender Ideologies and Gender Relations", in *Caribbean Portraits: Essays on Gender Ideologies and Identities*, ed. Christine Barrow (Kingston: Ian Randle, 1998), 82.
12. According to Joseph Moore, it was believed that God the Father did not attend Revival meetings, but remained in heaven. All the other spirits attended, although God the Son did not participate. Joseph Graessle Moore, "Religion of the Jamaican Negroes: A Study of Afro-Jamaican Acculturation" (PhD diss., Northwestern University, 1953), 79–80.
13. See also Austin-Broos, *Jamaica Genesis*, 62.
14. The Christian evangelical revival had started in the United States in 1858 and

spread to Britain and Ireland. The missionaries in Jamaica attempted to promote a similar movement from 1859 by having special prayer meetings. By late 1860 the revival began to generate public fervour that lasted well into 1862. See Curtin, *Two Jamaicas*, 170–71; Stewart, *Religion*, 139, 145–46; Schuler, *"Alas, Alas, Kongo"*, 104; and Shirley C. Gordon, *Our Cause for His Glory* (Kingston: The Press, University of the West Indies, 1998), 94. This interpretation of the revival is contested by Baptist historian Brian Stanley, who adopts the explanations of missionary James M. Phillippo to the effect that the revival "eliminated" Afro-creole practices such as obeah and Myal and reduced the incidence of funeral wakes. He also notes that the membership of the Baptist congregation increased during 1861. Hence, he concludes, "The revival was a reversion, not to African paganism, but to the black American Christian tradition from which the Jamaican Baptists sprang. As such, it inevitably evoked mixed reactions from European observers." See Brian Stanley, *The History of the Baptist Missionary Society, 1792–1992* (Edinburgh: T. and T. Clark, 1992), 96–97.

15. The 1874 Revival was reported mainly in St Thomas. See *Falmouth Post*, 2 April 1875; also Wesleyan Methodist Missionary Society, Report of the Religious State of the Societies, Synod minutes, 29 January 1875, MMS Box 163–1874. Bryan speaks about a revival in 1883, but does not produce any supporting references; Bryan, *Jamaican People*, 55. According to the *Daily Gleaner*, in 1886 "a woman appeared suddenly in some of the parishes and held Revival meetings in different centres". She said she had been converted in 1860, and had wandered into a forest and lived in a cave there until 1886, when she was discovered by a band of Revivalists. Her testimony that during her sojourn she was fed daily by an angel with locusts and honey was believed by some and rejected by others. In any event, according to the newspaper, she was partly responsible for the fresh start of Revival in Jamaica; *Daily Gleaner*, 3 November 1897.

16. *Jamaica Times*, 14 July 1906. In September four native evangelists, working under Rev. George Turner at Croft's Hill, Clarendon, began a mission; *Jamaica Times*, 22 September 1906. In October, at the Thompson Town and the Cedar Valley Baptist Churches, Clarendon, a series of special Revival meetings were held under the direction of Rev. George Turner and W.R. Phillips, an evangelist. Three meetings were held every day, and hundreds of persons professed to have been converted in the process; *Jamaica Times*, 20 October 1906. The Grantham Church in Clarendon was reportedly "attacked by the converts", and after a series of meetings "the whole church . . . surrendered to God. . . . The converts are very anxious for the conversion of others, and they go from house to house in some districts praying for them, and weeping over them, until they yield up themselves, and they get concerned about others"; *Jamaica Times*, 17 November 1906. In May and June 1907 there was a scene of Revival at York which began with a sixteen-year-old girl. The spirit of God took hold of her at home and she prayed, and

some on their way to their grounds or to the pond left those activities and gathered in her yard, where hundreds were assembled. The Revival also spread to Greenwick, Castle Mountain, Chester Castle, Lam's River, Baverant and Duckett where young converts were bringing in "lost souls"; *Jamaica Times*, 1 June 1907. In Clarendon and St Ann throughout 1907 there were "new victories" won every day; in Brown's Town "over 20 of the worse characters" professed conversion. *Jamaica Times*, 2 November 1907.

17. See *115th Report of the Baptist Missionary Society*, 1907, and *116th Report of the Baptist Missionary Society*, 1908, Angus Library, Regent's Park College, Oxford.
18. Edward Seaga, "Revival Cults in Jamaica: Notes towards a Sociology of Religion", *Jamaica Journal* 3, no. 2 (1969): 4; Chevannes, *Rastafari*, 20–21.
19. W.D. Townsley, "A Cousin of Myalism: Something About the Pokomaniac", *Jamaica Times*, 20 July 1912; see also Francis B. Isaacs to the editor, *Jamaica Times*, 10 August 1912. This failure to recognize the differences or linkages between Zion Revival and Pukumina was not confined to elite contemporaries. Patrick Bryan also speaks imprecisely about "African Zionism, Pukkumina, myalism and revivalism" without any attempt to explain their relationship (Bryan, *Jamaican People*, 34, 58).
20. Beckwith, *Black Roadways*, 176–83.
21. Makin, *Caribbean Nights*, 96.
22. Seaga, "Revival Cults in Jamaica", 10–11. According to Seaga, "The primary Zion criticism of the Pukkumina cult relates to the dealings of the latter with spirits of the dead. These are considered to be evil forces and their operators are said to be of a socially inferior status since they violate a fundamental moral law. On the other hand, Pukkumina followers consider all supernatural forces as capable of good and evil" (Seaga, "Revival Cults", 10–11). See also J.G. Moore, "Religion", 56–62, 70–109. Moore states that "Pocomania" was looked upon with disfavour by all other groups, including Cumina worshippers. In particular, Zionists saw "Poco" as devil worship; J.G. Moore, "Religion", 60.
23. Makin, however, did describe a Pukumina ceremony which revealed similarities to those of Zion, with a cloth-covered table on which were cups and saucers and an array of fruit. The devotees wore multicoloured turbans, and the leader (also called a "shepherd") was draped in a vermilion robe decorated with silver stars. In addition to his turban, he wore a silver cardboard crown and carried a huge, wooden scimitar "with which he cleaved the darkness in sudden, disconcerting fashion". The women (some of whom were called "shepherdesses") wore blue and pink headdresses which flowed down their backs, and children, dressed like brides, carried bouquets which contained lighted candles. Although various biblical intonations were made, and the congregation sang "Wash me in the Blood of the Lamb / An' I shall be whiter than snow", the focus was on the "Mystic Table" which contained many candles. " 'An' we begin, brethren, by lightin' the

great candle which represents God the Father. . . .' (A big, solitary red candle flickered into flame) 'followed by the Son, Jesus our Lawd' (a second white candle flickered) 'and then der Holy Ghost. . . .' (A black candle at the floor of the table was lit.)

"Twelve candles were lit for the disciples, and several for the prophets until the whole Mystic Table became a blaze of light. Women began to scream and convulse and very soon the announcement was made that the spirit had descended into their midst." Makin, *Caribbean Nights*, 98–106, 112.

24. J.G. Moore, "Religion", 56–57.
25. According to Joseph Moore, the leaders usually wore coloured turbans, while their assistants wore white; J.G. Moore, "Religion", 57.
26. Herbert George De Lisser, *In Jamaica and Cuba* (Kingston: Gleaner Co., 1910), 94–95. For a full description of a Revival service in the early twentieth century, see De Lisser, *Twentieth Century Jamaica* (Kingston: Jamaica Times, 1913), 134–47. While most Revivalists wore white, some were observed in turbans of white mixed with red; see R.W.T., "One of the Sights of a Suburb of Kingston: Rampant Revivalism", *Daily Gleaner*, 9 June 1914.
27. J.G. Moore, "Religion", 58. According to him, trumping was a dance done counterclockwise around the altar and having the appearance of a forward-moving two-step stomp: "With the step forward, the body is bent forward from the waist so sharply as to seem propelled by force. At the same time, the breath is exhaled or inhaled, with great effort and sound. The forcefulness of the action gives justification for the use of the word, 'labouring'. The word 'groaning' is used in connection with the heavy expulsion and sucking in of breath. In Revival and Pocomania the breath is exhaled when the body bends down and inhaled on the upswing; in Revival Zion, the process is reversed." He further noted that trumping and labouring referred to an unbroken process of worship and invitation to the spirits to come down and take possession of worshippers. J.G. Moore, "Religion", 70. For a graphic literary description of a private Revival service, see Brodber, *Myal*, especially chapter 11.
28. This was a collection of "gospel hymns" written and compiled by Americans Dwight L. Moody and Ira D. Sankey, which became popular in Jamaica and throughout the British Caribbean as American-style Pentecostalism spread in the late nineteenth and early twentieth centuries.
29. Beckwith, *Black Roadways*, 162.
30. Ibid., 162.
31. *Daily Gleaner*, 31 July 1897.
32. "Myalism Alias Revivalism in Kingston", *Jamaica Times*, 7 January 1899; and Williams, *Psychic Phenomena*, 90.
33. Moore, *Cultural Power*, 143; Law 21 of 1857, see "Myalism Alias Revivalism in Kingston", *Jamaica Times*, 7 January 1899.

34. "Obeah and Myal", *Daily Gleaner,* 18 October 1904.
35. According to Williams, "Myalism . . . was in reality the old tribal religion of the Ashanti with some modifications due to conditions and circumstances." He further argues that the age-old priestly antagonism to obeah was accentuated, "so that it came to form a part of the religious practice to dig up obeah". Put on the defensive after slavery by Myal, for self-protection the obeahman became more secretive and vindictive while at the same time assuming the role of Myalist and digging up perhaps the obeah that he himself had planted. This explains the confusion of obeah and Myal. Williams, *Psychic Phenomena,* 59–65, 72–75, 89–90, 98–99.
36. "Obeah and Myal", *Daily Gleaner,* 18 October 1904; Pullen-Burry, *Ethiopia,* 148. According to Williams, the practices were similar to the process used by the Asante; Williams, *Psychic Phenomena,* 40–43, 59, 65, 72–75.
37. A hard, yellowish, translucent resin normally used as an ornament.
38. The silk cotton tree formed an integral part of the Myal practitioner's spiritual environment, as a site for combating obeah as well as for shadow catching.
39. Banbury, *Jamaica Superstitions,* 13.
40. Ibid., 13–14; Moore, *Cultural Power,* 144–45.
41. " 'Unknown Tongues' and Other Things", *Jamaica Times,* 15 June 1901. To the Zionists/Myalists this may have been just another example of the conspiracy to "keep them down" and for evil to try to gain ascendancy. Persecution was, after all, part of the life of the disciples of Christ, and they were prepared to bear oppression in the name of the Lord; according to Jesus, "Blessed are ye, when men shall revile you, and persecute you, and shall say all manner of evil against you falsely, for my sake. Rejoice, and be exceedingly glad: for great is your reward in heaven: for so persecuted they the prophets which were before you." Matt. 5:11–12.
42. Stewart, *Religion,* 136–42.
43. Father James Splaine, SJ, Diary for 1872 (Jamaica), Society of Jesus, English Province, London, no. 515, entry for 13 June 1872.
44. Stewart, *Religion,* 136–42.
45. Banbury, *Jamaica Superstitions,* 19.
46. Ibid., 19 and 23.
47. *Jamaica Times,* 14 March 1903; Symmonett, *Jamaica,* 15; and "Curious", *Jamaica Times,* 29 November 1902.
48. A. McKay Smith, Lacovia, 28 November 1959, Jamaica Memories, JA 7/12/210.
49. *Jamaica Times,* 24 November 1900.
50. Report from Ritches, *Reports and Statistics of the Moravian Church in Jamaica,* 1908, JA 5/5.
51. Susan Gunter, 19 November 1959, Jamaica Memories, JA 7/12/70.
52. Pullen-Burry, *Jamaica as It Is,* 140–41.

53. Ibid., 141.
54. "Native Doctoring", *Daily Gleaner*, 18 May 1899.
55. *Daily Gleaner*, 9 November 1881.
56. Just what it would be used for and how it would be used were not revealed; *Jamaica Times*, 24 May 1902.
57. The root of horseradish and mustard seed were used to treat chronic rheumatism, paralysis and some forms of dropsy. Dyspepsia was treated with Jamaica Bitter Wood, while a tobacco infusion could be used as an enema. See C.A. Jeffrey-Smith to the editor, *Daily Gleaner*, 8 December 1897. Perhaps Jeffrey-Smith and other elite persons were only prepared to admit their use of herbal medicines publicly when it was validated by Western "authorities" like Professor Brown.
58. (Mrs) B. Jolly, n.d. [1959], Jamaica Memories, JA 7/12/120.
59. "Self-Doctoring", *Colonial Standard*, 21 September 1889.
60. *Jamaica Times*, 24 June 1899.
61. *Jamaica Times*, 8 July 1899.
62. *Jamaica Times*, 1 December 1900; *Daily Gleaner*, 11 August 1896.
63. *Jamaica Times*, 6 May 1905.
64. "Bush 'Doctoring' in Clarendon", *Daily Gleaner*, 30 October 1902.
65. "The Acting Governor and the Bush Doctor", *Daily Gleaner*, 30 October 1902.
66. *Jamaica Times*, 25 March 1899.
67. *Jamaica Times*, 13 May 1899.
68. *Morning Journal*, 1 July 1870. The claim of being "chosen", "holy" and "peculiar" set the Revivalists apart. They invoked the biblical description and label: "ye are a chosen generation, a royal priesthood, an holy nation, a peculiar people". 1 Peter 2:9.
69. "Among the Revivalists", *Daily Gleaner*, 17 July 1897.
70. "A Prophetess of Jamaica", *Jamaica Times*, 17 December 1898.
71. *Reports and Statistics of the Moravian Church in Jamaica*, 1901–2, JA 5/5.
72. Acts 2:4.
73. Waddell and Drummond cited in "Obeah and Myal", *Daily Gleaner*, 18 October 1904; see also "Revivalism Again", *Daily Gleaner*, 10 April 1905. Erna Brodber gives an excellent literary description of spirit possession in her novel *Myal*, 70–73. According to Joseph Moore, "Possession, for Revivalists, satisfies a dual purpose: the desire of the individual to invite the Holy Spirit and other saints and spirits to use his body and to teach him; and the desire of the Holy Spirit, the prophets and disciples, and ancestors, to return to the world by using individuals for their enjoyment and edification." He also notes that possession was "a mark of prestige, a criterion of spiritual knowledge, and a condition required for leadership". J.G. Moore, "Religion", 58, 78.
74. *Reports and Statistics of the Moravian Church in Jamaica*, 1901, JA 5/5.
75. Reports of the Friends Jamaica Mission (Spicey Grove), 1917–21, JA 5/8/4/570;

Report of the Friends Jamaica Mission (Prospect, Burlington and Fellowship), 1922–23, JA 5/8/55/3862.
76. "Tarrying" involved singing, drumming, "trumping" while waiting for the anointing of the Spirit.
77. Rampini presented much of this evidence from an interview that he had with a clergyman from Orange River; Rampini, *Letters*, 74–75, 84.
78. According to a correspondent from George's Plain, the "trooping" was hideous and was "harsh against the solemn stillness of the night"; *Jamaica Times*, 25 January 1902.
79. Wesleyan Methodist Missionary Society, Report of the Religious State of the Societies, Synod minutes, 29 January 1875, MMS Box 163–1874.
80. *Jamaica Times*, 14 August 1909.
81. *Reports and Statistics of the Moravian Church in Jamaica*, 1903, JA 5/5.
82. *Daily Gleaner*, 31 July 1897; "Report from Little London", *Jamaica Times*, 19 August 1899; R.W.T., "One of the Sights of a Suburb of Kingston: Rampant Revivalism", *Daily Gleaner*, 9 June 1914; and *Morning Journal*, 21 May 1875.
83. Acts 2:4.
84. See John Mbiti, *African Religions and Philosophy* (London: Heinemann, 1969), 54–55; Mbiti, *Introduction to African Religion* (Oxford: Heinemann Educational Books, 1991); Nadel, *Nupe Religion*, 90–91; M.J. Field, *Religion and Medicine of the Ga People* (Accra: Presbyterian Book Depot, 1961), 10–91; Robin Horton, *Patterns of Thought in Africa and the West: Essays on Magic, Religion and Science* (Cambridge: Cambridge University Press, 1993); Patrick Bellegarde-Smith, ed., *Traditional Spirituality in the African Diaspora* (Lexington, Ky.: Association of Caribbean Studies, 1992).
85. *Daily Gleaner*, 26 October 1895; *Jamaica Times*, 9 September 1899 and 7 October 1899.
86. See Olive Lewin, *Rock It Come Over: The Folk Music of Jamaica* (Kingston: University of the West Indies Press, 2000), 33–34.
87. *Daily Gleaner*, 5 July 1899; *Jamaica Times*, 12 August 1905; "Bedward Now Has a Rival", *Daily Gleaner*, 26 March 1906.
88. "The Bark Religion", *Jamaica Times*, 22 November 1902; R. Edward Foulkes, "The Bark Religion", *Jamaica Times*, 20 December 1902. Foulkes also declared that the worship of the revivalists, with all the "the barking and howling", was a "never-failing means of ensuring inmates for the Lunatic Asylum or the Public Hospital". R. Edward Foulkes to the editor, *Jamaica Times*, 12 August 1899.
89. *Falmouth Post*, 9 November 1860; "The Suppression of Revivalism", *Daily Gleaner*, 13 May 1899. See also "Revivalism and Lunacy", *Daily Gleaner*, 26 June 1899.
90. "Revivalism and Lunacy", *Daily Gleaner*, 26 June 1899.
91. Ibid.
92. Dr Williams further said that the majority of these cases came from the

"backwoods of Manchester, Westmoreland and Hanover"; "Revival Meetings and Ninth-Night Orgies Lead to Asylum", *Daily Gleaner*, 7 October 1919.
93. "A Review of Revivalism", *Jamaica Post*, 14 December 1898; Beckwith, *Black Roadways*, 161.
94. "Omega", "The Revivals in Kingston", *Morning Journal*, 23 January 1861.
95. *Falmouth Post*, 23 May 1862. Nor was the charge of sexual indiscretion made only against the women of the movement. In 1880 George Tisam Duaney, the "Shepherd of the Revivalists" in Allman Town, was charged with trespass when he was found in the bedroom of the wife of a follower at an unreasonable hour of the night. The case was eventually "compromised" when the complainant accepted a "salve" to his wounded honour in the shape of £1 10s. *Daily Gleaner*, 17 August 1880.
96. *Falmouth Post*, 23 May 1862.
97. "Revivalism Rampant in Kingston", *Daily Gleaner*, 3 November 1897.
98. These women, "of the very lowest class", were accused of disturbing the peace of the neighbourhood; the *Post* urged that they should be punished with hard labour in the house of correction, as examples. This would encourage their compatriots to "leave off making indecent exhibitions of their persons, and annoying respectable persons by shouting, yelling and using obscene and filthy language in the public streets"; *Falmouth Post*, 18 July 1862.
99. Within the Euro-Christian tradition where beliefs about Eve's inequality and sinful nature, as well as women's subordinate status, were firmly fixed, these spirit-filled women violated fundamental principles. That these Revival women should claim to speak as God's messengers and to be filled with the Holy Spirit threatened to stand "acceptable" gender roles on their heads. These trends were rejected by the dominant elite culture; the women who were involved in the services were vilified, while their morality and sanity were questioned.
100. R.E. Foulkes, "Revivalism", *Jamaica Times*, 20 May 1899.
101. *Periodical Accounts*, June 1879, Moravian Church Papers, JA 5/5. See also *Jamaica Times*, 26 August 1899.
102. "Revivalism Rampant in Kingston", *Daily Gleaner*, 3 November 1897.
103. *Jamaica Times*, 6 December 1902 and 21 February 1903; "Rows and Riots", *Jamaica Times*, 29 June 1901; Wesleyan Methodist Missionary Society, Report of the Religious State of the Societies, Synod minutes, 26 January 1872, MMS Box 162–1871.
104. Winifred James, *The Mulberry Tree* (London: Chapman and Hall, 1913), 47.
105. "Climaticus", "To Curb Street Preachers", *Jamaica Times*, 5 February 1910.
106. "Revivalism Rampant in Kingston", *Daily Gleaner*, 3 November 1897; and W.F. Elkins, " 'Warrior' Higgins: A Jamaican Street Preacher", *Jamaica Journal* 8, no. 4 (1974): 29–30.
107. *Jamaica Times*, 25 January 1902; Elkins, " 'Warrior' Higgins", 30.

108. The man assailed the priest "with words of one sort and another", and then resorted to assault and bodily injury. An angry crowd soon gathered, demanding that the wrathful Higginite be arrested, but although the priest was bloodied and battered, "the intelligent guardian of the peace could not see his way to arrest anything but his own action in the matter". Another priest and other officers of the law arrived on the scene when a vain attempt was made to arrest the offending assailant, who dispatched a message to "mass Charlie" to come and "bring his sword". Two men in the crowd were charged with disorderly behaviour after threatening any who touched their priest. Father Kayser decided not to press charges. "The Fanatic Rages", *Jamaica Times*, 29 June 1901. See also "Rows and Riots", *Jamaica Times*, 29 June 1901; and Elkins, " 'Warrior' Higgins", 30.
109. "Leaders of this band have located themselves in various localities in this city, making night and early morn hideous to the citizens. They indulge in yelling, loud beating of drums etc. which render the peaceful repose of the residents of these localities impossible." See "To Suppress Night Howlers", *Jamaica Times*, 11 March 1905; also Police Report, *Department Reports*, 1904–5, UWI Mona Library; and Elkins, " 'Warrior' Higgins", 31.
110. R.W.T., "Peculiar Folk Who Live in Smith's Village", *Daily Gleaner*, 21 July 1914. "Black art" referred to obeah. For an account of the trial to which Hewitt referred, see also "Duppy Catchers Follow the 'Messiah' From City Suburb", *Daily Gleaner*, 25 April 1914.
111. R.W.T., "Peculiar Folk Who Live in Smith's Village", *Daily Gleaner*, 21 July 1914; and R.W.T., "The 'Peculiar' People of Smith's Village", *Daily Gleaner*, 28 July 1914.
112. *Friends Jamaica Mission* 4 (7 July 1896).
113. Ibid.
114. "Dip Dem Bedward", Jamaican folk song and mento dance. See Lewin, *Rock It*, 33–34.
115. "The Healing Spring of Mona: A Visit to August Town I", *Daily Gleaner*, 14 and 19 September 1893. This dream encouraged Bedward to migrate to Colon. After two years there he received another "visitation" which urged him to return to Jamaica. After his return "the Spirit troubled him again" and his experiences were so violent that he was taken to see Drs Bronstorph and Ogilvia. He allegedly had to be violently restrained by eight men. He subsequently experienced yet another revelation, which indicated to him that "he was to be made a great power in the land and would be a servant of the Master".
116. "The Healing Spring of Mona: A Visit to August Town III", *Daily Gleaner*, 19 September 1893.
117. "The Healing Spring of Mona: A Visit to August Town I", *Daily Gleaner*, 14 September 1893.
118. "The Healing Spring of Mona: A Visit to August Town I", *Daily Gleaner*, 14 September 1893, "The Healing Spring of Mona: A Visit to August Town III", 8

October 1893; see also "Jamaica Parson" to the editor, *Daily Gleaner,* 15 September 1895. Also Pullen-Burry, *Ethiopia,* 142–47; Eustace Brown, August Town, n.d. [1959], Jamaica Memories, JA 7/12/71; Teresa Richards, Kingston, n.d. [1959], Jamaica Memories, JA 7/12/171; Reginald M. Murray, Comfort Castle, n.d. [1959], Jamaica Memories, JA 7/12/231; Rev. R.A.L. Knight, n.d. [1959], Jamaica Memories, JA 7/12/36; Florie Burkley, Kingston, n.d. [1959], Jamaica Memories, JA 7/12/161.

119. "The Healing Spring of Mona: A Visit to August Town I", *Daily Gleaner,* 14 September 1893; see also "The Healing Spring of Mona: A Visit to August Town II", *Daily Gleaner,* 15 September 1893, C.A. Lopez, Jr, to the editor, *Daily Gleaner,* 15 September 1893.

120. See "The Healing Spring of Mona: A Visit to August Town II", *Daily Gleaner,* 15 September 1893; "The August Town Fraud", *Daily Gleaner,* 26 September 1893.

121. See "Jamaica" to the editor, *Daily Gleaner,* 26 September 1893; "The August Town Fraud", *Daily Gleaner,* 26 September 1893.

122. *Daily Gleaner,* 2 October 1893.

123. "The Hope River Observances: Statement by the Primate of the West Indies", *Daily Gleaner,* 3 October 1893.

124. "Bishop Nuttall on the Hope River Proceedings", *Daily Gleaner,* 4 October 1893.

125. Bishop Charles Gordon to the editor, *Daily Gleaner,* 5 October 1893.

126. The private process of commitment involved certification by two medical men as to the individual's lunacy and "entering into a bond for the lunatic's maintenance in the Asylum". Dr Bronstorph said that the danger in Bedward's insanity lay in his belief that he heard from God, and that he might decide, at any point, that God had given him a message to kill someone; "The Proceedings at August Town: Medical Testimony as to Bedward's Mental Condition", *Daily Gleaner,* 4 October 1893.

127. *Daily Gleaner,* 30 November 1893.

128. "By the Banks of Mona Water: Bedwardism Still Flourishing at August Town", *Daily Gleaner,* 9 May 1895; *Jamaica Times,* 24 June 1899.

129. "The Bedward Craze: Still as Potent as Ever", *Daily Gleaner,* 25 May 1894.

130. "August Town Craze", enclosed in Blake to Ripon, 28 May 1895, no. 165, CO 137/566.

131. Ibid.; "Bedward's Trial", *Daily Gleaner,* 30 April 1895; "Bedward's Trial: The Verdict", *Daily Gleaner,* 2 May 1895; "By the Banks of Mona Water: Bedwardism Still Flourishing at August Town", *Daily Gleaner,* 9 May 1895; "Bedward's Trial: The Verdict", *Daily Gleaner,* 22 May 1895; "Prophet and People Again United", *Daily Gleaner,* 23 May 1895. See also Livingstone, *Black Jamaica,* 200–201.

132. As the Friends put it, "The 'Healing Spring' superstition of Bedward was not dead" in 1899 and people travelled from all over the island, congregating at August Town, hoping for a miracle. *Friends Jamaica Mission* 7, no. 9 (September

1899), JA 5/8/78/5934; and "The Recrudescence of Bedward", *Daily Gleaner*, 15 August 1899.

133. "Climaticus", *Jamaica Times*, 26 April 1902; "The Advance of Bedwardism", *Jamaica Times*, 27 April 1907; "W.A.S.", " 'Prophet' Bedward and His Amazing Prosperity", *Daily Gleaner*, 27 August 1910.

134. *Jamaica Times*, 6 April 1901, 13 June 1903 and 23 September 1905.

135. "A Well Wisher" to the editor, *Jamaica Times*, 10 May 1902. "Theo" disagreed, claiming that "the citadel of Bedwardism has its foundation not only in the deep ignorance and credulity of the lowest strata of Jamaicans, but also in a certain class of the more advanced" which included "A Well Wisher". The prayerful nature of the Bedwardites meant nothing, "Theo" said, since the heathen pray too – "bowing down to wood and stone". "Theo" to the editor, *Jamaica Times*, 31 May 1902. T.N. Wynter did not give Bedwardism any place "among Christ's true Church", and saw it as "a farce! a parody on Religion!! a huge burlesque". T.N. Wynter to the editor, *Jamaica Times*, 6 July 1907.

136. "I Cor. 13:13" to the editor, *Jamaica Times*, 11 May 1907. See also views of S.N. Tyson, Mr W.F. Mein, Sr, cited in "Sunday Notes: Advance of Bedwardism", *Jamaica Times*, 27 July 1907.

137. C.E.A. Roberts to the editor, *Jamaica Times*, 11 May 1907; "Leo the Saint" to the editor, *Jamaica Times*, 6 July 1907.

138. "Lord Bedward's Case", *Daily Gleaner*, 17 December 1920.

139. "After Friday", *Daily Gleaner*, 28 December 1920; "Bedward Fails to Go Up in the Air", *Daily Gleaner*, 3 January 1921; Beckwith, *Black Roadways*, 167–71.

140. "X.Y.Z.", "Bedward Sticks to the Earth", *Daily Gleaner*, 3 January 1921.

141. For a full examination of the rise and fall of Alexander Bedward, see Monica Schuler, "Alexander Bedward of Jamaica: A Black Nationalist?" (paper presented at the Sawyer Seminar, Department of History, Johns Hopkins University, 5 October 1998). See also *Jamaica Times*, 20 January 1906, 9 June 1906, 12 September 1908, 16 August 1913.

142. Matt. 3:4.

143. According to the *Falmouth Post*, from the 1860s the movement was most noticeable in "Altman Town", where "obscene and blasphemous language" was used under the auspices of "Revivalism"; *Falmouth Post*, 20 and 23 May 1862; also 19 May 1863, 6 January 1865 and 18 July 1873. A generation later, "A Sufferer" complained that every night in Allman Town there was a gathering of women and soldiers, with a sprinkling of civilians who held fanatical meetings which affected the sleep of those who had to "labour during the day for an honest living"; "A Sufferer" to the editor, *Daily Gleaner*, 16 July 1895. See also "Noisy Religionists", *Daily Gleaner*, 9 April 1883; *Jamaica Daily Telegraph*, 2 and 16 May 1899; Emerick, *Obeah*, 49; Report from Patrick Town, *Reports and Statistics of the Moravian*

Church in Jamaica, 1910, JA 5/5; Teresa Richards, Kingston, n.d. [1959], Jamaica Memories, JA 7/12/171; C. Wesley-Gammon to the editor, *Jamaica Times,* 24 November 1900; and *Report of the Wesleyan Methodist Missionary Society,* 1907, SOAS.

144. *Falmouth Post,* 16 January 1863.
145. Bishop of Kingston, encl. 1 in Grant to Carnarvon, 23 February 1867, no. 32, CO 137/422. See also Reginald Kingston, Bishop's Report, 23 April 1864, USPG D28a. For discussions of the claims of "blasphemy" see Aubrey Darrell, who spoke of the "evil spirit" of Revival which brought "obnoxious blasphemy" and "a spirit so remote from the mind of Christ and so akin to that of Satan" into public space. Aubrey Darrell (Friendship, Goshen), United Society for the Propagation of the Gospel in Foreign Parts, 31 December 1864, D Series.
146. Richard Chamberlaine (senior magistrate, St James) to Colonial Secretary, 21 December 1866; Inspector Scoine to Inspector General, 21 December 1866; Rev. D.R. Morris (St James) to Inspector Scoine, 21 December 1866; Rev. I. Davidson to Inspector Scoine, 20 December 1866; and Inspector General to Colonial Secretary, 31 December 1866; all enclosed in Grant to Carnarvon, 23 February 1867, no. 32, CO 137/422.
147. John Salmon (custos of St Elizabeth) to Colonial Secretary, 26 December 1866, enclosed in Grant to Carnarvon, 23 February 1867, no. 32, CO 137/422.
148. Rev. J. Aird to I.W. Fisher, 4 January 1867; I.W. Fisher (custos of Trelawny) to Colonial Secretary, 21 and 24 January 1867; all enclosed in Grant to Carnarvon, 23 February 1867, no. 32, CO 137/422.
149. The *Times* advocated that the "strong arm of the Law should intervene"; see *Jamaica Times,* 20 May 1899. "J.A.T." argued that some legal step in relation to the Revivalist movement would help the people morally and spiritually; "J.A.T." to the editor, *Jamaica Times,* 20 April 1901. According to a report from Croft's Hill, the activities of the "sheep" of Arthur's Seat had become more noticeable since a visit from their "shepherd". The correspondent asked what had become of the Vagrancy Law. *Jamaica Times,* 25 October 1902; see Law 12 of 1902. Also "Revivalism Again", *Daily Gleaner,* 10 April 1905; and "On Midnight Singing", *Daily Gleaner,* 7 March 1911.
150. *Falmouth Post,* 25 January 1867 and 8 November 1870. Likewise, Louisa Beckford and Joseph Brown of John's Lane, Kingston, were charged with disorderly conduct in 1880, found guilty, and fined 5s. each; *Colonial Standard,* 27 April 1880.
151. The fine was paid promptly; *Daily Gleaner,* 4 March 1890.
152. *Daily Gleaner,* 14 September 1904.
153. J.M. Morris, (Lilliput) United Society for the Propagation of the Gospel in Foreign Parts, 31 March 1864, D Series; *Colonial Standard,* 24 June 1881; *Daily Gleaner,* 26 March 1884.
154. "Silly 'Prophets' ", *Jamaica Times,* 2 February 1907.

155. North, *Recollections*, 93. See also *Daily Gleaner*, 21 March 1889; "Climaticus", *Jamaica Times*, 22 June 1901. The *Standard* disagreed with this stance, and expressed annoyance that the Revivalists were being "shielded" under "religious liberty"; *Colonial Standard*, 27 April 1880. The opinions of the *Gleaner*, however, tended to change with those of its editors, and consequently from time to time there were apparently contradictory positions taken by this newspaper. This explains its radically different stances on the issue of the law and Revival in 1889 and 1905. Over the period, a series of laws spoke to the concerns of the authorities about the belief in and practice of obeah. The laws against obeah included 19 Vict. c. 30; 21 Vict. c. 24; Law 1 of 1893; Law 5 of 1898; Law 18 of 1899 and Law 8 of 1903.
156. *Daily Gleaner*, 28 June 1876 and 7 July 1876.
157. *Daily Gleaner*, 21 March 1889.
158. Ibid. In the nineteenth century the term "Arab" was used pejoratively to signify a wild person.
159. *Daily Gleaner*, 17 July 1899. The Westmoreland board sought a legal definition of the word "revivalism" before it would contemplate taking any action against the bands; *Jamaica Times*, 29 July 1899 and 12 August 1899.
160. *Jamaica Times*, 1 April 1905 and 14 October 1905; "Silly 'Prophets' ", *Jamaica Times*, 2 February 1907; "Climaticus", "Blaspheming Against Piety", *Jamaica Times*, 26 June 1909.
161. *Daily Gleaner*, 16 July 1895.
162. See Edward L. Cox, "Religious Intolerance and Persecution: The Shakers of St Vincent, 1900–1934", *Journal of Caribbean History* 28, no. 2 (1994): 208–43; and Melville J. Herskovits and Frances S. Herskovits, *Trinidad Village* (New York: A. Knopf, 1947), 342–44.
163. See J.G. Moore, "Religion", chapter 5, 114 ff. Stewart made only passing references to Kumina (Stewart, *Religion*, 170, 197, 231). In addition to Moore, Schuler relies heavily on oral sources, and her analysis is bolstered by African historical and anthropological references; Schuler, *"Alas, Alas, Kongo"*, 70–80.
164. According to Schuler, a total of 8,205 African immigrants (both involuntary – so-called liberated – and voluntary) were brought to Jamaica between 1841 and 1867 from Sierra Leone and St Helena. Those who embarked at St Helena were Central Africans and were concentrated in St Thomas-in-the-East, although some were taken to other parts of the island as well. Schuler speculates that some of the latter might later have migrated to join their compatriots in St Thomas. Certainly, she says, "No other parish matched St Thomas-in-the-East's high concentration of people from a single culture area." The Kongos, therefore, were apparently able to reconstitute a fairly viable community. A significant number of Yoruba also settled in Westmoreland and, to a lesser degree, did likewise. Schuler, *"Alas, Alas, Kongo"*, 63, 68–69, and tables 1 and 2, 112–13.

165. Ibid., 71–72.
166. Ibid., 72–76; also J.G. Moore, "Religion", 135–60.
167. J.G. Moore, "Religion", 114–30.
168. Eph. 6:12.
169. Chevannes, *Rastafari*, 21.
170. Although Richard D.E. Burton recognizes the spirit of revolt and the subversive potential of Revival and its leaders, he argues that it did not constitute a concerted contestation of the status quo and its values, nor did it generate any fundamental changes in the structure of power. It thus remained a form of cultural "opposition and inversion", dependent on the existence of the dominant power structure in order to exist at all. Burton, *Afro-Creole*, 115–22, 263–64.

Chapter 4

1. Austin-Broos argues that Christian marriage and Christian forms of sexual restraint became "not only marks of civilization but also marks of assimilation to an orthodox Christian faith"; Austin-Broos, *Jamaica Genesis*, 35.
2. Karen Fog Olwig, "Cultural Complexity after Freedom: Nevis and Beyond", in *Small Islands, Large Questions: Society, Culture and Resistance in the Post-Emancipation Caribbean*, ed. Karen Fog Olwig (London: Frank Cass, 1995), 107, 109; also her *Global Culture, Island Identity: Continuity and Change in the Afro-Caribbean Community of Nevis* (Philadelphia: Harwood Academic Publishers, 1993).
3. Hall, *Civilising Subjects*, 122, 125 and 251.
4. Ps. 51:5.
5. In the twentieth century the unions, families and households that were formed along non-legal lines came under great sociological and anthropological scrutiny, with a view to discovering the reasons behind the "difference" in Caribbean family forms. There has consequently been a proliferation of literature on the black family. See, for instance, Fernando Henriques, *Family and Colour in Jamaica* (London: Eyre and Spottiswoode, 1953); Judith Blake, *Family Structure in Jamaica: The Social Context of Reproduction* (New York: Free Press, 1961); Edith Clarke, *My Mother Who Fathered Me* (London: George Allen and Unwin, 1957); M.G. Smith, *Kinship and Community in Carriacou* (New Haven: Yale University Press, 1962); and Raymond T. Smith, *The Negro Family in British Guiana: Family Structure and Social Status in Villages* (New York: Grove, 1956).
6. Bryan, *Jamaican People*, 92. The only thing that differentiated these unions from legal marriages was the fact that they did not enjoy the blessing of the church or the protection of the state (the law). But many were no less stable and long-

lasting than legal marriages. In strict terms, concubinage could only occur where legally married men had "illicit" sexual relationships with "outside" women. In Jamaica this was a predominantly middle- and upper-class phenomenon, and in many instances such white and brown men fathered "illegitimate" children by their concubines.

7. Jean Besson, "Reputation and Respectability Reconsidered: A New Perspective on Afro-Caribbean Peasant Women", in *Women and Change in the Caribbean: A Pan-Caribbean Perspective*, ed. Janet Momsen (Kingston: Ian Randle, 1993), 21.
8. Livingstone, *Black Jamaica*, 113–14, 210–15; Pullen-Burry, *Jamaica as It Is*, 16–17; De Lisser, *Twentieth Century*, 96; James, *Mulberry Tree*, 103; Report of the Jamaica Province of the Moravian Church (Carisbrook), 1912, JA 5/5/Periodicals; Mary White, Report of the Friends Jamaica Mission (Port Antonio), 1915–16, JA 5/8/2/431.
9. Stephen Sutton to General Secretaries, 8 July 1868, MMS Box 200 [microfiche 2418]. Sutton in fact did not think that his fellow clergymen were doing enough to preach and counsel against this "sin". See also Arthur Bourne to General Secretaries, 7 November 1877, MMS Box 201 [microfiche 2468]; and Annual Report of the Jamaica Baptist Union, *75th Report of the Baptist Missionary Society*, 1867. See also Splaine's account of a visit he made to a home where two couples were cohabiting "in sin" without shame; Splaine, diary, 26 and 27 February, 1872.
10. The comparative rates in 1878–79 were, for England and Wales 7.6 per 1,000, Scotland 6.5, France 7.5, Italy 7.1, Spain (1870) 6.2, Australian colonies 7.3, New Zealand 7.4, Ontario (Canada) 8.0; and for those West Indian colonies on record, St Vincent (1872–76) 6.3, Grenada (1871–78) 5.6, Dominica (1871–75) 6.9, while Barbados (1872–77) was just 3.7, and Trinidad (1871–75) 3.8. Figures for the United Kingdom in 1892–93 were: England and Wales 7.35 and Scotland 7.05. Only Ireland had comparably low rates: 4.7 in 1878 and 1893. See the Registrar General's Returns for 1879–80, 1882–83 and 1894–95 in the *Department Reports* of those years, UWI Mona Library.
11. Richard Harding to E. Hoole, 22 October 1867, MMS Box 200 [microfiche 2413]; George Lockett to W.B. Boyce, 21 October 1871, MMS Box 200 [microfiche 2438].
12. *Friends Jamaica Mission* 6, no. 2 (February 1898), JA 5/8/78/5906; *Friends Jamaica Mission* 7, no. 7 (July 1899), JA 5/8/78/5917; *Friends Jamaica Mission* 8, no. 1 (January 1900), JA 5/8/78/5944. Also Report of the Jamaica Province of the Moravian Church (Carisbrook), 1912, JA 5/5/Periodicals.
13. Livingstone, *Black Jamaica*, 214–15.
14. The number of legal marriages rose sharply, from 798 in the third (June) quarter of 1906 to 924 in the fourth (September) quarter. In the quarter coinciding with the January 1907 earthquake, the figure rose to 988, and then suddenly leapfrogged to 2,797 in the second (March) quarter of 1907 and 2,319 in the following quarter (June 1907), before declining to a still relatively high level of

1,278 in the first quarter of 1908. See the Registrar General's Report, *Department Reports*, 1907–8. See also the editorial in the *Daily Gleaner*, 12 May 1909. This newspaper argued that the increase in legal marriages was directly related to emigrants returning from Colon to get married.

15. Bryan, *Jamaican People*, 100. There is no indication as to who advanced these explanations, or whether they were contemporary or "modern".
16. *Friends Jamaica Mission* 6, no. 2 (February 1898), JA 5/8/78/5906; vol. 8, no. 1 (January 1900), JA 5/8/78/5944. Also Livingstone, *Black Jamaica*, 114, 210–11.
17. "An Old Minister" to the editor, *Daily Gleaner*, 5 June 1885; and C.H. Coles to the editor, *Jamaica Times*, 20 July 1901.
18. De Lisser, *Twentieth Century*, 96.
19. Splaine, diary, 27 February and 16 April 1872. Splaine noted that in one case no shame was attached to two "brown girls" who were living with men "in sin". Instead, "the fall of girls from Communicants to fornicators has given immense offence" (see his entry for 26 February 1872). On 2 April he observed that "As long as a man and woman live together married or unmarried, it gives little offence." When on 5 August he criticized one man for living in sin, he was told: " 'Es masa [*sic*], but God eye too pure fo' look upon sin." Beckwith noted that if a woman was faithful to her lover, she suffered no disrespect from her neighbours; Beckwith, *Black Roadways*, 63. See also Rampini, *Letters*, 81; and letter of Quaker missionary, M.S. Hinckle (Hector's River), Friends Jamaica Mission letters, 4 April 1919, JA 5/8/1/82.
20. Splaine, diary, 2 April 1872.
21. Livingstone, *Black Jamaica*, 114, 210–11; and Report of the Friends Jamaica Mission, first quarter 1920, JA 5/8/4/551.
22. Livingstone, *Black Jamaica*, 113–14 and 213. As late as 1909, the *Gleaner* was peddling this line. Black men, it said, "love to be free and are loth to assume their proper responsibilities" (16 October 1905). Also De Lisser, *Twentieth Century*, 96.
23. Bryan, *Jamaican People*, 100. Also James, *Mulberry Tree*, 103–4. Ford, too, claimed that "The vast majority of negro and coloured women prefer to have looser bonds than wedlock so that they can desert their homes, if the fathers of their children do not treat them well"; Isaac Newton Ford, *Tropical America* (London: Edward Stanford, 1893), 247. See also Pullen-Burry, *Jamaica as It Is*, 16–17.
24. Livingstone, *Black Jamaica*, 214. According to him, "The result of severance is not so hard on the woman as might be supposed. She continues working as before without the incumbrance of a husband, or adopts another in his place, and the children grow up or die as they would have grown up or died in any other circumstances."
25. See 1 Cor. 6:18–19, 7:2. Also Acts 15:20, 29; Rom. 1:29; 1 Cor. 5:1; 1 Cor. 6:13; Gal. 5:19; Eph. 5:3; 1 Thess. 4:3; Jude 1:7; and Heb. 13:4, among other biblical references.

26. Cundall, "West Indies", 92; Livingstone, *Black Jamaica,* 213; James, *Mulberry Tree,* 103–4.
27. B.W. Higman, "Household Structure and Fertility on Jamaican Slave Plantations: A Nineteenth Century Example", *Population Studies* 27, no. 3 (1973): 527–50; Michael Craton, "Changing Patterns of Slave Families in the British West Indies", *Journal of Interdisciplinary History* 10, no. 1 (1979): 1–35.
28. N. Solien, "Household and Family in the Caribbean: Some Definitions and Concepts", *Social and Economic Studies* 9, no. 1 (1960): 104–6; also Raymond T. Smith, *The Matrifocal Family: Power, Pluralism, and Politics* (London: Routledge, 1996), 41.
29. Smith, *Matrifocal Family,* 41–42.
30. Beckwith, *Black Roadways,* 62–63. Splaine was informed by a black cook named Moore that it was "considered very 'dirty' also for a man to sin with two cousins"; Splaine, diary, 2 April 1872.
31. For descriptions of life among the rural and urban lower classes in Jamaica in the late nineteenth and early twentieth centuries, see Moore and Johnson, *"Squalid Kingston",* and *Land We Live In.*
32. See, for instance, Cundall, "West Indies", 92.
33. Law 11 of 1879 allowed for separation and divorce in Jamaica for the first time, along the lines of the 1857 English divorce law. Before 1879 divorce was impossible in Jamaica. See Grant to Kimberley, confidential, 22 August 1871, CO 137/458.
34. Report of Anna M. Farr, *Friends Jamaica Mission* 7 (July 1897), JA 5/8/78/5987.
35. See James, *Mulberry Tree,* 103–4; and C.W. Willis, *"Buckra" Land: two weeks in Jamaica* (Boston: n.p., 1896), 24.
36. Beckwith, *Black Roadways,* 62–63.
37. Mary Lawrence, Hanover, n.d. [1959], Jamaica Memories, JA 7/12/207. According to C.G. Bailey, no child dared to pass an adult in the community without saying "Good morning" or "Good evening", or lifting his cap to a lady or gentleman; C.G. Bailey, Spanish Town, 18 November 1959, Jamaica Memories, JA 7/12/160.
38. See, for instance, *Daily Gleaner,* 25 March 1876, 7 May 1889, 9 September 1898, and 29 March 1916.
39. Naomi George (Swift), 4 November 1890, Friends Jamaica Mission letters, JA 5/8/10/941.
40. Olwig, *Small Islands,* 104–5.
41. William James Gardner, *A history of Jamaica from its discovery by Christopher Columbus to the present time: including an account of its trade and agriculture; sketches of the manners, habits, and customs of all classes of its inhabitants; and a narrative of the progress of religion and education in the island* (London: E. Stock, 1873), 377.
42. Bryan, *Jamaican People,* 97–98.
43. Morrissey, "Explaining", 82. See also Joycelin Massiah, *Women and Heads of*

Household in the Caribbean: Family Structure and Feminine Status (Paris: UNESCO, 1983).

44. Letter titled "Why our Young Men do not Marry?", *Daily Gleaner*, 11 February 1899.
45. "Bachelor" to the editor, *Daily Gleaner*, 18 October 1904.
46. Ronald Hyam, "Empire and Sexual Opportunity", *Journal of Imperial and Commonwealth History* 14, no. 2 (1986): 41–42; also Moore, *Cultural Power*, 39.
47. See, for instance, Charlotte Sussman, *Consuming Anxieties: Consumer Protest, Gender, and British Slavery, 1713–1833* (Stanford, Calif.: Stanford University Press, 2000); and Wendy Hamand Venet, *Neither Ballots nor Bullets: Women Abolitionists and the Civil War* (Charlottesville: University Press of Virginia, 1991).
48. See, for instance, Ian Tyrrell, *Woman's World/Woman's Empire: The Woman's Christian Temperance Union in International Perspective, 1880–1930* (Chapel Hill: University of North Carolina Press, 1991); Paul Slack, *From Reformation to Improvement: Public Welfare in Early Modern England* (Oxford: Clarendon; New York: Oxford University Press, 1999); and Bruce Dorsey, *Reforming Men and Women: Gender in the Antebellum City* (Ithaca: Cornell University Press, 2002).
49. See Jean V. Matthews, *The Rise of the New Woman: The Women's Movement in America, 1875–1930* (Chicago: Ivan R. Dee, 2003).
50. Letter titled "Why our Young Men do not Marry?", *Daily Gleaner*, 11 February 1899. According to the writer, "The earning of wages even less than that for which men could live on seems to give them a peculiar feeling of independence"; and working in the male sphere of business, they acquired "a mannish character very [different] from the womanly dignity which they ought always to preserve. Women shine best in the home, there they are the centre of attraction, there like guardian angels they carefully watch over their children and fashion the future of mankind for good or evil." The "new woman" did not conform to that ideal. Not only was her mannishness unattractive to the young men and turned them away from marriage, she was also instinctively disinclined to marry.
51. Ibid.
52. "Young Woman" to the editor, *Daily Gleaner*, 18 October 1904.
53. "Young Woman" to the editor, *Daily Gleaner*, 24 October 1904.
54. "Young Woman" to the editor, *Daily Gleaner*, 18 October 1904.
55. "Young Woman" to the editor, *Daily Gleaner*, 18 and 31 October 1904.
56. "A Married Woman" to the editor, *Daily Gleaner*, 7 November 1904.
57. While conceding that not all men deserved their wives, and that men could not conceive what it was to be a woman, he confidently asserted that a woman "cannot afford to remain single. There are cheerless days which only a loving husband can brighten – there are tedious nights of sleepless hours which a woman cannot bear alone, and, who can comfort her in those moments but her husband. . . . Yes: the general verdict is that a woman finds her suitable companion in man.

It is only the dogged clinging to wrong precedents that causes many unhappy marriages, but should a woman trust wholly to her intuitive powers, her spiritual guidance, defying custom and conventionalities, she may marry without fear of unhappiness." Moreover, he argued, "Young Woman" had been created a woman; she did not make herself one. "The serpent's head may be indeed bruised; but a woman is still a woman, and the penalty for the stolen fruit of Eden must be paid." His final wish was that "Young Woman", notwithstanding her selfishness, might one day "sacrifice anything – everything to marry the man she loves". "Amor" to the editor, *Daily Gleaner*, 24 October 1904 and 1 November 1904. Her response was appropriately terse: "As for paying Eve's penalty, I have no intention of doing any such thing. If other women choose to pay that old debt they are at liberty to do so. Times have changed since then, and there are many ways in which a woman may amuse herself. Poor Eve knew nothing of physical culture, never went to Cinderella's, had no bicycle and, lamentable fact, no Ruskin. Consequently she did not find the care of babies irksome." "Young Woman" to the editor, *Daily Gleaner*, 31 October 1904. See also "Experience" to the editor, *Daily Gleaner*, 2 November 1904; and S.R. Brathwaite to the editor, *Daily Gleaner*, 27 October 1904. The female responses are embodied in letters by "Young Woman", *Daily Gleaner*, 31 October 1904; and "A Married Woman", *Daily Gleaner*, 7 November 1904.

58. "Experience" to the editor, *Daily Gleaner*, 2 November 1904.
59. S.R. Brathwaite to the editor, *Daily Gleaner*, 27 October 1904; and "A Married Woman" to the editor, *Daily Gleaner*, 7 November 1904.
60. "Some Of It" to the editor, *Daily Gleaner*, 27 October 1904 and 2 November 1904.
61. Eloise A. Da Costa to the editor, *Daily Gleaner*, 25 October 1904 and 7 November 1904; and "A Mother" to the editor, *Daily Gleaner*, 24 October 1904.
62. *Daily Gleaner*, 29 October 1879.
63. Musgrave to Hicks Beach, 2 April 1879, no. 101, and encl., Report of the Attorney General, 31 March 1879, CO 137/489. The new law was No. 15 of 1879.
64. Church of England, Island Scraps No. 2, 1879, NLJ MST 51a; see also [Church of England] Memorandum on the Marriage Law of 1879; and Enos Nuttall to the editor, 31 October 1879, in *Daily Gleaner*, 3 November 1879. Also "Memorial on the New Marriage Law", *Daily Gleaner*, 1 December 1879.
65. Colonial Office minute of Edward Wingfield, 5 May 1880, appended to Newton to Hicks Beach, 10 April 1880, no. 88, CO 137/495. Further minor amendments were made by Laws 16 of 1893 and 3 of 1896. All these laws were consolidated by Law 25 of 1897. See Blake to Chamberlain, 10 June 1897, no. 236, CO 137/581.
66. "Azrael" to the editor, *Daily Gleaner*, 7 February 1898; and "Legitimacy" to the editor, *Daily Gleaner*, 26 March 1900. As late as 1918, "Young Bachelor" was making a similar proposal (see his letter, *Jamaica Times*, 10 August 1918).
67. "An Old Minister" to the editor, *Daily Gleaner*, 5 June 1885. But according to

C.H. Coles, "The publication of banns in such cases [people cohabiting out of wedlock] call[s] attention to their improper relation, and to produce the crowding and merry making and lavish expenditure which are most undesirable." See Coles to the editor, *Jamaica Times,* 20 July 1901.
68. Editorials, *Daily Gleaner,* 9 February 1889 and 25 April 1903.
69. See, for instance, *Jamaica Times,* 7 April 1900, 9 June 1900 and 20 July 1901. The Marriage Commission consisted of Justice E.A. Northcote (chair), Archbishop Enos Nuttall (Anglican), Bishop Gordon (Roman Catholic), T.B. Oughton (acting attorney general), Rev. T.B. Webb (member of the Legislative Council for Trelawny), Hon. J.V. Calder, Hon. Alexander Dixon, J.V. Leach (resident magistrate, St Catherine), S.P. Smeeton (Registrar General), Rev. Dr W. Clarke Murray, Rev. S.R. Brathwaite, W.H. Plant, Mrs Mary Macnee (the sole woman). Mr G.M. Wortley of the Colonial Secretary's office served as secretary to the commission. See *Daily Gleaner,* 9 May 1903; Hemming to Chamberlain, 28 July 1903, no. 434, JA 1B/5/18 vol. 57.
70. Olivier to Lyttelton, 15 September 1904, no. 471, and encl., Report of the Marriage Commission and Appendices, CO 137/641. The report was also printed in the *Daily Gleaner,* 29 July 1904. For the new law, see Swettenham to Lyttelton, 21 June 1905, no. 314, CO 137/645.
71. *Daily Gleaner,* 14 April 1905.
72. *Daily Gleaner,* 16 October 1905.
73. The comparable figures for 1902–3 were as follows: England 4 per cent, Scotland 7 per cent, Ireland 2.6 per cent, South Australia 2.49 per cent, New Zealand 3.2 per cent, Queensland 3.97 per cent, Victoria 5.09 per cent, Ontario 14.4 per cent, Bermuda 13.2 per cent. However, within the Caribbean Jamaica's 64.5 per cent in 1902–3 ranked favourably against Trinidad's 66.4 per cent, Antigua's 68.5 per cent, Dominica's 69.5 per cent and St Lucia's 71.32 per cent. Figures provided by the St Ann's Ministers Association in the *Jamaica Times,* 8 August 1903. Of course, the problem here lies in comparing colonies at different stages of development and periods. In early New South Wales, for instance, bastardy was quite common and the people, especially the convicts, were castigated as fornicators and prostitutes.
74. Mary White, Report of the Friends Jamaica Mission (Port Antonio), 1915–16, JA 5/8/2/431.
75. While noting that "All sections of the community have had a share in this evil", the 1903–4 Marriage and Registration Commission was quick to note that there were very few white "illegitimate" children in Jamaica and that nearly all the "illegitimate" children were either coloured or black (Report of the Commission, *Daily Gleaner,* 29 July 1904). Similarly, in the debate on the Registration Bill in 1900, acting Colonial Secretary Sydney Olivier viewed "illegitimacy" largely in racial terms, as essentially a black habit. See his speech in the Legislative Council on 4 April 1900, as reported in the *Daily Gleaner,* 5 April 1900. "R.W.B", in an

opinion column, compared Jamaica's 64 per cent "illegitimacy" in 1903 with an average of 8 per cent "for the Aryan races", and concluded that "All of us are anxious to alter this wide discrepancy"; *Daily Gleaner*, 30 April 1903.

76. See, for instance, R.E. Clarke, "The Social Condition of the People", in *Daily Gleaner*, 30 July 1904; Stephen Sutton to General Secretaries, 8 July 1868, MMS Box 200 [microfiche 2418]; and "An Anglican" to the editor, *Daily Gleaner*, 22 March 1900. "A Parishioner" writing from Westmoreland referred to a young man living less than five miles from the parish, who held a job in a respectable mercantile firm and was the reputed father of half-a-dozen "illegitimate" children whose mothers were all in their teens: "He makes this the business of his life, and the entire community knows it; and yet the young man passes muster, and in fact is the chief and honoured visitor at a clergyman's residence, and is sometimes seen, of an evening, cycling in company with the clergyman's wife." See "A Parishioner" to the editor, *Daily Gleaner*, 15 February 1898.
77. Clarke, "Social Condition".
78. Stephen Sutton to General Secretaries, 8 July 1868, MMS Box 200 [microfiche 2418]; and "An Anglican" to the editor, *Daily Gleaner*, 22 March 1900.
79. Clarke, "Social Condition"; and John H.H. Graham to the editor, 24 March 1900, *Daily Gleaner*, 3 April 1900. Several other clergymen made similar allegations about the officials, not least among them Rev. W. Graham of the Church of Scotland and Rev. C.H. Coles of the Church of England in April 1903. But the governors repeatedly defended their officers. In 1886 Governor Henry Norman dismissed such allegations as "mere gossip or rumours [which] should generally be disregarded". But while recognizing that he did everything to discourage profligacy in the civil service, a sceptical *Gleaner* nevertheless opined that he must have heard of several cases in which public officers of high standing had been guilty of sexual improprieties prejudicial to the public good; *Daily Gleaner*, 23 July 1886. Likewise Acting Governor Sydney Olivier in 1900 brushed aside these allegations as exaggerations (Olivier to Chamberlain, 24 September 1900, no. 466, CO 137/613); and Governor Hemming claimed in 1903 that "whilst no doubt there may be some black sheep in the flock, the majority of the Civil Service in Jamaica will bear favourable comparison with any other class of the community in correctness of life and conduct" (Hemming to Chamberlain, 15 April 1903, no. 212, CO 137/634). The Marriage and Registration Commission of 1903–4, too, asserted that "the allegation for the purpose of this enquiry may be disregarded, and that at no time in the history of the colony has a better example been set by such persons" (Report of the Commission, *Daily Gleaner*, 29 July 1904).
80. See Ronald Hyam, "Concubinage and the Colonial Service: The Crew Circular (1909)", *Journal of Imperial and Commonwealth History* 14, no. 3 (1986): 170–86.
81. Letter of Thomas Porter, SJ, VA, March 1887, *Letters and Notices* 19 (1887–88), Society of Jesus, English Province, London.

82. *Gall's News Letter*, 13 June 1881.
83. See Ronald Hyam, *Empire and Sexuality* (Manchester: Manchester University Press, 1990); also his "Empire and Sexual Opportunity", *Journal of Imperial and Commonwealth History* 14, no. 2 (1986): 34–90.
84. See, for instance, Presbyterian Church of Jamaica, minutes of the Western Presbytery, 23 June 1852, 17 March 1892, NLJ MST 2089; Presbyterian Synod Minutes, 1875, NLJ MST 2089; also Bishop of Kingston, 6 December 1861, USPG D28a; H.C. Williamson to A. Tidman, 5 October 1864, LMS 9/1; and Milo S. Hinckle, annual personal report, Friends Jamaica Mission, 1919, JA 5/8/4/544.
85. *Jamaica Advocate*, 4 April 1903; and Report of the Inspector General of Police, *Department Reports*, 1906–7, UWI Mona Library.
86. "An Anglican" to the editor, *Daily Gleaner*, 22 March 1900.
87. John A. Thomson, January 1863, USPG E14. The Wesleyan Conference advised their pastors to exercise great care to secure proper guarantee that the obligation of baptism was observed; see W. Clarke Murray to the editor, *Daily Gleaner*, 17 April 1900. However, this did not go down well with some people, who regarded the attitude of such churches as lax; see "St James" to the editor, *Jamaica Times*, 24 March 1900. But "A Woman of Jamaica" defended the Anglican Church for baptizing "illegitimate" children, and argued that those churches which excluded members for such lapses left them to drift and thus bore responsibility for the rising immorality; "A Woman of Jamaica" to the editor, *Daily Gleaner*, 11 April 1900. But in 1900 the Anglicans, too, tightened up on their church discipline as it related to baptism and other sacraments; Report of the Committee on Church Discipline, *Journal of the [31st] Synod of the Church of England in Jamaica*, 1900, appendix section 13, JA 5/1/11a/14.
88. As already noted, Jamaica's "illegitimacy" rate was lower than several of its sister colonies in the Caribbean; yet the Jamaican elites seemed to agonize about it far more than their counterparts in the other colonies. An article from the Demerara *Chronicle*, reprinted in the *Gleaner*, showed that none of the intense public debate on this issue was taking place in Guyana. In fact, the Guyanese elites were sitting back, awaiting the outcome of the Jamaican debate before taking action to deal with the problem; *Daily Gleaner*, 2 June 1903. Data from the other territories are sparse, but if the Jamaicans were indeed more concerned about this issue than their peers it raises questions about how they perceived themselves. Guyana, for instance, was (at least until the 1920s) very much a raw frontier colony, with its large and prosperous foreign-owned sugar plantations on which the labourers (largely immigrants) were regarded as no better than units of production, and the elites (mostly British expatriates) were temporary fortune-seekers. The Creole population had failed to develop a successful, settled small-farmer society to counterbalance the coarse sociocultural influences of the plantations. On the

other hand, Jamaica, with its larger population, declining plantation sector and burgeoning small-farming economy, probably conceived of itself as a young settled society, and thus paid more attention to the establishment of sociocultural institutions and issues of morality and civilization, however defined.

89. *Falmouth Post,* 14 December 1860.
90. Law 31 of 1869; *Falmouth Post,* 25 June 1869.
91. *Journal of the Synod of the Church of England in Jamaica,* 1885, and Reports of the Church of England Purity Society 1896, 1897, 1900 and 1901, both JA 5/1/11a; *Daily Gleaner,* 17 December 1886. The outspoken social reformer, Henry Clarke (an Anglican), also blamed the house tax for the state of "immorality" in the island: "on average, ten persons of all ages and both sexes have to sleep every night in each one of those delapidated [sic] one roomed huts which we see scattered over the whole island, no further evidence is required that our population must be reduced to the lowest state of poverty and degradation to which humanity can descend. And since this state of things has been brought about by the outrageous house tax, and by the general mismanagement of the last 30 years, it furnishes a formidable indictment against the Government which has held absolute power during the whole of that period." Clarke to the editor, *Daily Gleaner,* 12 March 1900.
92. Resolutions of the Synod of the Presbyterian Church of Jamaica, 2 March 1905, enclosed in Swettenham to Lyttelton, 12 April 1905, no. 167, CO 137/644. See also Presbyterian Synod Minutes, Memorial on Illegitimacy, appendix 5, 1912, NLJ MST 2089; and Presbyterian Synod Minutes, Life and Work Committee, 1912–15, NLJ MST 2089.
93. See, for instance, Methodist Church Western Annual Conference Journal, 1893, JA 5/6/7/2. Also William Clarke Murray to George Sergeant, 5 August 1897, and Thos. Geddes to G. Sergeant, 6 August 1897, both MMS Box 201 [microfiches 2467, 2468].
94. See for example the Presidential Address by J. Seed Roberts to the Jamaica Baptist Union 1885; Report of the Jamaica Province of the Moravian Church, JA 5/5/Periodicals; Minutes of the Congregational Union 1925, NLJ MST 2089; Reports of the Friends Jamaica Mission, 1920, JA 5/8/4/561. Successive issues of the newsletter *Friends Jamaica Mission* from the 1890s onwards also addressed this matter.
95. John Robson, "Christ's Great Commission and the Work in Jamaica: A Sermon Preached at the Opening of the Synod of the Presbyterian Church of Jamaica, at Lucea, January 24, 1899"; reprinted [by the Quakers as authored by] A.B. Robson, "The Hinderance" [sic], in *Friends Jamaica Mission* 7, no. 5 (May 1900).
96. Rampini, *Letters,* 81–82.
97. Robson, "Christ's Great Commission". For a biographical study of Henry Clarke, see James Walvin, *The Life and Times of Henry Clarke of Jamaica, 1828–1907* (Ilford, Essex: Frank Cass, 1994).

98. Henry Clarke to the editor, 25 October 1895, *Daily Gleaner*, 29 October 1895; and Clarke to the editor, *Daily Gleaner*, 20 March 1900.
99. William Simms to the editor, 13 March 1900, *Daily Gleaner*, 16 March 1900.
100. Clarke argued that "The only reason why the law, thou shalt not steal, is enforced with such vindictive punishment, while the law thou shalt not commit adultery, is not enforced at all, is that our rulers and legislators are tempted to break the one, while they have no temptation to break the other. If it were not so, adultery would be punished as severely as Praedial Larceny." Henry Clarke to the editor, 31 January 1898, *Daily Gleaner*, 3 February 1898.
101. Henry Clarke to the editor, *Daily Gleaner*, 3 February 1898, 20 March 1900 and 2 April 1900.
102. Hemming to Chamberlain, 15 April 1903, no. 212, CO 137/634.
103. Kissock Braham to the editor, 6 March 1900, *Daily Gleaner*, 9 March 1900; "W" to the editor, *Daily Gleaner*, 3 April 1895; "A Woman of Jamaica" to the editor, 9 April 1900, *Daily Gleaner*, 11 April 1900; and "Legitimacy" to the editor, *Daily Gleaner*, 26 March 1900.
104. "They have no rights and no wrongs. The law so orders it and public opinion condones it." *Daily Gleaner*, 9 March 1898. See also *Daily Gleaner*, 24 April 1903; and *Jamaica Post*, 19 October 1897. The *Gleaner* editorial argued that in the twenty years since the system of registration of births began, there had been an increase in the "illegitimacy" rate. Since this was the purview of the church, it had clearly failed in its mission against the evil. The paper supported Clarke's view that this was largely because the churches were not united or of one mind. With primarily the Anglican Church in mind, it stated, "Moral questions like this cannot be treated half-heartedly or dealt with in a compromising spirit. One cannot half-heal a disease. The churches should take an extreme stand; they should not recognize or countenance the existing state of things at all, but should ask for that which would at once, raise the country to a decent, self-respecting level." Editorial, *Daily Gleaner*, 7 March 1900.
105. *Daily Gleaner*, 24 April 1903. See also *Jamaica Post*, 19 October 1897.
106. Canon William Simms to the editor, 17 March 1900, *Daily Gleaner*, 21 March 1900; and reprint of an article written by Rev. W. Gillies, July 1886, in *Daily Gleaner*, 24 May 1900.
107. Enos Nuttall, Addresses to the 29th and 30th Synods of the Church of England, *Journal of the Synod of the Church of England in Jamaica*, 1898 and 1899, JA 5/1/11a/12 and JA 5/1/11a/13.
108. Memorials of the 31st Synod of the Church of England to Governor Hemming and to the Legislative Council, *Journal of the Synod of the Church of England in Jamaica*, 1900, appendix section 16, JA 5/1/11a/14; the Registration Law Amendment Law, No. 29 of 1900; and *Daily Gleaner*, 4 April 1900.
109. Clarke to the editor, 11 April 1900, *Daily Gleaner*, 14 April 1900.

110. Canon William Simms to the editor, *Daily Gleaner*, 15 and 16 March 1900. He argued that there was no connection between registration of the father's name and a purer family life, which was the church's critical objective. Simms to the editor, *Daily Gleaner*, 21 March 1900.
111. Enos Nuttall, Address to the 31st Synod of the Church of England, *Journal of the Synod of the Church of England in Jamaica*, 1900, JA 5/1/11a/14.
112. C.H. Coles to the editor, *Daily Gleaner*, 19 and 22 March 1900.
113. William Graham to the editor, 22 March 1900, *Daily Gleaner*, 27 March 1900.
114. Editorials, *Daily Gleaner*, 15, 16, 21 and 28 March 1900. The paper also refuted Rev. Coles's arguments, noting that intemperance and "illegitimacy" were incomparable. Drinking, it asserted, was not in itself a sin or an evil; see *Daily Gleaner*, 20 March 1900.
115. "An Anglican" to the editor, *Daily Gleaner*, 12, 13 and 22 March 1900.
116. *Jamaica Times*, 17 February 1900, 17, 24 and 31 March 1900.
117. Ibid.
118. *Jamaica Times*, 31 March 1900.
119. Sydney Olivier, speech in the Legislative Council, 4 April 1900, as reported in the *Daily Gleaner*, 5 April 1900.
120. Ibid. Both Henry Clarke and the newspaper were strongly critical of the government's position. See Clarke to the editor, 11 April 1900, *Daily Gleaner*, 14 April 1900; and editorial, *Daily Gleaner*, 18 April 1900.
121. *Jamaica Post*, 19 October 1897. The bill was cumbersome and would have been difficult and expensive to implement. Rev. C.E. Randall was just one of several persons who cynically thought that it was designed to frustrate women who might seek redress under its provisions. The mother first had to go to the registrar, who then put the case into the hands of the inspector of the poor. The latter would then initiate an inquiry into the alleged father, which the mother must attend: "This may involve a journey of many miles, after which there may be 'no time' to attend to the case that day." When the case was finally dealt with, the inspector of the poor would send it to the clerk of courts for the parish, who would decide if there was a "strong prima facie case" which warranted further proceedings. The impartiality of these officials was open to question, since many of them were highly compromised in this matter. But assuming that they did not act in a prejudicial manner, the next step was the resident magistrate's court, which could mean another long trip for the mother to face the alleged father, perhaps her hiring a lawyer at considerable expense, and her subjection to public examination in open court. Randall animadverted that "Where there is the slightest self-respect it will not be submitted to, but the complainant will rather bear the burden and the shame alone"; and the male perpetrators would continue to escape justice. He also observed that while the bill gave the male defendant the right of appeal of the magistrate's decision, no similar opportunity was given for

the mother if she knew her case had been wrongly adjudicated. See C.E. Randall to the editor, 6 April 1900, *Daily Gleaner,* 7 April 1900. Grave doubts were also expressed about the ability of the inspectors of the poor to perform these onerous additional duties; P. Williams to the editor, 9 April 1900, *Daily Gleaner,* 11 April 1900. One parochial board felt that the law would impose on these officers responsibilities that they could not undertake. Furthermore, as Olivier observed, additional fees and expenses had to be allowed to the inspectors of the poor for travel and other costs pursuant to the new duties. He in fact estimated that the new law would cost about £3,000 per annum to operate; Olivier to Chamberlain, 24 September 1900, no. 466, CO 137/613. The registration bill was passed along with a new Maintenance Law (No. 25 of 1900). For details see *Daily Gleaner,* 24 March 1900 and 4 April 1900.

122. R.V. Vernon argued that the operation of the law would be so costly that it would not have the effect of reducing the state's expense of supporting "illegitimate" children. In addition to costs, H.B. Cox raised the possibility of blackmail and the probability that many women would not be able to substantiate their allegations in court. A.A. Pearson expressed regret that the elected members had been absent and recommended that the law should be disallowed, saying that while the secretary of state did not altogether object to its provisions, he thought it required further consideration and that he would prefer that a law of this character, affecting the social conditions of the colony, should not be passed in the absence of the elected members. On the other side, C.P. Lucas advised that the law should be approved as an experiment. He argued that when faced with difficult problems like bastardy and praedial larceny in the West Indies, for which the remedies threatened to be worse than the disease, the tendency was to let things alone. But he felt that unless these communities were allowed to run risks, suitable remedies might never be found. In this particular instance, "If public opinion in Jamaica will sanction a law of this kind, and if the govt. can pay the expense involved, I should try it. If blackmailing ensues and the law is in consequence repealed, I do not see that the position will be made worse." Although Sir M. Ommanney objected to the "inquisitorial power" which he felt the law gave to the registrars and which could be abused ("the putative father may be exposed to a double system line of blackmailing"); and although he did not share Lucas's willingness to undertake risky experiments, he eventually recommended approval subject to a clear warning of possible dangers and requiring close supervision of the operation of the law. See minutes of R. Vernon, 2 November 1900, H.B. Cox, 5 November 1900, A.A. Pearson, 3 November 1900, C.P. Lucas, 16 and 29 November 1900, Sir M. Ommanney, 29 November and 1 December 1900, all appended to Olivier to Chamberlain, 24 September 1900, no. 466, CO 137/613; and Joseph Chamberlain, 3 December 1900, CO 137/613.

123. Enos Nuttall, Address to the 31st Synod, 1900, JA 5/1/11a/4.

124. Memorial of the Council of Evangelical Churches to Joseph Chamberlain, 1901, CO 137/621. See also *Jamaica Times*, 7 April 1900 and 9 June 1900, 20 July 1901.
125. See the Report of the Commission, *Daily Gleaner*, 29 July 1904. Some of the positions and recommendations made by the commission were not unanimous. For the dissenting riders of individual members, see *Daily Gleaner*, 30 July 1904.
126. H.B. Cox of the Colonial Office noted that legitimation was permitted in Quebec, New South Wales, Victoria, Queensland, South Australia, New Zealand, the Cape Colony, Natal, Transvaal, Orange River, Malta, Ceylon, Mauritius and Seychelles, in addition to three Caribbean colonies. See his minute of 13 October 1904, appended to Olivier to Lyttelton, 15 September 1904, no. 471, CO 137/641.
127. Cundall, "West Indies".
128. Henry Clarke to the editor, 1 August 1904, *Daily Gleaner*, 3 August 1904; and editorial, *Daily Gleaner*, 5 August 1904.
129. Minutes of H.B. Cox, 13 October 1904, and C.P. Lucas, 2 November 1904, appended to Olivier to Lyttelton, 15 September 1904, no. 471, CO 137/641; and Lyttelton to Governor, 9 November 1904, no. 366, CO 137/641.
130. Led by D.A. Corinaldi, the electives passed a resolution in April 1904 in favour of legitimation, but were resolutely opposed by the governor and the attorney general, who thought that this would put a premium on illicit connections and that one of the safeguards of morality and marriage would thus be destroyed; *Daily Gleaner*, 21 May 1904. See also minutes of H.R. Cowell, 14 July 1905, and A.A. Pearson, n.d., appended to Swettenham to Lyttelton, 21 June 1905, no. 314, CO 137/645.
131. "Young Bachelor" to the editor, 22 July 1918, *Jamaica Times*, 10 August 1918.
132. Editorial, *Daily Gleaner*, 21 May 1908.

Chapter 5

1. See Olwig, "Cultural Complexity", 104–5.
2. Robert E. Noble, "The True Gentleman", *Daily Gleaner*, 4 December 1915; Lena Kent, "True Gentlemanhood: A Letter Written Some Years Ago, but Left Unfinished at the Time", *Daily Gleaner*, 14 August 1909; A.P. Hanson, "Hitting the Bad Manners of Young Jamaica", *Jamaica Times*, 10 February 1917.
3. See Barbara Welter, "The Cult of True Womanhood: 1820–1860", *American Quarterly* 18, no. 2 (Summer 1966). Women were assigned the role of moral guardians of society, although as Amies notes, "not by confronting the corruption in the outside world with their moral virtue, but by retreating into the separate sphere of domestic life, cultivating self-denial, forbearance, and fidelity, and providing a cultured haven for their male relatives"; Marion Amies, "The Victorian Governess and Colonial Ideals of Womanhood", *Victorian Studies* 31, no. 4 (1988): 549–51. Also Joan Burstyn, *Victorian Education and the Ideal of*

Womanhood (London: Croom Helm, 1980); Deborah Gorham, *The Victorian Girl and the Feminine Ideal* (London: Croom Helm, 1982); Carol Dyhouse, *Girls Growing up in Late Victorian and Edwardian England* (London: Routledge and Kegan Paul, 1981).

4. *Jamaica Post*, 11 February 1890. Notwithstanding the touch of feminist sarcasm at the end, the following poem encapsulates perfectly what was expected of the cultured woman:

What a Girl Should Do

A girl should learn to cook and bake,
Make pies and puddings, soups and cake;
Learn rooms to dust, and beds to make:
This should she do – and more!

And she must sew as well as mend,
And learn to nurse the sick and tend;
While to the poor aid she must lend:
This should she do – and more!

The piano play, should sing a song,
Speak French and German – right or wrong;
Read recent books, both short and long:
This should she do – and more!

With fancy work should deck the chair,
Supply bazaars and shows and fairs
(It hurts her eyes, but no one cares):
This should she do – and more!

Soiled lace she should "do up" as new,
Cut out a dress, if sovs. be few –
To the latest style of course be true:
This should she do – and more!

Should letters write, and pictures scrawl,
Receive at home, go out to call,
Attend to brothers, big and small:
This should she do – and more!

In costume she should aye be neat,
Her temper "as the noontide sweet",
Howe'er depressed, aye smiling greet:
This should she do – and more!

Poor maid, the world asks much of thee!
Fain would I not put in a plea.
O mother, let your daughter be;
Tax not her youth so sore!

Teach her that life's not giv'n for jest;
Teach her to use her brains at best;
Her own good sense will do the rest –
Trust me, it will, and more!

5. Amies, "Victorian Governess", 549–51.
6. Hall, *Civilising Subjects*, 27.
7. See Rev. A. James's speech to the Men's Meeting at the Conversorium, as reported in the *Jamaica Times*, 13 June 1903; and W.B. Esson, "The High Road to True Manhood and How to Find It", *Jamaica Times*, 5 August 1911; Noble, "The True Gentleman"; and Kent, "True Gentlemanhood".
8. Noble, "The True Gentleman".
9. J.H. Aikman, "Home Life" (speech at the seventh Men's Meeting at the Conversorium), *Daily Gleaner*, 4 August 1903.

10. H. Crews (Stipendiary Magistrate, Clarendon), n.d., enclosed in Darling to Newcastle, 18 October 1860, no. 140, CO 137/351; censuses of 1844 and 1861, UWI Mona Library; and "The Women of Jamaica", *Daily Gleaner,* 28 February 1903 and 17 March 1903; "Our Women and Our Future", *Jamaica Times,* 27 July 1901.
11. Ann Laura Stoler, "Rethinking Colonial Categories: European Communities and the Boundaries of Rule", *Comparative Studies in Society and History* 31, no. 1 (January 1989): 144; also Moore, *Cultural Power,* 38–39.
12. Edgar Bacon and E.M. Aaron, *The New Jamaica* (New York: Walbridge and Co.; Kingston: Aston W. Gardner and Co., 1890), 74–75.
13. Edna Bradlow, "The Culture of a Colonial Elite: The Cape of Good Hope in the 1850s", *Victorian Studies* 29, no. 3 (1986): 391; also Moore, *Cultural Power,* 30–36.
14. Livingstone, *Black Jamaica,* 167–68.
15. "Respectability" (editorial), *Daily Gleaner,* 1 April 1905.
16. "The Critic", "Some Social Institutions: Mutual Admiration Societies", *Daily Gleaner,* 8 June 1906.
17. *Jamaica Times,* 13 May 1899.
18. "The Critic", *Daily Gleaner,* 30 May 1906.
19. Cundall, "West Indies", 180; "The Critic", "Some Social Institutions: 'At Homes' ", *Daily Gleaner,* 30 May 1906.
20. *Daily Gleaner,* 29 December 1909.
21. Livingstone, *Black Jamaica,* 167–68.
22. H.G.D., "Rowdyism", *Daily Gleaner,* 3 July 1897. The lecture in question was on "Movements of Plants" and was delivered by Professor McDougal. The commentator mentioned that a large portion of the audience were students from the Mico and other schools, and expressed regret that with their training and since they were "removed from the contaminating influences of vulgarity", the exemplary behaviour that had been expected of them was not in evidence.
23. "The Bad Manners of Audiences", *Jamaica Times,* 10 April 1909; "Public Behaviour", *Daily Gleaner,* 30 September 1913; "Manners and Theatre Goers", *Daily Gleaner,* 16 July 1919.
24. "The Bad Manners of Audiences", *Jamaica Times,* 10 April 1909.
25. The *Gleaner* said that the English newspapers had, in fact, objected to the terrible behaviour of the London audiences, and pointed to the American reaction to poor performances, of silently leaving the theatre, as a better path than the "cat-calls and objurgations and booings and similar vocal exercises [which] are not a pretty advertisement of our national manners"; "Public Behaviour", *Daily Gleaner,* 30 September 1913. Also "Manners and Theatre Goers", *Daily Gleaner,* 16 July 1919.
26. "Swearing", *Jamaica Post,* 28 July 1894.
27. Hall, *Civilising Subjects,* 6.
28. *Morning Journal,* 11 December 1873.

29. *Morning Journal*, 8 September 1875.
30. *Colonial Standard*, 17 August 1889.
31. *Daily Gleaner*, 25 October 1875 and 1 November 1875.
32. "Scene in Court: Two Lawyers Fighting", *Daily Gleaner*, 3 and 4 November 1875.
33. *Jamaica Post*, 19 March 1896.
34. In this instance, a batsman was adjudged "out" off an alleged no-ball, but the umpire called "no-ball" after the stump had been dislodged. One of the St James's players "made use of very insulting language respecting the Captain of the Falmouth Club", who attacked the offender and provoked the general disturbance. See *Falmouth Post*, 17 June 1870.
35. For instances of divorce cases see *Colonial Standard*, 10 February 1888; *Jamaica Times*, 9 September 1905, 22 April 1916, 9 December 1916 and 9 March 1918; *Jamaica Daily Telegraph*, 2 May 1899; *Jamaica Guardian*, 8 and 12 January 1909; *Daily Gleaner*, 4 September 1885, 1 and 2 July 1892, 1 October 1901, 30 January 1918, 25 April 1918 and 2 August 1918.
36. *Daily Gleaner*, 16 and 17 January 1902 and 22 April 1902.
37. *Daily Gleaner*, 20 and 21 July 1920.
38. Brackette F. Williams, *Stains on My Name, War in My Veins: Guyana and the Politics of Cultural Struggle* (Durham: Duke University Press, 1991), 127–74.
39. Livingstone, *Black Jamaica*, 227–31. Also Pullen-Burry, *Ethiopia*, 163; George Robson, *The story of our Jamaica Mission* (Edinburgh: Offices of the United Presbyterian Church, 1894), 95; Cundall, "West Indies", 95–98, 100; Mary Eliza Bakewell Gaunt, *Reflection in Jamaica* (London: Ernest Benn, 1932), 29; and Rampini, *Letters*, 80–81.
40. "The Civilization of Savages", *St James Gazette*, reprinted in the *Daily Gleaner*, 4 August 1885.
41. *Gall's News Letter*, 17 April 1875.
42. Frank Thomas Bullen, "Kingston, Jamaica 1905", *Cornhill Magazine*, February 1905, 190.
43. *Daily Gleaner*, 6 May 1876, 25 September 1880, 7 April 1885, 12 June 1886; *Colonial Standard*, 27 September 1890. In February 1886, according to the *Gleaner*, a set of "ruffians" took over the streetcars in Brown's Town (Kingston), cursing and swearing; they refused to respond to the pleas of the conductor and even the company's manager to tone down. Eventually, when one of the men also refused to pay his fare, the car was stopped, the mules taken out and the police summoned. The three ringleaders were arrested. *Daily Gleaner*, 18 February 1886.
44. In the district of Glengoffe in 1900, one "woman-offender" was fined 56s. or thirty days after she refused to attend court, being charged for using indecent language. When she was eventually brought before the magistrate, an additional 12s. or seven days was added to the penalty, and being unable to pay, she served thirty-seven days' imprisonment; *Jamaica Times*, 1 December 1900. See also the

Falmouth Post, 12 April 1870; *Morning Journal*, 12 and 13 September 1873; *Colonial Standard*, 4 October 1880 and 17 December 1894; *Daily Gleaner*, 11 June 1875, 15 March 1882 and 17 May 1882.

45. *Morning Journal*, 4 November 1871. This practice was not confined to the urban areas, but was noted throughout the island among men and women alike. See *Morning Journal*, 17 February 1871 and 19 April 1875; *Daily Gleaner*, 6 May 1876, 25 September 1880, 25 April 1882, 7 April 1885, 18 February 1886 and 12 June 1886; *Colonial Standard*, 2 October 1880 and 27 September 1890; *Jamaica Daily Telegraph*, 13 July 1899; *Jamaica Times*, 26 August 1899 and 29 March 1902.

46. *Daily Gleaner*, 2 June 1876, 17 May 1882, 10 December 1886; and H. Alma Swift, Report of the Friends Jamaica Mission (Orange Bay and Cedar Hurst), 30 June 1915, JA 5/8/2/420.

47. This newspaper mounted a public campaign against indecent language. See "Obscene Language", *Jamaica Advocate*, 12 December 1896; and "Suppression of Obscene Language in Public", *Jamaica Advocate*, 25 April 1903. Billingsgate was a fish market in East London which earned notoriety as a gathering place for the "dregs" of the city, whose language consisted primarily of "*sworn* statements".

48. *Morning Journal*, 4 November 1871; *Daily Gleaner*, 29 July 1875, 6 and 8 November 1884, 23 January 1885, 10 April 1885, 4 September 1885, 21 January 1886, 29 July 1887, 21 March 1892, and 18 May 1894; *Colonial Standard*, 16 October 1885 and 26 November 1890. See also "Noise in Kingston at Nights", *Daily Gleaner*, 2 June 1914.

49. *Daily Gleaner*, 5 December 1914.

50. "Black Diamond", "Plain Talk to the Masses", *Jamaica Times*, 22 February 1908.

51. For a discussion of the "Puritanical" world view, see Foster, *Long Argument*; also Zakai, *Theocracy*.

52. Only one arrest, that of a boy named Theophilus Brown, who struck a girl with a stick, was made. Brown was fined 21s. or thirty days' imprisonment. Nor was this behaviour limited to activities outside of the church. *Daily Gleaner*, 8 and 15 April 1884, 8 November 1884.

53. "Noise in Kingston at Nights", *Daily Gleaner*, 2 June 1914.

54. *Daily Gleaner*, 25 July 1878 and 25 September 1884; and *Jamaica Times*, 29 November 1902.

55. *Falmouth Post*, 15 August 1862; *Colonial Standard*, 23 April 1880 and 16 February 1892; *Daily Gleaner*, 13 August 1880.

56. Rampini, *Letters*, 15–16.

57. *Daily Gleaner*, 9 June 1876.

58. See, for instance, *Colonial Standard*, 21 May 1880, 11 June 1880 and 12 January 1881; *Daily Gleaner*, 31 May 1876, 16 July 1881, and 20 August 1885; *Morning Journal*, 13 November 1872 and 17 June 1873; and "Spread of Recklessness", *Jamaica Times*, 20 September 1902.

59. "Spread of Recklessness", *Jamaica Times*, 20 September 1902; *Morning Journal*, 12 September 1873; *Colonial Standard*, 30 April 1880 and 7 December 1892; *Daily Gleaner*, 1 May 1876 and 27 June 1888.
60. See Swithin Wilmot, "Females of Abandoned Character? Women and Protest in Jamaica, 1838–65", in *Engendering History: Caribbean Women in Historical Perspective*, ed. Verene A. Shepherd, Bridget Brereton and Barbara Bailey (Kingston: Ian Randle, 1995), 279–95.
61. *Daily Gleaner*, 9 June 1876. At times the street gatherings seemed to take on a gang character, such as the occasion in December 1894 when a "gang of roughs" composed of men and women took possession of the race course. *Colonial Standard*, 25 December 1894. See also *Jamaica Guardian*, 9 December 1909, and *Jamaica Times*, 9 May 1908; "Hooligans Terrorise People", *Daily Gleaner*, 28 January 1913.
62. See, for instance, *Daily Gleaner*, 29 April 1876 and 28 September 1878. Stick-licking is an integral part of Afro-creole culture and is found throughout the Caribbean. See, for instance, Downes, "Barbados"; Burton, *Afro-Creole*, 173–77; Brereton, *Race Relations*, 167–70; and David Vincent Trotman, *Crime in Trinidad: Conflict and Control in a Plantation Society, 1838–1900* (Knoxville: University of Tennessee Press, 1986), 181–82.
63. *Jamaica Daily Telegraph*, 24 and 31 August 1899; *Jamaica Times*, 11 May 1901. *Daily Gleaner*, 22 October 1902; *Daily Gleaner*, 8 March 1887, 24 March 1888, 6 April 1897, 2 June 1897 and 9 August 1898.
64. For a detailed account of living conditions in the slums of Kingston at the turn of the twentieth century, see Moore and Johnson, *"Squalid Kingston"*.
65. "The Gospel of Violence", *Jamaica Times*, 27 July 1907.
66. Similar concerns were expressed in Britain about the abuse (including sexual) of children. See Louise A. Jackson, *Child Sexual Abuse in Victorian England* (London: Routledge, 2000). Several studies have also been done on this social problem in the modern Caribbean; for example, Pauline Milbourn, *Child Abuse: A Collaborative Study in Jamaica, 1988 and 1989* (Kingston: Child Guidance Clinic, 1991); *Caribbean Regional Conference on Child Abuse and Neglect* (Port of Spain, 1989); and *Report of the Task Force on Child Abuse* (Kingston: Specialist Committee on Child Abuse, 1993).
67. See, for instance, *Falmouth Post*, 1 July 1865; *Morning Journal*, 8 June 1875; *Colonial Standard*, 24 November 1885; *Jamaica Post*, 14 June 1897; *Jamaica Times*, 29 August 1908; *Jamaica Guardian*, 18 and 19 March 1909; *Daily Gleaner*, 13 March 1893, 22 July 1893 and 19 October 1916.
68. There was a legal distinction between infanticide, which was the known murder of an infant, and "concealment of birth", which was a charge that originated in Britain in the seventeenth century that made secret childbirth a capital offence if the child died, even if there was no evidence of murder. Ann R. Higginbotham,

"'Sin of the Age': Infanticide and Illegitimacy in Victorian London", *Victorian Studies* 32, no. 3 (1989): 319–38.

69. *Falmouth Post,* 28 February 1865; *Daily Gleaner,* 26 January 1877, 16 June 1881, 28 February 1889, 7 July 1891, 10 June 1892. See the 1902 case of Englishwoman Anne Wheatle, discussed previously.
70. *Daily Gleaner,* 25 March 1876, 23 May 1890 and 27 March 1895.
71. Moore, *Cultural Power,* 107–8; Trotman, *Crime,* 174.
72. "Jamaican" to the editor, *Daily Gleaner,* 8 October 1894.
73. *Morning Journal,* 9 August 1871; *Daily Gleaner,* 15 September 1876; *Colonial Standard,* 28 July 1880.
74. Trotman, *Crime,* 176–77. See also Moore, *Cultural Power,* 105–6.
75. See V. Morgan, *Violence Against Women in Jamaica: The Situation and Who is Addressing It* (Kingston: Bureau of Women's Affairs, 1991); E. Hilberman and F. Munson, "Sixty Battered Women", *Victimology* 2 (1978); United Nations, *Violence Against Women in the Family* (Vienna: Centre for Social Development and Humanitarian Affairs, 1989).
76. *Colonial Standard,* 27 July 1880; *Daily Gleaner,* 14 January 1888; *Jamaica Daily Telegraph,* 10 July 1899. For other instances of domestic violence see, for instance, *Jamaica Times,* 14 March 1903; *Daily Gleaner,* 14 October 1901, 31 December 1910 and 20 July 1920.
77. *Daily Gleaner,* 18 June 1888 and 24 November 1905. For Guyana see Moore, *Cultural Power,* 106. The home as a site of violence was entirely in keeping with the experiences of explosive confrontation in the wider society. In the most intimate of spaces the contest over power occurred at a personal and intense level, and since the women in the community seemed willing to challenge the place prescribed by the Victorian ideology of gender, men (who were as aware of those prescriptions as the transgressing women were) felt compelled to exert their control. Inasmuch as many men in Jamaica could not exert the economic control that many of their European and American counterparts could (since so many women supported themselves, their families and even the men), many resorted to brute force to make their "manhood" and control clear. And they, no doubt, felt justified and supported in their actions since violence seemed to be an acceptable *modus operandi* in the society, and males were regularly encouraged to "be men".
78. Rampini, *Letters,* 78; *Colonial Standard,* 27 October 1881; *Daily Gleaner,* 4 August 1875 and 26 February 1888.
79. *Colonial Standard,* 8 and 12 July 1881; *Daily Gleaner,* 29 July 1881, 1 February 1888, 29 March 1888, 19 April 1888 and 20 April 1898; Rampini, *Letters,* 78.
80. A.P. Hanson, Agricultural Instructor, "Hitting the Bad Manners of Young Jamaica", *Jamaica Times,* 10 February 1917.
81. "A Criticism of Jamaica and Things Jamaican", *Daily Gleaner,* 14 March 1913.

82. President's Address, "Universal Negro Improvement Association", *Daily Gleaner,* 26 August 1915.
83. Downes, "Barbados", 212.
84. *Falmouth Post,* 2 April 1875; *Jamaica Times,* 12, 19 and 26 April 1902, 20 and 27 July 1918; *Daily Gleaner,* 27 February 1912, 10, 11, 12 and 13 July 1918; Probyn to Long, 22 July 1918, no. 283A, JA 1B/5/18 vol. 23; and 5 September 1918, no. 337 and encls., CO 137/727. For a detailed account of the 1902 riot in Montego Bay see Bryan, *Jamaican People,* 271–76. For an analysis of the anti-Chinese riots, see Johnson, "Anti-Chinese".
85. Vaughn Cornish, *The Travels of Ellen Cornish* (London: W.J. Ham-Smith, 1913), 274; and Alpheus Hyatt Verrill, *Jamaica of Today* (New York: Dodd, Mead and Co., 1931), 133 and 148–49. According to Maggie Jakes, referring to the situation at the turn of the twentieth century, "we never have so much self pride . . . we call white people angels"; Maggie Jakes, n.d. [1959], Jamaica Memories, JA 7/12/1.
86. Anonymous, quoted in Cundall, "West Indies", 102.
87. Scott, *To Jamaica,* 299; W. Bellows, *In Fair Jamaica* (Kingston: Educational Supply Co., 1907), 16.
88. Scott, *To Jamaica,* 299; Pullen-Burry, *Jamaica as It Is,* 23.
89. Cundall, "West Indies", 102; Cornish, *Travels,* 274; Margaret Newton, *Glimpses of Life in Bermuda and the Tropics* (London: Digby, Long and Co., 1897), 203, 205–6.
90. Verrill, *Jamaica of Today,* 148–49.
91. M.S. Hinckle, "Kisses and Curses – A few items from Jamaica", Report, Friends Jamaica Mission, Seaside, 18 July 1919, JA 5/8/1/102. See also Rampini, *Letters,* 27.
92. Alfred Leader, *Through Jamaica with a Kodak* (Bristol: John Wright, 1907), 41; Ella Wheeler Wilcox, *Sailing Sunny Seas* (Chicago: W.B. Conkey, 1909), 136; Splaine, diary, 19 February 1872.
93. Ernest Price, *Bananaland; pages from the chronicles of an English minister in Jamaica* (London: Carry, 1930), 145, 147, 148.
94. Arthur Swift to Susie J. Martin, 13 May 1897, Friends Jamaica Mission letters, JA 5/8/10/955.
95. Splaine, diary, 19 February 1872.

Chapter 6

1. Turner, *Slaves and Missionaries,* 10–11.
2. Stewart, *Religion,* 201 note 23. According to Stewart, the Scottish Missionary Society's start in 1800 proved abortive, and it was not until 1824 that they sent out another missionary. He also notes that two small American missions were established in Jamaica before 1865: the American Congregational (1837) and the United Christian Missionary Society (1856). In addition, the Roman Catholic

Church was served by Jesuits who were under the supervision of the English Province of the Society of Jesus until the 1890s.
3. Stewart, *Religion*, 52.
4. Turner, *Slaves and Missionaries*, 50 and 52.
5. Curtin, *Two Jamaicas*, 25.
6. Stewart, *Religion*, xix. Diane Austin-Broos makes a similar observation: "The Christian cosmology, anchored in God, presented an ontology in which evil was located in the person and addressed by moral discipline and rite. . . . Among Jamaicans with an African past, this encounter with sin was shaped by another practice antagonistic to the disciplined subject of Christian moral ontology. . . . The religions of West Africa brought a cosmology in which a multiplicity of spiritual forces, including ancestral living-dead, pervaded and defined the world. Their very presence in daily life brought different notions of good and evil which were not assigned to separate spheres but allowed to reside as ambivalent companions in the world." Austin-Broos, *Jamaica Genesis*, 6.
7. Stewart, *Religion*, xix; Turner, *Slaves and Missionaries*, 71.
8. Stewart, *Religion*, xviii–xix.
9. Turner, *Slaves and Missionaries*, 71–72.
10. Austin-Broos, *Jamaica Genesis*, 35.
11. Turner, *Slaves and Missionaries*, 73 and 75.
12. Curtin, *Two Jamaicas*, 172, 199–200; Stewart, *Religion*, 167–70.
13. Stewart, *Religion*, 147.
14. Ibid., 148, 167–74; see also Hall, *Civilising Subjects*, 251.
15. Law 30 of 1870. The government of the church along with church property rested in a synod which consisted of a bishop, clergy and lay representatives. See also *The Mission Field*, 1870. This was part of a wider imperial policy of the Gladstone government to disestablish the Church of England in colonies where Anglicanism was not the majority faith.
16. The missionary bodies were urging the Anglican Church in the island to indigenize the clergy, with a view to having the Jamaican church ultimately become independent. Hence they argued that "when the missionary is of another and superior race than his converts he must not attempt to be their *Pastor*; though they will be bound to him by personal attachment and by a sense of the benefits received from him, yet if he continues to act as their Pastor they will not form a vigorous Native Church, but as a general rule they will remain in a dependent condition and make but little progress in spiritual attainments." Rev. Henry Venn, Honorary Secretary of the Church Missionary Society, to the Lord Bishop of Kingston [Jamaica] on the state of the Negroes of Jamaica, January 1867, USPG D28a. Bryan notes that in 1892 the Church Army was established as an evangelizing agency of the Anglican Church; Bryan, *Jamaican People*, 61. Also Stewart, *Religion*, 5–6; Curtin, *Two Jamaicas*, 207–8. British-born Enos Nuttall

went to Jamaica as a Methodist, but joined the Church of England in 1866 and rapidly ascended through its hierarchy to become bishop of Jamaica in 1880, primate of the West Indies in 1894, and eventually archbishop in 1897. He died in 1916.

17. The ticket-and-class-leader system was started by the Wesleyans and then adopted by the Baptists. They would set up a class house in each area where church members lived and appoint a black member as class leader. Prayer meetings were held under the leader at these class houses. Tickets of different colours with biblical inscriptions, renewable quarterly, were issued as identification of either inquirer or full-membership status. Ticket holders often made voluntary contributions at the time of renewal. See Stewart, *Religion*, 8–9, 123–29.

18. London missionary James Milne argued that "I see more than ever the necessity for the European element in the Ministry of this country, for a long time yet. Few Natives have the wisdom, the courage, and the faithfulness to deal with the churches in their present condition. They succumb too easily to the difficulties they meet and resort too readily to measures of expediency rather than trust the efficiency of spiritual principles, and their applicability to all cases." James Milne to A. Tidman, 23 September 1864, LMS 9/1. This view, with its racist undertones, was endorsed by English negrophobe James Froude, who argued that "it seems unlikely that the political authority of the white race will be allowed to reassert itself, it must be through their minds and through those other qualities which religion addresses that the black race will be influenced by the white, if it is ever to be influenced at all"; J.A. Froude, *England in the West Indies or the Bow of Ulysses* (London: Longman, Green and Co., 1888), 232. The Society for the Propagation of the Gospel made the case for indigenization largely on racial grounds: "In their present ignorance, to which fornication is too often joined, the lower class in Jamaica cannot derive adequate benefit from the usual ministrations of the clergyman of the parish. Difference in race must also present, in many cases, another serious obstacle to the efficiency of an European clergyman among a coloured flock"; *Report: The Standing Committee of the Society for the Propagation of the Gospel in Foreign Parts and the Jamaican Clergy* (Kingston: M. DeCordova, McDougall and Co., 1867). Whether for similar reasons or not, the nonconformist churches slowly indigenized themselves. The Jamaica Congregational Union became wholly independent in 1884. The Methodist churches became independent in 1884 when the Methodist Church of the West Indies (or West Indian Conference) was formed. In 1904, however, the West Indian Conference surrendered its constitution and reverted to direct control from London. The Jamaica Baptist Union was self-governing by 1880 and became wholly self-supporting financially after 1905. See Charles Washington Eves, *West Indies* (London: Sampson Low, Marston and Co., 1889), 232; *113th Report of the Baptist Missionary Society*, 1905.

19. Bryan, *Jamaican People*, 60; Stewart, *Religion*, 187. Inasmuch as the Jamaican black and brown missionaries could not claim the privilege inherent in "whiteness" that the British missionaries did, they could aspire to other avenues of elevation: wholesale anglicization and Christianization, which both elevated them above the community from which they had emerged and operated as examples of the possibilities available in the dominant culture for one who "played by the rules". Evelyn Higginbotham notes that in the American South, similarly trained blacks were employed to spread the word and with it "civilization"; they too embraced white (American) culture in their own quest for social respectability. See Evelyn Brooks Higginbotham, *Righteous Discontent: The Women's Movement in the Black Baptist Church, 1880–1920* (Cambridge, Mass.: Harvard University Press, 1993), 43.
20. See Church of England, Jamaica Home and Foreign Missionary Society Reports, 1876–1920, JA 5/1/12/1–8.
21. Higginbotham, *Righteous Discontent*, 34. She observes that in the American South, blacks educated in Baptist training schools "adhered to the same beliefs of most white Baptists and rejected conjuring, beliefs in ghosts, voodoo, and practices of 'superstition' that carried over from slave religion. The educated ministry and laity in the late nineteenth century commonly encouraged a less demonstrative worship style than the 'shout', bodily movement, or moaning and clapping prevalent among the folk." Ibid., 44.
22. Decennial censuses 1881–1921, UWI Mona Library.
23. "Our Mission to Millions: The Work of the United Free Church in the Kingdoms Beyond the Seas. The Oldest Field – Jamaica", *United Free Church of Scotland Missionary Record* 16 (1916), Papers of the United Free Church of Scotland, New College Library, Edinburgh. The 1921 census listed fifteen, in addition to "others numbering less than 1,000 each". The missionaries who had served in the island for generations, along with those who joined the mission field in the later nineteenth century, shared a common belief in the need to save the souls of the descendants of the slaves. These were the world's most unfortunate beings, who, having been emancipated from physical bondage, were still threatened by the bonds of sin and the eternal damnation that resulted from non-acceptance of the doctrine of Christian salvation. As part of the spiritually enlightened community the missionaries had a duty, as had the disciples of Jesus, to "go out and preach that [wo]men should repent". For Jesus' instruction to his disciples regarding proselytization, see Mark 6:7–13.
24. Stewart, *Religion*, 167–68; *Periodical Accounts*, June 1866, Moravian Church Papers, JA 5/5; and John Mearns (Mount Fletcher/Gordon Town) to General Secretaries, 6 April 1866, MMS Box 200 [microfiche 2405]. The Society for the Propagation of the Gospel in Manchester complained that "some persons called Baptists came into the district creating great excitement, and many people, among whom there was then a very general impression that the Baptists had been

the great means of their freedom, went after them, and on more than one occasion I was left on Sunday with hardly any congregation". See John Morris (Keynsham), *The Mission Field,* 1865.
25. Eyre to Cardwell, 10 September 1864, no. 256, CO 137/384.
26. *The Church of Scotland Home and Foreign Missionary Record,* 4 (1 January 1866), and 5 (1 September 1866), Church of Scotland Papers, New College Library, Edinburgh.
27. Venn to the Lord Bishop of Kingston, January 1867, USPG D28a. In 1867, largely in response to the Morant Bay uprising, the standing committee of the Society for the Propagation of the Gospel in Foreign Parts conducted a "searching review" of the work of the clergy in Jamaica. Notwithstanding their presence in the island since 1824 and some signs of progress, there was "in spite of this, the very deplorable immorality prevailing in the island, the excessive violence of fanaticism evidenced in the recent outbreak". In the end, the standing committee "reluctantly" concluded that the Society's work was a failure in Jamaica; *Report: The Standing Committee of the Society for the Propagation of the Gospel in Foreign Parts* (1867). The bishop, in turn, responded that they had not failed, that slavery had only ended in 1834 and that the British government had not really helped the process by paying £26 for the body of each slave and 4s. 6d. for his education: "And was it really expected that for this or any other sum, a negro entering on a period of 12 years, with all the ingrained vices of centuries of servitude with him and around him, was to be produced at the end of that period (like an article manufactured to order, of the finest British texture of the nineteenth century) a freeman capable of fulfilling all the highest duties of citizenship, a conscientious juryman, an incorrupt voter, a moral vestryman and statesman, a faithful husband, a self-denying father?" See "Report of the Bishop of Kingston", in *Report: The Standing Committee of the Society for the Propagation of the Gospel in Foreign Parts* (1867); *Jamaica – Who Is to Blame? By a 30 Years' Resident* [written by a well-known Baptist missionary] (London: Effingham Wilson, n.d.).
28. William Reeve (Duncans) to General Secretaries, 23 April 1867, MMS Box 200 [microfiche 2410].
29. See *Periodical Accounts,* June 1868, Moravian Church Papers, JA 5/5; Wesleyan Methodist Missionary Society, Report of the Religious State of the Societies, Synod minutes, 26 January 1866, MMS Box 160–1866; and Thomas P. Russell (Duncans) to W.B. Boyce, "They must be followed", 23 June 1875, MMS Box 201 [microfiche 2458]. So important was the mission that when the difficult economic circumstances existing in the island after 1865 encouraged population movement, they also demanded that those who wanted to rescue, influence and control the people had to be prepared to make the sacrifice and move with them. However, once the missionaries had inserted themselves and their churches and schools in the hills of the island in order to be among the people, they became even more

important as the single sources of education, entertainment and community activities in these often isolated spots.

30. There were many examples of "free labour" in building churches. For instance, in 1877 "free labour" was used in the extension of Church of England churches in Santa Cruz, Mount Hermon, Woodford, Moore Town and Nain; *Jamaica Church Chronicle,* quoted in *The Mission Field,* 1877. In 1881 a massive effort among the Moravians at Mizpah went on for two months. These, said the missionary, were "anxious, toilsome days, from 5 a.m. to 10 p.m. . . . Every Monday forty or fifty persons were labouring gratis. . . . During the last three days the place was like a beehive, thronged with brethren and sisters, cleaning, clearing, plastering, whitewashing, painting, &c." Having participated in its construction, the people were also present at the opening of the building, with seven hundred persons crammed inside and three hundred outside. *Periodical Accounts,* June 1881, Moravian Church Papers, JA 5/5. At Carisbrook in 1890, every Friday a number of people carried stones, lime, water and other materials, and made lime kilns (Annual Report of the Moravian Church in Jamaica, 1890, JA 5/5); while at Moravia in 1906, when mules were in short supply to pull the cart loaded with stones, the workmen "laid hold on it, some before and others behind, and dragged it up the hill, with singing on the spot" (*Reports and Statistics of the Moravian Church in Jamaica,* 1906, JA 5/5). The Moravians also benefited from this system at Fulneck, Moravia, Beaufort and Dober in 1907–8 (*Reports and Statistics,* 1907–8). The Quakers, too, used "free labour" to build their chapel and to clear the bush from their premises at Amity Hall, while at Cedar Hurst one day in each month was set apart for "free labour" on the church and school premises. From the people's effort, an immense gully was filled in from a hill which was dug down, making the ground level. Report of the Friends Jamaica Mission (Cedar Hurst), 1918, JA 5/8/4/524.
31. *United Presbyterian Church Foreign Mission Report* 1885.
32. Church of Scotland [Rev. Maxwell], *Life and Work: The Church of Scotland Magazine and Mission Record* 29 (1907), Church of Scotland Papers, New College Library, Edinburgh, 54.
33. Letter of Father John Errington, SJ, 8 January 1893, *Letters and Notices* 22 (1893–94), Society of Jesus, English Province, London.
34. They moved to the courthouse, where there was prayer and singing, and they went to the old works at Prosper Estate for services. They then returned to Lucea, singing the doxology, after which they went on to the Baptist chapel for communion. The day's activities went on from six in the morning to after two in the afternoon. *Falmouth Post,* 16 August 1867.
35. See, for instance, *Daily Gleaner,* 11 and 19 June 1884, 23 May 1885, 12 May 1887, 1 October 1887 and 5 January 1888.
36. *Colonial Standard,* 24 November 1891.

37. *Jamaica Times*, 1 April 1899.
38. *Daily Gleaner*, 14 October 1893 *Jamaica Times*, 28 November 1903 and 10 April 1909; *Daily Gleaner*, 22 September 1892 and 14 December 1899.
39. Falmouth Wesleyan Chapel, *Daily Gleaner*, 19 August 1892; Fairfield Moravian Church, *Daily Gleaner*, 15 December 1896; Kingston Ebenezer Church, Savanna-la-mar Wesleyan Church, *Jamaica Times*, 3 December 1898; Mizpah Church at Above Rocks, Baptist Church in St Ann's Bay, St John's Church in Gayle, Mount Hermon Church, *Jamaica Times*, 10 June 1899, 19 August 1899, 23 September 1899, 9 December 1899, 16 December 1899; Wesley Chapel, *Jamaica Times*, 27 January 1900 and Coke Chapel, *Daily Gleaner*, 12 December 1900; Hope Bay Baptist Church, Negril Church of England and Presbyterian Churches, *Jamaica Times*, 22 June 1901, 2 November 1901; Fellowship Baptist Church, the Salvation Army corps in Allman Town, Whitefield Church in Porus, *Jamaica Times*, 24 May 1902, 15 November 1902, 6 December 1902; Elderslie Baptist Church in Ipswich, Falmouth Baptist Chapel, Falmouth Wesleyan Church, Falmouth Anglican Church, *Jamaica Times*, 4 April 1903, 18 April 1903, 2 May 1903, 28 November 1903; Bethlehem Moravian Church, St Matthew's in Allman Town, *Jamaica Times*, 13 February 1904, 24 September 1904; Buff Bay Wesleyan Church, Retreat Holy Trinity Church in St Mary, Moneague Christ Church, *Jamaica Times*, 9 September 1905, 21 October 1905; St Patrick's Church in Manchester, Hampstead Wesleyan Church, *Jamaica Times*, 3 February 1906, 19 May 1906; St James Church in Portland, *Jamaica Times*, 31 October 1909.
40. Hall, *Civilising Subjects*, 124–25.
41. According to the *Falmouth Post*, before 1860 they marched through the streets of the principal towns with bands of music and flags on which scriptural passages were written. These processions were led by clergyman, who were generally regarded as "Apostles of Liberty". Children were regaled with cakes and lemonade at well-decorated schoolrooms, and public meetings were held in the afternoon at which large sums of money were collected for various charitable purposes. But after the death of "the great liberator", William Knibb, the processions stopped in most parts of the island. This was interpreted as a growing sign of apathy towards the holiday. See, for instance, *Morning Journal*, 5 July 1873; also B.W. Higman, "Slavery Remembered: The Celebration of Emancipation in Jamaica", *Journal of Caribbean History* 12 (1979): 55–74.
42. William Knibb and James Phillippo were two of the leading British Baptist missionaries, both of whom went to Jamaica during the 1820s and worked tirelessly among the slaves, not only to christianize them, but also for their freedom. They came to symbolize the close identification of the Baptist Missionary Society with the emancipation of the black people of Jamaica, and that body of missionaries played a major role in organizing the annual celebrations of Emancipation Day through their churches and chapels.

43. *Jamaica Times*, 18 October 1902.
44. *Women's Missionary Magazine of the United Free Church of Scotland* 9 (1909), Papers of the United Free Church of Scotland, New College Library, Edinburgh.
45. H. Alma Swift, Report of the Friends Jamaica Mission, 1919, JA 5/8/4/533; Stephen Sutton (Savanna-la-Mar) to M.C. Osborn, 25 October 1887, MMS Box 203 [microfiche 2510].
46. *United Presbyterian Church Missionary Record*, n.s., 1 (1880), United Presbyterian Church of Scotland Papers, New College Library, Edinburgh.
47. Reports: West Indies 1868, LMS 1; and T.S. Penny, "Fair Jamaica", *Missionary Herald* 92 (1910), Baptist Missionary Society Papers, Angus Library, Regent's Park College, Oxford; Wesleyan Methodist Missionary Society, Report of the Religious State of the Societies, Synod minutes, 29 January 1875, MMS Box 163–1874.
48. Stewart, *Religion*, 177.
49. Splaine, diary. Splaine and others like him could or would not see that there was another competing culture in operation in Jamaica. Where he expected to find shame, there was none. In a culture that was nurtured in the open, where secrets were difficult to keep and privacy all but nonexistent, the people spoke and lived openly and were willing to share their concerns and their lives with anyone who showed an interest. This was very different from the dominant Victorian culture, which valued privacy very highly and whose products could not comprehend the Jamaican exuberance and "shamelessness".
50. *86th Report of the Baptist Missionary Society*, 1877, and *89th Report of the Baptist Missionary Society*, 1881; *United Presbyterian Church Missionary Record* 6 (1876–77). The Quakers, for instance, reported that members of their churches were expected to pay dues, one dollar a year for women, one dollar and fifty cents for men, but that many had "grown careless" in their obligations. The finance committee thus decided to send out letters, which had the surprising result of many paid balances and even tithing among a few members. See M.S. Hinckle, Report of the Friends Jamaica Mission, 1919, JA 5/8/4/536.
51. For instance, according to the Methodist pastor, Bunting, in 1867 there was much poverty, sickness and "hard life" which had caused church receipts to fall: "As we have travelled from place to place, throughout the parish we have been pleased to witness the apparent cheerfulness of the people in their straitened circumstances, and the noble manner in which many of them bear up against poverty, with its vexations and temptations." Rev. H. Bunting, Ocho Rios, *Wesleyan Methodist Magazine*, November 1867, Methodist Church Papers, JA 5/60/2/13.

The crisis was exacerbated by extremely low wages and a duty of 12.5 per cent on imported goods, which reportedly caused the price of clothing to increase by as much as 300 per cent, so that the effective duty was more like 37.5 per cent (Thomas Geddes to Elijah Hoole, 22 March 1865, MMS Box 199). Furthermore, the municipal authorities of the city and suburbs prohibited the keeping of small stock, thereby cutting off the resources of many poor people. Wesleyan Methodist Missionary Society, Report of the Religious State of the Societies, Synod minutes, 31 December 1867, MMS Box 160–1867; see also Report of the Religious State of the Societies, Synod minutes, 26 January 1866, MMS Box 160–1866. This was further exacerbated in 1881 by a new house tax and an additional penny per acre on land. The small settlers found this burdensome, and again, the church contributions were affected. Annual Report of the Moravian Church in Jamaica, 1890, JA 5/5.

52. *86th Report of the Baptist Missionary Society*, 1877, and *89th Report of the Baptist Missionary Society*, 1881.

53. See J.W. Rowbotham (Brown's Town) to E. Hoole, 7 November 1866, MMS Box 200 [microfiche 2408]; Alex W. Geddes, Pastoral Address, 1902, JA 5/6/7/2; and *Periodical Accounts,* June 1879, Moravian Church Papers, JA 5/5. Some also did not pay because prior to conversion they led "careless, improvident lives" and therefore had little, while others were newly married and could not give much from their slender means; see *Periodical Accounts,* June 1879. The age of the members of the congregation was also a factor, since the parents of those church members who were sixteen years did not think they were old enough to pay church subscriptions and so resisted the practice; *Reports and Statistics of the Moravian Church in Jamaica,* 1903, JA 5/5. The idea that the chronically poor should support their churches and ministers or else be labelled "careless" must have struck those who resisted as an attempt to make them pay for salvation (which they had been told had already been "paid for by the blood of the Lamb"). That they should support the pastor and his family, who were almost always in better material circumstances than themselves, must have seemed unfair to many and incongruous to others when they were told that the ministers were looking after *them*.

54. In the late 1860s the conditions in Lititz and Bethabara were so bad that many had to buy water or walk six to eight miles for water. Church attendance was affected because the people did not have water to wash clothes for church. *Periodical Accounts,* June 1866, June 1868, 1870, Moravian Church Papers, JA 5/5; John Atkins to George Osborn, 25 April 1865, MMS Box 199 [microfiche 2397]; and Thomas H. Clark, 24 February 1865, LMS 9/2. In Manchester in 1897 things were extremely bad; all the water had to be brought from Kingston in puncheons by the railway and sold to the people at halfpence per gallon; Report by Colonial Committee, Reports on the Schemes of the Church of Scotland, 1897, Church of Scotland Papers, New College Library, Edinburgh. See also *Reports and Statistics of the Moravian Church in Jamaica,* 1890 and 1907, JA 5/5; and Reports on the Schemes of the Church of Scotland, 1905–6, 1912, 1918. Still the people gave generously when they could; see, for instance, *78th Report of the Baptist Missionary*

Society, 1870; and Report by Colonial Committee, Reports on the Schemes of the Church of Scotland, 1903.
55. This was especially true in the face of disaster: droughts, floods, cyclones, and hurricanes in 1880, 1903, 1912, 1915–17. *73rd Report of the Baptist Missionary Society*, 1865, 14–15; Rev. W.M. Webb, Stewart Town, *Missionary Herald*, 1 April 1876; and the *87th* (1879), *89th* (1881), *92nd* (1884), *112th* (1904), *113th* (1905), and *121st* (1913) *Reports of the Baptist Missionary Society*. Of course, that the material deprivation of the people should be recognized primarily through their inability to "sustain their ministers in their usual comfort" simply confirmed what many suspected: that their condition (temporal and spiritual) was a secondary consideration to whether or not they could pay their way to heaven.
56. "There are idle persons about who live by plundering their neighbour's grounds", Report (Keynsham and Siloah), 1862–64, USPG E14.
57. *Periodical Accounts*, June 1881, Moravian Church Papers, JA 5/5. Penny savings banks were started in Jamaica in 1881 and spread rapidly all over the island, largely through the sponsorship of the churches. By 1886 nearly £20,000 had been deposited in these banks by ordinary Jamaicans. In addition, many people also had deposits in the Government Savings Bank. See *Colonial Standard*, 25 April 1881; *Daily Gleaner*, 29 November 1884 and 13 September 1886; and Report of the Government Savings Bank, *Department Reports*, 1883–84, UWI Mona Library.
58. *Life and Work* 26 (1904): 260.
59. Stewart, *Religion*, 177–78; *United Presbyterian Church Missionary Record* 7 (1878–79); *Daily Gleaner*, 18 May 1886 and 23 June 1900. The rates for persons above five years old who could *read only* were as follows: 1861, 31.3 per cent; 1871, 35 per cent; 1881, 45.7 per cent; 1891, 52.5 per cent; 1911, 62.3 per cent; and 1921, 60.9 per cent. See decennial censuses, 1861–1921, UWI Mona Library.
60. According to the proprietor of Aston Gardner and Co., "Every country person whether he or she be able to read or no, wants to have a bible." Likewise, Arthur Hylton listed Bibles among his top-selling books; *Daily Gleaner*, 30 May 1894.
61. *United Presbyterian Church Missionary Record* 6 (1876–77).
62. *Daily Gleaner*, 24 November 1886 and 9 December 1891.
63. *Periodical Accounts*, June 1881, Moravian Church Papers, JA 5/5; Henry Bunting (Ocho Rios) to Osborn, 22 November 1866, MMS Box 200 [microfiche 2408]; and William J. Lewis (Mount Fletcher) to General Secretaries, 20 May 1868, MMS Box 200 [microfiche 2417].
64. *Falmouth Post*, 1 June 1860 and 10 January 1865; *Morning Journal*, 22 and 28 November 1872.
65. *Colonial Standard*, 20 August 1888. At the Mount Olivet Church (Presbyterian) the children of the congregation raised £25 for the mission in Africa. Anne G. Johnstone, "A Visit to Jamaica", *Zenana Mission Quarterly*, n.s., 1 (1894), United Presbyterian Church of Scotland Papers, New College Library, Edinburgh.

66. There was a rally at the Kirk in Falmouth which featured an address on training the young to work. Christian Endeavour groups were formed at the Episcopal and Baptist churches in Cave Valley, St Ann. *Jamaica Times,* 11 July 1903; also *Reports and Statistics of the Moravian Church in Jamaica,* 1906, JA 5/5; Report by Colonial Committee, Reports on the Schemes of the Church of Scotland, 1904, New College Library.
67. *Daily Gleaner,* 7 April 1903; and *Reports and Statistics,* 1906.
68. Thomas Hosking (Montego Bay) to W.B. Boyce, 8 January 1873, MMS Box 201 [microfiche 2443]; and Wesleyan Methodist Missionary Society, Report of the Religious State of the Societies, Synod minutes, 29 January 1875, MMS Box 163–1874.
69. The "deserving poor" were generally "respectable" persons, morally erect Christians, who may even have been elites at one stage of their lives, but had for one reason or another (the death of a husband, lost fortune and so forth) fallen on hard times. The other category was the "chronic poor", of working-class origin, who were generally considered dissolute, vulgar, and potential whores and criminals.
70. *Daily Gleaner,* 9 August 1900.
71. For instance, on Christmas Eve 1886 the Kingston Catholic Association of Ladies of Charity put on a public exhibit of "Nascimiento" at St Martin's Church, East and Hanover Streets, with proceeds in aid of relieving the condition of the poor of Kingston. The same association celebrated the feast of St Joseph, their patron saint, with a dinner for the poor at the St Joseph schoolroom which was decorated with banners of many designs, wreaths of flowers and branches of beautiful creepers and plants. The event provided dessert, cakes and fruit and lively music, among other treats. The exhibition was described as a "wonderful sight, displaying great talent and taste in all its details . . . it is by no means a religious ceremony, but a representation, aided by artistic accompaniments, of the great event which took place in Bethlehem". *Daily Gleaner,* 28 December 1886. See also *Daily Gleaner,* 21 May 1886, 21 December 1886, 6 May 1887. For charitable work by the St Vincent de Paul Society, see *Daily Gleaner,* 12 and 20 July 1904; *Jamaica Times,* 28 January 1905 and 17 July 1909.
72. *Periodical Accounts,* June 1881, Moravian Church Papers, JA 5/5; Curate Aubrey Spencer Danell, Friendship, St Elizabeth, 31 March 1864, USPG D28a; and *United Presbyterian Church Missionary Record,* n.s., 1 (1880).
73. *Jamaica Times,* 6 May 1916. There was also a "rally of the 12 tribes" in the Methodist Free Church, Hanover Street, on Sunday 25 February 1917; *Daily Gleaner,* 23 February 1917.
74. See, for instance, *Falmouth Post,* 28 February 1865, 5 September 1871; *Morning Journal,* 22 July 1870, 18 August 1870, 7 August 1875; *Colonial Standard,* 19 November 1884, 4 December 1894; *Daily Gleaner,* 5 November 1889, 17 December

1889, 5 October 1912, 2 January 1919 and 27 December 1919; *Jamaica Post,* 28 May 1898; *Jamaica Times,* 8 April 1899, 9 September 1899, 30 May 1908, 24 April 1910, and 21 October 1911. Also H.S. Cambridge, report from Dober, *Reports and Statistics of the Moravian Church in Jamaica,* 1905, JA 5/5; and St Paul's Presbyterian Church, minutes of meetings, 5 April 1910 and 3 July 1911, NLJ MST 2089. Cricket in particular was promoted by the churches. Several clergymen played cricket in Jamaica; they also encouraged the formation of cricket clubs in the churches and schools for which they were responsible. See Brian L. Moore and Michele A. Johnson, "Challenging the 'Civilizing Mission': Cricket as a Field of Socio-cultural Contestation in Jamaica, 1865–1920", in *In the Shadow of the Plantation: Caribbean History and Legacy,* ed. Alvin Thompson (Kingston: Ian Randle, 2002). An Anglican clergyman, Rev. M.C. Clare, was also responsible for popularizing football in Jamaica after 1891.

75. Mabel Blanche Caffin, *A Jamaica Outing* (Boston: Sharwood Publishing, 1899), n.p. Many of the people in the rural areas lived in the mountainous districts and had to walk for miles (as far as eight miles) on Sunday mornings to attend church; Caleb Reynolds (Port Antonio) to W.M. Punshon, 29 March 1878, MMS Box 201 [microfiche 2470]. Church members in the Chapelton area walked four to six miles to church, crossing several rivers during rainy season; Reports: West Indies, 1865–66, LMS 1. According to the Presbyterians, Jamaica was "the oldest and one of the most successful of all [their] mission fields. . . . Fifty years ago it was a land of the most debasing idolatry. Mr Baillie [missionary stationed at Mount Olivet] showed the audience one of the ugly idols which the natives worshipped. But through the labours of the missionaries sent out by other Churches as well as our own, the dark land of Jamaica has become a land of light. The island now abounds in churches and schools, the Sabbath day is as well observed as in Scotland and the members of the churches will compare favourably with the members of Christian churches in Scotland as regards their liberality and missionary spirit." Report, Presbyterian Missionary meeting in Edinburgh, excerpt from *Jamaica Witness,* 3 January 1882, Church of England Scrapbook No. 1, NLJ MST 51. See also *Report of the Wesleyan Methodist Missionary Society,* 1906, SOAS.

76. Henry M.H. Cox (Black River) to W.M. Punshon, 23 March 1878, MMS Box 201 [microfiche 2470]. Even the Maroons, a group with strong African cultural elements, were largely brought into the fold. In 1876 those in St Elizabeth formally joined the Church of Scotland: "Nothing could exceed the gratitude of the people . . . to have a minister of the church of Scotland settled among them. The step they took of joining our Church was to many of them a very anxious one; and they were plied in all directions, especially the Maroons of Accompong, with every argument to shake them. . . . [But] the appearance of Mr Radcliffe

with the new minister was an event. It created quite an enthusiasm among them, and there was a long train of members of both congregations to meet us and escort us up the last three hours' journey or more." Even the Maroon congregations at Accompong and Retirement were described as "steadfast" in the Christian faith. Report by Colonial Committee, Reports on the Schemes of the Church of Scotland, 1876–77, 1882, 1885–86, New College Library. Also Albert H. Aguilar (Linstead) to General Secretaries, 6 July 1868, MMS Box 200 [microfiche 2418]; Henry Bunting (Beechamville) to General Secretaries, 6 November 1871, MMS Box 200 [microfiche 2439]; and E.C. Gardiner, Hope Bay, n.d. [1959], Jamaica Memories, JA 7/12/94.

77. Wesleyan Methodist Missionary Society, Report of the Religious State of the Societies, Synod minutes, 27 January 1871, MMS Box 161–1871.

78. Carlile, "38 years", 202–3. "Amid all . . . the gospel is certainly making progress, the ordinances of religion are appreciated by the body of the people, and there is a hope that many of the evils which we have to contend against will be generally made to give way. Civilization is generally slow in progress, especially among a people little more, as we would say, than a third of a century, removed from abject slavery." *United Presbyterian Church Missionary Record* 7 (1878–79). See also Wesleyan Methodist Missionary Society, Report of the Religious State of the Societies, Synod minutes, 26 January 1872, MMS Box 162–1871; S. Goodyer (Black River) to W.B. Boyce, 22 May 1875, MMS Box 201 [microfiche 2458]; *United Presbyterian Church Missionary Record*, n.s., 2 (1881); J.W. Rowbotham (Brown's Town) to General Secretaries, 23 May 1866, MMS Box 200 [microfiche 2405]; and Stephen Sutton (Ocho Rios) to General Secretaries, 7 August 1869, MMS Box 200 [microfiche 2427].

79. "Our Mission to Millions: The Work of the United Free Church in the Kingdoms Beyond the Seas. The Oldest Field – Jamaica", *United Free Church of Scotland Missionary Record* 16 (1916): 18–19.

80. *Church of Scotland Home and Foreign Missionary Record*, n.s., 20 (1895); and Stewart, *Religion*, 171.

81. Report of the Friends Jamaica Mission (Prospect), 1917–21, JA 5/8/4/570.

82. Wesleyan Methodist Missionary Society, Report of the Religious State of the Societies, Synod minutes, 26 January 1872, MMS Box 162–1871.

83. According to the Friends, in Port Antonio "[i]n place of the regulation three fights a week it has changed to one in three or more weeks". Mary E. White, Report of the Friends Jamaica Mission (Port Antonio), June 1915, JA 5/8/2/421.

84. See Brian L. Moore and Michele A. Johnson, "Celebrating Christmas in Jamaica, 1865–1920: From Creole Carnival to 'Civilized' Convention", in *Jamaica in Slavery and Freedom: History, Heritage and Culture*, ed. Kathleen E.A. Monteith and Glen Richards (Kingston: University of the West Indies Press, 2002), 144–78.

85. Excerpt from *Daily Gleaner,* n.d., in *Friends Jamaica Mission* 8, no. 5 (May 1900), JA 5/8/78/5955.
86. Leonard Tucker, "Baptist Work in Jamaica: The Centenary", *Missionary Herald* 96 (1914); T.S. Penny, "Fair Jamaica", *Missionary Herald* 92 (1910).
87. A. George Burkley, Kingston, n.d. [1959], Jamaica Memories, JA 7/12/195.
88. Report from Mizpah, Annual Report of the Moravian Church in Jamaica, 1890, JA 5/5. Among many, said missionary observers, there was "family discord – strife among brethren – evil speaking – a tenacious clinging to old superstitious beliefs and practices – and a sad lack of patient continuance in well-doing, a tendency to be led away into fanaticism. No wonder under such circumstances, many even those who did run well for a season, fell away, virtually renounced Christ, and by their walk declared that they no longer needed Him!" Report from Bethabara, *Reports and Statistics of the Moravian Church in Jamaica,* 1908, JA 5/5. The majority of missionaries acknowledged that "there still remain much ignorance, superstition . . . fanaticism" and indifference. *83rd Report of the Baptist Missionary Society,* 1875, 21, 95; United Free Church of Scotland, First Report on Foreign Missions, 1901, Papers of the United Free Church of Scotland, New College Library, Edinburgh.
89. "Address by Rev. James Watson, Chairman, 19 January 1887", LMS 3; and *United Presbyterian Church Missionary Record* 7 (1878–79).
90. Austin-Broos notes that marriage and the sanctification of sexuality have been a touchstone of what she calls "the politics of moral orders" in Jamaica, "that consumed the early missionaries and led many in the colonial middle class to see in Zion Revivalists merely an echo of the missionaries' 'African immoralist' ". Austin-Broos, *Jamaica Genesis,* 11.
91. Anonymous, Baptist Missionary Society, Box WI/18, n.d., Angus Library, Regent's Park College, Oxford University.
92. *Periodical Accounts,* June 1867, Moravian Church Papers, JA 5/5; and *Reports and Statistics of the Moravian Church in Jamaica,* 1900, 1901 and 1905, JA 5/5; *Daily Gleaner,* 26 November 1889.
93. *Reports and Statistics,* 1901.
94. United Free Church of Scotland, Report from Cedar Valley, in the Second Report on Foreign Missions, 1902, New College Library. The Springfield Moravian Church statistics, for instance, showed that over a forty-three-year period (1877–1919 inclusive), 178 members were suspended or excluded from membership for various offences including rape, carnal abuse and bestiality; stealing; obeah, revivalism and superstition; bad behaviour, fighting, drunkenness and other misdemeanours; and carelessness. But by far the largest number, 624 or 77.8 per cent of the total, were suspended or excluded for "fornication and living in sin". See Moravian Church, Register of Exclusions and Suspensions: Springfield, St Elizabeth, 1877–1919, JA 5/5 B/2.

95. The marriages at Bethabara and Patrick Town were mostly among the residents of Patrick Town; *Periodical Accounts,* June 1879, Moravian Church Papers, JA 5/5. In 1899, as a result of a series of evangelistic meetings at Mount Carey, twenty-four couples published their banns of marriage and declared their intention to stop "living in sin". *Jamaica Times,* 13 May 1899.
96. *United Presbyterian Church Missionary Record* 7 (1878–79).
97. *Periodical Accounts,* 1870, Moravian Church Papers, JA 5/5.
98. Ibid.; also *Reports and Statistics of the Moravian Church in Jamaica,* 1905 and 1913, JA 5/5. Also Mary E. White, Report of the Friends Jamaica Mission (Port Antonio), June 1915, JA 5/8/2/421.
99. 83rd Report of the Baptist Missionary Society, 1875, 21, 95; also Report of the Friends Jamaica Mission (Prospect, Burlington and Fellowship), 1922–23, JA 5/8/55/3862; Report on Foreign Missions 1911, United Free Church of Scotland Missionary Record 12 (1912).
100. "Drop-pan" (*chefa* in Guyana, *whe-whe* in Trinidad) was ostensibly simple, involving thirty-six Chinese characters painted on pieces of paper, each representing persons, animals, birds, reptiles or sea creatures (for example, an old man or woman, a horse, cow, sheep, dog, alligator, scorpion and so forth). One of these characters was selected at random and placed in a pan (or box, basket or cloth) which was then suspended from the roof by a string and pulley. The object was to wager on which character was in the pan. Each bet, for which a ticket was given, cost 3d. At an appointed time the pan was solemnly lowered ("dropped"), opened, the paper unrolled and shown to all. Seven shillings (twenty-eight times the value of the bet) was paid out on each winning ticket. In order to ensure the viability of these lotteries, they were officially recognized by the "Chinese Court", and every morning the amount of the bank was registered at the Chinese Club (located in the same compound as the temple), which served as insurer in the last resort. Furthermore, in no case was more money received from bettors than the bank could pay. "Our Chinese Colony", *Jamaica Times,* 26 November 1898; "Sunday at the Chinese Lottery", *Daily Gleaner,* 1 July 1897. Drop-pan became immensely popular among Jamaicans during the 1890s, and large crowds of working-class people congregated at the lottery shops day and night in a state of "lotto mania". According to the *Jamaica Post,* by 1896 there were twenty-five or more Chinese gambling dens flourishing in Kingston, frequented and mainly supported "by the lower orders – that large class of young men and women who have no visible means of support"; *Jamaica Post,* 11 April 1896.
101. See Law 25 of 1898. Also Annual Report of the Moravian Church in Jamaica, 1890, JA 5/5; and *Report of the Wesleyan Methodist Missionary Society,* 1912, SOAS.
102. *Reports and Statistics of the Moravian Church in Jamaica,* 1906, JA 5/5; "Annual Report of Jamaica Baptist Union for 1862", *Baptist Missionary Society Committees 1793–1914,* microfilm reel 18, Western Sub-Committee Minute Books; and M.S.

Hinckle, Report of the Friends Jamaica Mission (Amity Hall), 1918, JA 5/8/4/521.
103. M.S. Hinckle, Report of the Friends Jamaica Mission, 1919, JA 5/8/4/536.
104. From the 1890s, it became clear that Sunday was beginning to lose its exclusively religious significance for Jamaicans of all classes. By 1914 people were engaging in a wide range of leisure pursuits on Sunday, much to the chagrin of the churches, who urged the authorities, for instance, to stop the trains from operating and to close the cinemas. But even the conservative *Gleaner* was not sympathetic: "The idea of the special 'sanctity' of the Lord's Day has largely disappeared from the minds of the people; and, particularly in the region of amusements, both outdoor and indoor, there has been an increasing tendency to disregard old-time restrictions on freedom of action, and to utilise the weekly Day of Rest as also a day of healthy recreation." *Daily Gleaner*, 28 April 1914. The paper further argued that Jamaica no longer had a church establishment, "and it would not be safe for anyone to contend that Sunday must strictly be regarded as a religious institution on the ground that this is essentially a religious country. Not a third of the people are attached, either as members, as adherents or as Sunday scholars, to the several churches. . . . Nominally the people are Christian: effectively a good many of them are. But Christian peoples differ in their opinion as to how Sunday should be observed." *Daily Gleaner*, 30 April 1914. See also M.S. Hinckle, Report of the Friends Jamaica Mission (Amity Hall), 1918, JA 5/8/4/521; and H. Alma Swift, Report of the Friends Jamaica Mission, 1919, JA 5/8/4/533.
105. *Periodical Accounts*, June 1866, June 1868, September 1869, 1870, June 1870 and June 1871, Moravian Church Papers, JA 5/5. In addition, said the United Brethren, "From what we have seen, parental authority and home-training, as well as a good example on the part of the parents, are more or less wanting."
106. The same concerns were raised when work on a new road in the Beaufort and Cairn Curran area was carried out by "unprincipled men from distant places"; *Reports and Statistics of the Moravian Church in Jamaica*, 1917, 1920, JA 5/5. Also Edwin J. Southall, Pastoral Address, Methodist Church Western Annual Conference Journal, 1893, JA 5/6/7/2; Livingstone, *Black Jamaica*, 159.
107. "A Brief Report of the Societies in the Jamaica District 1907", Appendix A in: Minutes of the District Synod of the Jamaica District 1908, JA 5/6/7/2. Also United Free Church of Scotland, Report on Foreign Missions, 1910, New College Library. This was also the case in other circumstances of great dislocation, such as droughts and floods. According to the Baptists in 1882, at times of upheaval there was a "strengthening and deepening of the spiritual life of the church members; while a large number of both young and old have given up drink, fine dress, shop debts, and such things, and an earnest, quiet spirit of devotedness and zeal have been called into exercise". *90th Report of the Baptist Missionary Society*, 1882. In time, however, the "moral gains" would be eroded and the missionaries would resort to their usual litany of complaint and despair about the spiritual condition

of the Jamaican flock. This was the case in Hector's River in 1876, where the mission field was described as "good" but seasonal, since as soon as the ginger crop was over the migrants left and among them "the most horrible and flagrant wickedness prevailed". *84th Report of the Baptist Missionary Society,* 1876. This trend was also noted in the reports for the United Brethren mission stations at Aberdeen, Fairfield, New Eden, Irwin Hall, Lititz, Bethabara, Springfield, New Bethlehem, New Fulneck, New Hope/Salem, Nazareth, Beaufort, New Carmel, Bethany, Cheapside/Mizpah and Broadleaf. *Periodical Accounts,* June 1865, Moravian Church Papers, JA 5/5.

108. Father J. Woollett, Belmont, Santa Cruz Mountains, 26 November 1863, Jamaica Mission Letters, Society of Jesus, English Province, London; and *Daily Gleaner,* 5, 12 and 19 January 1901, 2 February 1901.
109. (Mizpah and Broadleaf) *Periodical Accounts,* 1870, Moravian Church Papers, JA 5/5.
110. According to the missionary at Fairfield, "too often the law of charity has been broken. Grievous words stir up anger and too many are ready to seek redress at law for supposed or real wrongs done to them"; Annual Reports of the Moravian Church in Jamaica, 1890 and 1900, JA 5/5.
111. Wesleyan Methodist Missionary Society, Report of the Religious State of the Societies, Synod minutes, 26 January 1872, MMS Box 162–1871; *United Presbyterian Church Missionary Record* 7 (1876–77); *Daily Gleaner,* 24 November 1886.
112. Gilbert Farr to Samuel Haworth, 4 August 1892, Friends Jamaica Mission letters, JA 5/8/10/932. The term "coolie" was applied to immigrant workers, more particularly of Indian origin, who were imported to work on the plantations after emancipation. It soon became a racist term of opprobrium.
113. Henry Bunting (Gordon Town) to W.B. Boyce, 7 May 1873, MMS Box 201 [microfiche 2447].
114. Reports: West Indies, 1868, LMS 1; *Reports of the London Missionary Society,* 1865–66, LMS; "Our Mission to Millions: The Work of the United Free Church in the Kingdoms Beyond the Seas. The Oldest Field – Jamaica", *United Free Church of Scotland Missionary Record* 16 (1916): 17.
115. Austin-Broos, *Jamaica Genesis,* 71.
116. Joseph S. Prior (Savanna-la-Mar) to M.C. Osborn, 8 April 1882, MMS Box 202 [microfiche 2486–87].
117. Report of the Friends Jamaica Mission, 1920, JA 5/8/4/555; and United Free Church of Scotland, Report on Foreign Missions, 1911, New College Library. Much earlier, Baptist missionary P. Williams had visited Alligator Pond, where he found "carousing and all kinds of debauchery [which] has long been the order of the day". Although he had been well received, he doubted if his visits would have any permanent effect. *81st Report of the Baptist Missionary Society,* 1873.

Chapter 7

1. See Ruby King, "Education in the British Caribbean: The Legacy of the Nineteenth Century", in *Educational Reform in the Commonwealth Caribbean*, ed. Errol Miller (Washington, D.C.: Organization of American States, 1999), 31 and 33. King labels elementary education "lower class education" because it was specifically geared to that class as distinct from the middle and upper classes. Education facilities for the different social classes were separate, but not equal.
2. In 1849 the Trinidadian government began to promote a policy of nondenominational education by establishing a system of secular government schools, financed out of local ward rates. This was in part designed to stymie the influence of the powerful Roman Catholic Church, which was promoting French religious culture. An educational law of 1870 formally introduced a dual system of education, whereby both government and denominational schools were funded out of the central budget. Thus, although religion was a key part of the syllabus of the church schools, it played a much smaller role in the curriculum of the government schools. But as Campbell notes, there was nevertheless consensus among clerics and government officials in Trinidad that religious instruction was a necessity for the moral education and character training of children. See Carl Campbell, *The Young Colonials: A Social History of Education in Trinidad and Tobago, 1834–1939* (Kingston: The Press, University of the West Indies, 1996), 5–40, 222.
3. See Ruby King, "Elementary Education in Early Twentieth-Century Jamaica", *Caribbean Journal of Education* 16, no. 3 (1989): 225. According to King's table 1, apart from twenty-two schools labelled "non-denominational", all the others (87 per cent of the total) were church schools.
4. *Wesleyan Methodist Magazine* (1871); and editions of the *Handbook of Jamaica* for 1883–99 (Kingston: n.p.), sections on elementary education.
5. This was a grant of £30,000 per year made by the British government in 1834, to the missionary bodies who were involved in the religious and moral "upliftment" of the slaves and to the Mico Trust, for the education of the freed people. It was subsequently to be progressively reduced each year over another five-year period until it ceased altogether.
6. Carlile, "38 years", 202–3; and *United Presbyterian Church Foreign Mission Report* 1894.
7. Campbell, *Young Colonials*, 222–23.
8. *The Sixth Report of the Jamaican Church of England Home and Foreign Missionary Society, 1866–67* (Kingston: George Henderson, 1868).
9. *United Presbyterian Church Missionary Record* 6 (1876–77).
10. *United Presbyterian Church Missionary Record* 7 (1878–79).

11. Campbell, *Young Colonials*, 223.
12. Moore and Johnson, *Land We Live In*, 90, 109.
13. Swettenham to Elgin, 23 April 1906, no. 217, JA 1B/5/18 vol. 61.
14. "The management of the schools is almost everywhere in the hands of the ministers." T.S. Penny, J.P., "Fair Jamaica: The Day and Sunday Schools", *Missionary Herald* 92 (1910); and *United Presbyterian Church Missionary Record* 7 (1878–79).
15. Swettenham to Elgin, 1 April 1905, no. 144, JA 1B/5/17 vol. 60; and *Daily Gleaner*, 23 May 1907.
16. Campbell, *Young Colonials*, 273–74.
17. King, "Elementary Education", 237–38. The same programme was conducted in other West Indian colonies. Thus Aviston Downes notes that in Barbados, for instance, children at the primary level were also expected to learn "obedience, honesty, industry, temperance, purity, good behaviour at home, in school, on the highway, in places of worship, avoiding evil and profane speaking, confession of wrong, forgiveness, truthfulness in word and deed, [and] cleanliness". Downes, "Barbados", 151.
18. See *Handbook of Jamaica* (1883), 128; *Missionary Herald* (September 1875): 169; and *Daily Gleaner*, 28 February 1885.
19. *Daily Gleaner*, 28 February 1885.
20. *Missionary Herald* (September 1875): 169.
21. See Brian L. Moore, *Race, Power and Social Segmentation in Colonial Society: Guyana after Slavery, 1838–1891* (New York: Gordon and Breach, 1987), 198; Brereton, *Race Relations*, 64–69; Campbell, *Young Colonials*, 87–88; and Downes, "Barbados", 151 ff.
22. See appendix 5, table 2.
23. Ibid.
24. See Brereton, *Race Relations*, 68; Campbell, *Young Colonials*, 88; and Moore, *Race*, 198. Also *United Presbyterian Church Missionary Record*, n.s., 2 (1881).
25. Immediately after the abolition of school fees, attendance at schools increased by as much as 9 per cent in 1893–94 and was higher than in any other British Caribbean colony and not far below the average in England and Wales; see Superintending Inspector of Schools, *Department Reports*, 1893–94, UWI Mona Library. But by the following year, it had deceased significantly; see appendix 5, table 2 and Superintending Inspector of Schools, *Department Reports*, 1894–95). Parents still did not like to send their children to school "unless they can make them look respectable, and unless they can give them a respectable luncheon to take with them"; Superintending Inspector of Schools, *Department Reports*, 1895–96. This was exacerbated by the hard times that many people endured in the period, and was especially marked in the 1915–16 period when a hurricane added to the difficulties of the war situation. According to Inspector Deerr, "The poorer

peasants whose ground crops were badly damaged, if not destroyed, and who in consequence have to procure their food from the shops cannot provide their children with food and decent clothes to go to school. I think that the latter consideration is regarded as the more important." Education Department, *Department Reports*, 1915–19.

26. *Friends Jamaica Mission* 7, no. 6 (June 1899).
27. *Periodical Accounts,* June 1867, Moravian Church Papers, JA 5/5. There was a belief that "as soon as a boy can earn a few pence or use the cutlass and hoe, he is taken away from school". This Inspector Deerr saw as "sheer disregard on the parents' part for the children's welfare". Inspector Mornan agreed, claiming that "many are kept away by their parents often for no adequate reason, while in other cases during the gathering of the pimento and other crops the attendance drops sometimes to 50 per cent or less than what it is at other times"; Education Department, *Department Reports*, 1915–16. This was also the experience of L.U. Williams, who claimed that at the turn of the twentieth century, "Few people send their children to school thay [sic] send them to work at the estate for 3d to 4½ a day." L.U. Williams, n.d. [1959], Jamaica Memories, JA 7/12/288. See also Moore, *Race*, 198; Brereton, *Race Relations*, 68–69; Campbell, *Young Colonials*, 88; and Downes, "Barbados", 151 ff.
28. In 1880 and 1881 school attendance was affected by both a hurricane and a drought; see Elementary Education, *Department Reports*, 1880–81. Time and again, there were references to the obstacles posed to school attendance by the influences of floods, droughts, hurricanes (cyclones) and the economic hardships that they caused. See Elementary Education, *Department Reports*, 1882–83; H.W. Norman, Governor's Report, *Department Reports*, 1882–83; and Education Department, *Department Reports*, 1908–9.
29. Elementary Education, *Department Reports*, 1882–83, UWI Mona Library. See also H.W. Norman, Governor's Report, *Department Reports*, 1882–83. In 1918–19 the attendance was severely affected by an epidemic of influenza; for the months of November and December 1918 there was a drop of 90 per cent in some schools, and several were ordered to be closed by the health authorities; Education Department, *Department Reports*, 1918–19. In 1920–21, over twenty schools were closed by the health authorities due to outbreaks of alastrim and measles; Education Department, *Department Reports*, 1920–21.
30. Elementary Education, *Department Reports*, 1880–81; *Jamaica Advocate*, 20 November 1897.
31. Elementary Education, *Department Reports*, 1882–83. In 1916 the inspector of schools remarked, "The ignorance of some teachers of the contents of their own school time-table would have been ludicrous, if it had not been distressing"; Education Department, *Department Reports*, 1915–16.
32. *Friends Jamaica Mission* 7, no. 6 (June 1899).

33. *Jamaica Advocate*, 20 November 1897.
34. Ibid.; see also *Periodical Accounts*, June 1867, Moravian Church Papers, JA 5/5.
35. Attorney General's Report, enclosed in Blake to Knutsford, 26 May 1892, no. 177, CO 137/549. Law 31 of 1892, sec. 23 stipulated that from 1 January 1894, no child fifteen years or older would be retained in any public elementary school; and from 1 January 1895, the maximum age would be lowered to fourteen. Law 9 of 1893, sec. 7 reinforced these age limits. Law 23 of 1899, sec. 5 fixed the age range at six to fourteen years. Hemming to Chamberlain, 28 July 1899, JA 1B/5/18 vol. 51.
36. By the 1894 law this provision was to end on 31 December 1897, but it was extended. In reality, the period when children up to sixteen years old were allowed to remain in school was extended by Laws 37 of 1897 and 23 of 1899 to 31 December 1900. Further attempts to clarify the issue of age in the schools were made by Law 6 of 1909 (see also Report of the Attorney General, 1 June 1909, enclosed in P.C. Cork to Crewe, 8 July 1909, no. 351, CO 137/672), Law 2 of 1911, and Law 35 of 1914, which stipulated that children could remain in school until age fifteen to comply with a requirement that they had eight years of elementary education.
37. Gilbert Farr (Seaside) to Susie J. Martin, 24 February 1893, Friends Jamaica Mission letters, JA 5/8/10/958. The Quakers further asserted that children who were excluded from school at fourteen were either obliged to stay at home or else their parents had to pay "at least US$200 per year" to send them to a boarding school which one or another of the denominations had established; *Friends Jamaica Mission* 7, no. 4 (April 1899), JA 5/8/78/5919. See Swettenham to Secretary of State for the Colonies, 14 September 1905, no. 453, JA 1B/5/18 vol. 60, for a different perspective.
38. Report of the Inspector of Schools, 20 April 1880, enclosed in Musgrave to Kimberley, 16 June 1880, no. 138, CO 137/495. While in broad concurrence with the inspector that compulsory education would fail, Inspector Savage thought that a limited experiment could be attempted in towns or estates, or in Kingston. See Kimberley to Musgrave, 11 September 1880, no. 104, CO 137/495. In Trinidad the cost of compulsory education also delayed its implementation until 1921. See Brereton, *Race Relations*, 68; and Campbell, *Young Colonials*, 46.
39. Rev. T.H. Clark said that several other London Missionary Society ministers agreed with his opposition to the proposition because they objected to the education tax that was proposed for its support. He argued that the amount paid over to education from the general revenue was "very considerable" and that the tax would remove the sense of personal responsibility for children's welfare from parents, and in turn would encourage the children to feel free from obligation to their parents. Further, the proposed education tax, which deceived the people into thinking that they had nothing to pay for education (while it compelled them to pay a tax), was unfair to those who had no children or whose children were

already educated, and made every teacher a government official, thereby changing the relationship of teachers with the (church) managers and parents. Clark said that he believed that the concept was wrong in principle and that the advantages of education would commend themselves to the people in time. Further, said Clarke, parents required the assistance of children in provision grounds and to help them pick their coffee, and they ought to be able to command this service but could not if compulsory education became law. See T.H. Clarke to R.W. Thompson, 25 June 1881, LMS 11/5.

40. Attorney General's Report, enclosed in Blake to Knutsford, 26 May 1892, no. 177, CO 137/549. Section 18 of Law 31 of 1892 made provision for the introduction of compulsory education from 1 January 1895 in areas to be designated; and section 19 imposed a tax on houses to pay for it. In 1893 a special law (Law 34) was passed to implement this school tax.

41. This argument was based on the opinion of the inspector general of police that it would cost £5,000 a year to enforce attendance. See Hemming to Chamberlain, 11 May 1899, no. 245, JA 1B/5/18 vol. 51.

42. Governor Musgrave expressed doubts as to whether any compulsory or "penal" system would work: "History does not show that penal laws in matters of faith and conscience have been very efficacious; and with an ignorant negro population education is almost a matter of faith and conscience, which I think they should be led and encouraged not driven." He added that to punish parents before a magistrate for the nonattendance of their children would be, among the black population, to run the serious risk of creating "very injurious disgust" at what was increasingly regarded as a privilege. And, after all, the "children may be forced to school, but they cannot be made to learn". See Musgrave to Kimberley, 10 October 1880, no. 283, CO 137/496.

43. Stewart, *Religion*, 177–78.

44. Minutes of I. Hales, 22 November 1880, and Edward Wingfield, 22 November 1880, appended to no. 283, CO 137/496. Also Kimberley to Musgrave, 11 September 1880, no. 104, CO 137/495.

45. *Daily Gleaner*, 27 October 1896.

46. Moore, *Race*, 198, 200; and Gillian Sutherland, *Policy-Making in Elementary Education, 1870–1895* (London: Oxford University Press, 1973).

47. See Deliverance of Synod of the Presbyterian Church of Jamaica, 27 February 1906, enclosed in Swettenham to Elgin, 21 March 1906, no. 128, CO 137/650; also Cork to Crewe, 8 July 1909, no. 351, CO 137/672. By Law 3 of 1910, sec. 12, the town and district school boards were empowered to enforce compulsory attendance at schools (see also Law 35 of 1914, sec. 12; Attorney General's Report, 14 May 1910, enclosed in Olivier to Crewe, 25 May 1910, no. 183, CO 137/678; and Law 35 of 1912). After the 1892 law was passed, guilty parents were liable to fines of 5s. for the first offence, 10s. for the second, and £1 for subsequent offences. If

they failed to pay, they could be imprisoned for up to seven days; see Law 31, sec. 18. These penalties were retained unchanged when compulsory education was finally introduced; see Laws 6 of 1913 and 35 of 1914; also Olivier to Harcourt, 30 September 1912, no. 350, CO 137/693. Law 6 of 1913, sec. 5 assumed, until proven to the contrary, that: (1) the incorrigible truant did not attend school, and (2) he or she was not exempt from attending school. Law 35 of 1914, sec. 36 stated that a certificate from the secretary of a school board "shall be conclusive evidence in any Court of Law as to any child having been declared an incorrigible truant"; while by section 25(4), the parent or guardian of a child who failed to attend school was "guilty of an offence". See also Attorney General's Report, 11 July 1913, enclosed in Manning to Harcourt, 9 August 1913, no. 298, CO 137/698. In Trinidad, although school fees were abolished in 1902, compulsory education was delayed to 1921 (even later than Jamaica), and restricted to the urban areas. Campbell, *Young Colonials*, 46; Brereton, *Race Relations*, 68.

48. So concerned was the governor with the operation of the law that he asked the director of education to report every six months on the number of whippings carried out under the law. See Manning to Harcourt, 9 August 1913, no. 298, JA 1B/5/18 vol. 68. Also Report of the Director of Education, 2 February 1914, enclosed in Manning to Harcourt, 11 February 1914, no. 47, CO 137/702; and Report of the Director of Education, 14 September 1914, enclosed in Manning to Harcourt, 23 September 1914, no. 416, CO 137/704.

49. Minutes of C.T. Davis, 30 August 1913, George Grindle, 2 September 1913, and C.A. Harris, 6 September 1913, all enclosed in Manning to Harcourt, 9 August 1913, no. 298, CO 137/698. T.C. Macnaghten was quite concerned about the whipping of the children with a "strap", and asked the Colonial Office Library to research in order to find some precedent for this action, as the "instrument" of the strap was new to him (minute of T.C. Macnaghten, 3 September 1913, no. 298, CO 137/698). The librarian assured him that "tamarind switches" had previously been used in Jamaica, and that a number of the other West Indian colonies prescribed the use of a light rod or cane (minute of the Colonial Office Librarian, n.d.). Also minute of George Grindle, 2 September 1913, appended to Manning to Harcourt, 9 August 1913, no. 298, CO 137/698.

50. As in Trinidad, "The main subjects of the ordinary primary school were reading, writing, arithmetic, English grammar, and geography. . . . A few schools did some singing and history; many did needlework; but the foundation of the curriculum involved the three R's." Campbell, *Young Colonials*, 89.

51. *Semi-Weekly Gleaner*, 17 May 1875.

52. (George Hicks, Assistant Inspector of Schools) Elementary Education, *Department Reports*, 1882–83, UWI Mona Library; see also Superintending Inspector of Schools, *Department Reports*, 1893–94.

53. The report mentioned two small publications which sought to answer the need

(one by Rev. W. Simms, MA, headmaster of the Jamaica High School, and the other by Messrs Fyfe and Sinclair, "well-known as the Compilers of the invaluable Jamaica Handbook"). Elementary Education, *Department Reports*, 1882–83.
54. King, "Elementary Education", 237–38.
55. *Colonial Standard*, 5 December 1893. See also Moore and Johnson, *Land We Live In*. There was almost universal agreement among the social elites throughout the island that industrial education was needed to teach the labouring population more scientific methods of agriculture. That they should remain manual labourers was not in doubt. Campbell notes that in Trinidad too the core subjects were always "bookish", following the metropolitan model, and he observes that the churches as school providers "were not organized to teach practical subjects; at any rate, everyone who was friendly to education agreed that basic literacy and character training . . . were the top priority for primary schools". Campbell, *Young Colonials*, 89.
56. *Colonial Standard*, 5 December 1893; *Jamaica Times*, 17 December 1898. The other aims included the provision of a thorough foundation in primary education; training the eye and hand; and forming accurate ideas of shape, distance and time.
57. Harry Goulbourne, *Teachers, Education and Politics in Jamaica, 1892–1972* (London: Macmillan Caribbean, 1988), 139–41. Among the founding members of the Jamaica Union of Teachers were Lt Col L.G. Gruchy (white, co-principal of Mico), Rev. James Balfour, Rev. William Gillies (white Anglican priest, co-principal of Mico), T.B. Stephenson (black teacher), A.L. Walcott, Robert Lindsay (Mico tutor), J.A. Mason (black, of Unity), A.J. Smith, W.F. Bailey (black, of Mount Olivet), E.N. Peart (of Bethany), Canon A.N. Thompson (black), W.H. Plant (brown, headmaster of Titchfield High School), Robert Bailey, J.C. Taylor, C.R. Taylor, W.E. Watson, W.W. Williams, C.A. Rennals, H.T. Cambridge (of Ritchies), W.C. Leslie and Miss Anna Cogle. L.G. Cruchy was elected as the first president. Further "respectability" was given to the union by its appointment of the following elite persons as honorary members: Enos Nuttall (white, Lord Bishop of Jamaica), Canon William Simms (white, headmaster of Jamaica College), Rev. S. Negus (white, principal of Shortwood College), Rev. Dr Jon Reinke (white), Hon Philip Stern (Jewish lawyer and mayor of Kingston), Hon. Rev. Henry Clarke (white), Rev. H. Kilburn (white), Rev. H. Seymour Isaacs (Jewish), J. DeCordova (white, proprietor of the *Gleaner*), William Morrison (white, headmaster of the Collegiate School), and Dr W. Clarke Murray (white, headmaster of York Castle School). Among the objects of the union were: to represent the interests of teachers and to improve the quality of education; and to establish provident, benevolent and annuity funds for members. Its agenda included the abolition of the payment-by-results system; compulsory education; the establishment of infant schools; raising the school-leaving age to fifteen; and the introduction of a pension scheme for teachers. For

a contemporary internal perspective, see W.F. Bailey, *History of the Jamaica Union of Teachers* (Kingston: Gleaner Co., 1937).
58. King, "Elementary Education", 239–40.
59. *Colonial Standard*, 5 December 1893.
60. *Daily Gleaner*, 11 December 1889.
61. Ibid.; and Education Department, *Department Reports*, 1907–8, UWI Mona Library.
62. *Daily Gleaner*, 18 October 1894; and Education Department, *Department Reports*, 1907–8.
63. Superintending Inspector of Schools, *Department Reports*, 1893–94; and Stewart, *Religion*, 171.
64. Elementary Education, *Department Reports*, 1880–81; and Campbell, *Young Colonials*, 222–23.
65. Superintending Inspector of Schools, *Department Reports*, 1893–94.
66. Superintending Inspector of Schools, *Department Reports*, 1892–93.
67. Elementary Education, *Department Reports*, 1880–81 and 1883–84.
68. Campbell, *Young Colonials*, 89.
69. Elementary Education, *Department Reports*, 1879–80, 1880–81, 1882–83, 1883–84.
70. Report from Eden, *Reports and Statistics of the Moravian Church in Jamaica*, 1913, JA 5/5.
71. *Daily Gleaner*, 11 December 1889. See also Campbell, *Young Colonials*, 222–23; Downes, "Barbados", 149–50; and Higginbotham, *Righteous Discontent*, 35.
72. See editions of the *Handbook of Jamaica* for 1883–1920, sections on education. St Joseph's College was run by the Franciscan Sisters of the Convent of the Immaculate Conception.
73. This was first provided for under Law 31 of 1892, sec. 26(2).
74. *Handbook of Jamaica* (1883–1920); and Moore and Johnson, *Land We Live In*, 86.
75. Campbell, *Young Colonials*, 228. Higginbotham further notes that Spelman students also gathered in social purity meetings, Christian Endeavour societies, converts' meetings, and the Young Women's Christian Association with its missionary and temperance bands. She adds that although teacher training formed the core of Spelman's academic work, its goals were hardly secular, as the students were taught to function in the dual capacity of teacher and missionary. Indeed, the Baptists regarded the two roles as inseparable. The same could be said of the teacher training colleges in Jamaica. See Higginbotham, *Righteous Discontent*, 34–35 and 43.
76. Law 32 of 1892, sec. 2; and *Handbook of Jamaica* (1883), 340.
77. W.J. Gardner to Joseph Mullens, 25 May 1869 and 8 June 1869, LMS 9/6; and *Handbook of Jamaica* (1883), 349. By the early 1890s this school had split into the Kingston Collegiate School and the Church of England Grammar School. See *Handbook of Jamaica* (1893), 340–41.

78. The Kingston University School also offered adult classes for foreigners wishing to learn English, and the confidential translation of foreign correspondence (*Morning Journal*, 12 September 1871). It should be noted that although Ford claimed to be setting up a school for children of both sexes, the programme of instruction seemed to have only boys in mind. *Morning Journal*, 25 August 1873.
79. Gardner to Mullens, 25 May 1869 and 8 June 1869, LMS 9/6. The Church of Scotland's Collegiate School was started by Rev. John Radcliffe. The Jesuit school (St George's) which catered to people of the same class and income bracket in Kingston had over one hundred pupils by June 1869. See also *Handbook of Jamaica* (1883), 348; and *Daily Gleaner*, 2 June 1877.
80. Wesleyan Methodist Missionary Society to George Sargeant, 28 December 1874, Methodist Church Papers, JA 5/6/10/3.
81. Andrew Kesson (principal, York Castle) to General Secretary, 21 September 1876, MMS Box 201 [microfiche 2464]. Kesson reported that the theological institution had three students in 1876, while in the high school, although arrangements had been made for twelve to sixteen pupils, there were thirty-nine boys being instructed. The pupils varied in age from eight to sixteen or seventeen years, and their work ranged from the basics to the matriculation examination of London University. The principal was pleased that the school's financial position was quite stable and that the annual expenditure, including teachers' salaries, was covered. There was, however, a need for more staff, to tackle areas which had either too few instructors or none at all. It was proposed that the headmaster be assisted by a classical and mathematics teacher, an English teacher and a "Native Teacher", and that provisions should be made for French, Spanish, music and drawing. See also the *Daily Gleaner*, 29 July 1885; *Handbook of Jamaica* (1920), 352.
82. Stanley, *History*, 85, 89, 99, 104–5, 243–46. Along with the theological college, Calabar had a normal day (elementary) school which offered reading, writing, arithmetic, writing from dictation, geography and scripture history. That was closed in 1891. The Baptist Missionary Society, however, continued to support Calabar financially after 1892. See also *Daily Gleaner*, 24 May 1884; *Handbook of Jamaica* (1913–1920).
83. This Beckford and Smith charity was comprised of monies bequeathed by Peter Beckford of Spanish Town in 1735, and Francis Smith, custos of St Catherine, in 1830; both had requested that their bequests should be used to establish free schools for the poorer classes. By Law 30 of 1869 the two schools were merged; *Handbook of Jamaica* (1883), 340.
84. King, "Education in the British Caribbean", 31–32.
85. Potsdam Boys' and Hampton Girls' Schools were established using funds from the estates of Robert Hugh Munro of St Elizabeth, bequeathed in 1797, and Caleb Dickenson, his nephew, for the purpose of educating poor children in the parish. All of these schools had been endowed by bequests from wealthy Jamaicans who

stipulated that admission should be free and open to poor Jamaican children; *Handbook of Jamaica* (1883–1920).

86. Attorney General's Report, 17 May 1892, enclosed in Blake to Knutsford, 26 May 1892, no. 178, CO 137/549; and *Handbook of Jamaica* (1913), 328.

87. The school moved first to temporary premises at Barbican in St Andrew, and thence to its new permanent home at Hope. The new premises, featuring buildings constructed in Gothic style and a cricket lawn, were opened by Governor Henry Norman with all the pomp and pageantry thought appropriate for the establishment of such an elite state institution. In 1885 the school had twenty- three boys on the Jamaica High School Foundation, ten boys on the Drax Foundation (with preference for residents of St Ann) and thirteen boys on the Open Foundation, "open to boys in the remaining parishes". These scholarships were only to be awarded to the children of parents "unable to pay the cost of a liberal education for their children"; *Daily Gleaner*, 10 and 11 July 1885. For similar schools in other Caribbean colonies, see Moore, *Cultural Power*, 58, 78; Brereton, *Race Relations*, 71–75; and Keith A.P. Sandiford, *Cricket Nurseries of Colonial Barbados: The Elite Schools, 1865–1966* (Kingston: The Press, University of the West Indies, 1998).

88. *Daily Gleaner*, 4 May 1912. From time to time during the war, the *Gleaner* printed the pictures and names of cadets who had died in battle.

89. Margaret Bryant, however, has argued that in reality the education of nineteenth-century English girls provided them with "snatches of disconnected information and the trivial or showy accomplishments which would educate them not for marriage but to get husbands". In short, it made them useless *wives*. Bryant, *The Unexpected Revolution* (London: University of London Institute of Education, 1979), 41. See also Sara Delamont, "The Contradictions in Ladies' Education", in *The Nineteenth-Century Woman,* ed. Sara Delamont and Lorna Duffin (London: Croom Helm, 1978), 135; and Burstyn, *Victorian Education.*

90. Amies, "Victorian Governess", 542. See also Dyhouse, *Girls Growing Up*; and Gorham, *Victorian Girl.*

91. *Morning Journal,* 8 June 1875; Campbell, *Young Colonials,* 237–38, 274; and King, "Education in the British Caribbean", 30.

92. This was probably a part of the St Mary's Convent complex established at Alpha Cottage in Kingston by the Sisters of Mercy. The girls who were admitted to the seminary were taught sewing, fancy work, shirt making, drawing, the pianoforte and the French language. *Daily Gleaner,* 29 September 1875.

93. S. Goodyer (Lucea) to M.C. Osborn, 22 May 1880, MMS Box 201 [microfiche 2478]. Part of the concern stemmed from the fact that some Catholic schools were taught almost exclusively by the Jesuits, who were men, and the "better class Christian parents" refused as a rule to send their girls to these schools beyond the age of nine or ten. As a consequence, there was a vast number of girls whose

parents could afford for them to have a suitable education to "fit them" for positions as wives of native teachers, or to become teachers themselves, but who were obliged to be content with the elementary education which they had received as children in the day schools. Sargeant thus called for an increased number of female teachers. See George Sargeant (Kingston) to W.M. Punshon, 9 June 1877, MMS Box 201 [microfiche 2467].

94. *Handbook of Jamaica* (1913), 361.
95. George Sargeant (Kingston) to W.M. Punshon, 9 June 1877, MMS Box 201 [microfiche 2467]; and Sargeant (Kingston) to M. Osborn, 9 September 1878, MMS Box 201 [microfiche 2471].
96. The Barbican High School's fees were: £35 per annum for girls under twelve years; £40 per annum for girls between twelve and fifteen years; £45 per annum for girls above fifteen years. Thomas Geddes (Kingston) to M.C. Osborn, 8 October 1881, MMS Box 202 [microfiche 2484]; Thomas Geddes (Kingston) to M.C. Osborn, 24 June 1885, MMS Box 202 [microfiche 2504]. See also *Handbook of Jamaica* (1883), 345.
97. *Handbook of Jamaica* (1913), 356–57.
98. Moore and Johnson, *Land We Live In*, 40.
99. Ibid., 39–43.
100. *Handbook of Jamaica* (1893), 341; (1920), 366.
101. *Handbook of Jamaica* (1883–1920).
102. *Daily Gleaner*, 6 March 1875.
103. The terms under which girls would be admitted to the institution were: for board, including an English education, £8 per quarter; washing cost £1 4s.; day pupils were asked to pay £1 10s.; music lessons on the pianoforte, £1 16s.; French, £1; drawing, £2; fancy work, £1. Each child was to be supplied with bedding, towels, spoons, knife and fork. A quarter's notice was to be given before a child was removed from the school, and each quarter's fees were to be paid in advance. *Daily Gleaner*, 25 September 1875.
104. This school catered primarily to girls in Kingston and after the move to the larger premises, it was expected that girls from the country would be able to live with the principal. *Daily Gleaner*, 29 April 1892.
105. "The Women of Jamaica – VII", *Daily Gleaner*, 9 April 1903; and M.M. Barrows, BA, "Our Elder Girls: Their Needs and How to Meet Them" (speech to the Mother's Union, June 1899), as printed in *Daily Gleaner*, 17 June 1899. M.M. Barrows was the headmistress of Wolmer's School. Also "High School for Girls", *Colonial Standard*, 22 December 1894.
106. Livingstone, *Black Jamaica*, 221.
107. Barrows, "Our Elder Girls".
108. "The Higher Education for Our Girls", *Daily Gleaner*, 30 March 1892; "The High School at Westwood", *Daily Gleaner*, 3 January 1910.

109. Manning to Harcourt, 9 June 1914, no. 235, CO 137/703; T. Gordon Somers, J. Kissock Braham and A.B. Lowe to the editor, *Daily Gleaner*, 3 March 1913; "Jamaica Scholarship for Girls and the Regulations Proposed for Governing It", *Daily Gleaner*, 3 March 1913; and "The Discussion Regarding the Girls' Scholarship", *Daily Gleaner*, 5 March 1913.
110. *Morning Journal*, 25 September 1873 and 15 October 1873.
111. *Handbook of Jamaica* (1883), 329.
112. *Handbook of Jamaica* (1893), 324–25, and (1920), 345–46.
113. *Handbook of Jamaica* (1893), 320.
114. *Handbook of Jamaica* (1920), 346–47.
115. *Handbook of Jamaica* (1883–1922). In 1922 the girls' scholarship was at last equalized in value with that of the boys, at £250 per annum.
116. *Handbook of Jamaica* (1893), 319.
117. *Handbook of Jamaica* (1913), 341–45.
118. Bryan, *Jamaican People*, 119; King, "Elementary Education", 237.
119. Campbell, *Young Colonials*, 267.

Chapter 8

1. Shepherd, *Transients*, 34. According to Walton Look Lai, the first batch of Chinese to be introduced into Jamaica arrived in 1854; Walton Look Lai, *The Chinese in the West Indies, 1806–1995: A Documentary History* (Kingston: The Press, University of the West Indies, 1998). Also decennial censuses 1881–1921, UWI Mona Library.
2. Warrand Carlile to the Scottish Missionary Society, 1884.
3. See Moore, *Cultural Power*, 207–8; and S. Vertovec, *Hindu Trinidad* (London: Macmillan Trinidad, 1992), 106. Brahmins or Brahmans form the highest social category in the hierarchical Hindu caste system. They are ascribed priestly responsibilities.
4. K.L. Gillion, *Fiji's Indian Migrants: A History to the End of Indenture in 1920* (Melbourne: Oxford University Press, 1962), 149.
5. David Brandon, *Some Amusing Reminiscences of a West Indian Barrister* (Kingston: Jamaica Times, 1911), 19; Marjorie Nelson, *How They Live: Sketches of Jamaican Life* (Kingston: W.I. Publishing, 1940), 16; *Jamaica Times*, 29 March 1902; and Martha Warren Beckwith, *The Hussay Festival in Jamaica* (Poughkeepsie: Vassar College, 1924), 7–8.
6. See Moore, *Cultural Power*, 237–38.
7. *Jamaica Times*, 26 November 1898.
8. W.A. Bell (St Dorothy), 7 February 1860, enclosed in Darling to Newcastle, 29 March 1860, no. 49, CO 137/349; Minute 2343, 28 June 1881, United Presbyterian

Church (UPC): Minutes of Foreign Mission Committee, 1881–82, United Presbyterian Church of Scotland Papers, New College, Edinburgh.

9. C.T. Boyd to General Secretaries, 20 December 1887, MMS Box 203 [microfiche 2510].

10. John Duff to Hoole, 23 December 1868, MMS Box 200 [microfiche 2422]; S. Goodyer to M.C. Osborn, 8 May 1878, and W. Westlake to M.C. Osborn, 28 July 1878, both MMS Box 201 [microfiche 2470]; Alfred Joyce to Joseph Mullens, 11 December 1871, LMS 10/2; Minute 1904, 6 September 1880, UPC: Minutes of Foreign Mission Committee, 1880–81; Minute 2343, 28 June 1881, UPC: Minutes of Foreign Mission Committee, 1881–82; and Rev. S.V. Robinson, Report, 5 July 1881, *Missionary Herald* (1 September 1881).

11. Minutes 1904, 6 September 1880, and 2017, 30 November 1880, in UPC: Minutes of Foreign Mission Committee, 1880–81; Minutes 3475, 26 June 1883, and 3525, 31 July 1883, UPC: Minutes of Foreign Mission Board, 1883–84; Minutes 4191, 29 July 1884, and 4339, *circa* August 1884, UPC: Minutes of Foreign Mission Committee, 1884–85; Minute 6132 (3), 25 October 1887, UPC: Minutes of Foreign Mission Board, 1887–88; and Robinson, Report, *Missionary Herald* (1 September 1881).

12. Letter of Henry B. Foster (Bath), 22 August 1860, in *Wesleyan Missionary Notices*, 3d ser., no. 70 (25 September 1860): 178. According to the Moravians, the Indians themselves used the language barrier as a reason for not attending church services. But it was also claimed that their singular focus on business – "they seem to have no thought for anything besides" – was another reason. Report of the Moravian Missions, *Periodical Accounts,* December 1881, Moravian Church Papers, JA 5/5; John Duff to Hoole, 23 December 1868, MMS Box 200 [microfiche 2422]; William Westlake to Osborn, 28 September 1878, MMS Box 201 [microfiche 2470]; Robinson, Report, *Missionary Herald* (1 September 1881); Sada F. Stanley, Report of the Friends Jamaica Mission (Annotto Bay), 30 September 1916, JA 5/8/2/436; Lora P. Arms, Report of the Friends Jamaica Mission, 1918, JA 5/8/55/3906.

13. Minute 544, 27 March 1894, UPC: Minutes of Foreign Mission Board, 1893–94; Rev. George McNeill, *United Free Church of Scotland; The Story of Our Missions; The West Indies* (Edinburgh: United Free Church, 1911), 55–56; and UPC *Report on Foreign Missions,* 1895; also *Daily Gleaner,* 5 August 1895.

14. Report on the East Indian Mission, Presbyterian Synod Minutes, 1901, NLJ MST 2089; Minute 2573, 27 July 1897, UPC: Minutes of Foreign Mission Board, 1897–98; also Minute 1792, 24 March 1896, UPC: Minutes of Foreign Mission Board, 1895–96.

15. "A Jamaica Friend", "Martha B. Croll", *Women's Missionary Magazine of the United Free Church of Scotland* 6 (1906): 237. It is puzzling that Verene Shepherd has made absolutely no mention of Martha Croll in her work, although Croll was

one of the principal Scottish missionaries, the only woman among them, and was mainly responsible for proselytizing Indian women for almost a decade. *Zenana* was the name given to the women's quarters in a Hindu home in India. No male stranger was allowed to enter it, not even to give medical attention. Because wives were required to move into the households of their husband's parents, their mothers-in-law ruled supreme in the zenanas. According to Martha Croll, they were generally "a dirty cheerless place, void of furniture, and always at the top of the house. The stair leading up to them is steep, dark, and narrow." The Presbyterians (and presumably other denominations as well) were obliged to send female missionaries in order to reach Indian women in the zenanas, hence the term "zenana missionaries". See Martha Croll, address at St Andrew's Kirk on 16 October 1899, as printed in the Daily Gleaner, 21 October 1899. Also reports of Mission to the East Indians, Presbyterian Synod Minutes, 1911 and 1912, NLJ MST 2089.

16. *Journal of the Synod of the Church of England in Jamaica*, 1892, 1895, 1896 and 1901, JA 5/1/11a; *Daily Gleaner*, 21 February 1894; *Jamaica Times*, 2 May 1908. The Anglicans also convened a special conference on missionary work among the Indians on 4–5 July 1917 at the Jamaica Church Theological College. The conference was attended by Bishop de Carteret, several leading canons, priests and catechists. *Daily Gleaner*, 7 July 1917.

17. Verene Shepherd made no use of the vast Quaker records in her book *Transients to Settlers*, despite the fact that they operated perhaps the largest mission to the Indian immigrants in Jamaica.

18. Mary E. White, Report of the Friends Jamaica Mission (Port Antonio), 1916–17, JA 5/8/2/442.

19. C.T. Boyd to General Secretary, 20 December 1887, MMS Box 203; Report of the Friends Jamaica Mission (Amity Hall), second quarter 1918, JA 5/8/4/522; Mary E. White, Report of the Friends Jamaica Mission, September 1919, JA 5/8/55/3838; Report of the Friends Jamaica Mission (Burlington), fourth quarter 1919, JA 5/8/4/542.

20. Methodist Church Western Annual Conference Journal, 1894, JA 5/6/7/2.

21. According to Shepherd, on one of his visits to rural churches Enos Nuttall interviewed a converted Indian at Lime Savannah; Shepherd, *Transients*, 155–56. For earlier conversions, see John Duff to Hoole, 23 December 1868, MMS Box 200 [microfiche 2422].

22. See S. Goodyer to M.C. Osborn, 8 May 1878, MMS Box 201 [microfiche 2470]; Report of the Moravian Missions, *Periodical Accounts*, December 1881, Moravian Church Papers, JA 5/5; Rev. John Stuart to the Convenor, 23 April 1884, in Church of Scotland, Report to the General Assembly by the Colonial Committee for 1883–84, Church of Scotland Papers, New College Library, Edinburgh. In 1885 the *Gleaner* reported that an Indian named Ramball presented a bell to the

Caymanas Presbyterian Church because the minister, Rev. James Robertson, cared for Ramball's sick wife. On her recovery Ramball reportedly felt that there were love and devotion in the Christian Church and thus was moved to make his donation; *Daily Gleaner*, 25 July 1885. Robertson was instrumental in establishing the Presbyterian Indian Mission at Ewing's Caymanas estate in 1894 (see UPC *Report on Foreign Missions* 1894).

23. UPC *Report on Foreign Missions* for 1894, 1896, 1897 and 1898; and the *Gleaner's* report (25 March 1899) of a meeting at the Susamachar East Indian Church, Caymanas estate. Also Superintendent's report on the East Indian Mission for 1904, Presbyterian Synod Minutes, 1905, NLJ MST 2089.

24. *Friends Jamaica Mission* 7, no. 12 (December 1899), JA 5/8/78/5937; [Mary White], *Friends Jamaica Mission* 8, no. 7 (July 1900), JA 5/8/78/5920; *Friends Jamaica Mission* 7, no. 10 (October 1899), JA 5/8/78/5935.

25. *United Free Church of Scotland Missionary Record* 2 (1902): 216. This view was also expressed by Rev. Dr Robson in a sermon at the Susamachar East Indian Church, Caymanas, in 1899 (see *Daily Gleaner*, 25 March 1899); Presbyterian Synod Minutes, 1906, NLJ MST 2089. Also Lora Arms, Report of the Friends Jamaica Mission (Fellowship), 1915–16, JA 5/8/2/432; Mary E. White, Report of the Friends Jamaica Mission (Port Antonio), 31 March 1916, JA 5/8/2/435; Alice I. Kennedy, Report of the Friends Jamaica Mission (Port Maria), 31 March 1917, JA 5/8/2/440; Report of the Friends Jamaica Mission, 1917–21, JA 5/8/4/570; Report of the Friends Jamaica Mission (Prospect, Port Antonio), 7 October 1920, JA 5/8/55/3859; and *United Free Church of Scotland Missionary Record* 21 (1921). From 1917 onwards the Presbyterians noted that in Vere, where they had hitherto encountered vigorous opposition from the Indians, "Prejudice is breaking down and the hope for the future is brighter" (1917); "The Catechist is well received everywhere he goes, and some are willing now to listen who would not do so before" (1918). See the Superintendent's reports on the Mission to the East Indians for 1917 and 1918, Presbyterian Synod Minutes, NLJ MST 2089.

26. Superintendent's report on the mission to the East Indians for 1910, Presbyterian Synod Minutes, NLJ MST 2089, 8; *United Free Church of Scotland Missionary Record* 1 (1901): 171–72; *United Free Church of Scotland Missionary Record* 10 (1910); United Free Church of Scotland, Second Report on Foreign Missions, 1901, New College, p. 81; *Daily Gleaner*, 24 January 1919; and report on the Mission to the East Indians, Presbyterian Synod Minutes, 1901, NLJ MST 2089, 21.

27. A full listing of all Indian catechists employed by the several Christian denominations in Jamaica is not available. However, the following have been identified (up to 1920). Presbyterian mission: Jonathan Rajkumar Lal[l], Simon Siboo, Samuel Kangaloo, F.W. Tar Mohammed [or Mahomed], Lal B[e/a/i]hari Singh, Pahar Singh, Phul Singh, Henry Kangaloo (son of Samuel), John Ghudar, Daniel Ch[a/e]dami, John Jones Subar[a]n, Mot[h]i, Joseph Shivdayal, Samuel

Joseph Rupert, Solomon M[u/a]ngaroo, James Adolphus, Henry Williams. A Miss Johnson served briefly as honorary catechist in Vere in 1913. Among those associated with the Quaker mission were Rufus King, Amir and Sehoda Williams, Terbaniesingh, D.D. Souri[e], J. Paraboosingh, U. and R. Amritt, Alexander Kura, R.C. Williams, Frederick Amir, J. Kissoon and Charles Byron. Two of the Anglican catechists were Suraj Parsad and Prabhn Singh Johnson.

28. United Free Church of Scotland, Sixth Report on Foreign Missions, 1905, 105; *Daily Gleaner*, 15 July 1904; Presbyterian Synod Minutes, 1913, NLJ MST 2089; Lora Arms, Reports of the Friends Jamaica Mission, March 1916, JA 5/8/2/435, and 31 March 1917, JA 5/8/2/440.

29. "Jamaica", in *United Presbyterian Church Missionary Record* 11 (1 November 1890): 334; *Friends Jamaica Mission* 8, no. 11 (November 1900), JA 5/8/78/5954. It was also argued that, in addition to persecution and ostracism, conversion might cause material loss for the Indian Christian; *Jamaica Times*, 10 July 1915. See also Superintendent's report for 1905 in Presbyterian Synod Minutes, 1906, NLJ MST 2089; and Report of the Friends Jamaica Mission (Fellowship), fourth quarter 1918, JA 5/8/4/526.

30. Census of 1921. In Trinidad Indians who had converted to Christianity amounted to 11.8 per cent in 1921. No statistics exist for Guyana before the 1931 census, but in that year the percentage of Indians who were Christians was just 6.9.

31. John Duff (Morant Bay) to General Secretaries, 23 October 1874, MMS Box 201 [microfiche 2455]; [Mary W. White], *Friends Jamaica Mission* 9, nos. 3 and 4 (March and April 1901).

32. Martha B. Croll, "A glance at my new field of labour", *Zenana Mission Quarterly*, n.s., 13 (1897): 297.

33. "Launching forth", *Women's Missionary Magazine of the United Free Church of Scotland* 1 (1901): 85–88; Mary E. White, *Friends Jamaica Mission* 9, no. 8 (August 1901), JA 5/8/78/5972.

34. Superintendent's report on the East Indian Mission for 1912, Presbyterian Synod Minutes, 1913, NLJ MST 2089; also Superintendent's report on the East Indian Mission for 1918, Minutes of the Synod, 1919, NLJ MST 2089; *Jamaica Times*, 2 May 1908; Report of the Friends Jamaica Mission (Prospect, Burlington and Fellowship), first quarter 1922, JA 5/8/55/3862. See also the 1923 report. The reality was quite different, for in fact greater inroads were made after 1920, resulting in about 80 per cent of the Indian population converting to Christianity by 1943.

35. Superintendent's report on the East Indian Mission for 1912, Presbyterian Synod Minutes, 1913, NLJ MST 2089.

36. *Jamaica Times*, 2 May 1908.

37. *Friends Jamaica Mission* 8, no. 10 (October 1900), JA 5/8/78/5928.

38. [H. Alma Swift], *Friends Jamaica Mission* 5, no. 4 (April 1897), JA 5/8/78/5916.

39. Report of the Friends Jamaica Mission, 1918, JA 5/8/4/528; Lora P. Arms, "Friends

in the Homeland", 9 April 1919, Friends Jamaica Mission, JA 5/8/55/3910; and Superintendent's report on the East Indian Missions for 1915, Presbyterian Synod Minutes, 1916, NLJ MST 2089.

40. See the Superintendent's reports on the East Indian Missions for 1911, 1913, 1914, 1918 and 1920, Presbyterian Synod Minutes, NLJ MST 2089; and "One of the East Indians" (Port Antonio, 5 March 1895) to the editor, *Daily Gleaner,* 13 March 1895.
41. Sada Stanley, *Friends Jamaica Mission* 9, no. 5 (May 1901), JA 5/8/78/5959.
42. *Friends Jamaica Mission* 5, no. 12 (December 1897).
43. *Jamaica Times,* 2 May 1908; Mary E. White, *Friends Jamaica Mission* 9, no. 8 (August 1901), JA 5/8/78/5972; *Friends Jamaica Mission* 9, no. 9 (September 1901), JA 5/8/78/5971; Superintendent's reports for 1911–14, Presbyterian Synod Minutes, NLJ MST 2089.
44. Sada F. Stanley, Report of the Friends Jamaica Mission (Annotto Bay), and Lora Harris, Report of the Friends Jamaica Mission (Port Antonio), both 1918, JA 5/8/4/521; and Superintendent's reports for 1920 and 1921, Presbyterian Synod Minutes, NLJ MST 2089.
45. By the 1940s it seems that about 80 per cent of the Indian population claimed to be Christians. See Shepherd, *Transients,* 166.
46. Sada F. Stanley, Report of the Friends Jamaica Mission (Annotto Bay), 31 March 1915, JA 5/8/2/416.
47. Jennie M. Hoover, annual personal report, Friends Jamaica Mission, 1915–16, JA 5/8/2/432.
48. See "School Manager" to the editor, *Daily Gleaner,* 4 May 1896; Immigration Department, *Department Reports,* 1892–93, 435 and 1910–11, 163, UWI Mona Library. Even though in 1894 the protector of immigrants, Philip Cork, thought that such race prejudice was on the wane because more Indians were sending their children to general elementary schools, he recognized that the high-caste Indians such as Brahmins and Rajputs would continue to object to such mixing. See also Report of the Protector of Immigrants, *Department Reports,* 1915–16; *Daily Gleaner,* 11 September 1916; Mary E. White to Mr Gregory, 3 May 1915, Friends Jamaica Mission letters, JA 5/8/84/6053; and Sada F. Stanley, Report of the Friends Jamaica Mission (Annotto Bay), 1914–15, JA 5/8/2/417.
49. Mary E. Allen, Report of the Friends Jamaica Mission, 30 June 1915, JA 5/8/2/418 and JA 5/8/2/426; Alice I. Kennedy, Report of the Friends Jamaica Mission (Trinity and Highgate), 30 June 1920, JA 5/8/55/3886; Jennie Hoover, Report of the Friends Jamaica Mission, 1915–16, JA 5/8/2/432. Also Immigration Department, *Department Reports,* 1880–81, 155.
50. Sada Stanley, Reports of the Friends Jamaica Mission, March 1915, JA 5/8/2/416. In April 1916 Kiffatula was fined in the police court for refusing to send his boy to school. For some months the Kingston School Board had been trying

unsuccessfully to persuade him to do so. He claimed that the boy was sickly (he was in fact being treated by a doctor for malarial fever), but the attendance officer stated that Kiffatula had openly refused to send the child to school, and that his action had influenced other Indians in Smith's Village. This suggests that there were many other Indian parents who simply refused to send their children to school. Kiffatula was fined 20s. or fourteen days' imprisonment for his intransigence. *Daily Gleaner*, 1 April 1916.

51. This reluctance to send their children to school was facilitated by the fact that education was not compulsory in Jamaica. See chapter 7, "Schooling for God and Empire".
52. Quoted in Immigration Department, *Department Reports*, 1880–81, UWI Mona Library, 155; "School Manager" to the editor, *Daily Gleaner*, 4 May 1896.
53. Mary E. White, Report of the Friends Jamaica Mission (Port Antonio), 1916–17, JA 5/8/2/442; Presbyterian Synod Minutes, 1904, 1909 and 1910, NLJ MST 2089; and Immigration Department, *Department Reports*, 1917–18, 166–67.
54. Immigration Department, *Department Reports*, 1910–11, 163 and 1915–16, 441. For details of the recommendations of the standing committee of the Board of Education, and the discussion of the board on this issue, see *Daily Gleaner*, 27 July 1910.
55. See Immigration Department, *Department Reports*, 1914–15 to 1920–21. The total number of Indian children between ages five and fifteen in 1921 was 5,470. The 20 per cent Indian attendance at school was, however, just 6.6 per cent below the national average. See census of 1921.
56. *Daily Gleaner*, 3 August 1912. This newspaper noted that the three special schools for Indians were doing well; while observing that the Indians were not yet in the habit of sending their children to school regularly, it noted also that they were beginning to see the benefits of schooling. See also Lora P. Arms, Report of the Friends Jamaica Mission (Fellowship), first quarter 1918, JA 5/8/55/3911; Lora Harris, Report of the Friends Jamaica Mission (Fellowship), 1918, JA 5/8/4/521; and Jennie Hoover, Report of the Friends Jamaica Mission, 1915–16, JA 5/8/2/432.
57. Lora Arms, annual personal report, Friends Jamaica Mission (Fellowship), 1918, JA 5/8/55/3906 and JA 5/8/4/523.
58. Mary E. Allen, Reports of the Friends Jamaica Mission (Happy Grove Industrial School, Orphanage Dept.), 1915–16, JA 5/8/2/416, JA 5/8/2/426, and JA 5/8/2/431.
59. C.J. Boyd (Morant Bay) to General Secretaries, 20 December 1887, MMS Box 203 [microfiche 2510].
60. *The Mission Field*, 1895. In less than ten years, roughly between 1865 and 1875, almost all the Chinese "converted" to Christianity in Guyana. Most became Anglicans. See Moore, *Cultural Power*, 278–81; and Moore, *Race*, 202.
61. Report by the Colonial Committee, in Reports on the Schemes of the Church of Scotland, 1900, New College Library; and *Jamaica Times*, 17 February 1912.

62. More than three hundred Chinese people turned out when the Roman Catholic section was opened in December 1911 by Bishop Collins; *Daily Gleaner*, 18 December 1911. Likewise there was "a large turn out of Chinese" for the Anglican dedication by Archbishop Nuttall in February 1912; *Daily Gleaner*, 14 February 1912.
63. *Jamaica Times*, 24 August 1918; *Daily Gleaner*, 25 February 1908. For a detailed analysis of the sociocultural integration of the Chinese into Jamaican society during the twentieth century, see Bryan, "Creolization", 173–272.
64. Brian L. Moore, "The Settlement of Chinese in Guyana in the Nineteenth Century", *Immigrants and Minorities* 7, no. 1 (March 1988): 41–56; reprinted in *After the Crossing: Immigrants and Minorities in Caribbean Creole Society*, ed. Howard Johnson (London: Frank Cass, 1988), 41–56.

Chapter 9

1. This was the case too in Australia where according to Ken Inglis, "She became in her own person an imperial symbol. . . . Unlike her predecessors in living memory, she was setting her people an example of respectable family life." Ken Inglis, *Australian Colonists: An Exploration of Social History, 1788–1870* (Melbourne: Melbourne University Press, 1974), 80.
2. Bradlow records this strong sense of the imperial idea and identification with the monarchy among British settlers in the Cape Colony; see Bradlow, "Colonial Elite", 391. Inglis likewise notes a similar loyalty to the crown among the settlers in Australia (see Inglis, *Australian Colonists*, 77–83); as does Moore for Guyana (see Moore, *Cultural Power*, 27); and Downes for Barbados (see Downes, "Barbados", 3).
3. Cannadine states that royal ceremony was not for the delight of the masses, but a group rite for the elite sections of society – the royal family, the aristocracy, and the church. The monarchy was thus not a symbol of national unity, but the head of the elite corporate groups. In fact celebrations focusing on national heroes such as Nelson and Wellington were far more popular than even coronations. The growth of the monarchy as a symbol of national and imperial unity was aided by Victoria's longevity, and the growth of a new empire, of a national press which made use of new photographic techniques, and of new modes of transportation (bicycles, tramcars, buses and cars). See David Cannadine, "The Context, Performance and Meaning of Ritual: The British Monarchy and the 'Invention of Tradition', *c.*1820–1977", in *The Invention of Tradition*, ed. Eric Hobsbawm and Terence Ranger (Cambridge: Cambridge University Press, 1983), 101–64.
4. For a detailed treatment of the Morant Bay Rebellion, see Hall, *Free Jamaica*, 245–53; Robotham, "*Notorious Riot*"; and Heuman, "*The Killing Time*".

5. Grant to Kimberley, 22 August 1871, no. 115, and encl., CO 137/458.
6. Robert Messias Bennett (Kensington, St Catherine) to the editor, *Daily Gleaner*, 21 February 1901.
7. See enclosures in Storks to Cardwell, 24 January 1866, no. 14; 29 January 1866, no. 17; 1 February 1866, no. 18; 7 February 1866, no. 22; 8 February 1866, no. 24; 19 February 1866, no. 29; 20 February 1866, nos. 33 and 34; and 22 February 1866, no. 39; all CO 137/399. Also 6 March 1866, no. 46, CO 137/401; 9 March 1866, nos. 50, 54, 58 and 60, CO 137/401; 23 March 1866, nos. 66 and 67, CO 137/402; and 4 May 1866, no. 104, CO 137/404.
8. During the 1860s and 1870s, whenever the mail packet arrived, local newspapers printed British news and some carried a special item entitled "The Royal Family", which provided news about their activities, birthdays, births, deaths, marriages, and so on.
9. See, for instance, the *Colonial Standard*, 10 November 1888.
10. See Thomas Richards, "The Image of Victoria in the Year of Jubilee", *Victorian Studies* 31, no. 1 (1987): 9–11. Richards notes that "Victoria was a domesticated monarch whose public image resided not in the trappings of the upper class but in the middle-class ethos of frugality, self-denial, hard work, and civic responsibility." In short, she lacked charisma.
11. The term "invented tradition" is used here in Hobsbawm's sense: "a set of practices, normally governed by overtly or tacitly accepted rules and of a ritual or symbolic nature, which seek to inculcate certain values and norms of behaviour by repetition, which automatically implies continuity with the past". Hobsbawm, "Introduction: Inventing Traditions", in *The Invention of Tradition*, ed. Eric Hobsbawm and Terence Ranger (Cambridge: Cambridge University Press, 1983), 1. Richards notes that while before Albert's death in 1861 royal events tended to be shabby and unrehearsed, for a time thereafter Victoria became a virtual recluse and such events became even more shabby. See Richards, "Image of Victoria", 8–9.
12. Moore, *Cultural Power*, 27.
13. See Inglis, *Australian Colonists*, 83–86; and Moore, *Cultural Power*, 27–28.
14. See *Falmouth Post*, 2 and 26 June 1865, 29 May 1866, 3 July 1866, 28 May 1867, 27 May 1870, 26 May 1871; *Morning Journal*, 26 May 1868, 29 May 1871; *Colonial Standard*, 18, 24, 25 and 26 May 1880, 17 May 1881, 23 and 27 May 1882, 20 June 1882, 22 and 26 May 1883, 29 May 1886, 27 May 1887, 22 and 25 May 1888, 25 and 30 May 1889, 27 and 29 May 1890, 26 May 1892; *Daily Gleaner*, 12 and 25 May 1877, 24 and 25 May 1881, 23 May 1883, 25 and 26 June 1884, 27 May 1885, 17, 22 and 31 May 1886, 26 May 1888, 28 and 31 May 1890, 21 May 1894, 12 November 1907; *Jamaica Times*, 27 May 1899, 3 June 1899, 9 and 16 November 1901, 20 December 1902, 14 November 1904, 18 November 1905, 17 November 1906, 2 November 1907, 14 November 1908. In 1884 the Queen's birthday celebrations

were postponed for a month because of the death of the Duke of Albany; *Colonial Standard*, 19 May 1884.

15. P.J. Rich, *Elixir of Empire* (1989; reprint, London: Regency, 1993), 18, 31, 73. Cannadine too notes the extensive use made of ritual in royal and imperial celebrations in late-nineteenth-century Britain itself. See Cannadine, "Context", 101–64. Bryan correctly points out that in Jamaica, the governor's dress served not only the ordinary functions of covering the body decently and fashionably, but "[a]s the representative of Her Majesty, the bureaucratic projection of Queen Victoria, his public attire was a symbolic representation of the might of the British empire". Bryan, *Jamaican People*, 86.

16. See *Morning Journal*, 30 June 1868, 30 June 1873; *Colonial Standard*, 28 and 29 June 1886, 20 June 1888, 20 and 28 June 1889, 21 June 1892.

17. See, for instance, Moore, *Cultural Power* for the celebrations in Guyana (p. 28). Richards, however, notes that certainly in the 1887 jubilee celebrations, Britons at home did not participate spontaneously out of a spirit of patriotic pride or loyalty to the royal family. Rather, most of the affair was driven by official and commercial advertising, and people had to pay for positions along the royal route to get a glimpse of the queen: "As consumers interested in remarkable sights, they turned out to 'see' the royalty just as they turned out to take in the industrial marvels of the Crystal Palace or the domestic marvels of the large London department stores." All that changed, however, by the diamond jubilee ten years later. By then the empire and its monarch had been successfully promoted by various institutions and the media, and Victoria's image was transformed into a grand imperial one. See Richards, "Image of Victoria", 11–13, 30–31.

18. Norman to Stanhope, 19 October 1886, no. 373, CO 137/528. The governor recognized this as "indicative of a warm feeling of loyalty to the British Crown and of strong attachment to our Most Gracious Sovereign" which actuated all classes, "none being . . . more thoroughly loyal than the great mass of the negro inhabitants".

19. Methodist Church Western Annual Conference Journal, 1887, JA 5/6/7/1; *Daily Gleaner*, 10 and 19 March 1887, 1 April 1887. In addition, several individuals wrote letters to the press making alternative proposals, such as to build docks at Kingston, a nursing hospital for pregnant women, a statue of the queen, an industrial orphan home and a sea wall in Kingston, among others.

20. Norman to Holland, 8 May 1887, no. 131, CO 137/530; *Colonial Standard*, 30 April 1887. During the two days of celebration the poor were regaled at several locations across the island. The *Gleaner* noted that many of these poor people were already grown men and women when Victoria acceded to the throne: "it was a touching sight to see the bent forms and wrinkled old faces gathered together in their 'Sunday best' to do honor to the celebration". See *Daily Gleaner*, 2, 5, 16, 22 July, and 6 August 1887; and *Colonial Standard*, 6 August 1887. Under the Poor Relief

system, two categories of poor were classified: the indoor poor were indigent people who had nowhere to live. They were offered accommodation in the parochial almshouses, clothing, two meals a day, and a weekly dole. The outdoor poor remained at their own homes but were provided with a weekly dole. See appendix 2 in Moore and Johnson, *"Squalid Kingston"*.

21. *Colonial Standard,* 30 May 1887; *Daily Gleaner,* 14 and 27 June 1887.
22. Bonfires were also lit in some places. *Daily Gleaner,* 27 June 1887, 2, 6, 8, 11, 16, 22 July 1887, and 6 August 1887; *Colonial Standard,* 7 July 1887.
23. *Colonial Standard,* 30 May 1887 and 21 June 1887; *Daily Gleaner,* 21 and 30 June 1887. The Royal Standard was also hoisted at Port Royal and at the garrison. The town hall was illuminated for the duration of the concert.
24. The sermon at the service at the parish church in Savanna-la-Mar was entitled "Fear God and Honor the King". See *Colonial Standard,* 7 July 1887; and *Daily Gleaner,* 30 June 1887.
25. *Daily Gleaner,* 2 July 1887.
26. The *Daily Gleaner,* 30 June 1887, described it as follows: "Upon the Altar was a most exquisite cross of red and white flowers which was of itself a perfect work of art. The standard gaseliers within the chancel were adorned with the graceful and delicate leaves of the Pointziana regia, and were bright with the scarlet blooms of that beautiful tree. In front of the lectern was a *Royal Crown* worked in flowers, all the jewels of the band, cross and archers being represented in flowers of brilliant hue. The hanging lamps were ornamented with drooping fringes of the 'old man's beard'. The seat reserved for His Excellency was marked at either end with a Royal Crown in scarlet and gold set upon wands.

    "The capitals of the pillars were most exquisitely decorated with living plants set in moss-covered boxes and following the angles of the abacus. The plants were principally ferns, caladiums, coleuses and crotons, and the mingling of the tender green of the delicate fronds with the harmonious colors of the ornamental-leaved plants produced an effect at once chaste and charming.

    "The font in the west-end was most beautifully adorned with stephanetis [*sic*], jessamine and moss, while the shaft was ornamented with blossoms of warmer hue."
27. The new stanzas were as follows (*Daily Gleaner,* 30 June 1887):

    Lift we both heart and voice,
    With one accord rejoice,
    On this glad day.
    On our Queen's Jubilee
    Bend we to God the knee,
    Singing right heartily,
    God save the Queen.

    God, hear our nation's prayer,
    Safe in Thy loving care,
    Guard Thou our Queen.
    Ruler of earth and sea,
    Through all eternity,
    In one blest Jubilee,
    Keep Thou our Queen.

28. Ibid.
29. *Daily Gleaner*, 30 May 1887, 2, 5, 6, 8, 11, 16, and 22 July 1887, and 6 October 1887; *Colonial Standard*, 30 May 1887 and 7 July 1887.
30. *Daily Gleaner*, 25 and 30 May 1887; *Colonial Standard*, 20 June 1887.
31. *Daily Gleaner*, 2 July 1887.
32. *Colonial Standard*, 10 and 25 June 1887, 7 and 9 July 1887; *Daily Gleaner*, 16 May 1887, 16 June 1887, 2, 5, 6, 8, 11, 16 and 22 July 1887. Marooned fireworks explode with a loud report.
33. *Daily Gleaner*, 2, 11 and 22 July 1887. See also the *Colonial Standard*, 7 July 1887.
34. *Colonial Standard*, 1, 9 and 30 June 1887, 8 July 1887; *Daily Gleaner*, 5 July 1887.
35. *Daily Gleaner*, 5 July 1897. See also Welter, "True Womanhood".
36. *Daily Gleaner*, 21 June 1897.
37. Blake to Chamberlain, 3 July 1897, no. 263, CO 137/582; *Daily Gleaner*, 25 June 1897 and 5 July 1897; and Ethel Scott, 12 November 1959, Jamaica Memories, JA 7/12/32.
38. Blake to Chamberlain, 3 July 1897, no. 263, CO 137/582; *Daily Gleaner*, 5 July 1897; *Jamaica Post*, 25 June 1897; Mrs Aubrey Baniff, 23 November 1959, Jamaica Memories, JA 7/12/157; Rev. R.A.L. Knight, n.d. [1959], Jamaica Memories, JA 7/12/36; Lawrence P. Peters, n.d. [1959], Jamaica Memories, JA 7/12/147; and A. McKay Smith, 28 November 1958, Jamaica Memories, JA 7/12/210.
39. *Jamaica Post*, 25 June 1897; *Daily Gleaner*, 5 July 1897; encl. in Blake to Chamberlain, 16 March 1897, no. 82, CO 137/580. Dennis Montague James, who was a former superintendent of parochial roads and works for St Elizabeth, also sent a poem to the Prince of Wales. See Blake to Chamberlain, 27 March 1897, no. 97, CO 137/580.
40. *Jamaica Times*, 2 February 1901.
41. *Jamaica Times*, 17 May 1902, 7 and 21 June 1902; *Daily Gleaner*, 12 July 1902. Jackass rope tobacco is strings of dried tobacco that look like coils of rope when put on display for sale. Khaki was used by the British military for field uniforms in the tropics. Perhaps in this instance, it signified the willingness of the people to enlist to defend their new king, country and empire, or at least to symbolize their loyalty to the monarchy.
42. *Jamaica Times*, 28 June 1902; *Daily Gleaner*, 12 July 1902.
43. *Daily Gleaner*, 12 July 1902. According to this paper, "Everybody in the crowd was in his or her 'Sunday best', an ill-clad person being a very rare exception. Ribbons and loyal favours were worn by nearly everybody." Besides, they were extremely well behaved: "Among the multitude who thronged the Race Course and the streets of Kingston during the past two days there was hardly a drunken man to be seen anywhere, and the popular excitement never ran into the excesses of disorder. The police had very little work to do on that score. . . . Although the streets were crowded and lively, any lady could walk along them in comfort and

enjoy the scene – so well-behaved were the people and so marked the absence of anything like riot or drunkenness."

44. According to the *Daily Gleaner,* 12 July 1902: "The Syrians participated in a very practical manner, several of their stores being nicely decorated, besides contributing largely to the Coronation Committee's funds. All the Syrians seemed to be having a most festive time.

    "The Cuban colony surpassed themselves. The stores of Messrs. B. & J.B. Machado and Loretto Chacon were beautifully decorated, and the former firm's car in the trades procession was splendidly got up.

    "Many of the Chinese took the holiday in their usual undemonstrative manner, taking in everything. Some of the younger ones were distinctly lively – for them."

45. The *Gleaner* published a special edition to commemorate Edward's coronation. The trooping of the colours is the military ceremony of mounting the guard in which the regimental colours (the flag) are received and paraded along the ranks of the soldiers. *Daily Gleaner,* 12 August 1902.

46. Ibid.

47. *Jamaica Times,* 24 June 1911; *Daily Gleaner,* 24 June 1911.

48. *Daily Gleaner,* 24 June 1911; also Butcher, *Peep,* 21–22. So, whereas there had been comments about the Chinese reticence to participate in things British in 1902, on this occasion they seemed more anxious to display evidence of their loyalty to their newly adopted land and empire. As foreigners and perhaps the ultimate "aliens", the Chinese did not want to be left out of this British moment, lest they be accused of not appreciating the hand of kindness that had been extended to them by "allowing" them to settle and even to succeed at their various enterprises.

49. "At Homes" were receptions held at the homes of the hosts where tea and other beverages and light snacks were served.

50. *Daily Gleaner,* 24 June 1911; Cork to Harcourt, 26 June 1911, no. 259, CO 137/685; Theophilus Wright, n.d. [1959], Jamaica Memories, JA 7/12/55; and Miss S.H. Brydson, n.d. [1959], Jamaica Memories, JA 7/12/10.

51. Darling to Newcastle, separate, 8 April 1861, CO 137/353.

52. *Daily Gleaner,* 13, 14, 16 and 18 February 1880, and 2 March 1880; *Colonial Standard,* 20 March 1880.

53. *Jamaica Post,* 6 May 1891. This was a time when elite Jamaicans were getting increasingly fed up with the crown colony administrations and wanted a greater say in running the colony. The constitutional changes of 1884, which introduced a minority of elected members (on a limited franchise) did not go far enough for some. See also the *Daily Gleaner,* 20 and 27 January 1891.

54. *Jamaica Times,* 22 March 1913.

55. *Jamaica Times,* 29 March 1913.

56. *Jamaica Times,* 24 January 1914 and 7 February 1914.

57. See minutes of meetings of the Kingston and St Andrew Committees, 6 and 13

August 1920, Colonial Secretariat Papers, JA 1B/5/76/3/365; *Daily Gleaner*, 15 September 1920.
58. This was also done, for example, in Guyana; Moore, *Cultural Power*, 28.
59. *Falmouth Post*, 20 March 1863; see also "A Spectator" to the editor, *Falmouth Post*, 16 March 1863; and Eyre to Newcastle, 26 May 1863, no. 149, CO 137/372. The Colonial Office admitted that the celebrations were testimony of the people's attachment to the queen's person and the throne. See Newcastle to Eyre, 10 July 1863, no. 636, CO 137/372.
60. *Daily Gleaner*, 6 and 7 July 1893.
61. See Darling to Newcastle, 23 January 1862, nos. 18 and 23; and 31 January 1862, nos. 29 and 30; and 1 February 1862, no. 31; all CO 137/364. Also Eyre to Newcastle, 1 May 1862, no. 13, CO 137/366; Eyre to Newcastle, 4 September 1862, no. 77, CO 137/367; *Falmouth Post*, 12 and 19 August 1862, 28 November 1862. In Spanish Town the proceeds of the first performance of a newly formed male Dramatic Association were presented as a subscription to the erection of a national monument for the prince consort.
62. *Daily Gleaner*, 31 March 1884, 3, 5, 7 and 8 April 1884, 15 and 21 January 1892.
63. *Jamaica Times*, 26 January 1901. See also the *Jamaica Advocate* of the same date. The *Daily Gleaner* of this date is missing from the microfilm in the National Library of Jamaica.
64. Henry Avis, 24 November 1959, Jamaica Memories, JA 7/12/57; and encl. in Hemming to Chamberlain, 31 August 1901, no. 529, CO 137/621.
65. *Daily Gleaner*, 21 February 1901.
66. Olivier to Chamberlain, 28 January 1901, no. 49, CO 137/617.
67. Hemming to Chamberlain, 5 February 1901, no. 59, CO 137/617; *Daily Gleaner*, 2 and 4 February 1901, 7, 9 and 21 May 1910; *Jamaica Times*, 14 May 1910.
68. Hemming to Chamberlain, 6 May 1901, no. 249, CO 137/619; 11 May 1901, no. 271, CO 137/619; and 28 May 1902, no. 293, CO 137/627; *Jamaica Times*, 27 April 1901 and 1 June 1901; *Daily Gleaner*, 10 May 1901 and 15 May 1903. The laws were Nos. 1 and 30 of 1902.
69. "Dark", perhaps, both in terms of colour and in terms of ignorance; the latter use is still current in Jamaican popular language.
70. *Daily Gleaner*, 8 May 1905. Arbor Day had been started in the United States in 1872 and spread to England and its white colonies, but was belatedly taken up in Jamaica in 1904.
71. *Daily Gleaner*, 26 May 1905, 27, 28, 29 and 31 May 1907, 25 May 1915; *Jamaica Times*, 27 May 1905 and 3 June 1905, 5 and 26 May 1906, 29 and 30 May 1909, 28 May 1910, 1 June 1912, 24 and 31 May 1913; also Alice I. Kennedy, Report of the Friends Jamaica Mission (Trinity and Highgate), 30 June 1920, JA 5/8/55/3886.
72. *Daily Gleaner*, 23 May 1907.
73. Olivier to Crewe, 24 June 1910, no. 234, CO 137/678, and appended Colonial

Office minutes; Olivier to Crewe, 26 September 1910, no. 389, JA 1B/5/18 vol. 65; and *Daily Gleaner,* 25 October 1910.
74. *Falmouth Post,* 28 March 1862; *Daily Gleaner,* 11 March 1889. Before the capital was moved to Kingston, governors had to travel by train to Spanish Town after docking at Kingston.
75. Musgrave to Carnarvon, 7 February 1878, no. 25, CO 137/486; *Morning Journal,* 8 November 1870; *Colonial Standard,* 20 April 1881, 20 and 22 December 1884, 27 April 1885, 14 May 1890; *Jamaica Times,* 14 January 1905, 7 November 1908, 16 January 1909, 8 March 1913.
76. Eyre to Cardwell, 10 September 1864, no. 256, CO 137/384.
77. Abigail B. Bakan, *Ideology and Class Conflict in Jamaica: The Politics of Rebellion* (Montreal: McGill–Queens University Press, 1990), 16–17.
78. See, for instance, Grant to Granville, 23 March 1870, no. 69, CO 137/448; and Olivier to Harcourt, 30 December 1911, no. 475, JA 1B/5/18 vol. 66. During the period under study, a statue was erected at the Parade in 1897 in memory of Victoria and several institutions were named after her, and a clock tower with the bust of Edward VII was erected in Half-Way Tree in 1913. *Daily Gleaner,* 27 February 1913; *Jamaica Times,* 5 April 1913. See also the *Daily Gleaner,* 26 February 1896.
79. Rich, *Elixir,* 18.
80. The *Gleaner* thought that an English warship was far superior to that of any other nation: "From truck to keelson, there is hardly a speck of dust to be seen. The brass and steel-work are made to shine until one can see one's face in them, the wonderful mechanism of the guns only equalled by the perfect condition which they are kept, while the human part of all this lethal machinery – the bluejackets and marines – is as spick-and-span as the rest." *Daily Gleaner,* 1 February 1899. See also the *Daily Gleaner,* 23 February 1894, 1 and 9 February 1899, 25 January 1900, 12 February 1901, 23 January 1904; *Daily Telegraph,* 16 January 1899 and 1 February 1899.
81. *Daily Gleaner,* 22 February 1895.
82. After the Morant Bay massacre Governor Eyre boasted: "The retribution has been so prompt and so terrible that is never likely to be forgotten"; Hall, *Free Jamaica,* 248. Memories of the brutality of the repression did, in fact, remain strong among the people. For instance, in 1871 one "negro" was heard to comment, "we no quite free yet. Look since dat time Gobernor Eyre been shot at all the people like a bud from tree, man life no come so? If we been really free like England people, dat no could ah come." *Morning Journal,* 5 June 1871.
83. J.G. Greenlee, "Imperial Studies and the Unity of the Empire", *Journal of Imperial and Commonwealth History* 7 (1979): 321.
84. *Jamaica Times,* 12 April 1913, 20 June 1914; *Daily Gleaner,* 18 January 1915. Education was the main thrust of the Victoria League. According to Greenlee, the

basic assumption of its programme of activities was that "the unity of the empire depended in the final analysis not on constitutional arrangements but on a deeply rooted mutual sympathy and sense of kinship among its peoples. Education, it was believed, would have to play a crucial role in tapping a large but latent reservoir of imperial sentiment before a political unification of the empire would be feasible." Greenlee, "Imperial Studies", 321–22.

85. *Daily Gleaner,* 1 and 19 February 1912, 26 March 1912.
86. *Jamaica Times,* 29 June 1901.
87. See *Jamaica Times,* 3 May 1902 and 18 October 1902.
88. *Daily Gleaner,* 13 December 1915.
89. David Whitelaw, "The Boy Scouts", *Life and Work* 32 (1910): 370–71; Baden-Powell visited Jamaica in January 1912. *Daily Gleaner,* 26 January 1912, 9 March 1912, 26 and 31 July 1913, 12 January 1914, 18 September 1915, 11 December 1915, 15 May 1916, 8 September 1920. Also H.M. Bell to the editor, *Daily Gleaner,* 7 January 1914.
90. *Daily Gleaner,* 10 July 1911.
91. *Jamaica Times,* 5 and 19 May 1906. Other objectives of the Imperial Order of the Daughters of the Empire were to provide an efficient organization by which prompt and united action could be taken when desired; to promote the study of the history of the empire; and to care for widows and orphans of British soldiers and sailors during war and peace, or in sickness, accident or reversals of fortune.
92. *Jamaica Times,* 7 April 1906. Its motto was: "What Britain holds she keeps; Jamaica second to none; they conquer who believe they can". The parent society was formed in England in 1900 and had links with the Victoria and Navy Leagues, and the Guild of Loyal Women of South Africa.
93. *Daily Gleaner,* 18 January 1900: "We learn that several householders are telling their servants about the facts of the war and encouraging them to subscribe amongst themselves to send a shilling to the fund for the relief of those absolutely dependent on the brave men who are fighting and falling for the Empire. This is a method of stimulating patriotism which may be commended to others." Concerts and other entertainments were also held to raise funds for the war effort. See *Jamaica Times,* 20 January 1900, 17 February 1900, 17 March 1900, 7 June 1902; Rev. A.L. Knight, n.d. [1959], Jamaica Memories, JA 7/12/36; and Ethel Scott, 12 November 1959, Jamaica Memories, JA 7/12/32.
94. *Daily Gleaner,* 9 and 13 August 1917, 1 February 1918. By 1917 there was a serious shortage of both saltfish and flour, as supplies from Canada dried up on account of German wartime attacks on commercial shipping. With tongue in cheek, the *Gleaner* warned that if no more saltfish came to Jamaica during the war, the people would realize what real sacrifice meant: "Our bitterness against the Germans will be increased a hundredfold, and men will go more gladly than ever

to the Contingent Camp with the resolute purpose of breaking the power of the Hun – acursed [*sic*] be he!"

95. Encl. in Manning to Harcourt, 9 October 1914, no. 435, CO 137/705.
96. Z.E. McFarlane to the editor, *Jamaica Times*, 17 October 1914; *Jamaica Times*, 3 October 1914. Rev. W. Graham of the Church of Scotland in Kingston observed, "A great wave of loyalty passed over the people." Some had gone to the front; others met twice a week for drill and held themselves ready at the governor's call for any emergency. Report by the Colonial Committee, Reports on the Schemes of the Church of Scotland, 1915, New College Library.
97. *Daily Gleaner*, 24 July 1915.
98. *Daily Gleaner*, 28 July 1915 and 14 October 1915. A second Flag Day was celebrated on 6 February 1918; *Daily Gleaner*, 6 February 1918.
99. *Daily Gleaner*, 17, 18, 19, and 20 October 1916, 16 April 1917. "Our Day" was again celebrated in 1917; see *Daily Gleaner*, 20 October 1917.
100. *Daily Gleaner*, 25 May 1917.
101. Probyn to Long, 11 December 1918, no. 458, JA 1B/5/18 vol. 73; *Daily Gleaner*, 21 July 1919.
102. Newton, *Glimpses*, 223–24; Etheline Nugent, November 1959, Jamaica Memories, JA 7/12/212; and Gladstone Burke, n.d. [1959], Jamaica Memories, JA 7/12/242.
103. Livingstone, *Black Jamaica*, 196.
104. "Climaticus" in *Jamaica Times*, 10 December 1904.
105. William Morrison, "Patriotism", *Jamaica Times*, 4 August 1900; *Daily Telegraph*, 26 May 1899 and 14 July 1899.
106. *Daily Telegraph*, 21 June 1899.
107. *Jamaica Times*, 25 April 1914, 5 September 1914 and 9 October 1914. The senior pledge of the league was as follows: "I promise to say no word nor do no deed which in my opinion will misrepresent Jamaica or Jamaicans; to promote the welfare of my country, and my countrymen by doing everything in my power to assist them to move onward; to discourage all forms of intemperance and other vices, and to endeavour specially to live a pure life in thought, word and deed." The junior pledge: "I promise to love Jamaica and Jamaicans, my country and my countrymen, and to do all I can to promote their welfare, and to show always a true spirit of patriotism; to endeavour to act always with true courtesy to those I meet; to be kind and gentle to all dumb animals. . . ."
108. *Handbook of Jamaica* (1921).
109. Bryan, *Jamaican People*, xii.
110. Patrick Bryan put it most succinctly: "For the rural black Jamaican it was Queen Victoria who had freed them; for middle and upper-class Jamaicans it was monarchy, armed with fleets and forts, which protected them from the people whom Victoria had 'freed'. The glitter of empire had a broad appeal . . . to reinforce a continued belief in white leadership." Bryan, *Jamaican People*, 18.

Chapter 10

1. Haiti was seen by most Europeans and white North Americans as a prime example of a barbarous "African" state in the New World. Ostracized by the "international community of civilized nations", Haiti's "savage" war of independence, followed by continuous political upheavals and killings, the demise of its once flourishing plantation economy and the consequent poverty and squalor of its people, and their widespread and "unchecked" belief and practice of Vodun, epitomized barbarism in the heart of the Western world. The British were determined that this should never happen in any of their West India colonies.
2. See Rudolf von Albertini, *European Imperial Rule, 1880–1940: The Impact of the West on India, Southeast Asia and Africa* (Oxford: Clio, 1982).
3. See Bryan, *Jamaican People*, 81–82. For a full analysis of the Jamaica Constabulary Force, see Anthony Harriott, *Police and Crime Control in Jamaica: Problems of Reforming Ex-colonial Constabularies* (Kingston: The University of the West Indies Press, 2000).
4. This forms the basis of another book being prepared by the authors.
5. See, for instance, C.L.R. James, *Beyond a Boundary* (London: Stanley Paul, 1980), 34.
6. For a description of *fin de siècle* conditions of life in rural Jamaican villages and the slums of Kingston, see Moore and Johnson, *Land We Live In*, and *"Squalid Kingston"*.
7. This complex situation of cultural adjustment to Victorian culture and retention of Afro-creole culture was also found among Afro-Guyanese after emancipation, although in Guyana the presence of a larger proportion of new immigrants seemed to encourage Afro-Guyanese to gravitate more towards the dominant culture in order to preserve their social pre-eminence *vis-à-vis* the aliens. See Moore, *Cultural Power*, 299–300.
8. de Certeau, "Oppositional Practices", 3–43.
9. Burton, *Afro-Creole*, 6–12.
10. Michel Foucault, *The History of Sexuality*, vol. 1, trans. Robert Hurley (London: Allen Lane, 1978), 95–96.
11. See Moore, *Cultural Power*; and Downes, "Barbados".
12. For Burton, power includes "both the external sources of power that from the beginning of European colonization have acted on and in large part determined the Caribbean's evolution . . . and the internal structures whereby that external power is transmitted and refracted"; Burton, *Afro-Creole*, 9. In this conceptualization, power is the monopoly of the local elites and their metropolitan backers.

Bibliography

Abbreviations

CO   Colonial Office Papers, Public Record Office, London

JA   Jamaica Archives

LMS   Papers of the London Missionary Society (Council for World Mission), School of Oriental and African Studies, University of London

MMS   Wesleyan Methodist Missionary Society Papers, School of Oriental and African Studies, University of London

NLJ   National Library of Jamaica

SOAS   School of Oriental and African Studies, University of London

UPC   United Presbyterian Church of Scotland

USPG   Papers of the Society for the Propagation of the Gospel in Foreign Parts, Rhodes House Library, Oxford University

Official Records

Colonial Office Papers, Public Record Office, London

CO 137   Original correspondence: governor. Vols. 349 (1860) to 746 (1921)
CO 139   Acts. Vols. 97 (1864–65) to 113 (1919–21)
CO 140   Sessional papers. Vols. 168 (1864–65) to 256 (1920)
CO 141   Government gazettes. Vols. 33 (1869–70) to 83 (1920)
CO 142   Miscellanea: *Blue Books of Statistics*. Vols. 79 (1865) to 134 (1920)

Government Records, Jamaica Archives, Spanish Town

EDUCATION: JA 1B/3

5/9–12   Bulletin of Education Department, 1895–1904

PROTECTOR OF IMMIGRANTS: JA 1B/9

41a   Correspondence, 1910–12

45	Annual report from British colonies, 1904–10
103	Annual report on immigration, 1910–16
134	General correspondence, 1907

Colonial Secretariat: JA 1B/5

18	Correspondence, governor to secretary of state, 1860–1920
26	Correspondence, secretary of state to governor, 1860–1920
75/1–111	Correspondence, general, 1867–1920
76/3	Colonial Secretary's Office: correspondence
78/1–2	Confidential and secret correspondence, 1889–1921
82/1/1–423	Colonial Secretary's letter books: out-letters, 1886–1920
84/1/1–12	Colonial Secretary: out-going circulars, 1867–1920

Miscellanea

Jamaica Archives: Private Archives

4/1/1	Diary of Thomas Witter Jackson, stipendiary magistrate, 1863–65
4/9/9	Diaries and notebooks: Rough diary, 1894–1902
4/12/3	Letters, etc. by Joseph Dussard Ormsby, 1881–98
4/26/2/4–13	Correspondence [Perkins], 1859–1916
4/26/2/124	Copy of Dr. V. Ffrench-Mullen, "Quashie's Lament"
4/64/1–2	Diary of Henry Plant, 1864–66, 1866–67
4/71/40–68	Miscellaneous letters and invitations

Jamaica Archives: Gifts and Deposits

7/12/1–312	Jamaica Memories [Collection of 312 essays by Jamaicans sent to the *Gleaner* (1959) about their recollections of Jamaica fifty years before]
7/28/422	Tropica: The Land of Sunshine, 1904
7/33	Photographs: Dr E.J. Sayword
7/74/1	*The Triffler Magazine,* October 1894
7/193/7	Diary of Mrs Stover, wife of a viticulturist employed by Lorenzo Baker Plantation, 1899
7/239/17	Journal 1893
7/239/18	Anthony Benn's diary, 1896
7/248/2	"An Adopted Son of Jamaica" [Colonel George Hicks]
7/251/5	Scrapbook, 1910–50
7/266/6–12	Photographs
7/314/1	Diary of William Browne, 1822–82

University of the West Indies (UWI Mona) Library, Kingston

Department Reports, 1879–1920

Laws of Jamaica, 1860–1920
Decennial censuses, 1861–1921

    SIR ARTHUR LEWIS INSTITUTE OF SOCIAL AND ECONOMIC STUDIES,
    UNIVERSITY OF THE WEST INDIES, MONA, KINGSTON

Brodber, Erna. "Life in Jamaica in the Early Twentieth Century: A Presentation of 90 Oral Accounts". Original transcripts.

Ecclesiastical Records
Jamaica Archives
CHURCH OF ENGLAND: JA 5/1

1/11	Journals of Synod
12/1–8	Jamaica Home and Foreign Missionary Society reports, 1876–1920
15/22	Kingston Parish Church: Register of Chinese members, c.1926
15/44	Trial of Rev. Henry Clarke, 1888
24/2	*Plummer's Magazine*, 1913

    UNITED CONGREGATION OF ISRAELITES: JA 5/4

4/2	Sepheb Ketubot, 1883
4/58	"The Jews of Jamaica"
4/82	"The Jews of Old Jamaica"
4/135	Bar Mitzvah of David De Souza
4/221	Analysed register of births and marriages, 1788–1918
4/225	Analysed register of births and marriages, 1809–1907

    MORAVIAN CHURCH: JA 5/5

A/7–8 Mizpah	Diary, 1887–94, 1908–10
B/2 Springfield	Register of exclusions and suspensions, 1877–1951
B/2 Irwin Hall	Register of exclusions and suspensions, 1877–1938
B/3 Nazareth	Exclusion list, 1861–76
B/17 Walder family	Rev. J.T. Dillon, "100 Years 1838–1938"
B/B Nazareth	Diary, 1863–65, 1889, 1911, 1913
C/3 Lititz	Register of exclusions and suspensions, 1877–1949
D/1 Salem	Register of exclusions and suspensions, 1887–1940
D/2 & 5 Nazareth	Candidates and excluded females/males, 1862–89
G/1–114	"The Breaking of the Dawn or Moravian Work in Jamaica 1754–1904"
M/12 Nazareth	List of Gifts for Harvest, 10 January 1895

Annual Report of the Moravian Church in Jamaica, 1890
Reports and Statistics of the Moravian Church in Jamaica, 1900–1913

[Annual] Reports of the Jamaica Province of the Moravian Church, 1915–21
Journal of the Provincial Synod of the Moravian Church in Jamaica, 1903, 1906, 1908, 1911, 1913, 1921
Periodical Accounts relating to the Missions of the Church of the United Brethren established among the Heathen. Nos. 267 (June 1865) to 340 (September 1883); 1886–99; and vols. 5 (1904) to 10 (September 1918).
The Messenger – A magazine of the Church of the United Brethren. Vols. 1 (1864) to 26 (1890).
Moravian Missions: An Illustrated Record of Missionary Work. Vols. 1 (1903) to 9 (1911).
The Jamaica Moravian – A Christian Monthly Magazine, 1888–93
Magazine (April 1920) of the Upward and Onward Society of the Women of Jamaica – Moravian Girls' Organization No. 2

Methodist Church: JA 5/6

5/60/2/11–18	*Wesleyan Methodist Magazine,* 1862–71
7/1	Western Annual Conference journal, 1885–92
7/2	Western Annual Conference journal, 1893–1909
10/3	Extracts and letters, 1872–83

Friends Jamaica Mission: JA 5/8

1/1–411	Letters: Milo S. and Addic Hinckle, 1911–23
2/412–455	Reports of the Friends Jamaica Mission, 1913–18
3/456–520	Minutes of the Executive Committee of the Friends Jamaica Mission, 1913–23
4/521–570	Reports of the Friends Jamaica Mission, 1918–21
10/932–963	Letters: Arthur Swift et al., c.1890
11/964–1109	Photographs, 1894–95, 1909, 1923
36/1949–2040	Letters: Farr et al., 1915–21
46/3093–3196	Statistics, 1916–22
47/3197–3198	Maps and clippings
55/3823–3918	Reports of the Friends Jamaica Mission, 1915–22
59/4163–4176	Letters: Lora P. Arms, 1915–34
60/4177–4220	Letters: Mary E. Allen, 1916–22
64/4530–4610	Letters: R.B. and Edith Michner, 1920–40
78/5906–5987	Monthly Publications of the Friends Jamaica Mission, 1892–1900
80/6032–6047	Annual Reports of American Friends Board of Foreign Mission, 1895–1908
82/6049	Notes re Sharpless Evi [b. 1844, d. 1913]
84/6051–6066	Letters: Mr Gregory, 1914–15
86/6098–6212	Letters: Charles S. Vincent, 1916–52
87/6213–6284	Letters: Charles S. and Mabel P. Vincent, 1916–31

National Library of Jamaica, Kingston

PRESBYTERIAN CHURCH/CONGREGATIONAL UNION OF JAMAICA: MST 2089

Minutes of the Synod of the Presbyterian Church of Jamaica, 1874–78, 1880, 1901–21
Western Presbytery, minutes, 1892–97, 1917–21
Northern Presbytery, minutes, 1895–1922
St Paul's Presbyterian Church, minutes of meetings, 1901–21
Mandeville Convention Council, minutes, 1903–5, 1906–10
Annual Reports of the Congregational Union of Jamaica, 1912–13

CHURCH OF ENGLAND

Scrapbook No. 1 General. MST 51.
Island Scraps No. 2. MST 51a.
Nuttall [Enos] Papers. MST 209a, d, and g.

School of Oriental and African Studies, University of London

WESLEYAN METHODIST MISSIONARY SOCIETY

West Indies: Correspondence – Jamaica

Boxes 199–203 (microfiche boxes 47–52), 1865–90
Boxes 740–743 (microfiche boxes 53–54), 1905–20

West Indies General: Synod Minutes

Boxes 159–180 (microfiche boxes 5–12), 1864–1921

West Indies: Correspondence – Conference

Boxes 144–145 (microfiche box 19), 1888–1902

Photographs and Additional Papers

Box 1200 West Indies
The Report of the Wesleyan Methodist Missionary Society. Vols. 14 (1858–60) to 35 (1918–22).
Wesleyan Missionary Notices. Vols. 16 (1860–62) to 31 (1903–4).
The Missionary Echo of the United Methodist Free Churches, 1894–1920/21.
The Foreign Field of the Wesleyan Methodist Church. Vols. 1 (1904–5) to 16 (1919).

LONDON MISSIONARY SOCIETY (COUNCIL FOR WORLD MISSION)

West Indies: Jamaica Correspondence. Boxes 9–12, 1864–94.
West Indies: Odds. Box 3, Jamaica Congregational Union Reports [printed], 1884–95.
Western Outgoing Letters: West Indies (letters from LMS Headquarters to
    Missionaries). Boxes 7–11, 1864–1925.
Reports: West Indies. Box 1, 1866–1901.

Reports of the London Missionary Society, 1865–84.

The Report of the Directors . . . of the Missionary Society usually called The London Missionary Society. Vols. 20 (1861–62) to 35 (1885).

The Missionary Magazine and Chronicle: chiefly relating to the London Missionary Society. Vols. 25 (1861) to 30 (1866).

The Chronicle of the London Missionary Society, 1867–1876/78.

Angus Library, Regent's Park College, Oxford University

BAPTIST MISSIONARY SOCIETY

Committee Minute Books

General Committee minute books, 1865–1914
Western Sub-Committee minute books, 1861–1921

West Indies General and Jamaica

Box WI/4 David Jonathan East, 1851–92
Box WI/5 [Other] Missionaries correspondence, 1840s–1899
Box WI/6 Statistics and printed material
Box WI/12 Miscellaneous material (uncatalogued), 1875–1939
Box WI/18 Miscellaneous uncatalogued papers
Box WI/19 Missionaries correspondence, 1898–1960s
Box WI/20 Unclassified reports and papers
Annual Reports of the Baptist Missionary Society, 1865–1921
The Missionary Herald, 1871–1921

New College Library, Edinburgh

CHURCH OF SCOTLAND

Reports on the Schemes of the Church of Scotland, 1865–1921
Reports to the General Assembly by the Colonial Committee, 1865–1921
Church of Scotland Home and Foreign Missionary Record, 1864–1900
Life and Work: The Church of Scotland Magazine and Mission Record. Vols. 5 (1883) to 43 (1921).

UNITED PRESBYTERIAN CHURCH OF SCOTLAND

United Presbyterian Church: Minutes and Reports of Foreign Mission Committee/Board, 1873–1900
United Presbyterian Magazine, 1865–87
United Presbyterian Church Missionary Record, 1864–1900
Zenana Mission Quarterly, 1887–1900
Illustrated Missionary News, 1877–92

UNITED FREE CHURCH OF SCOTLAND

Minutes of Foreign Mission Committee, 1900–1921
Foreign Mission Reports, 1900–13
United Free Church of Scotland Missionary Record, 1901–21
Women's Missionary Magazine, 1901–17

Rhodes House Library, Oxford University

SOCIETY FOR THE PROPAGATION OF THE GOSPEL IN FOREIGN PARTS

CLR Series, 1860–1920
CLS Series, 1860–1920
Committee on Women's Work, 1866–1920
D Series – Original letters received, 1860–1920
E Series – Missionaries' reports, 1860–1920

Partnership House, London

SOCIETY FOR THE PROPAGATION OF THE GOSPEL IN FOREIGN PARTS

The Mission Field: A Monthly Record of the Proceedings on the Society for the Propagation of the Gospel, at Home and Abroad. London: G. Bell and Sons, 1860–1920.

Society of Jesus, English Province, London

Correspondence, 1867, 1871, 1873–75, 1890
Correspondence, 1860–97
Copy of Declaration of Trust, 1901
Correspondence, 1877–88: Letters to Thomas Porter, SJ, Vicar Apostolic of Jamaica, from E.I. Purbrick, SJ; A.G. Knight SJ; and Joseph Johnson SJ.
Diary for 1872 (Jamaica): Father James Splaine, SJ.
Letters to Jamaica Mission from a number of Jesuit Fathers, 1872–1904
Jamaica Mission Letters, 1860–72
Letters and Notices. Vols. 1 (1863) to 35 (1919–20).
Litterae Annuae, Provinciae Angliae, Societatis Jesu, 1865–1913
Missio Jamaicensis, 1867–77

Manuscript Collections: National Library of Jamaica

Alexander, Leslie. Letters to Frank Cundall, 1896–97. MST 24.
Angell, F. Letter to L. Anderson, 15 November 1875. MST 908.
Biddlecombe, George. Letters and documents, 1831–76. MST 8.
Carpenter Smith, Thomas. "Three Weeks in Jamaica, 1901". MST 292.

Carter, Samuel James. "A trip to the tropics, January 6–April 7, 1887". MST 48.
Casserly papers. MST 317.
Colonial Literary and Reading Society. Minute books, 1849–91. MST 322.
Cork, Anne. "The true story of Louis Hutchinson", December 1897. MST 926.
Cundall, Frank. "The West Indies Today, 1908". MST 934.
———. "Jamaica in 1905". MST 931I.
Dixon, Harriet. Letter to Richard Smith, 21 May 1863. MST 1070d.
Fontabelle Estate documents, 1873–78. MST 1547.
Harvey, Lena (Mrs). "Chapelton in Early 1890–1920". MST 1998.
Jewish documents. MST 1870.
Joyce, A. Notebook, 1898–1908. MST 1511.
Letters and papers (miscellaneous). MST 54B.
Livingstone [W.P.] collection. MST 59.
McFarlane, J.E. Clare. Letters, clippings, postcards, photographs. MST 1949c.
Obeah broadsides with cases. MST 1842.
Olson [Rev George W.] collection, 1911–64. MST 1835.
Ormsby, M.T.M. Autobiography, 1869–1942. MST 1616.
Perkins [Lily] collection. MST 2019.
Samuel, L. Scrapbook, 1905–52. MST 1498.

Newspapers

Colonial Standard & Jamaica Despatch, 1864–95.
[Daily] Gleaner & De Cordova's Advertiser Sheet, 1865–1902.
Daily Gleaner, 1902–20.
Falmouth Post, 1860–74.
Gall's News Letter, 1871–72, 1875–99.
Jamaica Advocate, 1894–96, 1899–1905.
Jamaica Daily Telegraph & Anglo-American Herald, 1898–1909.
[Jamaica] Daily Telegraph & Jamaica Guardian, 1911–12.
Jamaica Guardian, 1861–72, 1908–9.
Jamaica Post & West Indian Advertiser, 1887–89.
Jamaica Post, 1889, 1891–99.
Jamaica Times, 1898–1920.
Morning Journal, 1861–75.

Contemporary Works

Bacon, Edgar, and E.M. Aaron. *The New Jamaica*. New York: Walbridge and Co.; Kingston: Aston W. Gardner and Co., 1890.
Bailey, W.F. *History of the Jamaica Union of Teachers*. Kingston: Gleaner Co., 1937.

Banbury, Rev. R. Thomas. *Jamaica Superstitions or the Obeah Book*. Kingston: Mortimer C. DeSouza, 1894.
Barrington, Ainsley Philip. *Reminiscences of a Scottish Gentleman*. London: Arthur Hall, Virtue and Co., 1861.
Beckwith, Martha Warren. *The Hussay Festival in Jamaica*. Poughkeepsie: Vassar College, 1924.
———. *Black Roadways: A Study of Jamaican Folk Life*. Chapel Hill: University of North Carolina Press, 1929.
———. *Jamaica Folklore*. New York: American Folklore Society, 1929.
Bellows, W. *In Fair Jamaica*. Kingston: Educational Supply Co., 1907.
Bengough, H.M. *Memories of a Soldier's Life*. London: Edward Arnold, 1913.
Blake, Sir Henry Arthur. "The awakening of Jamaica". *The Nineteenth Century* (1890).
Bleby, Henry. *Romance without Fiction*. London: Wesleyan Conference Office, 1877.
Bottle, Dorothy Mabel. *Reminiscences of a Queen's Army Schoolmistress*. London: Arthur Stockwell, c.1911.
Bradford, Mary F. *Side Trips in Jamaica*. Boston: Sherwood Publishing, 1902.
Brandon, David. *Some Amusing Reminiscences of a West Indian Barrister*. Kingston: Jamaica Times, 1911.
Bromley, Clare Fitzroy. *A Woman's Wanderings in the Western World*. London: Saunders, Otley and Co., 1861.
Bryce, Wyatt, ed. *Reference Book of Jamaica*. Kingston: n.p., 1946.
Bullen, Frank Thomas. "Kingston, Jamaica 1905". *Cornhill Magazine,* February 1905.
Burton, Capt. Reginald. *Tropics and Snows*. London: Edward Arnold, 1898.
Butcher, Mrs T.B. *A Peep at Jamaica and Its People*. London: Charles E. Kelly, 1902.
C.A.E. *Jamaica: A Health and Pleasure Resort*. Kingston: n.p., 1923.
Caffin, Mabel Blanche. *A Jamaica Outing*. Boston: Sharwood Publishing, 1899.
Caine, William Ralph. *The Cruise of the Port Kingston*. London: Collier and Co., 1908.
Capper, Samuel James. "Trip to the tropics". Extracts from newspapers, January–March 1887.
Carlile, Warrand. "38 years' Mission Life in Jamaica". *United Presbyterian Church Missionary Record,* January 1861. Reprinted as *Thirty-eight years' Mission Life in Jamaica*. London: J. Nisbet and Co., 1884.
Chapman, Esther Hyman. *A Scribbler in Jamaica*. Kingston: n.p., c.1925.
Chapple, Joe Mitchell. "Our Trip to Jamaica 1904". *National Magazine,* June 1904.
Clark, W.G. *Little Journeys from Constant Spring Hotel and Gordon Town*. Kingston: Sollas and Cocking, n.d.
Coaker, Sir William. *Sketches of Jamaica*. N.p.: R. Hibbs, 1928.
Cook, E.M. *Jamaica: The Lodestone of the Caribbean*. London: J.W. Arrowsmith, 1924.
Cornish, Vaughn. *The Travels of Ellen Cornish*. London: W.J. Ham-Smith, 1913.
Crommelin, May. "The mountain-heart of Jamaica". *The Ludgate,* October 1898.

Crone, Kennedy. "Jamaica, island jewel of the Caribbean". *Canadian Geographical Journal,* April 1932.
Cundall, Frank. *Jamaica in . . .[1895, 1896, 1897, 1901, 1905, 1912, 1920, 1922].* Kingston: Institute of Jamaica.
———. "Jamaica in the past and present". *Journal of the Society of Arts,* 3 January 1896.
———. *Life of Enos Nuttall.* London: Macmillan, 1922.
Curle, Richard Henry Parnell. *Wanderings, a book of travel and reminiscence.* London: Kegan Paul; New York: E.P. Dutton, 1920.
D'Arcy, C.E. *Old St Jago: Spanish Town – Past and Present.* N.p., 1903.
De Lisser, Herbert George. *In Jamaica and Cuba.* Kingston: Gleaner Co., 1910.
———. *Twentieth Century Jamaica.* Kingston: Jamaica Times, 1913.
Dingwall, Rev. R. *Jamaica's Greatest Need.* London: Lemmont and Co., 1892.
Dodsworth, Francis. *The Book of Jamaica.* Kingston: Sollas and Cocking, 1904.
East, D.J. *Elementary Education: Report of the Royal Commissioners: A Review.* Kingston: Gleaner Co., 1884.
Ellison, Rev. J., ed. *Church and Empire.* London: Longman, 1907.
Emerick, Abraham J. "Obeah and Duppyism in Jamaica". From *Woodstock Letters.* Woodstock, Md., 1915.
———. "Jamaica Duppies". From *Woodstock Letters.* Woodstock, Md., 1916.
———. "Jamaica Mialism". From *Woodstock Letters.* Woodstock, Md., 1916.
"An Evening Chat in Jamaica". *Cornhill Magazine,* 1895.
Eves, Charles Washington. *West Indies.* London: Sampson Low, Marston and Co., 1889.
Fenn, Annie Manville. "Housekeeping in Jamaica". *The Youth's Companion,* March 1893.
Feurtado, Walter. *The Jubilee Reign of Her Most Gracious Majesty Queen Victoria in Jamaica, 1837–1887.* Kingston: W.A. Feurtado, 1890.
Fiske, Amos Kidder. *The West Indies.* New York: G.P. Putnam's Sons, c.1899.
Ford, Isaac Newton. *Tropical America.* London: Edward Stanford, 1893.
Foulds, Elizabeth. *Sketches from the life of a Scotch Thistle.* London: A. Stockwell, n.d.
Fowler, Sir James K. *An Impression of Jamaica and the Panama Canal Zone.* London: Eyre and Spottiswoode, 1924.
Frank, Harry A. *Roaming through the West Indies.* New York: n.p., 1920.
Froude, J.A. *England in the West Indies or the Bow of Ulysses.* London: Longman, Green and Co., 1888.
Gardner, William James. *A history of Jamaica from its discovery by Christopher Columbus to the present time: including an account of its trade and agriculture; sketches of the manners, habits, and customs of all classes of its inhabitants; and a narrative of the progress of religion and education in the island.* London: E. Stock, 1873.
Gardner's Handy Guide to Jamaica, 1889. Kingston: Aston W. Gardner and Co., 1889.
Gaul, Gilbert. "Jamaica with pictures 1893". *Century Magazine,* March 1893.
Gaunt, Mary Eliza Bakewell. *Where the twain meet.* London: John Murray, 1922.
———. *Reflection in Jamaica.* London: Ernest Benn, 1932.

Gordon, Rev. R., et al. *Jamaica's Jubilee: or what we are and what we hope to be.* London: S.W. Partridge and Co., 1888.
Graham, Rev. William. *Woman: Her Sphere and Opportunities.* Kingston: Educational Supply Co., 1889.
Gurney, Emelia Russey. *Letters of Emelia Russey Gurney.* London: James Nisbet, 1903.
Hale, W.H. *The Island of Jamaica, an Illustrated Lecture.* Boston: United Fruit Steamship Co., 1914.
Handbook of Jamaica. Multiple editions, 1881–1922. Kingston: n.p.
Harvey, Thomas, and W. Brewin. *Jamaica in 1866.* London: A.W. Bennett, 1867.
Hawthorne, Julian. "Summer at Christmas-tide, 1897". *Century Magazine,* January 1897.
———. "A Tropic Climb, 1897". *Century Magazine,* February 1897.
Henderson, John. *The West Indies.* London: Adam and Charles Black, 1905.
———. *Jamaica.* London: Adam and Charles Black, 1906.
Henderson, George E. *Goodness and Mercy: A Tale of 100 Years.* Kingston: Gleaner Co., 1931.
Hope-Falkner, Mrs Percy. "A Few Notes on Jamaica". *Journal of the Royal Army Medical Corps* (1921).
Howe, E.W. *The Trip to the West Indies.* Topeka: Crane and Co., 1910.
Hurston, Zora Neale. *Voodoo Gods: An Enquiry into Native Myths and Magic in Jamaica and Haiti.* London: J.M. Dent and Sons, 1939.
Jamaica. Plymouth: W. Brandon and Son, 1877.
"Jamaica". *Blackwood's Magazine,* 1891. Reprinted as *Jamaica.* Edinburgh: n.p., 1890.
The Jamaica Times Tourist Guide. Kingston: Times Printery, 1909.
James, Winifred. *The Mulberry Tree.* London: Chapman and Hall, 1913.
Jay, E.A. Hastings. *A Glimpse of the Tropics, or Four Months Crossing in the West Indies.* London: Sampson Low, Marston and Co., 1900.
Jekyll, Walter. *Jamaica Song and Story: Anancy Stories, Digging Songs, Ring Tunes, and Dancing Times.* London: David Nutt for the Folklore Society, 1907.
Johnston, Sir Harry Hamilton. "In Jamaica". *Cornhill Magazine,* November 1909.
Johnston, James. *Jamaica: The New Riviera: A Pictorial Description of the Island and Its Attractions.* London: Cassell, 1903.
Kingsley, Charles. *At last: a Christmas in the West Indies.* London: Macmillan and Co., 1871.
Leader, Alfred. *Through Jamaica with a Kodak.* Bristol: John Wright, 1907.
Livingstone, William Pringle. *Black Jamaica: A study in evolution.* London: Sampson Low, Marston and Co., 1899.
Lucas, Edward Verrall. *A Fronded Isle and Other Essays.* London: Methuen and Co., 1927.
MacLean, Isabel Cranstoun. *Children of Jamaica.* Edinburgh: Oliphant, Anderson and Ferrier, 1910.

Makin, William James. *Caribbean Nights*. London: Robert Hale, 1939.
Malcolm, Ian. "Jamaica: an impression". *Blackwood Magazine,* February 1899.
Marsh, Florence L. *What I have seen in Jamaica: a lecture*. Kingston: M. de Cordova and Co., 1876.
Martin, T.M. *Jamaica, the Gem of the British West Indies*. Kingston: n.p., 1921.
Matthewman, L. de V. "Summering in Winter". *The Eva* 10, no. 6 (1902).
McNeill, Rev. George. *United Free Church of Scotland; The Story of Our Missions; The West Indies*. Edinburgh: United Free Church, 1911.
McQuade, James. *The cruise of the "Montauk" to Bermuda, the West Indies and Florida*. New York: Tomas R. Knox and Co., 1885.
Me: A Book of Remembrance. New York: Century, 1915.
Morris, M. *Memini; or, a mingled yarn*. London: Harrison, 1892.
Musgrave, Sir Anthony. "Jamaica: Now and Fifteen Years Since". *Proceedings of the Royal Colonial Institute* 11 (1879/80).
"My Holiday in Jamaica". *Chamber's Journal,* November 1880.
Nash, Francilla. *Jamaica, part of her history, climate, resources and general aspect: a lecture*. New York: Corlies, Macy and Co., 1877.
Nelson, Marjorie. *How They Live: Sketches of Jamaican Life*. Kingston: W.I. Publishing, 1940.
Newman, Arthur James. *Jamaica, the Island and Its People*. 5th ed. Kingston: Jamaica Times Press, 1948.
Newton, Margaret. *Glimpses of Life in Bermuda and the Tropics*. London: Digby, Long and Co., 1897.
North, Marianne. *Recollections of a happy life*. London: Macmillan, 1892.
Nuttall, Enos. "Characteristics of the Negro". In *Church and Empire,* edited by J. Ellison. London: Longman, 1907.
———. "The Negro Race". In *Church and Empire,* edited by J. Ellison. London: Longman, 1907.
Olivier, Sydney Haldane. *The West Indies Revisited*. London: The Times, 1931.
———. *Jamaica, the Blessed Island*. London: Faber and Faber, 1936.
———. *Letters and Selected Writings*. London: Allen and Unwin, 1948.
"Orange Hall". *The Leisure Hour,* December 1870.
Pleasant Glimpses of Jamaica. Kingston: Educational Supply Co., 1908.
Plowden, Alfred Chichele. *Grain or Chaff?* London: T. Fisher Unwin, 1903.
Poore, Ida Margaret. *An Admiral's Wife in the Making*. London: John Murray, 1917.
Price, Ernest. *Bananaland; Pages from the Chronicles of an English Minister in Jamaica*. London: Carry, 1930.
Pullen-Burry, Bessie. *Jamaica as It Is, 1903*. London: T. Fisher Unwin, 1903.
———. *Ethiopia in Exile: Jamaica Revisited*. London: T. Fisher Unwin, 1905.
Pyle, Howard. "Jamaica, New and Old". *Harper's New Monthly Magazine,* January/February 1890.

Rampini, Charles. *Letters from Jamaica*. Edinburgh: Edmonston and Douglas, 1873.
Reid, J.H. "The People of Jamaica Described". In *Jamaica's Jubilee: or what we are and what we hope to be*, edited by R. Gordon et al. London: Partridge and Co., 1888.
Robinson, Phil. "From Sea to Summit: a drive in the Jamaican hills, 1899". *Good Woods*, c.1899.
Robson, George. *The story of our Jamaica Mission*. Edinburgh: Offices of the United Presbyterian Church, 1894.
Robson, John. *Christ's Great Commission and the Work in Jamaica*. Kingston: Educational Supply Co., 1899.
Saville, S.E. "Jamaica". *Westminster Review*, March 1901.
Scholes, T.E.S. *The British Empire and Alliances: or Britain's duty to her Colonies and Subject Races*. London: E. Stock, 1899.
———. *Glimpses of the Ages or the "Superior" and "Inferior" Races So-called, Discussed in the Light of Science and History*. 2 vols. London: John Long, 1905.
Scotland, Horace. "Modern infidelity considered in respect to the middle and lower classes in the West Indies". *West Indian Quarterly*, 1886/87.
Scott, Sir Sibbald David. *To Jamaica and back*. London: Chapman and Hall, 1876.
Seithamer, G.O. "Negro Life in Jamaica". *Harper's New Monthly Magazine*, March 1872.
Sherlock, P.M. "Jamaica Superstitions". *Empire Review*, 1924.
Sibley, Inez Knibb. *Quashie's Reflections*. Kingston: Herald, 1939.
Smith, John Corson. *My Winter in the Tropics*. Chicago: n.p., 1897.
Spinner, Alice. *A Study in Colour*. London: T. Fisher Unwin, 1894.
———. *A Reluctant Evangelist and other Stories*. London: Edward Arnold, 1896.
St Johnston, T.R. *West India Pepper-Pot, or Thirteen "Quashie" Stories*. London: P. Allan and Co., 1928.
Stark, James H. *Stark's Jamaica Guide*. Boston: James H. Stark, c.1898.
Stuart, Villiers. *Adventures amidst the Equatorial Forests and Rivers of South America (and Jamaica Revisited)*. London: J. Murray, 1891.
Symmonett, Ethel Maud. *Jamaica: Queen of the Carib Sea*. Kingston: Mortimer C. DeSouza, 1895.
Thomas, Herbert Theodore. *Untrodden Jamaica*. Kingston: Aston W. Gardner and Co., 1890.
———. "Jamaica". *Journal of the Society of Arts*, February 1902.
———. *The Story of a West Indian Policeman or Forty Years in the Jamaica Constabulary*. Kingston: Gleaner Co., 1927.
Treves, Sir Frederick. *The Cradle of the Deep: An Account of a Voyage to the West Indies*. London: Smith, Elder and Co., 1913.
Tucker, Leonard, ed. *Glorious Liberty: The Story of a Hundred Years' Work of the Jamaica Baptist Mission*. London: Baptist Missionary Society, 1914.
Udal, J.S. *Obeah in the West Indies, Folklore*. London: n.p., 1915.
Verrill, Alpheus Hyatt. *Jamaica of Today*. New York: Dodd, Mead and Co., 1931.

Ward, C.J. *World's Fair: Jamaica at Chicago. An account descriptive of the colony of Jamaica*. New York: W.J. Pell, 1893.
Wilcox, Ella Wheeler. *Sailing Sunny Seas*. Chicago: W.B. Conkey, 1909.
Williams, Joseph John. *Whisperings of the Caribbean: Reflections of a Missionary*. New York: Benziger Bros., 1925.
———. *Voodoos and Obeah*. New York: Dial, 1932.
———. *Psychic Phenomena of Jamaica*. New York: Dial, 1934.
Willis, C.W. *"Buckra" Land: two weeks in Jamaica*. Boston: n.p., 1896.

Modern Works

Abrahams, Roger D. *The Man of Words in the West Indies: Performance and the Emergence of Creole Culture*. Baltimore: Johns Hopkins University Press, 1983.
Adorno, Theodor, and Max Horkheimer. "The Culture Industry: Enlightenment as Mass Deception". In *Dialectic of Enlightenment,* translated by John Cumming. New York: Seabury, 1972.
Alleyne, Mervyn C. *Roots of Jamaican Culture*. London: Pluto, 1988.
Amies, Marion. "The Victorian Governess and Colonial Ideals of Womanhood". *Victorian Studies* 31, no. 4 (1988).
Anstey, Roger. *The Atlantic Slave Trade and British Abolition, 1760–1810*. Atlantic Highlands, N.J.: Humanities Press, 1975.
Arnold, Matthew. *Culture and Anarchy*. London: Cambridge University Press, 1960.
Augier, Roy. "Before and After 1865". *New World Quarterly* 2, no. 1 (1966).
Austin-Broos, Diane J. *Jamaica Genesis: Religion and the Politics of Moral Orders*. Chicago: University of Chicago Press, 1997.
Bakan, Abigail B. *Ideology and Class Conflict in Jamaica: The Politics of Rebellion*. Montreal: McGill–Queens University Press, 1990.
Barrow, Christine. *Family in the Caribbean: Themes and Perspectives*. Kingston: Ian Randle, 1996.
Beckles, Hilary McD. *The Development of West Indies Cricket*. 2 vols. Kingston: University of the West Indies Press, 1999.
Behlmer, George K. *Child Abuse and Reform in England, 1870–1908*. Stanford: Stanford University Press, 1982.
Bellegarde-Smith, Patrick, ed. *Traditional Spirituality in the African Diaspora*. Lexington, Ky.: Association of Caribbean Studies, 1992.
Besson, Jean. "Reputation and Respectability Reconsidered: A New Perspective on Afro-Caribbean Peasant Women". In *Women and Change in the Caribbean: A Pan-Caribbean Perspective,* edited by Janet Momsen. Kingston: Ian Randle, 1993.
Besson, Jean, and Barry Chevannes. "The Continuity-Creativity Debate: The Case of Revival". *Nieuwe West-Indische Gids/New West Indian Guide* 70, nos. 3–4 (1996).

Bissoondoyal, U., ed. *Indians Overseas: The Mauritian Experience*. Moka, Mauritius: Mahatma Gandhi Institute, 1984.

Blake, Judith. *Family Structure in Jamaica: The Social Context of Reproduction*. New York: Free Press, 1961.

Bolland, O. Nigel. "Creolisation and Creole Societies: A Cultural Nationalist View of Caribbean Social History". *Caribbean Quarterly* 44, nos. 1–2 (1998).

Bradlow, Edna. "The Culture of a Colonial Elite: The Cape of Good Hope in the 1850s". *Victorian Studies* 29, no. 3 (1986).

Brathwaite, Edward. *The Development of Creole Society in Jamaica, 1770–1820*. Oxford: Clarendon, 1971.

———. *Contradictory Omens: Cultural Diversity and Integration in the Caribbean*. Kingston: Savacou, 1974.

Brathwaite, Edward Kamau. "Kumina: African Survival in Jamaica". *Jamaica Journal* 42 (1978).

Brereton, Bridget. *Race Relations in Colonial Trinidad, 1870–1900*. Cambridge: Cambridge University Press, 1979.

Brodber, Erna. *Myal: A Novel*. London: New Beacon, 1988.

Brody, Eugene B. *Sex, Contraception, and Motherhood in Jamaica*. Cambridge, Mass.: Harvard University Press, 1981.

Bryan, Patrick. *The Jamaican People, 1880–1902*. London: Macmillan Caribbean, 1991.

———. "The Creolization of the Chinese Community in Jamaica". In *Ethnic Minorities in Caribbean Society*, edited by Rhoda Reddock. St Augustine, Trinidad: Institute of Social and Economic Research, 1996.

Bryant, Margaret. *The Unexpected Revolution*. London: University of London Institute of Education, 1979.

Burstyn, Joan. *Victorian Education and the Ideal of Womanhood*. London: Croom Helm, 1980.

Burton, Richard D.E. *Afro-Creole: Power, Opposition, and Play in the Caribbean*. Ithaca: Cornell University Press, 1997.

Campbell, Carl. "Social and Economic Obstacles to the Development of Popular Education in Post-Emancipation Jamaica, 1834–1865". *Journal of Caribbean History* 1 (November 1970).

———. "Denominationalism and the Mico Charity Schools in Jamaica, 1835–42". *Caribbean Studies* 10, no. 4 (1971).

———. *Colony and Nation: A Short History of Education in Trinidad and Tobago, 1834–1986*. Kingston: Ian Randle, 1992.

———. *The Young Colonials: A Social History of Education in Trinidad and Tobago, 1834–1939*. Kingston: The Press, University of the West Indies, 1996.

Campbell, Mavis. *The Dynamics of Change in a Slave Society: A Socio-political History of the Free Coloreds in Jamaica, 1800–1865*. Rutherford, N.J.: Fairleigh Dickinson University Press, 1976.

Cannadine, David. "The Context, Performance and Meaning of Ritual: The British Monarchy and the 'Invention of Tradition', c.1820–1977". In *The Invention of Tradition*, edited by Eric Hobsbawm and Terence Ranger. Cambridge: Cambridge University Press, 1983.

Chevannes, Barry. *Rastafari: Roots and Ideology*. Syracuse: Syracuse University Press, 1995.

Clarke, Edith. *My Mother Who Fathered Me*. London: George Allen and Unwin, 1957.

Cox, Edward L. "Religious Intolerance and Persecution: The Shakers of St Vincent, 1900–1934". *Journal of Caribbean History* 28, no. 2 (1994).

Craton, Michael. *Searching for the Invisible Man: Slaves and Plantation Life in Jamaica*. Cambridge, Mass.: Harvard University Press, 1978.

———. "Changing Patterns of Slave Families in the British West Indies". *Journal of Interdisciplinary History* 10, no. 1 (1979).

Craton, Michael, and James Walvin. *A Jamaican Plantation: A History of Worthy Park, 1670–1970*. London: W.H. Allen, 1970.

Cumper, G.E. "The Jamaican Family: Village and Estate". *Social and Economic Studies* 7, no. 1 (1958).

Curtin, Philip. *Two Jamaicas: The Role of Ideas in a Tropical Colony, 1830–1865*. 1955. Reprint, New York: Atheneum, 1970.

Davis, Kortright, and Elias Forajaye-Jones, eds. *African Creative Expressions of the Divine*. Washington, D.C.: Howard University School of Divinity, 1991.

de Certeau, Michel. "On the Oppositional Practices of Everyday Life". *Social Text* 3 (1980).

———. *The Practice of Everyday Life*. Translated by Steven F. Rendall. Berkeley: University of California Press, 1984.

de Saussure, Ferdinand. *Course in General Linguistics*. Translated and annotated by Roy Harris. London: Duckworth, 1983.

Delamont, Sara. "The Contradictions in Ladies' Education". In *The Nineteenth-Century Woman*, edited by Sara Delamont and Lorna Duffin. London: Croom Helm, 1978.

Derrida, Jacques. *Writing and Difference*. Translated by Alan Bass. Chicago: University of Chicago Press, 1978.

Dorsey, Bruce. *Reforming Men and Women: Gender in the Antebellum City*. Ithaca: Cornell University Press, 2002.

During, Simon, ed. *Cultural Studies Reader*. London: Routledge, 1993.

Dyhouse, Carol. *Girls Growing up in Late Victorian and Edwardian England*. London: Routledge and Kegan Paul, 1981.

Eisner, Gisela. *Jamaica 1830–1930: A Study of Economic Growth*. London: University of Manchester Press, 1963.

Elkins, W.F. " 'Warrior' Higgins: A Jamaican Street Preacher". *Jamaica Journal* 8, no. 4 (1974).

———. *Street Preachers, Faith Healers, and Herb Doctors in Jamaica, 1890–1925*. New York: Revisionist Press, 1977.

Field, M.J. *Religion and Medicine of the Ga People*. Accra: Presbyterian Book Depot, 1961.

Fisher, Trevor. *Prostitution and the Victorians*. New York: St Martin's, 1997.
Foster, Stephen. *The Long Argument: English Puritanism and the Shaping of New England Culture, 1570–1700*. Chapel Hill: Published for the Institute of Early American History and Culture, Williamsburg, Va., by the University of North Carolina Press, c.1991.
Foucault, Michel. *The History of Sexuality*. Vol. 1. Translated by Robert Hurley. London: Allen Lane, 1978.
Gillion, K.L. *Fiji's Indian Migrants: A History to the End of Indenture in 1920*. Melbourne: Oxford University Press, 1962.
Gordon, Shirley. *A Century of West Indian Education: A Source Book*. London: Longman, 1963.
———. *Our Cause for His Glory*. Kingston: The Press, University of the West Indies, 1998.
Gorham, Deborah. *The Victorian Girl and the Feminine Ideal*. London: Croom Helm, 1982.
Goulbourne, Harry. *Teachers, Education and Politics in Jamaica, 1892–1972*. London: Macmillan Caribbean, 1988.
Gradussov, Alex, ed. *Jamaica Heritage*. Kingston: Government of Jamaica, 1969.
Gramsci, Antonio. *Selections from Prison Notebooks*. Edited and translated by Quintin Hoare and Geoffrey Nowell-Smith. London: Lawrence and Wishart, 1971.
Green, William A. *British Slave Emancipation: The Sugar Colonies and the Great Experiment, 1830–1865*. Oxford: Oxford University Press, 1976.
———. "The Creolisation of Caribbean History: The Emancipation Era and a Critique of Dialectical Analysis". *Journal of Imperial and Commonwealth History* 14, no. 3 (1986).
Greenlee, J.G. "Imperial Studies and the Unity of the Empire". *Journal of Imperial and Commonwealth History* 7, no. 3 (1979)
Hall, Catherine. *Civilising Subjects: Metropole and Colony in the English Imagination, 1830–1867*. London: Polity, 2002.
Hall, Douglas. *Free Jamaica 1838–1865: An Economic History*. New Haven: Yale University Press, 1959.
Hammerton, A. James. "Victorian Marriage and the Law of Matrimonial Cruelty". *Victorian Studies* 33, no. 2 (1990).
Henriques, Fernando. "West Indian Family Organization". *American Journal of Sociology* 55, no. 1 (July 1949).
———. *Family and Colour in Jamaica*. London: Eyre and Spottiswoode, 1953.
Herskovits, Melville J., and Frances S. Herskovits. *Suriname Folk-Lore*. New York: Columbia University Press, 1936.
———. *Trinidad Village*. New York: Alfred A. Knopf, 1947.
Heuman, Gad. *Between Black and White: Race, Politics, and the Free Coloureds in Jamaica, 1792–1865*. Westport, Conn.: Greenwood, 1981.

———. *"The Killing Time": The Morant Bay Rebellion in Jamaica.* Knoxville: University of Tennessee Press, 1994.
Higginbotham, Ann R. " 'Sin of the Age': Infanticide and Illegitimacy in Victorian London". *Victorian Studies* 32, no. 3 (1989).
Higginbotham, Evelyn Brooks. *Righteous Discontent: The Women's Movement in the Black Baptist Church, 1880–1920.* Cambridge, Mass.: Harvard University Press, 1993.
Higman, B.W. "Household Structure and Fertility on Jamaican Slave Plantations: A Nineteenth Century Example". *Population Studies* 27, no. 3 (1973).
———. "Slavery Remembered: The Celebration of Emancipation in Jamaica". *Journal of Caribbean History* 12 (1979).
———. "Domestic Service in Jamaica since 1750". In *Trade, Government, and Society in Caribbean History, 1700–1920.* Kingston: Heinemann, 1983.
———. *Slave Population and Economy in Jamaica, 1807–1834.* Kingston: The Press, University of the West Indies, 1995.
———. "Remembering Slavery: The Rise, Decline, and Revival of Emancipation Day in the English-Speaking Caribbean". *Slavery and Abolition* 19, no. 1 (1998).
Hill, Robert, ed. *The Marcus Garvey and Universal Negro Improvement Association Papers.* 10 vols. Berkeley: University of California Press, 1983–.
Hobsbawm, Eric. "Introduction: Inventing Traditions". In *The Invention of Tradition,* edited by Eric Hobsbawm and Terence Ranger. Cambridge: Cambridge University Press, 1983.
Hobsbawm, Eric, and Terence Ranger, eds. *The Invention of Tradition.* Cambridge: Cambridge University Press, 1983.
Hobson, Barbara Meil. *Uneasy Virtue: The Politics of Prostitution and the American Reform Tradition.* Chicago: University of Chicago Press, 1990.
Hoggart, Richard. *The Uses of Literacy.* Harmondsworth: Penguin, 1990.
Holt, Thomas C. *The Problem of Freedom: Race, Labor, and Politics in Jamaica and Britain, 1832–1938.* Baltimore: Johns Hopkins University Press, 1992.
Horton, Robin. *Patterns of Thought in Africa and the West: Essays on Magic, Religion and Science.* Cambridge: Cambridge University Press, 1993.
Hyam, Ronald. "Empire and Sexual Opportunity". *Journal of Imperial and Commonwealth History* 14, no. 2 (1986).
———. "Concubinage and the Colonial Service: The Crewe Circular (1909)". *Journal of Imperial and Commonwealth History* 14, no. 3 (1986).
———. *Empire and Sexuality.* Manchester: Manchester University Press, 1990.
Inglis, Ken. *Australian Colonists: An Exploration of Social History, 1788–1870.* Melbourne: Melbourne University Press, 1974.
Jackson, Louise A. *Child Sexual Abuse in Victorian England.* London: Routledge, 2000.
Jacoby, Robin Miller. *The British and American Women's Trade Union Leagues, 1890–1925: A Case Study of Feminism and Class.* Brooklyn: Carlson, 1994.
James, C.L.R. *Beyond a Boundary.* London: Stanley Paul, 1980.

James, Winston. *A Fierce Hatred of Injustice: Claude McKay's Jamaica and His Poetry of Rebellion.* Kingston: Ian Randle, 2001.
Johnson, Howard. "The Anti-Chinese Riots of 1918 in Jamaica". *Immigrants and Minorities* 2, no. 1 (1983).
Johnson, Michele A. "Intimate Enmity: Control of Women in Domestic Service in Jamaica, 1920–1970". *Jamaican Historical Review* 18 (1993).
———. "Decent and Fair: Aspects of Domestic Service in Jamaica, 1920–1970". *Journal of Caribbean History* 30, nos. 1–2 (1996).
———. "Young Woman from the Country: A Profile of Domestic Service in Jamaica, 1920–1970". In *Working Slavery, Pricing Freedom: The Caribbean and the Atlantic World since the Seventeenth Century,* edited by Verene Shepherd. Kingston: Ian Randle, 2002.
King, Ruby. "Elementary Education in Early Twentieth-Century Jamaica". *Caribbean Journal of Education* 16, no. 3 (1989).
———. "Education in the British Caribbean: The Legacy of the Nineteenth Century". In *Educational Reform in the Commonwealth Caribbean,* edited by Errol Miller. Washington, D.C.: Organization of American States, 1999.
Klass, Morton. *East Indians in Trinidad.* New York: Columbia University Press, 1961.
Lewin, Olive. *Rock It Come Over: The Folk Music of Jamaica.* Kingston: University of the West Indies Press, 2000.
Lewis, Rupert. "Claude McKay's Political Views". *Jamaica Journal* 19, no. 2 (1986).
———. "Garvey's Forerunners: Love and Bedward", *Race and Class* 28, no. 3 (1987).
Lewis, Rupert, and Patrick Bryan, eds. *Garvey, His Work and Impact.* Trenton, N.J.: Africa World Press, 1991.
Lewis, Rupert, and Maureen Warner Lewis. *Garvey: Africa, Europe, the Americas.* Trenton, N.J.: Africa World Press, 1994.
Look Lai, Walton. *Indentured Labor, Caribbean Sugar: Chinese and Indian Migrants to the British West Indies, 1838–1918.* Baltimore: Johns Hopkins University Press, 1993.
Lucas, J. *The Religion of the Yorubas.* Lagos: C.M.S. Bookshop, 1948.
Marshall, Woodville K. " 'We Be Wise to Many More Tings': Blacks' Hopes and Expectations of Emancipation". In *Caribbean Freedom: Society and Economy from Emancipation to the Present,* edited by Hilary Beckles and Verene Shepherd. Kingston: Ian Randle; London: James Currey, 1993.
Marti, Donald B. *Women of the Grange: Mutuality and Sisterhood in Rural America, 1866–1920.* New York: Greenwood, 1991.
Martin, Tony. *Race First: The Ideological and Organizational Struggles of Marcus Garvey and the Universal Negro Improvement Association.* Westport, Conn.: Greenwood, 1976.
Massiah, Joycelin. *Women and Heads of Household in the Caribbean: Family Structure and Feminine Status.* Paris: UNESCO, 1983.
Matthews, Jean V. *The Rise of the New Woman: The Women's Movement in America, 1875–1930.* Chicago: Ivan R. Dee, 2003.

Mbiti, John. *African Religions and Philosophy.* London: Heinemann, 1969.

———. *Introduction to African Religion.* Oxford: Heinemann Educational Books, 1991.

Milbourn, Pauline. *Child Abuse: A Collaborative Study in Jamaica, 1988 and 1989.* Kingston: Child Guidance Clinic, 1991.

Monteith, Kathleen E.A. "The Victorian Jubilee Celebrations of 1887 in Jamaica". *Jamaica Journal* 20, no. 4 (1987).

Moore, Brian L. *Race, Power and Social Segmentation in Colonial Society: Guyana after Slavery, 1838–1891.* New York: Gordon and Breach, 1987.

———. "The Settlement of Chinese in Guyana in the Nineteenth Century". *Immigrants and Minorities* 7, no. 1 (1988). Reprinted in *After the Crossing: Immigrants and Minorities in Caribbean Creole Society*, edited by Howard Johnson. London: Frank Cass, 1988.

———. *Cultural Power, Resistance and Pluralism: Guyana, 1838–1900.* Kingston: The Press, University of the West Indies, 1995.

Moore, Brian L., and Michele A. Johnson. " 'Fallen Sisters'? Attitudes to Female Prostitution in Jamaica at the Turn of the Twentieth Century". *Journal of Caribbean History* 34, nos. 1–2 (2000).

———. "Celebrating Christmas in Jamaica, 1865–1920: From Creole Carnival to 'Civilized' Convention". In *Jamaica in Slavery and Freedom: History, Heritage and Culture,* edited by Kathleen E.A. Monteith and Glen Richards. Kingston: University of the West Indies Press, 2002.

———. "Challenging the 'Civilizing Mission': Cricket as a Field of Socio-cultural Contestation in Jamaica, 1865–1920". In *In the Shadow of the Plantation: Caribbean History and Legacy,* edited by Alvin Thompson. Kingston: Ian Randle, 2002.

———. " 'Married but not Parsoned': Attitudes to Conjugality in Jamaica, 1865–1920". In *Control and Resistance in the Post- Emancipation Caribbean,* edited by Gad Heuman and David Trotman. London: Macmillan, 2004.

———, eds. *Land We Live In: Jamaica in 1890.* Kingston: Social History Project, Department of History, University of the West Indies, 2000.

———, eds. *"Squalid Kingston", 1890–1920: How the Poor Lived, Moved and Had Their Being.* Kingston: Social History Project, Department of History, University of the West Indies, 2000.

Moore, Brian L., and Swithin R. Wilmot, eds. *Before and After 1865: Education, Politics, and Regionalism in the Caribbean.* Kingston: Ian Randle, 1998.

Moore, Joseph G. "Music and Dance as Expressions of Religious Worship in Jamaica". In *African Religious Groups and Beliefs: Papers in Honor of William R. Bascom,* edited by Simon Ottenberg. Meerut, India: Published for the Folklore Institute by Archana Publications, *c.* 1982.

Morrissey, Marietta. "Explaining the Caribbean Family: Gender Ideologies and Gender Relations". In *Caribbean Portraits: Essays on Gender Ideologies and Identities,* edited by Christine Barrow. Kingston: Ian Randle, 1998.

Nadel, S.F. *Nupe Religion*. London: Routledge and Kegan Paul, 1954.
Odem, Mary E. *Delinquent Daughters: Protecting and Policing Adolescent Female Sexuality in the United States, 1885–1920*. Chapel Hill: University of North Carolina Press, 1995.
Olwig, Karen Fog. "The Struggle for Respectability: Methodism and Afro-Caribbean Culture on Nineteenth Century Nevis". *Nieuwe West-Indische Gids/New West Indian Guide* 64, nos. 3–4 (1990).
———. *Global Culture, Island Identity: Continuity and Change in the Afro-Caribbean Community of Nevis*. Philadelphia: Harwood Academic Publishers, 1993.
———, ed. *Small Islands, Large Questions: Society, Culture and Resistance in the Post-Emancipation Caribbean*. London: Frank Cass, 1995.
Osborne, Francis J. *History of the Catholic Church in Jamaica*. Chicago: Loyola University Press, 1988.
Parrinder, G. *West African Religion*. London: Epworth Press, 1949.
Pierson, Michael D. *Free Hearts and Free Homes: Gender and American Antislavery Politics*. Chapel Hill: University of North Carolina Press, 2003.
Pigou, Elizabeth. "A Note on Afro-Jamaican Beliefs and Rituals". *Jamaica Journal* 20, no. 2 (1987).
Porter, Andrew. " 'Cultural Imperialism' and Protestant Missionary Enterprise, 1780–1914". *Journal of Imperial and Commonwealth History* 25, no. 3 (1997).
Ranger, Terence. "The Invention of Tradition in Colonial Africa". In *The Invention of Tradition*, edited by Eric Hobsbawm and Terence Ranger. Cambridge: Cambridge University Press, 1983.
Rich, P.J. *Elixir of Empire*. 1989. Reprint, London: Regency, 1993.
Richards, Thomas. "The Image of Victoria in the Year of Jubilee". *Victorian Studies* 31, no. 1 (1987).
Robotham, Don. *"The Notorious Riot": The Socio-economic and Political Bases of Paul Bogle's Revolt*. Kingston: Institute of Social and Economic Research, 1981.
Sandiford, Keith A.P. *Cricket Nurseries of Colonial Barbados: The Elite Schools, 1865–1966*. Kingston: The Press, University of the West Indies, 1998.
Satchell, Veront M. *From Plots to Plantations: Land Transactions in Jamaica, 1866–1900*. Kingston: Institute of Social and Economic Research, 1990.
Savage, Gail. " 'The Wilful Communication of a Loathsome Disease': Marital Conflict and Venereal Disease in Victorian England". *Victorian Studies* 34, no. 1 (1990).
Schreuder, D.M. "The Cultural Factor in Victorian Imperialism: A Case Study of the British Civilizing Mission". *Journal of Imperial and Commonwealth History* 4, no. 3 (1976).
Schuler, Monica. "Myalism and the African Religious Tradition in Jamaica". In *Africa and the Caribbean: The Legacies of a Link*, edited by Margaret E. Crahan and Franklin W. Knight. Baltimore: Johns Hopkins University Press, 1979.

———. *"Alas, Alas, Kongo": A Social History of Indentured African Immigration into Jamaica, 1841–1865*. Baltimore: Johns Hopkins University Press, 1980.

Seaga, Edward. "Revival Cults in Jamaica: Notes towards a Sociology of Religion". *Jamaica Journal* 3, no. 2 (1969).

Shepherd, Verene. *Transients to Settlers: The Experience of Indians in Jamaica, 1845–1950*. Leeds: Peepal Tree, 1994.

Simpson, George Eaton. *Religious Cults of the Caribbean: Trinidad, Jamaica, and Haiti*. Caribbean Monographs, no. 18. Río Piedras: Institute of Caribbean Studies, University of Puerto Rico, 1980.

Slack, Paul. *From Reformation to Improvement: Public Welfare in Early Modern England*. Oxford: Clarendon; New York: Oxford University Press, 1999.

Smith, M.G. *Kinship and Community in Carriacou*. New Haven: Yale University Press, 1962.

Smith, Raymond T. *The Negro Family in British Guiana: Family Structure and Social Status in Villages*. New York: Grove, 1956.

———. "The Family in the Caribbean". In *Caribbean Studies: A Symposium*, edited by Vera Rubin. 2d ed. Seattle: University of Washington Press, 1960.

———. "The Matrifocal Family". In *The Character of Kinship*, edited by J. Goody. Cambridge: Cambridge University Press, 1973.

———. "Hierarchy and the Dual Marriage System in West Indian Society". In *Gender and Kinship: Essays toward a Unified Analysis*, edited by J.F. Collier and S.J. Yanagisako. Palo Alto, Calif.: Stanford University Press, 1987.

———. *Kinship and Class in the West Indies: A Genealogical Study of Jamaica and Guyana*. Cambridge: Cambridge University Press, 1988.

———. *The Matrifocal Family: Power, Pluralism, and Politics*. London: Routledge, 1996.

Stanley, Brian. *The History of the Baptist Missionary Society, 1792–1992*. Edinburgh: T. and T. Clark, 1992.

Stewart, Robert J. *Religion and Society in Post-Emancipation Jamaica*. Knoxville: University of Tennessee Press, 1992.

———. "A Slandered People: Views on 'Negro Character' in the Mainstream Christian Churches in Post-Emancipation Jamaica". In *Crossing Boundaries: Comparative History of Black People in Diaspora*, edited by Darlene Clarke Hine and Jacqueline McLeod. Bloomington: Indiana University Press, 1999.

Stoler, Ann Laura. "Rethinking Colonial Categories: European Communities and the Boundaries of Rule". *Comparative Studies in Society and History* 31, no. 1 (January 1989).

Storey, John. *An Introductory Guide to Cultural Theory and Popular Culture*. Athens: University of Georgia Press, 1993.

Sussman, Charlotte. *Consuming Anxieties: Consumer Protest, Gender, and British Slavery, 1713–1833*. Stanford, Calif.: Stanford University Press, 2000.

Sutherland, Gillian. *Policy-Making in Elementary Education, 1870–1895*. London: Oxford University Press, 1973.

Trotman, David Vincent. *Crime in Trinidad: Conflict and Control in a Plantation Society, 1838–1900*. Knoxville: University of Tennessee Press, 1986.

Turner, Mary. *Slaves and Missionaries: The Disintegration of Jamaican Slave Society, 1787–1834*. Urbana: University of Illinois Press, 1982.

Tyrrell, Ian. *Woman's World/Woman's Empire: The Woman's Christian Temperance Union in International Perspective, 1880–1930*. Chapel Hill: University of North Carolina Press, 1991.

Venet, Wendy Hamand. *Neither Ballots nor Bullets: Women Abolitionists and the Civil War*. Charlottesville: University Press of Virginia, 1991.

von Albertini, Rudolf. *European Imperial Rule, 1880–1940: The Impact of the West on India, Southeast Asia, and Africa*. Oxford: Clio, 1982.

Walvin, James. *The Life and Times of Henry Clarke of Jamaica, 1828–1907*. Ilford, Essex: Frank Cass, 1994.

Welter, Barbara. "The Cult of True Womanhood: 1820–1860". *American Quarterly* 18, no. 2 (Summer 1966).

Williams, Brackette F. *Stains on My Name, War in My Veins: Guyana and the Politics of Cultural Struggle*. Durham: Duke University Press, 1991.

Williams, Eric. *Capitalism and Slavery*. 1944. Reprint, New York: Russell and Russell, 1961.

Williams, Raymond. *Culture and Society*. Harmondsworth: Penguin, 1963.

———. "Base and Superstructure in Marxist Cultural Theory". In *Problems in Materialism and Culture*. London: Verso, 1980.

———. *Keywords*. London: Fontana, 1983.

Wilmot, Swithin. "Race, Electoral Violence and Constitutional Reform in Jamaica, 1850–54". *Journal of Caribbean History* 17 (1982).

———. "Females of Abandoned Character? Women and Protest in Jamaica, 1838–65". In *Engendering History: Caribbean Women in Historical Perspective*, edited by Verene A. Shepherd, Bridget Brereton and Barbara Bailey. Kingston: Ian Randle, 1995.

———, ed. *Adjustments to Emancipation in Jamaica*. Kingston: Social History Project, Department of History, University of the West Indies, 1988.

Zakai, Avihu. *Theocracy in Massachusetts: Reformation and Separation in Early Puritan New England*. Lewiston: Mellen University Press, c.1994.

Unpublished Theses/Dissertations/ Research Papers

Archer-Straw, Petrine. "Cultural Nationalism: Its Development in Jamaica, 1900–1944". MPhil thesis, University of the West Indies, 1987.

Brodber, Erna. "A Second Generation of Freemen in Jamaica, 1907–1944". PhD diss., University of the West Indies, 1985.

Brown, Marjorie E. "Rituals surrounding Death and Burial in Jamaica: African Retention or Inter-culturation?" MA thesis, University of the West Indies, 1986.

Campbell, Alistair. "The Life of Samuel Constantine Burke, 1836–1900". MPhil thesis, University of the West Indies, 1990.

Downes, Aviston DeC. "Barbados, 1880–1914: A Socio-Cultural History". PhD diss., University of York, 1994.

Gayle, Dorette Ethline. "The Moravian Church and Women's Roles in Post-Emancipation Jamaica, 1838–1865". MA thesis, University of the West Indies, 1988.

Grant, Robin L.F. "Class, Colour and Certain Social Concerns in Jamaica in 1865". MPhil thesis, University of the West Indies, 1985.

Grey, Kenneth. "The Image of the Elementary School Teacher, Jamaica, 1834–1980". MA thesis, University of the West Indies, 1983.

Kirkpatrick, J.W. "Protestant Missions in Jamaica (Being a Critical Survey of Mission Policy from 1754 to the Present Day)". PhD diss., University of Edinburgh, 1943.

Lawson, Winston. "Baptist, Methodist, and Anglican Churches in Jamaica, 1823–65". PhD diss., University of the West Indies, 1992.

Lumsden, Joy. "Robert Love and Jamaican Politics". PhD diss., University of the West Indies, 1988.

Moore, Joseph Graessle. "Religion of the Jamaican Negroes: A Study of Afro-Jamaican Acculturation". PhD diss., Northwestern University, 1953.

Schuler, Monica. "Alexander Bedward of Jamaica: A Black Nationalist?" Paper presented at the Sawyer Seminar, Department of History, Johns Hopkins University, 5 October 1998.

Speirs, Janet. "Poor Relief and Charity: A Study of Social Ideas and Practices in Post-Emancipation Jamaica". MPhil thesis, University of the West Indies, 2001.

Williams, Fay Aileen. "The Church of England and Education in Jamaica, 1838–1870". MA thesis, University of the West Indies, 1987.

Index

Aaron, E.M., 140
Afro-creole culture, xiv, 135, 170, 317, 324, 325
    Afro-creole world view, 133
    and "decency", 142
    cornerstone of creolization, 322
    cosmology, 318
    courtship, 104
    culture of resistance, xvii
    deplored, 321
    mainstream culture, xiii
    preservation of beliefs, 202
    persistence, 174
    revitalization, 321
    roots, xiv
    undermining by churches, 194–195
    war on, 176
Afro-Jamaican Christianity, regarded as blasphemy, 319
Albert Edward (Prince of Wales), 289
Amies, Marion, 139, 235
Anglicans. *See* Church of England
Anglicization, 320, 321
    contestation with creolization, 325
    retarded, 322, 323, 325
Anglo-creole culture, 321
Animals, treatment, 160–161
Arbor Day, 295
Arnold, Matthew, xiv
Assembly, self-abolition, 312
August Town, 79, 81
Austin-Broos, Diane, xii, 53, 170, 203

Bacon, Edgar, 140
Baden-Powell, Sir Robert, 301
Bakan, Abigail, 298
Baker, Capt. Lorenzo, 11, 252, 254
Baker, Moses, 51
Banbury, Rev. Thomas, 16, 21, 24, 35, 36, 38, 39, 45, 59, 61
Baptists
    Baptist Association Coolie Mission, 250
    Baptist Missionary Society, 168
    Calabar Institution (later College), 173, 227, 231
    disillusionment after Morant Bay, 5
    distancing from events at Morant Bay, 274
    Jamaican Baptist Union, 172
    Phillippo, Rev. James, 174
    Rally of Tribes, 191
    religious beliefs, 53–54
    rite of adult baptism, 186
    secondary education, 231
    teacher training, 227
    ticket system, 173
    Trelawny Girls' School, 236–237
    Underhill, Dr Edward, 174
Baptists, black American, 51, 168
Baptists, Native, 52, 55
Barbados, 294, 306
    behaviour of working classes, 162
    education in, 233
    marriage rates, 98
    queen's birthday, 274
    school attendance, 213

Barbarism, fear of reversion to, 2
Barrows, Miss M.M., 239
Bastardy, 97, 98, 103, 174, 320
    burden placed on women, 128
    fear of legitimizing, 130
    law of 1860, 125
    legitimization, 134–135
Beckwith, Martha, xii, 16, 21, 34, 42, 54, 56, 57, 58, 85, 104
Bedward, Rev. Alexander, 70, 72, 79–86
    allegation of insanity, 82
    confrontation with authorities, 85
    diagnosed insane, 79
    incarceration at Bellevue Asylum, 85–86
    millennium dream, 85
    preparations for ascension, 85
    second trial (1921), 85
    "seditious" speech, 83
    significance of, 86
    trial for sedition (1895), 83
Bedwardism
    August Town, 79
    Hope River, 79, 83
    spread, 84
Behaviour
    alleged influence of Africa and slavery, 148
    elite hypocrisy, 141–142
    lower classes, 148–165
    upper and middle classes, 140–148
Bell, Rev. Dr, 78
Bellows, W., 163
Besson, Jean, 98, 108
Black family
    conjugal relationship, 104–105
    divorce, 105
    household (definition), 103
    laws to regulate, 122
    living conditions, 104
    matrifocality, 103–104
    structure, 103
    women and child rearing, 106
Blacks
    alleged savagery, 149
    composition and status, 9–10
    intelligentsia, 9–10
Board of Education, 295, 308
Boer (South African) War, 181, 300
    interest in, 303
Bogle, Paul, 2, 7
Bolland, Nigel, xvi–xvii, xviii
Boston Fruit Company, 11
Boy Scouts Association, 301–302, 305, 306
Boys' Social League, 301
Brathwaite, Edward Kamau, xvi
Brazil, zumbi, 36
Brereton, Bridget, 12
British colonial subjects, moulding of, 273
British culture, 321
    alternative, xiii
    and colonial civilization, 245
    and Christian morality, 320
    importance, 12
    replication, xiv
    status, 322
British Empire, 272
British Empire Producers' Organization, 308
British flag, 181
British Guiana. *See* Guyana
British imperial ideology, 315
British military forces, 164, 314
    British Army regiments, 6
    British North American and West Indian Squadron (the Fleet), 6, 290, 298–299, 314
    ritualistic parades, 298
    West India regiments, 6
British monarchy, 271

loyalty to, 272, 274, 275, 276, 281, 289, 290, 291, 298, 303, 306, 307, 309, 314, 315, 320
  transformation into imperial institution, 272
Britishness, symbols of, 271
British rule, alleged impact, 164
Brodber, Erna, xix
Bryan, Patrick, xi, xii, 4, 6, 7, 8, 10, 12, 97, 102, 107–108, 173, 243
Bullen, Frank, 150
Burton, Richard D.E., 95, 323–324, 325
  resistance/opposition, xvii–xviii
Butcher, Mrs T.B., 20

Cadet corps, 301
Calabar Institution (later College), 173, 227, 231
Campbell, Carl, 207, 208, 210, 225, 227, 235, 243
Canadian Presbyterian Church (Trinidad), 251, 255
Cannadine, David, 272
Capper, Thomas, 225
Caribbean culture, and Gramscian theory of hegemony, xv
Carlile, Rev. Warrand, 21, 246
Chamberlain, Joseph, 133, 222, 299
Chevannes, Barry, xii, 55, 95
Children
  abandonment, 157
  abuse, 158
  care, 157–158
  conversion of Chinese, 268
  indecent language, 151–152
  infanticide and concealment of birth, 157–158
  methods of punishment, 106
  treatment, 106
Chinese, 319
  cemetery, 268
  Christianity, 267–269
  Confucian temple, 248–249, 268, 286–287
  Confucianism, 247, 268
  conversion of children, 268
  creolization, 270
  gambling dens/shops, 198, 247
  gambling, 249, 270
  immigration, 246
  opium, 249, 270
  participation in royal events, 285, 286–287
  population statistics, 246
  "uncultured" behaviour, 13
  See also Immigrants
Christianity
  africanization, 51
  and education, 205–206
  linkage with empire, 271, 273
  purpose of proselytization, 168
  See also Churches, and Nonconformist missionaries
Christmas, 195
Churches
  and Jamaican Christianity, 202–204
  anti-obeah activities, 197
  as community centres, 191
  attendance and clothing, 178, 183–184
  charity for deserving poor, 190
  Christian Endeavour, 188
  commemorating Emancipation Day, 180–181
  commemorating imperial events, 181, 316–317
  construction, 176
  converting Indians, 249–250
  dependence on offerings, 183
  desecration of the Sabbath, 199
  dominance in education, 206
  elite, 5
  female organizations, 188

Churches *(continued)*
    fight against gambling, 197–198
    fight against immorality, 196–201
    fight against non-legal marriage,
        196–197
    focus on sexual activity, 197
    funding Indian missions, 250
    harvest festivals, 179–180
    house visits, 182
    importance of services, 178–179
    "improving" Jamaican character, 140
    indifference among upper classes, 200
    indigenization of clergy, 172–173
    influences of, 192–195
    involvement in members' private
        lives, 182
    language barriers with Chinese, 267
    language barriers with Indians, 250
    links with state, 314, 317
    love feasts, 186–187
    male organizations, 188
    penny savings banks, 185, 190
    public cultural events, 191
    public rituals, 186–187
    quarrels among members, 200–201
    religious associations, 187–190
    religious indifference, 198–199
    religious publications, 185–186
    religious tracts, 182, 188
    services for 1887 jubilee, 277–278
    services for secular events, 180–181
    social entertainment, 180, 191–192
    social purity societies, 188, 197
    Sunday schools, 178
    support of empire, 181, 300, 316–317
    unruly members, 201
    use of "free labour", 176
    vanguard of civilizing process, 312
Church Missionary Society, 168, 172
Church of England, 5, 136, 167, 316
    and "illegitimacy", 120–121, 122, 126
    and Chinese, 267
    and Indians, 250, 251, 265
    British monarch head of, 271
    compulsory registration of paternity,
        127–129
    cynicism of lay members, 130–131
    disestablishment, 172, 212, 317
    opposition to 1879 Marriage Law, 114
    schools, 212
    secondary education for girls, 238
    Social Purity Society, 122
Church of God (Pentecostal), 174
Church of Scotland, 5, 167, 188
    and Chinese, 267
    and Indians, 250
    opposition to compulsory registration
        of paternity, 129–130
    See also Presbyterian churches
"Civilization", xiii, 2, 5, 167 ff, 245,
    and education, 214–215, 228, 243
    and Victorian Christianity, 97, 315
    apparent success, 166, 193
    Asian immigrants, 247, 249
    borne by browns and blacks, 173, 314
    despair of bearers, 325
    failure, 135, 312, 323
    Indian converts, 255–256, 261, 262
    missionary goal, 170
    objective, 137
    preservation, 313
    renewal after 1865, 171
    resistance to, 138, 264
    retarded, 320, 321, 325
    similarity in Britain and Jamaica, xv
Clarke, Rev. Henry, 124–128, 132, 134
Clerk, Astley, 9, 308
Coles, Rev. C.H., 100, 125, 129, 132, 133
Colonial government, building schools,
    206
Colonial Office, 134, 296, 313
    1909 "concubinage" circular, 119

attitude to flogging for obeah, 27, 32
compulsory education, 219–220
criticism of 1879 marriage law, 114
education policy, 218
political reform (1884), 4
power of, 3
Registration bill (1900),133
Colonial Subjects, attempts to transform Jamaicans, xiii
Coloureds
composition and status, 9
interest of, 7
Compulsory registration of paternity, 320
Anglican Synod, 127–128
arguments against, 131–132
elite opposition, 136
position of crown government, 132–133
Registration bill (1900), 127–128
"Concubinage", 98, 140, 174, 317, 321,
efforts to eradicate, 114–115
elite, 320
elite versus peasant, 107
"moral degradation", 113
old planter tradition, 133
See also Marriage (non-legal)
Confucianism, 319
Contestation, process of, xiii, xv
Cornish, Vaughn, 163, 164
Coronations, 272, 315
ball at King's House, 287
behaviour of people, 285
celebrations, 284–286
children's processions, 287
church services, 286, 287
decorations and illuminations, 286–287
governor's levee, 286, 287
postponement of Edward VII's, 284
Cosmology
Afro-creole, 318

Afro-Jamaican, 51
West African, 169, 318
Cotton tree, location for shadow catching, 61
Craton, Michael, 103
Creole culture. *See* Afro-creole culture
Creolization, 320, 322
contestation with Anglicization, 325
dialectical theory, xvi
Indian immigrants, 248
potency, 321
process, xv–xvi, 323
Croll, Martha B., 251, 254, 258
Crown colony government, 95, 206, 297
economic policies, 313
establishment, 3, 312
Cult of monarchy and empire, 295, 299, 300, 308, 309, 322
legitimization by churches, 316
Cult of true womanhood, 281
Cultural imperialism, 311, 320
Cultural nationalism, 95
Cultural policies, British, xiv
Cultural resistance, 136
Cultural self-determination, xiii, xv, 46, 94, 95, 136, 203, 319, 320, 322, 324
Cultural system
African based, 14
Afro-creole, 14
Culture
of exuberance, 153
of noise, 152–153
See also Afro-creole culture, Anglo-creole culture, British culture, Plantocratic cultural tradition, and Victorian culture
Cundall, Frank, 44, 102, 134, 163, 164, 231
Curtin, Philip, xii, 52, 53, 54, 168, 170, 171

Darling, Capt. Charles (governor), 140, 289

De Certeau, Michel, xviii, 323
De Lisser, H.G., 57, 100, 102, 127
Disturbances, 6, 163
Downes, Aviston, 162
Drinking, 197, 260, 317
Duff, John, 253, 258
Duppies, 36–43, 317
    definition, 36
    description and activities, 36–37
    Duppy Pumpkin, 39
    in Kumina, 93
    Myal/"Four-eye Man", 41
    propitiation of, 61
    rituals to protect children, 41–42
    stone throwing, 39–40
    types and forms, 38
    universal belief and fear, 37
    upper class beliefs, 41
    West African provenance, 36

Earl of Meath, 294, 295, 299
Earthquake of 1907, 99
    impact on religion, 200
Education, 205
    age restrictions for elementary education, 215
    agency for imperialism, 220, 244
    agricultural and industrial curriculum, 222
    and Christianity, 205–206, 207
    and civilizing mission, 214–215, 228, 243
    and social mobility, xiii, 222–223
    and system of domination, xiii
    attendance at school, 211–216
    Barbican School for Girls, 236
    basic skills, 209–210
    black lower classes, xiv
    Calabar Institution, 231
    church control of curriculum, 207
    Church of England and Indians, 265
    Church of England High School, 229
    Church of Scotland Collegiate School, 229
    church-state alliance, 208, 209
    class bias in education, 229, 231
    codes of regulations, 211, 221, 243
    competition among churches, 208
    compulsory education, 216–220
    control of teachers, 207
    delivery of moral education, 209, 211, 223
    denominational schools and teacher training institutions, 212
    Diocesan High School, 238
    Education Commission (1898), 217, 222
    education laws, 208, 215, 217, 219, 232
    education of Indians, 262–267
    endowed trust schools, 238
    expenditure, 211
    extension of education, 176
    external examinations, 232
    free schools (later high schools), 232
    Gilchrist Scholarship, 242
    girls in elementary schools, 215–216
    grants-in-aid, 211
    imported elementary curriculum, 220
    Indian girls, 263
    Indian non-attendance at school, 263–264
    Indians and Christian dogma, 262
    Indians in state schools, 265
    instilling discipline and industry, 223
    instilling imperial Christian ideologies, 206
    Jamaica High School (later College), 232, 234, 241
    Jamaica Scholarship for boys, 242
    Jamaica Scholarship for girls, 240
    Jamaica Schools Commission, 232, 241

Jamaica Union of Teachers, 216, 222
Kingston School Board, 219
lateness and truancy, 214
legal definition of secondary
    education, 228
Miss Long (Kingston High School
    for Girls), 239
Montego Bay High School, 232
Moravian teacher training colleges,
    227
Negro Education Grant, 206
objectives of education, 205, 243–244
penny savings banks in schools, 224
physical drills in curriculum, 211,
    223–224
private secondary schools for girls,
    238–240
promotion of Victorian ideology
    among girls, 235
Quakers and Indians, 265
Quakers in general education, 213
Queen's College, 240–241
reasons for non-attendance at school,
    213–214
religion in secondary curriculum, 228
religious instruction in teachers'
    colleges, 227–228
religious objectives and rituals, 207
Rhodes Scholarship, 242–243
role of Institute of Jamaica, 241–242
role of teachers, 224
Roman Catholic high schools for
    girls, 235–236
school fees, 211–212, 213
schools as extensions of churches, 318
schools promoting imperial loyalty,
    209
Scottish Presbyterians and Indians,
    265
secondary education for girls,
    234–240

secondary education, 228–240
separate schools for Indian children,
    264–265
Shortwood female teacher college,
    227
St George's College, 229–230
St Joseph's College, 227
St Mary's, 238
state and Indian children, 262
teacher training colleges, 227–228
teachers as moral messengers, 228
teachers, 224–227
tertiary education, 240–243
Trelawny Girls School / Westwood
    High School for Girls, 236
types of schools, 212
University College, 241
Victorian focus of curriculum, 207,
    220
Wesleyan Methodists and education
    for girls, 236
whipping for truancy, 219
York Castle High School, 230
Edward, Prince of Wales, 290–291
Eisner, Gisela, xi
Elites (cultural), xiv, 13, 135, 201, 322, 323
    attitude to non-legal unions, 320
    colonial mentality, 245
    composition, 12
    cultural power, 325
    frustration with Indians, 264
Elites (social), 8, 13, 176
    attitude to emancipation, 273
    clinging to Britain, 296–297
    fear of black insurrection, 274
    identification with crown and
        empire, 272
    meaning of imperial symbols, 310
    planters, 318
    preservation of hegemony, xiii
    promoters of new social order, xiii

Elites (social) *(continued)*
  psychological needs, 272
  royal celebrations, 316
  shared views with colonial officials, 313
Elkins, W.F., xii
Emancipation, 271, 309
  commemoration, 180–181
Emerick, Abraham, 31, 37, 87
Empire
  cult, 271, 277
  extolling virtues, 295
  loyalty, 294, 305
  promotion in schools, 209
Empire Day, 181, 294, 296, 300,
  catechism, 209, 295, 308
  celebrations, 295
  children's participation, 294
  promotion in schools, 209
  rituals, 296
  subverting creole culture, 295
Ex-slaves, post-emancipation struggles, 1
Eyre, Edward John, 4, 7, 171, 175, 273, 297, 298

Family
  male-headed nuclear model, 97
  See also Black family
Farquharson, 8, 308
Fiji, 247
First World War, 181, 303
Flag Day, 181–182, 304–305
Folk medicine. *See* Herbal medicine
Foucault, Michel, 324, 325
Franchise
  qualifications, 4
  women, 4–5
Fruit trade, 11

Gall, James, 273
Gambling, 197, 270, 317
  Chinese drop-pan lottery, 198

Gardner, William James, 107, 229
Garvey, Marcus Mosiah, xi, 9
  attitude to working class behaviour, 162
  embrace of Victorian moral culture, 320
  loyalty to British empire, 303–304
Gaunt, Mary Eliza Bakewell, 149
Gibb, George, 51
Gilchrist Scholarship, 242
Gillies, Rev. William, 127, 130
Gillion, K.L., 247
Girl Guides Association, 302, 305, 306
  and Victorian gender ideology, 302
Gordon, George W., 7
Gordon, Shirley, 54
Gordon, Charles (Roman Catholic Bishop), 81
Goulbourne, Harry, 222
Governor, 315
  autocratic power, 3, 297
  levees, 275, 279, 281
Graham, William, 129–130
Gramsci, Antonio, 322
Grant, Sir John Peter, 4, 88, 90, 122, 208, 211, 240
Green, William A., xvii
Greenlee, J.G., 300
Guyana, 10, 251, 267, 271, 275, 314
  assertiveness of women, 160
  Chinese converts, 268
  compulsory education, 218–219
  domestic violence, 159–160
  education, 213, 233
  elite male womanizers, 109
  Indian conversions, 257–258
  Indians and obeah, 248
  jumbi, 36
  legitimization of bastards, 134
  long bubbies and rolling calves, 38
  obeah, 15, 58, 60

"ole haig", 34
punishment of children, 158
queen's birthday, 274
school attendance, 213
Watermamma, 35

Haiti, fear of replication in Jamaica, 2, 312
    Vodun, 55
    zambi, 36
Hall, Catherine, xii, 5, 97, 139, 145, 181
Hallam, Arthur A., 251
Harrison (white Revivalist), 78–79
Healing, 62–67
    balm-yard, 62
    Myal/obeah practitioners, 62
    use of herbs, 62–63
    use of oils, 62
Hegemony
    Gramscian theory, xv
    preservation, 2
    role of education, 205
    ruling elites, xii, xiii
Hemming, Sir Augustus, 115, 126, 217, 294
    and obeah, 33
Herbal medicine, 62
    and the law, 65
    bush baths, 63
    general use of, 62–63
    popularity of bush doctors, 64–65
    use by upper classes, 63–64
Hewitt, Rev., 77–78
Higginbotham, Evelyn, 173, 228
Higgins, Charles "Warrior", 76–77
    Higginsism, 77
    relationship with Bedward, 76
Higman, B.W., 103
Hinduism, 317, 319
Holt, Thomas C., xi, 4, 11
Hyam, Ronald, 109, 119

Ideology of God and empire, 181
"Illegitimacy", 117–121, 140, 317, 319
    alleged consequences, 123
    and house tax, 122–123
    and the clergy, 119–120
    black lower class, 117
    child maintenance law 1869, 122
    Church of England Purity Society, 122
    considered a "social evil", 115
    efforts to compel paternal maintenance, 121–135
    hostility of churches, 117, 120–121, 123
    ideological basis of the law, 121
    old planter customs, 117
    racialized, 132
    rates, 117
    stigma, 117
    upper and middle class men, 117–118
Immigrants
    cultural complexity, xv
    differences from creole population, 246
    Germans, 8
    "uncultured" behaviour of Chinese, 13
    "uncultured" behaviour of Indians, 13
    See also Chinese and Indians
Imperial rituals, 275–276, 298, 309, 315
Imperial ethic, fostering, 299
Imperial Order of the Children of the Empire, 303, 308
Imperial Order of the Daughters of the Empire, 302
Indecent language
    children, 151–152
    lower classes, 150–152
    upper and middle classes, 145
    women, 150–152
Indian "Mutiny", 5, 312

Indians, 319
   and Church of England, 250, 251, 265
   and civilizing mission, 255–256, 261
   and Quakers, 251, 252, 265
   and Scottish Presbyterians, 250, 251, 265
   and Wesleyan Methodists, 252
   attempts to convert to Christianity, 249–262
   Brahmin priests, 247
   Canadian Presbyterian Church (Trinidad), 251, 255
   catechists, 251, 254–255, 261
   Christian converts, 253–254
   conversion of children in schools, 261, 263
   creole Jamaican participation in festivals, 248
   creolization, 260–261
   education and Christian dogma, 262
   education and role of the state, 262, 265
   education in English and Hindi, 264, 266–267
   education of girls, 263
   focus on boys' education, 266
   ganja, 248, 260, 270
   government assistance in Christian conversion, 254
   Hinduism, 247, 250, 257–258
   Hosay (Mohurrum) festival, 248, 263
   Immigration, 245
   intemperance, 248, 260–261
   Islam, 247–248, 250, 257–258
   Muslim imams, 247
   Obeah, 248
   participation in royal events, 285
   perceived benefits of education, 266
   persecution/ostracism of converts, 256–257
   population statistics, 245–246
   Presbyterian East Indian Mission, 251
   race prejudice towards creole Jamaicans, 252, 263
   reluctance to school children, 263
   resistance to Christianity, 258–259, 259–260, 261, 262, 270
   role of estates in Christian conversion, 254
   separate schools, 264–265
   teachers, 264
   "uncultured" behaviour, 13
   See also Immigrants
Institute of Jamaica, 282
   music and drawing examinations, 242
   role in tertiary education, 241–242
   University of Cambridge examinations, 241

Jamaica High School (College), 128, 223, 232, 241
Jamaica Scholarship, 240, 242
Jamaica Imperial Association, 308–309
Jamaica Union of Teachers, 216
   opposition to agricultural education, 222
Jamaica Memories, xix
Jamaica Baptist Union, 173
Jamaica Congregational Union, 173
Jamaica Exhibition, 290
Jamaican historiography, xi
Jamaican Patriotic League, 308
James, Winifred, 103
Jews, 8
Jordan, Edward, 121
Josephs, Hector, 9, 10
Jubilees
   Accession Day celebrations (1887), 277
   behaviour of people, 280, 282
   celebrations, 277–283
   children's participation, 278, 282

church services, 277–278, 281
Coronation Day celebrations (1887), 277
decorations and illuminations, 276–277, 279
governor's levee, 279, 281
imperial rituals, 281
Jubilee Market, 155, 279
ringing of church bells, 277

Kangaloo, Henry, 265
King Edward VII, 272
  birthday celebrations, 275
  coronation celebrations, 284–286
  death, 286, 294
  holiday to commemorate, 296
  installation, 284
King George V, 272, 290, 296
  birthday celebrations, 275
  coronation celebrations, 286–287
King, Ruby, 205, 211, 221, 222, 231, 243
King's House, 275, 289, 290, 297
  jubilee ball, 280
Kingston riot (1912), 6, 163
Kumina, 55, 92–94, 174, 317
  and obeah, 92, 93
  and Pukumina, 92
  and Zion Revival, 93
  beliefs of practitioners, 93
  Central African provenance, 92
  connection to Kongos, 92–93
  description, 93
  queen, 93
  shadow/duppy, 93
  use of drums, 93

Lads'/Boys' Brigades, 301
Leader, Alfred, 165
League of the Children of the Empire, 301
Legislative Council
  division over compulsory registration of paternity, 134
  establishment, 3
  jubilee planning, 276–277
  representation in, 4
Lisele/Leile, George, 51
Livingstone, W.P., 27, 99, 100, 101, 102, 103, 107, 124, 126, 127, 130, 141, 143, 307
London Missionary Society, 168
  compulsory education, 217
  Jamaica Congregational Union, 173
  secondary education, 229
Love, Dr Robert, xi, 9, 152, 162, 293
  embrace of Victorian moral culture, 320
Lower classes
  alleged respect for whites, 164
  assaults, 154
  culture of exuberance, 153
  culture of noise, 152–153
  domestic violence, 159–160
  etiquette, 165
  "free fights", 156–157
  indecent language, 150
  migration and crime, 157
  respect for law/authority, 163–164
  social deference, 165
  stick-licking, 156–157
  stoning, 157
  street brawls, 154–155
  urban slums, 157
Lumb, Charles F., 32–33

Makin, William, 41, 56
Manning, W.H., 219, 302, 306
Marriage (legal)
  attitudes of churches, 102–103
  attitudes of elites, 108–113
  attitudes of lower class women, 102
  benefits, 99

Marriage (legal) *(continued)*
   ideal of legal Christian monogamy, 96, 101
   middle-class male reluctance, 108–109
   rarity of mixed-race unions, 106–107
   rates, 98, 99–100
   reluctance of working-class males, 102
   sanctity, 319
Marriage (non-legal), 97ff
   and the law, 113–117
   assumed insecurity, 103
   stability and cordiality, 101, 105
   See also "Concubinage"
Marriage laws, 113–114, 116
   Scottish code, 114–115
Marriage and Registration Commission, 115–116, 134
McKay, Claude, xi, 9
Meath. *See* Earl of Meath
Methodists. *See* Wesleyan Methodists
Mico Institution (later Training College), 212, 227, 295
Middle class
   black, xiii
   coloured and black, emphasis on British cultural attributes, 12
   Victorian etiquette, 317
Military and police forces, use of, 312
Militias, 6
   disbandment, 314
   new Volunteer Militias, 314
Millennial Dawnists, 174
Missionaries. *See* Nonconformist missionaries
Mitchell, S.R., 251, 259, 261
Monarch's birthday, 181
   annual celebration, 315
   Edward VII, 275
   George V, 275
   invented tradition, 274
   Victoria, 274–275
Montego Bay High School, 232
Montego Bay riot (1902), 6, 163
Moore, Joseph G., 54, 56, 57, 92, 93
Morant Bay, xi, 1, 2, 3, 5, 6–7, 13, 163, 167, 171, 172, 174, 175, 205, 271, 272, 274, 296, 298, 309, 311, 312
Moravian Church, 168, 174, 186, 188
   attitude to obeah, 25
   teacher training colleges, 227
Morrison, William, 307, 309
Morrissey, Marietta, 108
Musgrave, Sir Anthony, 217, 218, 242
Myal. *See* Revival

Nadel, S.F., 34
Narcotics
   ganja, 246, 248, 270, 260
   opium, 246, 249, 270
National anthem, 275, 277, 306
   additional stanza for jubilee, 278
   in Empire Day celebrations, 295
Negotiation, process of, xiii, xv
Newton, Margaret, 164, 306
Nonconformist missionaries
   agents of "civilization", 167
   and civilizing mission, 5
   as educators, 206
   attitudes to freed people, 5
   distancing from events at Morant Bay, 274
   relations with Afro-Jamaicans, 171
   religious and moral values, 96
Norman, Sir Henry, 233
North, Marianne, 17, 90
Nuttall, Enos, 81, 126, 127, 129, 134, 172, 209, 251, 259, 267, 316

Obeah, 15ff, 59, 94, 174, 317, 319, 321, 322
   and Kumina, 92, 93
   associated with Africans, 17

attitude of Christian churches, 24–25, 197
beliefs, 15
connection to Myal/Revival, 58
attempts at control, 27–33
courts, 28–29
definition, 15
elite and Christian believers, 24–26
floggings, 29–33
functionality, 16
laws, 27–28
literature, 22–23
paraphernalia, 18–19
penalties, 28
police supervision, 29
practitioners, 15, 16–17, 22–23
prevalence, 26–27
services, 19–22
West African provenance, 15
Old hige, 34–35
Olivier, Sir Sydney, 65, 132–133, 293
attacked by rioters, 163
Olwig, Karen Fog, 97, 107
Our Day, 305–306
Overseas Club, 300

"Panya jars" (Spanish jars), 45
Patriarchal order, gender hierarchy, 96
Patriotic songs, 297
Peace Day, 306
Peasantry, 10–11
economic struggles, 313
loyalty to Queen Victoria, 273–274
Penny savings banks, 185
in schools, 224
Phillippo, Rev. James, 174
Plantations, revival of, 10–11
Plantocratic cultural tradition, xiv, 320
and "concubinage", 133
attitude to legal marriage, 107
characteristics, 137

survival, 136, 146, 148
Plymouth Brethren, 174
Police
and females offenders, 155–156
and obeah, 28–29
and Revival, 89–91
Jamaica Constabulary Force, 6, 314
Rural Police Force, 6, 314
strength, 164
targets of rioters, 163
Population statistics, 7
Praedial larceny, 185
Presbyterian East Indian Mission, 251
Presbyterian churches, 185
and Indians, 251, 265
attitude to "illegitimacy", 123
attitude to obeah, 25
secondary education, 229
See also Church of Scotland, United Presbyterian Church and United Free Church of Scotland
Price, Ernest, 165
Prince George Frederick, 289–290
Prince Albert, 290
Prince of Wales, birthday, 274
Prince Alfred, 289
Prince Albert Victor, 289–290
Princess Louise of Schleswig-Holstein, 290
Probyn, Lady, 4–5
Puk(k)umina. *See* Revival
Pullen-Burry, Bessie, 20, 27, 43, 59, 63, 102, 164

Quakers, 174
and Indians, 251
and the Chinese, 268
attitude to obeah, 24–25
education of Indian children, 265
in education, 213
Queen Victoria, 315

Queen Victoria *(continued)*
   association with emancipation, 273
   birthday celebrations, 274–275
   commemoration, 296
   imperial image, 272
   jubilees, 181, 272, 276–283, 315
   model of "true woman", 281
   mourning for, 284, 292–294
   personal loyalty to, 316

Racial stereotypes, 148–49
Rampini, Charles, 17, 37, 43, 68, 123, 154, 160, 161
Red Cross Society, 305
Registration bill (1900)
   disallowed, 133
   nonconformist reaction, 134
Resistance, 95, 166
   among Asian immigrants, 319
   among planters, 323
   resistance, cultural, xv
   resistance-opposition binary, xviii
   to churches' moral crusade, 197
Respectability, 317
   cult, 141, 143, 147
   ideology, 97
Revival, 16, 51ff, 94, 95, 174, 175, 317, 319
   Afro-creole, 5, 51
   allegations of insanity, 71–72
   and the law, 58, 76
   angels, 54
   anti-obeah ritual, 58–60
   attempts at control, 89–91
   attitude of Wesleyan Methodists, 87
   balm-yards, 66
   connection to Baptists, 55
   connection to obeah, 58, 61
   cultural elite/missionary response, 87
   definitions, 52–53
   duppy catchers, 62
   fountainists, 70
   "Four-eyed" man/woman, 41, 61
   Great Revival (1860–62), 54, 311
   hostility of Bishop of Kingston, 88
   missionary war against, 171
   Moody and Sankey hymns, 57, 73
   official position, 88–92
   political agitators, 75–76
   prophesying and warning, 69
   public and private services, 57
   public outbreaks, 54–55
   Pukumina, 55–56
   relationship with Kumina, 93
   religious beliefs, 52, 53–54
   rituals, 56–57
   rooting out evil, 58
   shadow catching, 60–62
   speaking in tongues, 69
   spirit possession, 51, 56, 67–70
   street preachers, 74–76
   tarrying for the Spirit, 68
   trumping/trooping, 57–58, 69
   upsurges, 55
   West African provenance, 59, 60–61
   women, 73–74
   Zion, 55–56
Rhodes Scholarship, 242–243
Rich, P.J., 275, 298
Riots, 6, 163
River Mumma, 35–36
Rolling calves, 38–39
Roman Catholic Church, 5, 178
   and "illegitimacy", 120
   and the Chinese, 268
   charity work, 190
   feasts, 179
   secondary education for girls, 235–236
   St George's College, 229–230
   teacher training at St Joseph's College, 227
Rosebery, Lord, 299
Royal birthdays, 274

Royal celebrations, 274–292, 315
Royal celebrities, interest in personal lives, 291
Royal Colonial Institute, 308
Royal deaths, 292–294
Royal events and churches, 316
Royal Jamaica Yacht Club, 275, 290
Royal marriages, local interest, 291–292
Royal visits, 289–291
Rum-shops, 197

Salvation Army, 174, 305
    charity work, 190, 285
Sargeant, George, 236
Satchell, Veront M., xi, 8, 10–11
Schuler, Monica, xii, 15, 53, 54, 92, 93, 170
Schwartz, Bill, xii
Scott, Sir Sibbald, 163, 164
Scottish Missionary Society, 168
Scottish Presbyterians. *See* Presbyterian churches
Seaga, Edward, 55, 56
Seventh Day Adventists, 174
Shepherd, Verene, xii, 252, 267
Simms, Canon William, 124, 128–129, 130, 131, 223, 226
Simpson, H.A. Leslie, 4, 9
Simpson, George Eaton, xii
Slave culture, 168
Smith, Raymond, 103
Society for the Propagation of the Gospel, 168, 172, 175
Society of Friends. *See* Quakers
Solien, Nancie, 103
Spinner, Alice, 36, 37, 41
Splaine, Father James, 61, 100, 101, 165, 166, 183
St Catherine (anti-Chinese) riot (1918), 6, 163
St Lucia, legitimization of bastards, 134
St Josephs' College, 227
St Vincent, Shakers outlawed, 92
Stewart, Robert, xii, 52, 54, 60, 61, 92, 168, 169, 170, 171, 173, 182, 185, 193, 218
Stoler, Ann, 140
Storey, John, xv
Street brawls
    lower classes, 154–155
    women, 154–155
"Superstitions", 43–44
    upper class, 44
Suriname, Watramamma, 35
Swettenham, Sir James, 134, 209, 216
Swift, Rev. Arthur, 252, 260
Symmonett, Ethel, 62

Teachers, 318
Trinidad, 314
    Chinese converts, 268
    domestic violence, 159–160
    education, 206, 207, 208, 213, 224, 225, 227–228, 233, 235
    Indian conversions, 257–258
    legitimization of bastards, 134
    marriage rates, 98
    Orisha/Shango, 55–56, 92
    punishment of children, 158
    school attendance, 213
    Shouters outlawed, 92
    "soucouyant", 34
    source of Indian catechists, 265
    stick-fighting, 156
Trotman, David, 158, 160
Turner, Mary, xii, 15, 52, 168, 169, 170

Underhill, Dr Edward, 174
United Brethren, attitude to obeah, 25
United Fruit Company, 11, 252, 254
United Presbyterian Church, 177
United Free Church of Scotland, 177

Upper classes
  and Victorian behaviour, 143–144
  crime, 147
  divorce, 147
  public brawling, 146
  religious indifference, 200
  rowdyism, 146–147
  use of indecent language, 145
Urban slums, 166
  conditions of life, 11
  poverty, 10
  crime, 157

Verrill, Alpheus, 163, 164
Victoria League, 300, 302
Victoria Day, 294, 296, 300
Victorian Christianity, 194, 319
  and civilization, 97, 315
  behavioural ethic, 172
  ideals, 96
  imposition, 176
  morality, 97
  morals and etiquette, 137
  role of churches, 191
Victorian culture
  embraced by black elites, 141, 320
  embraced by social elites, 323
  etiquette, 280
  importation, xiv
  "oppositional" to creole culture, 325
Victorian cultural agenda, xv
Victorian gender ideals
  image of gentleman (manliness), 139–140
  image of lady (true womanhood), 109, 138–139
  patriarchal society, 138
Victorian gender ideology, and secondary education for girls, 235

Waddell, Rev. Hope, 59, 67

Water rituals, 70–71
Watson, Rev. James, 175, 196
Wesleyan Methodists
  and Indians, 252
  and the Chinese, 268
  attitude to obeah, 25
  Barbican School for Girls, 236
  "illegitimacy", 120, 123
  Rally of Tribes, 191
  ticket system, 173
  Wesleyan Methodist Missionary Society, 168, 174, 206
  York Castle, 227, 230
West India Regiments, 85, 297, 306, 314
West India Committee, 308
Western medicine, deficiencies, 62
Whites
  preservation of dominance, 1
  crime, 147
  poor, 8
  middle class, 8
  composition and status, 7–8
  women, 8–9
Wilcox, Ella, 165
Williams, Brackette, 148
Williams, Joseph John, xii, 16, 35, 36, 59
Williams, Raymond, xiii
Women
  attitude to legal marriage, 102
  authority in the black family, 104–105
  burden of bastardy, 128
  child rearing, 106
  Chinese Christian converts, 267–268
  church organizations and activity, 188–189
  coloured, 9
  concubinary relationships with elite men, 107–108
  cult of true womanhood, 138, 188
  education of Indian girls, 263
  education, 215–216

exemption from flogging for obeah, 27
franchise, 4–5
heads of families/households, 103–104
hostility to "new woman", 112–113
in urban slums, 11
indecent language, 150–152
influence on elite male behaviour, 140
Moravian teacher training colleges, 227
music examinations, 242
"new woman", 109–112
old higes, 34
perpetrators of domestic violence, 160
resisting police, 155–156
Revival leaders, 73–74

secondary education, 232, 234–240
Shortwood teacher training college, 227
St Joseph's College, 227
street brawls, 154–155
Upward and Onward Society, 188
vanguard of patriotic movement, 304–306
victims of domestic violence, 159–160
Victorian gender ideals, 138–139
Victorian gender ideology, 234–235
white female population, 8–9, 140

York Castle, 123, 173, 227, 230

Zion. *See* Revival

www.ingramcontent.com/pod-product-compliance
Lightning Source LLC
Chambersburg PA
CBHW021812300426
44114CB00009BA/149